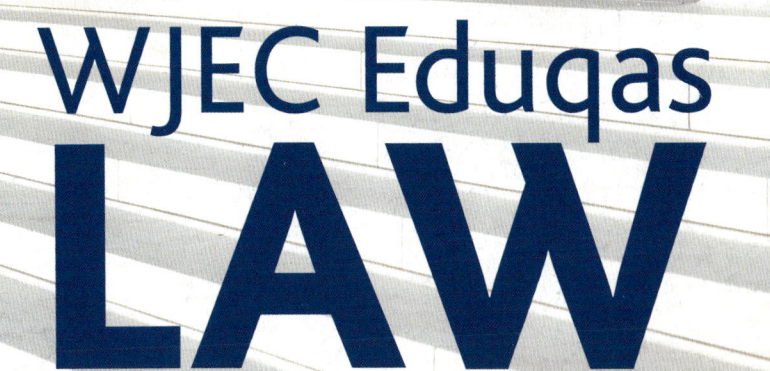

WJEC Eduqas
LAW
A Level   SECOND EDITION

> Sara Davies
> Karen Phillips
> Louisa Draper-Walters

Illuminate Publishing

Every effort has been made to trace all copyright holders, but if any have been inadvertently overlooked, the Publishers will be pleased to make the necessary arrangements at the first opportunity.

Although every effort has been made to ensure that website addresses are correct at time of going to press, Hodder Education cannot be held responsible for the content of any website mentioned in this book. It is sometimes possible to find a relocated web page by typing in the address of the home page for a website in the URL window of your browser.

Hachette UK's policy is to use papers that are natural, renewable and recyclable products and made from wood grown in well-managed forests and other controlled sources. The logging and manufacturing processes are expected to conform to the environmental regulations of the country of origin.

Orders: please contact Hachette UK Distribution, Hely Hutchinson Centre, Milton Road, Didcot, Oxfordshire, OX11 7HH. Telephone: +44 (0)1235 827827. Email education@hachette.co.uk. Lines are open from 9 a.m. to 5 p.m., Monday to Friday. You can also order through our website: www.hoddereducation.co.uk

ISBN: 978 1 3983 7950 3
© Sara Davies, Karen Phillips and Louisa Draper-Walters 2023

First published in 2023 by
Illuminate Publishing,
an imprint of Hodder Education,
An Hachette UK Company
Carmelite House
50 Victoria Embankment
London EC4Y 0DZ
www.hoddereducation.co.uk

Impression number 5 4 3 2 1
Year   2027 2026 2025 2024 2023

All rights reserved. Apart from any use permitted under UK copyright law, no part of this publication may be reproduced or transmitted in any form or by any means, electronic or mechanical, including photocopying and recording, or held within any information storage and retrieval system, without permission in writing from the publisher or under licence from the Copyright Licensing Agency Limited. Further details of such licences (for reprographic reproduction) may be obtained from the Copyright Licensing Agency Limited, www.cla.co.uk

Cover photo: © lazyllama – stock.adobe.com
Typeset by Integra
Produced by DZS Grafik, Printed in Slovenia

A catalogue record for this title is available from the British Library.

Contents

Introduction	iv

1 The Nature of Law — 1
1 Law making — 1
2 Law reform — 9
3 Delegated legislation — 19
4 Statutory interpretation — 26
5 Judicial precedent — 34
6 Civil courts — 42
7 Criminal process: Structure and sentencing — 55
8 Criminal process: Juries — 77
9 Legal personnel — 87
10 Access to justice and funding — 100

2 The Law of Tort — 108
11 Rules of tort — 108
12 Liability in negligence — 111
13 Torts connected to land — 123
14 Vicarious liability — 146
15 Occupiers' liability — 152
16 Defences: Tort — 159
17 Remedies: Tort — 163

3 Human Rights Law — 170
18 Rules, theory and protection of human rights law — 170
19 Specific provisions within the European Court of Human Rights — 176
20 Restrictions of the European Court of Human Rights — 183
21 The debate relating to the protection of human rights in the UK — 234

4 Contract Law — 239
22 Rules and theory of the law of contract — 239
23 Essential requirements of a contract — 241
24 Express and implied terms — 261
25 Misrepresentation and economic duress — 276
26 Discharge of a contract — 281
27 Remedies — 285

5 Criminal Law — 289
28 Rules and theory of criminal law — 289
29 General elements of criminal liability — 294
30 Offences against the person — 306
31 Property offences — 326
32 Capacity defences — 338
33 Preliminary offences of attempt — 364

Case index — 368

Glossary — 373

Index — 376

Introduction

How to use this book

The contents of this textbook are designed to guide you through the WJEC or Eduqas Law specification and lead you to success in the subject. It has been written by senior examiners who have pinpointed what is required of candidates, in terms of content, to achieve the highest marks. In addition, common errors have been identified, and support and advice given in how to avoid these errors, which will help lead to success in your AS/A Level examination.

The book covers:

- Eduqas AS Level components 1 and 2
- Eduqas A Level components 1, 2 and 3
- WJEC AS Level units 1 and 2
- WJEC A Level units 3 and 4.

This textbook covers the knowledge content that is required for each topic within the various specifications. There is also a selection of learning features throughout the topics.

Key terminology: important legal terms are emboldened in the main text and accompanied by a definition in the margin. They have also been compiled into a glossary at the end of the book for ease of reference.

Grade boost: gives you an insight into the examiner's mind and provides advice on things you should include to achieve the higher marks.

Stretch and challenge: these activities provide opportunities to research a topic further and give you advice on wider reading. These are usually additional cases, current affairs or areas under reform, knowledge of which should really impress your examiner.

Cases and key cases: examples of cases are highlighted to clarify the points of law they illustrate.

Exam skills: these give advice and guidance on how to prepare for your exams.

WJEC/Eduqas-only text: a minority of topics only feature on *either* the WJEC or Eduqas specification. This feature will identify these topics so that you can be sure you are covering all of the content that you need for the qualification you are studying towards. Grey-background text is WJEC only, and blue-background text is Eduqas only.

Summary: at the end of each topic there is a handy summary to help you structure your revision.

Test yourself: these summary questions at the end of each topic can be completed to test your knowledge of what you have just learnt. All the answers can be found in the main body of the topic.

Exam past paper questions: these show you how the topic has featured on actual past papers. Where applicable, a selection is shown across the different exam boards.

Note: following the death of Queen Elizabeth II in 2022, senior barristers switched their title from QC (Queen's Counsel) to KC (King's Counsel). In addition, the Queen's Bench Division of the High Court is now referred to as the King's Bench.

The Nature of Law

1 Law making

'Sources of law' refers to the way in which the law comes into existence (see Figure 1.1).

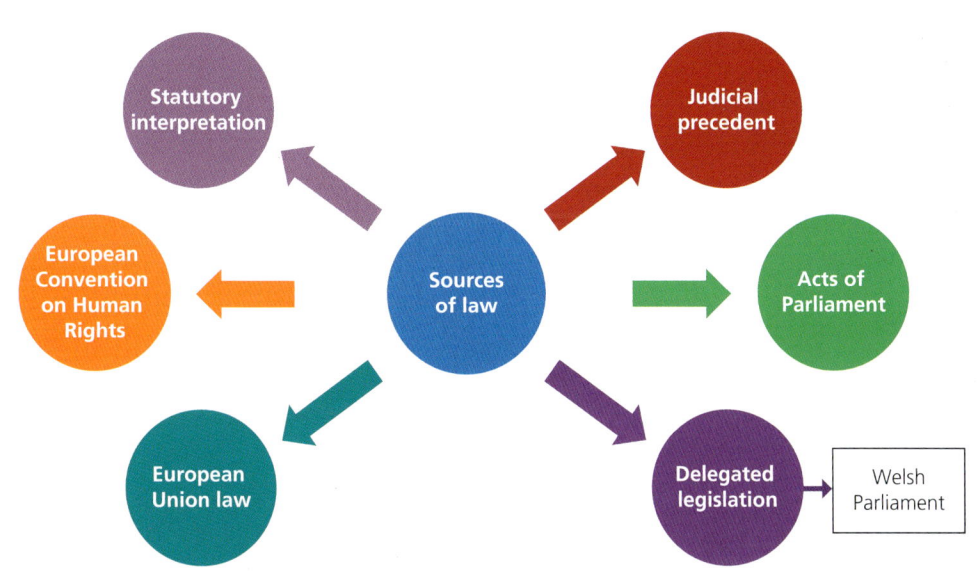

Figure 1.1 Sources of law in England and Wales

Acts of Parliament

Most United Kingdom (UK) law comes from the UK Parliament, which passes hundreds of laws every year. Parliament is composed of three institutions (see Figure 1.2).

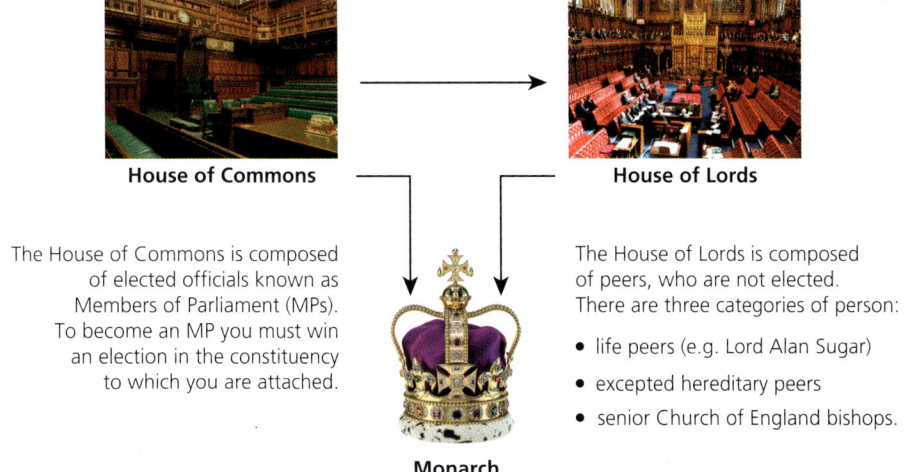

House of Commons

The House of Commons is composed of elected officials known as Members of Parliament (MPs). To become an MP you must win an election in the constituency to which you are attached.

House of Lords

The House of Lords is composed of peers, who are not elected. There are three categories of person:

- life peers (e.g. Lord Alan Sugar)
- excepted hereditary peers
- senior Church of England bishops.

Monarch

The monarch has to approve all laws passed by Parliament. The current monarch is King Charles III.

Figure 1.2 The three institutions of Parliament

The UK Parliament is based at the Palace of Westminster in London, so is sometimes referred to as 'the Westminster Parliament' or simply 'Westminster'. It consists of two debating chambers: the House of Commons and the House of Lords. The third element of the UK Parliament is the monarch, who is the head of state. The role of the monarch is hereditary: it normally passes from the present monarch to their eldest child when the reigning monarch dies.

All three parts of the UK Parliament must approve Acts of Parliament before they can become law.

Green and White Papers

The first stage of making a law is often to consult relevant people via a Green and/or White Paper.

Green Paper

A Green Paper is an intention to change the law and outlines the format this change could take. It is published on the internet for the public to comment on and copies are also distributed to interested parties. These individuals will then make comments and put forward suggestions on the proposal.

White Paper

Parliament will then publish a White Paper, which is a positive proposal on the format the new law will take. It often includes changes as a response to the opinions of the interested parties. There is then a further chance for consultation before the final Bill enters Parliament for consideration.

Bills

All Acts of Parliament begin life as a Bill, which is a draft law or a proposal for a change in the law. There are three types of Bill: Public Bills, Private Members' Bills and Private Bills.

Public Bills

A Public Bill involves matters of public policy that will affect the whole country or a large section of it. These Bills will sometimes reflect the manifesto of the government in power at the time. Most government Bills are in this category. Examples include:

- Children and Social Work Act 2017
- Juries Act 1974
- Finance Act 2017.

Private Members' Bills

Private Members' Bills are sponsored by individual Members of Parliament (MPs). At each parliamentary session, 20 members are chosen from a ballot to take their turn in presenting their Bills to Parliament. Relatively few Private Members' Bills become law, and the time available for debating them is very short. As they tend to cover issues that the individual MP is interested in, they rarely reflect the government's general agenda. Examples of Private Members' Bills that have become law are:

- Abortion Act 1967
- Marriage Act 1994
- British Sign Language Act 2022.

Private Bills

A Private Bill is a law that is designed to affect only individual people or corporations. Examples include:

- University College London Act 1996
- Whitehaven Harbour Act 2007.

> **GRADE BOOST**
>
> Public Bills currently being considered by Parliament can be found at www.parliament.uk/business/bills-and-legislation
>
> Recent legislation can be found at www.legislation.gov.uk/ukpga
>
> Go to www.parliament.uk/about/how/laws/flash-passage-bill and summarise in more detail what happens at each stage of the legislative process.

Legislative process

When a Bill is prepared, it is first presented to the UK Parliament and then has to go through a specific process before it officially becomes law (see Figure 1.3).

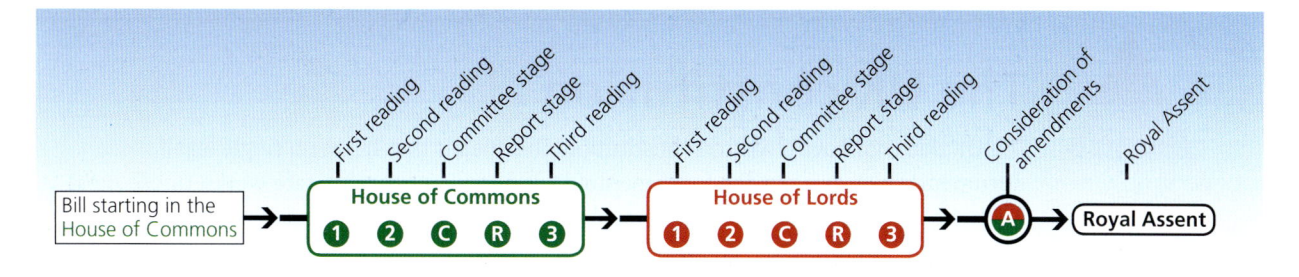

Figure 1.3 How a Bill progresses through Parliament (Source: www.parliament.uk/about/how/laws/flash-passage-bill. Crown Copyright)

The House of Commons can use powers under the **Parliament Acts 1911** and **1949** to make a law without the consent of the **House of Lords**. This rarely happens but is an available option if the House of Lords cannot reach an agreement. An example of the House of Commons using this power was when MPs passed the **Hunting Act 2004**, which outlawed the hunting of wild animals using dogs.

First reading
The title of the prepared Bill is read to the House of Commons. This is called the first reading and acts as notification of the proposed measure.

Second reading
The second reading is the first opportunity for MPs to debate the main principles of the Bill. At the end of the debate, the House of Commons votes on whether the legislation should proceed.

Committee stage
This is a detailed examination of the Bill where every clause is agreed to, changed or removed, taking into account the points made during the debates at the first and second readings.

Report stage
The committee will then report back to the House of Commons, and any proposed amendments are debated and voted upon.

Third reading
The third reading is a final chance for the House of Commons to debate the contents of a Bill but no amendments can be made at this stage. There is simply a vote on whether to accept or reject the legislation as it stands.

House of Lords
The Bill then goes to the House of Lords, where it travels through a similar process of three readings. If the House of Lords alters anything, the Bill returns to the Commons for consideration. This is known as 'ping pong'.

Royal Assent
In the majority of cases, agreement between the Lords and the Commons is reached and the Bill is then presented for Royal Assent. Technically, the King must give his consent to all legislation before it can become law but, in practice, that consent is never refused and is always granted.

The Bill is now an Act of Parliament and becomes law, although most Acts do not take effect the moment the King gives his consent, but on a specified future date. This is known as 'commencement'.

> **KEY TERMINOLOGY**
>
> **House of Lords:** the name of the Upper House in Parliament, which is the legislative chamber. Confusion arose before the establishment of the Supreme Court, as the highest appeal court was also called the House of Lords.

> **EXAM SKILLS**
>
> If you are asked to explain the legislative process, remember that you will need to do more than just list the different stages to achieve the full range of marks. Try to explain what happens at each stage, giving some examples if you can.

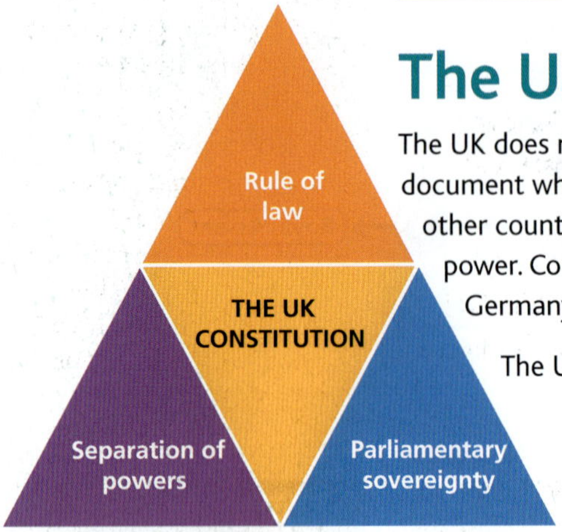

The UK constitution

The UK does not have a written constitution. This means that it has no single legal document which sets out the fundamental laws outlining how the state works. Unlike most other countries, there is no formal regulation of the organisation and distribution of state power. Countries which do have a written constitution include the USA, France and Germany.

The UK therefore relies on three key principles to underpin its unwritten constitution:

1. parliamentary sovereignty
2. the rule of law
3. separation of powers.

Figure 1.4 The three key principles of the UK's unwritten constitution

Parliamentary sovereignty

In its most simple form, sovereignty is the principle of absolute and unlimited power. An Act of Parliament can completely overrule any custom, judicial precedent, delegated legislation or previous Act of Parliament. This is because MPs are elected by the voters in their constituency in a democratic process, so each MP is participating in the legislative process on behalf of those voters.

Dicey's theory of parliamentary sovereignty

A.V. Dicey was a famous Oxford scholar and his traditional view has three main points that explain the concept of parliamentary sovereignty:

1. Parliament is sovereign

Parliament is sovereign and can make or unmake any law on any subject without legal constraints. This means that Parliament is the highest source of English law and has the right to make or unmake any law, and to override or set aside any existing legislation.

So, if Parliament decided that all dog owners also had to own a cat, there might be a public outcry, but the law would still be valid and the courts would be obliged to uphold it. The reason for this power is that Parliament is democratically elected and therefore has the upper hand when making the laws that every citizen has to follow.

2. No Parliament can bind another

No Parliament can bind another and an Act of Parliament passed by a previous Parliament can be repealed by the next Parliament. No Act of Parliament is entrenched, like the US Bill of Rights is.

> **KEY TERMINOLOGY**
>
> **parliamentary sovereignty:** Dicey's principle that Parliament has absolute and unlimited power, and that an Act of Parliament overrules any other source of law.
>
> **Act of Parliament (statute):** a source of primary legislation that comes from the UK legislature.
>
> **custom:** rules of behaviour which develop in a community without being deliberately invented.
>
> **judicial precedent (case law):** a source of law where past judges' decisions create law for future judges to follow.
>
> **delegated legislation (secondary or subordinate legislation):** law created by a body other than Parliament but with the authority of Parliament, as laid down in primary legislation.

3. No Act can be challenged

No Act can be challenged by a court nor its validity questioned. This means that, even if it were alleged that an Act has been passed by fraudulent means, it has to be upheld by the courts. It cannot be overruled by another 'arm' of the state. The only way to challenge the action of ministers, or any other law makers, is through judicial review, which is dealt with by the King's Bench Division of the High Court.

Threats to Dicey's theory

Dicey's theory of parliamentary sovereignty is a little outdated and does not reflect the UK's current legal position because there are three significant erosions of parliamentary sovereignty.

1. Membership of the European Union

European Union (EU) law overrides any UK law made before or after the UK joined the EU in 1972. However, since the 2016 Brexit referendum result, it remains to be seen how EU law will continue to influence the UK.

2. Human Rights Act 1998

The Human Rights Act 1998 made it a legal requirement that all public authorities must behave in a way that does not infringe on human rights. This means that under section 3 (s3) judges have to interpret every Act of Parliament in a way that upholds human rights.

If the law abuses human rights, they have to declare it incompatible under s4 and send the law back to Parliament to change.

3. Devolution

There have been changes to the UK constitution through devolution. The formation of the Welsh Parliament, Northern Ireland Assembly and the Scottish Parliament have had an impact on parliamentary sovereignty because these devolved institutions can now make laws, sometimes without the approval of the UK Parliament.

Rule of law

Dicey was also responsible for the second theory that underpins the UK's unwritten constitution. He said that the concept of the rule of law has three components:

1. No sanction without breach

No one should be punished unless they have broken a law. This means that there should be proper legal procedures and that all law should be public and cannot be secret. In principle, no law should have a retrospective effect; that is, a new law should not apply to past events.

In the English and Welsh legal systems, the actions of and decisions by government ministers can be challenged by judicial review. This element of the rule of law ensures that the state does not have wide discretionary powers to make arbitrary decisions.

2. One law should govern everyone

This means that everybody (including the government) is equal before the law. Dicey's idea was that court proceedings, the judicial mechanisms controlling society, would apply to the citizen and to the government and public bodies. However, some institutions of the state, such as the police, are given more powers than citizens to enable the state to function.

3. Rights of individuals are secured by decisions of judges

This engages with the idea of judicial precedent, which is that the highest courts can make a decision in a case which then has to be followed by the lower courts. In this way, no new

> **KEY TERMINOLOGY**
>
> **judicial review:** the process of challenging the legality of a decision, action or failure to act by a public body such as a government department or court.
>
> **devolution:** the transference of power from central government to regional or local government (e.g. the formation of the Welsh Parliament, the Northern Ireland Assembly and the Scottish Parliament).
>
> **rule of law:** the state should govern its citizens in accordance with rules that have been agreed upon.

Figure 1.5 The Human Rights Act 1998 has affected judges' interpretation of statutes

legal principles are created. Although most modern laws are created by Acts of Parliament and delegated legislation, judicial decisions do still create law.

Problems with Dicey's theory

Dicey's theory conflicts with the principle of parliamentary supremacy. This is the acknowledgement that Parliament has the right to make or unmake any law, including granting arbitrary power to the state. This is exactly the sort of arbitrary power that the rule of law seeks to forbid.

Dicey also considered equality before the law. This is often compromised because the cost of taking legal cases to court is very high, so may not be accessible to everyone.

Breaches of the rule of law

There have been many allegations in which the rule of law was alleged to have been breached. Here are some examples:

> John Hemming MP: Mr Hemming disclosed the name of a famous footballer subject to an injunction by using parliamentary privilege.
> Prisoners' vote: Conservative MPs proposed to ignore a ruling by the European Court of Human Rights (ECtHR) that gave UK prisoners the right to vote.
> Abu Qatada: the Human Rights Act 1998 protects people from torture, and Abu Qatada would have been tortured or received an unfair trial for terrorist crimes that he had allegedly committed if he had been deported to his home country of Jordan. In 2013, Abu Qatada left the UK after Jordan signed a treaty promising not to use evidence obtained by torture.

Upholding the rule of law

There are also examples which show judges upholding the rule of law:

> The Constitutional Reform Act 2005: this Act recognised the rule of law and the importance of the independence of the judiciary.
> Section 1 Constitutional Reform Act 2005: this states that the Act does not adversely affect 'the constitutional principle of the rule of law or the Lord Chancellor's existing constitutional role in relation to that principle'.
> Section 17(1) Constitutional Reform Act 2005: this outlines the oath to be taken by the Lord Chancellor to respect the rule of law and defend the independence of the judiciary. This is significant because it is the first time that the rule of law was recognised as a central issue in a statutory provision.

Separation of powers

Montesquieu was an 18th-century French philosopher. His theory of the separation of powers stated that the only way to safeguard the liberty of citizens is to keep the three arms of the state – legislature, judiciary and executive (see Figure 1.6) separate. This theory requires that individuals should not be members of more than one arm of the state, but in reality there is some overlap and we are increasingly seeing a fusion of the arms, rather than a separation.

The Prime Minister and their cabinet make up the Executive, but there are also MPs who sit in the legislature. The Executive is also influential on the legislative agenda, as proposed policies are often part of the government's manifesto. This may reflect a particular political viewpoint, as the Executive is usually formed by the party that won the most seats in the House of Commons at a general election. This is deemed acceptable, however, as the Executive is formed in a democratic way, having been elected by the public.

GRADE BOOST

Other theorists who have developed modern interpretations of the rule of law include Lord Bingham and Joseph Raz.

GRADE BOOST

Research these examples, which show judges upholding the rule of law:
- The Belmarsh Prisoners case
- Black Spider Memos case
- *Al Rawi and others* v *Security Service and others*

KEY TERMINOLOGY

separation of powers: state power is separated into three types, Executive, judicial and legislative, with each type exercised by different bodies or people.
Executive: the government.

1 Law making

LEGISLATURE
This is the UK Parliament.
It enforces the law.

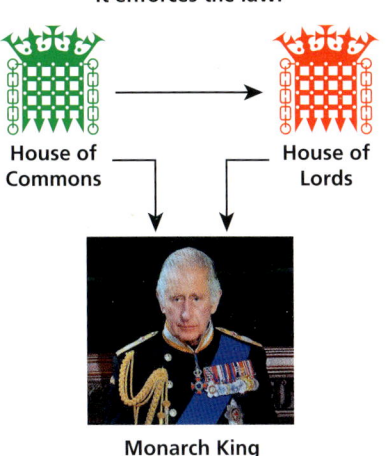

House of Commons → House of Lords

Monarch King Charles III

EXECUTIVE
This is the UK government.
It enforces the law.

Prime Minister Rishi Sunak

This is usually formed by the party that won the majority of seats in the House of Commons at a general election (at time of writing, the Conservative Party).

The Prime Minister is supported by senior Ministers who make up the Cabinet and each Minister has a role in a particular area, for example the Secretary of State for Education, the Secretary of State for Health, the Secretary of State for Justice.

JUDICIARY
These are the judges.
They apply and interpret the law.

Figure 1.6 Montesquieu's theory states that there are three functions of the state and that these should be kept separate

For a long time, there was also considerable overlap between the judiciary and the legislature. This is because the House of Lords was a legislative debating chamber as well as being the highest appeal court of the UK. This was deemed unsatisfactory because it goes against the theory of the separation of powers whereby the legislature has to be kept separate from the judiciary. As a result, the **Constitutional Reform Act 2005** created the UK Supreme Court, which is the highest appeal court in the UK, thus removing the most senior court from the legislature.

TEST YOURSELF

1. What are the three institutions that make up the UK Parliament?
2. What is the difference between a Private Bill and a Private Members' Bill?
3. What is the significance of the **Parliament Acts 1911** and **1949**?
4. Explain what happens at the Committee stage of the legislative process.
5. Explain what is meant by the 'ping pong' stage of the legislative process.
6. Outline Dicey's three principles of parliamentary sovereignty.
7. What are the three big erosions of parliamentary sovereignty?
8. Explain what is meant by the 'rule of law'.
9. Why is it important to uphold the doctrine of the separation of powers?
10. Explain how there may be overlap between the executive and the legislature.

> **SUMMARY: LAW MAKING**
>
> ➔ **Sources of law**: the UK has an unwritten constitution, so it is based on three principles:
>   1. **Parliamentary sovereignty** (Dicey): Parliament is supreme with absolute and unlimited power. Threats: EU, **Human Rights Act 1998**, devolution
>   2. **Rule of law** (Dicey): no sanction without breach, one law should govern everyone, rights are secured by the decisions of judges
>   - Examples of breaches: John Hemming MP, prisoners' vote, Abu Qatada
>   - Promotion: **Constitutional Reform Act 2005**, Black Spider Memos
>   3. **Separation of powers** (Montesquieu): three functions of the state should remain separate:
>   - Legislature: UK Parliament makes the law
>   - Executive: UK government enforces the law
>   - Judiciary: judges apply and interpret the law
>
> ➔ **UK Parliament**: the legislative arm of the UK
>
> Three elements:
> - House of Commons
> - House of Lords
> - Monarch
>
> All three must agree on a Bill before it becomes an Act, subject to the exceptions in the **Parliament Acts 1911** and **1949**.
>
> Three types of Bill can result in an Act of Parliament:
> - Public Bill
> - Private Members' Bill
> - Private Bill
>
> All potential Acts have to go through the legislative process: five stages in the House of Commons, five stages in the House of Lords and Royal Assent

> **EXAM PAST PAPER QUESTIONS**
>
> **WJEC – Unit 1 – May 2019**
> Explain the Rule of Law doctrine. [10]
>
> **Eduqas – AS Level Component 1 – May 2019**
> Explain what is meant by the separation of powers. [6]
>
> **Eduqas – AS Level Component 1 – May 2018**
> Explain the stages a Bill must go through in order to become an Act of Parliament. [6]

2 Law reform

Judicial change

The law does not, and cannot, stand still. It needs to keep up with society's changing attitudes and respond to events and media pressure.

Most legislation in the English and Welsh legal systems continues to apply until it is repealed. Where it is clear that the law is no longer reflective of society's needs, there is a number of ways in which it can be reformed (see Figure 2.1) and agencies that can put pressure on the government to change the law.

Case law can bring about some reform through the development of the common law, also known as judicial precedent.

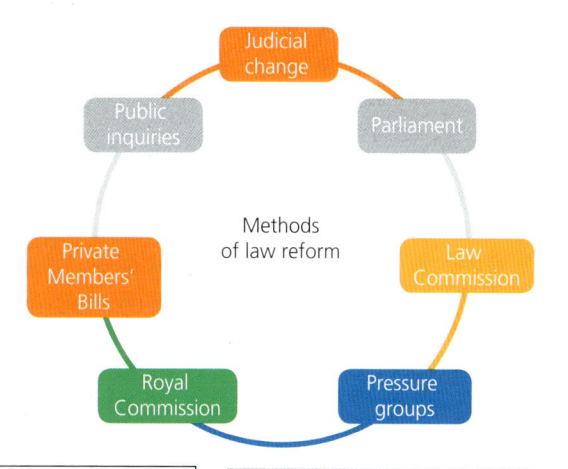

Figure 2.1 Many channels can be used to reform the law

R v R (1991)

A husband broke into the house where his estranged wife was staying with her mother and forced her to have non-consensual sex with him. The House of Lords declared that a husband who has non-consensual sexual intercourse with his wife can be guilty of rape on the basis that the status of women, and particularly of married women, has changed out of all recognition in various ways. As a result, the **Sexual Offences Act 2003** was amended to reflect the fact that non-consensual intercourse is rape regardless of marital status.

Ghaidan v Godin-Mendoza (2004)

Here the court held that homosexuals living in a long-term loving relationship should enjoy the same tenancy rights as heterosexual couples.

There are several reasons why judicial law making is rare, and why it should not regularly happen.

> Courts can only deal with cases that are brought to them so they are unable to enter into wide-ranging law reform.
> The parties involved in cases often do not have the money or interest to pursue the reform.
> Judges are usually unable to consult experts or commission research. They will be wary of reforming the law without this specific knowledge, as their decision will have future influence.
> Judges are unable to make changes where the doctrine of precedent applies, which inhibits any radical reforms.
> A precedent change is retrospective (that is, it covers something that has already happened), whereas a parliamentary reform is prospective (it takes effect only from the day it comes into force).
> Judges are unelected so it is often argued that their constitutional position is not to reform the law. The theory of separation of powers shows this.

However, judges are skilful at identifying issues to Parliament. Within their judgments, they are willing to point to areas of difficulty with a view to raising the profile of such issues and attracting the attention of Parliament to get reforms.

Parliamentary change

The government of the day has control over what ideas enter Parliament, even though they are often influenced by other bodies.

Much legislation reflects the political ideas of the government that is in power when the Act is passed. Such legislation may start as a political commitment in the manifesto of a political party. The government of the day will set out its legislative agenda in the King's Speech on the first day of a parliamentary session.

Parliamentary law reform happens in four ways

Repeal
> Old and obsolete laws are removed.
> Out-of-date laws will often stay on the statute books for a long time before they are repealed.

Creation
> Completely new laws are created, either in response to public demand or because of pressure from another group.
> Existing provisions can also be adapted to meet new needs.

Consolidation
> When a statute is created, problems may appear over time and new legislation may be enacted to amend it.
> It brings together successive statutes on the same subject.

Codification
> Where a particular area of law has developed over time, a large body of case law and statute can make the law confusing.
> Codification brings together all the rules into one statute to increase certainty.

New Acts of Parliament

A number of circumstances may provide the stimulus for a new Act of Parliament:

1. Events
Unexpected events can lead to an urgent need for law reform that the government may not have foreseen. For example, the attacks of 9/11 led to a tightening of the UK's terrorist laws through the creation of the **Anti-Terrorism, Crime and Security Act 2001**.

2. The Budget
Each year, the Chancellor of the Exchequer presents a Budget statement to MPs in the House of Commons. Once the Budget is agreed, a Finance Bill is presented to Parliament and will make its way through Parliament to give effect to the changes. Government expenditure changes in line with the needs of the country, so this law needs to be passed every year.

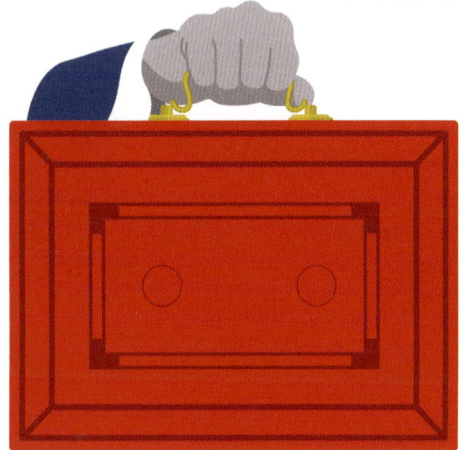

Figure 2.2 The famous red briefcase is said to contain the Budget recommendations

3. The media
Through the media, issues of public concern can be highlighted. Newspapers in particular often push a particular cause. For example, the *Daily Mail* often runs headlines on immigration

and asylum issues to try to achieve greater immigration controls and the *Sun* consistently campaigned against what it saw as the growing influence of the EU on British life.

An excellent example of media influence was the campaign run by the *News of the World* in 2000 following the murder of Sarah Payne by a known paedophile. The subsequent law change ('Sarah's law') was included in **s327 Criminal Justice Act 2003**, which places a duty on authorities to consider the disclosure of information about convicted sex offenders to parents in an area, if they consider that the offender presents a risk of serious harm to their children.

4. Law reform agencies
There are several formal agencies of law reform that put pressure on Parliament to change the law. They include:

- the Law Commission
- pressure groups
- Royal Commissions
- public inquiries.

5. Public opinion
If members of the public feel strongly about an issue, they can make their feelings known by writing to their MP or visiting their MP's surgery in their constituency. If the MP agrees, they can introduce the proposal to Parliament via a Private Members' Bill.

The **Dangerous Dogs Act 1991** was introduced because of public concern about dangerous dogs. The legislation was swiftly passed and is often criticised.

6. European Convention on Human Rights (ECHR)
Changes prompted by the requirements of the **ECHR** can also prompt parliamentary law reform.

> *Goodwin* v *UK* (2002)
>
> This case illustrated the inequalities in the law regarding transsexual rights. As a result of this case being heard in the European Court of Human Rights (ECtHR), the UK Parliament passed the **Gender Recognition Act 2004**.

> **STRETCH AND CHALLENGE**
>
> - **Clare's law**: research the law introduced as a result of a campaign by the father of Clare Wood, who was murdered by her ex-partner in 2009. A good starting point is the BBC News article '"Clare's law" introduced to tackle domestic violence', www.bbc.co.uk/news/uk-politics-26488011
> - **Natasha's law**: research the law introduced as a result of the parents of Natasha Ednan-Laperouse, who died because she ate a pre-packaged baguette that contained ingredients to which she was allergic.
>
> Can you find any more laws that have been introduced as a result of a media campaign?

Pressure groups

Pressure groups are those organisations that seek to influence the direction of law and policy on the basis of the views and opinions of their members.

If a pressure group begins to reflect the opinions of many members of the public, it can put a lot of pressure on Parliament. Remember that a pressure group cannot create law but can heavily influence Parliament. Parliament also consults with pressure groups to seek their views on law proposals.

There are two types of pressure groups: interest groups and cause groups.

1. Interest groups
These are sometimes also called 'sectional', 'protective' or 'functional' groups and represent a particular section of society, such as workers, employers, consumers, ethnic or religious groups, trade unions, business corporations, trade associations or professional bodies. Specific examples include the British Medical Association (BMA), the Law Society, the National Union of Teachers (NUT), the Confederation of British Industry (CBI) and the Trades Union Congress (TUC).

There are a few things to note about interest groups:

- They are concerned with the interests of their members.
- Membership of these groups is limited to those in a particular occupation, career or economic position.
- Members can be motivated by self-interest.
- Interest groups tend to be influential in the development of the law and are often consulted by Parliament in the early stages of law development.

2. Cause groups

These are sometimes called 'promotional', 'attitude' or 'issue' groups and are based on shared attitudes or values, rather than the common interests of their members. They seek to advance various causes ranging from charity activities, poverty reduction, education and the environment, to human rights, international development and peace. Specific examples include the Worldwide Fund for Nature (WWF), Amnesty International, Shelter, the Royal Society for the Protection of Birds (RSPB) and the Electoral Reform Society.

There are a few things to note about cause groups:

- They seek to advance particular ideals or principles.
- Membership is open to all.
- Members are motivated by moral issues.

The role of pressure groups as influential bodies

Pressure groups use a variety of tactics, including:

- letter writing
- protest marches
- lobbying MPs
- organising petitions
- gaining publicity and media attention
- attracting celebrities to support their campaign.

Some groups are more effective than others; size obviously helps, but other factors such as sheer persistence and headline grabbing can be very productive. Some groups use direct action, which in some cases can be illegal, such as violence or occupying land.

Figure 2.3 Another group that advocates direct action is Insulate Britain, which is campaigning for the UK government to fully fund and take responsibility for the insulation of all social housing in Britain by 2025. Its members have been campaigning by using violent protests, blocking the M25 and confronting drivers. Many members have been arrested and sentenced to time in prison.

The role of pressure groups as consultative bodies

Pressure groups also have a role as a consultative body. When an idea for a new law is proposed, Parliament may wish to begin with a consultation before it is presented to Parliament. This consultation can take the form of a Green Paper and White Paper (see page 2).

How effective are pressure groups?

Pressure groups can be effective and influential:

- They enhance democracy and encourage ordinary people to engage in politics.
- They facilitate public discussion on key issues.
- Their specialist knowledge can inform governments.
- They make political parties more responsive to the public.
- They enhance freedom of expression under Article 10 and freedom of assembly and protest under Article 11.
- They raise public awareness and educate the public on key issues.
- They often conduct their own specialist research, which can highlight important issues.

However, there are a few reasons why pressure groups should be regarded with care:

- They provide a one-sided view of an issue.
- If the group is small, their views can be distorted and not based on any substantial research.
- They are undemocratic in the sense that they are not elected but can still influence the government.
- Some groups advocate the use of direct action, which can be illegal.

> **STRETCH AND CHALLENGE**
>
> Research some key pressure groups, for example Fathers 4 Justice, Greenpeace, Shelter Cymru, National Union of Students, Amnesty International, Age UK, Friends of the Earth, Liberty, or No Dash for Gas. Find out:
> - their objectives
> - their methods
> - any successful attempts at law change.

Law Commission

The Law Commission is the only full-time law reform body in the UK.

It is an independent commission that comprises five members drawn from the judiciary, the legal profession and legal academics. The chairperson is a High Court judge. Members are appointed for a five-year term and are assisted by legally qualified civil servants and research assistants who are often law graduates.

The Law Commission was set up under the Law Commission Act 1965, and s3 of that Act states that its role is to:

> 'keep under review all the law ... with a view to its systematic development and reform, including in particular the codification of such law, elimination and anomalies, the repeal of obsolete and unnecessary enactments, the reduction of the number of separate enactments, the simplification and modernisation of the law.'

The Law Commission looks into laws and then seeks opinion on the possible reforms. The consultation paper describes the current law, sets out the problems and looks at the options for reform. Then the Law Commission will draw up positive proposals for reform in a report, which will also set out the research that led to the conclusions. Often there is a draft Bill attached to the report. This may then go to Parliament.

The Law Commission can reform law in the same four ways as Parliament: by repeal, consolidation, codification and creation.

The Law Commission Act 2009 is the most recent piece of legislation passed in relation to the Law Commission, to try to improve its success in reforming the law.

- It states that the Lord Chancellor must tell Parliament each year whether the government has decided to implement any of the previous year's Law Commission proposals, and if not, why not. This aims to hold ministers to account.

- It also introduced a new parliamentary procedure which reduces the time and resources required to implement non-controversial Law Commission Bills.
- The Act also sets out how the Law Commission and government departments should work together and a protocol has been agreed that the Law Commission will not take on a project without an undertaking from the relevant government minister that there is a serious intention to reform the law in that area.

Success of the Law Commission

1965–1975

The Law Commission was initially successful in reforming small areas of law. Its first 20 reform programmes were enacted within an average of two years, and included the **Unfair Contract Terms Act 1977**, **Supply of Goods and Services Act 1982** and **Occupiers' Liability Act 1984**.

Within ten years, it had a success rate of 85 per cent of its proposals for reform being enacted. Its reports led to the repeal of 2,000 obsolete statutes and partial repeal of thousands of others.

1976–2000

During this period, some academics argued that the process of law reform had stalled.

- In the 10–15 years from the late 1970s, only 50 per cent of its proposals became law.
- The rate hit an all-time low in 1990 when none of its proposed reforms were enacted.
- In 1992, there was a backlog of 36 Bills that Parliament had failed to consider.
- The lack of success during this period was put down to lack of parliamentary time and an apparent disinterest in Parliament of technical law reform.

One area highlighted by the Law Commission in 1989 was the need for criminal law to be codified. The government has failed to respond to the idea that the UK should mirror other jurisdictions where there is a single criminal code and there has been no sign of progress in implementing the suggestion of codification made by the Law Commission 2003: Halliday Review.

This review found that the main problem with law reform was the inability of government departments to accept reform proposals and create an opportunity for discussion in Parliament. In some cases, the delay in implementing the Law Commission reports was significant.

For example, the review found that the Law Commission's proposal for reform of the landlord's right of distress on the tenant's property was contained in its report on 'distress for rent', published in 1991. It took 16 years for those proposals to become part of the **Tribunals, Courts and Enforcement Act 2007**. Key factors in this delay can be traced to political issues, personnel changes and staffing.

The amount of annual legislation increased not only in numbers but also in length, adding further burdens to an already busy Parliament. Everyone from the Prime Minister and MPs to government departments sought to find a slot in which to introduce their legislation ideas.

Present day

In 2008, the Law Commission announced it would no longer seek to codify the criminal law but instead concentrate on simplifying specific areas of it, rather than repealing big chunks. Acts that have incorporated criminal law reform recommendations include:

- **Criminal Justice Act 2003**
- **Domestic Violence, Crimes and Victims Act 2003**
- **Fraud Act 2006**
- **Serious Crime Act 2007**
- **Coroners and Justice Act 2009**.

Figure 2.4 The Law Commission's law reform process
(Research → Consultation → Report of recommendations → Draft Bill → Parliament)

Since the Law Commission Act 2009, there have been annual reports to Parliament by the Lord Chancellor, resulting in varying levels of success. Implementation rates have improved, although there are still reports waiting to be made law. The Law Commission's Annual Report of 2020–21 showed that seven reports awaited implementation, and, since its inception in 1965, 64 per cent of Law Commission projects have been implemented in whole or in part.

An example of a current project being considered in the Law Commission's 14th Programme of Reform is regulating remote driving, so-called 'driverless cars' where a person outside a vehicle uses connectivity to control a vehicle on public roads.

GRADE BOOST

It is always good practice in an exam to show recent knowledge and an awareness of current issues. Here are some ideas in relation to the Law Commission:

- The Law Commission published a report in 2015 recommending reform of the Offences Against the Person Act 1861 (www.lawcom.gov.uk/project/offences-against-the-person). Summarise its main findings.
- In 2017 the Law Commission published a report recommending changes to the law surrounding wills (www.lawcom.gov.uk/project/wills). Summarise its proposals.

Two of the biggest successes of the Law Commission in recent years are:

- changes to offences surrounding jury conduct during trials, included in the Criminal Justice and Courts Act 2015.
- the consolidation of sentencing legislation in the Sentencing Act 2020, which was originally a Law Commission project.

STRETCH AND CHALLENGE

In order to keep on top of the progress of Law Commission proposals, it is a good idea to read the annual reports published by the Lord Chancellor's office, required by the Law Commission Act 2009. You can read the reports in full at www.gov.uk/government/collections/implementation-of-the-lawcommission-proposals.

Refer to these reports and draw on your learning to evaluate how successful the Law Commission has been since the implementation of the Law Commission Act 2009.

Advisory committees

Advisory committees are temporary law reform bodies. They are set up to research, consult and propose laws on a particular issue or to investigate where the law needs to be reformed following a tragedy or big event (such as the Hillsborough football stadium disaster or the Brixton Riots), or because of advances in science and technology that need to be reflected in the law.

Royal Commissions

Royal Commissions are temporary committees, set up by the government to investigate and report on one specific area of law. Once the report has been published, the Royal Commission is disbanded. Royal Commissions returned to popularity in the 1990s after not being used at all while Margaret Thatcher was Prime Minister in the 1980s. Examples include:

> Phillips Commission: resulted in the Police and Criminal Evidence Act 1984, which is key act for police powers and accountability
> Runciman Commission: established the Criminal Cases Review Commission, which investigates possible miscarriages of justice and can recommend a retrial at the Court of Appeal.

Public inquiries

Public inquiries are usually set up as a response to a significant event. They examine options for changing the law as a result of some failing by the government or the current law. The style and form of public inquiries is governed by the Inquiries Act 2005. In a public inquiry, three questions are asked:

1. What happened?
2. Why did it happen and who is to blame?
3. What can be done to prevent it happening again?

KEY TERMINOLOGY

institutional racism: when a public or private body's operation or policies and procedure are deemed to be racist.

STRETCH AND CHALLENGE

The Grenfell Tower inquiry is a highly publicised public inquiry into the fire at this block of flats in 2017. Find out more about the inquiry at this link: www.grenfelltowerinquiry.org.uk/news/prime-minister-announces-inquiry-terms-reference. Make a list of the priorities you think the inquiry should address.

Other recent inquiries concern:
- allegations of institutionalised child abuse spanning decades
- blood contamination, which led to the deaths of an estimated 2,400 people who were infected with hepatitis C and HIV (human immunodeficiency virus).

Look online for details of these inquiries and the progress that is being made in terms of changes to the law and/or any resulting prosecutions.

Examples include:

> **Stephen Lawrence inquiry:** concluded that the Metropolitan Police had been institutionally racist in its handling of the murder of black teenager Stephen Lawrence. Some recommendations were implemented, such as the requirement for a Racial Equality Scheme in all police forces.
> **Bloody Sunday inquiry:** British soldiers were found to have shot dead unarmed and already injured civilians in Ireland.
> **Leveson inquiry:** looked at the culture, practice and ethics of the press after allegations reporters were invading the privacy of celebrities, using tactics such as telephone hacking.

Other ad hoc committees

Other temporary committees are set up at the request of a particular government minister to investigate and produce a report about specific areas of law. Examples include:

> **Auld Review:** investigated the workings of the criminal justice system. Recommendations from this report resulted in the Criminal Justice Act 2003.
> **Woolf Report:** investigated the civil procedure system. Its recommendations resulted in one of the biggest changes to civil procedure in the form of the Access to Justice Act 1999.

Law reform in Wales

There are particular influences on law reform in Wales.

Welsh Language Society/Cymdeithas yr Iaith Gymraeg

This is a direct-action pressure group in Wales which campaigns for the rights of Welsh people to use the Welsh language in every aspect of their lives.

It has contributed to the passing of various Welsh Language Acts to increase opportunities to learn and use the Welsh language. These Acts also created the role of the Welsh Language Commissioner and the Welsh TV channel, S4C.

Yes Cymru

This is a pressure group campaigning for an independent Wales that has its own sovereign government and institutions.

Cymuned

This Welsh community pressure group was established in 2001 and campaigns on behalf of Welsh-speaking and rural communities, which it perceives to be under threat due to demographic changes.

What are the problems with law reform bodies?

> The Law Commission is the only full-time law reform body. So much law reform needs to happen that it may be not big enough to cope with the demand.
> There is no obligation for the government to consult permanent law reform bodies, or to set up Royal Commissions or other committees.
> Governments also have no obligation to follow any recommendations made by law reform bodies and are able to reject them entirely. Even where general proposals are implemented, the detailed proposals are often ignored or radically altered.
> Even where proposals are implemented, there may be insufficient funding to put them into practice.

› Legal professionals, such as judges and barristers, contribute to the consultation documents and their strong influence on any type of reform can defeat proposals even before they reach an official report or get to Parliament.
› The temporary committees are disbanded after they have produced their report and take no part in the rest of the law-making process, so this can be a waste of expertise.
› There is no single ministerial department responsible for law reform, so ministers are unlikely to make law reform their priority.

SUMMARY: LAW REFORM

→ **Judicial change**: judges can bring about law reform through judicial precedent
- Examples:
  - *R v R* (1991)
  - *Ghaidan v Godin-Mendoza* (2004)
- Judicial law making is rare because of constitutional position and judges not being elected to make laws

→ **Parliamentary change**: the main way to reform law, usually to reflect government manifesto or a political agenda
- Changes can be made in one of four ways:
  - **Repeal**: take old and obsolete laws off the statute books
  - **Create**: make completely new laws
  - **Consolidate**: bring together successive statutes on the same subject
  - **Codify**: bring together all the rules into one statute to increase certainty
- Influences on Parliament are media pressure, the annual Budget, significant events, recommendations from law reform agencies, public opinion and the European Convention on Human Rights
- Two types of pressure groups:
  1. **Interest groups**: a particular section of society, e.g. the British Medical Association, National Union of Teachers
  2. **Cause groups**: a shared attitude or value, e.g. Amnesty International, Fathers 4 Justice
- Pressure groups sometimes use illegal methods to attract attention, and are not always successful in forcing change
- Pressure groups are good at highlighting issues that Parliament may decide needs debate

→ **Law Commission**: its role under s3 Law Commission Act 1965 is to 'keep under review all the law':
- The Law Commission is the only full-time law reform body
- The Law Commission puts draft Bills before Parliament after a period of research and consultation
- Law Commission Act 2009 puts an obligation on the Lord Chancellor to report to Parliament whether the government has decided to implement any of the previous year's Law Commission proposals
- The Law Commission was successful at first, less so in the 1980s and 1990s, then more success since the 2009 Act

→ **Advisory committees**: temporary committees set up to review a particular area of law, e.g. Royal Commissions, public inquiries and ad hoc committees

EXAM SKILLS

If you are faced with an application question on law reform, copy and complete Table 2.1 to help structure your answer. Assess why it would/would not be a good idea to use each method of law reform. Remember to refer back to the scenario.

Table 2.1 Revision aid for law reform

Method	Definition	Example	Advantages	Disadvantages
Media campaigns				
Judicial change				
Private Members' Bills				
Pressure groups				
Parliamentary petitions				

TEST YOURSELF

1. Name five methods of law reform.
2. What are the four ways that Parliament can change the law?
3. Why is a media campaign unlikely to result in a change in the law?
4. Give two examples of interest pressure groups.
5. What is meant by a cause pressure group?
6. Give three reasons why pressure groups can be successful in reforming the law.
7. What is the significance of **s3 Law Commission Act 1965**?
8. Give two examples of current Law Commission projects.
9. Why might the Law Commission be seen as ineffective?
10. Define a public inquiry.

EXAM PAST PAPER QUESTIONS

WJEC – Unit 1 – May 2022
Explain the role of the Law Commission. [10]

WJEC – Unit 1 – May 2018
Explain the role of pressure groups in reforming the law. [10]

Eduqas – AS Level Component 1 – May 2022

A report recently published in the media claims that 23% of 18 to 24-year-olds crash their car within two years of passing their test. Luke is a 19-year-old student who has recently passed his driving test and feels strongly that a change in the law could reduce this statistic. He proposes that it should be law that new drivers should display a P plate for two years and that for the first two years, new drivers should not be permitted to carry more than one passenger between the hours of 8pm and 6am.

Advise Luke on the ways in which he could try to promote reform of the law on the use of P plates for learner drivers in England and Wales. [18]

3 Delegated legislation

What is delegated legislation?

Delegated, sometimes called secondary or subordinate legislation is a law made by a body other than Parliament but with authority given to it by Parliament. Parliament normally passes an enabling (or parent) Act to delegate the authority to make law to the other body, which has to stay within the terms and conditions set out in the enabling Act. If the enabling body does not, any law it makes may be declared ultra vires (this means void; see page 22 for further detail). Delegated legislation is often used to 'flesh out' a piece of legislation or make changes to an Act where it is not practical to pass a new Act. It can also be used for technical reasons such as changing the amount of a fine.

The Legislative and Regulatory Reform Act 2006 allows ministers to issue statutory instruments (SIs) to amend existing primary legislation. These are known as legislative reform orders. This is controversial as it is seen as shifting power from the elected Parliament to the Executive.

Forms of delegated legislation

There are three main forms of delegated legislation. In addition, you might also need to consider the role of secondary legislation and devolved legislatures.

Statutory instruments

Statutory instruments are made by government departments and make up most of the 3,000 or so pieces of delegated legislation passed each year. They are normally drafted by the legal office of the relevant government department, which will consult with interested bodies and parties. They are made via either affirmative resolution or negative resolution (see page 22 for more detail) as part of the parliamentary controls on delegated legislation.

Byelaws

Byelaws are made by local authorities, public corporations and companies, and usually concern local issues or matters relating to their area of responsibility. For example, county councils make byelaws that affect the whole county, while district or town councils only make byelaws for their particular area. The laws are made with awareness of the needs of that area. A local council may introduce a byelaw banning dogs from its beaches during certain months or imposing fines for littering.

The proposed byelaws must be advertised to allow local people to view and comment on them. They are accompanied by some sanction or penalty for their non-observance.

Orders in council

Orders in council are generally made in times of emergency (under the Emergency Powers Act 1920 and the Civil Contingencies Act 2004: the 'enabling Acts') and have to be approved by the Privy Council (a committee of the monarch's senior advisors) and signed by the King. They can also be used to amend law and to give effect to EU law. For example, the Misuse of Drugs Act 1971 (Modification) (No. 2) Order 2003 downgraded cannabis from a Class B to a Class C drug.

KEY TERMINOLOGY

delegated (secondary or subordinate) legislation: law created by a body other than Parliament, but with the authority of Parliament laid down in primary legislation.

primary legislation: law made by the legislature, which in the UK is Parliament. Acts of Parliament are primary legislation.

legislative reform order: a statutory instrument which can amend an Act of Parliament without the need for a parliamentary Bill.

Devolution

Devolution is the process of transferring power from central government to regional or local government (e.g. the Scottish Parliament, Welsh Parliament and Northern Ireland Assembly).

Following devolution, the Welsh Parliament initially only had the power to make secondary legislation (then called Assembly Orders) on certain matters such as education and agriculture. This power has since been increased to primary law making.

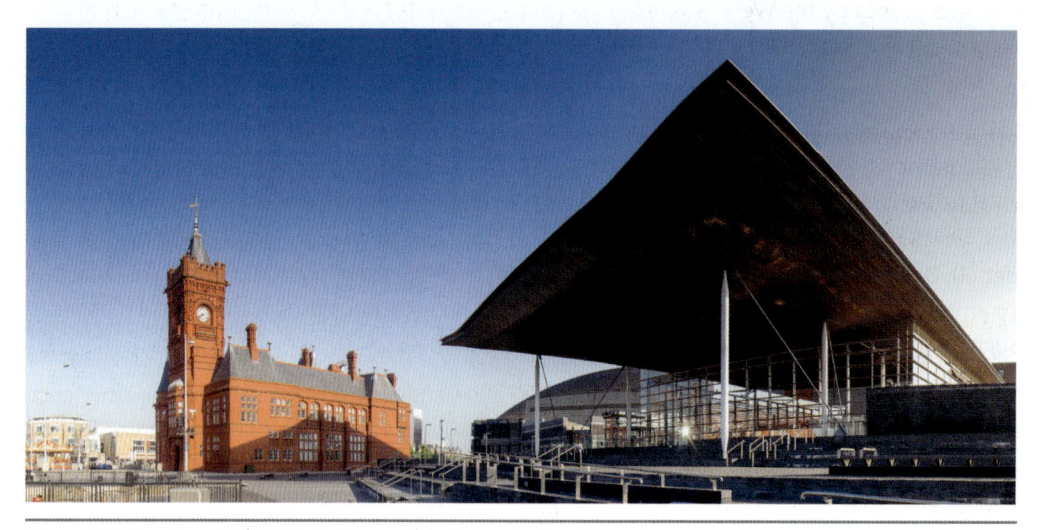

Figure 3.1 The Senedd (Welsh Parliament) building in Cardiff

Delegated legislation in Wales

The **Government of Wales Act 1998** established the Welsh Assembly (now known as the Welsh Parliament). The same Act created the National Assembly for Wales as a single corporate body. This provided the Assembly with the right to create secondary legislation; there are 60 Assembly Members (AMs). Parliament delegated 20 areas of law-making powers to Wales, for example, health, education and social services. Issues outside these 20 devolved areas are still governed by the UK Parliament (for example, defence and foreign policy).

The effects of the Government of Wales Act 2006

The **Government of Wales Act 2006** was passed in the UK Parliament, transferring power to the Welsh Assembly to make its own laws (primary legislation) within a number of specific areas, such as education and health. This means that the laws passed in the UK Parliament still apply to Wales but certain subject areas are now transferred to the Welsh Parliament.

Until 2010, the Welsh Assembly had to seek approval from Parliament for all the laws it passed. This created some conflict; for example, Parliament refused to let Wales pass the opt-out donor scheme.

The effects of the 2011 referendum

On 3 March 2011, a referendum took place in Wales to ask whether the Welsh Assembly should be allowed to pass its own legislation. The outcome of the referendum meant that the 20 devolved fields no longer needed further approval from the UK Parliament in order to create new laws.

It also means that the terminology has changed. Instead of using the phrase 'measures', the Welsh Assembly considers new legislation in the form of a Bill, which, if passed, will become a statute (an Act). This means that the Welsh Assembly has gained additional powers and reflects the same law-making process as carried out in the UK Parliament.

3 Delegated legislation

It also has the power to create subordinate (or delegated) legislation. The Assembly scrutinises subordinate legislation drawn up by the Welsh ministers under powers delegated by an Act or Measure of the Assembly or by an Act of Parliament. Subordinate legislation includes orders, regulations, rules and schemes as well as statutory guidance and local orders.

Legislative Competence Orders are no longer necessary, as these were requests to the UK Parliament to allow the Assembly to make laws in new subjects within the 20 devolved areas.

The laws passed by the Welsh Assembly are specific to Wales and those making the laws are democratically elected. For example, free prescriptions and the organ donation presumed consent scheme only applies to people in Wales.

The Silk Commission and the Wales Acts

The Commission on Devolution in Wales – also known as the Silk Commission – was established by the UK government in 2011 to review the future of the devolution settlement in Wales. It recommended the transferring of further powers such as tax raising, and the Wales Act 2014 made some provision for this.

The Wales Act 2017 is an Act of the Parliament of the United Kingdom. It sets out amendments to the Government of Wales Act 2006 and devolves further powers to Wales. The legislation is based on the proposals of the St David's Day Agreement, which were not included in the Wales Act 2014.

One of the most important provisions is that the Act moved Wales from a conferred powers model to a reserved powers model, which is used in Scotland under the Scotland Act 1998. The Act repealed the provision of the Wales Act 2014 for a referendum in Wales on devolution of income tax. A conferred powers model is where the Assembly has only the powers conferred on it by the UK Parliament, whereas a reserved powers model would allow the Assembly to legislate on any matter, provided that the matter in question has not been expressly reserved from its competence.

The role of the Supreme Court in devolution

The Supreme Court, established in 2009, is the UK's final court of appeal for civil cases. It also rules on devolution cases, where it is required to interpret devolution statutes in order to clarify the legal and constitutional meaning of the UK's devolution settlements.

The relevant devolution statute outlies the 'legislative competence' (legal competence) of each legislature, for example the Scotland Act 1998, Northern Ireland Act 1998 and Government of Wales Act 2006. These Acts also enable the Supreme Court to rule that primary legislation, made by each of the devolved legislatures, is outside their legislative competence. This was demonstrated in the case of the Agricultural Sector (Wales) Bill, where the UK government had challenged the legality of a National Assembly for Wales Bill on the basis that the Bill went beyond the powers specified in the Government of Wales Act 2006.

The Supreme Court ruled that the Bill was within the Assembly's legislative competence.

COVID-19 and delegated legislation

The (enabling) Coronavirus Act 2020 led to many statutory instruments being used in response to the evolving COVID-19 pandemic in 2020–22. These statutory instruments covered aspects such as: lockdowns, travel restrictions, employment and support allowances, and changes to statutory sick pay.

> **KEY TERMINOLOGY**
>
> **reserved powers model:** under this model, the Senedd is allowed to legislate on matters that are not reserved to the UK Parliament. Matters that remain reserved to the UK Parliament include defence and foreign affairs.

Figure 3.2 The Supreme Court is an important source of judgments relating to devolution

Control of delegated legislation

A huge amount of delegated legislation is passed each year by non-elected individuals and bodies. For that reason, it is important that the passing of this legislation is controlled. There are two types of control – parliamentary and judicial.

Parliamentary controls

There are several ways in which Parliament controls delegated legislation.

Affirmative resolution
This is where the statutory instrument has to be laid before both Houses of Parliament and they must expressly approve the measure. Where used, this is an effective control.

Negative resolution
This is where the statutory instrument is published but no debate or vote takes place. It may be annulled by a resolution of either House of Parliament.

About two-thirds of statutory instruments are passed via negative resolution and therefore are not actually considered before Parliament. They merely become law on a future specified date and so afford limited control over the delegated authority.

Super-affirmative procedure
This is sometimes required to oversee legislative reform orders issued under the **Legislative and Regulatory Reform Act 2006**. The super-affirmative procedure provides Parliament with more power to scrutinise the proposed delegated legislation. Reports must be produced and each House of Parliament must expressly approve the order before it can be made.

Consultation
Many enabling Acts require consultation with interested parties or those who will be affected by the delegated legislation. Consultation is an effective control but not all enabling Acts require consultation, which limits its usefulness. The enabling Act itself is a form of control as it sets the parameters and procedures for the delegated power.

Joint Committee on Statutory Instruments
All statutory instruments are subject to review by the Joint Committee on Statutory Instruments (JCSI), which reports to the House of Commons or House of Lords on any statutory instrument that it identifies as needing special consideration and could cause problems. Its control is limited by the fact that it can only make recommendations to the Houses of Parliament rather than compel it to take on board its suggestions.

Judicial controls

A statutory instrument can be challenged by someone who has been directly affected by the law. The process for challenge is called judicial review and takes place in the King's Bench Division of the High Court. The person making the challenge asks the judge to review the legislation and decide whether it is ultra vires ('beyond powers'). If so, the delegated legislation will be declared void (without legal force or binding effect).

Procedural ultra vires
Procedural ultra vires is where the procedures laid down in the enabling Act for making the statutory instrument have not been followed (e.g. consultation was required but not carried out).

> ### *Agricultural Horticultural and Forestry Industry Training Board* v *Aylesbury Mushrooms Ltd* (1972)
> The enabling Act required interested parties to be consulted before making the law. They were not and therefore the correct procedure had not been followed.
>
> The delegated legislation was therefore declared as procedurally ultra vires.

Substantive ultra vires
Substantive ultra vires is where the delegated legislation goes beyond what Parliament intended.

Customs and Excise v Cure and Deeley Ltd (1962)
The Customs and Excise Commissioners tried to impose a tax and decide the amount to be collected but this went beyond the power conferred by Parliament.

Unreasonableness
The delegated legislation can be challenged as being unreasonable if the person making it has taken into account matters which they ought not to have done or not taken into account matters which they ought to have done. Even if that test is passed, it still needs to be proved that it is a decision that no reasonable body could have come to.

Associated Provincial Picture Houses Ltd v Wednesbury Corporation (1947)
A cinema was allowed to open on Sundays but its licence barred under 15s from attending. The cinema challenged this on the grounds that it was unreasonable but the courts disagreed.

> **KEY TERMINOLOGY**
>
> **procedural ultra vires:** where the procedures laid down in an enabling Act for making a statutory instrument have not been followed (e.g. consultation was required but not carried out). Literal meaning: 'beyond the powers'.
>
> **substantive ultra vires:** where delegated legislation goes beyond what Parliament intended.

> **GRADE BOOST**
>
> Give a case for each of these judicial challenges:
> - procedural ultra vires
> - substantive ultra vires
> - unreasonableness.

> **STRETCH AND CHALLENGE**
>
> Look around your local area and see if you can spot any byelaws, for example banning ball games in the park. Make a list or take a picture on your phone. Why are these byelaws made at a local level?

Figure 3.3 Unreasonableness in delegated legislation can be challenged

When considering parliamentary controls, be aware of the **Legislative and Regulatory Reform Act 2006**. This gives the government wide powers to make delegated legislation. It allows ministers to issue statutory instruments to amend legislation. The Act is controversial because it is seen to be an enabling Act that removes the constitutional restriction on the Executive introducing and altering laws without assent or scrutiny by Parliament.

> **EXAM SKILLS**
>
> Exam questions on delegated legislation may require you to explain an aspect of the topic or you may be required to apply the law (e.g. the controls that could be used) to a hypothetical example to reach a conclusion.

Table 3.1 Advantages and disadvantages of delegated legislation

ADVANTAGES	DISADVANTAGES
Flexibility: delegated legislation is often used to amend existing legislation. It is easier to use delegated legislation than to pass a new Act of Parliament.	**Lack of control**: most SIs are passed using the negative resolution procedure. This is a loose control of delegated legislation. In addition, if consultation is not required it is not carried out, so is also a limited control.
Time: Parliament does not have time to debate and pass all the laws needed to run the country effectively. It barely has time for the 70 Acts per year it does pass.	**Undemocratic**: it is often argued that laws should be made by those elected to do so. Delegated legislation is made by unelected individuals/bodies.
Speed: it is far quicker to introduce a piece of delegated legislation than a full Act of Parliament. Orders in Council can be used in an emergency when a law is needed very quickly.	**Sub-delegation**: the power to make the delegated legislation is often sub-delegated to those not given the original authority to pass law, for example from a government minister to a department and then to a group of experts. This further distances it from the democratic process.
Expertise: delegated legislation is made by specialised government departments which have experts in the relevant field. MPs do not have that technical expertise.	**Volume**: so much delegated legislation (about 30,000 SIs) is made each year that laws can be difficult to find and keep up with.
Local knowledge: byelaws are made by local authorities that are familiar with the needs of their local area and people. Parliament does not have the same local awareness.	

SUMMARY: DELEGATED LEGISLATION

→ Parliament delegates power to make law to another person/body
→ Power delegated by an enabling Act
→ Main forms of delegated legislation are:
- statutory instruments (SIs) made via either affirmative resolution or negative resolution
- byelaws
- Orders in Council

→ **Devolution**: in Wales: Government of Wales Acts 1998, 2006, Wales Act 2014, Silk Commission, Wales Act 2017
→ Role of Supreme Court in devolution, e.g. Agricultural Sector (Wales) Bill
→ Control of delegated legislation: parliamentary:
- Affirmative resolution
- Negative resolution
- Consultation
- Joint Committee on Statutory Instruments (JCSI)

→ Control of delegated legislation (judicial):
- Procedural ultra vires
- Substantive ultra vires
- Unreasonableness

Advantages:
- Flexibility
- Time
- Speed
- Expertise
- Local knowledge

Disadvantages:
- Lack of control
- Undemocratic
- Sub-delegation
- Volume

3 Delegated legislation

TEST YOURSELF

1. What is the name of an Act that delegates the authority to make law?
2. Which type of delegated legislation is made at the time of an emergency?
3. Which type of delegated legislation is made by local authorities?
4. What does ultra vires mean?
5. Name one parliamentary control on delegated legislation.
6. Explain substantive ultra vires.
7. Which is a stronger control – affirmative or negative resolution procedure?
8. Name two advantages of delegated legislation.
9. Name two disadvantages of delegated legislation.
10. Who makes statutory instruments?

EXAM PAST PAPER QUESTIONS

WJEC Sample Assessment Materials

The Welsh Parliament has recently been concerned by the number of Welsh language protesters in and around the Senedd in Cardiff Bay. Some of the Welsh language protesters have also been defacing buildings and property around the area with Welsh graffiti and posters. The Welsh Parliament is asking for additional powers to be given by Parliament to enable the Senedd to introduce controls over protesters. Louisa Jones is a passionate protester in favour of increased use of the Welsh language and is seeking to challenge the delegated powers by way of judicial review so that she can continue protesting.

Advise Louisa on the ways in which the delegated powers could be controlled. [28]

Eduqas – AS Level – October 2020
Explain the judicial controls on delegated legislation. [6]

Eduqas – A Level – May 2018
Read the text below and answer part (a).

The Environment Department has recently become concerned by the increase in un-cleared dog mess across the country. Parents have also started to become quite vocal about the mess and a small group descended upon the Parliament to make a complaint and to stage a protest.

(a) Explain, with examples, what is meant by delegated legislation. [6]

And

Read the scenario below and answer part (b).

The Environment Department would like to pass a statutory instrument imposing a £5,000 fine for any dog owners who do not clean up their dog mess.

(b) Using the scenario above and applying your understanding of delegated legislation, advise the Environment Department on the ways in which their delegated powers could be controlled. [18]

4 Statutory interpretation

What is a statute?

A statute is a law made by Parliament, otherwise known as an Act of Parliament. It is primary legislation and is the highest source of law.

What is statutory interpretation?

Parliament makes the law and judges apply it. In doing this they create precedents for future cases to follow. Statutory interpretation is the procedure by which a judge works out the meaning of words in an Act of Parliament and how this applies to the facts of the case before them. In most cases, the meaning of statutes is clear and a judge's role is simply to determine how this law applies to the facts of the case before them.

However, occasionally words require interpreting. There are a number of reasons why judges need to interpret statutes.

- A broad term is used. This may be deliberate if it covers more than one possibility and to allow the judge some flexibility. The judge still has to decide the meaning to be applied to the case before them. An example is the word 'type' in the Dangerous Dogs Act 1991, which means dogs of the 'type' known as the pit bull terrier, which the court held to include not only pedigree pit bull terriers but also dogs with a substantial number of characteristics of pit bulls. The Act was also interpreted in *Brock v DPP* (1993).
- Changes in the use of language. Language use changes over time, for example 'gay'. The issue of how language has changed was also the subject of the interpretation in *Cheeseman v DPP* (1990).
- Ambiguous words. Some words have more than one meaning and the judge has to decide which meaning applies, for example 'bar' or 'wind' are words with more than one meaning.

Figure 4.1 The Supreme Court is the final court of appeal for all UK civil cases, and criminal cases from England, Wales and Northern Ireland

GRADE BOOST

Think of some further reasons why judges may need to interpret statutes.

› A drafting or other error. An error in the drafting of a statute may not have been picked up during the Bill stage.
› New developments. Changes in technology can sometimes mean that an older Act of Parliament does not seem to cover a modern situation, for example *Royal College of Nursing* v *DHSS* (1981), when subsequent medical methods and advances may not have been foreseen at the time the Act was passed.

Approaches to statutory interpretation

Judges use four different rules or 'approaches' when dealing with a statute that requires interpretation. They are free to use any of the four approaches in combination with the other aids to interpretation discussed in this section.

Literal rule

The judge gives the words contained in the statute their ordinary and plain meaning even if this causes an absurd result. Many people think this should be the first rule applied by judges in the interpretation of an unclear statute.

Figure 4.2 *Whiteley* v *Chappel* (1968) demonstrates the literal rule

Whiteley v *Chappel* (1868)

In this case, it was an offence to 'impersonate anyone entitled to vote' at an election. The defendant had pretended to be a dead person and taken their vote. He was found not guilty of the offence as the judge interpreted the word 'entitled' literally. As a dead person is no longer 'entitled' to vote, the defendant had done nothing wrong.

Golden rule

If the literal rule causes an absurd result, the judge can take a more flexible approach to rectify the absurdity. Courts can take either a narrow or a wide interpretation considering the statute as a whole. With both the golden and literal rules, judges use internal (intrinsic) aids (anything within the Act itself, such as its titles and headings; see page 29).

Adler v *George* (1964)

s3 Official Secrets Act 1920 states that it is an offence to obstruct a member of the armed forces 'in the vicinity of' a 'prohibited place'. The defendant in the case had obstructed an officer in an army base (a 'prohibited place') and argued that the natural meaning of 'in the vicinity of' means in the surrounding area or 'near to' and not directly within. Had the judge applied the literal rule, the defendant could have escaped prosecution, but the judge used the golden rule to reasonably assume the statute to include both within and around the prohibited place.

Mischief rule

Laid down in **Heydon's Case (1584)** to allow the judge to look for the 'mischief' or problem the statute in question was passed to remedy. It directs the judge to use external (extrinsic) aids (elements beyond the Act, such as case law; see page 30) and look for Parliament's intention in passing the Act.

Elliot v Grey (1960)

It is an offence under the **Road Traffic Act 1930** to 'use' an uninsured car on the road. In this case, a broken-down car was parked on the road but could not be 'used' because its wheels were off the ground and its battery had been removed. The judge decided that the **Road Traffic Act 1930** was passed to remedy this type of hazard and, even though the car could not be 'used' on the road, it was indeed a hazard to other road users.

Figure 4.3 *Elliot* v *Grey* (1960) demonstrates the mischief rule

Purposive approach

Purposive approach is similar to the mischief rule in that it looks for the intention or aim of the Act. This approach has become more common since the UK joined the EU, due in part to the different way that European laws are drafted. While UK laws are wordier and suit a literal interpretation, EU laws are more vaguely written, requiring the judge to construct a meaning. Lord Denning was a supporter of the use of the purposive approach and giving judges more discretion when interpreting Acts. Judges look for the 'purpose' of the Act or, as Lord Denning said, the 'spirit of the legislation'.

STRETCH AND CHALLENGE

Look up the case of *Isle of Wight Council* v **Plat (2017)**. Summarise the facts of the case. In this case the magistrates and the High Court initially used the literal rule to decide the father had not committed an offence. When the case went to the Supreme Court on appeal, how did they use the purposive approach to overrule those decisions and decide the father had committed an offence?

Magor and St Mellons Rural District Council v Newport Corporation (1950)

Lord Denning, sitting in the Court of Appeal, stated 'we sit here to find out the intention of Parliament and of ministers and carry it out, and we do this better by filling in the gaps and making sense of the enactment than by opening it up to destructive analysis'.

Lord Simmons criticised this approach when the case was appealed at the House of Lords, calling this approach 'a naked usurpation of the legislative function under the thin disguise of interpretation'. He suggested that 'if a gap is disclosed, the remedy lies in an amending Act'.

> **STRETCH AND CHALLENGE**
>
> Think of an advantage and disadvantage for each of the four rules, to help you to consider how to evaluate them. Here are some examples:
>
> **Literal rule**
> **Advantage:** respects parliamentary sovereignty.
> **Disadvantage:** can cause absurd results.
>
> **Golden rule**
> **Advantage:** gives judges discretion and puts right absurdities caused by literal rule.
> **Disadvantage:** judges given power to interpret what is constitutionally the role of the legislator.
>
> **Mischief rule**
> **Advantage:** the most flexible of the rules and allows judges flexibility when dealing with statutes.
> **Disadvantage:** this approach was developed when parliamentary supremacy was not fully established and common law was the primary source of law. It is felt that the mischief rule gives too much power to the unelected judiciary to interpret the 'will of Parliament'.
>
> **Purposive approach**
> **Advantage:** flexible and seeks the purpose or reason why the Act was passed.
> **Disadvantage:** described by Lord Simonds as 'a naked usurpation of the judicial function, under the thin disguise of interpretation'.

> **GRADE BOOST**
>
> When answering a question on statutory interpretation, it is important to apply all four rules and give a case example for each. Other aids to interpretation may also be necessary to give a complete answer to a problem scenario style question.

Aids to interpretation

As well as the four main approaches to statutory interpretation, a judge can use other aids to help determine the meaning of a statute. These can also be divided into internal (intrinsic) aids and external (extrinsic) aids.

Presumptions

These may be regarded as intrinsic, as they refer to presumptions of the Act itself, but they can also be seen as neither intrinsic nor extrinsic. The court will start with the presumption that certain points are applicable in all statutes, unless explicitly stated otherwise. Some of the main presumptions are:

- Statutes do not change the common law.
- Mens rea (guilty mind) is required in criminal cases.
- The Crown is not bound by any statute.
- Statutes do not apply retrospectively.

Internal (intrinsic) aids

Intrinsic aids are found within the Act itself. Examples are:

- the long title to the Act
- preamble: normally states the aim of the Act and intended scope
- headings
- schedules
- interpretation sections.

Rules of language

Judges can use other words in the statute to help give meaning to specific words that require interpretation.

Ejusdem generis

Ejusdem generis means 'of the same kind'. Where general words follow a list of specific words, the general words are limited to the same kind/class/nature as the specific words.

> ### *Powell v Kempton* (1899)
> A statute stated that it was an offence to use a 'house, office, room or other place for betting'. The defendant was using a ring at a racecourse. The court held that the general term 'other place' had to include other indoor places because the specific words in the list were indoor places and so the defendant was found not guilty.

Expressio unius est exclusio alterius

Expressio unius est exclusio alterius means 'express mention of one thing is the exclusion of all others'.

> ### *R v Inhabitants of Sedgley* (1831)
> In this case, it was held that, due to the fact the statute stated 'lands, houses and coalmines' specifically in the Act, this excluded application to other types of mine.

Noscitur a sociis

Noscitur a sociis means 'a word is known by the company it keeps'. Words in a statute must be read in context of the other words around them.

> ### *Muir v Keay* (1875)
> A statute required the licensing of all venues that provided 'public refreshment, resort and entertainment'. Defendant argued his café did not fall within the Act because he did not provide entertainment. Court held the word 'entertainment' in the Act referred to refreshment houses, receptions and accommodation of the public, not musical entertainment, and therefore did include the defendant's café.

STRETCH AND CHALLENGE

Try to think of your own hypothetical example for each of the rules of language.

External (extrinsic) aids

With both the mischief and purposive approach, the judge is directed to use external or extrinsic aids. These are found outside of the Act and include:

- dictionaries and textbooks
- reports, for example from the Law Commission
- historical setting
- treaties
- previous case law.

Hansard

Perhaps the external aid that has caused the most problems is Hansard – the daily record of parliamentary debate during the passage of legislation. Some argue that it acts as a good indicator of Parliament's intention; however, its use has been subject to limitations.

Traditionally, judges were not allowed to consult Hansard to assist them in the interpretation of statutes to reinforce the separation of powers. Lord Denning disagreed with this approach and said in the case of Davis v Johnson (1979) that: 'Some may say, and indeed have said, that judges should not pay any attention to what is said in Parliament. They should grope about in the dark for the meaning of an Act without switching on the light. I do not accede to this view.' The House of Lords disagreed with him and held that the prohibition on using Hansard should stand. However, the key case of Pepper v Hart (1993) finally permitted the use of Hansard, albeit in limited circumstances. This was confirmed in the case of Three Rivers District Council v Bank of England (No. 2) (1996).

Figure 4.4 Hansard, the daily record of parliamentary debate during the passage of legislation

> ### Wilson v Secretary of State for Trade and Industry (2003)
> The House of Lords stated that Hansard could be used to look for the meanings of words but not to read the general debates to look for Parliament's intention. The House of Lords was also of the opinion that the statements of one or two ministers in a debate did not necessarily represent the intention of Parliament. Therefore, the Wilson case has restricted the use of Hansard so that only statements made by an MP or other promoter of legislation can be looked at by the court, and other statements recorded in Hansard must be ignored.

Human Rights Act 1998

The Human Rights Act 1998 (HRA) incorporates into UK law the European Convention on Human Rights. Under s3 HRA, courts are required 'so far as it is possible to do so, primary and subordinate legislation must be read and given effect in a way which is compatible with convention rights'. If the statute cannot be interpreted to be compatible then the court can issue a declaration of incompatibility under s4. This asks the government to change the law to bring it in line with the convention. They can use the fast-track procedure to make amendments quickly but there has to be a 'compelling reason' to do so and, under s10(2), the issuing of a declaration of incompatibility is not necessarily a compelling reason.

Section 2 also requires judges to take into account any previous decision of the European Court of Human Rights (ECtHR), though they are not bound by it.

GRADE BOOST
Look carefully at what the question is asking. Some exam questions ask for all the aids available to judges, whereas others focus on just one or two types of aid such as Hansard. Remember to include as many case examples as you can, not just for the rules of interpretation but the other aids too.

Be prepared to discuss s3 and s4 Human Rights Act 1998 in a statutory interpretation question and the implications for statutory interpretation of these sections.

GRADE BOOST
Make sure you cite s3 and s4 Human Rights Act 1998 and understand how they apply to this topic. In addition, be sure to know some cases on the use of Hansard. Examiners are looking for a range of case law and an understanding of how the law has evolved.

KEY TERMINOLOGY
declaration of incompatibility: issued under s4 Human Rights Act 1998, this gives senior judges the power to question the compatibility of legislation with human rights. The declaration is sent to Parliament. It does not allow judges to strike out laws.

SUMMARY: STATUTORY INTERPRETATION

→ Judges sometimes need to interpret Acts of Parliament (statutes) due to:
  - ambiguous terms
  - broad terms
  - changes in the use of language
  - error
→ Judges can use four approaches to interpretation:
  - **Literal rule**: *Whiteley v Chappel* (1968)
  - **Golden rule**: *Adler v George* (1964)
  - **Mischief rule**: *Elliot v Grey* (1960)
  - **Purposive approach**: *Magor and St Mellon's Rural District Council v Newport Corporation* (1950)

Judges use other 'aids' to help them interpret statutes:
→ **Intrinsic aids**:
  - The long title to the Act
  - Preamble
  - Headings
  - Schedules
  - Interpretation sections
→ **Extrinsic aids**:
  - Dictionaries and textbooks
  - Reports, e.g. from the Law Commission
  - Historical setting
  - Treaties
  - Hansard
  - Previous case law: *Pepper v Hart* (1993), *Three Rivers* (1996), *Wilson* (2003)
  - Rules of language: *ejusdem generis*, *noscitur a sociis*, *expressio unius est exclusio alterius*
  - Presumptions
→ **Human Rights Act 1998 (HRA)**:
  - **Section 2**: judges must 'take into account' precedents of the ECtHR (persuasive precedent only)
  - **Section 3**: interpret statutes' compatibly 'so far as possible'
  - **Section 4**: declaration of incompatibility
  - **Section 10**: Parliament can change an incompatible law using a fast-track procedure if there is a compelling reason

---

STRETCH AND CHALLENGE

Research and find the case of *Ghaidan v Godin-Mendoza* (2004) regarding the issue of human rights when interpreting statutes. What happened in the case and how did human rights apply? What is the current approach regarding interpreting statutes' compatibly with human rights?

EXAM SKILLS

Exam questions on statutory interpretation may require you to 'explain' an aspect of the topic or you may be required to 'apply' the rules to a hypothetical example to reach a conclusion.

Use Table 4.1 as a guide on how to approach the rules of statutory interpretation.

Table 4.1 Approaching the rules of statutory interpretation

Literal rule	Golden rule
Explain the rule	Explain the rule
Give a case example	Give a case example
Advantage	Advantage
Disadvantage	Disadvantage
APPLY to the scenario	APPLY to the scenario
Mischief rule	**Purposive approach**
Explain the rule	Explain the rule
Give a case example	Give a case example
Advantage	Advantage
Disadvantage	Disadvantage
APPLY to the scenario	APPLY to the scenario
Intrinsic aids and extrinsic aids	**CONCLUSION**
Identify and explain some intrinsic and extrinsic aids and apply them	Decide which rule you would apply

4 Statutory interpretation

TEST YOURSELF

1. State four reasons for statutory interpretation.
2. What is the literal rule?
3. To which rule does the *Elliot v Grey* (1960) case apply?
4. Name a case in which the golden rule was applied.
5. What is the correct approach when dealing with an 'apply' question on this topic?
6. What are the three questions applied for the mischief rule?
7. What is the purposive approach?
8. What power does s3 Human Rights Act 1998 give judges in respect of statutory interpretation?
9. If judges cannot 'stretch the meaning' of words far enough under s3, what power do they have?
10. When can a judge use the golden rule?

KEY TERMINOLOGY

charge: the decision that a suspect should stand trial for an alleged offence.

EXAM PAST PAPER QUESTIONS

WJEC – AS Level – Unit 1 – May 2019
Read the fictitious statute and the scenario below and answer the question that follows.

Following concerns raised in Parliament about the importation of some wildlife products from countries where those species are endangered, Parliament passed the Protection of Endangered Species (Fictitious) Act 2017.
Section 1 of the Act makes it an offence for 'any person to knowingly be in possession in the United Kingdom of any wildlife product that has been imported into the United Kingdom unless he has possession of a sales licence'.
Section 2 makes it an offence for any person to 'import or seek to import into the United Kingdom any wildlife product unless he has an import licence'.
Derek owns a shop in which he sells artefacts from abroad. His premises are raided by police officers and several products are seized. The products seized are found to contain fur from an endangered Brazilian monkey, which is a protected species under the Act. Derek is **charged** under Section 1. Derek has no sales licence but claims that he did not know that the products contained this fur, however, the customs officials note that the accompanying papers written in Portuguese refer to the fur. Derek does not read or speak Portuguese. Derek used a trader called Ronaldo, based in London, to import the products from Brazil.

Using the rules of statutory interpretation, advise Derek and Ronaldo as to whether any offences have been committed in this situation. [28]

Eduqas – AS Level – May 2019
1. Explain the mischief and purposive rules of statutory interpretation. [6]
2. Read the text to the right and answer part (a).

'In addition to the main rules of interpretation there are a number of secondary aids to the construction of statutes available to a judge and these are often neglected.'

(a) Explain the rules of language available to a judge when interpreting a statute. [6]

Read the scenario below and answer part (b).

Police Powers (fictitious) Social Media Surveillance Act 2017 reads as follows:
Section 1 'If the police suspect an individual to be, about to be or to have been involved in the commission of a crime, they can use surveillance techniques to monitor all social media accounts of the suspect.'
Section 2 'If the police uncover incriminating evidence against the individual on their social media accounts, they may be granted a warrant to arrest that person and/or search their property.'
Carol was convicted of theft of a designer bag 10 years ago. She paid a fine for the offence and carried out community service. She has been searching online for a new designer bag to buy and has contacted Jenny, a fashion blogger, via social media, asking her advice on which bag to 'snatch before it's gone'. The police have arrested Carol on suspicion of planning another theft and have applied for a warrant to search her property.

(b) Using your knowledge of statutory interpretation, advise Carol as to whether the actions of the police are lawful. [18]

Eduqas A Level Law May 2019
Explain the literal and golden rules of statutory interpretation. [5]

33

5 Judicial precedent

Elements of precedent

Figure 5.1 The common law has evolved over time

KEY TERMINOLOGY

stare decisis: to stand by the previous decisions.

original precedent: a decision in a case where there is no previous legal decision or law for the judge to use.

The English legal system is a common law system. This means that much of the law has been developed over time by the courts, through cases. The basis of this system of precedent is the principle of *stare decisis*. This requires a later court to use the same reasoning as an earlier court where the two cases raise the same legal issues, which in turn ensures a just process.

When a case comes to court and its issues have never been decided before, judges will create a new precedent, which future judges will follow in similar cases. This is called original precedent.

1. The court hierarchy

This establishes which decisions are binding on which courts. Decisions of higher courts are binding on lower courts.

Supreme Court
The highest appeal court on civil and criminal matters, the Supreme Court binds all other English courts. It was bound by its own decisions as the House of Lords until 1966 (see House of Lords 1966 Practice Statement on page 36).

Court of Appeal
It has criminal and civil divisions that do not bind each other. The Supreme Court and the House of Lords (which was the highest court in the UK before 2009) bind both divisions. The Criminal Division is not usually bound by its previous decisions.

High Court
The High Court consists of the divisional courts: King's Bench Division (criminal appeals and judicial review), Chancery Division and Family Division, and the ordinary High Court. The Court of Appeal, the Supreme Court and the old House of Lords bind the High Court.

5 Judicial precedent

Crown Court
All the courts above bind this court. Decisions from the Crown Court do not form **binding precedent** but can form **persuasive precedent**; they are not bound by their previous decisions.

Magistrates' and county courts
Bound by the High Court, Court of Appeal, old House of Lords and Supreme Court. They do not produce precedents; they are not bound by their previous decisions.

European Court of Human Rights
Under **s2 Human Rights Act 1998**, English courts must take into account decisions from the European Court of Human Rights (ECtHR) but they are not bound by them.

2. Accurate law reporting
This allows legal principles to be collated, identified and accessed. The earliest form of law reporting was in Year Books from around 1272. Modern reporting dates from the Council on Law Reporting, established in 1865. There are also private series of reports, for example the All England Law Reports (All ER), as well as reporting in journals (such as the *New Law Journal*) and newspapers (such as *The Times*). More recent innovations include online systems (such as LEXIS) and the internet.

> **KEY TERMINOLOGY**
>
> **binding precedent:** a previous decision that has to be followed.
>
> **persuasive precedent:** previous decision that does not have to be followed.
>
> *ratio decidendi:* 'the reason for the decision'. This is the binding element of precedent, which must be followed.
>
> *obiter dicta:* 'things said by the way'. This is not binding and is only persuasive.

Figure 5.2 Law reports are now available in print and online

3. The binding element
The judgment contains four elements:

- Statement of material (relevant) facts.
- Statement of legal principle(s) relevant to the decision (the *ratio decidendi:* 'the reason for the decision').
- Discussion of legal principles raised in argument but not relevant to the decision (*obiter dicta:* 'things said by the way').
- The decision or verdict.

The binding element in future cases is the *ratio decidendi*. This is the part of the judgment that future judges, depending on their position in the court hierarchy, have to follow. The *obiter dicta*, while never binding, may have strong persuasive force. This is known as persuasive precedent, and it is particularly persuasive if it comes from the higher courts such as the Court of Appeal, the Supreme Court and the old House of Lords.

Other forms of persuasive authority include:

> decisions of other common law jurisdictions (especially from Australia, Canada and New Zealand)
> decisions of the Privy Council: see *Attorney General for Jersey v Holley* (2005)
> writing of legal academics.

4. Flexibility and certainty

The system of binding precedent, sometimes referred to as the doctrine of judicial precedent, does create the certainty needed to allow people to plan and lawyers to advise. It also creates flexibility, as precedent enables the common law to develop.

How judicial precedent works

Normally, judges will follow an earlier precedent. The other options of overruling, reversing, distinguishing and departing are means of avoiding having to follow a difficult (awkward) precedent.

> **Following**: if the facts are similar, the precedent set by the earlier court is followed.
> **Overruling**: higher courts can overrule lower courts.
> **Distinguishing**: where a lower court points to material differences that justify the application of different principles.
> **Departing**: where, in certain circumstances, a court can depart from its previous decision.
> **Reverse**: on appeal, a higher court may change the decision of a lower court.

KEY TERMINOLOGY

per incuriam: 'made by mistake'. Before the 1966 Practice Statement this was the only situation in which the House of Lords could depart from its previous decisions.

House of Lords Practice Statement 1966

Until 1966, the House of Lords was bound by its own previous decisions (see *London Street Tramways v LCC* (1898)) unless the decision had been made *per incuriam* (by mistake). In 1966, the House of Lords issued the Practice Statement. This stated that the House of Lords will normally be bound by its previous decisions but may depart, as well as on the grounds of *per incuriam*, when it is right to do so.

The cases in Table 5.1 show where the House of Lords departed from previous decisions.

Table 5.1 Cases where the House of Lords departed from previous decisions

Case	Significance regarding the Practice Statement
Conway v Rimmer (1968)	This first use of the Practice Statement only involved technical law on discovery of documents.
Herrington v British Railways Board (1972)	The first major use of the Practice Statement, on the duty of care owed to child trespassers.
Anderton v Ryan (1985)	This precedent was overruled in *R v Shivpuri* (1986).
Rondel v Worsley (1969)	This precedent was overruled in *Hall v Simons* (2000).
R v Caldwell (1982)	The Practice Statement was later used in *R v G and another* (2003) to overrule the decision in Caldwell on recklessness in criminal law.
R v R (1991)	This set a new precedent for the law on rape within marriage, overruling a precedent set hundreds of years before.
Pepper v Hart (1993)	The Practice Statement was used to allow the courts to look at Hansard for the purpose of statutory interpretation.
Austin v London Borough of Southwark (2010)	The Supreme Court stated that the Practice Statement applied to it.

Court of Appeal (Civil Division)

While normally bound by its own previous decisions, it can depart from such decisions if any of the exceptions established in *Young v Bristol Aeroplane Co* (1944) and *R (on the application of Kadhim) v Brent London Borough Housing Benefit Review Board* (2001) apply. It can depart when:

> the previous decision was made *per incuriam*
> there are two previous conflicting decisions
> there is a later, conflicting House of Lords decision
> a proposition of law was assumed to exist by an earlier court and was not subject to argument or consideration by that court.

The Court of Appeal (Criminal Division) is also not bound to follow its previous decisions where, in the previous case, the law was misapplied or misunderstood resulting in a conviction (*R v Taylor* (1950)); extra flexibility is given to the Criminal Division because it deals with the liberty of the citizen.

The Privy Council
The Privy Council is the final appeal court for Commonwealth countries. The general rule is that decisions of the Privy Council do not bind English courts but its decisions do have strong persuasive authority.

> **KEY TERMINOLOGY**
>
> **Privy Council:** the final appeal court for most Commonwealth countries.

R v James and Karimi (2006)
The Court of Appeal applied the Privy Council's judgment in *Attorney General for Jersey v Holley* (2005) rather than the House of Lords' judgment in *R v Smith (Morgan)* (2001).

Judges as law makers
Are judges making law, or are they simply interpreting existing law? Should judges make law or should this be left to Parliament? The following cases clearly support the view that judges do make law.

Airedale NHS Trust v Bland (1993)
The House of Lords stated that this case raised wholly moral and social issues that should be left to Parliament to legislate for; nevertheless, they had no option but to give a decision.

R v Dica (2004)
The Court of Appeal overruled a previous decision and held that a defendant could be criminally liable for recklessly infecting another person with HIV. The court gave this decision despite Parliament refusing to introduce legislation to impose such liability.

Kleinwort Benson Ltd v Lincoln City Council (1998)
In this case, the House of Lords changed a long-standing rule regarding contract law, despite the Law Commission's recommendations that this rule should be changed by Parliament.

Director of Public Prosecutions (DPP) v Jones (1999)
The House of Lords concluded that statutory highway laws replaced unrealistic restrictions on the public.

Fitzpatrick v Sterling Housing Association Ltd (2000)
The House of Lords held that same-sex partners could establish a familial link for the purposes of the Rent Act 1977, overruling the Court of Appeal's decision that this should be left to Parliament to determine.

Gillick v West Norfolk and Wisbech Area Health Authority (1985)
The House of Lords, faced with no lead from Parliament on the issue in this case, held that a girl under 16 could be given contraceptive services without her parents' consent, if she is mature enough to make up her own mind.

Donoghue v Stevenson (1932)
In this famous case, Lord Aitken developed the law of negligence, that is the principle that those who harm others should pay compensation for damage done.

R v R (1991)
The House of Lords established that rape within marriage was a crime, overruling a precedent set hundreds of years before, and after pleas from the House of Lords for several years to Parliament to change the law in this area.

Simmons v Castle (2012)
The Court of Appeal stated in this case that judges should change the law if Parliament intended them to do so, and a failure to do so would be a breach of faith. This case concerned changes to the Legal Aid, Sentencing and Punishment of Offenders Act 2012.

Figure 5.3 *Fitzpatrick* v *Sterling Housing Association Ltd* (2000) allowed same-sex partners to establish a familial link for the purposes of the Rent Act 1977

Advantages and disadvantages of judicial precedent

Table 5.2 Advantages and disadvantages of judicial precedent

Advantages	Disadvantages
A just system: like cases will be treated the same.	Developments contingent on accidents of litigation: case law only changes if someone is determined enough to pursue a case through the courts.
Impartial system: treating like cases in similar ways promotes impartiality.	Retrospective effect: unlike legislation, case law applies to events which took place before the case came to court (see *SW* v *UK* (1996); *R* v *C* (2004)).
Practical rules: case law is always responding to real-life situations. As a result, there is a large body of detailed rules that give more information than statutes.	Complex: while case law gives us detailed practical rules it also means that there are thousands of cases, and identifying relevant principles and the *ratio decidendi* can be difficult and time consuming.
Certainty: claimants can be advised that like cases will be treated in a similar way and not by random decisions of judges.	Rigid: depending on the place of the court in the hierarchy, precedent can be very rigid, as lower courts are bound to follow decisions of higher courts even where they think the decision is bad or wrong.
Flexibility: case law can change quickly to meet changes in society.	Undemocratic: judges are not elected and should therefore not be changing or creating laws, unlike Parliament that has been elected to do so.

> **KEY TERMINOLOGY**
>
> **retrospective effect:** laws that operate on matters taking place before their enactment, i.e. they change what was legal or illegal yesterday.

The Supreme Court and precedent

The Constitutional Reform Act 2005 established the Supreme Court to replace the House of Lords. The aim was to achieve a complete separation between the UK's senior judges and the Upper House of Parliament, which is also called the House of Lords, emphasising the independence of the law lords and removing them from the legislature.

In August 2009, the justices moved out of the House of Lords (where they sat as the Appellate Committee of the House of Lords) into their own building. They sat for the first time as the Supreme Court in October 2009.

The Supreme Court is the highest appeal court in the UK. It also took over from the Privy Council the role of hearing cases concerned with the devolution of Wales, Scotland and Northern Ireland. The impact of Supreme Court decisions extends far beyond the parties involved in a case, shaping society and affecting our everyday lives. However, the Supreme Court does not have the power to strike out legislation.

> **STRETCH AND CHALLENGE**
>
> Research the two cases of *Balfour* v *Balfour* (1919) and *Merritt* v *Merritt* (1970) to see how distinguishing works in practice.
>
> Research the following cases and debate the effect of s2 Human Rights Act 1998 on judicial precedent:
> - *Morris* v *UK* (2002)
> - *R* v *Boyd* (2002)
> - *R* v *Horncastle* (2009)
> - *Al-Khawaja and Thaery* v *UK* (2009)
> - *Kay* v *Lambeth London BC* (2006)
> - *Manchester City Council* v *Pinnock (No. 2)* (2011)

> **GRADE BOOST**
>
> In the exam you are often required to apply the principles of precedent to a scenario-type question, so you must fully understand how it works and be able to apply the principles with supporting legal authority.
>
> It is also important that you are up to date with the functions of the Supreme Court and recent cases decided there. You can find Supreme Court decisions at the following link: www.supremecourt.uk/decided-cases.

SUMMARY: JUDICIAL PRECEDENT

→ Precedent is based on *stare decisis* ('let the decision stand')
→ Courts must follow precedents set by courts higher in the hierarchy
→ The Supreme Court is usually bound by its own decisions, but since the 1966 Practice Statement it can depart from a previous decision where it is right to do so
→ The Court of Appeal (Civil Division) is bound by its previous decisions, unless any of the exceptions in Young's case apply
→ *Ratio decidendi* is the reason for the decision and creates a binding precedent for future cases
→ *Obiter dicta* ('things said by the way'). It is the rest of the judgment and does not create a binding precedent
→ Judges in later cases do not have to follow precedent if they can use an avoidance technique: distinguish; overrule; reverse
→ Advantages of precedent: creates certainty; flexibility; consistency; saves time
→ Disadvantages of precedent: can be rigid; complex and slow

EXAM SKILLS

An exam question on precedent may require you to do one of the following:
- explain an aspect of the topic for AO1, or
- apply the law on precedent for AO2 (e.g. to a hypothetical scenario) and reach a conclusion.

TEST YOURSELF

1. What is judicial precedent?
2. What is the *ratio decidendi*?
3. What is *obiter dicta*?
4. How can judges avoid precedent?
5. Why did the House of Lords feel it was necessary to issue the Practice Statement?
6. Is the Court of Appeal bound by its own decisions?
7. What does *stare decisis* mean?
8. Name two advantages of precedent.
9. Name two disadvantages of precedent.
10. What effect does **s2 Human Rights Act 1998** have on judicial precedent?

5 Judicial precedent

EXAM PAST PAPER QUESTIONS

WJEC – AS Level – Unit 1 – 2019 and 2022
1. Explain the techniques used by judges to avoid an awkward precedent. [10]
2. Explain what is meant by the *ratio decidendi* and *obiter dicta* of a judgment. [10]

WJEC – AS Level – Unit 1 – May 2018
Read the information below and answer the question that follows.

In 1998 a case was heard in the Civil Division of the Court of Appeal. In the case, a husband and wife had tried to enter into a binding contract together where she agreed to pay him £100 a month in return for him cleaning their marital home. The Civil Division of the Court of Appeal held that married couples are not able to enter into binding contracts of this nature together. In 2018, the High Court is due to hear a case involving Tom and Dan who have a civil partnership. They have been separated, living apart for 2 years. Tom wishes to enter into a binding contract with Dan for him to do the gardening in Tom's new home.

Using the doctrine of judicial precedent, advise Tom as to the possible outcomes of this case. [28]

Eduqas – AS Level – Component 1 – October 2020
Explain the use of the Practice Statement in relation to judicial precedent. [6]

Eduqas – A Level – Component 1 – June 2019
Read the text below and answer the question that follows.

In 2013 the Supreme Court in the (fictitious) case of *R* v *Phillips* held that the defence of self-defence for the crime of murder was only available where the defendant had been put in an unavoidable and imminent situation where life was at stake. In 2016, Miriam killed her husband, Wyn. She had planned to do so over a period of months because she had been repeatedly physically abused by him over many years. The prosecution claimed that on a basis of the (fictitious) Supreme Court decision in *R* v *Phillips* that the defence of self-defence was not available to her. Miriam's case has now reached the Court of Appeal and they are considering the options available to them.

Using your knowledge of judicial precedent, advise the Court of Appeal as to the possible outcomes for Miriam's case. [15]

6 Civil courts

Civil process, structure, courts and appeals

The civil justice system is used to settle disputes between private individuals or organisations.

> The person bringing the action is called the **claimant**.
> The person defending the action is known as the **defendant**.

The case has to be proved **on the balance of probabilities** (the standard of proof), and the burden to prove the case is on the claimant. The claimant is normally seeking some form of **remedy**, which could be the payment of compensation or an injunction. Often, these cases are settled out of court.

KEY TERMINOLOGY

claimant: the person bringing the action. Before 1 April 1999, this person was known as the plaintiff.

defendant: the person defending the action (e.g. the person accused of a crime).

on the balance of probabilities: the standard of proof in a civil case where the burden is on the claimant to establish that it is more likely than not the defendant did what they are claiming.

remedy: a solution in a civil case to 'right the wrong'. Examples are an injunction or the payment of damages.

first instance (trial court): a court in which the first hearing of a case takes place. It is distinguished from an appellate court, which hears appeal cases.

litigation: the process of taking a case to court.

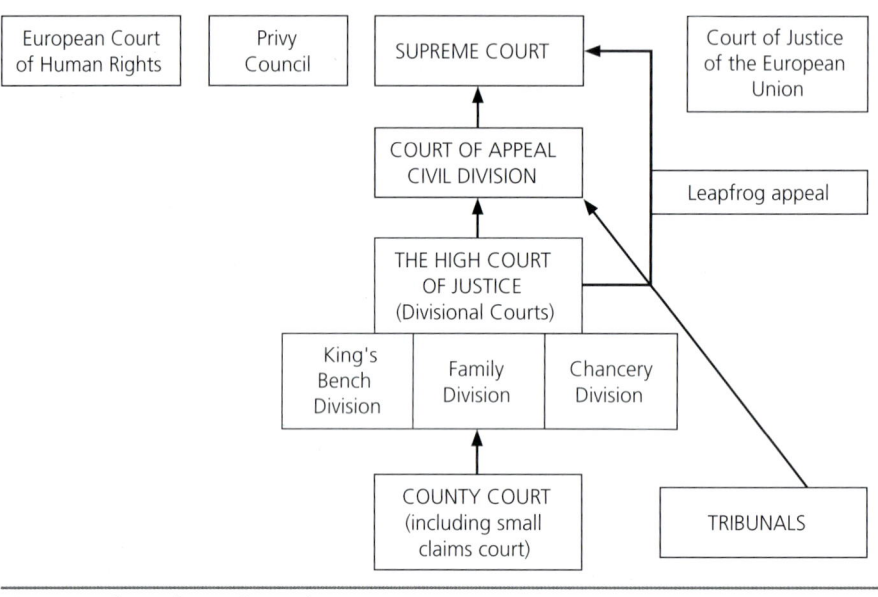

Figure 6.1 The civil court hierarchy

Civil court structure

The county court and the High Court are the two **first instance** civil courts, which means that **litigation** for civil cases is started in one of these courts.

Since the implementation of reforms proposed by Lord Woolf in the mid-1990s, civil cases fall into three categories, called tracks. The allocation of a case to a particular track determines where it will be tried and the process under which it is dealt with.

> The small claims track (tried in the small claims court):
> - cases up to £10,000, but
> - £1,500 for personal injury claims, or
> - £1,000–£5,000 for personal injuries arising from a road traffic accident, or
> - £1,000 for housing cases.
> The fast track (cases between £10,000 and £25,000): tried in the county court.
> The multi-track (cases above £25,000): tried in either the county court or the High Court.

County court
County courts have jurisdiction over:

> claims under contract and tort
> cases for the recovery of land
> disputes over partnerships, trusts and inheritance up to a value of £30,000.

High Court
All civil cases not dealt with in the county court are dealt with in the High Court. Cases in the High Court are organised according to case type and are heard in one of the three separate courts, called divisions. Each division has separate functions and differing jurisdictions. The three divisions are:

> King's Bench Division
> Family Division
> Chancery Division.

Appeals in civil law

High Court
Each division of the High Court has an appellate division called a divisional court (e.g. the King's Bench Divisional Court). A first instance case in a High Court division is heard by a single judge, whereas an appeal case in a divisional court is heard by three judges. The divisional courts hear appeals from the county court. The King's Bench Divisional Court can also hear appeals from the (criminal) Magistrates' Court and Crown Court as well as conducting judicial review proceedings.

Court of Appeal Civil Division
The head of this division is called the Master of the Rolls. The Court of Appeal (Civil Division) hears appeals from the three divisions of the High Court, divisional courts and county courts. It also hears appeals from the Tribunal Service. Usually, a minimum of three judges will sit, although this can increase to five. All appeals need 'leave to appeal' (permission).

Supreme Court
The Supreme Court replaced the House of Lords as the top of the hierarchy of English courts, providing a second level of appeal. There are 12 judges, with at least one from Scotland and one from Northern Ireland. They must sit as an uneven panel, so three, five, seven, nine, or, in rare cases, such as ruling on Brexit, judges can hear an appeal. A case will only be heard in this court if leave to appeal is granted, either by the Supreme Court or by the court against whose decision the appeal is being sought (usually the Court of Appeal). The court hears only 50 cases on average every year. Permission to appeal is only granted if the case is certified as involving a point of law of general public importance. From a decision of the Court of Appeal, there is further appeal to the Supreme Court, but only if the Supreme Court or Court of Appeal gives permission to appeal.

Leapfrog appeals
These go directly from the High Court to the Supreme Court ('leapfrogging' over the Court of Appeal). They can only be made on the granting of a certificate by the High Court judge and where the case involves a point of law of general public importance, which either concerns the interpretation of a statute or involves a binding precedent of the Court of Appeal or Supreme Court that the trial judge must follow. In addition, the Supreme Court must give permission to appeal.

Civil appeal process
Either party to a dispute may make an appeal. Permission to appeal will be granted where the appeal has a realistic chance of success or where there is a compelling reason why the appeal should be heard. Appeals are generally made to the next level of judge in the court hierarchy.

GRADE BOOST
1. Find out some features of each of the three tracks. How do they try to remedy the three main problems Woolf found of cost, delay and complexity?
2. Find out about Money Claim Online.

Civil procedure before the 1999 reforms

Before the Woolf reforms in April 1999, there were two separate sets of civil procedure, depending on where the case commenced. Cases in the High Court used the 'White Book' and cases in the county court used the 'Green Book' (these are the rules of civil procedure and practice and had either a white cover or a green cover). There were also different procedures for commencing a case. A case in the county court was started with a summons, but a case in the High Court was started with a writ. The system could be confusing for plaintiffs because of the differing rules of procedure and evidence.

Lord Woolf was tasked with reforming the civil justice system. This culminated in 'Access to Justice: Final Report', which was published in 1996 and soon became known as the Woolf Report. He concluded that the civil justice system of the time had some key flaws:

- Expensive: his report found that costs often exceeded the amount in dispute.
- Delays: cases took an average of three to five years to reach the trial stage.
- Complex: with differing procedures for the county and High courts, litigants found the system complex. As a result, more lawyers would be hired, increasing costs for plaintiffs.
- Adversarial: there was an emphasis on exploiting the system rather than cooperation between parties.
- Unjust: there was an imbalance of power between the wealthy represented party and the underrepresented party. This was a particular problem with out-of-court settlements, with one party under pressure to settle more than the other.
- Emphasis on oral evidence: most evidence did not need to be presented orally and could have been pre-assessed by the judge. This made trials slow and inefficient and led to an increase in costs, with expert witnesses charging high fees.

As a result of the findings of the Woolf Report, the main recommendations were put into effect in the **Civil Procedure Rules 1998**, which came into force in April 1999.

They represent one of the biggest reforms of the civil justice system, with some people questioning whether such wide reforms were needed. Rule 1.1(2) states:

> *Dealing with a case justly and at proportionate cost includes, so far as is practicable –*
> *(a) ensuring that the parties are on an equal footing;*
> *(b) saving expense;*
> *(c) dealing with the case in ways which are proportionate –*
>   *(i) to the amount of money involved; (ii) to the importance of the case; (iii) to the complexity of the issues; and (iv) to the financial position of each party;*
> *(d) ensuring that it is dealt with expeditiously and fairly; and*
> *(e) allotting to it an appropriate share of the court's resources, while taking into account the need to allot resources to other cases; and*
> *(f) enforcing compliance with rules, practice directions and orders.*

STRETCH AND CHALLENGE

Find more out about the civil appeals process. This is another area that can be examined and it is important to understand the appeal routes and what can happen as a result of an appeal.

The Woolf reforms

Several significant changes were made as a result of the **Civil Procedure Rules 1998**.

Simplified procedure
The overriding aim of this reform was to provide a common procedural code for the county and High courts. Some terminology was changed to make it more accessible for claimants (previously plaintiffs).

Pre-action protocols
One of the biggest themes of the reforms was to encourage parties to cooperate. Pre-action protocols are designed to encourage parties to exchange information as early as possible, be in contact with each other and cooperate over the exchange of information. Their overall aim was to encourage parties to settle out of court, reducing costs and delay.

Case management
One of the most important reforms has been judges becoming the managers of cases, with proactive powers to set timetables and sanction parties that do not cooperate. The overall aim of this reform was to pass the management of the case to the court and not the parties, to improve efficiency and reduce costs.

Alternative dispute resolution
Parties can postpone proceedings for one month to attempt to settle the case using alternative dispute resolution (ADR) (see page 47). Courts should also actively promote its use. However, in *Halsey v Milton Keynes General NHS Trust* (2004), the Court of Appeal said the courts cannot force parties to ADR as it might be against Article 6 European Convention on Human Rights (the right to a fair trial).

Sanctions
The overriding aim of the reforms was to ensure that cases are as efficient and cost effective as possible. With judges taking on the role of case managers, they have been given powers to issue sanctions where parties do not follow the timetables they set or delay unnecessarily. Two main sanctions are:

- adverse award of costs
- order for a case to be struck out (in part or full).

In *Biguzzi v Rank Leisure plc* (1999) it was held that striking out a case would only happen if it was proportional and there were other options available to deal with delay. In *UCB v Halifax (SW) Ltd* (1999), however, it was stressed that a lax approach should not be used for serious cases and courts should use the new powers available to them.

Briggs Review
The latest review was undertaken by Lord Briggs in 2016. His report outlined five main weaknesses afflicting the civil courts:

- Lack of adequate access to justice for ordinary individuals and small businesses. This is due to excessive costs associated with taking a civil case to court along with the risk that the losing party pays some or all of the winner's costs. In addition, civil courts can be intimidating for litigants in person, therefore necessitating the use of expensive legal representation.
- Inefficiencies arising from excessive paperwork and outdated IT facilities.
- Unacceptable delays in the Court of Appeal, caused by its excessive workload.
- Serious under-investment in provision for civil justice outside London.
- Widespread weaknesses in the processes for the enforcement of judgments and orders.

Lord Briggs put forward several proposals: the main one was for setting up an online court. The COVID-19 pandemic and the need for remote hearings means that this proposal has already started to develop already.

Flexible operating hours of courts
His Majesty's Courts and Tribunal Service have piloted flexible opening hours (between 8.30am and 8.30pm) in some civil courts to see if this will provide greater flexibility and accessibility for litigants and other court users.

Civil courts and the COVID-19 pandemic
To help ensure the court service continued during the pandemic, His Majesty's Courts & Tribunals Service (HMCTS) permitted hearings to be conducted via phone and video. Digitisation of the courts and online hearings have developed rapidly since March 2020. The Law Society reported in July 2021 that:

'Feedback from our members suggests that some cases can be dealt with perfectly well remotely, and this should remain a permanent feature of the justice system.'

For example, the Law Society contends that remote hearings are working well in simple hearings such as procedural matters, directions and case management hearings where the hearing is limited to judges and lawyers. In more complex or contested cases (e.g. family or criminal law where witnesses or live evidence needs to be given), remote hearings are less appropriate and a more traditional hearing remains more suitable.

Nightingale courts were also set up to tackle the backlog of cases that built up during the pandemic and prior due to court closures. Judges and magistrates sat for additional days and hours.

Civil procedure

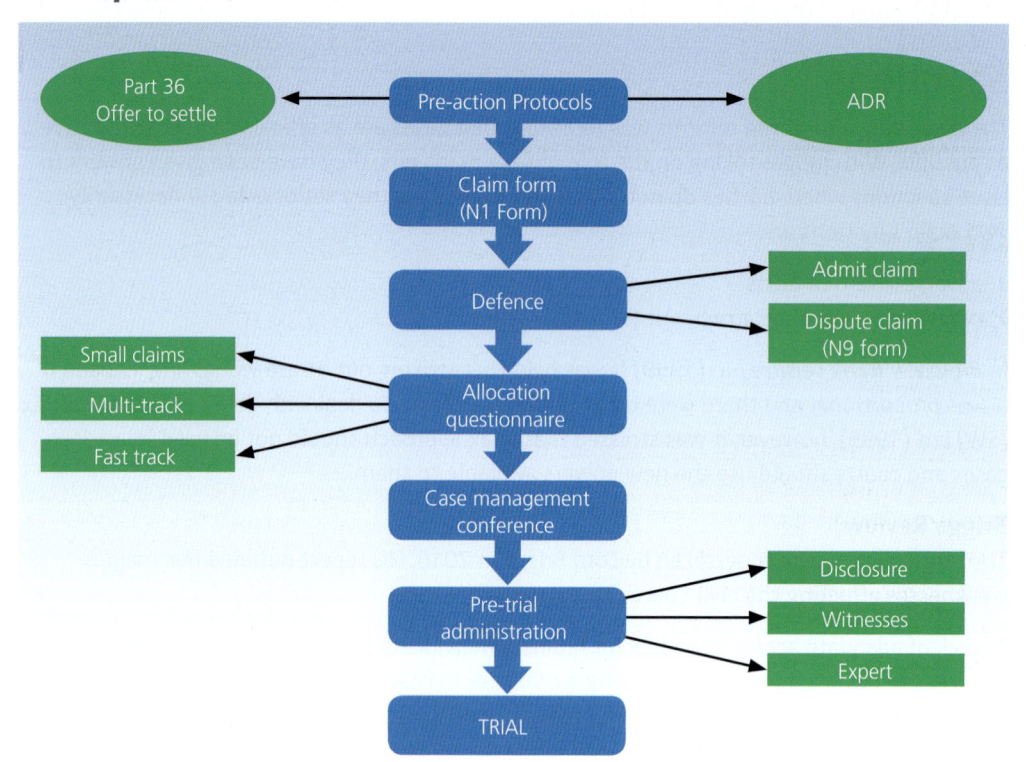

> **EXAM SKILLS**
>
> Exam questions on civil procedure may require you to 'explain' an aspect of the topic such as the three tracks, civil appeals or the main features of civil justice. You may also be required to 'analyse and evaluate' for a higher order response. This is more likely to be on the sub-topics of ADR or tribunals that follow.

Figure 6.2 The civil procedure

Juries in civil cases

Juries are used in less than 1 per cent of civil cases. They decide whether or not the claimant has proved their case 'on the balance of probabilities' (the standard of proof) and they also decide the amount of damages the defendant should pay the claimant if they decide in favour of the claimant.

Parties have the right to jury trial only in the following cases, according to **s69 Senior Courts Act 1981** for High Court cases and **s66 County Courts Act 1984** for cases in the county court:

> false imprisonment
> malicious prosecution
> fraud.

S11 of the Defamation Act 2013 removed the presumption of a trial by jury for defamation cases. Defamation cases are therefore tried without a jury unless the court orders otherwise.

Why are juries used rarely in civil cases?
- They tend to award excessive damages.
- They do not have to give reasons for their decisions.
- Excessive cost.

Juries in personal injury cases

In personal injury civil cases in the King's Bench Division of the High Court, the parties can apply to the judge for a jury trial but it is rarely granted. The Court of Appeal in the case of *Ward* v *James* (1966) laid down guidelines for personal injury cases, which, in effect, stopped the use of juries for personal injury cases. They said that personal injury cases should normally be tried by a judge sitting alone, because such cases involve assessing compensatory damages that need to relate to conventional scales of damages, with which the judge will be familiar.

Singh v *London Underground* (1990) and *H* v *Ministry of Defence* (1991) show how the courts have proved reluctant use juries in personal injury cases.

Alternative dispute resolution

Reasons for alternative dispute resolution

Alternative dispute resolution (ADR) is a method of resolving issues out of court. Litigation is not always the most appropriate means of resolving a dispute because of the:

- complexity of legal procedures
- delay it causes in resolution
- cost of court action
- intimidating atmosphere of the courts
- public nature of court action
- adversarial nature of court action, which can result in a deterioration of the relationship between the parties.

ADR is encouraged by Part 1 of the Civil Procedure Rules 1998 (CPR), where it is part of a judge's role in active case management (where the judge plays an active role in resolving the case) to encourage ADR where appropriate. ADR is only used in civil cases. This is because in criminal cases, there is too much at risk to justify an alternative to the criminal justice system. ADR has grown in popularity over the last 50 years, and is now increasingly seen as a compulsory step in the process rather than an alternative. Indeed, some parties have been 'punished' with an adverse costs order (where one party pays the other's costs) for refusing to cooperate in a method of ADR.

GRADE BOOST

Make the connection between the Civil Procedure Rules 1998 (CPR) and the promotion of ADR in order to encourage more settlements out of court. CPR, which were introduced following Lord Woolf's Report, require active case management and include 'encouraging parties to use an ADR procedure if the court considers it to be appropriate'. Rule 26.4 allows judges to stay (i.e. suspend) court proceedings where they feel that ADR should be attempted. The judge can make this decision with or without the agreement of the parties.

Under Rule 44.5 of CPR, if a court believes that a case could have been more effectively settled via ADR it can punish the party who insisted on a court hearing by penalising them in costs. So, for example, even if a claimant wins the case, they might not have their costs paid by the losing party. The application of this rule is demonstrated in the case of *Dunnett* v *Railtrack* (2002).

GRADE BOOST
A further case demonstrating the reluctance to use juries in personal injury cases is *Singh* v *London Underground* (1990). The request was refused on the basis it involved wide issues and technical points.

EXAM SKILLS
Juries have three roles – in the criminal, civil and coroners' courts. You need be familiar with all aspects of a jury's role as you could both be asked a question on the role of the jury (requiring you to explain all three roles) or asked about just one of the jury's roles. The other roles are covered within the topic of criminal process on page 57.

Figure 6.3 Mediation : the mediator's role is to facilitate rather than to actively shape the outcome

GRADE BOOST
Halsey v *Milton Keynes General NHS Trust and Steel* v *Joy and Halliday* (2004) are also important. Research the Court of Appeal judgment given in these two appeals.

47

Forms of ADR

Table 6.1 Forms of ADR, with advantages and disadvantages

TYPE OF ADR	DESCRIPTION
ARBITRATION Commonly used in commercial and contract cases, and most notably in high-profile sports cases. 	This is the most formal method and is adjudicative (disputes are resolved through a neutral third party who has the authority to bind the parties to the terms of a decision). The parties agree to let an independent arbitrator make a binding decision. Many contracts include a *Scott* v *Avery* clause to agree pre-contractually to arbitrate in the event of a dispute. The decision of the arbitrator is called an 'award'. There can be a hearing but many cases are conducted using 'paper arbitration', when parties submit their arguments and evidence in writing to the arbitrator as opposed to making oral submissions at a hearing. An award can be appealed only on the basis of serious irregularity in the proceedings or on a point of law (s65 Arbitration Act 1996). The European Directive on Alternative Dispute Resolution (which came into force in July 2015) requires all EU countries to have ADR available for consumer disputes. It also requires ADR providers to meet certain standards.
MEDIATION Commonly used in family disputes or any area where a relationship needs to be maintained. 	The parties are encouraged to come to their own settlement with the help of a neutral third party or mediator who acts as a go-between. The mediator's role is to facilitate rather than to actively shape the outcome. The Ministry of Justice funds the Civil Mediation Online Directory. Individuals can search the directory for a mediation provider that is local to them. The cost of mediation is based on a fixed fee, depending on the value of the dispute. Not automatically binding unless a contract is drawn up.
CONCILIATION Commonly used in industrial disputes. 	The third party plays a more active role in the proceedings to push towards a settlement.
NEGOTIATION Used in most cases at the outset of a dispute. 	Resolving the dispute between the parties themselves; can involve solicitors. Can be completed using letters, email, phone, meeting, etc. At its most basic, it involves returning faulty goods to a shop; at its most complex, it involves solicitors and settlement offers being exchanged.

6 Civil courts

LEGAL AUTHORITY/EXAMPLE	ADVANTAGES	DISADVANTAGES
Arbitration Act 1996 Institute of Arbitrators *Scott* v *Avery* (1855) European Directive on Alternative Dispute Resolution	The parties have discretion over the choice of arbitrator via the Institute of Arbitrators. The hearing procedure is left to the discretion of the parties; they can choose the venue, date, number of witnesses, etc. There is rarely any publicity. The award is binding and can be enforced by the courts. The arbitrator is an expert in the field.	Public funding is not available, so one party may have an advantage from the outset. Appeals are restricted in the arbitration process. Parties may feel they do not get their 'day in court'. If a legal point arises, there is not always a legal professional in the hearing.
Dunnett v *Railtrack* (2022) *Halsey* v *Milton Keynes NHS Trust* (2004) Neighbour disputes Mediation in divorce cases: under **s10 Child and Families Act 2014**, in most cases involving a dispute over finances or children, the parties are required to attend a Mediation Information and Assessment Meeting (MIAM) Small Claims Mediation Service Court of Appeal Mediation Scheme Online dispute resolution is available (e.g. www.mediate.com/odr) Centre for Effective Dispute Resolution (CEDR): commercial mediators	A private and confidential process. The parties enter into mediation voluntarily. Quick, cost effective and accessible. A good chance that the parties can maintain a relationship. CEDR reports 80% of cases are settled at mediation.	The dispute may end up going to court anyway if mediation fails, resulting in greater costs. Increasingly seen as a compulsory step in the process. Where parties are forced into mediation, there is a half-hearted commitment, decreasing the chances of success.
Advisory, Conciliation and Arbitration Service (ACAS) Early conciliation via ACAS	A cheaper option than litigation. A private and confidential process. ACAS adopts a 'prevention rather than cure' approach to dispute resolution. Process identifies and clarifies the main issues in the dispute. Conciliator plays an active role.	Heavily relies on the skills of the conciliator. The dispute may go to court anyway if conciliation fails, resulting in greater costs.
N/A	Completely private. Quick resolution, maintaining relationships. Relatively informal method of resolution.	Involving solicitors can make the process costly. Offers are often exchanged and are not agreed until the day of court, wasting time and money. People see it as a 'halfway house' and think that they are not receiving as much as if they had gone to court.

STRETCH AND CHALLENGE	GRADE BOOST

STRETCH AND CHALLENGE

In cases involving dispute over finances or children, divorcing couples are required to attend Mediation Information and Assessment Meetings (MIAMs). Do you think this causes resentment towards the system, or encourages people to be more amicable in their disputes? Will it eventually replace solicitors?

GRADE BOOST

When an examination question asks you about the **Civil Procedure Rules 1998** or **CPR** remember to talk about ALL the Woolf Reforms, not just ADR.

It is a common mistake for students to only discuss ADR in a civil procedure question.

In preparation for the examination, it is worth mentioning any recent cases you have researched that have involved ACAS, as examiners are always impressed by knowledge of current affairs. Also make sure that you mention all relevant sections of the **Arbitration Act 1996**.

Tribunals

Tribunals are an important part of the legal system and act as specialist courts for disputes in specialised areas, mainly welfare and social rights. For example, employment disputes are often resolved using a tribunal, as are immigration and social security disputes.

Tribunals are frequently seen as another alternative to the courts, but the biggest difference is that if the case fails at the tribunal stage, there is no redress to the courts, whereas if any other form of ADR fails, the parties still get the option of going to court to resolve their dispute.

There are three different types of tribunal:

› **Administrative**: these deal with disputes between individuals and the state over rights contained in social welfare legislation, such as social security, immigration and land.
› **Domestic**: these are internal tribunals used for disputes within private bodies, such as the Law Society and the General Medical Council.
› **Employment**: these are the most common use of tribunals. They deal with disputes between employees and employers over rights under employment legislation.

Tribunals date back to the birth of the welfare state and were established to give people a way of making sure their rights were enforced. When they were first introduced, there were more than 70 different tribunals, all with different procedures and administration. This led to over-complication and many users felt intimidated and confused by the system.

History of tribunals

1957: The Franks Committee recommended that tribunal procedures should be an example of 'openness, fairness and impartiality'. The recommendations were implemented in the **Tribunals and Inquiries Act 1958**.

1958: The Council on Tribunals was set up to supervise and review tribunal procedures. The Council would deal with complaints and submit recommendations for improvement. However, some people regarded it as a 'watchdog with no teeth', meaning it had very little power to make changes.

2000: Sir Andrew Leggatt: 'Tribunals for Users – One System, One Service'. This report marked a radical reform of the tribunal system, since Leggatt reported that tribunals lacked independence, coherence and were not user-friendly (see Table 6.2 for details).

2007: The **Tribunals, Courts and Enforcement Act** formalised and implemented most of Leggatt's reforms and contributed to the most radical shake-up of the tribunal system seen for many years.

Table 6.2 Leggatt recommendations

Leggatt recommendation	Explanation
A single Tribunal Service to be responsible for the administration of all tribunals.	This makes the Tribunal Service independent of its government department. The support that it gives to tribunals is unified both in procedure and administration.
Tribunals should be organised into divisions grouping together similar tribunals.	The divisions that were created are Education, Financial, Health and Social Services, Immigration, Land and Valuation, Social Security and Pensions, Transport, Regulatory and Employment. Each division is headed by a registrar who takes on case management duties in line with the Civil Procedure Rules (CPR) 1998.
The system should be user-friendly.	Users are encouraged to bring their own cases without legal representation. Written judgments should be given in plain English. Information about procedures, venues, etc. should be made freely available.
Single route of appeal.	Each division has a corresponding appeal tribunal, and only then will there be a redress to the Court of Appeal.

Tribunals, Courts and Enforcement Act 2007

This Act implemented many of Leggatt's reforms. In particular, Part 1 established a Tribunal Service that unified all the procedures and created a new structure that addressed many of Leggatt's concerns. There are now only two tribunals: the First Tier Tribunal and the Upper Tribunal, within which are chambers, or groups of tribunals with similar jurisdictions. The Upper Tribunal has the power to conduct a judicial review of a case that has been heard in the First Tier Tribunal, minimising the need for the courts to get involved in the case. All members are appointed by the Judicial Appointments Commission and are thus recognised as judges, which increases the status of tribunals. Further appeal from the Upper Tribunal is available to the Court of Appeal, but this is rare because of the well-structured system.

The whole system is headed by the Senior President of Tribunals who is responsible for assigning judges to the chambers, looking after their general welfare and helping with any issues. The president has the power to issue practice directions in order to help tribunal judges maintain a unified procedure across all the chambers.

Composition

Cases in the First Tier Tribunal are heard by a tribunal judge. Also, for some types of case, two specialist non-legal members sit with the judge to make the decision. These specialist members have expertise in the particular field of the tribunal, such as social care or housing. In employment tribunals there are also two lay members (e.g. one from an employers' organisation and one from an employees' organisation). One lay member represents the employer, the other represents the employee. The lay members are experts in their field and will have a clear understanding of employment issues.

The benefit of the lay members is that the tribunal judge has a clear and balanced understanding of the issues in the case. All non-legal members and judges are appointed by the Judicial Appointments Commission and are recognised as judges, which increases the status of tribunals. The system is headed by the Senior President of Tribunals who is responsible for assigning judges to their chambers and can issue practice directions (rules for tribunals to follow) to maintain a unified process.

The Wales Act 2017 established the role of a President of Welsh Tribunals to oversee devolved tribunals such as the Education Tribunal for Wales.

> **KEY TERMINOLOGY**
>
> **First Tier Tribunal:** part of the legal system that aims to settle the 'first instance' stage of legal disputes. It is split into seven chambers or specialist areas.
>
> **Upper Tribunal:** hears appeals from the First Tier Tribunal, and in some complex cases will act within a first instance jurisdiction.
>
> **lay (person):** someone who is not legally qualified.

Procedure

The procedure in tribunals is generally less formal than in the ordinary courts. Both sides must be given an opportunity to put their case. In some tribunals, such as employment and immigration tribunals, this is done in a formal way with the witness giving evidence and being cross-examined. Other tribunals operate in a less formal way.

There is now one clear appeal route under the **Tribunals, Courts and Enforcement Act 2007** from the First Tier Tribunal to the Upper Tier and then to the Court of Appeal. The grounds for appeal must relate to a point of law.

COURT OF APPEAL						
UPPER TRIBUNAL						
Administrative Appeals Chamber		Tax and Chancery Chamber		Lands Chamber	Asylum and Immigration Chamber	
FIRST TIER TRIBUNAL						
Social Entitlement Chamber	Health, Education and Social Care Chamber	War Pensions and Armed Forces Compensation Chamber	General Regulatory Chamber	Taxation Chamber	Land, Property and Housing Chamber	Asylum and Immigration Chamber

The employment tribunal operates separately from the First Tier tribunals.

The Council on Tribunals has now been replaced by the Administrative Justice and Tribunals Council, which is much more powerful in terms of reviewing the system, keeping it under control and advising the government on future reforms of the Tribunal Service. Tribunals are overseen by His Majesty's Court and Tribunal Service.

Employment tribunals

Employment tribunals are not included in the structure because it was felt that the types of disputes dealt with by employment tribunals were very different from the other tribunals, so the employment tribunal and the employment appeals tribunal remain distinct from the structure. From July 2013, fees were charged for both employment tribunals and employment appeal tribunals; however, these fees in employment cases have been removed following the case of **R v Lord Chancellor (2017)**, which adds to the cost effectiveness of employment tribunals.

Figure 6.4 A lay person is someone who is not legally qualified

Advantages and disadvantages of tribunals

Table 6.3 Advantages and disadvantages of tribunals

Advantages	Disadvantages
• Speed: there is a duty on the tribunal judges to take on case management duties, so they are able to impose strict timetables to ensure that most cases can be heard within one day. • Cost: parties are encouraged to take their own cases without the need for representation. This has been made even easier with the availability of application forms online and a more transparent Tribunal Service since the reforms. • Expertise: at least one member of the tribunal will be an expert in the relevant field, so this saves time explaining complex technicalities to a judge in court. • Informality: tribunals are much less formal than a court hearing, though they are more formal than other methods of ADR. The parties benefit from a private hearing and have the chance to maintain a relationship after the case is over. • Independence: because of the involvement of the Judicial Appointments Commission in appointing tribunal judges, the tribunal system is more transparent, independent and fair. The unified set of procedures and rules minimises the risk of inconsistencies between tribunals.	• Lack of funding: legal funding is available for some disputes; for example, a trade union may pay for your case if you are a member. However, funding is not always available, which can be detrimental to a person taking on a big company that has the benefit of expensive representation. In addition, fees for claims in the employment tribunal or employment appeal tribunal may prevent some people from pursuing a claim. • Delay: if the case is complex, there can be a delay in getting it heard. • Intimidated parties: parties may still feel intimidated and daunted at the prospect of taking a case to 'court', particularly without the comfort of having a legal representative. • Lack of precedent: tribunals do not operate a strict system of precedent, so the outcome of cases can be unpredictable. • Lack of legal representation: Hazel Genn, in 'The Effectiveness of Representation at Tribunals' (1989), found that those who did not use a lawyer had a success rate of 28% compared to 49% if they had used a lawyer. She also discovered that applicants lost most often when they appeared without representation against a legally represented respondent. Also, the average amount of award was higher in cases where the applicant had representation (£1,084) as compared to cases where applicant received no advice (£449).

6 Civil courts

SUMMARY: CIVIL COURTS

→ Civil justice settles disputes between private individuals and companies
→ Cases are claimant versus defendant; the claimant is seeking a remedy
→ Case depends on the standard of proof (balance of probabilities)
→ First instance courts are the county and High Courts
→ High Court has three divisions:
  - King's Bench
  - Family
  - Chancery
→ Three tracks for civil hearings:
  - Small claims
  - Fast track
  - Multi-track
→ Appeals happen at High Court Divisional Courts, Court of Appeal and Supreme Court
→ All appeals need leave to appeal
→ Leapfrog appeals go straight from the High Court to the Supreme Court
→ Lord Woolf's 'Access to Justice: Final Report' (1996) identified key flaws in the justice system:
  - Expensive
  - Delays
  - Complex
  - Adversarial
  - Unjust
  - Emphasis on oral evidence
→ Woolf Report's main recommendations were put into effect in the **Civil Procedure Rules (CPR) 1998**. Main reforms:
  - Case management
  - Three tracks
  - Increased ADR
  - Sanctions
  - Pre-action protocols
→ Lord Briggs Review of Civil Justice 2016 highlighted five key issues with civil justice and suggested establishing an online court
→ **Juries in civil cases**: less than 1 per cent of civil cases use juries
  - Juries decide for or against the claimant and amount of damages
  - **s69 Senior Courts Act 1981** and **s66 County Courts Act 1984** state that cases in the county court can allow for jury trial in cases of false imprisonment, malicious prosecution and fraud
  - Juries are no longer used in defamation cases (**s11 Defamation Act 2013**)
  - Juries are rarely used in personal injury cases: see *Ward v James* (1966)
→ **Alternative dispute resolution (ADR)**: alternative to litigation. Encourages settlements out of court
  - Four main methods of ADR:
    · Arbitration: binding decision. **Arbitration Act 1996**. *Scott v Avery* arbitration clause
    · Mediation: facilitative third party, e.g. MIAMs, Small Claims Mediation
    · Conciliation: active third party, e.g. ACAS, early conciliation
    · Negotiation: with or without lawyers; phone, email, letter, meeting

GRADE BOOST

When you are writing an essay on tribunals, make sure you include a little about the history of the tribunal system. More importantly, you need to show your knowledge of the current system and be able to cite the **Tribunals, Courts and Enforcement Act 2007** and its provisions.

Be prepared to talk about tribunals both as a topic in its own right, and as a form of ADR.

EXAM SKILLS

Exam questions on civil justice may require you to 'explain' an aspect of the topic such as the three tracks, civil appeals or the main features of civil justice. You may also be required to 'analyse and evaluate' for a higher order response. This is more likely to be on the sub-topics of ADR or tribunals.

→ **Tribunals**: specialist 'courts': an alternative to courts but the only avenue for some cases
- Three types: administrative, domestic, employment
- Franks Committee report recommended openness, fairness, impartiality
- Leggatt report led to **Tribunals, Courts and Enforcement Act 2007**, which introduced:
  - First Tier
  - Upper Tier
  - appeals to Court of Appeal
  - tribunal judges
- Organised by His Majesty's Courts and Tribunal Service
- Overseen by Administrative Justice and Tribunals Council
- Employment tribunals now charge a fee
- **Advantages**: cost, expertise, speed, independence
- **Disadvantages**: lack of funding, lack of precedent, delay, intimidated parties, lack of legal representation

TEST YOURSELF

1. What is the overriding objective in the Civil Procedure Rules?
2. What does it mean that cases should be dealt with 'justly' and with 'proportionate cost'?
3. What are the names of the two parties in civil disputes?
4. What is the standard of proof in a civil case?
5. Who bears the burden of proof in a civil case?
6. What are the three tracks to which a civil case can be allocated at first instance?
7. Which is the most formal method of ADR?
8. Which method of ADR involves the use of an active third party?
9. What are the two tribunal tiers?
10. What is the composition of tribunals?

EXAM PAST PAPER QUESTIONS

WJEC – AS Level – Unit 1 – May 2018
(a) Explain the composition and role of tribunals.   [8]
(b) Analyse and evaluate the advantages and disadvantages of the main methods of Alternative Dispute Resolution (ADR).   [24]

Eduqas – AS Level – May 2019
Analyse and evaluate the advantages and disadvantages of tribunals.   [18]

Eduqas – A Level – October 2020
Explain the main methods of alternative dispute resolution.   [10]

7 Criminal process: Structure and sentencing

The law lists many criminal offences to which a suspect can plead guilty or not guilty, but the procedure that follows arrest varies depending on the classification of offence that has been committed. Remember that, throughout the process, the suspects are innocent until proven guilty and at all times their **Article 6 ECHR** right to a fair trial should be upheld, and the courts have a duty under the **Human Rights Act 1998** to make sure this happens.

In terms of criminal procedure, every case has an initial hearing in the Magistrates' Court, even if it is only for the official passing over to the Crown Court. This is known as the **early administrative hearing**. The **Criminal Procedure Rules 2013** govern the pretrial and trial process in England and Wales.

Table 7.1 shows the three categories of offence in the English and Welsh legal system.

KEY TERMINOLOGY

Early administrative hearing: the first appearance at Magistrates' Court for all defendants suspected of a summary or indictable offence. This hearing considers legal funding, bail and legal representation.

Triable either way: mid-level crimes (e.g. theft, assault causing actual bodily harm) that can be tried in either the Magistrates' Court or Crown Court.

Table 7.1 Three categories of offence

Category of offence	Place of trial	Examples of offence
Summary	Magistrates' Court	Driving without a licence
		Taking a vehicle without consent
		Common assault
Triable either way	Magistrates' Court or Crown Court (the defendant chooses)	Theft
		Assault occasioning actual bodily harm
		Obtaining property by deception
Indictable	Crown Court	Murder
		Manslaughter
		Rape
		Robbery

Summary offences

Early administrative hearing at Magistrates' Court deals with administration such as:
- whether defendant should be bailed or remanded in custody
- what legal funding provisions are in place
- pre-sentence reports

↓ PLEAD GUILTY → Sentencing at Magistrates' Court

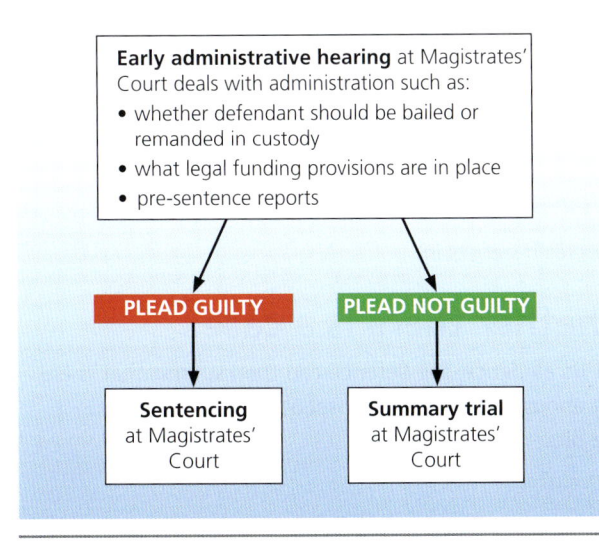

↓ PLEAD NOT GUILTY → Summary trial at Magistrates' Court

Figure 7.1 Process for summary offences

Indictable offences

Early administrative hearing at magistrates' court but **s51 Crime and Disorder Act 1998** stipulates that the magistrates must immediately send the case to Crown Court using committal proceedings

↓ PLEAD GUILTY → Sentencing at Crown Court

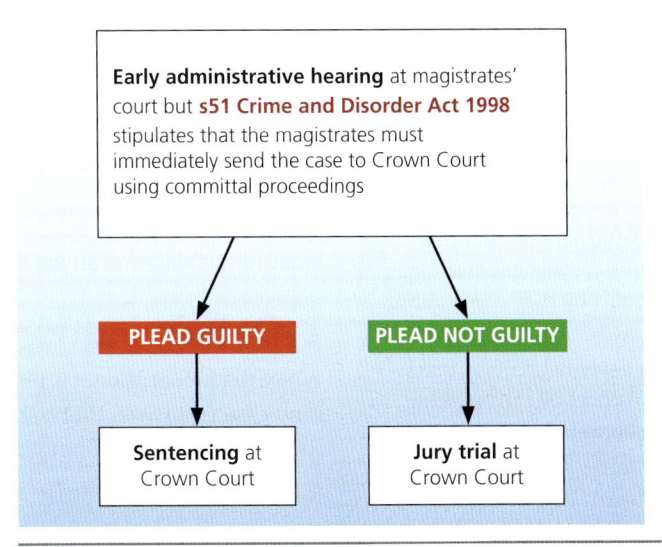

↓ PLEAD NOT GUILTY → Jury trial at Crown Court

Figure 7.2 Process for indictable offences

Triable either way offences

> **STRETCH AND CHALLENGE**
>
> In triable either way offences, the defendant has the option to choose whether or not they wish to have a trial by jury. Research the implications of choosing a trial by jury, and the arguments for and against abolishing the right to choose a trial by jury.

> **GRADE BOOST**
>
> Remember that magistrates have limited sentencing powers; they can sentence up to a one-year custodial sentence and an unlimited fine. The ability to sentence for up to one year for a single triable either way offence was introduced by the Judicial Review and Courts Act 2022. This was introduced in the hope that fewer cases would be referred to the Crown Court to alleviate some of the backlog of cases created by the pandemic. However, the sentencing powers for summary offences remains at a maximum of six months custody.

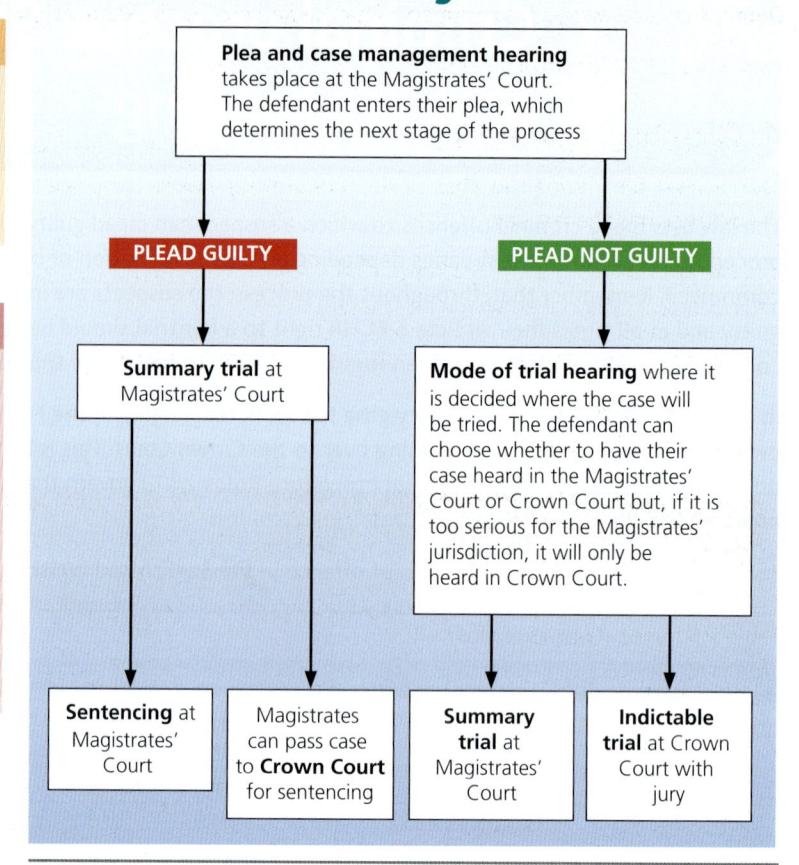

Figure 7.3 Process for triable either way offences

- **Plea and case management hearing** takes place at the Magistrates' Court. The defendant enters their plea, which determines the next stage of the process.
  - **PLEAD GUILTY** → **Summary trial** at Magistrates' Court
    - **Sentencing** at Magistrates' Court
    - Magistrates can pass case to **Crown Court** for sentencing
  - **PLEAD NOT GUILTY** → **Mode of trial hearing** where it is decided where the case will be tried. The defendant can choose whether to have their case heard in the Magistrates' Court or Crown Court but, if it is too serious for the Magistrates' jurisdiction, it will only be heard in Crown Court.
    - **Summary trial** at Magistrates' Court
    - **Indictable trial** at Crown Court with jury

> **KEY TERMINOLOGY**
>
> **burden of proof:** the responsibility placed on one party in a case to prove the allegation or claim. In criminal cases, this lies with the prosecution to prove that the defendant is guilty.
>
> **beyond reasonable doubt:** the standard of proof that is required in criminal cases. For a defendant to be guilty, the judge or jury must be convinced that there is no doubt that the defendant is guilty.
>
> **examination in chief:** the defence or prosecution questioning a witness in court by their own counsel.
>
> **cross-examination:** questioning of a witness in court by the opposing counsel.

The trial process

In both the Magistrates' and Crown Courts, the burden of proof lies with the prosecution, who have to prove beyond reasonable doubt that the defendant is guilty.

The procedure in the Magistrates' and Crown courts is essentially the same. However, there is no jury in the Magistrates' Court, and the magistrates are guided on the law by their clerk, as magistrates are not legally qualified.

1. Prosecution case

Prosecution delivers its opening speech to outline facts.

Prosecution calls its witnesses to support its case and conducts examination in chief.

Defence then cross-examines those witnesses.

Prosecution will re-examine those witnesses if necessary.

2. Determination of whether there is a case

When the prosecution has presented all its evidence, the defence can then submit that there is no case to answer; that is, there is not enough evidence to prosecute. If this submission is successful, a verdict of not guilty will be directed.

3. Defence case

Defence calls its witnesses to support its case and conducts examination in chief.

Prosecution then cross-examines those witnesses.

4. Closing speeches

Both sides make closing speeches to the jury or magistrates. The prosecution goes first so that the defence has the last say.

If in the Crown Court, the judge sums up the legal and factual issues, which should be balanced, and offers clear advice for the jury.

The jury or magistrates retire (leave the court) to aim for a unanimous verdict.

If the defendant is found not guilty, they are acquitted. If they are found guilty, the judge or magistrates deliver their sentence.

> **KEY TERMINOLOGY**
>
> **sentence:** the punishment given to someone who has been convicted of an offence. It can be imprisonment, a community sentence or a suspended sentence or discharge.

Figure 7.4 The Old Bailey is probably the most famous Crown Court, and is also known as the Central Criminal Court

Role of the Crown Court

The Crown Court hears serious, indictable cases such as rape, murder, manslaughter and robbery. The Courts Act 1971 established the Crown Court but its jurisdiction is now contained in the Supreme Court Act 1981.

Trials in the Crown Court are heard before a judge and a jury. Although the Crown Court is always described as singular, there are 77 court centres across England and Wales, for example in large towns.

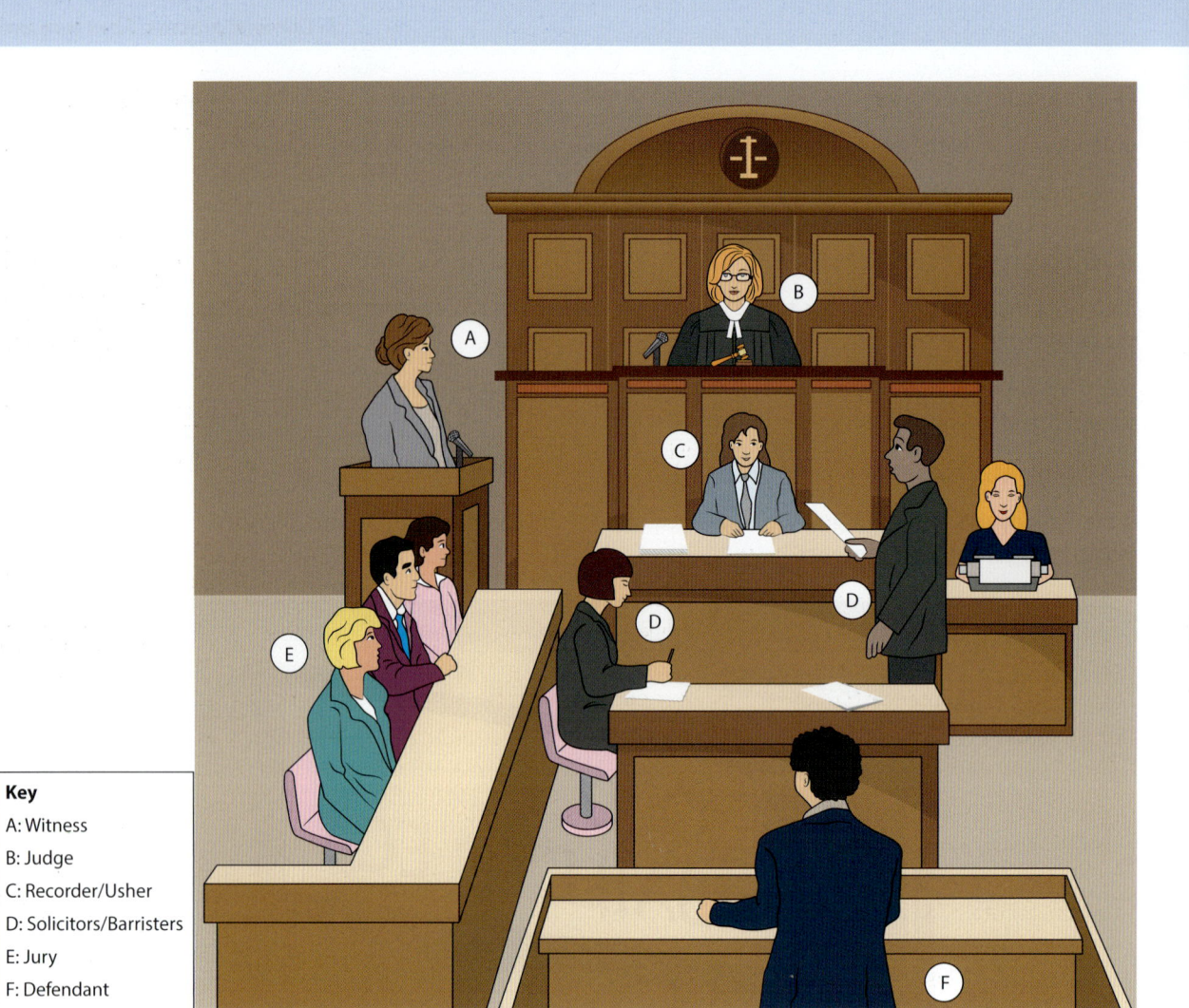

Key
A: Witness
B: Judge
C: Recorder/Usher
D: Solicitors/Barristers
E: Jury
F: Defendant

Figure 7.5 The layout of a court

The Crown Court has four basic duties:

> To try serious, indictable criminal offences such as murder, rape and robbery. Where the defendant pleads guilty, there will be no need for a jury; the judge will sentence.
> To carry out jury trials for the most serious offences, where the defendant has pleaded not guilty.
> To hear appeals from Magistrates' Courts; these will usually be summary offences.
> To sentence defendants from the Magistrates' Court where the defendant has had their trial there but the magistrates have passed the case to the Crown Court to sentence because a sentence greater than their powers is required.

The **Police, Crime, Sentencing and Courts Act 2022 (PCSC)** modernised the delivery of criminal justice by encouraging greater use of technology in courts, where appropriate. This makes permanent some of the temporary measures that were introduced by the **Coronavirus Act 2020**, which enabled court users to participate in and observe court proceedings via video and audio technology to improve the accessibility of courts.

GRADE BOOST

You should refer to the ECHR in every question on criminal process. Relevant articles for criminal process are:

- **Article 5 ECHR**: Right to liberty
- **Article 6 ECHR**: Right to a fair trial.

7 Criminal process: Structure and sentencing

Criminal appeals

Criminal cases, in the first instance, are heard either in the Magistrates' Court or the Crown Court. After several high-profile miscarriages of justice, the appeal system was reformed significantly under the **Criminal Appeal Act 1995**.

Appeals from Magistrates' Courts

Following a trial in the Magistrates' Court, two routes of appeal are open to a defendant, depending on what basis they want to appeal.

1 If the defendant wishes to appeal against conviction or sentence, they can appeal to the Crown Court as of right. This automatic right of appeal is open to the defence only if they pleaded not guilty. The appeal must be lodged within 28 days of the case finishing.

- Appeal against **conviction**: the procedure is the same as in the Magistrates' Court but is heard by a judge sitting with two magistrates.
- Appeal against sentence: the prosecution read out the facts and the defence can put forward mitigating factors relating to the offence or the offender. The Crown Court can then impose any sentence the magistrates could have given.

2 If they wish to appeal by way of **case stated**, they must appeal to the Divisional Court of the King's Bench Division of the High Court. This method can be used by the defence against a conviction, or by the prosecution if the defendant has been acquitted. This appeal route is based on a mistake having been made in the application of the law. This route of appeal is infrequently used. The divisional court can either allow or dismiss the appeal. They can also re-order a hearing before a new bench of magistrates.

3 A further appeal from the High Court is available to the Supreme Court but this will only happen if the matter is one of public importance.

> ### C v Director of Public Prosecutions (DPP) (1994)
> This case considered the issue of children having criminal responsibility. It was held that it was not to be presumed that children aged between 10 and 14 knew the difference between right and wrong, and therefore criminal activity will not always result in prosecution. The Divisional Court of the Queen's Bench Division (as it was then called) had wanted to change the law so that it was always presumed that a child aged 10–14 knew the difference between right and wrong, but the Supreme Court held that they were bound by precedent and were not at liberty to change the law.

Figure 7.6 Hierarchy and appeal routes of the criminal courts

KEY TERMINOLOGY

conviction: the defendant has been found guilty and the case will proceed to the sentencing stage.

case stated: appeals on the grounds that there has been an error of law or the magistrates have acted out of their jurisdiction. Can be used by both the prosecution and defence.

Appeals from the Crown Court

1. By the defence
Appeals from the Crown Court to the Court of Appeal (Criminal Division) are the most common route of appeal by the defence against conviction and/or sentence. However, the defendant must have leave to appeal, and a request must be made within 28 days of the defendant being convicted. If leave is granted, the Court of Appeal has the following powers available to them:

- Allow the appeal, so the conviction will be quashed (rejected as invalid).
- Dismiss the appeal, so the conviction will stand.
- Decrease the sentence given.

> Reduce the conviction to a lesser offence (such as murder to manslaughter).
> Order a retrial in front of a new jury at the Crown Court.

2. By the prosecution

Appeals by the prosecution against an **acquittal** are rare, and can only be made with the permission of the Attorney General, who can:

> refer a point of law to the Court of Appeal; or
> can apply for leave against an unduly lenient sentence.

In 2016, 146 cases out of 190 applications had their sentences increased after the Court of Appeal found the sentences unduly lenient.

A further appeal from the Court of Appeal (Criminal Division) to the Supreme Court is extremely rare but is available to the prosecution and defence. Leave to appeal is rarely granted and then only on legal points of 'general public importance'.

Leave to appeal

This is permission to appeal by a Court of Appeal judge. The rules for granting leave to appeal are contained in the **Criminal Appeal Act 1995** where it is stated that the Court of Appeal shall:

> allow an appeal against conviction if they think that the conviction is unsafe
> dismiss such an appeal in any other case.

Common examples of this are misdirections by the judge, or evidence that should have been admitted.

Sentencing

A sentence is the punishment given to a defendant who has been convicted of an offence. The type of sentence they receive will depend on the type of offence they have committed and whether they are an adult or a youth offender.

The judge is responsible for sentencing in the Crown Court and the magistrates decide the sentence in the Magistrates' Court. The sentencing powers of each court are shown in Table 7.2.

Table 7.2 Sentencing powers

Magistrates' Court	Crown Court
Unlimited fine. Maximum 12 months in prison for adult offenders for a single triable either way offence. Maximum six months in prison for a single summary offence. Youth Detention and Training Order for up to two years.	Unlimited fine. Maximum life imprisonment.

The tariff (or length) of the sentence will be determined by the court, who will look at the:

> age of the offender
> seriousness of the offence
> likelihood of further offences being committed
> extent of harm likely to result from further offences.

STRETCH AND CHALLENGE

Often new evidence coming to light will prompt leave for appeal to be granted based on the fact that the conviction is unsafe. This is important on the grounds of **Article 6 ECHR**; however, the courts are not always as lenient in their interpretation of unsafe.

Look at the case of Simon Hall, who had his appeal against murder dismissed. Do you think there has been a breach of his **Article 6** right to a fair trial, since he alleged that new evidence could prove his innocence?

KEY TERMINOLOGY

acquittal: the defendant has been found not guilty and will go free.

Aims of sentencing

People often assume the one aim of sentencing is to punish individuals, but other factors need to be considered, such as the effect on the community and the long-term rehabilitation of the offender.

Section 57 Sentencing Act 2020 outlines five aims of sentencing:

1. Retribution (punishment)
This is the classic aim of sentencing, and it is a way of punishing the defendant because it has been established that they have committed a crime and an element of blame rests with them. The punishment must fit the crime, so the sentence given must be proportionate to the crime that has been committed.

2. Deterrence
Individual deterrence is where the individual offender is deterred from offending again.

General deterrence aims to deter others from committing a crime, showing society the potential consequences of committing a crime and making an example of the offender. Obviously, the harsher the sentence, the more likely it is to act as a deterrent.

3. Protection of society
Protection of society is where the sentence given will protect the public from the offender. For example, a dangerous driver could be given a driving ban, or a convicted burglar could be given an electronic tag to stop them from leaving their house after dark.

4. Rehabilitation
Rehabilitation is where the offender is given a sentence that will help rehabilitate their behaviour and prevent them from offending again. This is particularly effective for youth offenders, as a wide belief is that a period of imprisonment is not effective in preventing reoffending. For this reason, the Sentencing Act 2020 offers community sentencing, which can be tailored to help the offender and the community as a whole. Following the PCSC Act 2022 it is now the case that community sentencing should offer an appropriate level of punishment as well as address the underlying causes of offending by providing early interventions to deflect people away from future offending.

5. Reparation
Reparation essentially means paying back to society what you have taken away, for example in the form of compensation or through unpaid community work. For example, someone who has been convicted of criminal damage may be ordered to remove graffiti or repair any damage they have caused.

Types of sentencing

The Sentencing Act 2020 came into force in December 2020, and consolidated all previous legislation on sentencing into one 'Sentencing Code'. The Act covers both youth and adult sentencing and applies to all defendants convicted after 1 December 2020. The new Act does not change any maximum sentence or any mandatory minimums.

Sentencing of youth offenders

Offenders aged between 10 and 17 are classed as youth offenders, and are usually tried in the youth court, unless the case is so serious that it is tried in the Crown Court. Youths can also be tried in the Crown Court if they are being tried alongside an adult offender. The role of the youth court was consolidated in the case of *Thompson and Venables* v *UK* (1999).

> ### Thompson and Venables v UK (1999)
> The European Court of Human Rights (ECtHR) upheld complaints by the boys convicted of the murder of Jamie Bulger that their trial in the Crown Court violated their right to a fair trial. According to Article 6 ECHR, the formality of a jury trial in open court would have rendered most of the proceedings incomprehensible to them.
>
> The ECtHR ruled that the trial of a young person should be held in a courtroom in which everyone is on the same level and the defendants should be permitted to sit with their family. Wigs and gowns should not be worn, and public and press attendance should be restricted if necessary.

KEY TERMINOLOGY

appropriate adult: a parent, guardian or social worker who must be present when a youth under the age of 17 is being interviewed in police custody or is on trial at the youth court. Their role is to make sure the young person understands legal terminology, is aware of their rights and is comforted and reassured.

The youth court is usually located in the same building as the Magistrates' Court. It is not open to the public and is more informal; for example, the district judges do not wear wigs and there is only limited access for the press. Young offenders are also entitled to have an appropriate adult with them at all times, and this is provided for under s57 Police and Criminal Evidence Act 1984 and Code C PACE.

Several types of sentences are available for youths, but the primary aim of youth sentencing, according to s58 Sentencing Act 2020, is to prevent reoffending and to rehabilitate the offender so that they change their behaviour while compensating, or 'repairing', society for the damage that has been caused.

> **EXAM SKILLS**
> If an examination question asks about the aims of sentencing, it is good practice to give examples of types of sentences that support that aim.

Pre-court sentencing
Table 7.3 shows disposals available in the youth justice system for those offenders who have committed a first offence or plead guilty to an offence.

Table 7.3 Disposals available in the youth justice system

Youth restorative disposal (YRD)	Youth caution	Youth conditional caution
This is used for 10- to 17-year olds who have committed minor crimes. The offender must admit fault and there has to be the option for them to apologise or put right the harm they have caused. It aims to strike the balance between addressing the offence and providing support for young people by encouraging them not to commit further crimes or anti-social behaviour.	Youth cautions and youth conditional cautions were introduced by the Legal Aid, Sentencing and Punishment of Offenders Act 2012 in April 2013, to replace police reprimands and final warnings.	This is for a more serious first offence or for a subsequent offence. It is a caution with conditions attached to it that the young person must adhere to. Young people who receive a youth conditional caution will be referred to Youth Offending Service (YOS).

Youth rehabilitation order
Youth rehabilitation orders (YROs) are now covered by s173 Sentencing Act 2020. They are a type of community sentence imposed by the court, a flexible order that aims to reduce reoffending and the number of youths in custody. The order can last for a maximum of three years and can be applied to any criminal offence that has been committed by an individual under the age of 18.

The following requirements can be attached to a YRO:

- activity
- unpaid work
- curfew
- prohibited activity

- exclusion
- electronic monitoring
- local authority residence
- supervision
- education
- intoxicating substance
- mental health treatment
- drug testing.

A full list of the requirements that can be attached to a YRO is contained in **s174 Sentencing Act 2020**.

Supervision of the youth will be carried out by the Youth Offending Team (YOT), and the youth will be required to visit their case worker who will work out a YRO plan with them, to address their behaviour and help them move forward. If a youth offender breaches the order three times, they will have to return to court and could face a period in custody.

Youth fines

Youth fines should reflect the offender's ability to pay. If the youth is under 16, paying the fine is the responsibility of a parent or guardian, and it is their ability to pay that is taken into consideration when the level of fine is being set.

First tier sentencing

These are community sentences that are designed to act as a deterrent from committing further crime and provide a way in which the offender can attempt to rehabilitate, so preventing reoffending in the future (see Table 7.4).

Table 7.4 First tier sentences

Referral order	Reparation order	Parenting order
s83 Sentencing Act 2020	s109 Sentencing Act 2020	s23 Police and Justice Act 2006
This is given for a first offence, when the offender pleads guilty. The young person will be referred to a youth offender panel, which will draw up a contract that will last between three and twelve months, aiming to address the causes of the offending behaviour and giving the offender an opportunity to repair the damage they have caused.	This allows the offender to take responsibility for their behaviour and express their remorse to society by repairing the harm caused by the offence. For example, they may be required to meet their victim, clean up graffiti or undertake some form of unpaid work.	These can be given to parents for up to a year. Conditions attached may be having to attend counselling sessions and the order will contain a list of items their offending child must and must not do, for example attend school or be at home between certain hours. They are intended to support the parents in dealing with their child's behaviour. If a parent breaches the order, they can be fined up to £1,000. The aim is to prevent reoffending, and the order will only be granted if the court is satisfied that it will help prevent further crime.

Discharges

Discharges are the same for adults and youth offenders.

- Conditional discharge – **s80 Sentencing Act 2020**: This sentence is rarely used, but is a way of giving the offender a 'cooling off' period. The youth will receive no punishment on the condition that they do not reoffend.
- Absolute discharge – **s79 Sentencing Act 2020**: an offender is released without punishment and nothing further is done.

Custody

Custody will only be granted to a youth in very serious cases (see Table 7.5).

Table 7.5 Types of custody for youths

Type of custody	Explanation
Detention and Training Order s233 Sentencing Act 2020	This is a period in custody for a youth offender, and the length can vary between four months and two years. The first half of the sentence is served in custody, and the second half is served in the community under the supervision of the Youth Offending Team. During this community element, the offender will have to undertake reparation work and adhere to any targets contained in the training and supervision plan, which will have been agreed with their youth offending team worker. These orders are only given to those youths who are a particularly high risk, or are persistent offenders, or have committed a particularly serious offence, because custody is not usually the most appropriate solution for a youth offender. Any breach of the order at any stage of the process could result in a fine or continued detention in custody.
Detention for Life s258 Sentencing Act 2020 s250 Sentencing Act 2020	If the conviction is for one of the serious offences outlined in Schedule 19, the court will impose a sentence for life under s250. Examples of offences under Schedule 19 include manslaughter, kidnapping and s18 Offences Against the Person Act 1861. This section deals with youths who have committed offences for which an adult offender would serve at least 14 years. The length of the sentence can be anywhere up to the adult maximum, life imprisonment. The young offender can be released automatically at the halfway point and also up to a maximum of 135 days early on a home detention curfew. The offender, once released, will also be subject to a supervisory licence until their sentence expires. This is a sentence that can only be given by the Crown Court. This is usually given for offences such as sexual assault, child sex offences and offences related to firearms.

GRADE BOOST

Read the judge's sentencing report for *R v Lavinia Woodward* (2017) and outline the aggravating and mitigating factors in his judgement when passing a suspended sentence.

R v Lavinia Woodward (2017)

The defendant struck her partner in the leg with a bread knife in a drunken rage and was charged with unlawful wounding under s20 Offences Against the Person Act 1861.

EXAM SKILLS

When you are talking about youth sentencing, you should attempt to evaluate the theories of sentencing and the different types of sentence. For example, the youth rehabilitation order deals with reparation, rehabilitation and deterrence.

STRETCH AND CHALLENGE

The Lammy Review was published in September 2017 by the MP David Lammy.

It reviewed the treatment of, and outcomes for, black, Asian and minority ethnic individuals in the criminal justice system. One of the key recommendations was to adopt an American principle of 'sealing' (expunging or deleting) spent criminal convictions, which enables the offender to apply to have their case heard by a judge or independent body, such as the Parole Board, to prove they have reformed. This would enable them to gain employment in the future and to have a second chance, as their criminal convictions would not have to be disclosed.

Read all of Lammy's recommendations in the full report, available at www.gov.uk/government/news/lammy-publishes-historic-review

KEY TERMINOLOGY

Parole Board: a body set up under the Criminal Justice Act 1967 to hold meetings with an offender to decide whether they can be released from prison after serving a minimum sentence. They complete a risk assessment to determine whether it is safe to release the person back into the community. If they are safe to be released, they will be released on licence with conditions and close supervision.

7 Criminal process: Structure and sentencing

Sentencing of adult offenders

Table 7.6 Differences between out-of-court disposals and court disposals

OUT-OF-COURT DISPOSALS	Penalty Notice for Disorder (PND) (Criminal Justice and Police Act 2001)	A fixed penalty given to offenders who have committed one of 24 minor offences, such as theft from shops, minor criminal damage, dropping litter and drunkenness, as well as possession of khat or cannabis. Once the penalty notice has been served, the offender must either pay the penalty or elect to go to court within 21 days. Police community support officers (PCSOs) are able to issue PNDs.
	Caution	Cautions can be given to anybody aged ten or over for minor crimes, for example graffiti. Offenders have to agree to be cautioned and can be arrested and charged if they don't. Although a caution is not a criminal conviction, it can be used as evidence of bad character if a defendant goes to court for another crime. Cautions can show on standard and enhanced Disclosure and Barring Service (DBS) checks.
	Conditional caution	This caution has certain conditions or restrictions attached to it, such as an agreement to attend alcohol or drug rehabilitation or to fix damage caused.
COURT DISPOSALS	Absolute discharge (s79 Sentencing Act 2020)	The court feels that the offender has received enough punishment by going through court and so discharges the offender with no further action.
	Conditional discharge (s80 Sentencing Act 2020)	The offender will receive no punishment on the condition that they do not reoffend for a specified period.
	Fine	The most common sentence given to adults, mostly administered for minor offences. Both Magistrates' and Crown courts can give unlimited fines.
	Suspended sentence order (s286 Sentencing Act 2020)	The offender does not go to prison but has to comply with conditions set out by the court. The suspended period can be between 14 days and one year (or six months in the Magistrates' Court). Breach of the conditions can result in the offender being sent to prison for the remainder of their sentence. The court can attach any of 12 requirements to the sentence.
	Community order (s200 Sentencing Act 2020)	A court can impose a community order with any number of the requirements contained in the **s201 Sentencing Act 2020**. A community order encompasses both punishment and reparation to the community. It is usual to only have one requirement in less serious cases, but a more intensive package would be required for more serious offences. Requirements can include: unpaid work — residence an activity — mental health treatment a programme (e.g. anger management or drug rehabilitation) — drug rehabilitation a prohibited activity — alcohol treatment curfew — supervision exclusion — an attendance centre requirement. Following the **Crime and Courts Act 2013**, every community sentence must contain a punitive element such as unpaid work or a curfew.

Custodial sentences

This is the most severe sentence for the most serious of offences.

Determinate sentence

A determinate sentence is when the court fixes the amount of time an offender must stay in prison. It is the most common custodial sentence, although the length of sentence is usually a maximum, as the offender will not always serve this amount of time.

For sentences of more than a year, the offender is likely to only serve half of their sentence and the other half will be served in the community on licence with conditions attached and under supervision. The **Legal Aid, Sentencing and Punishment of Offenders Act 2012** created a new 'extended sentence' for criminals convicted of serious sexual or violent offences, meaning they have to serve at least two-thirds of their sentence before they will be considered for parole.

Indeterminate sentence

An indeterminate sentence is when the court sets a minimum period that the offender has to serve in prison before they are eligible for early release by the Parole Board.

65

Imprisonment for life

Imprisonment for life is covered under **s321 Criminal Justice Act 2003** and suggests that an offender should serve a sentence of imprisonment for life, when:

› the offender is convicted of a serious offence (defined as carrying a maximum sentence of life imprisonment or at least ten years)
› in the court's opinion, the offender poses a significant risk to the public of serious harm by carrying out further specified offences
› the maximum penalty for the offence is life imprisonment
› the court considers that the seriousness of the offence, or the offence and one or more associated offences, justifies the imposition of imprisonment for life.

Mandatory life sentence

This compulsory sentence is given in two circumstances:

› Offenders who have been found guilty of murder. If they are considered for release by the Parole Board then they will be on a licence for the rest of their lives.
› The **Legal Aid, Sentencing and Punishment of Offenders Act 2012** introduced a 'two strikes' policy, which means that a mandatory life sentence will also be given to anyone convicted of a second serious sexual or violent crime.

Whole life orders

Whole life orders are extremely rare and are given to the most serious or persistent offenders. These prisoners can only be released on compassionate grounds with the permission of the Secretary of State. There are currently very few prisoners serving whole life orders in England and Wales. However, the **PCSC Act 2022** provided that a whole life order should be the starting point for the premeditated murder of a child.

Sentencing Council

The Sentencing Council was set up as part of the **Coroners and Justice Act 2009**, and replaced the Sentencing Guidelines Council with the aim of encouraging transparency and consistency in sentencing.

When deciding what sentence to impose on an offender, several factors are taken into consideration, depending on whether the offender is an adult or a youth. These factors may be relevant in determining the type of sentence as well as its length. Each case is decided on the facts of the individual case. The judge or magistrate will often also consider a **pre-sentence report**, which will outline the perceived risk the defendant poses and provide some recommendations for sentencing.

Table 7.7 Differences between youth and adult sentencing

Youth offenders	Adult offenders
The main aim of the system is to prevent reoffending. The welfare of the child must be considered.	Sentence must reflect the five purposes of sentencing.
When deciding the appropriate sentence, the judge shall consider:	
the offender's age and maturity the seriousness of the offence their family circumstances any previous offending history whether they admitted the offence.	the seriousness of the offence the offender's previous convictions any **aggravating factors** any **mitigating factors** personal mitigation whether the offender pleaded guilty the maximum sentence available for the offence.
The judge will then look at any relevant sentencing guidelines relevant to the offence.	

GRADE BOOST

The Sentencing Council website (www.sentencingcouncil.org.uk) has all the information you need to know about how offenders are sentenced in England and Wales.

KEY TERMINOLOGY

pre-sentence report: a report written by the Probation service, social worker or Youth Offending Team that helps the court to decide whether any factors in the defendant's history should affect the sentencing.

aggravating factor: a factor relevant to an offence that has the effect of increasing the sentence. Examples include the defendant having previous convictions, or if a weapon was used in the offence.

mitigating factor: a factor relevant to the offence that has the effect of decreasing the sentence or reducing the charge. Examples include it being the defendant's first offence, or if the defendant pleaded guilty.

7 Criminal process: Structure and sentencing

Bail

Eduqas: Bail features on Component 1 of both AS and A Level in Section B.

WJEC: Bail features on both Unit 3 and Unit 4 of A Level only in Section C: Criminal Law.

An important pretrial matter is whether the defendant should stay in custody while awaiting trial or whether **bail** should be granted. A person can be released on bail at any point after being arrested by the police. Being given bail means a person is allowed to be at liberty until the next stage in the case, in line with **Article 5 ECHR** – Right to liberty.

Police bail

The police can grant bail (see Figure 7.7) in three circumstances.

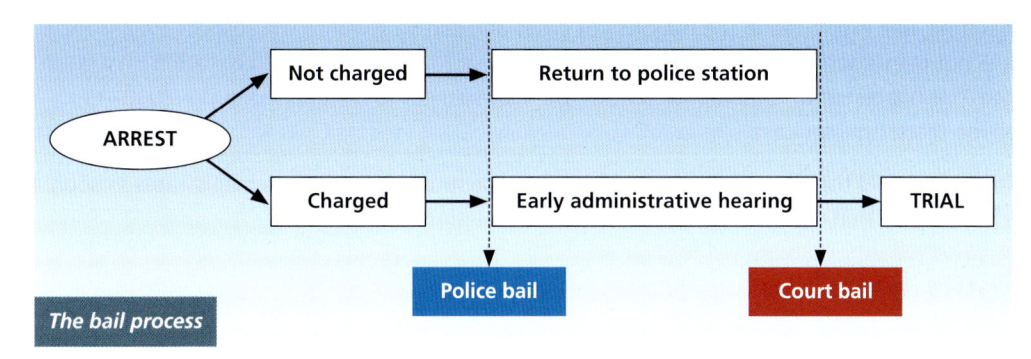

The bail process

Figure 7.7 Circumstances for bail

> **KEY TERMINOLOGY**
>
> **bail:** the defendant is allowed to be at liberty rather than in prison before their court hearing, as long as they agree to particular conditions, such as regularly reporting to a police station.

1. When a person is released without charge on the condition that they return to the police station on a specific date. This is provided for in **s37 Police and Criminal Evidence Act 1984**.
   The law governing pre-charge bail has experienced changes with recent legislation. This legislation resulted in too many people being released under investigation and bail not being used when appropriate, for example to prevent individuals from committing an offence while on bail or interfering with victims and witnesses. Conversely, the suspect is left in limbo with no updates on their case, and the average length suspects are released under investigation is over 200 days in some areas. This lack of time limit and the number of suspects released under investigation can also cause victims of crime serious anxiety and concern.
   As a consequence of the death of Kay Richardson at the hands of her ex-partner who had been released under investigation, rather than on bail, the law was changed. The so called **Kay's law** was introduced in the **Police, Crime, Sentencing and Courts Act 2022**.
2. When a defendant has been charged with an offence until their early administrative hearing at the Magistrates' Court. This is provided for in **s38 Police and Criminal Evidence Act 1984**.
3. Police can grant street bail for minor offences, without the need to take them to the police station. This is provided for by **s30A Police and Criminal Evidence Act 1984**.

> **GRADE BOOST**
>
> An evaluation question on bail will often ask how the law on bail addresses the balance between protecting the public and upholding the rights of the defendant. Understanding the changes in law relating to pre-charge bail will give you some good evaluation points in terms of how victims and witnesses are better protected.

67

> **STRETCH AND CHALLENGE**
>
> 1. The government announced proposals to reduce sentences by 50 per cent for those who plead guilty. Research these proposals and discuss the implications on the prison population. Do you think this supports the sentencing theory of retribution?
> 2. Whole life orders are extremely controversial and have been challenged in the ECtHR by groups of defendants on the grounds that they breach **Article 3 ECHR**. The defendants include Jeremy Bamber and Peter Moore, and the full case is **Vinter v UK (2013)**. Evaluate the outcomes of this or similar challenges.

The decision to grant bail is taken by the custody officer. The police can only refuse bail if:

- the suspect does not give a name and address; or
- if the name and address given is thought not to be genuine.

Therefore, bail is granted in the majority of cases and can be given to the suspect even if they have not been charged, on the agreement that they will return to the police station on a given date. This happened to Christopher Jeffries, the first suspect to be arrested in the 2010–11 Joanna Yeates murder case.

If the police feel that they cannot grant bail, the case must be put before magistrates as soon as possible, so that they can make the decision in relation to bail.

Court bail

The court's powers to grant bail are governed by the **Bail Act 1976**, where **s4** contains a presumption in favour of bail (and bearing in mind **Article 5 ECHR**: Right to liberty), but other considerations may prevent a suspect from being granted bail. **Schedule 1 Bail Act 1976** outlines factors that need to be taken into consideration when deciding whether or not to grant bail:

- The nature and seriousness of the offence.
- The character, past record, associations and community ties of the defendant.
- The defendant's previous record of surrendering to bail.
- The strength of the evidence against them.

Bail need not be granted if there are substantial grounds for believing that the suspect would:

- commit another offence while on bail
- fail to surrender to bail
- interfere with witnesses or otherwise obstruct the course of justice; or
- the suspect needs to be kept in custody for their own protection.

There is a further exception under the **Legal Aid, Sentencing and Punishment of Offenders Act 2012**, when there are substantial grounds for believing that the defendant would, if released, commit an offence against an 'associated person' in a domestic violence case.

Conditional bail

The police **or** the courts can grant conditional bail under powers given to them by **s3 Bail Act 1976** and the **Criminal Justice and Public Order Act 1994**. These conditions are imposed to minimise the risk of the defendant committing another offence while on bail or otherwise interfering with the investigation and, in some circumstances, for their own protection. Conditions that can be imposed include:

- curfew
- electronic tagging
- surrendering their passport
- reporting to a police station at regular intervals
- residing at a **bail hostel**
- getting someone to stand **surety** for them.

> **KEY TERMINOLOGY**
>
> **bail hostel:** a place of residence for people on bail who cannot give a fixed address, run by the Probation Service.
>
> **surety:** a sum of money offered to the court by a person known to the suspect, which guarantees the suspect's attendance at court when required.

The conditions that can be imposed are under the wide discretion of the police and courts, and there is no limit or restrictions on the conditions that can be imposed. Here are two high-profile examples.

> **Dave Lee Travis (2014)** was charged with 11 counts of indecent assault and one count of sexual assault. His conditional bail stated that he had to live at home in Bedfordshire and should not contact his alleged victims.
> **Ryan Cleary (2012)** was charged with attempting to hack the website of the Serious Organised Crime Agency. His conditional bail was extensive and stated that he should observe a curfew between 9pm and 7am every night, wear an electronic tag and only leave the house in the company of his parents. He also had to live and sleep at his home address and have no access to the internet or possess any devices capable of internet access.

Restrictions on bail

There have been many amendments over the years to the **Bail Act 1976**, because of concern that bail was being given too freely, and those who were granted bail often committed further offences. Table 7.8 shows the main amendments.

> **STRETCH AND CHALLENGE**
>
> Look at the following cases. Do you agree with the decision that was made in relation to bail?
> - Julian Assange (2011)
> - Gary Weddell (2008)
> - Michael Donovan (2008)

Table 7.8 Amendments to the Bail Act 1976

Section from the Bail Act 1976	Explanation
s25 Criminal Justice and Public Order Act 1994	The courts were barred from granting bail in cases of murder, manslaughter and rape, where the defendant had already served a custodial sentence for such an offence.
	However, this was held to be a breach of **Article 5 ECHR** in the case of *Caballero v UK* (2000).
s56 Crime and Disorder Act 1998	A defendant can only be granted bail in serious cases if the court is satisfied that there are exceptional circumstances.
s24 Anti-Terrorism, Crime and Security Act 2001	All bail applications from suspected international terrorists should be made to the Special Immigration Appeals Commission.
s14 Criminal Justice Act 2003	If the defendant was on bail for another offence at the date of the offence, bail should be refused unless the court is satisfied that there is no significant risk that they will commit another offence.
s18 Criminal Justice Act 2003	The prosecution can appeal against the granting of bail for any imprisonable offence.
s19 Criminal Justice Act 2003	Bail will not be granted for an imprisonable offence where the defendant has tested positive for a Class A drug and where the offence is connected with Class A drugs.

> **GRADE BOOST**
>
> You should demonstrate an awareness of both court bail and police bail. It is a common mistake in examinations for candidates to omit police bail and just concentrate on court bail.

Section 90 Legal Aid, Sentencing and Punishment of Offenders Act 2012 introduced the 'no real prospect test', where the court's power to refuse bail is restricted if it appears that there is no real prospect that the defendant would receive a custodial sentence if convicted.

There should be a balance in terms of upholding the defendant's human rights and protecting the public. This is especially important because at this point the suspect is still innocent until proven guilty, so should not be treated as a convicted criminal.

> **STRETCH AND CHALLENGE**
>
> Research and conduct an evaluation into the effectiveness of conditions being attached to bail, particularly in light of the case of *Weddell* (2008).

Advantages and disadvantages of bail

> **GRADE BOOST**
>
> Wherever possible, you need to show knowledge of the amendments to the **Bail Act 1976** as these are part of the factors that are taken into consideration when deciding a bail application.

Table 7.9 Advantages and disadvantages of bail

Advantages	Disadvantages
There is a reduction in the number of defendants on remand, which means less cost to the government.	There is a risk that the defendant will interfere with witnesses or otherwise obstruct the course of justice. In the case of *Shannon Matthews (2008)*, had the suspects been granted bail, they might have further concealed evidence and impeded the investigation.
The Home Office suggests that up to 20 per cent of people in prison are awaiting trial and may go on to be found innocent or given non-custodial sentences.	There seems to be disparity in the interpretation of the **Bail Act 1976** in different courts.
The defendant can maintain employment and spend time with their family during their bail period.	Home Office statistics state that 12 per cent of bailed suspects fail to appear at their trial, so there is a risk of them absconding or not surrendering to bail.
The defendant is not restricted in the time available to prepare for trial by meeting with their legal representatives.	It is thought a third of burglaries are committed by people who are on bail for another offence.

> **STRETCH AND CHALLENGE**
>
> Discuss the way in which the courts seek to balance safeguarding a suspect's human rights with protecting the public from a potentially dangerous criminal.

The Crown Prosecution Service

Eduqas: CPS features on Component 1 of both AS and A Level in Section B.

WJEC: CPS features on both Unit 3 and Unit 4 of A Level only in Section C: Criminal Law.

When a suspect is arrested, they will not automatically be prosecuted. The decision to prosecute rather than caution or drop the case lies with an independent body known as the Crown Prosecution Service (CPS). Before the CPS was established in 1986, the decision to prosecute was taken by the police.

> **GRADE BOOST**
>
> This background to the history and role of the CPS provides a useful introduction to an essay about the CPS.

Establishment of the CPS

› **1970** Justice Report identified problems with the police making the decision to prosecute. These were prosecution bias, potential infringement of right to a fair trial after miscarriages of justice involving police tampering with evidence, and conflict of interest, as the same body investigating and prosecuting was seen as inappropriate.
› **1978** Phillips Royal Commission recommended the establishment of an independent agency to take charge of prosecuting suspects.
› **1985** **Prosecution of Offences Act** established the CPS.

Structure and aims of the CPS

The CPS is headed by the Director of Public Prosecutions (DPP), who is answerable to the Attorney General. Max Hill KC took up the post in November 2018. The CPS generally takes control of a case as soon as the police have finished collecting evidence and conducting the investigation. It has five main roles, to:

› advise police on the charge that should be brought against the suspect, using the CPS charging standards (see page 311)
› review cases
› prepare cases for court
› present cases in court, as CPS lawyers have rights of audience
› decide whether to bring a prosecution against the suspect. (This is the CPS's main role.)

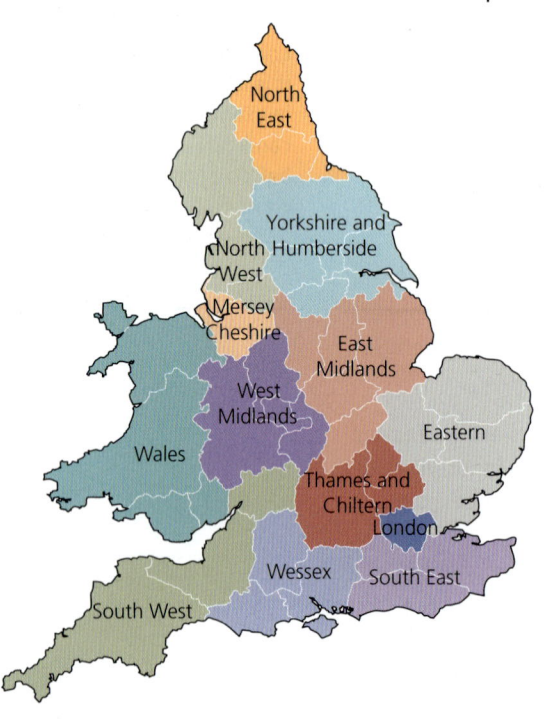

Figure 7.8 The 14 areas of the CPS (London is split into North and South)

7 Criminal process: Structure and sentencing

Structure of the CPS

The CPS operates across 14 areas in England and Wales. Each area is headed by a Chief Crown Prosecutor. Each of the 14 areas is further split into branches, which usually correspond to the police forces, and each branch is headed by a Branch Crown Prosecutor. An additional 'area' is CPS Direct, which provides an out-of-hours service to the police on charging advice.

CPS Inspectorate

The CPS Inspectorate was set up under the **Crown Prosecution Service Inspectorate Act 2000** and is an independent body answerable to the Attorney General. Its role is to enhance the quality of justice through independent inspection and assessment of prosecution services, and, in doing so, to improve effectiveness and efficiency after a recommendation by Sir Iain Glidewell in his 1999 report. Its website is www.hmcpsi.gov.uk.

The CPS uses two key documents to outline its role, how it makes decisions and what service the public can expect.

Code for Crown prosecutors

This is the code of practice that Crown prosecutors use to determine whether to charge a suspect with an offence. The code is contained in **s10 Prosecution of Offences Act 1985**.

The full code test is based on two aspects relating to whether the suspect will be charged:

1. Evidential test: is there a realistic prospect of conviction?
2. Public interest test: is it in the public interest to prosecute?

A case has to pass the evidential test before it moves on to the public interest test; if it fails the evidential test, the case will proceed no further.

1. Evidential test

In order to pass the evidential test, the CPS must be satisfied that there is a realistic prospect of conviction: a judge or jury is more likely than not to find the suspect guilty. It is an objective test and having a lot of evidence is not enough; the evidence has to be sufficient, reliable and **admissible**.

Table 7.10 Evidence must be admissible

Unreliable evidence	Reliable evidence
Blurred CCTV	DNA
Confession obtained by oppression	Eyewitness from the scene of a crime
Hearsay	Voluntary confession
Eyewitness testimony of a child	

An example is in the **Damilola Taylor case (2002)**, when unreliable witnesses and inadmissible evidence made the case the centre of an investigation.

If the evidential test is not passed then the case must be discontinued under **s23 Prosecution of Offences Act 1985**. If the evidential test is passed, the case passes on to the next stage, which is the public interest test.

2. Public interest test

Prosecutors use a series of questions to determine whether charging is in the public interest. The questions are:

a) How serious is the offence committed?
b) What is the level of culpability of the suspect?
c) What are the circumstances of the crime and the harm caused to the victim?

Attorney General
↓
DPP
↓
Chief Crown prosecutors, e.g. Wales
↓
Branch Crown prosecutors, e.g. South Wales, Dyfed Powys, North Wales, Gwent
↓
Lawyers and support staff

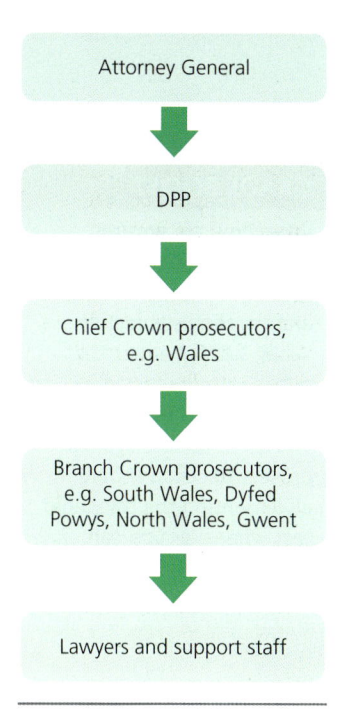

Figure 7.9 Structure of the CPS

KEY TERMINOLOGY

admissible: useful evidence which cannot be excluded on the basis that it is immaterial, irrelevant or violating the rules of evidence.

hearsay: second-hand evidence which is not what the witness knows personally but is something they have been told.

d) Was the suspect under the age of 18 at the time of the offence?
e) What is the impact on the community?
f) Is prosecution a proportionate response?
g) Do sources of information require protecting?

The last three questions take into account the findings of the 'Public Prosecution Service – Setting the Standard' (2009), which emphasises a holistic approach to looking at the offence and the circumstances surrounding it. Crucially, this includes taking into account the feelings of the victims, witnesses and other affected parties.

When considering the public interest test, the prosecutor may also consider whether an out-of-court disposal would be more appropriate (see Sentencing of adult offenders, page 65).

The threshold test

Sometimes, the CPS decides that the full code test has failed and there is not enough evidence to charge the suspect, but the suspect is still believed to be too much of a risk to be released. In these cases, the CPS will apply the threshold test relating to whether the suspect will be charged:

> Is there a reasonable suspicion that the person arrested has committed the offence in question?
> Can further evidence be gathered to provide a realistic prospect of conviction?
> Does the seriousness or circumstances of a case justify the making of an immediate charging decision?
> Are there continuing substantial grounds to object to bail in accordance with the **Bail Act 1976** and in all the circumstances is it proper to do so?
> Is it in the public interest to charge the suspect?

A decision to charge a suspect under the threshold test must be kept under review and the full code test must be applied as soon as the anticipated further evidence is obtained.

Casework Quality Standards

This is a document published by the CPS in October 2014, which outlines the standards that the public can expect from the CPS and are important in holding the CPS to account if it fails to provide the service outlined by the standards. Each standard contains benchmarks of quality that the CPS must achieve:

> Standard 1: Victims, witnesses and communities
> Standard 2: Legal decision making
> Standard 3: Casework preparation
> Standard 4: Presentation

The complete document, including the benchmarks of quality, can be found at www.cps.gov.uk/publications/docs/cqs_oct_2014.pdf

Reforms of the Crown Prosecution Service

The CPS has been the subject of much criticism and reform since its establishment and it has often been accused of not achieving what it set out to do.

Narey Review (1998)

Criticism	Reform
Lack of preparation and a considerable delay in bringing the cases to court.	Caseworkers were employed and trained to review files and present straightforward guilty pleas in court, which freed up CPS lawyers to deal with more complex cases.

GRADE BOOST

When you are writing about the evidential test, give examples of reliable and unreliable evidence. When writing about the public interest test, give at least three factors for and three factors against prosecution. You should also mention the threshold test whenever you can.

STRETCH AND CHALLENGE

The DPP published guidelines on shaken baby cases in February 2011 because of the difference in opinion among medical experts. Do you think it is always in the public interest to prosecute such cases because of the debate?

Glidewell Report (1999)

Criticism	Reform
12% of cases were being discontinued by the CPS where the police had charged.	The 14 areas were divided into 42 areas, to correspond with the police forces, each with a Chief Crown Prosecutor and each with the responsibility to decide to prosecute.
Charges were downgraded in an alarming number of cases.	
Tense working relationships between the police and the CPS, with a hostile 'blame culture', led to inefficiency and poor preparation.	The CPS is now based in police stations, and 'joined up working' is encouraged, with an emphasis on the police and CPS to collaborate on shared issues. This also helps cut the delay in bringing cases to court. The introduction of Criminal Justice Units has attempted to make the working relationships more amicable.
Long delays were reported between arrest and sentence, along with a distinct lack of preparation.	
Many witnesses were unreliable in court, and sometimes did not turn up at all.	A revised code for Crown prosecutors was published with detailed guidance on the application of the evidential test.

Macpherson Report (1999)

This was the report written after the murder of Stephen Lawrence, through which the Metropolitan Police Service was investigated for potential institutional racism.

Criticism	Reform
The police were institutionally racist, and there were serious criticisms of the investigation because the victim was black.	Every police force is now under a legal obligation to publish a racial equality policy to protect victims and defendants. Regular inspections are carried out to ensure that these rules are being followed.

Auld Review (2001)

This review recommended the introduction of statutory charging. This scheme has been running since 2006, giving the CPS the responsibility of determining the charge for a suspect in all but the most minor routine cases, for which the police still retain the charging responsibility. This ensures the correct charge is brought and that only those that are strong enough to stand trial get to court. It reduces the number of cases that are discontinued, in line with the recommendations from Glidewell. This was later implemented in the **Criminal Justice Act 2003**.

> ### *Abu Hamza* (2006)
> This case involved a Muslim cleric who was jailed for inciting murder and racial hatred. The police complained on several occasions that they had put evidence before the CPS but the CPS had continually refused to prosecute. This suggests that working relationships between the police and the CPS were still hostile.

'The Public Prosecution Service – Setting the Standard' (2009)

This is a report published by the former DPP, Keir Starmer, on his vision for the CPS. He envisaged an enhanced role for public prosecutors in engaging with their communities to inform their work and address their concerns. Broadly speaking, he set out three main aims, to:

- protect the public
- support victims and witnesses
- deliver justice.

He saw the CPS being able to achieve these aims by:

- addressing offending and using out-of-court disposals where appropriate
- deciding the charge in all but the most routine cases
- taking the views of the victims into account
- taking decisions independently of any improper influence
- recovering assets from criminals
- ensuring that witnesses can give their best evidence
- presenting their own cases in court
- helping the court to pass an appropriate sentence.

Victim's Code (updated April 2021)

This is a Code of Practice for all victims of crime and outlines the minimum standards that victims can expect from the justice system. As well as the people who have actually suffered harm, the Code also protects their close relatives and, if the victim is under 18 years of age, their parents or guardians.

Examples of rights under this Code are:

- to be able to understand and be understood
- to be provided with information when reporting the crime
- to be provided with information about compensation
- to be able to make a Victim Personal Statement.

Victims' Right to Review Scheme (updated May 2021)

This is a scheme that provides a victim with a process to exercise the right to review certain CPS decisions, not to start a prosecution. This is only a right to review and does not guarantee a charge will be brought. Cases where the CPS may overturn a decision not to prosecute or the discontinuance of a prosecution could include:

- Where the prosecution was stopped because of a lack of evidence, but significant new evidence has been discovered.
- Where a prosecution is now needed in order to maintain confidence in the criminal justice system.
- Where the original decision not to prosecute was wrong because of, maybe, an incorrect application of the law or the public interest test.

(Source: www.cps.gov.uk/legal-guidance/victims-right-review-scheme)

> **GRADE BOOST**
>
> View the Victims' Code at the following link:
> tinyurl.com/jw2d463r

> **EXAM SKILLS**
>
> If you are asked to evaluate or consider the effectiveness of the CPS, make sure that you include as much as you can from the various reports and initiatives and remember to develop a balanced argument.

> **STRETCH AND CHALLENGE**
>
> 1. www.independent.co.uk/news/uk/home-news/police-crown-prosecutionservice-disclosure-lawyerstrial-a7846021.html is a 2017 article about some failings of the CPS. Do you think these findings are reflective of an improved service, or are we still seeing the problems identified by Glidewell?
> 2. It is not only the CPS that can charge a suspect; individuals are able to bring a private prosecution. Research the limitations on private prosecutions, paying particular attention to the case of *Whitehouse v Lemon* (1976).
> 3. Look at the case involving *Lord Janner* (2015), where DPP Alison Saunders was under pressure to step down as she deemed Lord Janner, a House of Lords peer, unfit to stand trial for child sex offences because he had dementia. Even though there was enough evidence to proceed with charges, Ms Saunders decided it was not in the public interest to prosecute. Could this decision be damaging to the reputation of the CPS?
> 4. It is often reported that celebrities who have been accused of sex offences are usually acquitted (e.g. William Roache and Michael Le Vell). Is this a misapplication of the full code test? Could these acquittals also be attributed to pressure from the media and the government?
> 5. Look up the CPS Defendants: Fairness for All Strategy 2025. This is a strategy which deals with challenges faced by suspects and defendants entering the justice system in relation to mental health, youth justice and the proportionality of decision making. Summarise this strategy and discuss how the action plan will improve the effectiveness of the CPS.

7 Criminal process: Structure and sentencing

> **SUMMARY: CRIMINAL PROCESS : STRUCTURE AND SENTENCING**
>
> → Sentencing powers:
>   - Magistrates' Court: unlimited fine; maximum six months' imprisonment
>   - Crown Court: unlimited fine; maximum life imprisonment
> → Aims of sentencing (**s142 Criminal Justice Act 2003**):
>   - Retribution
>   - Deterrence (individual and general)
>   - Protection of society
>   - Rehabilitation
>   - Reparation
> → Young offenders are aged 10–17 and tried in the youth court
> → Youth sentencing: primary aim is to prevent reoffending and rehabilitate the offender
> → Out-of-court youth sentencing:
>   - Youth restorative disposal
>   - Youth caution
>   - Youth conditional caution
> → Youth rehabilitation order: a community sentence with requirements, e.g. activity, unpaid work or drug testing requirements
> → First tier youth sentencing:
>   - Referral order
>   - Reparation order
>   - Parenting order
>   - Conditional discharge
>   - Absolute discharge
> → Youth custody: detention and training order; life imprisonment
> → Adult sentencing: primary aim is punishment and protection of society
> → Out-of-court disposals:
>   - Penalty notice for disorder
>   - Conditional cautions
>   - Cautions
> → Court disposals:
>   - Absolute discharge
>   - Conditional discharge
>   - Fine
>   - Suspended sentence order
>   - Community order
> → Custodial sentences:
>   - Determinate sentences
>   - Indeterminate sentences
>   - Mandatory life sentences
>   - Whole life orders
> → Bail: following arrest, either:
>   - Charged: **s38 Police and Criminal Evidence Act 1984**: police bail then early administrative hearing at Magistrates' Court; court bail then trial
>   - Not charged: **s37 Police and Criminal Evidence Act 1984**: police bail; return to police station; released under investigation
> → Bail need not be granted if there are substantial grounds for believing that the suspect would:
>   - commit another offence while on bail
>   - fail to surrender to bail
>   - interfere with witnesses or otherwise obstruct the course of justice
>   - be required to stay in custody for own protection
> → **s90 Legal Aid, Sentencing and Punishment of Offenders Act 2012**: 'No real prospect test'
> → Factors taken into consideration for bail: **Schedule 1 Bail Act 1976**:
>   - Nature and seriousness of the offence
>   - Defendant's character, past record, associations and community ties of the defendant
>   - Defendant's previous record of surrendering to bail
>   - Strength of the evidence against defendant
> → Conditional bail: granted under the **Criminal Justice and Public Order Act 1994**
> → Restrictions on bail: mainly contained in the **Criminal Justice Act 2003** to balance protecting the public and upholding the defendant's rights

TEST YOURSELF

1. Explain the three categories of criminal offence.
2. What is an early administrative hearing?
3. What is meant by a 'case stated' appeal?
4. Outline the route of appeal available for the defence from the Crown Court.
5. What are the five main aims of sentencing?
6. What is the primary aim of youth sentencing?
7. Name three requirements that can be attached to a youth rehabilitation order.
8. What is the difference between a conditional discharge and an absolute discharge?
9. Name the Act that consolidated all the existing sentencing legislation.
10. What is the difference between a mandatory life sentence and a whole life order?
11. What does it mean for a suspect to be released under investigation?
12. What is the significance of **s4 Bail Act 1976**?
13. Give three advantages of bail.
14. Where would you find the full code test used by the Crown Prosecution Service?
15. Outline three questions considered under the public interest test.
16. Summarise the Victims' Right to Review Scheme.
17. How did the MacPherson Report improve the effectiveness of the CPS?

EXAM PAST PAPER QUESTIONS

WJEC – Unit 1 – May 2022
(a) Explain the process of appeal from the Crown Court. [8]
(b) Analyse and evaluate whether jury trial should be abolished in Wales and England. [24]

WJEC – Unit 4 – June 2022
'The Crown Prosecution Service provides quality, efficiency and justice.' Analyse and evaluate this statement. [50]

WJEC – Unit 4 – June 2019
Analyse and evaluate the extent to which the law relating to bail contains ample safeguards to ensure that the public is not put at risk from suspected offenders. [50]

Eduqas – A Level – Component 1 – June 2022
(a) Explain the process of appeal for a criminal case. [10]
(b) Analyse and evaluate whether trial by jury should be abolished in England and Wales. [15]

Eduqas – AS Level – Component 1 – June 2018
(a) Explain the role of the Crown Prosecution Service. [6]
(b) Analyse and evaluate the success of the Crown Prosecution Service. [18]

8 Criminal process: Juries

The criminal process depends on the participation of two critical groups of lay people: the jury and magistrates. This chapter focuses on the role of the jury; see Chapter 9 for information on magistrates.

The history of jury trials

Trial by jury is an ancient and democratic institution within the legal system, dating back to the Magna Carta. It is based on the principle of 'trial by one's peers' and provides an opportunity for the lay person to participate in the administration of justice. This means that 12 members of the public, selected at random, can see for themselves that justice is being done. The jury also acts as a restraining influence on judges as it takes the decision of guilt or innocence out of the judge's hands.

A major milestone in the history of the jury was *Bushell's case* (1670). Before this, judges would try to bully juries into convicting the defendant but, in this case, it was established that the members of the jury were the judges of fact, with a right to return a verdict based on their conscience. The judge can thus never direct a jury to return a guilty verdict and this point was more recently upheld in the House of Lords in the case of *R v Wang* (2005).

The importance of this power is that juries may acquit a defendant, even when the evidence demands a guilty verdict. This situation arose in *R v Ponting* (1985) and in the *GM Crops* case in 2000. In both cases, the jury sympathised with the defendants, believing them to have acted fairly and thereby acquitting them. This power, also known as jury equity, is quite controversial.

1215	1670	1985	2001	2005
The Magna Carta included recognition of a person's right to trial by 'the lawful judgment of his peers'	**Bushell's case** Jurors cannot be punished for their verdict because they are independent	***R v Ponting*** Juries may acquit a defendant even when evidence demands a guilty verdict (jury equity)	**Auld Review** Juries should 'have no right to acquit defendants in defiance of the law or in disregard of the evidence'	***R v Wang*** The judge cannot direct a jury to return a guilty verdict

Figure 8.1 Significant milestones in the history of jury trials

Role of the jury

> **STRETCH AND CHALLENGE**
>
> **R v *Cilliers* (2017)** concerned a man who was on trial for attempting to murder his wife by tampering with her parachute. The jury in the case were discharged for failing to reach a verdict and there were also allegations of bullying among the jury.
>
> Research this case and make a note of the problems with jury trials highlighted by this case.

In criminal cases, the jury sits in the Crown Court and listens to the evidence presented by both the prosecution and defence counsel. Jury members also examine exhibits such as photographs of the crime scene and alleged weapons. They have to weigh up all the facts and decide for themselves what actually happened. They observe how each witness performs during examination and cross-examination in an effort to judge the credibility of that person.

They listen to the judge who will sum up the evidence for them and direct them on relevant points of law. They must then retire to consider their verdict. They must aim to reach a unanimous verdict but if, after a reasonable time (not less than two hours), they cannot agree, the judge can inform them that they can reach a majority verdict of 11–1 or 10–2 under the **Juries Act 1974**. Anything less than 10–2 is known as a hung jury.

Table 8.1 details the role of the jury in criminal and civil cases, and in the coroners' court.

Table 8.1 Role of the jury in criminal and civil cases, and the coroners' court

	Criminal cases	Civil cases	Coroners' court
Function of jury	Jury members have a dual function in the administration of justice: They consider the facts and return a verdict. They represent society and symbolise democracy.	The jury sits in the county court or High Court and members have a dual role: They decide the liability of the defendant. They decide the amount of damages if they find in favour of the claimant.	The jury sits in the coroners' court to decide a cause of death where a death has occurred in suspicious circumstances.
Legal authority of the jury	Juries Act 1974.	High Court: s69 Supreme Court Act 1981. County court: s66 County Courts Act 1984.	
Types of case	Criminal juries usually sit on indictable cases in the Crown Court. This includes cases such as murder, manslaughter and rape.	Fraud. False imprisonment. Malicious prosecution. Defamation (the right to a trial by jury in defamation cases was removed by the Defamation Act 2013, and use of a jury in these cases is now subject to the courts' discretion).	Deaths in police custody. Deaths in prison. Deaths caused by an industrial accident. Deaths where the health and safety of the public is involved, such as the Hillsborough football stadium disaster and the death of Princess Diana.

> **STRETCH AND CHALLENGE**
>
> Research the jury selection for the Hillsborough Inquest, when the judge outlined specific requirements for the jury. This link may help: www.bbc.co.uk/news/uk-englandmerseyside-26783600. What were these criteria? Think about the impact this would have had on the random and representative nature of the jury.

Figure 8.2 Juries are required at the coroners' court when deaths have occurred in suspicious or unusual circumstances, such as the Hillsborough football stadium disaster

Jury eligibility

The Juries Act 1974 as amended by the Criminal Justice Act 2003 and the Criminal Justice and Courts Act 2015 provides that potential jurors must be:

- aged 18–75
- on the electoral register
- a UK resident for at least five years since their 13th birthday.

Many categories of person used to be considered ineligible or excused from jury service. However, following the Auld Review of the criminal justice system (see page 73) and the subsequent Criminal Justice Act 2003, the Juries Act 1974 has been amended. This is because the Auld Review advised that jury service was too easily avoided and that the jury should be far more representative. The general principle behind the Criminal Justice Act 2003 is to ensure that every eligible person between 18 and 70 (now 75) should perform this public duty if called upon. The revised rules mean that anyone can now serve on a jury, including members of the legal profession, clergy, judges and police officers. However, a member of the armed forces may be excused from jury service if their commanding officer provides a statement that certifies that their absence from service would be prejudicial to the efficiency of the service.

Figure 8.3 shows the history of jury eligibility and how the pool of potential jurors has widened massively since 2001.

Under the PCSC Act 2022, a judge is permitted to appoint a British Sign Language interpreter if they consider it would enable a deaf person to act effectively and for them not to be prevented from participating in jury service.

The Jury Central Summoning Bureau is responsible for ensuring that members of the public serve as required. It deals with requests for being excused but can only allow individuals to defer their service rather than fully excusing them from it. It is not possible to be fully excused because the Auld Review found that the same categories of people kept being excused, resulting in an unrepresentative jury pool.

Computers produce a random list of potential jurors from the electoral register. It is necessary to summon more than 12 jurors for a particular trial, and bigger courts tend to summon up to 150 people every fortnight.

Jurors receive a set of notes briefly explaining the procedure and the functions of the juror. The normal length of jury service is two weeks although it can be longer for complex cases. Jury service is compulsory and failure to attend or to be unfit because of alcohol or drugs is a criminal offence; this is known as contempt of court (see page 80).

R v Abdroikov (2007)

In two cases, serving police constables were on the jury, and in the third, a CPS solicitor. The House of Lords held that this could give an appearance of bias, contrary to the right to fair trial where police evidence is being challenged. It allowed two appeals and the convictions were quashed.

Hanif and Khan v UK (2011)

The ECtHR held that the presence of police officers on the jury could breach Article 6 ECHR (right to a fair trial). In this case, the police officer knew a police witness in a professional capacity.

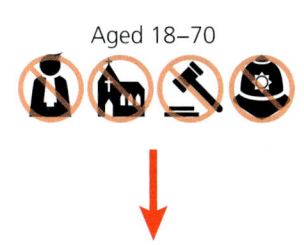

Aged 18–70

Auld Review (2001)
- Jury service too easily avoided.
- Pool of jurors needs to be widened to increase representation.

Criminal Justice Act 2003
Aged 18–70
Deferrals only
Jurists are barred if they:
- have serious criminal convictions
- are currently on bail
- have been diagnosed with a mental health condition

Criminal Justice and Courts Act 2015
Aged 18–75
Four new offences barring jurists are added.

Figure 8.3 Legislation for eligibility of juries

KEY TERMINOLOGY

contempt of court: a criminal offence punishable by up to two years' imprisonment for anyone who is disobedient or discourteous to a court of law.

Contempt of court

The courts take participation in jury service very seriously, and failure to attend if a juror is called is a criminal offence known as contempt of court.

> ### R v Banks (2011)
> Matthew Banks was jailed for 14 days for contempt of court after missing jury service to see a musical in London. He was in the middle of a trial and the case had to be postponed for a day as a result.
>
> ### R v Fraill (2011)
> Joanna Fraill was jailed for eight months for contempt of court after sitting on a jury and contacting the defendant on Facebook to discuss the case.
>
> ### AG v Davey and Beard (2013)
> Two jurors were each jailed for two months for contempt of court.
>
> Mr Davey posted a strongly worded message on Facebook during the trial of a man for sex offences, suggesting he was going to find the defendant guilty. His defence was that he was just expressing shock at the type of case he was on.
>
> Mr Beard was on a fraud trial. He researched the case on Google and gave his fellow jurors extra information about the number of victims of the alleged fraud.

The Criminal Justice and Courts Act 2015 created four new offences in relation to jury deliberations and researching a case. Conviction of any of these offences can result in up to two years in prison.

s71 (s20A Juries Act 1976 as amended) created an offence of 'researching' a case during the trial period. 'Researching' means intentionally seeking information that the juror knows will be relevant to the case. Means of research include asking a question, searching the internet, visiting or inspecting a place or object, conducting an experiment or asking another person to seek information.

s72 (s20B Juries Act 1976 as amended) created an offence for a juror to intentionally disclose information obtained under s71 to another member of the jury.

s73 (s20C Juries Act 1976 as amended) created an offence for a juror to engage in 'prohibited conduct', which is defined as trying the case other than on the basis of the evidence presented in the proceedings.

s74 (s20D Juries Act 1976 as amended) created an offence for a juror to intentionally disclose information about statements made, opinions expressed, arguments advanced or votes cast by members of the jury during their deliberations. The exception is for the purposes of an investigation by the court into whether an offence or contempt of court has been committed by a juror in the proceedings.

> ### R v Smith and Deane (2016)
> This case was brought under the Criminal Justice and Courts Act 2015 for what the judge deemed a 'serious' contempt of court.
>
> Mr Smith carried out internet research on a case he was trying. He was given a nine-month term suspended for 12 months.

Ms Deane disclosed contents of jury deliberations after her jury service. She was jailed for three months, suspended for 12 months.

R v Dallas (2012)
University lecturer Theodora Dallas was jailed for six months for researching the criminal defendant while serving on a jury. She said she had been checking the meaning of 'grievous bodily harm' on the internet then added the word 'Luton' to a search, which produced a newspaper report that mentioned the defendant had previously faced an allegation of rape. It showed he had been acquitted of the charge but it did include information not disclosed during his trial.

Jury challenging

As members of the jury are called, and before they are sworn in, they can be challenged in several ways.

Challenge for the cause

Challenge by either defence or prosecution
This is a request that a juror be dismissed because there is a reason to believe that they cannot be fair, unbiased or capable. This may include bias on the grounds of race, religion, political beliefs or occupation. Examples include:

- knowing someone in the case
- prior experience in a similar case
- an obvious prejudice
- ineligibility or disqualification.

R v Gough (1993)
This case held that where a juror is challenged on the grounds of bias, the test is whether there is a 'real danger' that they are biased.

There were concerns in the *United States v Ghislaine Maxwell* (2022) sex trafficking case in New York that one of the jurors had not disclosed his own childhood sexual abuse. It was claimed that he could not be unbiased and should have been challenged.

Challenge to the array

Challenge by either prosecution or defence
This is where the whole jury panel is challenged on the grounds that the summoning officer is biased or acted improperly.

Romford Jury (1993)
Out of a panel of 12 jurors, nine came from Romford, with two of them living within 20 doors of each other in the same street.

R v Fraser (1987)
Although the defendant was from a minority ethnic background, all the jurors were white (also note the case of *R v Ford* (1989) below).

Stand by the Crown

Challenge by prosecution or judge

This is rarely invoked and only in cases of national security or terrorism, and where vetting has been authorised. Where it is used, the permission of the Attorney General is required.

Racial challenges

Despite the recent reforms to make the jury more representative and to remove the middle-class 'opt out', the jury is still not racially representative. The issue of racism in the criminal justice system has been of public concern mainly due to the murder in 1993 of the black teenager Stephen Lawrence.

Groups such as the Commission for Racial Equality have argued that where race is an issue in a trial, the jury should contain at least three minority ethnic individuals. This had been proposed by the Runciman Royal Commission in 1993 but was rejected by the government at that time.

The same proposal was included more recently in the Auld Review (see page 73) but was again rejected by the government, on the grounds that it would undermine the random principle.

> ### R v Ford (1989)
> It was held that there is no power for a judge to order a multiracial jury.
>
> ### Sander v UK (2000)
> This case went before the ECtHR, and it was held that the judge should have discharged the jury and ordered a retrial when a note was sent to the judge alleging racism within the jury room.
>
> ### R v Smith (2003)
> The defendant argued that s1 Juries Act 1974 contravened his right to a fair trial under the Human Rights Act 1998. This argument was rejected by the court, which held that 'personal impartiality must be presumed'.

> **STRETCH AND CHALLENGE**
>
> The Lammy Review (see page 64) found that juries were not generally biased in their verdicts and that they were consistent in their decision making, regardless of the ethnicity of the defendant. Judges, however, according to the review, are a different story. Read more at www.theguardian.com/public-leaders-network/2017/sep/15/racial-bias-criminaljustice-system-lammy-reviewmagistrates-courts-jury
>
> What could be the implications of these findings?

Jury tampering

Sometimes, friends of the defendant might try to interfere with the jury. This might be bribing jury members to bring in a not guilty verdict or making threats against jury members so that they are too afraid to find the defendant guilty. In such cases, the police may be used to try to protect the jurors but this may not be effective. It is also expensive and removes the police from their other work.

To combat this, s44 Criminal Justice Act 2003 provides that where there has already been an effort to tamper with a jury in the case, the prosecution can apply for the case to be heard by the judge alone.

> ### R v Twomey and others (2009)
> This is the first and only case where trial without a jury was approved. The defendants were charged with various offences connected to a large robbery from a warehouse at Heathrow. Three previous trials had collapsed and there had been 'a serious attempt at jury tampering' in the last of them. The prosecution applied to a single judge for the trial to take place without a jury. The judge refused but the Court of Appeal overturned this decision, ordering that the trial should take place without a jury.

Alternatives to the jury

- A single judge sitting alone would save time through not having to explain everything to a jury. This would also reduce the number of verdicts that are in defiance of the law because the judge would feel it their duty to uphold the law even if it is harsh.
- A bench of judges consisting of three or five on a panel would give a more balanced view but would be far more expensive and again would stop the element of public participation.
- A specially trained jury selected from non-lawyers would ensure that the panel was capable of fulfilling its functions. However, if they were full time, they might reflect the magistracy too closely and consist of only older, middle-class people.
- A mixed panel consisting of a judge and two lay members is used in Scandinavian countries. This speeds up the trial process as the judge is involved in all discussions. Community participation is retained but it could be argued that the judge might have too much influence on the lay members, who might be intimidated or defer to the experienced judge.

Figure 8.4 Jury trials remain a standard procedure, but there are many alternatives that could be used

Evaluation of the jury concept

Advantages

- Juries allow ordinary people to participate in the justice system, so verdicts are seen to be those of society rather than the judicial system. The verdict is more likely to be acceptable because the panel should include members of the defendant's social class and ethnic background. There is an impression that justice has not only been done but is seen to be done as seen in the Magna Carta (the right to be tried by one's peers).
- Juries may be less prosecution-minded than judges or magistrates, considering the mix of social backgrounds.
- Juries offer protection against harsh or unjust laws since they often come to a verdict that is fair rather than legally correct.

> ### R v Owen (1992)
> The defendant's son had been killed by a lorry driver who had a long criminal record for drink driving and violence. The driver showed no remorse for killing the boy.
>
> He was convicted of a driving offence, sentenced to 15 months imprisonment and released after a year. He then resumed driving his lorry unlawfully. After contacting the authorities about getting proper justice for his son, and getting nowhere, the defendant took a shotgun and injured the lorry driver. He was charged with attempted murder, but despite the evidence against him, the jury found him not guilty.

- The jury is not 'case hardened' in the way that some judges might be. Jurors have not become jaded and cynical about defence arguments because, for most of them, this is the first time they have served.
- It is argued that 12 opinions of the jury are safer than one single judge. Also, due to **s8 Contempt of Court Act 1981** and the new offences introduced by the **Criminal Justice and Courts Act 2015**, discussions within the jury room are secret and thus the jury is protected from outside influence and pressure.

- Juries are fully capable of making common-sense decisions based on fact, which does not require specialist legal training. They should also be impartial since they are not connected to anyone in the case. This is known as jury equity and was demonstrated in *Ponting* (1985), where the jury refused to convict even though the judge ruled there was no defence.
- The jury is an ancient institution and the entire trial system is founded upon it. Professor Blackstone said 'it is the bulwark of our liberties' and Lord Devlin described it as 'the lamp that shows freedom lives'.

Disadvantages

- McCabe and Purves, in 'The Shadow Jury at Work' (McCabe and Purves, 1974), reported that a jury can be dominated by two or three strong-minded individuals, or be persuaded by a forceful foreperson when locked in the jury room.
- Compulsory jury service can cause resentment or strain, which might lead to some jurors being keen to get away as soon as possible, and they will thus go along with the majority to bring the trial to an end.
- Jurors might also be too easily convinced by the manner and presentation of barristers, the courtroom becoming more of a theatre, with the jury easily manipulated and distracted. Appearances and prejudicial views can also be a deciding factor.

Figure 8.5 A jury is representative of society and is diverse in terms of gender and ethnicity

Jurors may not understand the case presented to them and are often unable to weigh evidence correctly and appreciate the significance of certain matters.

R v *Alexander and Steen* (2004)

This is known as the 'amorous juror' case; the defendants appealed because a female juror had bombarded the prosecution barrister with romantic proposals.

R v *Pryce* (2013)

The trial collapsed in the case of Vicky Pryce, the ex-wife of MP Chris Huhne, when the judge realised that the jury was struggling to understand the basics when they asked ten questions that revealed 'fundamental deficits' in understanding.

Media influence can also be seen as a disadvantage on the grounds of Article 6 ECHR.

R v *Taylor and Taylor* (1993)

Two sisters were charged with murder. Some newspapers published a still video sequence which gave a false impression of what was happening. After conviction, leave of appeal was granted because of the possible influence this picture could have on the jury's verdict.

Juries are very difficult to research because the Contempt of Court Act 1981 and the Criminal Justice and Courts Act 2015 prevent jurors from discussing the case or their reasoning. This was discussed in R v *Mirza* (2004) and R v *Connor and Rollock* (2002), where it was held that s8 is compatible with Article 6 ECHR (right to a fair trial). An exception to this was in R v *Karakaya* (2005) where it was discovered that a juror had conducted internet searches at home and brought the notes into the jury room. See also more recent cases such as *Dallas* (2012) and *Deane* (2016).

8 Criminal process: Juries

> ### EXAM SKILLS
> When answering an evaluation question on juries, you will only achieve the higher mark bands if you can support your points with legal authority, so cases are very important in this topic. Also, make sure you are answering the question posed and not the rehearsed answer that you have prepared. For example, if the question asks about representativeness of the jury, focus your answer on that and not general advantages and disadvantages, as this would give the impression that you have just learned a stock answer and are not answering the question posed.

SUMMARY: CRIMINAL PROCESS: JURIES

- Criminal
  - Role: to decide verdict of guilty or not guilty in Crown Court
  - Types of cases: indictable offences where the defendant pleads not guilty and some either way offences where defendant has elected for a Crown Court trial
  - Aims to reach a unanimous verdict (12–0) or a majority if the judge agrees (10–2, 11–1)
  - Governed by the *Juries Act 1974* amended by the *Criminal Justice Act 2003*
- Civil
  - Dual role: to decide liability of defendant and to decide amount of damages
  - Types of cases: fraud, false imprisonment and malicious prosecution
  - Governed by *s67 Supreme Courts Act 1981* and *s66 County Courts Act 1984*
- Coroners' court
  - Role: to decide cause of death in suspicious circumstances
  - Types of cases: death in prison, death in police custody, death through an industrial accident or a death where the health and safety of the public is at risk
  - Examples: Hillsborough Inquest, Princess Diana death
- Potential jurors must be:
  - aged 18–75
  - on the electoral register
  - a UK resident for at least five years since their 13th birthday
- Potential jurors cannot be:
  - currently on bail
  - diagnosed with a mental health condition
  - convicted of a serious criminal offence (and served more than five years in prison)
  - convicted of an offence under the *Criminal Justice and Courts Act 2015*
  - a member of the armed forces if their commanding officer has provided a statement to certify that their absence from service would be prejudicial to the efficiency of the service
- Jury challenging:
  - For cause: a request that a juror be dismissed because there is a reason to believe that they cannot be fair, unbiased or capable: *R v Gough* (1993)
  - To the array: a request that the whole jury is challenged because the summoning officer is biased or acted improperly: *Romford Jury* (1993)
  - Stand by the Crown: only used in cases of national security or terrorism, and with the permission of the Attorney General
- Racial challenges:
  - There is no entitlement to a multiracial jury: *R v Ford* (1989)
  - There is an entitlement to a jury that is not racist: *Sander v UK* (2000)
  - Jury tampering: interfering with the jury: *s44 Criminal Justice Act 2003* provides that if this happens, the prosecution can apply for the case to be heard by the judge alone: *R v Twomey and others* (2009)

- Alternatives to the jury:
    - A single judge
    - A bench of judges
    - A specially trained jury selected from non-lawyers
    - A mixed panel of a judge and two lay members
- Advantages of juries
    - Allow ordinary people to participate in the justice system (the right to be tried by one's peers)
    - May not be biased towards prosecution
    - Protect against harsh or unjust laws as may prioritise fairness: *R v Owen* (1992)
    - Less cynical than legal profession
    - 12 opinions of the jury are safer than one single judge
    - s8 Contempt of Court Act 1981 and s69–77 CJCA 2015 protect secret deliberations
    - Jury equity: *Ponting* (1985)
    - Lord Blackstone: 'It is the bulwark of our liberties' and Lord Devlin: 'The lamp that shows freedom lives'
- Disadvantages of juries
    - Can be dominated by strong-minded individuals or a forceful foreperson
    - Compulsory jury service can lead to some jurors being keen to end the trial without thorough consideration
    - Jurors might also be influenced by appearances: *R v Alexander* and *Steen* (2004)
    - Lack of legal knowledge: *R v Pryce* (2013)
    - Media influence on the grounds of Article 6 ECHR: *R v Taylor and Taylor* (1993)
    - Contempt of Court Act 1981 and CJCA 2015 prevent jurors from discussing the case: *R v Mirza* (2004), *R v Connor and Rollock* (2002), *R v Karakaya* (2005)

TEST YOURSELF

1. What is the significance of *Bushell* (1670)?
2. Why is it said that juries have a dual role in criminal trials?
3. Name the cases in which juries sit in civil cases.
4. Give an example of where a jury sat in the coroners' court?
5. Outline the changes in eligibility brought about by the Criminal Justice and Courts Act 2015.
6. Summarise the four new offences introduced by the Criminal Justice and Courts Act 2015.
7. Give two examples of cases where jury members have been convicted of contempt of court.
8. What is meant by 'challenge for the cause'?
9. Give three advantages of jury trial, with case law to support each point.
10. Give three disadvantages of jury trial, with case law to support each point.

EXAM PAST PAPER QUESTIONS

Eduqas – A Level – Component 1 – June 2019
(a) Explain the role of the jury in trials in England and Wales. [10]
(b) Analyse and evaluate the advantages and disadvantages of trial by jury. [15]

Eduqas – AS Level – Component 1 – May 2019
Analyse and evaluate whether juries are representative of society. [18]

9 Legal personnel

This chapter looks at the different personnel involved in the English and Welsh legal system. Some of these personnel are paid, such as barristers and solicitors, legal executives and professional judges, while others, such as magistrates, are essentially unpaid.

Barristers and solicitors

The legal profession in England and Wales is divided into two separate branches: barristers and solicitors. Each branch does similar work (e.g. both do advocacy and legal paperwork), but they differ in the amount of time dedicated to this work, with barristers spending more of their time in court. A simple analogy is with the medical profession, by thinking of the barrister as the consultant or the specialist, and the solicitor as the general practitioner.

The legal profession also includes paralegals and legal executives.

Role of solicitors

There are approximately 143,000 solicitors, with 80 per cent being in private practice. The Solicitors Regulation Authority (SRA) regulates solicitors.

What types of work do solicitors do?
Most solicitors' work and income comes from commercial, conveyancing, family or matrimonial and probate work. In 1985, solicitors lost their monopoly on conveyancing work.

Solicitors do almost all their advocacy work in the Magistrates' Court. Until 1999, solicitors did not have full **rights of audience** upon qualification, a right barristers have always had. However, the **Courts and Legal Services Act 1990** and **Access to Justice Act 1999** changed this, and solicitors now acquire full rights of audience when they are admitted to the roll, and can exercise this right upon completion of extra training.

Solicitors' offices range from large firms to sole practitioners. Solicitors can form business partnerships, including limited liability partnerships. Most law firms are small, with 85 per cent having four or fewer partners, and 50 per cent having only one partner.

Qualifications for a solicitor
Training to be a solicitor has several stages. Prior to the introduction of the Solicitors Qualifying Examination (SQE) in 2021, the education and training route for a solicitor involves completing a 'Qualifying Law degree', which means passing exams in Legal Foundations, Contract, Tort, Public, Criminal, Trust & Equity, EU, or, for those with a non-law degree, completing the Graduate Diploma in Law, which is a conversion course. The next step is the one-year Legal Practice Course. After passing this course and undertaking a period of two years recognised training, you would be a qualified solicitor.

This traditional route to qualifying is, however, being gradually phased out, and transition from the Legal Practice Course route to the SQE route will be complete by 2032.

To qualify as a solicitor through the SQE, you must have a degree or equivalent in any subject. In addition, you will need to pass the character and suitability assessments as laid down by the Solicitors Regulation Authority. You will also need to pass both stages of the SQE and

> **KEY TERMINOLOGY**
>
> **rights of audience:** the right to appear as an advocate in any court.

complete two years' qualifying work experience (QWE). This is perhaps the most significant change to qualifying as a solicitor: under the SQE, QWE trainees will be able to work at up to four different solicitor firms to gain the overall two-year work experience. Formal training contracts, working as a paralegal and volunteering in legal advice clinics will all count towards the work experience requirements.

Anyone who started a law degree, Graduate Diploma in Law (GDL) or Legal Practical Course (LPC) before the SQE was introduced in 2021 can choose which route to qualify. As stated, there will be a long transition period from 2021, running until 2032, in which candidates who are already on one of the former courses will be able to qualify as solicitors in the 'traditional' way.

Figure 9.1 The solicitors' governing body is called The Law Society. In 2005 membership of The Law Society became voluntary

Complaints against solicitors

› The Solicitors Regulation Authority (SRA) deals with complaints about professional misconduct of solicitors. If there is evidence of serious misconduct, the SRA can put the case before the Solicitors' Disciplinary Tribunal, which can reprimand, fine, suspend or, in very serious cases, strike a solicitor off the roll. If the complainant is not happy with the decision of the SRA then they can take the matter further to the Legal Service Ombudsman.
› The Legal Service Ombudsman was set up by the Office for Legal Complaints. The Ombudsman can, among other things, order a legal professional to apologise to a client, refund or reduce legal fees or pay compensation of up to £30,000.
› Action for negligence can go through the courts; for example, *Arthur JS Hall and Co* v *Simons* (2000).

Promotion to the judiciary

Before 1990, solicitors were only eligible to apply for junior judicial appointments (e.g. circuit judges). Since the Courts and Legal Services Act 1990 they are eligible for appointment to the higher courts.

Role of barristers

There are approximately 16,500 barristers, known collectively as the Bar. The governing body of barristers is the General Council of the Bar. The Bar Standards Board is responsible for regulating the Bar.

What types of work do barristers do?

Their main role is advocacy (presenting cases in court). A great deal of their work is pretrial work, opinions (considered assessment of cases), and conferences with solicitors and clients.

A key difference to solicitors is that barristers must be self-employed and cannot form partnerships. Instead, they share offices called chambers with other barristers, and the sets of chambers are managed by the clerk who arranges meetings with solicitors and negotiates barristers' fees.

Not all barristers work as advocates: some barristers work for law centres, the government and private industry.

Before 2004, members of the public were not allowed to directly contact a barrister; they had to be appointed through a solicitor. In 2004, direct access was introduced, so members of the public can now contact a barrister without going through a solicitor.

Barristers work according to the cab rank rule. This means that a barrister is obliged to accept any work in a field in which they profess themselves competent to practise, at a court at which they normally appear and at their usual rates.

> **KEY TERMINOLOGY**
>
> **chambers:** office space where barristers group together to share clerks (administrators) and operating expenses.
>
> **cab rank rule:** a barrister is obliged accept any work in a field in which they are competent to practise, at a court at which they normally appear and at their usual rates.

9 Legal personnel

Qualifications for a barrister

Training to be a barrister has several stages:

- Law degree or, for non-law graduates, the Graduate Diploma in Law (GDL).
- Join one of the four Inns of Court.
- Bar Professional Training Course (one year).
- Called to the Bar.
- Pupillage (one year).
- Tenancy in chambers.
- Continuous professional development.

Barristers remain 'junior' unless made King's Counsel (KC). This was known as Queen's Counsel (QC) prior to the death of Queen Elizabeth II. Barristers are eligible to become a KC after ten years in practice and they are appointed by The General Council of the Bar and Law Society. On appointment, they 'take silk'. KCs can command higher fees for their recognised expertise and status.

> **KEY TERMINOLOGY**
>
> **Inns of Court:** barristers must join Inner Temple, Middle Temple, Gray's Inn or Lincoln's Inn. The Inns provide accommodation and education, and promote activities.
>
> **pupillage:** a one-year apprenticeship in which a pupil works alongside a qualified barrister, who is known as the pupil master.
>
> **tenancy:** a permanent place for a barrister in chambers.
>
> **King's Counsel (KC):** an appointed senior barrister who has practised for at least ten years. They can wear silk gowns, hence 'to take silk'.

Figure 9.2 The Honourable Society of Lincoln's Inn is one of four Inns of Court in London, where barristers are called to the Bar. The other three are Middle Temple, Inner Temple and Gray's Inn

Complaints against barristers

- Barristers are no longer immune from liability for negligent work in court – *Rondel* v *Worsley* (1969) overruled by *Arthur JS Hall* v *Simons* (2000).
- However, see *Moy* v *Pettman Smith* (2005). This concerned the lenient treatment of a barrister by the House of Lords compared to other professionals.
- The Bar Standards Board deals with disciplinary matters and also oversees the training and education of barristers. The Board can discipline any barrister who is in breach of the Code and can refer serious matters to a disciplinary tribunal. If the complainant is unhappy with the decision of the Board, the matter can be taken to the Legal Ombudsman.

Promotion to the judiciary

Barristers are eligible for appointment to all judicial posts, provided they have the necessary experience.

Figure 9.3 Criminal barristers rally as part of strike action over legal aid fees

Representation issues surrounding barristers and solicitors

Those in the legal profession are often accused of not representing wider society. Accusations include that they are mainly middle-class and that women and people from minority ethnic groups have traditionally been underrepresented. Access may be improving but the higher positions are still dominated by white males and there is still discrimination. In 2021, only 15 per cent of practising barristers were from minority ethnic groups (Bar Standards Board Figures 2021 Diversity at the Bar).

Reforms and the future of the legal profession

Should the two professions merge and become one? This is a question that has been asked for many years. Moves towards fusion include:

- **1990**: Courts and Legal Services Act
- **1992**: Solicitor-advocates were introduced
- **1999**: Access to Justice Act when all barristers and solicitors acquired full rights of audience
- **2004**: Clementi Report advocated regulation of the profession
- **2007**: Legal Services Act allowed for alternative business structures. It is often called the 'Tesco law' because it aimed to make legal work such as will writing or conveyancing as accessible for consumers as buying a tin of beans from a supermarket, and enabled big companies to buy law firms. Other reforms included allowing:
  - legal businesses to include lawyers and non-lawyers
  - legal businesses to include barristers and solicitors
  - non-lawyers to own legal businesses
  - alternative business structures (ABS) (e.g. in 2012, the Co-operative Society gained a licence from the Legal Services Board to offer legal services).

Other legal personnel

Legal executives and paralegals

- There are approximately 20,000 legal executives who perform professional work under solicitors. They tend to specialise, for example in conveyancing.
- They can go on to qualify as solicitors.
- Their governing body is the Institute of Legal Executives.
- Under the Tribunals, Courts and Enforcement Act 2007, legal executives were given the right to apply for junior judicial appointments.

There are an estimated 100,000 paralegals, who assist solicitors in their work but do not give advice to clients on legal services.

Licensed conveyancers

The Courts and Legal Services Act 1990 abolished solicitors' monopoly on conveyancing.

> **EXAM SKILLS**
>
> This topic could feature on the Unit 1 exam, Section B of WJEC AS Law, Eduqas component 1 exam AS and A Level component 1 exam.
>
> Part (a) questions will require you to use your skills for explaining an aspect of the topic covering AO1 knowledge and understanding.
>
> Part (b) questions require you to use your analysis and evaluation skills on an aspect of the topic covering AO3 skills.

9 *Legal personnel*

Figure 9.4 There are many routes to entering the legal profession

STRETCH AND CHALLENGE

1. Look at the Legal Ombudsman's website, www.legalombudsman.org.uk. Find a case study of a complaint, discuss it with your class and give a presentation based on what you have learned.
2. Research whether KC status is a reliable indicator of excellence and expertise.

GRADE BOOST

It is important that you can show the examiner that you are fully aware of all proposals and reforms to the legal profession, for example the **Legal Services Act 2007**, alternative business structures and so on. Examination questions sometimes focus on the unmet need for legal services, so ensure that you are able to discuss this fully.

SUMMARY: LEGAL PROFESSION

→ Solicitors
  - Can work in a firm or organisation
  - Mostly do office work but can present cases in the Magistrates' Court and county court. They can also qualify for rights of audience in the higher courts
  - To qualify, they must pass the Legal Practice Course or, since 2021, the SQE and do QWE
  - Represented by the Law Society and regulated by the Solicitors Regulation Authority

→ Barristers
  - Usually self-employed but can work for an organisation
  - Mostly do court work, with full rights of audience upon qualification
  - Must be a member of one of the four Inns of Court
  - To qualify and practise, they must pass the Bar Professional Training Course and undertake a pupillage
  - To apply for King's Counsel, barristers must have been practising for at least ten years

→ Legal executives
  - Work in solicitor's firms or other legal organisations
  - Carry out straightforward matters
  - Have limited rights of audience

Judiciary

Role of judges

The independence of the judiciary is a fundamental principle of the rule of law. Judges have a key role in controlling the exercise of power by the state through judicial review and through the **Human Rights Act 1998**, with the power to issue **Section 4 declarations of incompatibility** (*A and X and others* v *Secretary of State for the Home Department* (2004)).

Hierarchy of judges

Superior judges

Head of the Judiciary is the President of the Courts of England and Wales (in practice the Lord Chief Justice) (**Constitutional Reform Act 2005**).

The most senior judges are the Justices of the Supreme Court and Privy Council (**Constitutional Reform Act 2005** replaced the House of Lords with the Supreme Court in 2009).

Lord and Lady Justices of Appeal at the Court of Appeal. Head of Criminal Division is the Lord Chief Justice; Head of Civil Division is the Master of the Rolls.

Judges in the three divisions of the High Court.

Inferior judges

Circuit judges at the Crown Court and county court.

Recorders (part-time) at the Crown Court and county court.

District judges at the Magistrates' Court and county court.

The Lord Chancellor

The role of the Lord Chancellor has existed for over 1,400 years but recently it has been seen to conflict with the doctrine of separation of powers. In 2003, the government announced the intention to abolish the role but, at time of writing, this has not yet happened. The **Constitutional Reform Act 2005** has maintained the role but the powers of the Lord Chancellor have been severely curtailed.

> **KEY TERMINOLOGY**
>
> **secret soundings:** the old appointments process whereby information on a potential judge would be gathered over time, informally, from leading barristers and judges.

Table 9.1 Changes to the role of the Lord Chancellor by the Constitutional Reform Act 2005

The Lord Chancellor no longer:	The Lord Chancellor is now:
sits as a judge in the House of Lords	head of the Ministry for Justice
heads the judiciary	responsible for legal aid, the Law Commission and the court system
takes a role in judicial appointments process	potentially drawn from a background other than law (**s2 Constitutional Reform Act 2005**). In 2012, Chris Grayling became the first non-lawyer to hold this post for 400 years
is required to be a member of the House of Lords	
automatically becomes Speaker of the House of Lords	

Table 9.2 Judicial appointments process

Old procedure	New procedure
Lord Chancellor took a central role in appointments.	**Constitutional Reform Act 2005** established Judicial Appointments Commission (JAC).
Secret soundings.	Judicial Appointments Commission (JAC): 14 members (five lay, five judges, two legal professionals, a lay magistrate and a tribunal member) appointed by the King on the recommendation of the Law Commission.
No advertisements for judicial appointments.	The Commission is not involved in appointing judges to the Supreme Court.
Secretive: eligibility to become a judge was based on numbers of years of rights of audience.	**Tribunals, Courts and Enforcement Act 2007**: eligibility to become a judge is based on number of years of post-qualification experience.

Other countries have different systems for appointing judges:

> In France, judges choose at the beginning of their career to be a judge, rather than being a lawyer first, and follow a judicial career path.
> In the United States, judges are appointed by two methods: appointment and election.

Training, dismissal, termination and promotion of judges

Training

Judges receive little formal training. The training they do receive is organised by the Judicial College.

Dismissal and termination

There are five ways a judge may leave office:

> Dismissal (High Court judges and above: Act of Settlement 1700, Courts Act 1971 and Constitutional Reform Act 2005).
> Suspension from office (Constitutional Reform Act 2005 set up disciplinary procedures).
> Resignation.
> Retirement (judges usually retire at 70).
> Removal due to infirmity.

Promotion

There is no formal system for promoting judges, as it is believed that the desire to be promoted may affect their decision making. Any promotion is dealt with in the same way as the initial appointment process, through the Judicial Appointments Commission (JAC).

Judicial independence

Judicial independence is of paramount importance: it is a necessary condition of impartiality and, therefore, of a fair trial. Judges should:

> be independent from the Executive, interest groups and litigants
> have an independent pay review
> have no other paid appointment or profession or business
> not sit on a case in which they have or appear to have personal interest/bias (e.g. Lord Hoffmann in *Re Pinochet Ugarte* (1999)).

Figure 9.5 Judicial independence is vital

Threats to judicial independence

Ideally, judges are independent arbitrators of the law but this is not always the case.

> Judges are subordinate to the will of Parliament.
> Judges have been to seen to show political bias (see *McIlkenny v Chief Constable of the West Midlands* (1980); *R v Ponting* (1985)).
> Some cases tend to show a bias towards the right wing of the political spectrum (see *Bromley London Borough Council v Greater London Council* (1982); *Council of Civil Service Union v Minister for the Civil Service* (1984); *Thomas v NUM* (1985)).
> Some judges' attitudes towards women are out of date and stereotypical. This is of particular concern in cases involving a sexual offence such as rape.

Criticisms of the judiciary

Judges are often criticised for mostly being white and male, and having attended public school and/or Oxford and Cambridge universities. They are perceived as out of touch with everyday society. They may also have limited training and lack specialisation, so approaches to cases may be inconsistent.

Part 2 of the **Crime and Courts Act 2013** deals with courts and justice, and attempts to address these criticisms. Some of the reforms that relate to judges include:

- improving the organisation of court hours
- enabling flexible working in the High Court and above, with opportunities to work flexibly clearly highlighted in each Judicial Appointments Commission (JAC) selection process
- flexible deployment, which enables judges to more easily move between courts and tribunals, to help their career development
- new selection processes, including the introduction of an 'equal merit provision' to clarify that where two persons are of equal merit, a candidate can be selected on the basis of improving diversity. This is to encourage the appointment of more female and minority ethnic judges.

Role of the Supreme Court and reasons for its establishment

The **Constitutional Reform Act 2005** established the Supreme Court, which replaced the House of Lords to completely separate the UK's senior judges, and the Upper House of Parliament, which is also called the House of Lords. This is to emphasise the independence of the Law Lords and to remove them from the legislature. The Supreme Court is the highest appeal court in the UK.

In August 2009, the justices moved out of the House of Lords (where they sat as the Appellate Committee) into their own building. They sat for the first time as the Supreme Court in October 2009.

Appointing judges to the Supreme Court

Under **s23 Constitutional Reform Act 2005**, to qualify for appointment to the Supreme Court, a judge must have held high judicial office for at least two years or been a qualifying practitioner for at least 15 years in, for example, the Court of Appeal or House of Lords.

Twelve judges are appointed to the Supreme Court by the King on the recommendation of the Prime Minister. The Lord Chancellor recommends these judges to the Prime Minister following a selection commission set up by the Lord Chancellor. The number of judges can be increased.

The senior Lord of Appeal is called the President of the Court.

GRADE BOOST

It is a common examination error when discussing the appointment process to only discuss the old procedure.

It is vital that you can fully discuss both the old and new procedures and that you can evaluate the new procedure. You must also be able to discuss whether judges are representative of society; this is affected by factors such as their social class and ethnic background.

A judiciary question could also focus on the independence of the judiciary, so ensure you are aware of the importance of having an independent judiciary, the threats to independence, and political implications on cases.

A judiciary question could also ask you to discuss the role of the Supreme Court and the reasons for its establishment.

9 Legal personnel

> **EXAM SKILLS**
>
> This topic could feature on Unit 1 exam, Section B of WJEC AS Law, Eduqas component 1 exam AS and A Level component 1 exam.
>
> Part (a) questions will require you to use the skills of explaining an aspect of the topic covering AO1 knowledge and understanding.
>
> Part (b) questions require you to use the skills of analysis and evaluation on an aspect of the topic covering AO3 skills.

> **SUMMARY: JUDICIARY**
>
> → The role of judges differs depending on what court they sit in, and there are different types of judges in each level of the courts
>
> → Judges are selected by the Judicial Appointments Commission (JAC), which was established by the **Constitutional Reform Act 2005**. JAC makes recommendations to the Lord Chancellor
>
> → To ensure judicial independence and for judges to be able to act without fear of repercussions, they must have security of tenure, be independent in all cases, and be independent from the government

> **STRETCH AND CHALLENGE**
>
> 1. Research ways in which judges can be more representative of society, for example by looking at the Lord Chancellor's Diversity Strategy (2006).
> 2. Consider more reforms to the appointment process. You could start by researching the findings of the government's 2007 consultation paper, 'Constitutional Reform: A New Way of Appointing Judges'.
> 3. Research the **Crime and Courts Act 2013**. Will the Act improve the efficiency, transparency and diversity of judicial appointments?

Magistrates

> **GRADE BOOST**
>
> Magistrates are another example of how lay people are involved in the criminal justice system. You may get a question that asks you about 'lay participation' in the law. This would require you to discuss both magistrates and juries. Remember to include both (see Chapter 8 for information on the role and function of juries).

Magistrates are lay people who volunteer to hear cases in the Magistrates' Court. They are not paid; volunteering as a magistrate is seen as a way of giving back to the community and gaining valuable skills. In addition to magistrates, professional judges, known as district judges (see page 98), sit alone in Magistrates' Courts.

The role of a magistrate or justice of the peace was established with the **Justices of the Peace Act 1361**. Today, magistrates' powers and functions are governed by the **Justices of the Peace Act 1997** and **Courts Act 2003**.

There were approximately 12,650 magistrates in 2021; the number has fallen steadily in recent years, decreasing by 50 per cent from 25,000 in 2012.

Magistrates must be able to commit at least 26 half-days per year to sit in court. An employer is required by law to allow reasonable time off work for an employee's service as a magistrate. Although this time off does not have to be paid, many employers allow for time off with pay. If a magistrate suffers loss of earnings they can claim a set rate for this loss. Expenses are also paid for travel and subsistence.

Cases in the Magistrates' Courts are usually heard by a panel of three magistrates, called a bench, supported by a legally qualified justices' clerk and legal advisor. The magistrate who sits in the centre is called the Presiding Justice, or more informally the Chair, as they have had additional training to do this.

Appointment of magistrates

- Appointed from the age of 18.
- Must retire at 75, although they generally won't be appointed if they are over 70.
- Since 2013, magistrates are appointed by the Lord Chief Justice on behalf of the Crown, assisted by local advisory committees who vet and recommend suitable candidates.
- Potential magistrates need to demonstrate six key characteristics, which were outlined by the Lord Chancellor in 1998:
  - Good character
  - Commitment and reliability
  - Social awareness
  - Sound judgement
  - Understanding and communication
  - Maturity and sound temperament
- Individuals can apply to become a magistrate by completing an online application form, which includes a series of questions on their eligibility and suitability. This application has to be accompanied by two references. If the applicant is successful at this stage, they will be invited for an interview, at which they will be assessed on whether they meet the six key characteristics and their motivations for applying.
- Selection is based on merit.
- Applications are welcome from all sections of the community regardless of gender, ethnicity, religion or sexual orientation.
- Magistrates should live within 15 miles of the bench's area. Up to 2003, it was necessary for lay magistrates to live within 15 miles of the commission area for the court they sat in. In 2003, the **Courts Act** abolished commission areas. Instead, there is now one commission area for the whole of England and Wales. However, the country is divided into local justice areas. These areas are specified by the Lord Chancellor and lay magistrates are expected to live or work within or near to the local justice area to which they are allocated.
- Applications are welcome from those with a disability, so long as their health does not prevent them from carrying out their duties.
- No legal or academic qualifications are required and full training is provided.
- Certain individuals are excluded from appointment, such as police officers and traffic wardens, and those with serious criminal convictions.

Role of magistrates

Criminal jurisdiction

Magistrates play an important role in the criminal justice system, dealing with approximately 95 per cent of cases. They hear summary and some triable either way offences. Their role is to decide the guilt or innocence of the defendant and to sentence them. They also issue warrants for arrest and decide on bail applications, and are involved in appeals to the Crown Court.

They have a limited sentencing jurisdiction. They cannot order sentences of imprisonment that exceed six months (or 12 months for consecutive sentences).

However, in May 2022, the **Judicial Review and Courts Act 2022** increased sentencing powers for magistrates to help ease the backlog of cases in the Crown Court. Magistrates will now be able to issue prison sentences of 12 months for a single offence.

The maximum fine allowed in a Magistrates' Court has generally been £5,000, but for offences committed on or after 12 March 2015, the fines in a Magistrates' Court are unlimited in most cases. In triable either way cases, the offender may be committed by the magistrates to the Crown Court for sentencing if a more severe sentence is thought necessary. They also try cases in the youth court if the defendants are aged 10 to 17.

Civil jurisdiction

Magistrates have a limited role in civil cases. They are responsible for issuing licences to betting shops and casinos, and they also hear appeals from Local Authority decisions regarding the issuing of pub and restaurant licences.

Magistrates no longer deal with adoption and domestic matters. Since 2014, the Family Proceedings Court has jurisdiction over various family law matters such as orders for protection against violence, maintenance orders and proceedings concerning the welfare of children.

The justices' clerk

Justices' clerks assist the magistrates with the law. They are qualified lawyers with a minimum five-year Magistrates' Court experience. Their role is to advise and guide the magistrates on questions of law, procedure and practice, as set out in the **Justices of the Peace Act 1979**. They have to give their advice in open court and cannot influence the magistrates' decision. This is an important role and some have recommended increasing the role of the clerk to aid the efficiency of magistrates.

Training for magistrates

As lay magistrates are rarely from a legal background, they receive mandatory training. They are also assisted by a justices' clerk and legal advisor. Magistrates' training is based on competences or what a magistrate needs to know and be able to do so that they can carry out the role. The Magisterial Committee of the Judicial College is responsible nationally for training, and at a local level this responsibility lies with the Magistrates' Association and the Justices' Clerks' Society.

Training in the first year

- Initial training covers the understanding of the organisation, administration, and roles and responsibilities of those involved in the court.
- Core training allows new magistrates to acquire and develop legal skills, knowledge and understanding.
- Ongoing training and development involves activities, observations of court sittings and visits to prisons and probation offices.
- Appraisals: during the first two years magistrates will be mentored, and an appraisal will take place to check if the magistrate has acquired the necessary competencies.

After the first year, ongoing training and development involves activities, observations of court sittings, and visits to prisons and probation offices, as well as updates on new legislation and procedures.

Continuation training

Magistrates continue training throughout their magisterial career. They receive additional training for youth court work.

Background of magistrates

There is an argument that magistrates do not represent the people whom they serve. They face similar criticisms to the judiciary in that they are 'middle class, middle aged and middle minded'. There are reasons why they tend to come from professional or middle-class backgrounds, such as availability to sit as a magistrate. Similarly, they tend to be middle aged or older as a result of the impact on their career of taking time to sit as a magistrate.

As at 1 April 2022:

- 57 per cent of magistrates identified as female
- 14 per cent of magistrates identified as BAME
- 79 per cent of magistrates were 50 and over
- 44 per cent of magistrates were 60 and over.

According to the Magistrates' Association, there is a crisis, as the number of magistrates has halved in the last decade, and between 1 April 2019 and 31 March 2020, 1,440 people left the magistracy. In January 2022, a huge recruitment campaign was launched, aiming to recruit 4,000 new magistrates, including young people and people from all social backgrounds. It is also hoped that the new online application system will modernise the candidate experience and enable diversity to be more closely monitored.

District judges (Magistrates' Court)

There are also approximately 130 professional judges who sit in the Magistrates' Court. They act as a sole judge and usually sit in Magistrates' Courts in large cities. Since the **Constitutional Reform Act 2005**, the Judicial Appointments Commission (JAC) is involved in their appointment. They receive a salary of around £90,000.

Advantages of magistrates

- Lay involvement: an example of public participation in the justice system.
- Local knowledge: community concerns and interests are represented.
- Balanced view: a bench of three magistrates should provide a balanced view.
- Cost: as volunteers, they are relatively cheap but do take longer to make decisions than professional judges. The average direct cost of a lay magistrate is £500 per year, whereas that of a district judge is £90,000.

Disadvantages of magistrates

- Not representative: as with the judiciary, most magistrates are from middle-class and professional backgrounds.
- Inconsistent: Magistrates' Courts tend to come to different decisions and sentences for the same crime.
- Inefficient: magistrates can be slow to reach a decision, often retiring to consider their verdict when a professional district judge would come to a decision straight away.
- Bias towards the police: sitting in local areas, magistrates get to know the police officers that give evidence in court and tend to be more sympathetic to them than the defendant.
- Cost: despite the low average direct cost, lay magistrates incur more indirect costs than paid judges, as they are slower, and they need support from the justice's clerk and also administrative support, so in reality there is very little difference between the costs of lay magistrates and district judges.

SUMMARY: MAGISTRATES

→ Magistrates' powers and functions are governed by the **Justices of the Peace Act 1997** and **Courts Act 2003**

→ Lay people aged 18–75

→ Appointment based on merit by the Lord Chief Justice on behalf of the Crown

→ Applications welcome from all sections of the community regardless of gender, ethnicity, religion or sexual orientation

→ Exclusions include police officers and traffic wardens, and those with a serious criminal conviction

---

STRETCH AND CHALLENGE

In 2012, the government issued a consultation paper called 'Swift and Sure Justice'. One proposal was to set up local community justice centres and some are now being piloted. The centres seek to bring together the courts and other agencies to tackle the underlying problems of crime in a community.

Research the consultation document. Do you think these centres will achieve the aims set out in the paper? What role will magistrates play in the centres?

GRADE BOOST

There have been calls to remove lay participation in the legal system. Investigate and discuss these main reform proposals:

- Increase the role of the justices' clerk.
- Replace lay magistrates with professional judges.
- Set up a District Division (Auld Review 2001 recommendation).
- Increase the representativeness of magistrates. How could this be achieved?

9 Legal personnel

- **Criminal jurisdiction**:
  - Hear summary and some triable either way offences
  - Decide the guilt or innocence of the defendant and sentence them
  - Limited sentencing jurisdiction
- **Civil jurisdiction**:
  - Limited role in civil cases
  - Issue licences to betting shops and casinos, and hear appeals on pub and restaurant licences
- **Justices' clerks**: qualified lawyers who advise and guide the magistrates on questions of law, procedure and practice, give advice in open court and cannot influence decisions
- **Training**: mandatory training based on competences or what they need to know and do for the role
- **Background**: 'middle class, middle aged and middle minded', although more representative in regards to gender and ethnicity
- **District judges (Magistrates' Court)**: professional judges who sit in city Magistrates' Courts
- **Advantages**: lay involvement; local knowledge; balanced view; lower direct cost
- **Disadvantages**: not representative; inconsistent; inefficient; biased towards the police; high indirect cost

TEST YOURSELF

1. What does KC mean?
2. What are the new requirements under the SQE to qualify as a solicitor?
3. What does cab rank rule mean?
4. What is the name of the body that appoints judges?
5. What are the four Inns of Court called?
6. What Act of Parliament reformed the role of the Lord Chancellor?
7. What types of criminal cases are magistrates involved with?
8. What are the sentencing powers of magistrates?
9. What is the role of the justices' clerk?
10. What is the correct title for legally qualified magistrates?
11. List four eligibility criteria required to become a magistrate.
12. Name the six key characteristics required to become a magistrate.
13. How has the Magistrates' Association tried to attract younger people to the magistracy?
14. Explain the training process for magistrates.
15. What is the role of magistrates in civil cases?

EXAM PAST PAPER QUESTIONS

WJEC – AS level – Unit 1 – May 2018
Section B
(a) Explain the education and training of solicitors and barristers in England and Wales. [8]
(b) Analyse and evaluate the independence of the judiciary. [24]

Eduqas – A Level – Component 1 – May 2019
Section B
(a) Explain the eligibility criteria required to become a judge. [10]

WJEC – AS Level – Unit 1 – May 2019
(a) Explain how magistrates are appointed. [8]

Eduqas – AS Level – Component 1 – May 2022
(a) Explain the role of magistrates in the criminal courts of England and Wales. [6]

10 Access to justice and funding

Many people have an unmet need for legal services, which simply means that they have a problem which could be solved by going to a solicitor or a court, but they are not able to get help from the system. This could be for a number of reasons:

> People fail to see that their problem has legal implications.
> People choose not to pursue their case because of implications such as cost, or they see solicitors as unapproachable.
> People do not know of the existence of a legal service or cannot find one that could help.

It is therefore clear that most people would not be able to gain access to justice unless there was some form of state-funded scheme. Equal access to legal services is a fundamental principle of the rule of law, as advocated by A.V. Dicey (see page 5).

The principle of the rule of law promotes the principle of equality before the law, equal access to justice and the right to a fair trial.

History of legal aid

1949: Welfare state

The first legal aid system was established after the Second World War as part of the welfare state. It worked by providing public funding to cover assistance with the cost of litigation and representation in court. The Legal Aid Board administered legal aid and people were assessed based on their means to pay and whether the case merited public funding.

1980s: Different types of legal aid

The system had developed into six different schemes, still administered by the Legal Aid Board. These were:

> legal advice and assistance scheme (the 'green form' scheme)
> assistance by way of representation (ABWOR)
> civil legal aid
> criminal legal aid
> duty solicitor – police stations
> duty solicitor – Magistrates' Courts.

1999: Access to Justice Act

This was introduced by the Labour government following its report, 'Modernising Justice'. The legal aid system was seen as needing a dramatic overhaul as it was not delivering access to justice. The new system had four clear aims:

> improve quality
> improve accessibility
> tighter control of the budget
> promote competition between providers. Solicitor firms had to apply for a contract for legal services, on the satisfaction of certain quality criteria.

The Legal Aid Agency was replaced by the Legal Services Commission, which administered two schemes: the Community Legal Service for civil legal aid, and the Criminal Defence Service for criminal cases.

2011: Lord Jackson, 'Review of Civil Litigation'

This report recommended a further overhaul of the legal aid system and has been extensively criticised. Many of Lord Jackson's recommendations were contained in the **Legal Aid, Sentencing and Punishment of Offenders Act 2012**, which has resulted in further austerity cuts and made access to justice further out of reach for many.

Legal Aid, Sentencing and Punishment of Offenders Act 2012

This Act came into force in April 2013 and created the publicly funded legal aid system that we use today. Its biggest criticism has been the removal of significant categories from the scope of legal aid, as well as the more stringent eligibility criteria and the reduction of the amount paid to legal professionals for undertaking legal aid work.

The system is overseen by the Legal Aid Agency, which replaced the Legal Services Commission, and is an executive agency sponsored by the Ministry of Justice.

The **Legal Aid, Sentencing and Punishment of Offenders Act 2012** also created the statutory office of the Director of Legal Aid Casework, who takes decisions on the funding of individual cases.

Civil legal aid

The **Legal Aid, Sentencing and Punishment of Offenders Act 2012** removes some cases from legal aid funding, and states that other cases will only qualify when they meet certain criteria. Now, the only cases or people that qualify for legal aid under **Schedule 1** are:

> clinical negligence in infants
> debt, mortgage repayment, repossession of home, orders for the sale of home and involuntary bankruptcy where the person's estate includes their home
> discrimination relating to the **Equality Act 2010**
> special educational needs (relating to young people)
> child protection and abduction
> domestic violence
> family mediation
> forced marriage
> housing issues that are a risk to health or life and homelessness
> welfare benefits (appeals on a point of law only)
> immigration (in limited cases).

In addition, **s10 Legal Aid, Sentencing and Punishment of Offenders Act 2012** provides that 'exceptional funding' can be granted in exceptional circumstances, where a failure to provide funding would result in a breach of the **European Convention on Human Rights**.

The reforms apply across all civil litigation and the most notable omission to the eligible cases is personal injury cases, where no win, no fee arrangements or conditional fee arrangements and damages-based agreements are the only options available (see below). Other notable omissions include employment cases, divorce and custody cases, immigration, debt (if there is no risk to the home) and many housing issues.

Only those solicitors' firms with a contract with the Legal Aid Agency can offer civil legal aid services. This introduces competition and improves standards between firms. This is a principle that was first introduced by the **Access to Justice Act 1999**.

CIVIL LEGAL AID
s8
Legal Aid, Sentencing and Punishment of Offenders Act 2012

Legal Aid Agency

CRIMINAL LEGAL AID
s16
Legal Aid, Sentencing and Punishment of Offenders Act 2012

Figure 10.1 Provisions in the Legal Aid, Sentencing and Punishment of Offenders Act 2012 relating to Legal Aid

A telephone gateway service was set up for clients who need debt, special educational needs and discrimination advice. They can only obtain this assistance via the phoneline, which is open from 9am to 8pm on weekdays and 9am to 12.30pm on Saturdays.

Means test

In order to qualify for civil legal aid, a means test and a merits test must be satisfied, found under **s4 Legal Aid, Sentencing and Punishment of Offenders Act 2012** and under **the Civil Legal Aid Regulations 2013**.

All clients will first be subject to a capital assessment, regardless of whether they are in receipt of certain benefits. Some people are automatically eligible through the passport system, that is, if they are in receipt of income support, jobseeker's allowance, universal credit, pension credit and employment and support allowance.

Income limit: to receive legal aid, the client's gross monthly income must be less than £2,657, with a disposable income of less than £733 per month.

Capital limit: the client can have capital of no more than £8,000.

The Legal Aid Agency waives all upper eligibility limits if the client is applying for legal aid for an order for protection from domestic violence or forced marriage, though a contribution may be required.

Merits test

The person/s making the assessment for legal aid (usually the solicitors) will consider the following:

> Prospects of success: how likely it is that the person applying will obtain a successful outcome. Usually, the chance of a successful outcome needs to be more than 50 per cent.
> Public interest: the case must benefit an identifiable class of individuals and be of a significant wider public interest.
> Proportionality test: whether the benefit to be gained from funding the case justifies the projected costs.
> Likely damages: the amount of damages the client is likely to receive if they are successful. High is more favourable because the solicitor will potentially receive more money.

Citizens Advice

Previously called the Citizens Advice Bureau, this is a national body and registered charity that provides free, easily accessed legal advice, making it an option as an alternative to legal aid. Face-to-face advice is offered at community centres, doctors' surgeries, courts and prisons, and also via phone and email services, and online.

GRADE BOOST
Legal advice and funding changes all the time, and although you would not be expected to include any legal reforms from the year before your exam, it is useful to demonstrate current and up-to-date knowledge.

Civil legal aid: Evaluation of Legal Aid, Sentencing and Punishment of Offenders Act 2012

> Civil legal aid is now only available in a limited number of cases, so that the government saves money.
> Access to legal aid has dramatically fallen under the reforms, and some categories of cases are completely inaccessible for legal funding. Dame Hazel Genn notes that these cuts will lead to an 'inevitable deterioration in effective access to justice' (Source: www.lawgazette.co.uk/analysis/dame-hazel-genn-warns-of-downgrading-of-civiljustice/48739.article).

10 Access to justice and funding

- Lord Neuberger: 'the most vulnerable in society are going to be affected by the cuts' (Source: www.bbc.co.uk/news/uk-21665319).
- Many people have to pay privately, find charitable help or represent themselves.
- People representing themselves put an increased burden on the courts as the hearing will last longer.
- The telephone gateway service provision has been criticised for a lack of public awareness as well as fewer referrals than expected for face-to-face advice.
- Some solicitors' firms are going out of business because there are not enough legally aided cases.
- Two-thirds of family cases going through the family courts have at least one side with no lawyer.
- Cuts to civil legal aid mean people are encouraged to look for an alternative to court: mediation, arbitration, tribunals, out-of-court settlements, etc.
- Alternative sources of funding have seen an increase in business.
- Applications to the Bar Pro Bono Unit (a charity that helps people to find free legal assistance from volunteer barristers) have doubled since 2012. This has led to a serious strain on this service and similar charitable organisations; it is questionable how long they will be able to cope with the increased demand. Successes such as *Heather Ilott* (2017) have raised the profile of the Bar Pro Bono Unit.

'No win, no fee' arrangements

The Legal Aid, Sentencing and Punishment of Offenders Act 2012 provides for two types of 'no win, no fee' arrangements. These arrangements are particularly useful for personal injury cases but also provide access to justice for those who do not qualify for civil legal aid.

Conditional fee arrangements		Damages-based agreements	
WIN	**LOSE**	**WIN**	
Legal representative gets paid the usual fee, plus an uplift/success fee.	Legal representative does not get paid.	Legal representative gets paid a percentage of the damages recovered.	

Figure 10.2 Outcome of CFA and damage-based agreements

Conditional fee arrangements

Conditional fee arrangements (CFAs) were first introduced by the Courts and Legal Services Act 1990 and then more widely in the Access to Justice Act 1999. They are not part of the legal aid system and are an entirely private agreement between the legal representative and the client. They are available for personal injury cases, as these cases are no longer funded by the legal aid system.

A notable change made by s44 Legal Aid, Sentencing and Punishment of Offenders Act 2012 was that the losing side no longer has to pay the costs of the winning party. The winning party typically pays out of the damages recovered. The legislation did provide for damages to be increased by 10 per cent to cover the additional fees that claimants face.

The uplift or success fee can be up to 100 per cent of the basic fee, except in personal injury cases, where the success fee cannot exceed 25 per cent of the damages, excluding damages for future care and loss. This is designed to protect claimants' damages, and ensures that any damages for future care and loss are protected in their entirety.

> **KEY TERMINOLOGY**
>
> **no win, no fee:** an agreement between a solicitor and a client whereby the client only pays the legal fees if the case is won.
>
> **uplift fee/success fee:** additional fee in a no win, no fee case of up to 100 per cent of the legal representative's basic fee, which is payable if the case is won. If the case is not won, the losing party does not have to pay any fees.

Damages-based agreements

Damages-based agreements (DBAs) work in a similar way to CFAs, as legal representatives are not paid if the case is not successful, but if their case is successful, they are entitled to take a percentage of their client's damages. These agreements have only been widely available for civil cases since 1 April 2013; before this, they were used mainly in employment tribunals.

The maximum payment that the legal representative can recover from the claimant's damages is capped at 25 per cent of the damages in personal injury cases, excluding damages for future care and loss, 35 per cent of the damages in employment tribunal cases and 50 per cent of damages in all other civil cases.

Evaluation of CFAs and DBAs

- CFAs and DBAs provide access to justice for those who do not qualify for legal aid and for cases (e.g. personal injury) for which civil legal aid is not available.
- They are a private agreement, so do not cost the taxpayer anything.
- Preparation and performance may be improved on the part of the legal professional because there is a financial incentive to win the case.
- Only 'cast-iron' cases are taken on and solicitors can essentially cherry-pick cases that have the highest chance of success.
- People can be subjected to high-pressure sales tactics by so-called claims farmers who use inappropriate marketing techniques and intimidating salespeople. They are known to approach people in hospital beds.
- Some people think these cases are literally 'no win, no fee', when in reality there are often hidden, unpredictable charges. In civil litigation, the loser normally pays the winner's costs, so individuals often have to take out expensive insurance premiums to cover the cost of losing and paying the other side's legal costs, which may not be affordable to everyone. In some cases, clients end up owing money.

Criminal legal aid

Similar principles apply for criminal legal aid as to civil legal aid; that is, the solicitors' firm has to have a contract to provide legal aid.

At the police station

Under **s58 Police and Criminal Evidence Act 1984** suspects have the right to access a **duty solicitor** at the police station.

> ### R v Samuel (1988)
> Access to a duty solicitor cannot be delayed after a suspect has been charged.

Under **s58(8) Police and Criminal Evidence Act 1984**, the suspect's right of access to a solicitor can be delayed by a police superintendent or above if the suspect has not been charged, if there is reasonable belief that access to a solicitor will lead to the alerting of other suspects.

> **KEY TERMINOLOGY**
>
> **duty solicitor:** solicitors who work in private practice but have secured a contract with the Legal Aid Agency to provide criminal advice to people who have been arrested. The person in custody will have the assistance of whoever is on the rota for that day.

> **STRETCH AND CHALLENGE**
>
> In October 2017, the Justice Secretary, David Liddington, announced a review into the cuts to legal aid imposed by the **Legal Aid, Sentencing and Punishment of Offenders Act 2012**. The consultation's focus is on whether the anticipated £450 million savings have been achieved and whether access to justice has been restricted, as critics of the reforms have suggested.
>
> Keep track of the progress of the review as it may offer key recommendations for reform.

10 Access to justice and funding

A duty solicitor is free for everyone at the police station, regardless of income. This is provided for by **s13 Legal Aid, Sentencing and Punishment of Offenders Act 2012**.

The Legal Aid Agency oversees a number of different agencies responsible for legal aid at the police station (see Table 10.1).

Table 10.1 Agencies responsible for legal aid

Agency	Explanation
Defence Solicitor Call Centre (DSCC)	All requests for publicly funded police station work must be made through the DSCC, which is manned by paralegals. The DSCC records the basic details of the alleged offence before deciding whether to pass the case to Criminal Defence Direct for telephone advice or whether to pass it to a duty solicitor, who will provide the suspect with a physical presence at the police station.
Criminal Defence Direct	Due to duty solicitors sometimes not turning up to police stations, Criminal Defence Direct was established to provide telephone advice to suspects at police stations. It is now the preferred method of contact for drink-driving offences, non-imprisonable offences, breach of bail and warrants.
Police station representative	In addition to duty solicitors, police station representatives can attend police stations to give advice and assistance to suspects. These are non-solicitors who are accredited to give legal advice and assistance to people detained at police stations. The standards that have to be met are available at www.sra.org.uk.
Public Defender Service (PDS)	The PDS is a department of the Legal Aid Agency, which operates alongside private providers to deliver legal services, advice and representation at the police station and Magistrates' Court through to advocacy in the higher courts.

At the Magistrates' Court

Two tests need to be satisfied to qualify for a representation order, which is criminal legal aid at the Magistrates' Court; this is provided for by **s14 Legal Aid, Sentencing and Punishment of Offenders Act 2012**. It is a way of capping the availability of criminal legal aid to those suspects who could afford to pay for their own defence.

Means test

This is a financial test that takes into account household income, capital and outgoings.

> Initial means test: if your calculation of household income is between £12,475 and £22,325 then a full means test is carried out.
> Full means test: this takes into account annual costs such as childcare, housing and maintenance, as well as essential spending on items like food, clothing and fuel. The outcome determines whether or not the suspect's costs of representation are covered in full.

If you are on certain benefits, you can passport your claim to be automatically granted criminal legal aid. The same benefits apply here as for civil legal aid (see page 101).

Merits test: Interests of justice test

In general, the more serious the charge and consequences, the more likely it is the person will qualify. The test considers previous convictions, the nature of the offence and the risk of custody. The solicitor must consider the Widgery Criteria, by taking into account the suspect agreeing to one or more of these statements:

> It is likely that I will lose my liberty.
> I have been given a sentence that is suspended or noncustodial. If I break this, the court may be able to deal with me for the original offence.
> It is likely that I will lose my livelihood.
> It is likely that I will suffer serious damage to my reputation.
> A substantial question of law may be involved.
> I may not be able to understand the court proceedings or present my own case.
> I may need witnesses to be traced or interviewed on my behalf.
> The proceedings may involve expert cross-examination of a prosecution witness.
> It is in the interests of another person that I am represented.
> Any other reasons.

> **EXAM SKILLS**
>
> If a question on legal funding doesn't specify civil or criminal, then it is crucial that you discuss both to achieve maximum marks.

At the Crown Court

A financial eligibility threshold was introduced for Crown Court trials from 27 January 2014. A defendant's household disposable income must be under £37,500 in order to be granted legal aid, then a means test will be applied and the defendant may be liable for contributions towards the case. If a client is refused legal aid, they will be expected to pay privately for the cost of their defence.

Criminal legal aid: Evaluation of Legal Aid, Sentencing and Punishment of Offenders Act 2012

> - Challenges in relation to criminal legal aid mean that apart from having a duty solicitor, defendants need to pass a means and a merits test to get help to be represented in court. This has huge implications for the undermining of the rule of law.
> - In 2014, solicitors challenged a government proposal to further cut criminal legal aid by 8.75 per cent and to reduce the number of contracts providing 24-hour cover at a police station in local communities from 1,600 to 527. They lost their case and the cuts went ahead.
> - The cuts also saw solicitors participate in strikes and walkouts, and they refused to take on any more legal aid clients.

> **GRADE BOOST**
>
> Criminal barristers in England and Wales have taken strike action over a pay dispute and access to legal services. Research this issue by reading the article at this link:
>
> www.theguardian.com/law/2022/oct/10/barristers-in-england-and-wales-vote-to-end-strike-action
>
> Summarise the impact the strike has had on the legal system. Do you agree with the barristers' motive for striking?

> **STRETCH AND CHALLENGE**
>
> Review the following articles, which highlight the effect that cuts to criminal legal aid had on legal professionals.
>
> 'Criminal defence call centres may work but are they justice?', *The Law Society Gazette*, 5 February 2009, www.lawgazette.co.uk/analysis/criminal-defence-call-centres-may-work-but-are-they-justice/49227.article
>
> 'Criminal legal aid fee cuts for lawyers confirmed by justice secretary', *The Guardian*, 27 February 2014, www.theguardian.com/law/2015/jul/27/criminal-barristers-stop-taking-new-crown-court-cases-legal-aid-protest
>
> 'Criminal barristers stop taking new Crown Court cases in legal aid protest', *The Guardian*, 27 July 2015, http://qrs.ly/ve5sg73

> **TEST YOURSELF**
>
> 1. What is meant by an 'unmet legal need'?
> 2. Name three categories of civil case that qualify for legal aid under the **Legal Aid, Sentencing and Punishment of Offenders Act 2012**.
> 3. What is the significance of **s10 Legal Aid, Sentencing and Punishment of Offenders Act 2012**?
> 4. Explain the difference between a conditional fee arrangement and a damages-based agreement.
> 5. What is meant by a 'no win, no fee' arrangement?
> 6. Outline four reasons why there is still an unmet legal need in civil cases.
> 7. What are the criticisms of conditional fee arrangements and damages-based agreements?
> 8. How is it decided whether a suspect qualifies for criminal legal aid at the Magistrates' Court?
> 9. Outline four reasons why there is still an unmet legal need in criminal cases.
> 10. Under which section of the **Police and Criminal Evidence Act 1984** is a suspect entitled to a duty solicitor at the police station?

SUMMARY: ACCESS TO JUSTICE AND FUNDING

→ 1949–1999:
- Welfare state
- Demand-led system led to 'unmet need for legal services'

→ 1999–2012:
- Set budget
- Franchising legal services
- Introduction of conditional fee arrangements
- Administered by Legal Services Commission

→ **Legal Aid, Sentencing and Punishment of Offenders Act 2012 (LASPO)**

→ **Legal Aid Agency**: Director of Legal Aid Casework takes decisions on individual cases

→ **Civil legal aid**:
- **s8 LASPO Act 2012**: Means test and merits test:
  - Child protection
  - Special educational needs
  - Welfare benefits
  - Domestic violence
  - Family mediation
  - Clinical negligence in infants
  - Loss of home
- **s10 LASPO Act 2012**: 'exceptional funding' where a failure to provide finding would breach human rights
- **Contracts**: only those with a contract with the Legal Aid Agency can offer civil legal aid (introduces competition and improves standards)

→ **Criminal legal aid**:
- **s16 LASPO Act 2012**: criminal advice and representation is delivered through a mixed system, e.g. public defender service, lawyers in private practice with contracts with the Legal Aid Agency
- **s13 LASPO Act 2012**: duty solicitor scheme at the police station: free for everyone, not means tested
- **s14 LASPO Act 2012**: legal aid for representation in court: only available subject to means and merits (interests of justice) test

EXAM PAST PAPER QUESTIONS

WJEC – AS Level – Unit 1 – May 2019
(a) Explain the sources of funding available to access justice in England and Wales.   [8]
(b) Analyse and evaluate the importance of conditional fee agreements.   [24]

Eduqas – AS Level – Component 1 – May 2022
(b) Analyse and evaluate the extent to which there is still a lack of funding to meet legal needs.   [18]

The Law of Tort

11 Rules of tort

What is a tort?

A **tort** is a civil wrong committed by one individual against another. There are various torts covering a wide range of situations such as claims by:

- an injured road user
- a patient injured by a negligent doctor
- someone who has suffered due to excessive noise
- someone injured when visiting a premises
- a celebrity libelled by a magazine
- a landowner whose land has been trespassed on.

The tort of negligence is most commonly associated with this area of law but there are several other torts.

A claimant to a tort action is normally seeking some form of **remedy**. This is usually in the form of damages (monetary compensation) paid by the **tortfeasor** in order to compensate for the tort. However, there are other remedies available such as well as or instead of damages, such as an injunction.

To win some tort cases, the victim needs to prove that the tort has caused some harm; however, some torts are actionable per se (in themselves). In these cases, the victim only has to prove that the relevant tort has been committed, not that any damage has been done. An example is the tort of trespass, where the landowner can claim damages from somebody trespassing on their land, even though no harm has been done by the **trespasser**.

Competing theories surround the purpose of the remedy in the law of tort:

- On the one hand, corrective (or restorative) justice supports the view that the purpose of damages in tort is to 'right the wrong'. It provides a civil recourse to put things back as they were, as far as this is possible.
- On the other hand, retributive justice, more commonly associated with the criminal law, can also play a role. This theory is associated with punishment, with the intention of dissuading the defendant and others from future wrongdoing. In the law of tort, the knowledge that one might be sued for a tortious act might serve as a deterrent or encourage a higher standard of care when performing certain acts. However, the fact that insurance premiums rather than the defendant's savings are, in many cases, used to pay compensation means that the deterrent value is reduced, despite the knowledge that premiums may increase.

KEY TERMINOLOGY

tort: a civil wrong committed by one individual against another, such as injury caused by negligence.

remedy: what the claimant is seeking to 'right the wrong'.

tortfeasor: someone who has committed a tort.

trespasser: a visitor who has no permission or authority to be on the occupier's land.

GRADE BOOST

The word 'tort' is French for 'wrong'. A person who commits a tort is referred to as a tortfeasor.

The difference between a tort and a crime

A tort is a private law action committed against an individual (e.g. negligence or nuisance), whereas a crime is a public law action committed against the state (e.g. theft, grievous bodily harm or murder). The aim of a tort action is to compensate the victim for the harm done, whereas the aim of a criminal prosecution is to punish the wrongdoer.

There are some areas of overlap; for example, high-level damages in tort arguably 'punish' the defendant and there are also provisions in criminal law for the wrongdoer to financially compensate the victim. In some areas, one incident may result in both a criminal prosecution and proceedings for tort; for example, where a victim suffers injury as a result of someone else's dangerous driving.

> **STRETCH AND CHALLENGE**
> There are also differences between tort and contract law. Research what these are.

Fault-based liability and strict liability

The general principle in law is that there can be no liability without fault. Liability in tort is based on the idea that the defendant is, in some way, at fault. Fault has been given a wide meaning in the law of tort and includes situations like negligence (where a defendant's behaviour has fallen below an accepted standard), intentionally causing harm and trespass (where the defendant is infringing another's rights). Fault-based liability deters others as they are aware that, if found to be at fault, they may be liable to pay compensation.

Some torts, known as strict liability torts, can be committed without the defendant being at fault in any way. These have the potential to be unfair, as the defendant can be liable to pay damages even though they may not have been able to prevent the harm. The case of *Rylands v Fletcher* (1868) is an example of a strict liability tort.

Strict liability offences also exist in criminal law and are contrary to the presumption of mens rea (see page 296) being required for the commission of a criminal offence. Find some case examples of these.

> **STRETCH AND CHALLENGE**
> Research *Rylands v Fletcher* (1868) and explain why it is significant in tort law.

Justifications for tort law

> The victim can be compensated for the damage caused by the wrongdoer. They can be put back in the position they would have been in (as far as possible) had the wrong not occurred (corrective or restorative justice).
> Individuals are deterred from committing acts or omissions that might hurt others in the knowledge that they may have to pay compensation. Tort law aims to make people and companies be more careful with their acts or omissions and therefore make society safer.
> In the absence of a tort system people who suffer injuries would be unable to claim compensation so instead may have to claim social security benefits, at the cost of the taxpayer.
> It is supported by the concept of the rule of law. For instance, a claimant unlawfully detained by the police can bring an action for unlawful imprisonment.
> Although the law of tort is largely based on corrective justice, there are elements of retributive justice. For example, in some circumstances a court can award damages to punish the tortfeasor in the form of exemplary damages.

Criticisms of tort law

- Some people believe that tort law is creating a compensation culture.
- Claims of negligence brought against state bodies such as the NHS still cost the taxpayer money.
- There is a lack of equality in the tort system. Many potential claimants may not have the financial means to bring an action in tort, and legal aid is rarely available for tort.
- Strict liability torts, as in the case of *Rylands* v *Fletcher* (1868), have been criticised for not requiring fault on the part of the tortfeasor.
- The system may be abused by people making fraudulent claims.

SUMMARY: RULES OF TORT

- A tort is a civil wrong (private law action) committed by one individual against another
- The aim of a tort action is to compensate the victim for the harm done, not to punish the wrongdoer
- A person who commits a tort is a tortfeasor
- A claimant to a tort action normally seeks a remedy such as damages or an injunction
- Corrective or restorative justice provides a civil recourse to put things back as they were, as far as possible
- Retributive justice is more common in criminal law, when the defendant is punished, but can apply to tort, e.g. exemplary damages
- Fault-based liability: no liability without fault, e.g. negligence or trespass
- Strict liability torts can be committed without the defendant being at fault: *Rylands* v *Fletcher* (1868)
- **Criticisms of tort law**:
  - May create a compensation culture
  - Claims against state bodies cost the taxpayer
  - Only those who can afford it bring action
  - Strict liability torts do not require fault
  - May encourage fraudulent claims

TEST YOURSELF

1. Which torts require no proof of fault?
2. What does the term 'remedy' mean?
3. What is a person who commits a tort known as?
4. Who are the two parties to a civil claim?
5. What is the standard of proof for a civil claim such as negligence?
6. Which party bears the burden of proof?
7. Name two remedies in the law of tort.
8. What is a tort?
9. Explain corrective justice in the law of tort.
10. In what way can the criminal theory of retributive justice apply to the law of tort?

12 Liability in negligence

Figure 12.1 Trips and falls can lead to claims for negligence

The tort of negligence is the most common tort. It covers a wide range of situations including medical negligence, road traffic accidents and faulty workmanship. Someone is negligent if they act carelessly to another person to whom they are legally obliged to act carefully, and if the carelessness causes the other person to suffer some harm or loss.

Negligence was defined in the case of *Blyth v Birmingham Waterworks Co* (1856) by Baron Alderson as 'failing to do something which the reasonable person would do or doing something which the reasonable person would not do'. According to this definition, negligence can come from either an act or an omission.

Negligence essentially protects against three different types of harm:

› personal injury
› damage to property
› economic loss.

The elements of negligence

For a claimant to succeed in a negligence case against a defendant, three elements need to be proved:

› The defendant owes the claimant a duty of care.
› The defendant was in breach of that duty of care.
› The claimant suffered damage as a result of the breach and that damage was not too remote.

Element 1: Duty of care

Only those who are owed a duty of care by a defendant will be able to claim a remedy for negligence. The tort of negligence has developed through case law and one of the first landmark rulings on the matter was in *Donoghue v Stevenson* (1932).

> ### *Donoghue* v *Stevenson* (1932)
> Mrs Donoghue's friend bought her a bottle of ginger beer in a café. She drank some of it but then discovered a decomposing snail in the bottle. As a result, she suffered gastroenteritis. Mrs Donoghue could not sue the café as she had not bought the drink herself; therefore, she brought an action against the manufacturer of the ginger beer for not ensuring the bottles were cleaned properly. In deciding whether the manufacturer owed Mrs Donoghue a duty of care, the House of Lords established the neighbour principle. Lord Atkin said that the manufacturers owed a duty of care to 'anyone who could be affected by their actions' (their neighbours). Therefore, they did owe Mrs Donoghue a duty of care and her claim succeeded.

Lord Atkin said: 'You must take reasonable care to avoid acts or omissions which you can reasonably foresee would be likely to injure your neighbours.' He defined 'neighbour' as 'anyone who would be so directly affected by your act that you ought reasonably to have them in your contemplation'.

The neighbour principle has since been used in situations such as:

> a lift repairer owing a duty of care to anyone using their lift
> a solicitor owing a duty of care to a client who suffers financially following the negligent drafting of a legal document.

Several different approaches have been formulated by the courts since *Donoghue v Stevenson* (1932) for deciding when a duty of care is owed, including the three-stage test in *Caparo v Dickman* (1990) and most recently the approach taken in *Robinson v Chief Constable of West Yorkshire Police* (2018). This case is important because it is a UK Supreme Court decision which reformulates the approach to establishing a duty of care. It does not overrule *Caparo*, but rather it states that it has been misunderstood and should now be viewed and applied differently.

> ### KEY CASE
> *Robinson* v *Chief Constable of West Yorkshire Police* (2018)
> An elderly woman was knocked over by two police officers as they attempted to arrest a drug dealer. They were found liable for her injuries as it was reasonably foreseeable that the police officers' actions would cause the claimant harm, based on the *Donoghue v Stevenson* (1932) neighbour principle.

The court set out the approach that the courts should take when addressing questions of whether a duty of care exists. In the exam, you should outline the approach following *Robinson* (2018), as this is now established law.

1. Follow precedent if possible

'Follow precedent if possible' – the court should always follow precedent if one exists. The court will ask if the case involves issues that are the same or similar to existing, established case examples. Examples include:

> Doctor – patient (*Montgomery v Lanarkshire* (2015))
> Lawyer – client (*Arthur JS Hall v Simons* (2000))

GRADE BOOST

In *Robinson* v *Chief Constable of West Yorkshire* (2018), Elizabeth Robinson's claim failed in the Court of Appeal on Parts 2 and 3 of the Caparo test.

However, the Supreme Court drew a distinction between positive acts and omissions of the police. Mrs Robinson won her claim on the basis that a police officer is liable in negligence where the injury results from a negligent action by a police officer, as long as that injury was a reasonably foreseeable consequence. They concluded that Part 3 of the Caparo test would be satisfied where a public body's action risks causing harm that would not otherwise have existed. This case has also changed the approach of the courts with regard to duty of care (see above).

- Driver – passenger (*Nettleship v Weston* (1971))
- Manufacturer – consumer (*Donoghue v Stevenson* (1932))

2. If no precedent exists...

'If no exact precedent exists, develop case law incrementally from analogous (similar) cases' – if no exact precedent exists, the court should seek analogous (similar) cases to inform their decision, but always aim to keep the law consistent and avoid distinguishing precedents unnecessarily. If the law can be extended, based on existing precedent, the court can consider whether this would be just and reasonable.

> **KEY CASE**
>
> ***Darnley v Croydon Health Services NHS Trust* (2018)**
> This case was decided post-*Robinson*. Although no exact precedent existed for injury caused by the negligence of a hospital receptionist, or non-medical staff, the court held that this case fell within the same established category of duty as *Barnett v Chelsea and Kensington* (1969), a duty not to cause physical injury to the patient. The court also considered analogous cases such as *Kent v Griffiths* (2001).
>
> Based on this, the court held that there was no distinction between medical and non-medical staff: they all owed a duty of care to patients not to provide misleading information.

3. If no analogous cases exist...

'If no analogous cases exist and the situation is completely novel only then revert to the Caparo test' – the court should only use the three-part Caparo test if a case involves a relationship between the parties or set of facts that has never been seen before. The three part-test is set out below.

The Caparo test

The basic concept of the neighbour principle was redefined in the key case of *Caparo Industries plc v Dickman* (1990). This is known as the Caparo test (or incremental approach) and is considered to be wider than the neighbour test. The test consists of three elements. It has to be shown that:

- the damage was **foreseeable**
- there is a sufficiently **proximate relationship** between the claimant and defendant
- it is just, fair and reasonable to impose a duty of care.

Lord Bridge, in the *Caparo* case, also suggested that the law of the duty of care should develop on an incremental basis (step-by-step) as new situations arise, rather than assuming it exists in all situations.

Each of the elements of the Caparo test will now be considered in turn.

1. Foreseeability

For a duty of care to exist, it must be reasonably foreseeable that damage or injury would be caused to the particular defendant or to a certain group of people (rather than people in general).

> **KEY TERMINOLOGY**
>
> **foreseeable:** events the defendant should be able to have predicted could happen.
>
> **proximate relationship:** (in tort law) how close the defendant and victim are physically or emotionally.

> ***Kent v Griffiths* (2000)**
>
> A doctor called for an ambulance to take a patient suffering from a severe asthma attack to hospital immediately. The ambulance failed to arrive within a reasonable time and there was no good reason for the delay. The patient suffered a heart attack, which would not have happened if the ambulance had arrived on time. It was held that it was reasonably foreseeable that the claimant would suffer some harm from this delay.

Figure 12.2 *Kent* v *Griffiths* (2000) demonstrated the foreseeability element of the Caparo test

> **GRADE BOOST**
>
> What would the impact be of a culture where the emergency services can be sued? Is it in the public interest for police to owe a duty of care to individuals?
>
> Research *Michael* v *Chief Constable of South Wales Police* (2015). What was Lord Keith's position in relation to the application of tort to police officers?

> **STRETCH AND CHALLENGE**
>
> Look up the case of *Haley* v *London Electricity Board* (1965). What damage was reasonably foreseeable?

2. Proximity

Proximity means 'closeness' in terms of physical space, time or relationship. This test is quite similar to the neighbour test. If there is not a sufficiently proximate relationship between the claimant and defendant, the defendant cannot reasonably be expected to have the claimant in mind since they are not likely to be affected by the defendant's acts or omissions.

> **KEY CASE**
>
> **Bourhill v Young (1943)**
> The claimant, a pregnant Mrs Bourhill, was descending from a bus when she heard a motor accident. She did not actually see it but later saw blood on the road and suffered shock and her baby was stillborn. Although it was reasonably foreseeable that someone would suffer harm as a result of the defendant's negligent driving, injury to the specific claimant was not foreseeable as she was not in the immediate vicinity of the accident and she only heard but did not see the accident. Her action therefore failed.

> **STRETCH AND CHALLENGE**
>
> Look up the case of *McLoughlin* v *O'Brien* (1983) on the issue of proximity. In what other ways can there be a 'proximate' relationship?

3. It is just, fair and reasonable to impose a duty of care

This is also known as the policy test, as judges are able to limit the extent of the tort through judicial discretion. One of the main reasons for this is the floodgates argument, where there is the risk of opening up a potential claim to a huge number of claimants. An American judge, Benjamin N. Cardozo, referred to this danger when he warned of 'liability in an indeterminate amount for an indeterminate time to an indeterminate class'.

Mulcahy v Ministry of Defence (1996)
The claimant was a soldier who had served in the Gulf War, where he had suffered damage to his hearing. The Court of Appeal held that although both factors of foreseeability and proximity were present, the facts required it to consider this a policy issue. The Ministry of Defence did not, therefore, owe a duty of care to servicemen in such battlefield situations.

Alcock v Chief Constable of South Yorkshire Police (1991)
This case involved people who suffered 'nervous shock' as a result of witnessing the Hillsborough stadium disaster, when 95 people were killed as a result of a crush. It was decided that it would not be just, fair and reasonable to impose a duty of care on the police in respect of a claimant who was at the other end of the ground to the crush, in which his brother-in-law was involved.

Element 2: Breach of duty of care

Once a duty of care has been established, it needs to be proved that it has been breached: in other words, that the defendant has not fulfilled their duty of care. The standard of care to be expected is that of the 'reasonable man', which assumes that a reasonable person is 'average', not perfect. This is generally an objective test, asking 'What would a reasonable person have foreseen in this particular situation?' rather than 'What did this particular defendant foresee in this particular situation?' However, it has been developed through case law to take account of special standards of care for defendants with a professional skill (see examples below), and other relevant factors such as the magnitude of risk.

The reasonable man test derived from *Alderson B in Blyth v Birmingham Waterworks* (1865), which defined it as 'the omission to do something which a reasonable man would do, or doing something which a prudent and reasonable man would not do'.

For example, in the case of *Nettleship v Weston* (1971), when a learner driver's passenger was injured when she crashed, it was established that a learner driver is expected to meet the same standard as a qualified and competent driver.

The courts have established various tests in determining if a defendant has breached their duty of care.

1. Degree of probability that harm will be done
If the risk is very small then it may be decided that the defendant is not in breach. Care must also be taken in respect of a risk where it is reasonably foreseeable that harm or injury may occur. In *Roe v Minister of Health* (1954), two claimants had been paralysed after being given contaminated anaesthetic for minor operations. The anaesthetic had been contaminated in storage, but this storage method was common at the time. The hospital was not liable as they had not diverted from standard practice at that time.

Bolton v Stone (1951)
The claimant had been hit by a cricket ball while standing on the road outside the cricket ground. In 35 years, a cricket ball had only been hit out of the ground on six occasions and no one had ever been injured. In addition, the wicket was 100 yards from the road and there was a 17-foot-high fence between the ground and the road. It was held that the defendant was not in breach of his duty of care.

> **GRADE BOOST**
> In *Hill v Chief Constable of West Yorkshire* (1988), the family of a victim of serial killer Peter Sutcliffe brought a claim for negligence against the police for failing to catch the killer quickly enough. They argued that the police had been negligent in their duty. The court held that there was no duty of care because it would not be 'fair and reasonable' to impose one on a police force for this omission.

2. The magnitude of likely harm

In this test, the courts consider not only the risk of harm but also how serious the injury could foreseeably be.

> ### Paris v Stepney Borough Council (1951)
> In this case, Paris was a mechanic who was blind in one eye. His employers were aware of this, yet failed to provide him with protective goggles for his work. He was blinded in his 'good' eye by a piece of metal that went into it during his work. His employers tried to argue that it was not usual to provide goggles for such activities, but it was counter-argued that, as they were aware he was blind in one eye, they should have taken greater care of his safety than for employees without that disability. The magnitude of potential harm was greater for Paris, so the greater risk to the claimant meant that more precautions than normal should have been taken. The employer was found to be liable.

3. The cost and practicality of preventing risk

With this test, the court is looking at whether the defendant could have taken precautions against the risk. If the cost of taking such precautions to eliminate the risk is disproportionate to the extent of the risk itself, the defendant will not be held liable.

> ### Latimer v AEC Ltd (1953)
> The owner of a factory used sawdust to reduce the effects of a recent flood but the factory floor remained slippery, and as a result, an employee fell and was injured. It was held that there was no breach of duty as the only way to have avoided the risk was to close the factory altogether, which was not proportionate to the level of risk involved.

4. Potential benefits of the risk

There are some situations where the risk has a potential benefit for society.

> ### Daborn v Bath Tramways (1946)
> The claimant was injured after being hit by a left-hand drive ambulance without indicators during wartime. The Court of Appeal held that a lower standard of care than usual applied because the ambulance driver was acting in the public good, and it would have been unreasonably expensive to have converted the ambulance to right-hand drive.

Lord Justice Asquith said: 'If all the trains in this country were restricted to a speed of five miles an hour, there would be fewer accidents, but our national life would be intolerably slowed down. The purpose to be served, if sufficiently important, justifies the assumption of abnormal risk.'

However, the nature of the work of the emergency services does not make them immune from negligence claims, as can be seen in the case of *Armsden v Kent Police* (2000), when a driver was killed in a collision with the defendant's police car. The police car did not have its siren on and was driving fast to attend an incident when it collided with the other car when approaching a junction with a side road. The Court of Appeal found the driver of the police car had breached his duty of care by failing to use the siren.

Special characteristics of the defendant

In some situations, the standard is not a purely objective one and the courts are able to take into account certain special characteristics of the defendant. Interestingly, in the case of drivers, the standard is that of the ordinary, normal driver (ignoring their experience and years qualified). This was confirmed in the case of *Nettleship v Weston* (1971) (see page 115).

Professional persons

Where the defendant has a professional skill, the court will expect them to show that they have the degree of competence usually expected of a typical skilled member of that profession. This means, for example, that a GP will only be expected to exercise the normal level of skill of a GP, not that of a senior consultant or surgeon.

> **STRETCH AND CHALLENGE**
>
> What did the courts say regarding the standard of care to be expected where the defendant is exercising special skill or knowledge, as in the case of *Bolam* v *Friern Hospital Management Committee* (1957)?

Figure 12.3 A defendant with a professional skill, where relevant to the case, is expected to only demonstrate the normal level of skills for their job

Children

Where the defendant is a child, the standard of care is that of an ordinarily careful and reasonable child of the same age.

> ### *Mullin* v *Richards* (1998)
> Two 15-year-olds were fighting with plastic rulers. One ruler broke and fragments blinded one of the girls in one eye. It was held that their behaviour was reasonable for their age, so the defendant was not negligent.

Element 3: Resulting damage

There has to be some sort of damage (e.g. physical injury or damage to property) resulting from the defendant's negligence. The claimant must be able to prove both that the damage was caused by the defendant's breach of duty and that the damage was not too remote; that it was reasonably foreseeable. This can be broken down into two issues:

› causation
› remoteness of damage.

Causation is decided using the 'but for' test: 'But for (i.e. if it wasn't for) the defendant's breach of duty, would damage or injury have occurred?'

Barnett v Chelsea & Kensington Hospital Management Committee (1968)

The claimant's husband attended the defendant's hospital, complaining of severe stomach pain and vomiting. The doctor in A&E refused to examine him and he was sent home with the advice to see his own GP. Some hours later, he died of arsenic poisoning. The defendant (the A&E doctor) clearly owed the deceased a duty of care and was also in breach by failing to examine him. However, the doctor was held not liable because the evidence showed that, by the time he attended the hospital, the man would have died anyway and the doctor could not have done anything to save him. As the deceased would have died regardless of the breach, the hospital was held not to be the cause of his death.

It must also be established that the damage was not too remote, i.e. that it is not too removed from the defendant's negligence. The test for remoteness is whether there is a direct, foreseeable causation.

KEY TERMINOLOGY

causation (or chain of causation): the connection of the negligent act with the corresponding result.

KEY CASE

Wagon Mound (No. 1) (1961)
The defendant, a ship owner, negligently discharged fuel from his ship into Sydney Harbour. The oil drifted across to a wharf where welding works were taking place. The claimants were advised that there was no risk of this heavy oil catching fire on the water and as a result carried on welding. But the oil did ignite, damaging the claimants' property. On appeal, it was held that the defendants were not liable for the damage to the claimant's property because the major damage to the property caused by the ignition of the oil was too remote from the original discharge of oil.

Another issue to consider is foreseeability of damage. This relates to the kind, and extent, of damage suffered. For example, a defendant may still be liable even if the extent of the injury was not foreseen. This can be seen in the case of *Smith v Leech Brain & Co* (1962) where the defendant was found liable for the death of a man who was burned on the lip by hot metal due to the defendant's negligence. The burn caused cancer and the man died. This case also illustrates the legal principle of the 'thin skull test', which states that the defendant must take the victim as they find them as regards their physical characteristics. This means that the defendant will be liable where injuries to the claimant are more serious than might have been anticipated because of factors that are particular to the victim.

GRADE BOOST

The case of *Wagon Mound (No. 1)* (1961) overruled a previous case (*Re Polemis & Furness, Withy & Co Ltd* (1921)) in that the defendant would be liable for all damage that was a direct consequence of their breach of duty. This test was considered too wide and would have the potential for too many claims to succeed.

Intervening causes

Sometimes the law will not impose liability for negligence if there is an intervening cause that breaks the chain of causation; for example, a natural event or the actions of a third party. The phrase *res ipsa loquitur* (Latin for 'the facts speak for themselves') is associated with this idea.

Where, in negligence cases, it is clear that the harm could not have arisen unless the defendant was negligent, the court may be prepared to infer that the defendant was negligent without hearing detailed evidence of what was or was not done. A classic example of a *res ipsa loquitur* situation is leaving a train door open as it departs the station, as in *Gee v Metropolitan Railway* (1873).

STRETCH AND CHALLENGE

Look up the cases of *Hughes v Lord Advocate* (1963) and *Jolley v Sutton* (2000) and explain how they illustrate the issue of foreseeability.

Psychiatric injury: Primary and secondary victims

Psychiatric damage is injury to the mind rather than the body; it can also be referred to as nervous shock. To claim damages, a claimant must show, using medical evidence, that they have a recognised psychiatric injury that goes beyond normal grief or distress.

Primary victims

A primary victim has either suffered physical injury as a result of another person's negligence or suffered a psychiatric injury where it was reasonably foreseeable that they could have been physically injured as a result of another person's negligence; for example, a person who is involved in a workplace accident and is not physically injured but develops a serious psychiatric condition.

Secondary victims

A secondary victim has suffered psychiatric injury as a result of another person's negligence but was not exposed to danger. Several other conditions need to be met to be classified as a secondary victim.

Alcock v *Chief Constable of South Yorkshire Police* (1992) demonstrates the law surrounding secondary victims relates to the Hillsborough disaster in 1989. Following the Hillsborough disaster, ten claimants brought a case against the South Yorkshire Police.

> ### *Alcock* v *Chief Constable of South Yorkshire Police* (1992)
> The claimants were attempting to claim for nervous shock resulting in psychiatric injury which they claimed had been caused by the experience of witnessing the Hillsborough football stadium disaster. To claim they had to be classed as secondary victims. Robert Alcock, one of the claimants, was in a different stand to where the disaster unfolded but witnessed distressing scenes. On leaving the ground, he went to meet his brother-in-law, who did not arrive. Alcock then had to identify his brother-in-law's heavily bruised body in the mortuary. The other claimants had similar experiences.
>
> It was held that the claimant must usually show a sufficiently proximate relationship to the victim. This is often described as a 'close tie of love and affection'. Such ties are presumed to exist between parents and children, spouses and fiancés. This means other relations, including between siblings (e.g. brothers), must prove their ties of love and affection. Robert Alcock had lost a brother-in-law and the court held that there was no evidence of particularly close ties of love or affection. It was held that it must be proved that it was reasonably foreseeable that the claimant would suffer psychiatric damage. Therefore, the case did not succeed.

GRADE BOOST
Research the Hillsborough football stadium disaster. Where did it take place? What happened and do you think anyone was negligent in causing the disaster?

Figure 12.4 Memorial to those who died in the Hillsborough football stadium disaster

Reasonable foreseeability depends upon establishing a sufficiently proximate relationship. The closer the tie between the plaintiff and the victim, the more likely it is that they would succeed in showing that the psychiatric damage was reasonably foreseeable.

In addition, *Alcock* v *Chief Constable of South Yorkshire Police* (1992) held that to be a secondary victim, a claimant must witness the event with their own unaided senses, hear the event in person or view its immediate aftermath: the claimant must be in close physical proximity to the event. Therefore, those who witness such an event on television, hear it on the radio or are informed about it from a third party are unlikely to be classified as secondary victims. This applied to some of the other claimants in the case.

The House of Lords did hint that a person with no sufficiently proximate relationship may be classed as a secondary victim in exceptional circumstances. Lord Keith said:

> 'The case of a bystander unconnected with the victims of an accident is difficult. Psychiatric injury to him would not ordinarily, in my view, be within the range of reasonable foreseeability, but could not perhaps be entirely excluded from it if the circumstances of a catastrophe occurring very close to him were particularly horrific.'

STRETCH AND CHALLENGE

Research what happened to the other claimants in the *Alcock* (1992) case and what this meant for tort law.

EXAM SKILLS

You might be asked to explain an individual element of negligence for a lower mark question. With a scenario question involving negligence, you would be required to explain and then apply all three elements in turn in order to reach a conclusion.

GRADE BOOST

When applying the law to a problem question, take each element of the offence and apply it to the problem question. Work your way methodically through the list of elements for liability in negligence, applying each to the scenario and remembering to use appropriate legal authority throughout.

Also, make sure you apply each element of a relevant test (e.g. the Caparo test).

12 Liability in negligence

> **SUMMARY: LIABILITY IN NEGLIGENCE**
>
> → **Duty of care:** neighbour test: *Donoghue v Stevenson* (1932)
> → **Duty of care:**
>   - *Robinson v Chief Constable of West Yorkshire Police* (2018):
>   - Apply precedent
>   - If no precedent, use analogous case law
>   - If no analogous case, apply Caparo test
>   - Caparo (incremental) test: *Caparo Industries plc v Dickman* (1990)
>   - Damage foreseeable: *Kent v Griffiths* (2000)
>   - Proximity: *Bourhill v Young* (1943)
>   - Just, fair and reasonable: *Mulcahy v Ministry of Defence* (1996)
> → **Breach of duty of care:**
>   - Standard of care: reasonable man: *Nettleship v Weston* (1971)
>   - Probability of harm: *Bolton v Stone* (1951)
>   - Magnitude of likely harm: *Paris v Stepney Borough Council* (1951)
>   - Cost and practicality of preventing risk: *Latimer v AEC* (1953)
>   - Potential benefits of risk: *Daborn v Bath Tramways* (1946)
> → **Special characteristics** of defendant, e.g. professional persons, children: *Mullins v Richards* (1998)
> → **Resulting damage not too remote:**
>   - Causation: 'but for' test: *Barnett v Chelsea & Kensington Hospital Management Committee* (1968)
>   - Remoteness of damage: is the loss a reasonably foreseeable consequence of the defendant's negligence? *Wagon Mound (No. 1)* (1961)
>   - Foreseeability of damage: *Smith v Leech Brain* (1962) ('thin skull test')
> → Intervening causes can break the chain of causation
> → *Res ipsa loquitur*: the facts speak for themselves
> → Psychiatric injury: nervous shock; medical evidence
>   - Primary victims
>   - Secondary victims: proximate relationship (close ties of love and affection); unconnected bystanders: *Alcock v Chief Constable of South Yorkshire Police* (1992)

> **TEST YOURSELF**
>
> 1. What are the three elements of a negligence claim?
> 2. Name and explain the facts of the case that has superseded *Caparo* (1990) for proving a duty of care exists in the tort of negligence.
> 3. Name the three Caparo tests for duty of care, and include a case for each.
> 4. What is the Latin for a 'new intervening act'?
> 5. The case of *Nettleship v Weston* (1971) established that the standard of care for learner drivers is that of a ...?
> 6. Who can claim for psychiatric harm?
> 7. Explain the 'but for' test.
> 8. Name and explain three risk factors in relation to breach of duty of care. Include a case for each.
> 9. What does the Latin doctrine of *res ipsa loquitor* mean?
> 10. Define a secondary victim.

EXAM PAST PAPER QUESTIONS

NB: you will need to have also read the information on damages in Chapter 17 Remedies: tort before being able to attempt some of these questions.

WJEC – AS Level – Unit 2 – May 2019

1. Explain, with relevant case law, the Caparo three-part test used to decide whether a duty of care is owed. [8]

Cerys owns a pop-up food stall that she sets up at festivals and events. Noah, a freelance journalist, bought a chicken burger from Cerys' stall during a concert and became very unwell shortly after consuming the burger. Tests revealed that it was food poisoning and environmental health also discovered poor hygiene conditions in Cerys' stall. Noah has a stomach condition that means he is much more likely to suffer serious long-term conditions if he experiences food poisoning. As a result, he is hospitalised for a month and loses out on £3,000 of work. In addition, he suffers long-term stomach pain which affects his ability to work and socialise.

4. Advise Noah as to whether Cerys is liable in the law of negligence for his injuries. [18]
5. Analyse and evaluate the different types of damages in the law of negligence. [18]

Eduqas – AS Level – Component 2 – October 2020

1. Assess the differences between primary and secondary victims. [9]
2. Read the scenario below and answer part (d).

Chris, a chemistry teacher, liked making his own fireworks. He took a firework he had just finished to show his neighbour Ben, who invited Chris into his living room. Chris put the firework on Ben's coffee table so that they could admire it. Unfortunately, the fuse on the firework was not secured properly and the firework exploded, wrecking the living room and severely injuring Ben who can no longer work and requires constant care. His life expectancy is greatly reduced as a result. The explosion also damaged an expensive painting hanging on the wall in the living room, which cost £3,000 to repair. In addition, the cost of repairing the living room was £10,000.

(d) Assume that Chris was found liable in negligence. Advise Ben how the court would calculate his award of damages. [9]

Eduqas – A Level – Component 2 – June 2019

After several weeks of persistent rain, Sara noticed a leak coming through her bedroom ceiling so she rang a roofing company and arranged for Jim, a roofing contractor, to come and have a look to see if any of the roof tiles were loose. Jim said that there were five tiles that were damaged and loose, and that he would have to come back and replace them. A week later, when Jim was replacing the tiles on the roof, he used the wrong nails, which did not secure the new tiles properly. As a result, some of the tiles came loose and fell on Julie, a delivery driver, as she was delivering a parcel to Sara, causing her to suffer a broken leg. Julie had thought that the tiles were loose and might fall, but had decided to ignore the risk and go ahead and deliver the parcel anyway.

Advise Julie if Sara could be held liable in tort for her injuries, applying your knowledge and understanding of legal rules and principles. [25]

13 Torts connected to land

Trespass to land

Trespass to land is a tort that can be defined as the unjustifiable interference with land that is in the immediate and exclusive possession of another. This topic is not relevant to the WJEC specification.

The essential elements of trespass to land

This topic is not relevant to the WJEC specification and is Eduqas only.

There are four essential elements:

- There is direct interference with the land.
- The interference must be voluntary.
- There is no need for the defendant to be aware they are trespassing.
- There is no need for the claimant to experience harm or loss.

Figure 13.1 Common warning sign placed on private property

1. Direct interference

Trespass requires direct interference with land, such as physical entry, throwing something onto the land, or if given the right to enter the land, remaining there when the right has been withdrawn.

For instance, if a person plants a tree that overhangs a neighbouring property, it is indirect interference and likely to be a private nuisance rather than trespass. However, if someone

123

cuts down a tree and throws the branches into their neighbour's garden, that is direct interference and is likely to be a trespass.

> ### KEY CASE
>
> **Southport Corporation v Esso Petroleum (1954)**
> A small oil tanker ran aground in poor weather conditions, due to carrying a heavy load and having a steering fault. Oil was deliberately discharged to free the tanker. The oil drifted onto the claimant's land. The claimant brought an action for nuisance, negligence and trespass. The Court of Appeal decided by 2 to 1 that the defendants were liable for negligence, not trespass. Denning LJ stated that the defendants were not liable for trespass because:
>
>> '(t)his discharge of oil was not done directly on to their foreshore, but outside in the estuary. It was carried by the tide on to their land, but that was only consequential, not direct. Trespass, therefore, does not lie.'

2. Voluntary interference with land
It can only be trespass if the person has voluntarily entered the land. In *Stone v Smith (1647)*, it was held that a person who was forcibly carried or thrown onto land by others was not trespassing.

3. Awareness of trespassing is not needed
An innocent trespass is still a trespass. Mistake is no defence in trespass.

> ### KEY CASE
>
> **Conway v George Wimpey & Co (1951)**
> One of the defendant's lorry drivers had given a lift to the claimant, who worked for another company. Both were working on an aerodrome. This was expressly prohibited by company rules. The claimant claimed that while dismounting from the lorry, he was injured due to the negligence of the driver.
>
> The Court of Appeal held that because there was no proof that the defendant knew or must have known that passengers from other companies were being given lifts, the claimant was a trespasser while on the lorry and as a result the defendants were not under any duty of care to him. Therefore, the Court of Appeal held that a person could be liable for trespass even if they were mistaken about the ownership of land or wrongly believed they had permission to enter the land.

4. No need for the claimant to experience harm or loss
Trespass to land is actionable per se (in itself). This means that there is no need for the defendant to have caused the claimant any damage or loss.

Trespass above or below the land

Cuius est solum, eius est usque ad coelum et ad inferos is Latin for 'who owns the land owns to the heavens and down to hell'. It is controversially used to explain the common law principle that ownership of land includes the air above it and the ground below it. This principle has been restricted through precedent and statute.

Lord Hope in *Star Energy Weald Basin Limited v Bocardo SA (2010)* stated that the above Latin phrase 'still has value in English law as encapsulating, in simple language, a proposition of law which has commanded general acceptance'.

Trespass in airspace

Bernstein v Skyviews and General Ltd (1977)

The defendants had flown over the claimant's land to take an aerial photograph of his property, which they then offered to sell to him. The High Court stated that there was no trespass because the claimant did not have an unlimited right to all the airspace above his land but only the right to that airspace as was necessary for the ordinary use and enjoyment of his land and buildings.

Griffiths J said:

> 'The problem in this case was to balance the rights of a landowner to enjoy the use of his land against the rights of the general public to take advantage of all that science now offered in the use of airspace. The best way to strike that balance in our present society was to restrict the rights of an owner in the airspace above his land to such height as was necessary for the ordinary use and enjoyment of his land and the structures upon it, and to declare that above that height he had no greater rights in the airspace than any other member of the public.'

Figure 13.2 Trespassing in airspace

Trespass below the surface of land

Star Energy Weald Basin Limited v Bocardo SA (2010)

The Supreme Court held that the defendant had trespassed when, from adjacent land, it had vertically drilled oil wells that were 244 to 853 metres below the surface of the claimant's land.

However, since **s43 Infrastructure Act 2015**, land that is 300 metres or more below the surface ('deep-level land') can be exploited for 'the purposes of exploiting petroleum or deep geothermal energy' without liability for trespassing.

Figure 13.3 One of the reasons why fracking is controversial is because the Infrastructure Act 2015 allows companies to drill into land without liability for trespass, even if they do not have the landowner's permission

Trespass *ab initio*

Ab initio is Latin for 'from the beginning'. This is a form of trespass that occurs when a person who has entered land with the authority given by law, rather than with the permission of the person possessing the land, subsequently commits an act that is an abuse of that authority. The authority is cancelled retrospectively and the entry is deemed to have been a trespass from the beginning.

This type of trespass action was often used in cases against the police when they had exceeded the authority given to them with a search warrant while seizing stolen goods during a search of premises. Such an action often meant damages were assessed on the tortious nature of the police's whole conduct, rather than just the abuse of authority. However, precedent and statute law have increased the power of the police when searching premises, so such actions are rarely successful today and, therefore, some textbooks regard *trespass ab initio* as having little relevance to English and Welsh law today.

Actions for *trespass ab initio* are more common in other common law jurisdictions such as the USA.

> **STRETCH AND CHALLENGE**
>
> Research the **Infrastructure Act 2015**. Why is **s43** controversial?

Defences to trespass to land

The following are the main defences to trespass to land.

1. Legal authority (or justification by law)

A person is not liable for trespass if they have legal authority permitting them to be on that land. Here are four examples:

> The **Countryside and Rights of Way Act 2000** gives the public certain rights of access to land, provided that they comply with certain statutory restrictions.
> The **Police and Criminal Evidence Act 1984** gives the police certain rights to enter land to make arrests and to search premises.

- Rights of way established under the common law. Rights of way are recorded on 'definitive maps' prepared by a local authority.
- Common land, which is land where although it might be owned by someone else, certain people have rights of access through custom for a particular purpose, such as to graze livestock or cut peat for fuel.

Figure 13.4 Public footpaths are considered common land

2. Consent (licence) including contractual licence

A licence to enter land can be received with either the express or implied consent of the person possessing the land. Implied consent can be given in a number of ways. For instance, at the front of a house is a pathway to the front door, and the door has a letterbox and a doorbell. This gives implied consent for persons to walk on the path and come to the front door to deliver a letter or ring the bell to attract the attention of those who live there.

A contractual licence to enter land covers situations when a purchaser receives permission to be on land as part of a purchase. For instance, if you buy a cinema ticket to see a film, you receive a contractual licence to go into the cinema.

A person becomes a trespasser once express or implied permission is withdrawn or if a person exceeds the limits of the permission. The defence of consent (or licence) can no longer be used once permission is withdrawn.

For instance, although there may be implied permission for someone to come to up to a front door and deliver a letter, there is no implied permission for that person to go into the back garden or enter the property.

Even if there is a contractual licence, this can be withdrawn. If, having bought a cinema ticket, you are asked to leave the cinema, you will become a trespasser if you stay. (Of course, if having paid you are asked to leave, you might have a remedy under the law of contract!)

> #### Wood v Leadbitter (1845)
> A man was removed from a racecourse despite having bought a ticket. It was held that his contractual licence could be revoked, making him a trespasser.

3. Necessity

Necessity has two forms: private and public necessity:

> Private necessity involves an act needed to protect your own property against the threat of harm.
> Public necessity involves an act to protect the wider public against harm.

The case law of necessity when applied to trespass is uncertain. The general rule seems to be that there must be an actual danger and the acts of the defendant must be reasonable in light of all the facts.

Remedies to trespass to land

> Damages and injunctions are the usual remedies for trespass to land.
> Orders for Possession are court orders and covered by the **Civil Procedure Rules Part 55**. They are issued by a court following a successful 'possession claim against trespassers'. The order instruct the defendants to leave the land by a particular date.
> Self-help (sometimes known as 'abatement') involves the common law right of a land owner or occupier to remove the trespasser themselves. This 'remedy' consists of a person using 'reasonable force' to remove trespassers. It is not available if the trespass is on a residential property.

Possession claim against trespassers

The **Civil Procedure Rules Part 55.6** state:

'Where, in a possession claim against trespassers, the claim has been issued against "persons unknown", the claim form, particulars of claim and any witness statements must be served on those persons by:

(a)

(i) attaching copies of the claim form, particulars of claim and any witness statements to the main door or some other part of the land so that they are clearly visible; and

(ii) if practicable, inserting copies of those documents in a sealed transparent envelope addressed to 'the occupiers' through the letter box; or

(b) placing stakes in the land in places where they are clearly visible and attaching to each stake copies of the claim form, particulars of claim and any witness statements in a sealed transparent envelope addressed to "the occupiers".'

KEY CASE

Rigby v Chief Constable of Northamptonshire (1985)
The police had fired a CS gas canister into a shop to force out a dangerous suspect. The gas canister caused the shop to catch fire. The police had not arranged for adequate firefighting equipment to be available, so the shop was burned out. A claim was brought for negligence, under the rule in *Rylands v Fletcher* (1868) (see page 141), and trespass.

The High Court held that the police were liable for negligence for failing to provide adequate firefighting equipment. However, the judge rejected liability for trespass, arguing that the defence of necessity was available in an action for trespass because there was no negligence on the part of the police in creating or contributing to the necessity. They did not create the suspect.

The judge also rejected liability under the rule in *Rylands v Fletcher* (1868) because the rule applies only to an 'escape' and 'probably' does not apply to the intentional or voluntary release of a dangerous thing.

Figure 13.5 Rights of way can be indicated by signs

> **GRADE BOOST**
> Note that US case law is relatively more decided than English law on the defence of necessity. When searching for information on the internet, make sure you know which country case law applies to.

Trespass in criminal law

Trespass originates in civil law. After Parliament grew concerned about many incidents of trespass by protestors, hunt saboteurs, squatters and those attending open-air raves, it created several statutory offences involving trespass, such as the offences of aggravated trespass and squatting in a residential building.

Aggravated trespass

Under **s69 Criminal Justice and Public Order Act 1994**, a person commits the offence of aggravated trespass if they trespass on land and, in relation to any lawful activity which persons are engaging in or are about to engage in on that or adjoining land, does anything there which is intended by them to have the effect of:

- intimidating any of those persons to deter them from engaging in that activity
- obstructing that activity, or
- disrupting that activity.

Offence of squatting in a residential building

Under **s144 Legal Aid, Sentencing and Punishment of Offenders Act 2012**, a person commits a criminal offence (of squatting) if they:

- are in a residential building as a trespasser, having entered it as a trespasser
- know or ought to know that they are a trespasser
- are living in the building or intend to live there for any period.

Figure 13.6 Hunt saboteurs can be prosecuted for committing aggravated trespass

Public nuisance

A public nuisance 'materially affects the reasonable comfort and convenience of life of a class of Her Majesty's subjects' (*Attorney General v PYA Quarries Ltd* (1958) per Romer LJ). Archbold's definition:

> 'A person is guilty of a public nuisance (also known as common nuisance), who (a) does an act not warranted by law, or (b) omits to discharge a legal duty, if the effect of the act or omission is to endanger the life, health, property or comfort of the public, or to obstruct the public in the exercise or enjoyment of rights common to all Her Majesty's subjects.'

A public nuisance differs from a private nuisance on the basis of who is affected by the nuisance. It affects a representative cross-section of a society in a neighbourhood.

Public nuisance is a crime. Under **s17(1)** and **s1 Magistrates' Courts Act 1980**, public nuisance is an offence which is triable either way.

There is no requirement of intention or recklessness in the offence of public nuisance. The fault element is one of foreseeability of the risk of the type of nuisance. The defendant is liable if they knew or ought to have known of the risk of the type or kind of nuisance that in fact occurred.

This type of foreseeability was established in the key case *Wagon Mound (No. 1)* (1961) and reiterated in *Cambridge Water Co v Eastern Counties Leather plc* (1994).

Cambridge Water Co v Eastern Counties Leather plc (1994)

The defendant owned a leather-tanning business. Small quantities of solvents were spilled over a long period of time, seeping through the floor of the building into the soil below. These solvents made their way to the borehole owned by the claimant water company. The borehole was used for supplying water to local residents. The water was contaminated beyond a level that was considered safe and Cambridge Water had to cease using the borehole. Cambridge Water brought actions based on negligence, nuisance and the rule in *Rylands v Fletcher* (1868) (see page 141). Eastern Counties Leather was not liable as the damage was too remote. It was not reasonably foreseeable that the spillages would result in the closing of the borehole.

The foreseeability of the type of damage is a prerequisite of liability in actions of nuisance and claims based on the rule in *Rylands v Fletcher* (1868) in the same way as it applies to claims based in negligence.

R v Goldstein (2006)

The defendant had enclosed some salt in an envelope together with a cheque. It was intended as a joke both because of the age of the debt he was paying and as a reference to a recent anthrax outbreak in the USA, which he had discussed with the intended recipient. The salt leaked out of the envelope in a sorting office, creating an anthrax scare and the evacuation of the sorting office.

The House of Lords held that there was no public nuisance because it was not proved that the defendant knew or reasonably should have known that the salt would escape from the envelope in the sorting office and cause a nuisance.

It is the same type of foreseeability as in private nuisance. Note that the term 'fault element' is often referred as the mens rea in criminal law.

13 Torts connected to land

> **KEY CASE**
>
> ### Wagon Mound (No. 1) (1961)
> The defendant's vessel, *The Wagon Mound*, leaked furnace oil at a wharf in Sydney Harbour. Some cotton debris became entangled in the oil and sparks from some welding works ignited the oil. The fire spread rapidly, destroying some boats and the wharf.
>
> In this case, a test of remoteness of damage was substituted for the direct consequence test. The test is whether the damage is of a kind that was foreseeable. If a foreseeable type of damage is present, the defendant is liable for the full extent of the damage, whether or not the extent of damage was foreseeable. The Privy Council found in favour of the defendant, agreeing with the expert witness who provided evidence that the defendant, despite the furnace oil being innately flammable, could not reasonably expect it to burn on water.

Figure 13.7 An injunction was granted in *Attorney General* v *PYA Quarries Ltd* (1958)

> **KEY CASE**
>
> ### Attorney General v PYA Quarries Ltd (1958)
> An injunction was obtained to prevent the defendant from emitting quantities of stones, splinters, dust and vibration from their quarry, which was disturbing local residents. The defendants unsuccessfully appealed to the Court of Appeal to have the injunction removed. The injunction was granted as the result of a 'relator action'. This is when an injunction is sought to stop a person committing a public nuisance. Relator actions are brought in the name of the Attorney General. They are very rare today.

In relation to *Attorney General* v *PYA Quarries Ltd* (1958), Romer LJ stated:

> 'The sphere of the nuisance may be described generally as "the neighbourhood"; but the question whether the local community within that sphere comprises a sufficient number of persons to constitute a class of the public is a question of fact in every case. It is not necessary, in my judgement, to prove that every member of the class has been injuriously affected; it is sufficient to show that a representative cross-section of the class has been so affected.'

Denning LJ stated:

'I decline to answer the question how many people are necessary to make up Her Majesty's subjects generally. I prefer to look to the reason of the thing and to say that a public nuisance is a nuisance which is so widespread in its range or so indiscriminate in its effect that it would not be reasonable to expect one person to take proceedings on his own responsibility to put a stop to it, but that it should be taken on the responsibility of the community at large.'

A class of people

The facts of the case will determine if the persons affected by a nuisance amount to a class of people.

Class of people: Local communities

R v Ruffell (1991)

- The defendant had pleaded guilty to causing a public nuisance. The nuisance had consisted of an 'acid house' party. A side road to the site had been blocked by traffic. Very loud music played all night and the woodlands around the site were littered with human excrement.
- The class of people affected by the nuisance were the local residents.
- The defendant unsuccessfully appealed to the Court of Appeal against the custodial sentence imposed in the Crown Court.

Figure 13.8 Sports spectators can be classed as a group of people

Class of people: Group with a common interest

R v Ong (2001)
- The defendant and others were planning to interfere with the floodlights during a Premier Division football match between Charlton Athletic and Liverpool.
- They pleaded guilty to conspiracy to commit a public nuisance (and another offence).
- The class of people that would have been affected by the nuisance were the football spectators.
- The defendants unsuccessfully appealed to the Court of Appeal against the custodial sentences imposed in the Crown Court.

Class of people: Impact on the community

R v Lowrie (2004)
- The defendant, who had made a number of hoax calls to the emergency services, pleaded guilty to causing a public nuisance.
- The class of people that would have been affected by the nuisance were those who were in genuine need of help from the emergency services but could not get help because the emergency services had been diverted by the hoax calls.

Sending abusive letters

R v Rimmington (2006)
The House of Lords held that sending racially offensive materials to members of the public was not a public nuisance. The reasoning was that sending individual letters to individual people did not constitute a nuisance affecting a class of people.

The House of Lords also stated that common law offences such as public nuisance should not be used for conduct covered by a statutory offence unless there was a good reason. Rimmington could have been prosecuted under the Malicious Communications Act 1988.

Making obscene telephone calls

R v Johnson (1997)
The Court of Appeal held that making obscene telephone calls to several women in a geographic area was a public nuisance. However, the House of Lords indicated in *R v Rimmington* (2006) that such behaviour is unlikely to amount to a public nuisance as they were separate calls made to separate people rather than to a class of people.

Making obscene telephone calls can now be prosecuted under statutory provisions such as the Communications Act 2003.

Law Commission Report No. 358

The Law Commission indicated in 2015 that:

- prosecutions for public nuisance were still occurring despite relevant statutory provisions
- some nuisance telephone call cases were still being prosecuted as a public nuisance.

Both of the above cases indicate that limitations on prosecution imposed in *Rimmington (2006)* were not being 'reflected in practice'.

STRETCH AND CHALLENGE

Read the Law Commission's report, 'Simplification of Criminal Law: Public Nuisance and Outraging Public Decency' (Law Com No. 358, 2015; https://s3-eu-west-2.amazonaws.com/lawcom-prod-storage-11jsxou24uy7q/uploads/2015/06/lc358_public_nuisance.pdf). You need only read the parts concerning public nuisance. You will find that the report gives a good insight into public nuisance.

1. What criticisms does the Law Commission make of the law on public nuisance?
2. How does the Law Commission suggest that the law on public nuisance could be reformed?

Civil actions against public nuisance

Civil actions can be brought against those committing a public nuisance in three ways. The remedies sought will be damages and a prohibitory injunction.

1. By a realtor action. These are brought in the name of the Attorney General on behalf of a private citizen who has persuaded the Attorney General to agree to the action. Such actions are rare. Possible reasons for this include the following:
   - There are statutory bodies, such as local authorities, who will usually bring the actions.
   - The Attorney General is unlikely to agree to a realtor action unless there is special damage and, if there is special damage, private citizens can bring actions in their own name without the permission of the Attorney General.
   - Most nuisance that affects the citizen can be prosecuted under statutory provisions rather than public nuisance.
   - The Attorney General will often receive no applications for a realtor action in any particular year.
2. By a local authority under **s222 Local Government Act 1972**.
3. By an action for tort by a private citizen who can show that they have suffered special damage beyond that experienced by the others of 'His Majesty's subjects'.

Private nuisance

A private nuisance is an interference with a person's enjoyment and use of their land. It is a civil action.

When courts and law reports refer to a 'nuisance', they are usually referring to a private nuisance and not a public nuisance.

When statute law refers to a 'nuisance', it usually means both public and private nuisance unless otherwise stated.

Figure 13.9 Noisy music that disturbs your neighbours could be regarded as a private nuisance

Types of private nuisance

There are three kinds of private nuisances:

> Nuisance by encroachment on a neighbour's land. For example, the roots from a tree in a garden grow under the ground and into a neighbour's garden, damaging the foundations of the neighbour's house.
> Nuisance by direct physical injury to a neighbour's land. For example, driving a car over a neighbour's garden, damaging their garden.
> Nuisance by interference with a neighbour's quiet enjoyment of their land. For example, playing Justin Bieber music all night, every night, and stopping a neighbour from sleeping.

Lord Lloyd in *Hunter and Others* v *Canary Wharf Ltd* (1997) and *Hunter and Others* v *London Docklands Corporation* (1997) stated that just because something is an annoyance does not mean it is actionable in private nuisance. For example, a building interfering with television signals is an annoyance but is not actionable as a private nuisance.

Hunter and Others v *Canary Wharf Ltd* (1997)

The claimants sought damages for private nuisance in respect of interference with the television reception in their homes caused by the construction of Canary Wharf. The House of Lords stated by a majority decision that no action lay in private nuisance for interference with television caused by the mere presence of a building. Lord Lloyd stated: 'The annoyance caused by the erection of Canary Wharf and the consequential interference with television reception must have been very considerable. But, unfortunately, the law does not always afford a remedy for every annoyance, however great.'

Figure 13.10 Buildings at Canary Wharf interfered with local television reception

Characteristics of a private nuisance

A private nuisance has three key elements.

1. The claimant must have an interest in the land

A claimant must have an interest in the land affected by the nuisance in order to make a claim of private nuisance. In effect, an 'interest in land' means a person must own or have a right over the land. Owners, leaseholders or tenants have an interest in the land and can make a claim of private nuisance. Visitors, family members and lodgers do not have an interest in the land and cannot make a claim of private nuisance. In effect, a person who is in exclusive possession of the land is regarded as having an interest in the land.

Figure 13.11 A claimant can have interest in the land if they have exclusive possession of it

Foster v *Warblington UDC* (1906)

The claimant was an oyster merchant who for many years had occupied oyster beds artificially constructed on the foreshore. The claimant excluded everybody from the oyster beds, and nobody interfered with his occupation of the oyster beds or his removal and sale of oysters from them. However, he could not prove ownership of the oyster beds.

Despite this, the claimant could bring an action in the private nuisance caused by the defendants discharging sewage into the oyster beds because he was in exclusive possession of the land.

Malone v *Laskey* (1907)

A company had rented a house for one of its managers to live in. The wife of the manager was injured when a bracket in a toilet fell on her head because of the vibrations of machinery on the defendant's property. The Court of Appeal decided that the wife could not make a claim of nuisance because she had no interest in the property.

Khorasandjian v *Bush* (1993)

The daughter of a property owner brought a claim to obtain an injunction against a man who was harassing her, including making nuisance telephone calls. The county court granted an injunction preventing the defendant from 'harassing, pestering or communicating' with the claimant. It was argued by the defence that the injunction could prevent the defendant from assaulting or threatening to assault the claimant because that was covered by the tort of trespass to the person. However, it was argued by the prosecution that the current wording of the injunction did not reflect any known tort. The Court of Appeal held that the wording of the injunction should remain unaltered. As part of its reasoning, it argued that the telephone harassment was covered by the tort of private nuisance because it was an actionable interference with the woman's ordinary and reasonable use and enjoyment of property where she is lawfully present.

The Court of Appeal was particularly concerned that, at the time of *Khorasandjian* v *Bush* (1993), there was no alternative action available for the woman to take. The woman could now obtain protection under the **Protection From Harassment Act 1997**.

In *Hunter and Others* v *Canary Wharf Ltd* (1997) and *Hunter and Others* v *London Docklands Corporation* (1997) the claimants included not only property owners and tenants but also members of their families and lodgers. Both cases were heard by the House of Lords at the same time. *Hunter and Others* v *London Docklands Corporation* (1997) concerned damage caused by dust created during the construction of a road. Both cases included actions for nuisance.

The House of Lords had to decide which persons could bring an action in private nuisance. They decided that only householders with a right to land could commence an action in private nuisance. In doing this, the House of Lords rejected the decision in *Khorasandjian* v *Bush* (1993) but upheld the decision in *Malone* v *Laskey* (1907).

2. There must be unreasonable use of the land which is the source of the nuisance

The use of the land which is the source of the nuisance must be unreasonable for a claim of private nuisance to succeed. In deciding whether the use of land is unreasonable, the courts will consider several factors:

> The sensitivity of the claimant: the standard of tolerance is that of the reasonable person and ordinary land use. Abnormally sensitive claimants or using land for an unusual purpose that makes it sensitive to disruption are unlikely to succeed in a claim for private nuisance.

Robinson v *Kilvert* (1888)

The defendant let a floor of his property to a tenant to be used as a paper warehouse, retaining the cellar immediately below. The tenant brought an action to prevent his landlord from heating the cellar, on the grounds that the rising heat dried his special brown paper, making it less valuable. Ordinary paper would not have been damaged. There was no private nuisance. Lopes LJ at the Court of Appeal argued that a:

'man who carries on an exceptionally delicate trade cannot complain because it is injured by his neighbour doing something lawful on his property, if it is something which would not injure anything but an exceptionally delicate trade'.

> The duration and time of the nuisance can determine whether a private nuisance has been created. In *Halsey* v *Esso Petroleum Co Ltd* (1961) the High Court held that a private nuisance was created by noise at night from boilers and road tankers. Generally, the courts require a private nuisance to be a continuing state of affairs. However, there are exceptions to this requirement. For example, in *Crown River Cruises Ltd* v *Kimbolton Fireworks Ltd* (1996), a firework display that set fire to some moored barges was held to be a private nuisance.

Figure 13.12 Fireworks were held to be a private nuisance in *Crown River Cruises Ltd* v *Kimbolton Fireworks Ltd* (1996)

> The character of the area in which the alleged nuisance occurred is relevant in deciding whether there is a private nuisance.

St Helen's Smelting Co v *Tipping* (1865)

Damage caused by vapours from a factory was held to be a private nuisance even though there were many other factories in the neighbourhood that also emitted vapours. It was held that, although the character of the area is important, it did not prevent a successful action in private nuisance for damage to property.

Wheeler v *Saunders Ltd* (1994)

The claimant owned a house next to a farm. He claimed that a private nuisance had been created by the granting of planning permission for two new pig houses because the smell of the pigs was interfering with his use and enjoyment of his house.

The defendants argued that the granting of planning permission changed the character of the area so that what would have once been a private nuisance was no longer one. The Court of Appeal decided that the granting of planning permission for a pair of pig houses did not alter the character of the area and therefore what was once a private nuisance is still a private nuisance. The granting of planning permission does not authorise the creation of a private nuisance. The defendants were liable for private nuisance.

> The reasonable foreseeability of the type of damage: to succeed in an action for private nuisance, it does not need to be shown that the defendant has taken reasonable care to avoid causing a nuisance (i.e. harm, damage or inconvenience). However, it does need to be shown that the type of nuisance was reasonably foreseeable. This type of foreseeability was established in *Wagon Mound (No. 1)* (1961).
> Any act of malice on the part of the defendant can lead to a successful action for private nuisance even though the defendant might be abnormally sensitive or if the act would not usually amount to an unreasonable use of land.

Hollywood Silver Fox Farm Ltd v Emmett (1936)
The claimant company was a fox fur farm. The defendant, an adjoining landowner, maliciously caused his son to discharge a shotgun on his own land as near as possible to the fox pens to interfere with the female foxes during the breeding season. The court held the claimant was entitled to an injunction and damages for the private nuisance. Although it was not unreasonable for a farmer to use a shotgun on his own land, and the keeping of a fox fur farm might not be an ordinary use of land, the defendant had acted maliciously. It was also irrelevant in this case that the female foxes were unusually sensitive to noise during the breeding session.

3. The claimant must suffer some harm
Private nuisance is not actionable per se. There must be some damage, harm, injury or inconvenience.

Liability for private nuisance: Occupier
An occupier is liable in private nuisance if they bear some personal responsibility for it. This means that if the private nuisance was created by an act of:

- a stranger
- nature
- the previous occupier, the current occupier is liable if they know or ought to know about it.

Liability for private nuisance: Landlord
A landlord is liable in private nuisance if:

- the landlord authorises the tenant to commit a private nuisance
- at the date of letting, the landlord knows or ought to know of the private nuisance
- the private nuisance is created during the tenancy and there is no agreement between the landlord and tenant making the tenant responsible for such repairs needed to remove the nuisance.

Defences to private nuisance
There are two main defences to a private nuisance.

1. Statutory authority
It is a defence to private nuisance if the claimant can show that their conduct was authorised by law. For example, s76 Civil Aviation Act 1982 states:

> 'No action shall lie in respect of trespass or in respect of nuisance, by reason only of the flight of an aircraft over any property at a height above the ground which, having regard to wind, weather and all the circumstances of the case is reasonable, or the ordinary incidents of such flight, so long as the provisions of any Air Navigation Order ... have been duly complied with.'

2. Prescription
The defence of prescription is a claim by the defendant that they have acquired the right to act in a particular way because they have done so for 20 years. It is sometimes referred to as an 'easement by prescription'. However, this defence is based on property law and can be difficult to use in practice.

Sturges v Bridgman (1879)
Prescription could not be used as a defence because although the defendant had used noisy equipment for more than 20 years, it only became a nuisance the moment the claimant doctor built his consulting room nearby. In other words, the 20 years is not based on how long the act has been going on but rather on how long the act has been a nuisance.

KEY TERMINOLOGY

maliciously: interpreted as meaning with intention or subjective recklessness.

GRADE BOOST

Read Lord Neuberger's judgment in *Coventry and Others* v *Lawrence* (2014) where the Supreme Court stated there will be occasions when the terms of a planning permission may be of some relevance in a nuisance case.

STRETCH AND CHALLENGE

Find out the facts and decisions in *Sturges* v *Bridgman* (1879) and *Miller* v *Jackson* (1977). Do you think that the decisions in both cases were fair?

Remedies for private nuisance

The main remedies for a private nuisance are damages and injunctions.

The overlap between private nuisance and negligence

There is an overlap between nuisance and negligence. In many cases, claimants bring an action for both private nuisance and negligence. Both require injury or harm to the claimant and require foreseeability of the type of damage. There are, however, differences between the two. A private nuisance does not need to involve a negligent act. The remedies for a private nuisance are usually damages and an injunction to stop the nuisance. The remedy for negligence is damages.

In *Miller* v *Jackson* (1977) Denning MR stated:

> 'The tort of nuisance in many cases overlaps the tort of negligence ... But there is at any rate one important distinction between them. It lies in the nature of the remedy sought. Is it damages? Or an injunction? If the plaintiff seeks a remedy in damages for injury done to him or his property, he can lay his claim either in negligence or nuisance. But, if he seeks an injunction ... I think he must make his claim in nuisance. The books are full of cases where an injunction has been granted to restrain the continuance of a nuisance. But there is no case, so far as I know, where it has been granted so as to stop a man being negligent.'

Figure 13.13 The emission of fumes can establish liability in nuisance and negligence

Hunter and Others v *Canary Wharf Ltd* (1997) and *Hunter and Others* v *London Docklands Corporation* (1997) quoted the statement from *Wagon Mound (No. 1)* (1961):

> 'Nuisance is a term used to cover a wide variety of tortious acts or omissions and, in many, negligence in the narrow sense is not essential. An occupier may incur liability for the emission of noxious fumes or noise although he has used the utmost care in building and using his premises ... On the other hand, the emission of fumes or noise or the obstruction of the adjoining highway may often be the result of pure negligence on his part: there are many cases ... where precisely the same facts will establish liability both in nuisance and in negligence.'

13 Torts connected to land

> **KEY CASE**
>
> **Rylands v Fletcher (1868)**
> Fletcher had a reservoir built on his land. Sometime later the reservoir burst and flooded a neighbouring mine run by Rylands. The House of Lords held that if someone, for their own purposes, brings, collects and keeps on their land anything likely to do mischief, they must do so at their peril. If it escapes, they are *prima facie* (on the face of it) answerable for all the damage which is the natural consequence of its escape.
>
> Blackburn J in the Court of Exchequer quoted by Lord Cairns in *Rylands v Fletcher* (1868):
>
> > 'The person whose grass or corn is eaten down by the escaping cattle of his neighbour, or whose mine is flooded by the water from his neighbour's reservoir, or whose cellar is invaded by the filth of his neighbour's privy, or whose habitation is made unhealthy by the fumes and noisome vapours of his neighbour's alkali works, is damnified without any fault of his own; and it seems but reasonable and just that the neighbour who has brought something on his own property (which was not naturally there), harmless to others so long as it is confined to his own property, but which he knows will be mischievous if it gets on his neighbour's, should be obliged to make good the damage which ensues if he does not succeed in confining it to his own property.'

> **EXAM SKILLS**
>
> Always check the wording of the question. Many acts can involve possible liability in negligence, private nuisance or trespass to land. You will only gain limited marks if the question asks you to consider liability for private nuisance and you write an answer on negligence or trespass.

The rule from *Rylands v Fletcher* (1868)

The essential parts of the rule are as follows, although some of these essential parts have been modified, refined and added to by precedent over the years:

- Something must have been collected and kept on the land.
- The use of the land must be non-natural. Lord Cairns in *Rylands v Fletcher* (1868) suggested that if water had naturally accumulated on or below the surface of the land then liability would not have arisen.
- The thing brought onto the land must be likely to do mischief if it escaped.
- The thing brought onto the land must have escaped and caused damage.

The development of the rule

Although the main principles of the rule have remained, precedent has adapted the rule in several ways. In particular, the courts have examined the following questions:

- Does the thing collected and kept have to escape?
- What is the meaning of non-natural use of land?
- To what extent must the thing be likely to cause mischief?
- Is foreseeability of harm needed?

The thing collected and kept

The thing collected and kept on land need not be the thing that escapes. Something collected and kept on land that causes something else to escape can lead to liability.

> **GRADE BOOST**
>
> Research *Coventry and Others v Lawrence and another* (2014) and *Coventry and Others v Lawrence and another (No. 2)* (2014). In these cases, the Supreme Court needed to consider various issues concerning private nuisance. Read the Supreme Court press release, which summarises both cases and the law on private nuisance:
> https://www.burges-salmon.com/-/media/files/publications/open-access/fundamental_change_to_law_of_nuisance_coventry_v_lawrence.pdf

> **Miles v Forest Granite Co (Leicestershire) Ltd (1918)**
> Explosives kept on land were detonated to break up some rocks. Some of the rocks were forced into the air, escaped the defendant's property and injured the claimant. The explosives caused the rocks to escape the property. The defendant was held to be liable.

Non-natural use of the land

Rickards v Lothian (1913)

Water had escaped from an overflow pipe connected to a washbasin where the tap had been left running and the washbasin's waste pipe had been blocked by an unknown person. The Judicial Committee of the Privy Council held that the water from the overflow pipe did not involve the non-natural use of land. It was also accepted that damage was caused by a third party (i.e. the person who deliberately turned the tap on and blocked the wastepipe).

Non-natural use and likelihood of mischief

Transco plc v Stockport Metropolitan Borough Council (2004)

A water pipe took water to a block of flats owned by the council. Unknown to anyone, the pipe had failed and water was escaping, eventually causing an embankment to collapse and leave a gas main exposed and unsupported. The gas company took the council to court to recover the cost of repairing the gas main. It was accepted by the House of Lords that the council had not been negligent. The case was decided using the rule in *Rylands v Fletcher (1868)*. The House of Lords decided in favour of the council because the supply of water through the pipes was normal and did not create any special hazard.

Non-natural use and foreseeability of harm

Cambridge Water Co Ltd v Eastern Counties Leather plc (1994)

The Cambridge Water Company provided water to Cambridge. In 1976, it purchased a borehole. In 1980, a European Directive was issued, which controlled the presence of PCE (a chemical) in water. The borehole was found to be contaminated with PCE that had come from a tannery owned by Eastern Counties Leather. The contamination was caused by occasional small spillages, which soaked through a concrete floor until eventually entering an underground water supply. The House of Lords accepted that the storage of PCE by the defendants was a non-natural use of the land. The House of Lords decided that the claimants needed to show that the defendant should have foreseen the potential contamination of the water supply. It was held that they could not have foreseen it because, at the time of the spillages, the factory supervisor would have expected any spillage to evaporate rapidly in the air and would not have been expected it to seep through the floor of the building into the soil below. This type of foreseeability was established in *Wagon Mound (No. 1) (1961)*.

Read v J Lyons & Co Ltd (1947)

Some explosives detonated in a munitions factory, killing one person and injuring others. There was no evidence of negligence and the case was decided using the rule in *Rylands v Fletcher (1868)*. It was held by the House of Lords that no liability arose because the persons injured were on the premises and there was no escape from the factory.

Defences: *Rylands* v *Fletcher* (1868)

Possible defences that can be used in *Rylands* v *Fletcher* (1868) include:

- consent
- *vis major* or an act of God
- act of a stranger
- statutory authority
- contributory negligence.

A review of the rule in *Rylands* v *Fletcher* (1868)

- The rule was decided at a time when there was growing public concern over bursting reservoir dams damaging property.
- Australia no longer follows the rule: *Burnie Port Authority* v *General Jones Pty Limited* (1994).
- The rule is not followed in Scotland: *RHM Bakeries* v *Strathclyde Regional Council* (1985).
- In English and Welsh law it is increasingly seen as part of the tort of nuisance rather than a separate tort itself.

> ### *Stannard* v *Gore* (2012)
>
> Stannard owned a tyre fitting business on an industrial estate. He kept about 3,000 tyres on the premises. In February 2008 a fire broke out due to a faulty wire and spread to the tyres. The fire was so fierce that it totally destroyed Gore's neighbouring property.
>
> Gore argued that Stannard was liable in negligence for allowing the fire to escape from his land. Alternately, he was strictly liable under the rule in *Rylands* v *Fletcher*. The negligence claim failed at first instance but the *Rylands* v *Fletcher* claim succeeded. Stannard appealed the second finding.
>
> Ward LJ considered the proper approach in an ordinary *Rylands* v *Fletcher* case, having regard to *Transco plc* v *Stockport Metropolitan Borough Council* (2004):
>
> (a) The defendant must be the owner or occupier of the land.
> (b) He must bring or keep or collect an exceptionally dangerous or mischievous thing on his land.
> (c) He must have recognised or ought reasonably to have recognised, judged by the standards appropriate at the relevant place and time, that there is an exceptionally high risk of danger or mischief if that thing should escape, however unlikely an escape may have been thought to be.
> (d) His use of his land must, having regard to all the circumstances of time and place, be extraordinary and unusual.
> (e) The thing must escape from his property into or onto the property of another.
>
> Reversing the decision at first instance, Ward LJ held the rule of strict liability does not apply unless the 'thing' which escapes is that which is collected on the land. Stannard kept tyres. The tyres did not escape; only the fire which came from them. Tyres are not exceptionally dangerous things and the use of the land as a tyre fitting business was neither 'extraordinary' nor 'unusual'.

Ward LJ did not discount the possibility that *Rylands* v *Fletcher* (1968) could apply in a fire case, but that would be very rare. This case highlights how, and more importantly why, the rule in *Rylands* v *Fletcher* has been continually eroded by the developing tort of negligence.

KEY TERMINOLOGY

vis major: Latin for 'a superior force'. Used in civil cases to denote an act of God or loss resulting from natural causes, such as a hurricane, tornado or earthquake, and without the intervention of human beings.

STRETCH AND CHALLENGE

To fully understand the rule in *Rylands* v *Fletcher* (1868), read the House of Lords judgment in *Transco plc* v *Stockport Metropolitan Borough Council* (2004). Five law lords explored the development of the rule and their reasoning and insights can help you prepare for your examination.

Also read the more recent case of *Stannard* v *Gore* (2012) where the Court of Appeal reviewed the following question: will a landowner be liable for the damage caused by fire which (through no fault of his own) 'escapes' from his land? The judgment in this case is over 62 pages long and concludes with 'no never ... well, hardly ever'.

GRADE BOOST

For possible defences, research the following cases or statute law.

Defence of consent: *Peters v Prince of Wales Theatre* (1943)

Defence of vis major or an act of God: *Nichols v Marsland* (1876)

Defence of act of a stranger: *Perry v Kendrick's Transport Ltd* (1956)

Defence of statutory authority: *Charing Cross Electric Supply Co v Hydraulic Power Co* (1914)

Defence of contributory negligence: s1(1) Law Reform (Contributory Negligence) Act 1945

SUMMARY: TORTS CONNECTED TO LAND

Trespass to land

→ Four essential elements:
  - Direct interference with the land
  - Interference must be voluntary
  - No need for defendant to be aware they are trespassing
  - No need for claimant to experience harm or loss

→ Three main defences:
  - Legal authority (justification by law)
  - Consent
  - Necessity

→ Remedies:
  - Damages and injunctions
  - Orders for possession
  - Self-help ('abatement')

→ Trespass in criminal law:
  - Main offences:
    - Aggravated trespass
    - Squatting

Public nuisance

→ A criminal nuisance which materially affects the reasonable comfort and convenience of life of a class of His Majesty's subjects

→ Affects a representative cross-section of a class of society in a neighbourhood

→ No requirement of intention or recklessness in the offence of public nuisance – the fault element is foreseeability of the risk of the type of nuisance

→ Defendant liable if they knew or ought to have known of the risk of the type or kind of nuisance: *Wagon Mound (No. 1)* (1961)

→ Civil actions can be brought by:
  - a realtor action
  - a local authority under **Local Government Act 1972**
  - an action for tort by a private citizen who can show that they suffered special damage beyond that experienced by other Her Majesty's subjects

Private nuisance

→ An interference with a person's enjoyment and use of their land

→ A civil action

→ Nuisance is by:
  - encroachment on a neighbour's land
  - direct physical injury to a neighbour's land
  - interference with a neighbour's quiet enjoyment of their land

→ Key elements:
  - claimant must have an interest in the land
  - must be unreasonable use of the land which is the source of the nuisance
  - claimant must suffer some harm or inconvenience

→ Main defences to a private nuisance are statutory authority and prescription

→ Main remedies are damages and injunctions

→ Key case and defences: *Rylands v Fletcher* (1868): essential parts and development of the rule

144

TEST YOURSELF

1. What criticisms can you think of the rule in *Rylands v Fletcher* (1868)?
2. What are the rules that came from *Rylands v Fletcher* (1868)?
3. What are the essential elements of trespass to land?
4. What are the possible defences that can be used in *Rylands v Fletcher* (1868)?
5. What happened in the *Wagon Mound* (1961) case?
6. What are the different types of private nuisance?
7. What are the main remedies for trespass to land?
8. What are the defences to trespass to land?
9. Explain the types of private nuisance.
10. What are the characteristics of public nuisance?
11. What happened in the case of *Transco plc* v *Stockport Metropolitan Borough Council* (2004)?

EXAM PAST PAPER QUESTIONS

Eduqas – A Level – Specimen Assessment Materials

The rule in *Rylands* v *Fletcher* has no place in modern tort law. It is both unfair and wrong to impose strict liability in tort'. Discuss. [25]

Andy bought a large yard in a quiet, rural area. He used the yard to keep and maintain coaches to provide transport for school children and holidaymakers. Sam, who owned the house next to the yard, was fed up with the persistent noise and diesel fumes coming from the coaches. After four months, Sam complained to Andy, who responded by causing even more disturbance by noise and fumes. In addition, Andy's coaches were often parked in a narrow public road next to the yard, causing obstruction to motorists. Andy bought a large supply of diesel oil. He kept the oil in a tank in his yard. The tank was situated near to Sam's garden. One night some of the oil leaked from the tank and caught fire. The fire immediately spread to Sam's garden and destroyed his fence and shed.

Advise Sam of any legal action he may be able to take against Andy under the law of tort, applying your knowledge of legal rules and principles. [25]

14 Vicarious liability

What is vicarious liability?

Vicarious liability is the term used to explain the liability of one person for the torts committed by another. There must be a legal relationship between the two parties and the tort should be connected to that relationship. It mostly arises in employment when an employer might be liable for the torts of their employee. Vicarious liability is a form of **strict liability**.

This topic is not relevant to the WJEC specification and is Eduqas only.

Does vicarious liability apply?

Vicarious liability is sometimes justified by the idea that if someone over whom an employer has a degree of authority makes a mistake, then the employer bears some responsibility for this. Vicarious liability has become a practical tool to help compensate victims, as employers are often insured against such losses. Vicarious liability is, therefore, a form of joint liability. This means that both the person who committed the tort and their employer can be sued (although in practice it is usually only the employer that is sued, because they are most likely to have insurance).

There are two questions to determine if vicarious liability applies to an employer:

1. Is the person who committed the tort an employee?
2. Was the tort committed in the course of that person's employment?

Primarily there has to be a tort committed by the employee and, therefore, the claimant must prove the elements of whichever tort is alleged. For example, if the claimant is suing for negligence, they need to establish duty, breach and resulting damage.

1. Who is an employee?

To establish vicarious liability against an employer, a claimant must show, first, that the employee has 'employee status'. An employer is not generally responsible for the actions of an independent contractor. This seems like an obvious answer, as an employee is someone who performs services in return for payment, but it is not such a straightforward question when considering the complexities of modern working arrangements. The courts have, therefore, had to distinguish between employees and independent contractors along with other employee/employer relationships, such as agency workers, casual workers, freelancers and those working on commission. In such cases, the courts have had to determine the 'employment status' of the worker and have developed several tests to do so.

The control test
This is the test traditionally used to determine if someone is an employee or an independent contractor. Dating back to the Victorian era and *Yewens v Noakes* (1880), it uses the concept of the master–servant relationship.

A person would be considered an 'employee' if the employer had control over the work, and was in a position to lay down how and when tasks should be done.

KEY TERMINOLOGY

vicarious liability: a third party (e.g. an employer) is held responsible for a tort committed by another (e.g. an employee).

strict liability: crimes where the prosecution does not have to prove mens rea against the defendant.

STRETCH AND CHALLENGE

Strict liability has the potential to be unfair but there are justifications for the imposition of such liability, for example improving safety standards. Research some other justifications for the imposition of strict liability.

A person would be considered an independent contractor if they were engaged by the employer to do a particular task, but were allowed discretion as to how and when to do it (*Walker v Crystal Palace Football Club* (1909)).

However, as many types of work became increasingly skilled and specialised, the test became less useful. The control test is still used, but it has faults when dealing with highly skilled or professional workers. The level of control is now, therefore, only one of the circumstances considered by the courts when determining employee status.

The organisation (or 'integration') test

This test looks at how closely the worker is involved with the core business of the employer. Lord Denning introduced the 'integration' or 'organisation test' in *Stevenson, Jordan and Harrison v MacDonald and Evans* (1952), where it was held the more the worker is integrated into the organisation, the more likely they are to be employed.

Figure 14.1 Determining the status of employer/employee is an essential element of vicarious liability

The multiple test

The modern test is the multiple test (also referred to as the 'economic reality test'), which involves the court considering all the facts of the case and the overall impression of whether the worker is an employee or an independent contractor. It can be uncertain, as each case will involve varying factors. This test was established in *Ready Mixed Concrete Ltd v Minister of Pensions* (1968) and, although each case will be decided on its own facts, three conditions have emerged:

1. Employee agrees to provide skill in return for a wage.
2. Employer exercises a degree of control.
3. Nothing in the terms of work is inconsistent with employment (e.g. the worker cannot delegate their job to someone else).

There has been a recent decision on the nature of the relationship between an organisation and an individual. In *Cox v Ministry of Justice* (2016), the Supreme Court had to decide whether the prison service was liable for an injury to a catering supervisor caused by a prisoner working in the kitchen. The prison service was held to be liable even though it did not technically 'employ' the prisoner, as the relationship between the prisoner and the prison service was sufficiently close to an employment relationship. Engaging prisoners to work in the kitchen was a key part of the prison service activities, creating a risk that the claimant (the catering supervisor) could be injured.

STRETCH AND CHALLENGE

Which of these are employees and which are independent contractors? What are the differences?
- Taxi driver
- Chauffeur
- Manager of a shop
- Nurse
- Teacher
- Teaching assistant
- Plumber carrying out work in someone's house

> **STRETCH AND CHALLENGE**
>
> Research *Ready Mixed Concrete Ltd* v *Minister of Pensions* (1968). Why did the courts consider Ready Mixed to be independent contractors and not employees? Consider the potential implications for zero-hours contract workers.

2. Was the tort committed in the course of employment?

For an employer to be liable for torts committed by their employees, the employee must be acting in the course of their employment. This also applies where the employee is carrying out their duties in an unauthorised or undesired manner.

Century Insurance v *Northern Ireland Road Transport* (1942)

The worker, the driver of a petrol tanker, was unloading petrol from his tanker in the claimant's garage when he lit a cigarette and discarded the match onto the ground. This caused a fire and explosion, damaging the claimant's property. The defendants (the driver's employers) were found to be vicariously liable for the driver's negligence, on the basis that what he was doing at the time was part of his authorised duties, even if he was doing it in a negligent way. It was, therefore, within the course of his employment.

> **STRETCH AND CHALLENGE**
>
> Compare *Century Insurance* v *Northern Ireland Road Transport* (1942) with the decision in *Iqbal* v *London Transport Executive* (1973). Why did the court, in this case, decide that the employee was acting outside the course of his employment?

Figure 14.2 A small action can have serious consequences

'A frolic of his own'

An employer is not liable for the torts committed by an employee who is on 'a frolic of his own'. This means that they will not be liable if an employee does something unauthorised and separate from their duties if a tort is committed during the 'frolic'. This can be seen in *Storey* v *Ashton* (1869).

Storey v *Ashton* (1869)

The defendant employer sent two employees to deliver some wine, but on their way back, they went on a diversion to do some business of their own. While doing this, the employees ran over the claimant, owing to the negligence of the employee driving the horse and cart. It was held that the defendant was not liable for the negligence of his employee because he was on 'a frolic of his own'.

Doing authorised work in a forbidden manner

An employer may still be vicariously liable for torts committed by employees even if the act is unauthorised and the employee has been expressly forbidden to carry out the act, if the prohibition relates to the way the job is done rather than the scope of the job itself. This can be seen in *Limpus v London General Omnibus* (1863).

> ### *Limpus v London General Omnibus* (1863)
> A bus driver had been expressly prohibited to race with or obstruct other buses. He disobeyed and caused a collision with the claimant's bus while racing another bus. It was held that he was doing an act which he was authorised to do (driving a bus), which meant that he was within the course of his employment, even though the way he was doing the job was improper and had been prohibited. The defendants were held to be vicariously liable.

Travelling to work

Commuting to and from work is not normally considered to be 'in the course of employment' and so an employer will not be liable for any torts committed by employees during these journeys. However, if the employee who is travelling, for example, between sites during working hours, detours from a route or gives a lift to an unauthorised person then the employer may be liable. Cases that demonstrate these principles are: *Conway v Wimpey* (1951), *Hilton v Thomas Burton (Rhodes) Ltd* (1961) and *Rose v Plenty* (1975).

STRETCH AND CHALLENGE

Compare *Storey v Ashton* (1869) with the decision in *Beard v London General Omnibus* (1900). Why, in this case, did the courts decide the employer was not vicariously liable?

GRADE BOOST

Lord Lowry clarified the issue of liability arising from journeys in *Smith v Stages* (1989).

Figure 14.3 Employers can be liable for their employees for travel during working hours, but not commuting

Independent contractors

An employer is not generally responsible for the torts of independent contractors, only for those of employees. There are exceptions to this rule which make the employer jointly liable along with the independent contractor. The tests above (control, organisation and multiple) help determine if a worker is an employee or independent contractor.

Vicarious liability will take place where an employee commits an unlawful act if there is a close connection between the employment and the unlawful act, such as a store detective who uses unreasonable force in the course of their employment: *Lister and Others* v *Helsey Hall* (2002).

Evaluation of the law on vicarious liability

It is also important to be able to evaluate the law in this area. Here are some of the main points of evaluation on the topic of vicarious liability.

> Employers are in a stronger financial position to pay compensation than the employee, as they will usually be insured.
> Employers are in control of the conduct of employees and so should be responsible for their actions. Problems with this argument arise when considering more modern and flexible working arrangements. It must be 'in the course of employment', which is fair and appropriate.
> Employers profit from the work done by their employees so arguably should be liable for their torts and losses.
> Employers have control over who they employ and are in control of who is dismissed. They should be deterred from employing those known to create a 'risk'.
> Employers are encouraged to take care to prevent resulting accidents and to provide a safer working environment and better health and safety practices.
> The test to establish if a person is an employee takes into account a common-sense approach by considering aspects such as does the employer exercise a degree of control, level of independence and responsibility for providing equipment.
> There can be confusion over whether a person is an independent contractor or an employee even despite case law and legal tests.
> Is it fair if there is no liability on an employer when an employee is on 'a frolic of his own'?
> Is it fair that employers can be liable for the unlawful acts of employees even when they are unaware that the employees are committing crimes? *Catholic Church Welfare Society* v *Institute of the Brothers of the Christian Schools* (2012)

EXAM SKILLS

This topic is frequently examined as a problem scenario but can also feature as an essay question. For problem questions, you will need to be able to explain and/or apply the liability of the parties involved. For essay questions, you will need to be able to analyse and evaluate the effectiveness of the law in this area and consider proposals for reform.

TEST YOURSELF

1. What is vicarious liability and what form of liability does it impose?
2. What does the prosecution not have to prove for a strict liability offence?
3. Why should an employer be held responsible for acts of their employees?
4. What are the two questions to determine if vicarious liability applies to an employer?
5. Who is considered an employee? Why does this cause difficulties?
6. What case established the control test?
7. Explain the organisation or 'integration' test. Include some case law to support.
8. Explain the multiple test. What is it used to decide?
9. What was decided in the case of *Cox v Ministry of Justice* (2016)?
10. For there to be vicarious liability, when must the tort be committed by the employee?

14 Vicarious liability

SUMMARY: VICARIOUS LIABILITY

→ Liability of one person for torts committed by another:
  - Requirement of legal relationship between the two parties and a connected tort
  - Form of strict liability and joint liability
→ Two questions to determine if vicarious liability applies
  1. **Is the tortfeasor an employee?** Employees v independent contractors:
     - Control test: *Yewens v Noakes* (1880)
     - Organisation (or 'integration') test: *Stevenson, Jordan and Harrison v MacDonald and Evans* (1952)
     - Multiple test: *Ready Mixed Concrete Ltd v Minister of Pensions* (1968)
  2. **Was the tort committed in the course of employment** or on 'a frolic of his own'?
     - Part of authorised duties: *Century Insurance v Northern Ireland Road Transport* (1942)
     - Frolic: *Storey v Ashton* (1869)
     - Doing authorised work in a forbidden manner: *Limpus v London General Omnibus* (1863)
     - Travelling to work: *Conway v Wimpey* (1951), *Hilton v Thomas Burton (Rhodes) Ltd* (1961) and *Rose v Plenty* (1975)
→ **Reasons for imposing vicarious liability**: Employers:
  - have adequate insurance/finances
  - can control conduct of employees
  - profit from work of employees
  - should take care when recruiting
  - may be encouraged to provide a safe work environment and policies

EXAM PAST PAPER QUESTIONS

Eduqas – A Level – Component 3 – June 2022
Discuss whether or not vicarious liability is fair on employers.   [25]

Eduqas – A Level – Component 2 – June 2020
Ashley was a semi-professional rugby player employed by Ridgeway Rugby Club. The club had the final league match coming up in a week's time against their old rivals Grange Rugby Club. Ridgeway Rugby Club were desperate to win the title as they had lost to Grange Rugby Club on three previous occasions. During the course of the match, the referee had to warn several of the players on both sides about their unreasonable behaviour and language. Ashley got angry, at what he thought was unwarranted warnings from the referee, and lashed out at the player who he felt was responsible for all the trouble. He ran over to Geraint, a player on the opposite team, and punched him, causing a serious head injury.

Advise Geraint as to whether the club is vicariously liable for the consequences of Ashley's tort in injuring him, applying your knowledge and understanding of legal rules and principles.   [25]

15 Occupiers' liability

The tort of negligence comes from the common law. However, occupier's liability comes from both statute law and the common law. This area of tort involves the liability of an occupier to both visitors and persons other than visitors on their premises. There are two key statutes:

> The Occupiers' Liability Act 1957, which covers visitors.
> The Occupiers' Liability Act 1984, which covers persons other than visitors.

Occupiers' Liability Act 1957: Visitors

This Act concerns the duty owed to visitors. (A visitor is often referred to as a 'lawful visitor' to distinguish them from unlawful visitors or trespassers.)

Figure 15.1 An occupier is one who has occupational control over the premises

Who is an occupier?

The Occupiers' Liability Act 1957 does not define who is the occupier, but s1(2) does state that the rules of common law shall apply. The test is occupational control: who has control over the premises?

In *Wheat* v *Lacon & Co* (1966), four categories of occupier were identified.

1. If a landlord lets premises then the tenant will be the occupier.
2. If a landlord who lets part of a building retains certain areas (such as an entry hall) then the landlord will be the occupier in respect of those areas.

STRETCH AND CHALLENGE

Research the following cases and explain how they apply to the Occupiers' Liability Act 1957:
- *Haseldine* v *Daw* (1941)
- *Phipps* v *Rochester* (1955)
- *Wheat* v *Lacon & Co* (1966)
- *Glasgow Corporation* v *Taylor* (1992)
- *Bailey* v *Armes* (1999)

3. If an owner licenses (allows) a person to use premises but reserves the right of entry then the owner remains the occupier.
4. If contractors are employed to carry out work on the premises, the owner will generally remain the occupier, although there may be circumstances where the contractor could be the occupier.

Who is a visitor?

Under the common law, a visitor is a person who has express or implied permission to enter the premises.

The common duty of care

Section 2 Occupiers' Liability Act 1957 imposes a common duty of care that is owed to lawful visitors:

› An occupier of premises owes the same duty (the common duty of care), to all their visitors, but they can extend, restrict, modify or exclude this duty to any visitor or visitors by agreement or otherwise.
› The common duty of care is to take reasonable care in all circumstances to see that the visitor is reasonably safe when using the premises for the purposes for which they are invited or permitted by the occupier.

The **Occupiers' Liability Act 1957** lays down guidelines in applying the common duty of care:

› **S2(3)(a)** An occupier must be prepared for children to be less careful than adults.
› **S2(3)(b)** An occupier can expect a person, in the exercise of their calling, to appreciate and guard against any special risks ordinarily incident to it (i.e. if the person is there to perform a particular role that has particular risks, the occupier can assume they will take care).
› **S2(4)(a)** A warning may discharge the duty of care (i.e. it is sufficient for the occupier to warn the visitor about any dangers).
› **S2(4)(b)** The occupier is not liable for the fault of an independent contractor if they acted reasonably in entrusting the work to that contractor and took reasonable steps to ensure that the contractor was competent and the work was properly carried out.

There are a number of references in the **Occupiers' Liability Act 1957** (as there are in other Acts and in the common law) to 'reasonable'.

Figure 15.2 Under the Occupiers' Liability Act 1957, persons who have a right to enter premises conferred by law (e.g. fire fighters and police officers) are lawful visitors

Occupiers' liability to children

Children do not form a special category on their own, but the **Occupiers' Liability Act 1957 s2(3)(a)** states that occupiers 'must be prepared for children to be less careful than adults (and as a result) the premises must be reasonably safe for a child of that age'.

Standard of care is measured subjectively, according to the age of the child.

The occupier should guard against any kind of 'allurement' or attraction which places a child visitor at risk of harm; for example, poisonous berries on a council park tree (*Glasgow Corp* v *Taylor* (1922)).

Where very young children are injured, the courts are reluctant to find the occupier liable as the child should be under the supervision of a parent or other adult. No age limit is set on parental supervision requirement.

> ### *Phipps* v *Rochester Cor* (1955)
> A five-year-old boy playing with his sister fell down a trench in a council-owned ground. The Court held that the parents should have been supervising their child so the council was not liable.

If an allurement exists, there will be no liability on the occupier if the damage or injury suffered is not foreseeable.

> ### *Jolley* v *London Borough of Sutton* (2000)
> An abandoned boat had been there for two years and the council was aware of it. Children regularly played on it. This was foreseeable that someone would be injured.

Occupiers' liability to people carrying out a trade or calling

The occupier will owe a tradesperson coming onto the premises the common duty of care. However, by **s2(3)(b)** of the 1957 Act, an occupier can expect that a person in the exercise of his calling will 'appreciate and guard against any special risks ordinarily incident to it so far as the occupier leaves him free to do so'. The effect of this provision is that an occupier will not be liable where tradespeople fail to guard against risks which they should know about or be expected to know about.

> ### *Roles* v *Nathan* (1963)
> Chimney sweeps died after inhaling carbon monoxide. They should have appreciated the risk as it was part of their 'job'.

This rule, which acts as a defence to an occupier, only applies where the tradesperson visitor is injured by something related to their trade or calling. If they are injured by something different (e.g. a frayed carpet in the defendant's home), the occupier will still owe the common duty of care.

Occupiers' liability for the torts of independent contractors

As before, a lawful visitor will be owed the common duty of care while on the occupier's land. However, if the visitor is injured by a worker's negligent work, the occupier may have a defence and be able to pass the claim to the worker. This is set out in **s2(4)** of the 1957 Act. There are three requirements:

1. It must be reasonable for the occupier to have given the work to the independent contractor. The more complicated and specialist the work, the more likely it will be for the occupier to have given the work to a specialist.

> ### *Haseldine* v *Daw & Son Ltd* (1941)
> A lift plunged, but the occupier was not liable as lift work is highly specialised.

2. The contractor hired must be competent to carry out the task. Occupiers should check they are competent to carry out the work and that the contractor is properly insured. If the contractor fails to carry appropriate insurance cover, this could indicate that the contractor is not competent.

> ### Bottomley v Todmorden Cricket Club (2003)
> A firework display caused injuries to visitors. The occupier did not check that they were competent contractors to carry out a firework display, so the occupier was liable.

3. The occupier must check the work has been properly done. The more complicated and technical the work, and the less expert the occupier, the more likely that this condition will require the occupier to employ an expert, such as an architect or surveyor.

Defences to a claim by a lawful visitor

There are two possible defences:

- Contributory negligence – partial defence. Defendant is partly responsible for his injuries and so damages will be reduced accordingly.
- Consent (*volenti*) – complete defence; defendant not liable.

Warning notices

These offer a complete defence to a claim of occupiers' liability. The warning can be oral or written. By **s2(4)** of the 1957 Act, 'a warning is ineffective unless in all the circumstances it was enough to enable the visitor to be reasonably safe'.

What amounts to a sufficient warning will be a question of fact in each case and will be decided by the judge on the evidence. If the premises have extreme danger or they are unusual, the occupier may be required to erect barriers or additional warnings to keep visitors safe.

> ### Rae v Marrs (1990)
> There was a deep pit inside a dark shed, so a warning alone was not sufficient.

If the danger is obvious and the visitor is able to appreciate it, no additional warning is necessary.

> ### Staples v West Dorset District Council (1995)
> The danger of wet algae on a high wall was obvious so no additional warning was required.

Exclusion clauses

Section 2(1) of the 1957 Act states that an occupier is able 'to restrict, modify or exclude his duty by agreement or otherwise'. This means that the occupier will, in any warning, be able to limit or exclude completely their liability for any injury caused to the visitor. This is the case for residential occupiers, though whether an exclusion clause would work against a child visitor may depend on the child's age and ability to understand the effect of the exclusion.

In addition, **s65 Consumer Rights Act 2015** provides that 'A trader cannot by ... a consumer notice exclude or restrict liability for death or personal injury resulting from negligence.' These provisions mean that if there are such clauses in a warning notice, they are ineffective and cannot operate as a defence to an occupier.

> **STRETCH AND CHALLENGE**
>
> Find out the facts of the case and the decision of the House of Lords in:
> - *Adie* v *Dumbreck* (1929)
> - *British Railways Board* v *Herrington* (1972)

Occupiers' Liability Act 1984: Persons other than visitors

This Act concerns the duty owed to persons other than visitors. A 'person other than a visitor' is often referred is an 'unlawful visitor' or trespasser.

Who is an occupier?

Anybody who would be classified as an occupier under the Occupiers' Liability Act 1957 is an occupier under the Occupiers' Liability Act 1984.

Trespassers

The common law was very harsh towards trespassers, including children. In *Addie* v *Dumbreck* (1929) it was held that there was no duty of care owed by occupiers to trespassers to ensure that they were safe when coming onto the land. The only duty was not to inflict harm wilfully.

However, in *British Railways Board* v *Herrington* (1972), the House of Lords used its 1966 Practice Statement and departed from its precedent in *Addie* v *Dumbreck* (1929) to hold that a duty of care could be owed to trespassers. The decision in this case eventually led to Parliament introducing the Occupiers' Liability Act 1984.

The statutory duty of care

> **KEY CASE**
>
> ***Tomlinson* v *Congleton Borough Council* (2003)**
> Tomlinson was aged 18. He visited an artificial lake that was part of a country park in Congleton, Cheshire. Canoeing and windsurfing was permitted in one area of the lake and angling in another, but swimming and diving were not permitted. Tomlinson ignored warning signs not to enter the lake (which stated 'Dangerous water. No swimming') and dived into it. He hit his head on the bottom, causing him to break his neck and become tetraplegic. He brought proceedings against Congleton Borough Council claiming for loss of earnings, loss of quality of life and the cost of the care he would require as a result of his injuries.
>
> Tomlinson may have been a visitor when he arrived at the lake but it was accepted that he was a trespasser when he entered the water as he was aware that he was not permitted to dive in the lake. The council was aware of the danger and had introduced patrols and warning signs to stop swimming and diving. The House of Lords dismissed Tomlinson's claims.

Under s1(3) Occupiers' Liability Act 1984 an occupier of premises owes a statutory duty of care to an unlawful visitor if:

› they are aware of the danger or have reasonable grounds to believe that it exists; and
› they know, or have reasonable grounds to believe, that the unlawful visitor is in the vicinity of the danger concerned or that they may come into the vicinity of the danger; and
› the risk is one against which, in all the circumstances of the case, the occupier may reasonably be expected to offer the unlawful visitor some protection.

> **GRADE BOOST**
>
> What is the meaning of 'reasonable'? Read Lord Reed's explanation of the 'reasonable man' test in *Healthcare at Home Limited* v *The Common Services Agency* (2014)?

Under s1(4) Occupiers' Liability Act 1984 the duty owed to persons other than visitors is to take reasonable care in all the circumstances to see that they are not injured on the premises by the danger concerned.

15 Occupiers' liability

Table 15.1 shows the difference between the duty imposed under the Occupiers' Liability Act 1984 from that imposed under the Occupiers' Liability Act 1957.

Table 15.1 Difference between occupiers' duty under the two Acts

Occupiers' Liability Act 1957	Occupiers' Liability Act 1984
To take such care as is reasonable to see that the **visitor** will be reasonably safe in using the premises for the purposes for which they are invited or permitted by the occupier to be there.	To take care as is reasonable to see that the **non-visitor** is not injured on the premises by the danger concerned.

Lord Hoffmann was one of the House of Lords judges in the *Tomlinson v Congleton Borough Council (2003)* case. He said: 'Parliament has made it clear that, in the case of a lawful visitor, one starts from the assumption that there is a duty, whereas in the case of a trespasser one starts from the assumption that there is none.'

This means that, under the Occupiers' Liability Act 1957, a duty of care is owed to all visitors, whereas under the Occupiers' Liability Act 1984, a duty is owed only if certain conditions are met (such as the occupier being aware of the danger).

Figure 15.3 A warning sign can discharge the duty of care owed by an occupier

GRADE BOOST

Research Lord Hoffman's judgment in *Tomlinson v Congleton Borough Council (2003)*, described above. Was the council liable under the Occupiers' Liability Act 1957? Was the council liable under the Occupiers' Liability Act 1984?

Research the cases of *Keown v Coventry Healthcare NHS Trust (2006)* and *Baldaccino v West Wittering (2008)* regarding child trespassers.

EXAM SKILLS

An exam question on occupiers' liability may require you to explain an aspect of the topic for AO1; or apply an aspect of the topic, for example to a hypothetical scenario, for AO2; or evaluate an aspect of the topic for AO3.

SUMMARY: OCCUPIER'S LIABILITY

→ Occupier's liability comes from statute law and the common law
→ **Occupiers' Liability Act 1957**:
  - Concerns the duty of care owed to visitors
  - Does not define who is the occupier, but the rules of common law apply (**s1(2)**). Who has control over the premises? *Wheat v Lacon & Co (1966)*
  - A visitor is a person with express or implied permission to enter the premises
  - **S2(3)(a)** Be prepared for children to be less careful than adults
  - **S2(3)(b)** Visitors should be expected to guard against special risks associated with the reason for their visit
  - **S2(4)(a)** A warning may discharge the duty of care
  - **S2(4)(b)** The occupier is not liable for the fault of an independent contractor if they took reasonable steps to ensure that the contractor was competent and the work was properly carried out
  - 'Reasonable man': Lord Reed: *Healthcare at Home Limited v The Common Services Agency (2014)*
  - *Haseldine v Daw (1941)*, *Phipps v Rochester (1955)*, *Wheat v Lacon & Co (1966)*, *Glasgow Corporation v Taylor (1992)*
→ **Occupiers' Liability Act 1984**:
  - Concerns the duty of care owed to persons other than visitors (unlawful visitors or trespassers)
  - **Trespassers:** *Addie v Dumbreck (1929)* but *British Railways Board v Herrington (1972)*
  - **S1(3)** An occupier of premises owes a statutory duty of care to an unlawful visitor if they are aware of the danger, they know that the unlawful visitor is in the vicinity of the danger and the occupier may reasonably be expected to offer some protection against the risk
  - **S1(4)** The occupier's duty to persons other than visitors is to take reasonable care that they are not injured
→ *Tomlinson v Congleton Borough Council (2003)*
→ Lord Hoffmann: under the **Occupiers' Liability Act 1957**, a duty of care is owed to all visitors, but under the **Occupiers' Liability Act 1984** a duty is owed only if certain conditions are met

TEST YOURSELF

1. What are the two statutes governing occupiers' liability?
2. What is the difference between the two statutes?
3. What is an 'occupier'? Give a case to illustrate.
4. What is the definition of 'premises'?
5. What is the effect of a warning sign on the liability of the occupier? Are there any conditions on this?
6. What is the duty of care owed to adult lawful visitors?
7. Does the occupier have to make the visitor completely safe?
8. What is the liability of an occupier for an independent contractor under **s2(4)**? What are the three requirements? Include a case for each.
9. What does **s2(3)** provide for? What is the reasoning behind this?
10. What is an 'allurement', and why is it relevant to child visitors?

EXAM PAST PAPER QUESTIONS

WJEC – AS Level – Unit 2 – May 2018

David decided to go swimming in the lake in his local park run by the local council. He ignored signs informing visitors to the park that swimming in the lake is both dangerous and not permitted. Unfortunately, when he dived in, he hit his head on the bottom of the lake and broke his neck. David has been told that he will never walk again.

Advise David as to whether the council is liable for his injuries. [18]

Eduqas – AS Level – Component 1 – May 2019
Explain what is meant by occupier's liability. [6]

Eduqas – A Level – Component 2 – June 2022

Bao runs a small museum specialising in Egyptian artefacts. There are several signs displayed prominently that read 'Please do not touch the exhibits'. Sally, a visitor to the museum, having left her glasses in her car, fails to notice the signs and wanders into the roped off area where she cuts her hand badly on an ancient Egyptian hunting knife. Lily works in the newly refurbished coffee shop, which was fitted out by Lennox, a local handyman. Lennox struggled with some of the wiring, not being experienced with electrical work, and this caused a power surge during which the coffee machine explodes, causing Lily to suffer severe burns.

Advise Lily if Bao could be held liable in connection with her injuries under the tort of occupiers' liability, applying your knowledge and understanding of legal rules and principles. [25]

16 Defences: Tort

Once all elements of a tort have been proved, the defendant may escape liability by relying on a defence. The Eduqas specification requires knowledge of three defences: consent (*volenti non fit injuria*), contributory negligence and the defences specific to claims connected to nuisance and *Rylands v Fletcher* (1868) (see page 141).

This topic is not relevant to the WJEC specification and is Eduqas only.

The burden of proving a defence rests with the defendant, on the balance of probabilities.

> **KEY TERMINOLOGY**
>
> **burden of proof:** the responsibility of a party to prove the issue to the court to a particular standard.

Consent: *Volenti non fit injuria*

The Latin term *volenti non fit injuria* translates as: 'there can be no injury to one who consents', although it is often said to mean 'voluntary assumption of risk'.

The principle behind this defence is that if the claimant consented to behaviour that carries a risk of harm, then the defendant is not liable in tort. Successfully claiming this defence means that the defendant is not liable for any of the claimant's losses.

This is a subjective not an objective question: did that particular claimant know of the risk? It is a complete defence, therefore, and the claimant receives no damages.

The use of this defence can be seen in *Morris v Murray* (1991).

Figure 16.1 In *Morris v Murray* (1991), the claimant agreed to go on a drunken joyride

> ### *Morris* v *Murray* (1991)
> The claimant agreed to go for a drunken joyride in his friend's (the defendant's) aircraft. The aircraft crashed and the defendant was killed. An autopsy revealed a huge amount of alcohol in his system. The claimant was seriously injured and brought an action for damages against the defendant's estate. On appeal, the defence successfully argued that as the claimant was aware of the risk he was taking and consented to it, there was no liability in negligence.

To argue this defence, it must first be shown that the defendant has committed a tort. Once this is proved, the defendant must prove that the claimant knew of the risk involved (nature and extent of risk) and that they voluntarily accepted that risk (it was the claimant's free choice).

Passengers in vehicles

The courts have been reluctant to allow the *volenti* defence in cases of negligent driving, even if a passenger accepts a lift with an obviously drunk driver.

Section 149(3) Road Traffic Act 1988 states:

> *'The fact that a person so carried has willingly accepted as his, the risk of negligence on the part of the user shall not be treated as negativing any such liability of the user.'*

There may, instead, be a defence of contributory negligence.

Sporting activities

Individuals who voluntarily participate in a sporting activity by implication consent to the risks of that particular sport. The 'risk' varies with different sporting activities, for example rugby tackles, cricket ball impact, boxing injuries, etc. The general principle is that provided the activity is within the rules of the game, then an injured player cannot sue (see *Smoldon* v *Whitworth and Nolan* (1997)).

Figure 16.2 Participants accept that boxing is a contact sport and therefore carries risk of injury

Some sports carry risks for spectators, such as being hit by a rugby ball while watching a match. The approach by the courts seems to be that an error of judgement or lapse of skill does not give rise to liability, as the spectator has accepted the risks of going to watch the live activity.

Figure 16.3 Attending a high-speed car race is an example of accepting the risks of being a spectator – *Hall* v *Brooklands Auto Racing Club* (1933)

Contributory negligence

Unlike *volenti*, which is a complete defence, the defence of contributory negligence allows a court to apportion blame (and therefore damages) between the two parties in a way that it considers to be just and equitable.

It means that the claimant and defendant are both partly to blame for the damage, for example when a negligent driver hits someone who had stepped into the road without looking.

Section 1(1) Law Reform (Contributory Negligence) Act 1945 states:

> 'Where any person suffers damage as the result partly of his own fault and partly of the fault of any other person or persons, a claim in respect of that damage shall not be defeated by reason of the fault of the person suffering the damage, but the damages recoverable in respect thereof shall be reduced to such extent as the court thinks just and equitable having regard to the claimant's share in the responsibility for the damage.'

This means that the claimant can still make a claim against the defendant, but any damages awarded will be reduced by the amount the claimant was to blame. This can be seen in *Sayers* v *Harlow UDC* (1957).

> **KEY TERMINOLOGY**
>
> **equitable:** an outcome that represents fairness.

Sayers v *Harlow UDC* (1957)

Sayers got locked in a public toilet that was owned by Harlow Urban District Council. She stood on the toilet roll holder to try to climb out but was injured in the process of doing so. She won damages after the defendants were found liable for negligence, but her damages were reduced by 25 per cent for her own 'blameworthiness' for standing on the toilet roll holder.

GRADE BOOST

Another case that illustrates contributory negligence is *Froom* v *Butcher* (1976). The claimant was not wearing a seat belt when sitting in the front seat of the defendant's car. He suffered injuries when he was thrown through the windscreen during an accident. He was not the driver, and was therefore not liable, but his damages were reduced by 20 per cent to reflect the contribution his negligence (not wearing his seatbelt) made to the injuries he sustained.

For a defence of contributory negligence to succeed, it must be proved that:

› the claimant failed to take care of their own safety in a way that at least partially caused their injuries, **and**
› the claimant failed to recognise that they were risking their own safety even though 'the reasonable person' would.

SUMMARY: DEFENCES: TORT

Consent
→ *Volenti non fit injuria*: voluntary assumption of risk: *Morris* v *Murray* (1991)
→ Complete defence
→ Requirements:
  • Tort
  • Knowledge of extent and nature of risk
  • Voluntary acceptance of risk
→ Passengers in vehicles: courts reluctance to allow *volenti*: s149(3) Road Traffic Act 1988
→ Sporting activities/spectators:
  • Rules of the game: *Smoldon* v *Whitworth and Nolan* (1997)

Contributory negligence
→ Apportionment of blame and damages: s1(1) Law Reform (Contributory Negligence) Act 1945 and *Sayers* v *Harlow UDC* (1957)

EXAM SKILLS

Defences are likely to be needed as part of a scenario on negligence or occupiers' liability if the specification includes defences.

TEST YOURSELF

1. What is the principle behind the defence of consent?
2. What is the effect of the defence of consent on the defendant's liability?
3. What happened in the case of *Morris* v *Murray* (1991), and what principle was established in relation to the defence?
4. What is the law surrounding individuals who voluntarily participate in sporting activity and get injured?
5. Can spectators sue?
6. What is the effect of a successful defence of contributory negligence?
7. What must be proved for a defence of contributory negligence to succeed?

EXAM PAST PAPER QUESTIONS

Eduqas – A Level – Component 3 – June 2019
Analyse and evaluate the extent to which the defences of consent and contributory negligence are fair and effective. [25]

17 Remedies: Tort

The main remedies for tort are:

- damages: the aim is to put the injured party in the same position they would have been in if the tort had not occurred. Damages are the main remedy for tort
- injunctions: a court order instructing a party to do or refrain from doing something. In tort, injunctions are mostly used in cases of nuisance.

Damages

Mitigation of loss

A claimant who has suffered a loss as a result of a tort is entitled to damages for any losses. However, the claimant is expected to take reasonable steps to mitigate any losses.

Types of damages payable

The following are the main categories of damages payable for tort:

- general
- special
- nominal
- contemptuous
- aggravated
- exemplary.

General damages

This term covers all losses that are not capable of exact quantification and they are further divided into pecuniary damages and non-pecuniary damages.

Pecuniary damages

The courts calculate pecuniary damages using the multiplicand (a sum to represent the claimant's annual net lost earnings) and the multiplier (a notional figure that represents a number of years for which the claimant was likely to have worked). These are multiplied together in order to calculate the future losses.

The multiplier is arbitrary – it can never be precise and is calculated by looking at previous cases. Even in the case of a young wage earner, the maximum multiplier used is 18 because it is intended to take into account the possibility that the claimant may lose their job or retire early.

The expectation is that the claimant will invest any money received as a lump sum and use the income and possibly some of the capital to cover living expenses during the years when they would have been earning, so that by the time of retirement the whole of the sum awarded will be exhausted.

As victims of accidents often receive financial support from several sources in addition to tort damages (e.g. social security benefits, sick pay and private insurance), amounts are deducted from the damages award to account for these. This is known as off-setting.

> **KEY TERMINOLOGY**
>
> **Pecuniary damages:** damages that can be easily calculated in money terms.
>
> **Non-pecuniary damages:** damages that are not wholly money-based.

However, the claimant is entitled to an award to cover the cost of future care, such as nursing requirements and physiotherapy.

Non-pecuniary damages
Pain and suffering
Compensation for pain and suffering is subjective as they are impossible to measure in terms of money. However, an award will be made to cover nervous shock and physical pain or suffering.

It is important to achieve consistency between the award made to different claimants who suffer similar injuries. The Judicial College sets tariffs to govern the fixing of the appropriate figure. However, each tariff provides for a range of possible awards, and a claimant who can show that the injury has had a particular impact upon their life may be able to recover at the high end of the range.

Loss of amenity
The claimant is entitled to claim damages if their injury has led to the inability to carry out everyday activities and to enjoy life. This includes, for example, the inability to run or walk, play sport or play a musical instrument, and impairment of the senses. Such awards are assessed objectively and are thus independent of the victim's knowledge of their fate.

> ### *West* v *Shepherd* (1964)
> The claimant was 41 when she suffered a severe head injury. Although she could not speak, there was evidence from her eye movements that she understood her predicament and so she received a high award for loss of amenity.

Damages for the injury itself
Injuries are itemised and specified sums are awarded for these on the basis of precedents.

Special damages
These are damages that are capable of being calculated at the time of the trial. Examples are loss of both past and future earnings and medical expenses before trial.

Medical expenses
These cover any services, treatment or medical appliances, or the unpaid services of relatives or friends. Only such expenses as are considered reasonable by the court are recoverable.

> ### *Cunningham* v *Harrison* (1973)
> The claimant said that he needed a housekeeper and two nurses to live in his home and look after him. The court refused to allow this claim as it was considered unreasonably large.
>
> ### *Donnelly* v *Joyce* (1972)
> The claimant was successful in claiming the financial loss that his mother had suffered as a result of her having to care for him.

Expenses to cover special facilities
These can cover the cost of special living accommodation. The measure of damages here is the sum spent to obtain the special facility and its running costs. A large amount of money can be spent to adapt a house for people with particular disabilities.

Povey v Rydal School (1970)
The claimant received an award to cover the cost of a special hydraulic lift to take a wheelchair in and out of a car.

Nominal damages
These damages are awarded when there has been little or no harm caused and the court wishes to award a very small amount. They are only used for torts that are actionable per se. This means the tort does not require proof of damage to be actionable: damages are payable just because the tort has happened. Defamation and trespass are torts that are actionable per se.

Contemptuous damages
These damages are awarded when the level of harm has been low and the court believes that an action should not have been taken, even though the defendant has been liable under tort. These damages can be as low as one pence. Unlike nominal damages, they can be awarded for any tort.

Aggravated damages
These are damages awarded over and above that needed to put the claimant back in the position that they would have been in had the tort not occurred. They represent an additional sum of money because the initial harm was made worse due to some aggravating factor. They are mostly awarded in cases of defamation and trespass to the person.

Exemplary damages
Sometimes called 'punitive damages', these are damages whose purpose is to punish the defendant for committing the tort. They are only awarded in certain circumstances.

> **KEY CASE**
>
> **Rookes v Barnard (1964)**
> This case is important because, when it was heard on appeal in the House of Lords, Lord Devlin explained the purpose of exemplary damages and the circumstances when they could be awarded. He said:
>
> > 'Exemplary damages are essentially different from ordinary damages. The object of damages in the usual sense of the term is to compensate. The object of exemplary damages is to punish and deter.'

Lord Devlin identified three circumstances when exemplary damages could be imposed:

> Oppressive, arbitrary or unconstitutional action by the servants of the government.
> Where the defendant's conduct was calculated by them to make a profit for themselves, which may exceed the compensation payable to the claimant.
> Where a statute authorises the paying of exemplary damages.

Evaluation of an award of damages in negligence
Criticisms
In some cases, people who suffer serious injuries will not be adequately compensated by an award of damages, no matter how generous the award. The award of damages simply cannot put them in the position they would have been in had the negligent act not happened.

GRADE BOOST

A ship called *The Barracuda* was sunk by another ship, which had negligently collided with it, causing damage. *The Barracuda* refused any offer of aid after the collision and it sank.

Can *The Barracuda* make a claim against the other vessel for the sinking of their ship?

If *The Barracuda*'s refusal of aid is regarded as negligent, the owners can only recover the damage caused by the collision and not the sinking of the ship.

Figure 17.1 The claimant's actions might bar them from making a successful claim

Guidelines issued by the Judicial College for general damages are not always overly generous. Compensation ranges from a few hundred to many thousands of pounds, depending on the type and severity of the injury. For example, a minor hand injury receives general damages ranging from £737 to £3,509 under the Judicial College Guidelines (JCG). For people with serious injuries, general damages may offer no more than a token award. In many cases, the bulk of a personal injury claim is made up of special damages, particularly where the injury is life-changing.

In addition, the **Civil Liability Act 2018** has now limited the amount of damages for whiplash-type injuries.

Many large awards ordered by the courts are for cases where the bulk of the claim is made up of awards for past and future loss of earnings. In cases where, for example, the negligence has led to the death of a child, the award is comparatively low as there will not be claims on behalf of dependents. This can be extremely difficult for grieving parents to understand and appears unjust.

Many criticisms can be made of the process in achieving an award of damages:

- Cases can take several months, if not years – some cases may not be concluded until the claimant's medical position has settled. It could be argued that this may encourage some claimants to exaggerate their symptoms to maximise their damages award.
- There is also the difficulty of financing a civil action. There is no state funding (legal aid) for personal injury matters and most will be financed by conditional fee agreements. These often require an 'after the event' insurance premium to be paid.
- An award of damages from the court or through an out-of-court settlement does not necessarily mean that the claimant will automatically receive their compensation. Unless the defendant has sufficient assets to pay an award or is insured, the claimant will not receive any compensation.

> **STRETCH AND CHALLENGE**
> Some people argue that exemplary damages should not be allowed because the purpose of civil law is not to punish. Punishment, it is argued, should be the purpose of the criminal law. Do you think exemplary damages should be payable in cases of tort?

Benefits

- An award of damages can improve a victim of negligence's quality of life. Money can make a difference – for example, their home can be adapted for their needs, or specialist nursing care can be paid for. The award can cover past and future losses.
- Bringing a negligence claim can alert defendant organisations to certain individuals who need more support and training. In addition, lessons can be learnt – for example, in medical negligence cases, areas where medical practice needs to improve can be highlighted and appropriate steps taken. This may save another family going through the same traumatic experience as the victim.
- A sense of justice may be achieved through bringing an action – individuals are held to account.

Injunctions

An injunction is a court order that requires the defendant to behave in a certain way. Injunctions can take two forms:

- Prohibitory injunctions instruct the defendant to not behave in a certain way (i.e. to stop committing the tort).
- Mandatory injunctions instruct the defendant to take an action to rectify the situation created by the tort. They are rarely granted in tort actions.

Injunctions tend not to be used for torts such as negligence or occupier's liability. They are mostly used for the torts of nuisance, trespass to land and defamation.

KEY CASE

Fletcher v Bealey (1884)
The judge, Pearson J, said:

> 'There must, if no actual damage is proved, be proof of imminent danger, and there must also be proof that the apprehended damage will, if it comes, be very substantial. I should almost say it must be proved that it will be irreparable, because, if the danger is not proved to be so imminent that no one can doubt that, if the remedy is delayed, the damage will be suffered, I think it must be shown that, if the damage does occur at any time, it will come in such a way and under such circumstances that it will be impossible for the plaintiff to protect himself against it if relief is denied to him in a quia timet.'
>
> Quoted in *London Borough of Islington* v *Elliott and Morris* (2012), paragraph 30.

Quia timet injunction

This is an injunction which is obtained prior to the commission of a tort. *Quia timet* is Latin for 'because he fears'. The circumstances when a *quia timet* may be granted were stated in **Fletcher v Bealey (1884)**: the danger must be imminent, the potential damage must be substantial and the only way the claimant can protect themselves is through a *quia timet*.

Interim injunction

This is also known as an interlocutory injunction and may be granted once an action has begun but before the main court hearing. The injunction will instruct the defendant to not behave in a certain way.

The conditions for granting an interim injunction were stated in **American Cyanamid v Ethicon (1975)**:

› There must be a serious issue to be tried.
› The 'balance of convenience' must favour the granting of the injunction. If there is no imbalance then no injunction should be issued so as to preserve the status quo.

Figure 17.2 An injunction is a legal and equitable remedy in the form of a court order that compels a party to do or refrain from specific acts

The balance of convenience

An interim injunction is only granted if the claimant undertakes to pay damages to the defendant for any loss sustained as a result of the injunction, if it is held that the claimant had not been entitled to restrain the defendant from doing what they were threatening to do. However, these damages may not be adequate compensation if the defendant is made to stop doing something. The courts must try to balance the need for the injunction against the effects on the defendant.

Lord Diplock stated that the court must weigh one need against another and determine where the balance of convenience lies.

Injunctions as an equitable remedy

Injunctions are an equitable remedy (actions that a court prescribes that should resolve a dispute). They are therefore at the discretion of the court and not a right. The maxims (general principles) of equity determine when they might not be awarded.

One who seeks equity must do equity. Injunctions will not be granted if the claimant acted unfairly (e.g. if they encouraged the defendant to commit the tort).

Equity does nothing in vain. The court will not award an injunction if the defendant will be unable to comply with its terms.

Delay defeats equity. The court is unlikely to award an injunction where there has been an unreasonable delay in asking for an injunction.

> **SUMMARY: REMEDIES: TORT**
>
> → **Damages**: aim to put the injured party in the same position they would have been in if the tort had not occurred
> - **Mitigation of loss**: a claimant is entitled to damages for losses but must take reasonable steps to mitigate such losses
> - **General damages**: cannot be calculated before the trial, e.g. loss of future earnings, pain and suffering
> - **Special damages**: can be calculated at the time of the trial, e.g. loss of earnings, existing medical expenses
> - **Pecuniary damages**: relating to money, those damages that can be quantified in financial terms
> - **Non-pecuniary damages**: these damages generally include pain and suffering, loss of amenity and mental distress
> - **Nominal damages**: small amounts for actionable per se cases where there was little or no harm and no proof of damage needed, e.g. defamation, trespass
> - **Contemptuous damages**: minimal damages following low level of harm and the court believes that an action should not have been taken
> - **Aggravated damages**: additional damages awarded because an aggravating factor made the initial harm worse, e.g. defamation, and trespass to the person
> - **Exemplary (punitive) damages**: punish and deter the defendant: *Rookes v Barnard* (1964)
>
> → **Injunctions**: a court order instructing a party to behave in a certain way; mostly used for nuisance, trespass to land and defamation
> - **Prohibitory injunctions**: instruct the defendant to not behave in a certain way (i.e. to stop committing the tort)
> - **Mandatory injunctions**: instruct the defendant to take an action to rectify the situation
> - *Quia timet* **injunction**: obtained before the tort is committed if danger is imminent, damage would be substantial and no other protection available: *Fletcher v Bealey* (1884)
> - **Interim (interlocutory) injunctions**: instruct the defendant to not behave in a certain way and may be granted once an action has begun but before the main court hearing (balance of convenience): *American Cyanamid v Ethicon* (1975)
> - Injunctions are an equitable remedy not a right

17 Remedies: Tort

> **EXAM SKILLS**
>
> An exam question on remedies may require you to explain an aspect of the topic for AO1; or you may be required to apply an aspect of the topic, for example to a hypothetical scenario, for AO2; or evaluate an aspect of the topic for AO3.

> **TEST YOURSELF**
>
> 1. What are damages? How does this differ from 'damage'?
> 2. What is included in special damages?
> 3. What is included in general damages?
> 4. What are pecuniary damages?
> 5. Explain 'mitigation of loss'.
> 6. What is contributory negligence, and if successfully established, what effect does this have on the award of damages?
> 7. Explain three criticisms of damages in negligence.
> 8. Explain three benefits of damages in negligence.
> 9. What is an injunction?
> 10. When might an injunction be granted?

> **EXAM PAST PAPER QUESTIONS**
>
> **WJEC – AS Level – Unit 2 – May 2019**
> Analyse and evaluate the different types of damages in the law of negligence.   [18]
>
> **WJEC – AS Level – Unit 2 – May 2018**
> Explain the terms general and special damages.   [8]
>
> **Eduqas – A Level – Component 2 – June 2022**
>
> Richard runs a hotel and golf course. Juan is a regular player at the golf course every week. Juan suffered injuries to his leg following an accident in a golf buggy. He was a passenger when Richard drove the buggy downhill on a cliff-side golf course. Juan claimed that he was thrown out of the buggy when the driver lost control of it. He broke his left leg, and lost some flesh when the broken bone stuck out of his leg. As a result, he suffered severe pain and had to undergo complex surgery at a private medical facility, where he also received plastic surgery to repair the skin. Juan was unable to work for over a year because of his injuries. He was self-employed. Juan is no longer able to play golf due to the lasting damage to his leg.
>
> Advise Juan whether he is eligible for any damages for injuries suffered, applying your knowledge and understanding of legal rules and principles.   [25]

Human Rights Law

UNIT 3

18 Rules, theory and protection of human rights law

> **KEY TERMINOLOGY**
>
> **entrenched:** a firmly established piece of law which is difficult, or unlikely, to change (e.g. the US Bill of Rights). The UK has no laws that are entrenched.

Citizens in the UK are fortunate to live in a country where human rights are protected. The UK has an 'unwritten constitution' and, presently, no **entrenched** Bill of Rights, but certain rights and freedoms have been guaranteed by the UK's membership of various international institutions such as the United Nations and the Council of Europe. This section will explore the nature of human rights protection in the UK.

Human rights theory

Human rights are often described as inalienable, universal and interdependent. They emphasise the belief that common humanity is shared across the globe. All people everywhere in the world are entitled to human rights.

> - Inalienable means that that they cannot be taken or given away.
> - Universal human rights theory says that they apply to everyone simply by being human.
> - Interdependent means that each human right, in some way, contributes to a person's dignity. Each right relies on the others.
>
> They are also described as indivisible. Human rights are inherent to the dignity of every human person, and cover civil, cultural, economic, political and social issues. Therefore, all human rights are considered to have equal status and are not positioned in a hierarchical order. Denying a person one right invariably hinders their enjoyment of other rights.

Figure 18.1 Everyone is entitled to protection under human rights law

Civil liberties

There is a debate about the difference between human rights and civil liberties.

To many people, the difference is largely semantic, and the terms are often used interchangeably with some overlap between the meaning of 'rights' and 'liberties'. However, the key difference is why a person has them. Human rights arise just by being a human, whereas civil rights arise by citizens being granted that right; for example, the rights given to American citizens by the US Constitution. The UK does not have a written constitution but is a signatory to the **Universal Declaration of Human Rights (UDHR)** and the **European Convention on Human Rights (ECHR)**, the latter being incorporated into domestic law via the **Human Rights Act (HRA) 1998**. However, the UK does not have a Bill of Rights.

> **STRETCH AND CHALLENGE**
>
> Explain some advantages and disadvantages of entrenched laws.

18 Rules, theory and protection of human rights law

European Convention on Human Rights

Following the atrocities of the Second World War, the international community came together to collectively agree to protect human rights and promote peace. They formed the United Nations (UN), which subsequently adopted the **UDHR** in 1948. This is seen as the inception of modern human rights protection. This was followed by the formation of the Council of Europe, which, in turn, adopted the **European Convention on Human Rights (ECHR)**. This is separate to the European Union and covers more countries; its aim is to uphold peace and protect human rights within Europe. The UK has since incorporated most of the **ECHR** into domestic law via the **Human Rights Act 1998**.

The Council of Europe oversees states' adherence to the **ECHR**. Other institutions overseeing the **ECHR** are the Committee of Ministers and the Parliamentary Assembly.

As society evolves, human rights also evolve and the **ECHR** (along with other human rights treaties) is considered to be a living instrument. For example, when the **ECHR** was written in 1950, modern technologies did not exist that today influence the interpretation of, for example, the right to privacy.

The rights and freedoms protected by the **ECHR** are shown in Table 18.1.

Table 18.1 Rights and freedoms protected by the ECHR

Article	Right
2	Right to life
3	Freedom from torture, inhuman or degrading treatment
4	Freedom from slavery and forced labour
5	Right to liberty and security of the person
6	Right to a fair trial
7	Freedom from retrospective law
8	Right to respect for private and family life, home and correspondence
9	Freedom of thought, conscience and religion
10	Freedom of expression
11	Freedom of assembly and association
12	Right to marry and start a family
14	Prohibition of discrimination

> **GRADE BOOST**
>
> Research the role of each of the institutions overseeing the **ECHR**.

The rights contained within the **ECHR** can be categorised as absolute, limited or qualified.

- **Absolute rights**: these are the strongest rights. The state cannot deviate from these rights and they can never legally be breached. Example: the right to a fair trial (**Article 6**).
- **Limited rights**: the state can deviate from these rights but only in the prescribed limitations laid down in the right. Example: the right to liberty (**Article 5**).
- **Qualified rights**: most human rights are qualified rights. These are the weakest rights and can be removed when 'prescribed by law, necessary and proportionate in a democratic society in order to fulfil a legitimate aim'. They may be restricted to protect the rights of others or for the public interest. Example: freedom of expression (**Article 10**). They often involve balancing one human right against another.

There are times when a state may avoid its obligations, which is known as derogation. Derogation from some articles (e.g. **Articles 8**, **10** and **11**) is allowed under **Article 15** in times of 'war or other public emergency threatening the life of the nation' and to the extent derogation is 'strictly required' by the situation.

> **KEY TERMINOLOGY**
>
> **margin of appreciation:** the discretion given to each EU member state to interpret ECHR rights.

The ECHR has been signed by 47 states, each with varied social and legal histories. A 'margin of appreciation' is used to allow individual state discretion with the interpretation of Convention rights taking account of their individual histories, cultural, political and moral differences. It aims to respect the sovereignty of each state by allowing for a degree of divergence between the states, and recognises that the individual states are better placed to make decisions with regard to, for example, public morals. The Court gives the state some discretion when making the initial decision as to whether restricting a person's human rights is necessary to pursue a legitimate aim.

The margin of appreciation can be either wide (in most cases) or narrow, where there is a consensus across most European states (see Handyside v United Kingdom (1976)).

Proportionality is also important when considering qualified rights in particular. This gives the court the power to balance competing rights, for example, Article 10 against Article 8. Absolute rights do not lend themselves to proportionality as they cannot be deviated from.

The distinction between rights and residual freedoms or liberties

> **GRADE BOOST**
>
> The UK is a dualist system in respect of incorporating international law into the UK legal system. This means that Parliament must pass legislation to make provisions in a treaty or convention with another country or organisation part of UK, law and so directly enforceable in a UK court.

Citizens' rights in the UK have traditionally been thought of as residual. This means that what a citizen is not allowed to do is set out by law and what they can do (rights and freedoms) is not. This is evidenced in Malone v Metropolitan Police Commissioner (1979). Residual freedoms are quite easy to remove and difficult to enforce, so protection in the UK, before the Human Rights Act 1998 (HRA) incorporated the ECHR into domestic law, was weaker.

Before the HRA, the ECHR, not being part of domestic law, was not always binding as a source of law by judges in UK courts. In R v Secretary of State ex parte Brind (1990), Lord Ackner said that, while unincorporated, the treaty 'cannot be a source of rights and obligations'. Similarly, in Derbyshire County Council v Times Newspapers (1993), the ECHR was considered useful as an extrinsic aid.

> **STRETCH AND CHALLENGE**
>
> Consider the difference between a 'right' and a 'liberty'.

European Court of Human Rights

The ECHR also established the European Court of Human Rights (ECtHR), which sits in Strasbourg and is the final court of appeal for individuals who feel their human rights have been violated. The ECtHR is the primary enforcement mechanism of the ECHR. The UK may be brought before the ECtHR by individuals alleging that their rights have been violated. Before the HRA, individuals had to use the right of individual petition, granted in 1966, in order to appeal to the ECtHR. All domestic remedies had to have been exhausted first, which was both time-consuming and expensive. However, when the ECtHR declared the UK had illegally removed human rights, the country did usually respond positively to the judgment. While the UK was not under a legal obligation to amend the law, it was under a moral obligation. For example, the Contempt of Court Act 1981 was passed as a result of Sunday Times v UK (1979), when the ECtHR held that the common law offence of contempt of court breached Article 10 of the ECHR.

Figure 18.2 The European Court of Human Rights (ECtHR) is based in Strasbourg

> **GRADE BOOST**
>
> The UK did not incorporate Article 13 'the right to an effective remedy'.

An example of a case where an individual petitioned the ECtHR is McCann v UK (1995) on the matter of the UK's 'shoot to kill' policy and a breach of Article 2 (the right to life).

Human Rights Act 1998

The Human Rights Act 1998 (HRA) provided citizens in the UK with positive rights and strengthened their protection domestically. It incorporated the majority of the ECHR into domestic law and provided UK judges with additional powers and duties to uphold citizens' human rights.

> **GRADE BOOST**
>
> An example of the UK responding to a judgment of the ECtHR is by passing the Contempt of Court Act 1981 following the ruling in Sunday Times v UK (1979) (known as the 'Thalidomide case').

> **KEY TERMINOLOGY**
>
> **declaration of incompatibility (DOI):** where a judge is declaring that a piece of UK law illegally removes human rights and is therefore incompatible with the protection of that right in the ECHR.

The Impact of the Human Rights Act

There are several key sections of the HRA that need to be considered, as outlined in Table 18.2.

It is important to include examples and/or case law and/or evaluation to support your answer.

As well as the sections considered in the table below, residual freedoms became positive rights. The moral obligation to uphold human rights became a legal one.

Table 18.2 Key sections of HRA 1998

Section	Detail	Case law/example/evaluative point
s7	The ECHR is now directly applicable in the UK courts; a citizen who believes that their human rights have been removed is able to take the case to a national court. Citizens can still take their cases to the ECtHR at Strasbourg on appeal.	A free-standing human rights case must be brought within the time limit of one year.
s2	When deciding on a case involving alleged breaches of human rights, courts in the UK must take into account the precedents of the ECHR. They are not binding, but they are strongly persuasive.	Leeds City Council v Price (2006) demonstrates that UK courts can choose a UK precedent over a ECHR decision. If there is a conflicting UK precedent, then the UK precedent will be used instead. If the ECHR precedent is clear and there is no UK precedent, then the ECHR precedent should be followed (Ullah (2004)). However, case law appears to suggest that the Supreme Court will normally apply the principles that are clearly established by the ECtHR. For example, in Re P and Others (2009) the House of Lords declared a rule exempting unmarried couples from adopting was a breach of Article 8 and Article 14. Here the court held that a recent ruling from the ECtHR appeared to override its previous decision. The court did again note that they were not bound by the decision and it was their choice to follow it. Evaluative point: power given to unelected judges under ss2 and 3, particularly when combined with s6.
s3	When deciding a case involving human rights, judges must interpret a law 'so far as is possible to do so' compatibly with human rights.	R v A (2001): Lord Steyn said the duty under s3 goes beyond the purposive approach. A 'declaration of incompatibility' should be a measure of last resort. Ghaidan v Godin-Mendoza (2004) provides the current approach for the use of s3.
s4	If a statute cannot be interpreted broadly enough to ensure compatibility with ECHR rights, judges can issue a declaration of incompatibility (DOI). The legislation can then be sent back to Parliament, on a fast track procedure (s10 HRA), where it should be altered quickly by Parliament to make sure it does not illegally remove human rights.	Bellinger v Bellinger (2003) Anderson (2003) Belmarsh detainees (A and Others (2004)) R v Mental Health Tribunal ex parte H (2001) In Steinfeld and Keidan v Secretary of State for International Development (2018), the Supreme Court issued a unanimous landmark judgment declaring that the provisions in the Civil Partnership Act 2004 preventing opposite sex couples from entering into a civil partnership is incompatible with Articles 8 and 14 of the European Convention on Human Rights. Evaluative point: to comply with the doctrine of Parliamentary Sovereignty the court cannot get rid of an Act of Parliament. Instead, the court, under s4 HRA, can make a declaration of incompatibility. Parliament then decides whether or not to change it.

173

Section	Detail	Case law/example/evaluative point
s6	Individuals can sue 'public authorities' for breaches of human rights. These are bodies whose functions are 'public' or 'partly public'. Courts and tribunals are considered public authorities.	'Standard' public authorities (e.g. NHS, armed forces, prison service). 'Functional' public authorities can be classed as either public or private depending on the nature of their work and the proximity of their relationship with the state (see *Poplar* (2001) and *YL* v *Birmingham City Council* (2008)).
		Implied horizontal direct effect: if a human rights issue is raised in a private case, the public authority (e.g. the court which hears the case) is under a duty to protect these rights (see *Douglas and Jones* v *Hello! Ltd* (2005)).
s10	If a declaration of incompatibility has been issued, Parliament has the power to change this quickly using a fast-track procedure.	Evaluative point: under s10(2), Parliament can change the law using the fast-track procedure if there is a 'compelling reason'. However, merely issuing a DOI is not necessarily a 'compelling reason'.
s19	All legislation that is passed after the HRA came into force should have a statement of compatibility. Before the second reading of a Bill, a Minister must make a statement as to whether it is compatible with Convention rights.	Evaluative point: under s19(1)(b) a law can be passed without a statement of compatibility. Ministers are not saying the law is 'incompatible', just that they are unable to declare it 'compatible'. Two Bills that did not have a statement of compatibility are the Local Government Bill 2000 and the Communications Bill 2003. Both are now Acts of Parliament.
s8	A court may grant 'any just and appropriate remedy within its powers'.	Evaluative point: the UK chose not to incorporate Article 13, which would have required courts to provide an 'effective remedy'.

> **STRETCH AND CHALLENGE**
>
> Research the cases listed under s4, and search for further cases on declarations of incompatibility.
>
> Did the UK change its law?

A British Bill of Rights

There are ongoing proposals to replace the Human Rights Act 1998 (HRA) with a British Bill of Rights. The HRA is simply an Act of Parliament and could be removed at any time; it is not entrenched and neither is the ECHR. The UK is one of only a couple of developed Western countries without a Bill of Rights.

Some positive impacts of the HRA are evidenced by the sections and case examples in Table 18.2 but there are also limitations and criticisms (for further details on the drawbacks of the HRA, please see Chapter 21). One of these came following the ECtHR decision to block the deportation of the radical Muslim cleric Abu Qatada in the case of *Othman (Abu Qatada)* v *UK* (2012).

Repealing the HRA would not necessarily mean leaving the Council of Europe and the protection of the ECHR.

A commission was established by the Conservative–Liberal Democrat coalition to consider replacing the HRA with a Bill of Rights. The commission published its final report in 2012, entitled 'A UK Bill of Rights? The Choice Before Us'. Although its findings were largely inconclusive, a majority of the commission's members supported establishing a Bill of Rights. The main reason cited was lack of public support for the HRA. The Bill of Rights issue featured in the Conservatives' 2015 election manifesto, but was suspended due to Brexit. On 14 December 2021, the UK Government published the long-awaited Independent Report on the Human Rights Act written by the Panel of the Independent Human Rights Act Review (IHRAR), along with its own consultation, 'Human Rights Act Reform: a Modern Bill of Rights'.

The IHRAR, established in December 2020, looked at the relationship between domestic courts here in the UK and the ECtHR, and the impact that the HRA has had on the relationships between the judiciary, the government and Parliament. The report summarises the panel's findings and looks at how the HRA works in practice, who it protects and how it is used, and makes suggestions for how it should work in the future. The government's consultation sets out wide-ranging plans to replace the HRA with a Bill of Rights. This goes much further than the IHRAR recommended.

Figure 18.3 The Human Rights Act 1998 could be replaced with a British Bill of Rights

18 Rules, theory and protection of human rights law

The government introduced the Bill of Rights Bill to Parliament on 22 June 2022. If passed, it would repeal the HRA, but its passage has been suspended at the time of writing. It has provided an indication of what could be different if a Bill of Rights replaced the HRA. See Chapter 21 for details on the proposed changes to the law.

SUMMARY: RULES, THEORY AND PROTECTION OF HUMAN RIGHTS LAW

- Human rights: inalienable, universal and interdependent
- Civil liberties
- European Convention on Human Rights (ECHR) agreed following Second World War
- Council of Europe oversees States' adherence to the ECHR
- ECHR as a 'living instrument':
  - Absolute, limited and qualified rights
  - Pre-Human Rights Act 1998 (HRA) use as an 'extrinsic aid: *Derbyshire County Council v Times Newspapers* (1993)
  - *R v Secretary of State ex parte Brind* (1990): ECHR 'not domestic law'
- Margin of appreciation: *Handyside v UK* (1976)
- Proportionality
- Residual freedoms: *Malone v MPC* (1979)
- European Court of Human Rights (ECtHR): right of individual petition 1966
- *McCann v UK* (1995)

- HRA incorporated the majority of ECHR into domestic law:
  - s7: applicable in UK courts
  - s2: ECHR rulings are strongly persuasive but not binding: *Leeds City Council v Price* (2006), *Ullah* (2004)
  - s3: judges under a duty to interpret laws compatibly with human rights 'so far as possible to do so': *Ghaidan v Godin-Mendoza* (2004)
  - s4: declaration of incompatibility: *Bellinger v Bellinger* (2003)
  - s10: incompatible legislation can be changed quickly using a fast-track parliamentary procedure
  - s6: individuals can sue 'public authorities' for breaches of human rights. Standard, functional and courts/tribunals. Implied horizontal direct effect: *Douglas and Jones v Hello! Ltd* (2005)
  - s19: statement of compatibility required: Communications Act 2003
  - s8: a court may grant 'any just and appropriate remedy within its powers'
- British Bill of Rights introduced as Bill to Parliament June 2022 but suspended at time of writing

TEST YOURSELF

1. What does it mean for a law to be 'entrenched'?
2. Human rights are described as inalienable, universal and interdependent. What do these words mean in this context?
3. List as many of the rights under the ECHR as you can.
4. What are the three categories of human rights, and what is the effect of each?
5. What is the 'margin of appreciation'?
6. What was the right of 'individual petition'?
7. What have residual freedoms become under the HRA?
8. Explain the impact of the following sections of the HRA: s7, s2, s3, s4, s6, s7, s10, s19 and s8.
9. Explain some case law in relation to s4 declarations of incompatibility.
10. In relation to s6 HRA, what is the concept of implied horizontal direct effect?

EXAM PAST PAPER QUESTIONS

WJEC – A Level – June 2019 – Unit 3
Analyse and evaluate whether the protection of human rights within the United Kingdom would be strengthened by the introduction of a Bill of Rights. [50]

19 Specific provisions within the European Court of Human Rights

The rights contained within the **European Convention on Human Rights (ECHR)** can be categorised as either absolute, limited or qualified:

Absolute rights: these are the strongest rights. The state cannot deviate from these rights and they can never legally be breached. Example: the right to a fair trial (**Article 6**).

Limited rights: the state can deviate from these rights but only in the prescribed limitations laid down in the right. Example: the right to liberty (**Article 5**).

Qualified rights: most human rights are qualified rights. These are the weakest rights and can be removed when 'prescribed by law, necessary and proportionate in a democratic society in order to fulfil a legitimate aim'. They may be restricted to protect the rights of others or for the public interest. Example: freedom of expression (**Article 10**). They often involve balancing one human right against another.

This section will explore **Articles 5**, **6**, **8**, **10** and **11**.

Article 5: The right to respect for liberty and security of the person

Figure 19.1 Article 5 offers the right to respect for liberty and security of the person

5(1)
Everyone has the right to liberty and security of person. No one shall be deprived of their liberty save in the following cases and in accordance with a procedure prescribed by law:

(a) the lawful detention of a person after conviction by a competent court

(b) the lawful arrest or detention of a person for non-compliance with the lawful order of a court or in order to secure the fulfilment of any obligation prescribed by law

(c) the lawful arrest or detention of a person effected for the purpose of bringing them before the competent legal authority on reasonable suspicion of having committed an offence or when it is reasonably considered necessary to prevent them committing an offence or fleeing after having done so

(d) the detention of a minor by lawful order for the purpose of educational supervision or their lawful detention for the purpose of bringing them before the competent legal authority

(e) the lawful detention of persons for the prevention of the spreading of infectious diseases, of persons of unsound mind, alcoholics or drug addicts or vagrants

(f) the lawful arrest or detention of a person to prevent them effecting an unauthorised entry into the country or of a person against whom action is being taken with a view to deportation or extradition.

5(2)
Everyone who is arrested shall be informed promptly, in a language which they understand, of the reasons for their arrest and of any charge against them.

5(3)
Everyone arrested or detained in accordance with the provisions of paragraph 1(c) of this Article shall be brought promptly before a judge or other officer authorised by law to exercise judicial power and shall be entitled to trial within a reasonable time or to release pending trial. Release may be conditioned by guarantees to appear for trial.

5(4)
Everyone who is deprived of their liberty by arrest or detention shall be entitled to take proceedings by which the lawfulness of their detention shall be decided speedily by a court and their release ordered if the detention is not lawful.

5(5)
Everyone who has been the victim of arrest or detention in contravention of the provisions of this Article shall have an enforceable right to compensation.

Summary of Article 5
In essence, **Article 5** states that everyone has the right to liberty and security of person. This is a limited right: there are prescribed limitations provided for in the Article.

Article 5(1) provides that any arrest or detention must be lawful and 'in accordance with a procedure prescribed by law'. An exhaustive list for when the right can be overridden is given in **Article 5** and includes things such as detention after conviction by a court, detention following lawful arrest (remand), detention of those who breach court order, detention of those with mental health issues and detention of minors.

EXAM SKILLS
Article 5 links to the topic of police powers. Make sure you put your answer into context, referring to the human right(s) it relates to and the nature of that right (e.g. absolute, limited or qualified).

STRETCH AND CHALLENGE
Look up each right covered in **Article 5** on https://rightsinfo.org and summarise what each means in plain English. Make a note of landmark cases regarding the application of each right. Also make a note of any interesting statistics about each right.

Article 6: The right to a fair trial

6(1)

In the determination of their civil rights and obligations or of any criminal charge against them, everyone is entitled to a fair and public hearing within a reasonable time by an independent and impartial tribunal established by law.

Figure 19.2 Article 6 gives the right to a fair trial

Judgment shall be pronounced publicly but the press and public may be excluded from all or part of the trial in the interests of morals, public order or national security in a democratic society, where the interests of juveniles or the protection of the private life of the parties so require, or to the extent strictly necessary in the opinion of the court in special circumstances where publicity would prejudice the interests of justice.

6(2)

Everyone charged with a criminal offence shall be presumed innocent until proved guilty according to law.

6(3)

Everyone charged with a criminal offence has the following minimum rights:

(a) To be informed promptly, in a language which they understand, and in detail, of the nature and cause of the accusation against them.

(b) To have adequate time and facilities for the preparation of their defence.

(c) To defend themselves in person or through legal assistance of their own choosing or, if they have not sufficient means to pay for legal assistance, to be given it free when the interests of justice so require.

(d) To examine or have examined witnesses against them and to obtain the attendance and examination of witnesses on their behalf under the same conditions as witnesses against them.

(e) To have the free assistance of an interpreter if they cannot understand or speak the language used in court.

Summary of Article 6

Article 6 is an absolute right and can never be deviated from by the state. It provides for the right to a fair trial and covers both civil and criminal situations. There are three essential components to Article 6: a fair and public hearing, which should take place within a reasonable time and be made by an independent and impartial tribunal established by law.

It allows for the exclusion of the press and/or public if the case involves morals, public order or national security. This also applies if the exclusion is in the interests of juveniles, to protect the private life of the parties or in special circumstances if the court believes publicity would prejudice the interests of justice.

Articles 6(2) and (3) provide that, in any criminal case, the accused shall be considered innocent until proven guilty. They set out some minimum rights; for example, the right to be assisted by a lawyer.

Articles 8, 10 and 11 are all qualified rights. They are all structured similarly, with part 1 of each Article providing for the basic right, and part 2 providing that the right may be removed in some circumstances (the 'qualifications').

Qualified rights can be removed when:

> prescribed by law
> it is necessary in a democratic society and proportionate
> it fulfils a legitimate aim; for example, the protection of the rights and freedoms of others.

Case law generally centres on whether the removal of the right is justifiable and often involves balancing one right against another.

> **GRADE BOOST**
>
> Article 6 links with all instances where a person would face a civil hearing or criminal trial. It is not limited to situations involving human rights so would also link with topics within the other specification options: criminal, contract and tort.

> **EXAM SKILLS**
>
> In an evaluative essay on Articles 8, 10 and 11, the focus is on the balance between these often competing rights. They are all qualified rights, so your essay should explore the extent to which the case law tends to support one right over another and the reasons for this.

Article 8: The right to respect for private and family life, home and correspondence

Figure 19.3 Article 8 protects the right to respect for private and family life, home and correspondence

8(1)

Everyone has the right to respect for their private and family life, their home and their correspondence.

8(2)

There shall be no interference by a public authority with the exercise of this right except such as is in accordance with the law and is necessary in a democratic society in the interests of national security, public safety or the economic well-being of the country, for the prevention of disorder or crime, for the protection of health or morals, or for the protection of the rights and freedoms of others.

Summary of Article 8

The parts outlined in **Article 8(2)** are the 'legitimate reasons' when the right can be interfered with by a public authority. The other aspects of a qualified right (prescribed by law and necessary in a democratic society and proportionate) also apply.

There are four expressly protected interests under **Article 8**:

> private life
> home
> family
> correspondence.

Article 8 contains both negative and positive obligations. The state is under a negative obligation not to interfere with privacy rights but **Article 8** includes a positive obligation on the state to act in a manner which protects an individual's right to private and family life: see *Y v the Netherlands* (1985).

Case law suggests that an individual's right to private life extends to situations that might at first appear to be relatively public situations. The court asks whether the person has, in all the circumstances, a reasonable or legitimate expectation of privacy. There is a clear link to the topic of privacy.

Article 10: Freedom of expression

Figure 19.4 Article 10 protects freedom of expression

10(1)

Everyone has the right to freedom of expression. This right shall include freedom to hold opinions and to receive and impart information and ideas without interference by public authority and regardless of frontiers. This Article shall not prevent states from requiring the licensing of broadcasting, television or cinema enterprises.

10(2)

The exercise of these freedoms, since it carries with it duties and responsibilities, may be subject to such formalities, conditions, restrictions or penalties as are prescribed by law and are necessary in a democratic society, in the interests of national security, territorial integrity or public safety, for the prevention of disorder or crime, for the protection of health or morals, for the protection of the reputation or rights of others, for preventing the disclosure of information received in confidence, or for maintaining the authority and impartiality of the judiciary.

Summary of Article 10

As with Article 8, the parts outlined in Article 10(2) are the 'legitimate reasons' when the right can be interfered with by a public authority. The other aspects of a qualified right (prescribed by law and necessary in a democratic society and proportionate) also apply. This provision is frequently in the news as the 'freedom of the press' and other media is related to the courts deciding whether the media have been acting appropriately in the dissemination of certain information. There are clear issues with the regulation of information distributed via social media and the Internet, yet the right to freedom of expression is crucial in any democracy. Part of ensuring that freedom of expression and debate is possible is protection of a free press and journalistic sources.

Where freedom of expression is at risk of being taken away, s12 Human Rights Act 1998 provides that the courts must have 'special regard' to the right of freedom of expression in any case where it is in issue, and the public interest in disclosure of material which has journalistic, literary or artistic merit is to be considered. It has been used in cases involving the issuing of injunctions and super injunctions. Section 12 had been considered to give 'special protection' to freedom of expression, though this has been called into question following the Supreme Court ruling in the 'Celebrity Threesome' case of *PJS v News Group Newspapers (2016)*. They held that neither Article 10 (freedom of expression) nor Article 8 (privacy) has preference over the other.

The following are considered areas of law where freedom of expression is protected or taken away:

> Defamation
> Breach of confidence
> Contempt of court
> Obscenity
> Freedom of assembly (right to protest).

> **KEY TERMINOLOGY**
>
> **super injunction:** a type of injunction that prohibits the publication of information and also prohibits the reporting of the fact that the injunction even exists.

> **GRADE BOOST**
>
> There are links with the topic of defamation, breach of confidence, freedom of assembly, interception of communication and obscenity. Article 10 is often balanced against Article 8 and also Article 6 when considering contempt of court laws.

Article 11: Freedom of assembly and association

11(1)
Everyone has the right to freedom of peaceful assembly and to freedom of association with others, including the right to form and to join trade unions for the protection of their interests.

11(2)
No restrictions shall be placed on the exercise of these rights other than such as are prescribed by law and are necessary in a democratic society in the interests of national security or public safety, for the prevention of disorder or crime, for the protection of health or morals or for the protection of the rights and freedoms of others. This Article shall not prevent the imposition of lawful restrictions on the exercise of these rights by members of the armed forces, or the police, or of the administration of the state.

Summary of Article 11

Article 11 has two elements: the right to freedom of assembly and the right to freedom of association.

The right to freedom of assembly covers peaceful protests, demonstrations and public and private meetings. Being a qualified right, it can be restricted for the legitimate reasons outlined above. There is a clear balance to be struck between **Articles 10** and **11**.

The right to freedom of association permits individuals to join with others for a particular objective; for example, the right to join a trade union or political party. Freedom of association also provides for a negative right for individuals who may not be compelled to join an association. There is also a positive obligation on the state to provide legal safeguards for those who associate with other states that are also under a positive obligation to provide legal safeguards for individuals who associate with others.

Figure 19.5 Article 11 protects freedom of assembly and association

GRADE BOOST
There is a link with the topics of public order and freedom of expression. There is a clear balance to be struck between **Articles 10** and **11**.

TEST YOURSELF
1. What are the three categories of human rights?
2. What is the effect of an absolute right?
3. What is the effect of a limited right?
4. What is the effect of a qualified right?
5. What does **Article 5 ECHR** provide for?
6. What does **Article 6 ECHR** provide for?
7. What does **Article 8 ECHR** provide for?
8. What does **Article 10 ECHR** provide for?
9. What does **Article 11 ECHR** provide for?
10. What does it mean that rights are 'balanced' against each other?

20 Restrictions of the European Court of Human Rights

Public order

Obviously, there is a close connection between freedom of expression (**Article 10 ECHR**) and freedom of assembly (**Article 11 ECHR**). People may wish to come together for the purposes of expressing opinions and ideas. This means that constraints on this freedom may also be constraints on freedom of expression.

Some degree of order and control is necessary for freedom to be meaningful in any society, but a society characterised by excessive concern for order and control would stifle healthy debate and criticism, repress a freedom and probably lack imagination and dynamism. Any attempt to encourage freedom carries dangers of lawlessness and disorder. Yet, ultimately, attempts to repress are also likely to end in protest and violence. Many incidents which threaten or involve breaches of public order are associated with events and activities that have a serious purpose in society. For instance, these could be protests about major social and political issues, concerns with questions of employment, or concerns with the pursuit of alternative lifestyles that do not easily fit in with the way communities are usually organised and run. When public order is threatened by these kinds of events and activities rather than by ordinary acts of violence, disorder and vandalism, there is a need to balance the preservation of order against the need to preserve and support fundamental freedoms.

The most effective way to maintain public order may be to prevent the trouble arising in the first place by strictly controlling or even prohibiting related activities and events. Yet there is a danger that this may be seen as the easy way out of the problem, with the result that freedom of expression and assembly are effectively repressed. The court resisted this temptation in *Beatty* v *Gillbanks* (1882) when holding that marchers behaving peacefully and lawfully should not be prohibited from marching merely because another group of marchers would oppose them and thus threaten the peace. Effectively, the authorities had to control the other group.

Nevertheless, there are now many preventive powers which may be used to restrict otherwise lawful activity.

The **Human Rights Act 1998 (HRA)** gives effect to the rights protected by **Articles 11** and **10** by requiring the police (as a public authority under **s6 HRA**) to act in a way that is compatible with a person's human rights and, if a violation of the right is suspected, to allow the person to bring a claim in a domestic court (**s7 HRA**).

Both **Articles 10** and **11** are 'qualified rights', which means that they can be lawfully restricted by the police ONLY when it is:

› prescribed by law (e.g. within the powers granted under the **Police, Crime, Sentencing and Courts Act 2022 (PCSC)**);
› for a legitimate aim (e.g. for the prevention of crime or disorder, the protection of public health or the protection of the rights of others); and **proportionate**.

EXAM SKILLS

This topic includes several sub-topics that could be examined as either an essay-style question or as a problem-style question.

The sub-topics covered in this chapter are:
- Public order
- Police powers
- Interception of communication
- Duty of confidentiality
- Obscenity
- Defamation

GRADE BOOST

The police relied on the legitimate aim of protecting public health to lawfully restrict protests during the COVID-19 pandemic from 2020.

183

KEY TERMINOLOGY

proportionate: relates to the concept of 'proportionality'. This means that the restriction on the human right must be the least restrictive option to meet the legitimate aim.

Public Order Act 1986

Figure 20.1 The Public Order Act 1986 covers both marches/processions and assemblies

Marches/processions

Section 11: duties of organiser. This concerns organisers of a march, not a meeting. The police must be given six days' notice of a procession intended to show support for, or opposition to, the views or actions of a person or group, to publicise a cause or campaign, or to mark or commemorate event (the aim is to target political processions). The notice must specify the date, time and proposed route, along with the organiser's name. The notice requirement is not required if it is 'not practical' to give such notice. Otherwise, it is an offence to fail to give notice, or to deviate from the details given in the notice (**s11(7)**, and **ss11(8)** and **(9)**). A defence for the organiser is if they can show that the march deviated and they (a) did not suspect it had occurred or (b) it was beyond their control.

Section 11 creates a criminal offence but prosecutions are rare. The **s11** notice requirement causes confusion as it states that notice is not required if it is not practical to give any notice (permitting spontaneous protest). This is not to be interpreted to mean that a phone call five minutes before a spontaneous demonstration will always be sufficient, as the section does refer to written notice.

Section 12: conditions on marches/processions. This section has been amended by the **PCSC Act 2022**. The police are given power to impose conditions regarding time and place of a procession if they think that it might result in:

> serious public disorder
> serious damage to property
> serious disruption to the life of the community
> in the case of a 'noisy protest', the noise generated by persons taking part in the procession disrupting the activities of an organisation in the vicinity of the procession
> the noise generated by the protest by persons taking part in the procession having a significant impact by causing harassment, intimidation, alarm or distress to people in the area
> a belief in the presence of intimidation or coercion for any of the above.

If any of the above 'triggers' exist, then a senior police officer 'may give directions imposing on the persons organising or taking part in the procession such conditions as appear to him necessary to prevent such disorder, damage, disruption, impact or intimidation, including conditions as to the route of the procession or prohibiting it from entering any public place specified in the directions.'

The **PCSC Act 2022** gives examples of what might amount to 'serious disruption to the life of the community'. These include:

› significant delay to the delivery of a time-sensitive product to consumers of that product
› prolonged disruption of access to any essential goods or services, such as money, food, water, energy or fuel.

Evaluative points

› The new definition of disruption gives the police very broad powers to decide what constitutes 'serious disruption'. Consequently, protestors are at greater risk of being caught by the new definition and, subsequently, having their **Article 11** freedom of assembly limited by the police. The aim of many protests is to draw attention to an issue, and causing disruption is one tactic to achieve this.
› The new 'noise triggers' arguably limit protestors' right to **Article 10** freedom of expression and consequently their freedom of assembly under **Article 11**. Noise is often a key part of an effective protest and the Act also provides that the more people that attend a protest, generating more noise and therefore likely to affect more people in the vicinity, the more likely they are to face restrictions. This means that well-supported protests are more likely to have conditions imposed on them.

The above situations are known as 'triggers'. Factors taken into account include the time and place of the procession and the route. It is an offence to break the conditions imposed. The sixth trigger in the list above is a political statement: 'the intimidation of others with a view to compelling them not to do an act they have a right to do or to do an act they have a right not to do'. This might be, for example, an anti-immigration march through an area where many immigrants live, which might be regarded as intimidating but not coercive; however, this would fall under the third trigger, disruption to community life.

According to *Reid* **(1987)**, the triggers should be interpreted strictly, and the words not diluted. The defendants shouted, raised their arms and waved their fingers, which might cause discomfort but not intimidation. In *Newsgroups Newspapers v Sogat* **(1982)**, abuse and shouting did not amount to a threat of violence.

The police can, however, invoke conditions as they see fit to deal with a situation. The courts may be unlikely to find police decisions unlawful in this regard, but note the effect of the **Human Rights Act 1998**. According to *Kent v Metropolitan Commissioner* **(1981)**, a challenge would only succeed if it were held to be unreasonable (e.g. no trigger existed).

Section 13: banning order. On the application of the police, the local authority, with the Home Secretary's consent, can impose a 'blanket ban' on marches. A ban must be imposed if it is thought that it may result in serious public disorder. The ban would cover any march within the time and area specified, which could include a peaceful march. The ban can stay in force up to three months. **Section 13** is used where the police believe the powers under **s12** are inadequate. Anyone who organises a march knowing of a ban commits an offence.

Meetings/assemblies

Section 14: powers of police to impose conditions on public assemblies now uses the same six triggers as for **s12** (following the **PCSC Act 2022**). Before this Act, the rules around a static assembly were more relaxed as they were considered less disruptive and easier to manage, but they are now subject to the same triggers and therefore could have the same conditions imposed upon them as a protest march.

> **STRETCH AND CHALLENGE**
>
> Think back to Chapter 19 Specific provisions within the European Convention on Human Rights. What categories of right are **Articles 8**, **10** and **11**? What does this mean?

> **STRETCH AND CHALLENGE**
>
> Research *Beatty v Gillbanks* **(1882)**. What happened in this case concerning the right to peaceful assembly?

The police are given the power to impose conditions on static assemblies, held wholly or partly in the open air, and then to arrest those who fail to comply. Conditions include the place it is held, its duration and the maximum number of people.

The **PCSC Act 2022** now also includes one-person protests in this definition, whereas before the Act two or more people had to be present.

An assembly is not subject to the notice requirement found in **s11**.

Evaluative points

> Protestors who now try to be less disruptive by choosing a static or one-person assembly may now find themselves subject to police restrictions.
> The new Act gives the police additional powers but does not grant any additional rights to protestors.
> The new Act has also changed the level of knowledge needed to commit an offence: a person is guilty of an offence if they '*know or ought to know*' that the condition has been imposed. The punishments have also increased for these offences.
> Overall, the new **PCSC Act 2022** gives the police more power to arrest protestors and punish them more harshly. This, combined with the fact that conditions can be imposed in a wider range of circumstances, means that freedom of expression and freedom of assembly are being restricted.

The Public Order Act 2023

The Public Order Act 2023 received Royal Assent on 2 May 2023 and introduced a range of new offences and powers aimed at trying to limit the disruption (particularly the 'nuisance') caused by protests. Some have argued that this legislation disproportionately limits freedom of assembly under **Article 11** and restricts freedom of expression under **Article 10**. Some of the powers were used for the first time during the King's Coronation in May 2023.

The key new elements within the 2023 Act are as follows:

> New offences under:
> - Sections 1 and 2 – Locking-on and going equipped to lock-on.
> - Section 6 – Obstructing major transport works.
> - Section 7 – Interference with key national infrastructure.
>
> Additional stop and search powers for the police under **Sections 10 and 11** (amending **s.1** of the **Police and Criminal Evidence Act 1984**) for the police to search for and seize objects (such as locking-on devices) that may be used in the commission of a protest-related offence.
>
> Serious Disruption Prevention Orders under **Sections 20–29** allows for requirements to be placed by the courts to prevent someone from causing serious disruption.
>
> **Section 16** amends the **Public Order Act 1986** and extends the powers to manage public assemblies to the British Transport Police and Ministry of Defence Police, including, in certain circumstances, the power to place conditions on public assemblies and single person protests.
>
> **Section 18** enables a Secretary of State to bring civil proceedings in relation to the potential disruption caused by a protest and where the court grants an injunction in the context of those proceedings, the measure enables the court to attach a power of arrest.
>
> Abortion clinic safe access zones (150m zone) and provides the police with powers to enforce the safe access zone.

KEY TERMINOLOGY

'Locking-on' is a technique used by protesters to make it difficult to remove them from their place of protest. They have been known to attach themselves to a place of protest using chains or even superglue, for example.

Criminal Justice and Public Order Act 1994

Section 14A–C: trespassory assemblies. On the application of the police, **s14A** gives power to the local authority (with the Home Secretary's consent) to prohibit the holding of all trespassory assemblies for a specified period of not more than four days in the whole, or part of, the district, but not exceeding an area represented by a circle with a five-mile radius from a specified centre.

Under **s14B**, it is an arrestable offence to organise, participate in or incite an assembly which you know breaches a banning order.

The first case interpreting **s14A** was *DPP v Jones* (1998).

> ### *DPP v Jones* (1998)
> The police had obtained an order from the local authority under **s14A** prohibiting for four days all assemblies within a four-mile radius of Stonehenge. The respondents had taken part in a peaceful, non-obstructive gathering of about 20 people on the grass verge of a road running along the perimeter fence of the historical site, as part of a demonstration for access to the monument. This gathering contravened the order and the demonstrators were arrested on failing to disperse at the request of the police. They were convicted but on appeal the Crown Court stated that any assembly on the highway is lawful provided it is peaceful and non-obstructive. The Director of Public Prosecutions (DPP) appealed to the Queen's Bench Division, which held that the Crown Court had misstated the law and the respondents had committed an offence by breaching the banning order. On a further appeal to the House of Lords, this was reversed, and the Crown Court judgment approved.

In *Windle v DPP* (1996), it was found that an offence had been committed under **s14B** when the respondents had run after a hunt, intending to disrupt it when they were sufficiently close.

Section 61: at the request of an occupier, the police have power to require trespassers to leave land on which they were intending to reside if they have damaged the land, caused damage or distress, or used threatening, abusive or insulting behaviour to the occupier, their family or their employees or agents, or have brought at least six vehicles on the land.

The new **PCSC Act 2022** now makes it a criminal offence to fail to comply with the order to leave the land or to return.

Section 63: the police have the power to break up or prevent open-air gatherings of 20 or more people at which loud music is likely to cause serious distress to neighbours. (The numbers were lowered from 100 by the **Anti-Social Behaviour Act 2003**.)

Section 68: aggravated trespass. The main targets for this offence were hunt saboteurs. However, it covers any trespasser who disrupts a lawful activity taking place on land.

Section 69: police can direct trespassers whom they reasonably believe to have committed, or are about to commit, an offence under **s68** to leave the land and can arrest, without a warrant, those whom they reasonably suspect to be committing an offence.

Public order offences under the Public Order Act 1986

Section 1: riot. This is defined as 12 or more people threatening or using unlawful violence, acting together for a common purpose. The conduct of the 12 must be such that would cause a person of reasonable firmness to fear for their safety.

Section 2: violent disorder. This is similar to riot but only three or more people are required, and they do not have to be acting for any common purpose.

Section 3: affray. A person commits affray by using or threatening unlawful violence so that someone of reasonable firmness would fear for their safety. No minimum number of people is required.

Section 4: fear or provocation of violence. An offence is committed by using threatening, abusive or insulting words or behaviour towards another person, or by distributing any writing, sign or other visible representation which is threatening, abusive or insulting. There must be an intention to provoke or to cause fear of immediate unlawful violence. According to *R v Horseferry Road Justices, ex parte Siadatan* (1990), the threat of violence must be immediate.

Section 4A: intentional harassment, alarm or distress. This offence is identical to that in **s5** except that the accused must intend to cause harassment, alarm or distress and must actually do so. The maximum penalties are far higher than those in **s5**.

Section 5 is similar to **s4** but of a lower level. This section covers harassment, alarm or distress and disorderly behaviour taking place within the hearing or sight of a person likely to be caused harassment, alarm or distress. *DPP v Orum* (1988) confirmed that police officers can be victims of **s5** Public Order Act 1986 caused by swearing and other abusive/threatening behaviour.

> ### *DPP v Fiddler* (1992)
> It was confirmed that an offence had been committed under **s5** when an anti-abortion protester shouted and talked to people attending an abortion clinic and displayed plastic models and photographs of human foetuses.
>
> ### *DPP v Clarke* (1992)
> Holding up pictures of aborted foetuses was found to be both abusive and insulting.

Section 57 Crime and Courts Act 2013 has now removed the term 'insulting' from **s5** and is designed to offer better protection to **Article 10** – freedom of expression.

Section 6: mens rea requirement. There must be intention or awareness that they are being threatening or abusive. If not, they should be acquitted.

Incitement to racial hatred

This is defined in **s17** as 'hatred against any group of persons defined by reference to colour, race, nationality or ethnic or national origins'.

- Firstly, words and behaviour must be 'threatening, abusive or insulting'.
- Secondly, the actions of the person charged must either have been intended to stir up racial hatred or be likely to do so.
- **Sections 18–22** are publication offences.
- **Section 18** deals with speeches at meetings or demonstrations. It is an offence to use words or behaviour, or display written material, which fulfils the elements outlined in **ss16** and **17**.
- **Section 19** covers publishing or distributing written material. It can be used against racist organisations that circulate newsletters and leaflets intended or likely to stir up racial hatred.

- Section 20 deals with the performance of plays.
- Section 21 deals with showing or playing films, videos or records.
- Section 22 deals with broadcasting and cable services.
- Section 23 makes it an offence to simply possess racist material.

Proceedings for any of these sections can only be brought with the consent of the Attorney General.

The Racial and Religious Hatred Act 2006

This Act added a Part 3A to the Public Order Act 1986 (POA).

- Section 29A: religious hatred is defined as 'hatred against a group of persons defined by reference to religious belief or lack of religious belief'.
- The offences cover speech, publications, plays, recordings and broadcasts and possession of inflammatory material.
- The offences are limited to threatening behaviour.
- Prosecution has to prove that the defendant intended to stir up religious hatred.
- Comedians who joke about a particular religion should not be affected.
- In 2006, a Danish newspaper published cartoons showing the Prophet Mohammed and caused offence to Muslims. According to s29J, a publisher who reprinted the cartoons in England would be unlikely to commit an offence under Part 3A POA.

Other offences relating to racial and religious hatred

- Crime and Disorder Act 1998 increased penalties for racially aggravated offences.
- Anti-Terrorism, Crime and Security Act 2001 extended previous Acts to include religious aggravation.
- Football (Offences) Act 1991 introduced the offence of 'indecent or racialist chanting' at a designated football match.

Private law remedies

Apart from control by the police, private persons can seek injunctions.

> ### Hubbard v Pitt (1976)
> Protesters handed out leaflets and carried posters outside the claimant's estate agency, who claimed they were trespassing over the public footpath outside. The claimant was awarded an injunction to prevent their demonstrations. The defendants appealed but the injunction was upheld. The question of rights to use the highway was irrelevant as the court was concerned only with the private law rights of the claimant in relation to an alleged private nuisance.

Denning MR gave a dissenting judgment, saying: 'The public have a right of passage over a highway but the soil may belong to someone else. The owner of the soil may sue if a person abuses the right of passage so as to use it for some other and unreasonable purpose, such as where a racing tout walked up and down to note the trials of the race horses (see Hickman v Maisey (1900)). But those cases do not give Prebble and Co a cause of action here, because Prebble and Co do not own the pavement; it is a highway. The surface is vested in the local authority and they have not complained, nor could they, since no wrong has been done to them or their interest. The courts should not interfere by interlocutory injunction with the right to demonstrate and to protest any more than they interfere with the right of free speech; provided that everything is done peaceably and in good order' and 'the right to demonstrate and the right to protest on matters of public concern … are rights which it is in the public interest that individuals should possess' and that 'history is full of warnings against suppression of these rights.'

Protests in the vicinity of Parliament

Figure 20.2 Protesting near Parliament is subject to tighter restrictions

The **Police Reform and Social Responsibility Act 2011** contains a number of measures that have severely restricted the freedom to protest near Parliament and other 'sensitive' sites. For example, within the 'controlled area' (Parliament Square and the adjoining pavements), amplified noise equipment, putting up tents and using sleeping equipment were restricted. The **PCSC Act 2022** has extended the 'controlled area' to include more of the surrounding roads and so restrictions now apply to a broader area. In addition, it adds a new restriction of not being allowed to obstruct a vehicle from entering or exiting parliamentary buildings. If a protestor does, they commit an offence.

> **GRADE BOOST**
>
> Research the case of *R (on the application of Haw) v Secretary of State for the Home Department* (2006) and also the case of *Maya Evans* (2010).

> **STRETCH AND CHALLENGE**
>
> The lawfulness of any particular exercise of the power can be tested in the courts of England and Wales usually by judicial review. The Metropolitan Police issued numerous conditions on the Extinction Rebellion protests in April 2019 and October 2019. The use of these powers in October 2019 was challenged in *R (on the application of Baroness Jenny Jones and others) v the MPC* (2019). The High Court concluded that the decision by the police to impose the October 14 order was unlawful. Liberty and Amnesty International both welcomed the judgment. Liberty said the ruling would 'help safeguard future protests from police overreach'. Amnesty International said there must now be 'no repeats of this attempt to suppress legitimate non-violent protest'.
>
> Now give your view and evaluate it. Do you think the powers of the police to impose conditions on meetings adequately balances rights of freedom of assembly and freedom of expression with the need to protect public order?

Breach of the peace

In common law, the police have the power to arrest without warrant if a breach of the peace has been committed, if there is reasonable belief that a breach of the peace will be committed, or if they think it will be repeated. This was widely used during the 1984–85 miners' strike to prevent access to picket areas. This power to arrest for breach of the peace was technically abolished by the **Serious Organised Crime and Police Act 2005 (SOCPA)**, which makes all offences arrestable if it is necessary to arrest according to one of the necessity factors.

Moss v McLachlan (1985)

There had been violent conflict between members of different trade unions during the 1984–85 miners' strike and the police had found it difficult to maintain the peace. The defendants were four of about 60 striking miners who were intent on a mass demonstration at a nearby colliery. They were stopped by the police less than five minutes away from the nearest pit. The police feared a violent episode would occur if they went there. The men tried to push past the police and were arrested.

The miners lost their appeal. The court accepted that the police had acted correctly; a test of 'close proximity both in place and time' and a breach of the peace was held to be 'imminent and immediate'.

Figure 20.3 The police can arrest without a warrant for breach of the peace

Foy v Chief Constable of Kent (1984)

Striking miners were held up more than 200 miles from their destination, suggesting that the requirement of proximity stated in *Moss v McLachlan* (1985) was now unnecessary. In assessing whether a real risk existed, the police took into account news about disorder at previous pickets. There did not appear that there was anything about these particular miners to suggest that they might cause a breach of the peace. Therefore, the police were able to deny them their freedom of movement and assembly on no more substantial grounds than that other striking miners had caused trouble in the past.

Note the difference in proximity of the miners between *Moss v McLachlan* (1985), where they were two to four miles away from the collieries they intended to picket, and *Foy v Chief Constable of Kent* (1984), where they were over 200 miles from their intended place of picket.

KEY CASE

R (Laporte) v Chief Constable of Gloucestershire (2007)

In March 2003, officers from seven police forces, acting under the direction of Gloucestershire Police, stopped three coaches from London carrying 120 anti-Iraq War protesters. The protesters had been planning to join thousands of people in a demonstration at RAF Fairford. Some of the protesters, including Laporte, had purely peaceful intentions, but some items suggesting violent intent were discovered on the coaches by the police. The coaches were returned to London under police escort, without any opportunity for the passengers to get off.

Laporte sought a judicial review of the actions of the Chief Constable in preventing her from attending the protest and forcibly returning her to London. The court rejected her first complaint but upheld her second. The Court of Appeal upheld that decision. Both parties appealed. The issue was whether the Chief Constable's actions were prescribed by law and necessary in a democratic society.

The House of Lords allowed Laporte's appeal. The House of Lords found that the Chief Constable's actions were not prescribed by law, neither was there a power to take action short of arrest to prevent a breach of the peace which was not sufficiently imminent to justify arrest. The Chief Constable's actions were disproportionate because they were premature and indiscriminate. It was disproportionate to restrict Laporte's exercise of her rights of freedom of expression and the right to peaceful protest under **Articles 10** and **11 ECHR** because she was with some people who might, in the future, breach the peace.

KEY CASE

Austin and Another v Commissioner of Police of the Metropolis (2007)

Figure 20.4 The police must act proportionately when exercising their powers

This case involved the May Day demonstrations in London, when police surrounded about 3,000 people in Oxford Circus and did not allow them to leave for seven hours to prevent the spread of violence. One claimant, who had simply been there on business and was not one of the protesters, sought damages for false imprisonment and unlawful detention.

The claimant's case failed. The court said that the police have powers to act out of necessity to defend property. It was reasonable for the police to have treated all those in Oxford Circus as demonstrators until they came forward with their personal circumstances. Less intrusive action would not have been appropriate or effective. In exceptional circumstances, it was lawful for the police to act in this way to prevent an imminent breach of the peace.

Obstruction of the highway

Under **s137 Highways Act 1980**, it is an offence 'if a person without lawful authority or excuse in any way wilfully obstructs the free passage along a highway'. For the purposes of this crime the highway includes the pavement as well as the road. If a police officer orders a speaker, distributor, vendor or audience to move along, and they refuse to do so, they are likely to be arrested for obstruction of the highway or obstruction of a constable in the execution of their duty.

Lord Esher in *Harrison v Duke of Rutland* (1893) considered access to be a right to pass or repass, for any reasonable or usual mode of using the highway as a highway. In *Arrowsmith v Jenkins* (1963), a pacifist meeting was held in a street which linked two main roads. The meeting blocked the street and the organiser cooperated with the police in unblocking it. The road was blocked completely for five minutes, and partly for fifteen. Although the police had notice of the meeting, the organiser was arrested and convicted. In *Nagy v Weston* (1966), reasonable use of the highway constituted a lawful excuse. The test of reasonableness will consider length of obstruction, purpose and whether there is actual or potential obstruction.

The **PCSC Act 2022** has amended **s137** of the **Highways Act 1980** to increase the maximum penalty for obstruction of the highway, from a fine to up to six months' imprisonment. It has also become a recordable offence, meaning the police can take fingerprints, photographs and DNA if needed and the offence will show up in Disclosure and Barring Service checks.

It is also now easier to commit the offence: it no longer matters if the road was already blocked when the protestors blocked it.

Obstruction of the police

Obstruction of the police is a statutory offence under **s89 Police Act 1996**. The courts have been willing to uphold a wide use of this offence, even where its use restricts freedom of assembly. In *Duncan v Jones* (1936), a speaker addressing a crowd from a box on the highway was told to stop because the police feared a breach of the peace. Although the only grounds for this fear was that a disturbance had occurred in the same place a year earlier, the courts upheld the arrest of the speaker for obstruction after she refused to stop speaking.

GRADE BOOST

Was there an imminent and immediate breach of the peace in *Foy v Chief Constable of Kent* (1984)? Were the miners in 'close proximity in both time and place'? Research *Nicol v DPP* (1996), *Steel v UK* (1998), *Redmond-Bate* (1999) and *Bibby* (2000). What do these cases tell us about the police's powers to arrest for breach of the peace?

STRETCH AND CHALLENGE

Compare *R (Laporte) v Chief Constable of Gloucestershire* (2007) with *Austin and Another v Commissioner of Police of the Metropolis* (2007).

SUMMARY: RESTRICTIONS OF THE ECHR: PUBLIC ORDER

→ **Public Order Act 1986**: riot: **s1**; violent disorder: **s2**; affray: **s3**; fear or provocation of violence: **s4**: *R v Horseferry Road Justices, ex parte Siadatan* (1990); harassment, alarm or distress: **s4A**; **s5**: *DPP v Orum* (1988); *DPP v Fiddler* (1992); *DPP v Clarke* (1992); mens rea requirement: **s6**; marches/processions: **ss11–13**; meetings/assemblies: **s14**; **s16**; incitement to racial hatred: **s17**; **s23**; publication offences: **ss18–22**

→ **Criminal Justice and Public Order Act 1994**:
  • Trespassory assemblies: **s14A**: *DPP v Jones* (1998); **s14B**: *Windle v DPP* (1996); **s14C**; **s61**; **s63**
  • Aggravated trespass: **s68**; **s69**

→ Racial and religious hatred: **Racial and Religious Hatred Act 2006: s29A**; **Crime and Disorder Act 1998**; **Anti-Terrorism, Crime and Security Act 2001**; **Football (Offences) Act 1991**

→ Private law remedies: *Hubbard v Pitt* (1976); *Hickman v Maisey* (1900)

→ **Sections 128–138 Serious Organised Crime and Police Act 2005 (SOCPA)** restrict the freedom to protest near Parliament and other 'sensitive' sites: *R (on the application of Haw) v Secretary of State for the Home Department* (2006)

→ Breach of the peace: *R (Laporte) v Chief Constable of Gloucestershire* (2007); *Austin and Another v Commissioner of Police of the Metropolis* (2007); *Moss v McLachlan* (1985); *Foy v Chief Constable of Kent* (1984); *Nicol v DPP* (1996); *Steel v UK* (1998); *Redmond-Bate* (1999); *Bibby* (2000)

→ Obstruction of the highway: **s137 Highways Act 1980**: *Harrison v Duke of Rutland* (1893); *Arrowsmith v Jenkins* (1963); *Nagy v Weston* (1966)

→ Obstruction of the police: **s89 Police Act 1996**: *Duncan v Jones* (1936)

TEST YOURSELF

1. What two articles of the **ECHR** are considered when discussing public order offences?
2. Regarding marches/processions, what are the requirements under **s11 Public Order Act 1986**?
3. When may the police impose conditions on marches/processions according to the **Public Order Act 1986** as amended?
4. According to the **PCSC Act 2022**, what might amount to 'serious disruption to the life of the community'?
5. What is obstruction of the highway under **s137 Highways Act 1980**?

Police powers

Police powers are considered in the context of human rights as they sometimes involve the deprivation of a suspect's liberty (**Article 5**) and invasion of their privacy (**Article 8**).

The main Act governing police powers is the **Police and Criminal Evidence Act 1984 (PACE)**, although others also give the police powers over citizens. Within **PACE** and other Acts, police are given discretion with the ways they exercise their powers and remedies are available for breach of these powers.

A remedy is a solution in a civil case (e.g. payment of compensation). In this context it can also refer to a claimant taking a civil action against the police or making a complaint against the police force in question that may result in disciplinary action or an apology. (You can read more about police complaints on page 201.) Codes of Practice run alongside **PACE** and provide guidelines for the exercise of certain powers.

Breach of the codes cannot give rise to legal action but, if there is a 'serious and substantial' breach, evidence could be excluded.

The Royal Commission on Criminal Procedure (RCCP or Philips Commission) concluded in 1981 that a balance needed to be reached between 'the interests of the community in bringing offenders to justice and the rights and liberties of persons suspected or accused of crime'. **PACE** was passed following these findings and consolidated police powers into one Act.

The powers of the police can be broken down into five main sections:

- Stop and search (persons, vehicles and premises)
- Arrest
- Detention and interrogation
- Admissibility of evidence
- Complaints against the police and remedies

GRADE BOOST

It is crucial when discussing police powers to accurately refer to the sections of **PACE** or other Acts that provide the police with the power to carry out a particular act or that guide their conduct. In the exam, remember with a problem-style question to identify and define the law, apply the law to the facts and reach a conclusion as to whether the power was correctly used. Even if an action has been done correctly, you still need to discuss the law that gives them that power.

20 Restrictions of the European Court of Human Rights

The test for authorising **s47A** powers is that the senior police officer giving it must:

> reasonably suspect that an act of terrorism will take place
> consider that the powers are necessary to prevent such an act.

1a. Stop and search of persons and vehicles

Section 1 PACE
Police can stop and search persons or vehicles in a public place or a place to which the public has access if there are reasonable grounds to suspect they will find stolen or prohibited articles. This search must take place in a public place, which is defined as a place to which the public have access and is not a dwelling.

Section 23 Misuse of Drugs Act 1971
Police can stop and search any person or vehicle if they have reasonable suspicion that they will find controlled drugs.

Section 1(3) Criminal Justice Act 2003
Police have extended powers to stop and search for articles intended to be used to cause criminal damage.

Section 1(6) PACE
Police may seize any stolen or prohibited articles.

Code of Practice Code A paragraph 2.2
This gives guidance on 'reasonable suspicion'. There is a two-stage test:

1. The officer must have genuine suspicion that they will find the stolen or prohibited object.
2. The suspicion that the object will be found must be reasonable. This means that there must be an objective basis for that suspicion, based on facts, information and/or intelligence or some specific behaviour. Reasonable grounds for suspicion cannot be supported by personal factors alone (e.g. physical appearance), or with regard to any of the protected characteristics under the **Equality Act 2010** such as age, disability, race, religion or gender. Generalisations or stereotypical images that certain groups are more likely to be involved in criminal activity will not give grounds for reasonable suspicion, and nor will a person being known to have previous convictions.

There are powers where the police do not need reasonable suspicion, such as under **s44 Terrorism Act 2000** and **s60 Criminal Justice and Public Order Act 1994**.

Section 60 Criminal Justice and Public Order Act 1994 (CJPOA)
If a police officer of or above the rank of inspector reasonably believes that serious violence will take place in an area, they can authorise the stop and search of persons and vehicles in that area for up to 24 hours to look for dangerous instruments or offensive weapons.

The use of the power to conduct **s60** searches without reasonable suspicion was unsuccessfully challenged as breaching **Article 8 ECHR** (right to a private life) in *R (Roberts)* v *Commissioner of the Police of the Metropolis* (2015).

Section 60AA CJPOA (1994)
This gives powers to require the removal of face coverings. However, the officer must reasonably believe that someone is wearing such an item wholly or mainly to conceal their identity.

The power in **s44 Terrorism Act 2000** was successfully challenged in *Gillan and Quinton* v *the UK* (2010). The European Court of Human Rights (ECtHR) ruled that the powers were an illegal breach of **Article 8 ECHR** as they were so broad they failed to provide safeguards against abuse. Following this decision, the government announced that it was suspending the power to stop and search a person without suspicion under **s44**. The power was replaced with

> **STRETCH AND CHALLENGE**
> 'Reasonableness' is a tricky concept and depends on what the individual deems reasonable and acceptable. This provides the police with some measure of discretion in the exercise of their powers.

new stop and search powers in **s47A Terrorism Act 2000** as amended by **ss59–62 Protection of Freedoms Act 2012**.

The maximum authorisation length was cut from 28 to 14 days and should be authorised for no longer than is necessary.

Section 117 PACE
Reasonable force can be used in carrying out the stop and search. This also applies to the arrest. It is a 'floating section'.

Section 2 PACE
Before carrying out a stop and search, police officers must take reasonable steps to follow the correct procedure and bring five things to the attention of the suspect, for example, the police officers should identify themselves, the station at which they are based and the grounds for carrying out the search. In *R v Bristol* (2007), a failure to provide the necessary information rendered a stop and search unlawful because the PC had failed to give his name and station. Evidence found could be ruled inadmissible in court.

Section 2(3): police officers not in uniform must provide documentary evidence of their ID.

Section 2(9): a suspect can be asked to remove their outer coat, jacket and gloves in public. Headgear and footwear can be removed but in private and in the presence of an officer of the same sex.

Section 3 PACE
After the search, the police must make a written record of the search unless this is not practicable and there are exceptional circumstances. If it is not practicable straight away, it should be done as soon as practicable. A **s3** record must include five items such as the person's ethnic origin, the object of the search, the grounds for making it, the date, time and place, and the outcome of the search.

Figure 20.5 The police can use reasonable force in the exercise of their powers

> **KEY CASE**
>
> *Osman* v *DPP* (1999)
> Officers failed to give their name or station, making the search unlawful.

GRADE BOOST
When studying this topic, make the connections with human rights. Many of the cases above were challenged on the basis of human rights.

Section 4 PACE
An officer of the rank of superintendent or above can authorise in writing the setting up of road checks to see if the vehicle is carrying a person who has committed an offence other than a road traffic offence, a person who is a witness to such an offence, a person intending to commit such an offence or a person who is unlawfully at large.

1b. Search of premises

Searches of premises can be carried out with or without a warrant. Any property can be searched if a person consents to it.

Search with a warrant
The main provisions are found in **s8 PACE**. This gives the police the power to apply to a magistrate for a search warrant. The magistrate must be satisfied that the police have reasonable grounds to believe that an indictable offence has been committed and that there is material on the premises which is likely to be of substantial value to the investigation and that the material is likely to be relevant evidence. It must be impractical for the search to be made without a warrant (because, for example, they cannot communicate with the occupier, they have not consented to entry or they need immediate entry to the premises).

Search without a warrant

There are four key sections:

1. **Section 17:** police may enter to make an arrest with or without a warrant, capture a person unlawfully at large or to protect people or prevent damage to property.
2. **Section 18:** after an arrest for an indictable offence, police can search premises occupied or controlled by the suspect if they reasonably believe there is evidence of the offence or other offences on the premises.
3. **Section 32:** after an arrest for an indictable offence, an officer can enter and search the premises where the person was arrested or where they were just before being arrested, if the officer reasonably suspects it contains evidence relating to the particular offence.
4. **Section 19:** once lawfully on the premises, the police can seize and retain any relevant evidence.

Code B

This provides important guidelines for the exercise of the power to search premises. It provides that searches of premises should be carried out at a reasonable time with reasonable force and showing due consideration and courtesy towards the property and privacy of the occupier(s).

2a. Arrest with a warrant

Arrest can be carried out with and without a warrant. Police must apply to the magistrates for an arrest warrant. The name and details of the offence should be specified to the police and, once granted, provides the power to a constable to enter and search premises to make the arrest if required.

2b. Arrest without a warrant

This is covered by **s24 PACE** as amended by **s110 Serious Organised Crime and Police Act 2005**. An arrest without a warrant can be made if a constable has reasonable grounds to believe that a person is committing, has committed or is about to commit an offence or has reasonable grounds to suspect the defendant is guilty and, importantly, that an arrest is necessary.

Figure 20.6 Police can make an arrest with or without a warrant

'Necessary' to arrest
Under **s24(5)**, a constable must have reasonable grounds for believing it is necessary to arrest the person for reasons given in **s24(5)**. These grounds are:

(a) to enable the name of the person in question to be ascertained (where it is not known or where the constable believes the one provided to be false)

(b) to enable the address of the person in question to be ascertained as in (a)

(c) to prevent the person in question—

    (i) causing physical injury to himself or any other person

    (ii) suffering physical injury

    (iii) causing loss of or damage to property

    (iv) committing an offence against public; or

    (v) causing an unlawful obstruction of the highway

(d) to protect a child or other vulnerable person from the person in question

(e) to allow the prompt and effective investigation of the offence or of the conduct of the person in question

(f) to prevent any prosecution for the offence from being hindered by the disappearance of the person in question.

Code of Practice G
This governs the power of arrest. In recognition of the **HRA 1998** and the right to liberty, the power of arrest should be fully justified and the police have to prove that it is necessary. Police officers using this power should consider whether their objectives could be met in any other way.

The ECtHR case of *O'Hara* v *UK* **(2000)** confirmed the two-part test for 'reasonable suspicion'. The officer must have actual suspicion (subjective) and there must be reasonable grounds for that suspicion (objective).

Section 117 PACE
Officers can use reasonable force to make the arrest.

Section 28 PACE
For an arrest to be valid, certain procedural elements must be complied with. Even if it is obvious, the suspect must be told in accessible language that they are being arrested and the grounds for the arrest.

Code of Practice C
The suspect must be cautioned on arrest: 'You do not have to say anything. But it may harm your defence if you do not mention when questioned something which you later rely on in court. Anything you do say may be given in evidence.'

Section 24A PACE as amended by SOCPA
This provides a power to a person other than a constable to arrest without a warrant anyone who is in the act of committing an indictable offence, or anyone they have reasonable grounds for suspecting is committing an indictable offence. They must have reasonable grounds for believing an arrest is necessary and that it is impracticable for an officer to make the arrest. The term indictable within **SOCPA** not only means the most serious offences but also crimes that are triable either way.

> **GRADE BOOST**
>
> **Code A** also applies to arrest. Reasonable suspicion can never be based on personal factors alone, such as gender, ethnicity, age, previous convictions and other general stereotypes.
>
> **Article 5 ECHR** provides that everyone has the right to liberty. Arrest interferes with this right and must be exercised lawfully.

Section 32 PACE
A constable may search an arrested person at a place other than a police station if they have reasonable grounds for believing that the arrested person may present a danger to themselves or others, are in possession of evidence or present a danger.

3. Detention and interrogation

Section 30 PACE
The suspect must be taken to the police station as soon as possible after arrest unless they are required elsewhere.

Section 36 PACE
On arrival at the police station, the custody officer decides whether there is enough evidence to charge the suspect.

Section 37 PACE
If there is not sufficient evidence to charge a suspect, police will assess whether such evidence might be obtained through questioning and, if so, a suspect may be detained for these purposes. If not, the suspect should be released. If enough evidence exists to charge on arrest, the suspect should be granted bail under s38 PACE.

Once detention has been authorised, the custody officer must begin a custody record for the detainee which must record the reasons for detention (Code C and s37).

Section 40 PACE
A person detained but not yet charged should have their detention reviewed after first six hours and then every nine hours by the custody officer.

Section 41 PACE
Police could authorise detention without charge for up to 24 hours. This was increased to 36 hours (s42) following the Criminal Justice Act 2003.

Section 44 PACE
The maximum period of detention is 96 hours, on approval of magistrates.

Section 54 PACE
Police may conduct an ordinary search on an arrested person on arrival at the police station and seize any item they believe the suspect might use to cause physical injury to themselves or any other person, to damage property, to interfere with evidence, or to assist them to escape; or any item the constable has reasonable grounds for believing may be evidence relating to an offence.

Intimate searches and samples
Section 55: intimate search: the police, on the authorisation of an inspector or higher, have the power to carry out an intimate search of a suspect's body's orifices where the superintendent has reasonable grounds for believing that the suspect has concealed something they could use to cause physical injury to themselves or others while in police detention or in the custody of a court; or that such a person may conceal a Class A drug. The search must be carried out by a registered medical professional or a registered nurse.

A search of the mouth used to be classed as an intimate search. Drug dealers would frequently hide drugs in their mouths in the knowledge that the police could not search them. This gave them time to dispose of the evidence. Section 65 PACE as amended by CJPOA 1994 now provides that a search of the mouth is a non-intimate search.

Also relevant are the following sections of PACE:

> Section 62: intimate samples such as blood, saliva and semen can be taken from the suspect.
> Section 63: non-intimate samples such as hair and nail clippings can be taken if authorised by an inspector or above.

KEY TERMINOLOGY
custody officer: a constable of at least the rank of sergeant who is present in the custody suite of a police station and is responsible for the welfare and rights of people brought into custody. They keep a custody record.

STRETCH AND CHALLENGE
The Terrorism Act 2006 allows detention to be extended to 14 days where the offence relates to terrorism.

> **Section 64**: DNA information can be extracted from the samples and placed indefinitely on the national DNA database. In *S and Marper* v *UK* (2008), the ECtHR ruled that it was a breach of Article 8 ECHR to retain DNA indefinitely if there was no conviction. The Protection of Freedom Act 2012 allows for the indefinite retention of DNA profiles only where a person has been convicted of a recordable offence. The DNA sample of anyone arrested but not charged or charged and later acquitted of most offences cannot be retained.
> **Section 65**: a person may also be identified by intimate samples as defined by s65 (i.e. bodily samples, swabs and impressions).
> **Sections 61 and 27**: police can take fingerprints from suspects.
> **Section 61A** as amended by SOCPA (2005): impressions of footwear can be taken.

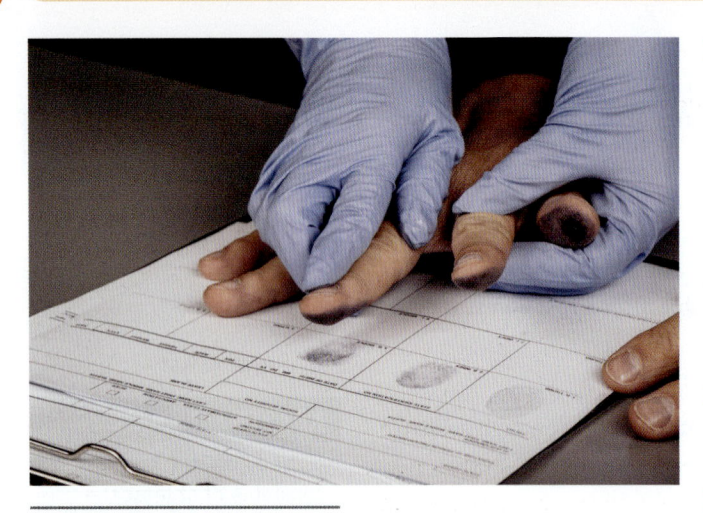

Figure 20.7 Police can take fingerprints from suspects

Rights and treatment of suspects during detention and interrogation

Section 60: the police must make a record of the interview and keep it on file. Interviews should be tape-recorded. However, it has been found that interviews can take place outside the police station, for example on the way to the police station. In some areas, the police also video interviews.

Section 56: the suspect has the right to have someone informed of their arrest. This right can be suspended for up to 36 hours if it is felt that the person chosen by the suspect may interfere with the investigation in some way (e.g. by alerting other suspects or destroying evidence).

Section 58: the suspect has the right to consult a solicitor privately and free of charge. Again, this right can be suspended for up to 36 hours for the reasons mentioned in s56. This advice can be given over the telephone by Criminal Defence Service Direct.

Section 57: vulnerable suspects (those under 17 or those who are mentally disordered or disabled) must have an appropriate adult with them during questioning. This right is in addition to the s58 right. The absence of this person may render any confession inadmissible in court.

Code C: the suspect must be cautioned on arrest and before each interview. Suspects have the right to read the Codes of Practice. Code C also deals with conditions of detention. Suspects must be given adequate food, refreshment, sleep and breaks. The interview room must be adequately lit, heated and ventilated, and a suspect must be allowed to sit. Interviews should not exceed two hours in length. Persons under the age of 16 should not be kept in police cells.

GRADE BOOST

Under Code of Practice E, interviews are tape-recorded in the case of offences triable on indictment, including those triable either way.

Note Article 8 ECHR: the right to respect for a person's private and family life, their home and their correspondence.

KEY CASES

R v *Samuel* (1988)
The suspect was detained and questioned for armed robbery but was refused access to a solicitor on several occasions, as police felt there was a danger that other suspects could be warned. It was held that this was unjustified and, although Samuel confessed to the offence, the confession could not be used in court.

R v *Grant* (2005)
Interference by the police in a person's right to consult with a solicitor was held to be so serious that Grant's conviction for murder was quashed.

20 Restrictions of the European Court of Human Rights

Admissibility of evidence

It is essential that police powers are exercised correctly for the evidence obtained to be used in court (is admissible). The courts can refuse to admit evidence that has not been properly obtained.

The following sections of **PACE** are relevant.

Section 76(2)(a)
Confession evidence may be excluded at trial if it is obtained by oppression. If this is raised, it is up to the prosecution to prove beyond reasonable doubt that the confession was not obtained by oppression. According to **s76(8)** oppression means torture, inhuman or degrading treatment or the use of threat or violence.

Section 76(2)(b)
Confession evidence may be excluded at trial if it was obtained in circumstances which make it unreliable. In the cases of *R v Samuel* (1988) and *R v Grant* (2005), failure to provide access to legal advice rendered the confessions inadmissible.

Section 78
Any evidence, including a confession, may be excluded on the ground that it would adversely affect the fairness of the trial. This includes situations such as not writing up the interviews straight after they had finished, as in *R v Canale* (1990).

Other relevant points
Breaches of the Codes of Practice must be 'serious and substantial' for the evidence obtained to be considered for exclusion.

Under **s57** vulnerable suspects (those under 17 and mentally disordered or disabled people) must have an appropriate adult with them during questioning. The absence of this person may render any confession inadmissible in court. Under **s77**, the jury would be warned that a confession was made by a mentally disordered person.

The police have wide-ranging powers that must be exercised with discretion. There is always the risk of misinterpretation of a situation and errors being made, but the powers are essential in order to keep the public safe. Where there have been errors, remedies may be available.

Complaints against police and remedies

According to the rule of law, no one is above the law and everyone is equal under it. This also applies to the police. Even though the police have the power to lawfully infringe a person's human rights, such as the right to liberty under **Article 5 ECHR**, they must do so within the powers they have been given and without breaking any law. They should also adhere to the **PACE** Codes of Practice.

Anyone can make a police complaint. The complainant does not need to be a 'victim' of police misconduct. They might, for example, have witnessed an incident which they feel should be the subject of a complaint. The complaint should be made within one year and must be against a particular officer, group of officers or civilian staff. It is therefore important for a complainant to get as many details about the officer(s) as they can to file the complaint. General complaints about police policy and practice or local police may be made to the Home Office via a local MP or the Local Police Authority.

To ensure the police act within the law, an aggrieved citizen can either make a complaint or sue through the civil courts. The police complaints procedure used to be overseen by the Police Complaints Authority (PCA) but, due to wide criticisms, it was abolished by the **Police Reform Act 2002**, which replaced it with the Independent Police Complaints Commission (IPCC). Its role was to investigate, supervise or manage complaints against the police and make sure they were dealt with effectively. The IPCC aimed to be more independent, open

> **EXAM SKILLS**
>
> When answering a question on this topic, be sure to include as many sections of relevant legislation as you can and apply them to the facts of a scenario-style question. Remember to identify, define and apply the law to reach a conclusion on that point of law before moving on to the next point. Even if the police appear to have exercised their powers correctly, it is still important to discuss this in the same way, just concluding that it was correctly done. This is a very common topic at A Level.

and accessible than the PCA, so that individuals feel more willing to make a complaint. An alternative or additional option is for the aggrieved person to take a civil action and sue the police. In January 2018, the Independent Office for Police Conduct (IOPC) was established to continue the IPCC's work under a new structure with strengthened powers.

This section is going to explore the procedure for making a complaint, the role of the IOPC and the possibility of taking a civil action against the police.

Complaints procedure: Civil actions against the police

An individual may bring a civil action against the police and seek damages for the injuries and loss sustained. In a civil case, the standard of proof is 'on the balance of probabilities' and the burden lies with the claimant.

The police have been sued successfully several times. *Goswell v Commissioner of Police for the Metropolis* (1998) is an example of a successful claim against the police.

Goswell v Commissioner of Police the Metropolis (1998)

Mr Goswell was waiting in his car for his girlfriend when he was approached by PC Trigg who, without making any check upon the car, asked him to get out of his car. Mr Goswell began shouting, swearing and complaining that the police were unfairly troubling him and instead should have been out investigating a recent arson attack on his home. PC Trigg twice told Mr Goswell to calm down but he failed to do so. The officers then took hold of Mr Goswell and handcuffed him behind his back. PC Trigg struck Mr Goswell over the forehead with a police truncheon, causing a wound which bled profusely. Mr Goswell was put into a police car and taken to Woolwich Police Station. Only on arrival was he told why he had been arrested. He sued the police in the civil courts for assault and false imprisonment, and was awarded the considerable damages of £120,000 for assault, £12,000 for false imprisonment and £170,000 exemplary damages for arbitrary and oppressive behaviour. On appeal, this was reduced to £47,600.

The Commissioner of Police for the Metropolis v *Thompson and Hsu* (1997)

The Court of Appeal laid down important guidelines on the award of damages in civil cases against the police. Kenneth Hsu was originally awarded £220,000 in damages for wrongful arrest, false imprisonment and assault by the police but this was reduced on joint appeal (Thompson) to £35,000. Following these cases, the compensation awards have been limited due to concerns that the large awards given by juries diminished the budget available for policing. There is a current ceiling of £50,000 for exemplary damages for 'oppressive, arbitrary or unconstitutional behaviour' by the police.

STRETCH AND CHALLENGE

Look up the incidents mentioned here, and any other relevant cases investigated by the IPCC and the IOPC. Compile a report on what happened and the IPCC's conclusions.

Remedies for breach of police powers

It is important that there are adequate remedies in place to deter similar behaviour and to provide the complainant with some form of resolution. Among the outcomes of both local resolution and other types of investigation are:

- an apology by the police force
- an explanation
- a change in policy or procedure
- a referral to the CPS
- a recommendation that disciplinary action be taken
- judicial review.

20 Restrictions of the European Court of Human Rights

SUMMARY: RESTRICTIONS OF THE ECHR: POLICE POWER

→ **Section 1 Police and Criminal Evidence Act 1984 (PACE)**: stop and search of persons and vehicles
→ **Code A paragraph 2.2**: two-stage test for 'reasonable suspicion'
→ Reasonable force: **s117, s2(3), s3 PACE**
→ Search of premises with a warrant: **s8 PACE**
→ Search without a warrant: **s17**: *Osman* v *DPP* (1999); **s18**; **s19**; **s32**; **Code B**
→ Arrest with a warrant: police must apply to a magistrate
→ Arrest without a warrant: **s24 PACE** as amended by **s110 SOCPA 2005**
→ Reasonable grounds to believe that a person is committing, has committed or is about to commit an offence and an arrest is necessary
→ Detention and interrogation: **ss30, 36–38, 40, 41, 44, 54 PACE**
  - Fingerprinting, intimate searches and samples: **ss27, 55, 61–64** (*S and Marper* v *UK* (2008)), **65** as amended by **CJPOA 1994**
  - Rights and treatment of suspects during detention and interrogation: **ss56–58, 60**; **Code C**
  - Admissibility of evidence: courts can refuse to admit evidence that has not been properly obtained: **s76(2)(a)(b)**; *R* v *Samuel* (1988); *R* v *Grant* (2005); **s78 PACE**: *R* v *Canale* (1990)
→ Complaints against and police and remedies
  - No one is above the law and everyone is equal under it, including the police
  - Complaints to the Home Office via an MP or the Local Police Authority
  - In January 2018, the Independent Office for Police Conduct (IOPC) was established to continue the IPCC's work under a new structure with strengthened powers.
  - Professional Standards Department (PSD) of relevant police authority deals with general complaints
  - Civil actions against the police: the standard of proof is 'on the balance of probabilities' and the burden lies with the claimant: *Goswell* v *Commissioner of Police for the Metropolis* (1998); *Commissioner of Police for the Metropolis* v *Thompson and Hsu* (1997)

STRETCH AND CHALLENGE

Judicial review in the High Court oversees the decisions of public bodies such as the police. An application is made by an individual who feels their rights have been infringed. If a public body breaches its powers, it may have breached individuals' rights and therefore the right to review the exercise of powers is an important remedy.

Find out more about the following cases:
- Protesters at the G20 demonstrations who complained of being beaten and unlawfully restrained by the police won a judicial review of the tactics used by the officers.
- Politician John Prescott won a judicial review into the police inquiry into the phone-hacking scandal.
- High-profile supporters of the Extinction Rebellion protests in London successfully challenged a banning order issued by the Metropolitan Police using judicial review.

TEST YOURSELF

1. What is the main Act governing police powers?
2. Explain the power of the police to arrest suspects under **s24 PACE 1984** as amended by **s110 SOCPA 2005**.
3. What does **Code G** say in relation to the exercise of the powers of arrest?
4. When can the police stop and search a suspect?
5. What does **Code A** say in relation to the exercise of stop and search powers?
6. What rights does a suspect have under **s58** and **s56** of **PACE 1984**?

203

Interception of communications

Article 8 ECHR provides that everyone has 'the right to respect for his private and family life, his home and his correspondence'. Respect for correspondence under **Article 8** covers all forms of communication including phone calls, letters, text messages, emails and other communication methods.

Article 8 is of course a qualified right, so can be removed under **Article 8(2)** if it:

> is in accordance (i.e. set down) in law
> is necessary and proportionate
> fulfils a legitimate aim, such as in the interests of national security.

History of state surveillance

Agents of the state may invade privacy with the aim of promoting internal security or preventing or detecting crime. Such aims are legitimate; the question is whether the safeguards against unreasonable or arbitrary intrusion are adequate. Safeguards should include a clear remedy for the citizen, and strict control over the power of such interception, with proper authorisation for it. Proper authorisation is crucial since the citizen will not probably be aware of the surveillance.

Before 1985, there was no requirement to follow a legal procedure when authorising the tapping of telephones or the interception of mail. The conditions for issuing warrants for interception of postal or telephone communications were laid down in administrative rules, which had no legal force. Under these rules, the interception could be authorised to assist in a criminal investigation only if the crime was serious, normal methods had been tried and had failed, and there was good reason for believing that the evidence gained would lead to a conviction. If the interception related to security matters, it could only be authorised in respect of major subversion, terrorism or espionage, and the evidence obtained had to be directly useful to the security services in compiling the information it needed to carry out its function of protecting state security.

Figure 20.8 Surveillance can take many forms

The Interception of Communications Act 1985

The **Interception of Communications Act 1985 (ICA)** made the use of telephone and mail intercepts subject to certain controls. It was introduced partly as a direct result of the ruling in the ECtHR in *Malone* v *UK* (1985) that the existing warrant procedure violated the **Article 8** guarantee of privacy.

Figure 20.9 Technology facilitates growing methods of electronic surveillance

Bugging devices

Surveillance techniques are an important way for the police and security services to maintain law and order and protect national security. However, as said in the Supreme Court of Canada, 'one can scarcely imagine a state activity more dangerous to individual privacy than electronic surveillance' (*Duarte* (1990)). Despite the development of such devices and their increased use by the state, they have continued to operate outside the control of the courts. Their use by the police was, until recently, authorised only under administrative guidelines. These guidelines failed to provide an element of independent scrutiny. The use of surveillance devices by the police has been in question in several cases, such as *Khan (Sultan)* (1996).

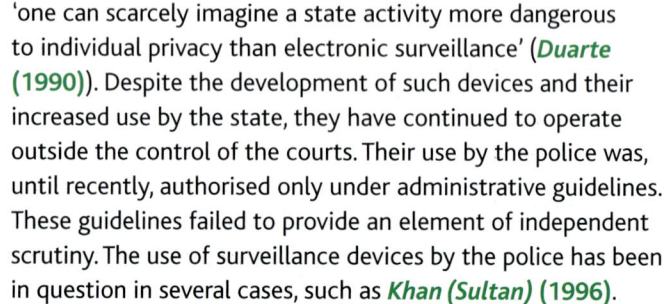

20 Restrictions of the European Court of Human Rights

Khan (Sultan) (1996)

A bugging device had been secretly installed on the outside of a house that Khan had been visiting. Khan was suspected of involvement in importing drugs, and the tape-recording from the bug showed that he was involved. The defence argued that the tape was inadmissible as evidence because the police had no statutory authority to place bugs on private property and that therefore there had been a trespass, and the bug amounted to a breach of Article 8 ECHR. The Court of Appeal held that trespass and damage to the building had occurred, and that there had been an invasion of privacy. However, the court said these were of slight significance and were outweighed by the fact that the police had largely complied with Home Office guidelines, and that the offences were serious. Khan's appeal was therefore turned down. The House of Lords recommended legislation taking into account that the regime governing the use of bugging devices was not on a statutory basis, and therefore might not comply with requirements under the ECHR.

Police Act 1997

This Act places current practice on a statutory basis. The basis for allowing the use of bugging is very broad. An authorisation may be issued if the action is expected to be of substantial value in the prevention and detection of serious crime and the objective cannot reasonably be achieved by other means (s93(2)).

KEY CASE

Malone v UK (1985)

In 1979, Mr Malone was on trial for receiving stolen goods. During his trial, evidence that his phone had been tapped came to light, and that the intercept had been authorised by the Home Secretary. Malone sought a declaration in the High Court that it was unlawful for anyone to intercept another's telephone conversation without consent (*Malone* v *MPC* (1979)). This line of argument failed, as did the argument based on Article 8 that there was a right to privacy that had been violated by the tapping. The judge, Megarry, concluded that the ECHR did not give rise to any enforceable rights under English law and that therefore there was no direct right of privacy (HRA would obviously now alter that position.) However, Megarry commented that, 'I find it impossible to see how English law could be said to satisfy the requirements of the Convention... This is not a subject on which it is possible to feel any pride in English law ... Telephone tapping is a subject which cries out for legislation.'

Malone took his case to the ECtHR, arguing that Article 8 had been violated. Article 8(2) reads: 'There shall be no interference by a public authority with the exercise of this right except such as in accordance with the law.' The ECtHR held that UK law did not regulate the circumstances in which telephone tapping could be carried out sufficiently clearly or provide any remedy against abuse of that power. However, the decision only required the UK government to introduce legislation to regulate the circumstances in which the power to tap could be used, rather than giving guidance on what would be acceptable limits on the individual's privacy.

The UK government responded by passing the Interception of Communications Act 1985. This has now been replaced by Part 1 Regulation of Investigatory Powers Act 2000 (RIPA), which in turn has been amended by the Investigatory Powers Act 2016.

Covert surveillance

Covert surveillance is now regulated by ss26–48 Regulation of Investigatory Powers Act 2000 as amended by the Covert Human Intelligence Sources (Criminal Conduct) Act 2021.

Surveillance is defined in s48 to include:

> - monitoring, observing or listening to persons, their movements, their conversations or their other activities or communications

205

> recording anything monitored, observed or listened to in the course of surveillance
> surveillance by or with the assistance of a surveillance device.

Section 26 identifies different types of behaviour covered by the Act: directed surveillance, intrusive surveillance, the conduct and use of covert human intelligence sources and criminal conduct in the course of, or otherwise in connection with, the conduct of covert human intelligence sources.

Section 26: intrusive surveillance. Intrusive surveillance occurs when a device or an individual is present on residential premises or in a vehicle, or where it is carried out in relation to such premises or vehicle. If the device is not on the premises, it is not intrusive unless the device consistently provides information of the same quality and detail as might be expected from a device actually on premises or in a vehicle.

Section 26(2) states that covert but not intrusive surveillance is directed surveillance if 'it is undertaken for the purpose of a specific investigation and in order to obtain private information about a person'.

Section 26(8) defines what is meant by a covert human intelligence source. Such a source will establish or maintain a relationship with a person for the covert purpose of using the relationship to obtain access to information, or provide access to another, or for the covert purpose of disclosing information obtained from the relationship.

Section 26(8) is most likely to cover the actions of police informers. Authorisations are granted under ss28–32. Sections 28 and 29 cover directed surveillance, which may be authorised on the same grounds as those in the Police Act 1997. A superintendent can authorise it, it must be necessary and proportionate, the grounds include national security and the economic well-being of the UK, and the crime to be prevented or detected does not have to be serious. Section 28 also includes 'public safety', 'public health' and tax collection.

Section 32: authorisations for intrusive surveillance are granted by the Secretary of State or senior authorising officers (e.g. chief constables). Requirements of necessity and proportionality apply but the grounds are limited to national security, the economic well-being of the UK and serious crime. Notice must be given to Surveillance Commissioner and authorisation will not take effect until it has been approved.

Figure 20.10 Covert and intrusive surveillance are controversial issues when it comes to infringement of human rights

STRETCH AND CHALLENGE

Research the cases of *R v Hall* (1994) and *R v Stagg* (1994). The police actions in both cases would clearly fall within the definition found in s26 RIPA.

Investigatory Powers Act 2016

The Investigatory Powers Act 2016 (IPA) brings together and updates existing powers (RIPA 2000 will continue until expressly repealed). The IPA introduced:

> a 'double-lock' for the most intrusive powers, so that warrants issued by a Secretary of State will also require the approval of a senior judge
> new powers and restated existing ones, for UK intelligence agencies and law enforcement to carry out targeted interception of communications, bulk collection of communications data, and bulk interception of communications
> a powerful new Investigatory Powers Commission to oversee how the powers are used
> new protections for journalistic and legally privileged material
> a requirement for judicial authorisation for acquisition of communications data that identify journalists' sources
> harsh sanctions, including the creation of new criminal offences for those misusing the powers.

Key points from the Investigatory Powers Act 2016

Interception of an individual's communications (Part 2 IPA)
From 27 June 2018, the interception of communications operations became authorised under a new regime set out in the **Investigatory Powers Act 2016 (IPA)**. This covers the actual content of communications — listening to the actual words spoken on a phone call or reading the text of an email.

The heads of the intelligence agencies, some police forces and HMRC can intercept communications if they have a warrant. The Home Secretary (personally) can grant a warrant under **s19** if he deems it necessary on certain, limited grounds, and that the interception is proportionate to what it seeks to achieve. The grounds are set out in **s20** and are for national security, to fight serious crime, or to protect the economy at a national security level.

Except in urgent cases, the Home Secretary's decision then has to be approved by a Judicial Commissioner from the Investigatory Powers Commissioner's Office (**s19**) ('double-lock' safeguard). The post of Judicial Commissioner is only open to people who have been a senior judge (High Court or above). Communications data (**Parts 3** and **4** of **IPA**).

'Communications data' is information about someone's communications rather than the contents of it. So, in the case of an email, the communications data would be who sent it, who received it, the time and date — but not the actual text of the email.

A range of public bodies, from GCHQ to the Food Standards Agency, can get access to communications data. A request needs to be authorised by a senior figure within that organisation. They can only authorise it if the request is necessary for one of ten purposes, the first of which is 'national security'.

Communications data includes records of which websites someone has visited, although there are more restrictions on accessing these records.

Phone and internet companies that have people's communications data can be told to hold on to it for up to 12 months.

Equipment interference (Part 5 of IPA)
This is about hacking into computers or other devices to mess with or get information out of them. The Home Secretary can grant interference warrants to the intelligence services for the same reasons as for interception of communications (national security, serious crime, economy). Various 'law enforcement chiefs', for example the police, can grant warrants to prevent serious crime, or to ward off death or serious injury. But in both cases, Judicial Commissioners also have to approve the warrant under **s108**, unless it's urgent.

Bulk personal datasets
This refers to databases containing information on lots of people when someone the authorities are interested in might be among them. An example might be a Home Office database of everyone who has a UK passport.

The intelligence services generally need a warrant to keep or look at bulk personal data. Again, these are granted by the Home Secretary on national security, serious crime or economic grounds, with sign-off from a Judicial Commissioner. There are extra protections for health records in particular.

Bulk interception, acquisition and hacking powers
As well as targeted snooping, it allows 'bulk warrants' to be granted.

These give the state access to communications en masse — this is done either by intercepting them directly during transmission or by forcing communication companies to hand over swathes of data.

A bulk warrant can also be given to authorise the widespread hacking of electronic devices.

These warrants can only be granted to the UK's intelligence agencies, upon the approval of both a minister and a Judicial Commissioner and on certain specified grounds, namely in the interests of national security, for the purpose of preventing or detecting serious crime or in the interests of the economic well-being of the UK.

Evaluation of surveillance in the UK

> Are further reforms needed or is the IPA 2016 enough?
> Should surveillance evidence be admissible in court? Britain's security services fear that allowing intercept evidence to be used in a court of law would undermine its work, but globally the UK's stance on this issue is an exception. The USA, Canada, New Zealand, Ireland, Australia, Hong Kong and South Africa all allow certain kinds of intercept evidence in their courts of law. A judge and not a politician has the power to authorise telephone interception in all those countries (except Ireland).
> Why is the UK reluctant to follow what other countries do?
> England has perhaps the first instance of interception being used in a court of law when, in 1586, Mary, Queen of Scots, was convicted of treason on the basis of intercepted mail.
> There is also a loophole in the law which allows taped conversations from prison, mandatory for Category A prisoners, to be used in evidence. Phone calls the Soham killer Ian Huntley made to his girlfriend, Maxine Carr, and his mother were used to secure a conviction in 2003.

> **STRETCH AND CHALLENGE**
>
> The Chilcott Review 2008 was in favour of the use of intercept evidence in court in some cases. Research this report.
>
> Read this article and summarise the five arguments put forward to allow intercept evidence in court:
>
> www.libertyhumanrights.org.uk/news/blog/5-reasons-why-we-need-intercept-evidence-court
>
> What is your view on the issue? Should intercept evidence be allowed in court?

> **SUMMARY: RESTRICTIONS OF THE ECHR: INTERCEPTION OF COMMUNICATIONS**
>
> → Interception of Communications Act 1985 (ICA): introduced following *Malone* v *UK* (1985) to use telephone and mail intercepts, subject to controls
> → Use of bugging devices: *Khan (Sultan)* (1996); Police Act 1997
> → Regulation of Investigatory Powers Act 2000 (RIPA): it is an offence to intentionally and without lawful authority intercept communications by a postal service or telecommunications system
> → Covert surveillance: ss26–48 RIPA: *R* v *Hall* (1994); *R* v *Stagg* (1994)
> → Investigatory Powers Act 2016 (IPA): brings together and updates existing powers (RIPA 2000 continues until repealed)

> **TEST YOURSELF**
>
> 1. Summarise the case of *Malone* v *UK* (1994) in relation to interception of communication.
> 2. What is Article 8 ECHR and when can it be removed in relation to interception of communication?
> 3. Which law covers covert surveillance?
> 4. What is the difference between covert and intrusive surveillance?
> 5. What is the 'double-lock' safeguard?

Duty of confidentiality

Breach of confidence and privacy

Do citizens under English and Welsh law have a right to privacy? Lord Justice Glidewell in *Kaye* v *Robertson* (1991) stated that 'it's well known that in English law there is no right to privacy, and accordingly there is no right of action for breach of a person's privacy'. In the UK, unlike in the USA, there is no overarching, all-embracing course of action for 'invasion of privacy'.

Wainwright v Home Office (2003)

The claimants, a mother and son, were strip-searched for drugs on a prison visit in 1997, in breach of the prison rules, and were humiliated and distressed. The second claimant, who was mentally impaired and suffered from cerebral palsy, developed post-traumatic stress disorder. The judge held that trespass to the person, consisting of wilfully causing them to do something to themselves which infringed their right to privacy, had been committed against both claimants and that trespass to the person, consisting of wilfully causing a person to do something calculated to cause them harm, had been committed against the second claimant in addition to a battery. They were awarded basic and aggravated damages. The Court of Appeal allowed the Home Office's appeal against the finding of trespass, dismissing the first claimant's claim and reducing the award of damages to the second claimant.

The issue in *Wainwright v Home Office* (2003) was whether English common law recognises a cause of action for invasion of privacy. The court held that there was no common law tort of invasion of privacy and that creation of such a tort required a detailed approach, which could only be achieved by legislation.

This was the first time the House of Lords had been asked to declare whether an action for invasion of privacy exists in English law. The case confirmed the widely held view that declaration of a general right to privacy is beyond the acceptable limits of judicial development of the common law. However, protection of various aspects of privacy is a fast-developing area of the law. The decision of the Court of Appeal of New Zealand in *Hosking v Runting* (2004) is an example of this.

Hosking v Runting (2004)

The claimants were a celebrity couple who had had twin girls in 2001 and declined to give interviews about them or allow them to be photographed. They separated in 2002. The first defendant, a photographer, was commissioned by the second defendant, a publisher, to photograph the claimants' 18-month-old twins. He took the photos in a street, while they were with their mother but without her knowledge. The claimants brought proceedings to prevent publication of the photographs, on the basis that their publication would amount to a breach of the twins' privacy. Randerson J held that New Zealand courts should not recognise privacy as a distinct cause of action. The claimants appealed.

The issues in the cases were whether:

- there was a freestanding tort of privacy in New Zealand
- any other cause of action could prevent the publication of the photographs.

On appeal, the court held by a majority of 3–2 that there is a freestanding tort of invasion of privacy in New Zealand. It was held that the expansion of breach of confidence, as has happened in the UK courts, might lead to the same outcome, but greater clarity was achieved by analysing breaches of confidence and privacy as separate causes of action. Privacy and confidence are different concepts. There are two fundamental elements for a successful claim for interference with privacy:

- The existence of facts in respect of which there is a reasonable expectation of privacy.
- Publicity given to those private facts that would be considered highly offensive to an objective, reasonable person.

The New Zealand Court of Appeal revived the privacy debate in New Zealand and beyond by recognising a common law tort of privacy. The cases contain a helpful review of English and commonwealth cases. In the UK, the development of the law has been spurred by enactment of the **Human Rights Act 1998**.

Breach of confidence

As explained in the previous section, there is no tort of invasion of privacy in England and Wales. However, legal controls can be used against the media and others. There is also competition between freedom of expression and respect for an individual's privacy. Both are vitally important rights.

What is privacy? The Calcutt Committee (1990) defined it as 'the right of the individual to be protected against intrusion into his personal life or affairs, or those of his family, by direct physical means or by publication of information'.

What, therefore, is breach of confidence? It is a civil remedy giving protection against the disclosure or use of information which is not generally known, and which has been entrusted in circumstances imposing an obligation not to disclose it without authorisation.

The use of the civil law of breach of confidence to protect privacy can be traced back to *Prince Albert* v *Strange* (1849).

Figure 20.11 Queen Victoria and her husband Prince Albert were the subjects of an early example of breach of confidence

Prince Albert v *Strange* (1849)

Both Queen Victoria and Prince Albert sketched as a hobby. Sometimes they showed their drawings to friends or gave them away. Strange obtained some of these sketches and arranged a public viewing of them. He also published a catalogue listing them. Prince Albert filed a claim for the return of the sketches and a surrender of the catalogue for destruction. The court awarded Prince Albert an injunction, restraining Strange from publishing a catalogue describing Prince Albert's sketches.

Another example is *Argyll* v *Argyll* (1967), where it was held that the Duchess of Argyll could obtain an injunction to prevent newspapers from revealing secrets about her marriage, which had been disclosed to the newspaper by her husband, the Duke.

The three traditional elements of breach of confidence were summarised in the key case of *Coco* v *AN Clark (Engineers) Ltd* (1968):

1. The information must have the necessary quality of confidence about it.
2. The information must have been given in circumstances importing an obligation of confidence.
3. There must be unauthorised use of that information.

What is 'information', for the purposes of the law of confidence?

It can include information concerning an individual's sexual orientation, as in *Stephens* v *Avery* (1988), photographs, as in *HRH Princess of Wales* v *MGN Newspapers Ltd* (1993) and photos from a film set, as in *Shelley Films Ltd* v *Rex Features Ltd* (1993).

Stephens v Avery (1988)

The parties had been friends and had discussed their sex lives. The defendant took the information to a newspaper editor, who published it. The claimant sought damages, saying the conversations and disclosures had been confidential. The court held that the defendants had published knowing that the material was disclosed in confidence. Information about sexual activities could be protected under a duty of confidence, where it would be unconscionable for someone who had received information on an expressly confidential basis to disclose it.

HRH Princess of Wales v MGN Newspapers Ltd (1993)

The court had no hesitation in granting injunctions to prevent the *Daily Mirror* and others from publishing photographs of Princess Diana exercising in a gymnasium, taken by the gym owner without her knowledge or consent.

Shelley Films Ltd v Rex Features Ltd (1993)

The defendant was restrained by injunction from publishing photographs that had been taken on set of a forthcoming film, *Frankenstein*, photographs of which the producers had taken steps to keep confidential. The court held that the photographer knew that the occasion was a private one and that the taking of photographs by outsiders was not permitted.

Figure 20.12 As a high-profile public figure, Princess Diana often fought to protect her privacy

Since *Stephens v Avery* (1988), the basic principle appears to be that confidentiality will be enforced if the information was received on the basis that it is confidential. The fact that information is given in confidence may be expressly communicated to the defendant, but can be implied from the circumstances surrounding the communication, as in *Fairnie (Deceased) and Others v Reed and Another* (1994).

Fairnie (Deceased) and Others v Reed and Another (1994)

Confidential information about the format of a board game, which the claimant wished to sell, was mentioned by him in passing during a conversation with a virtual stranger. The stranger was not told that it was given in confidence. The Court of Appeal held that the information was given in confidence due to the clear commercial value of the information.

Public interest defence

Confidential information will not be protected if the public interest outweighs the interest in preserving confidentiality. In *AG v Guardian Newspapers Ltd (No. 2)* (1990), the interest in maintaining confidentiality was outweighed by the public interest in knowing the allegations in the book *Spycatcher*.

> ### *AG* v *Guardian Newspapers Ltd (No. 2)* (1990)
> A retired secret service spy sought to publish his memoirs. At the time of publication, he was living in Australia. The British government sought to restrain publication in Australia, and the defendant newspapers sought to report those proceedings, which would involve publication of the allegations made in the book. The Attorney General sought to restrain the publications.
>
> The court held that a duty of confidence arises when confidential information comes to the knowledge of a person in circumstances where they have notice, or are held to have agreed, that the information is confidential, with the effect that it would be just in all the circumstances that they should be precluded from disclosing the information to others.

The principle of confidentiality only applies to information to the extent that it is confidential. In particular, once it has entered what is usually called the public domain, as it had in this case, then generally the principle of confidentiality can have no application to it.

Note that what is of interest to the public may not be in the public interest.

Breach of confidence and privacy after the Human Rights Act 1998

Article 8 ECHR (the right to privacy) is now incorporated by the Human Rights Act 1998. How quickly or how far will judges move the law in the direction of the protection of privacy?

Individual privacy cannot be considered in isolation. Privacy must be weighed alongside freedom of speech and expression, which is also an important right under Article 10 ECHR.

Technically, there is no such thing as a privacy claim in English and Welsh law, but this name has come to be used for claims set down in *Campbell* v *MGN* (2004), where supermodel Naomi Campbell sued the *Daily Mirror* over stories about her being a recovering drug addict and attending Narcotics Anonymous meetings. In that case, the House of Lords created a new form of claim, which they called 'misuse of private information'. This is a separate action to breach of confidence.

In *OBG Ltd* v *Allan* (2007), Lord Nicholls asserted that the action 'now covers two distinct causes of action, protecting two different interests: privacy, and secret ("confidential") information. It is important to keep these two distinct'.

The Court of Appeal confirmed in *Vidal-Hall* v *Google* (2015) that the action for misuse of private information was a separate tort. Therefore, in reality, privacy rights can be enforced against anyone, not just public authorities.

In *Campbell* (2004) the House of Lords held that to decide whether to grant a claim for misuse of private information, a court has to use a two-stage test:

› Stage 1: does the claimant have a reasonable expectation of privacy with respect to the information or material disclosed? If they do,
› Stage 2: is the claimant's right to privacy more important, in all the circumstances than the defendant's right to freedom of expression?

20 Restrictions of the European Court of Human Rights

KEY CASES

Venables and Thompson v News Group Newspapers (2001)
The claimants, the convicted murderers of toddler James Bulger, applied for indefinite injunctions to restrain publication of their new identities and their whereabouts. The issue was whether the court had the authority to protect an adult's identity in circumstances where there was a serious risk to physical safety. It was argued that the court should exercise its equitable jurisdiction to make the orders sought by the claimants. The claimants were notorious and at risk of serious physical harm then and in the future. The claimants' rights under **Article 2 ECHR** (the right to life) demanded protection, which could be provided by extension of the law of confidence. An injunction was granted restraining publication of the claimants' identities and their whereabouts.

Associated Newspapers Ltd v Prince of Wales (2006)
The *Mail on Sunday* published extracts of a diary by Prince Charles, Prince of Wales. The extracts published from the diary, titled 'The Great Chinese Takeaway', were personally embarrassing to the Prince. They had been written on a flight back from Hong Kong to the UK after the transfer of sovereignty of Hong Kong to China, and had been handed out to Prince Charles's friends. The Prince described the Hong Kong handover ceremony as an 'awful Soviet-style' performance and 'ridiculous rigmarole' and likened Chinese officials to 'appalling old waxworks'. The Prince sought to claim confidentiality and copyright in them when the *Mail on Sunday* tried to publish them. The Prince won the case and gained an injunction, which prevented the *Mail on Sunday* from publishing further extracts from the diary.

STRETCH AND CHALLENGE

Research the following cases to see how the law of breach of confidence was considered in these cases:

- *Woodward v Hutchings* (1977)
- *Lion Laboratories v Evans and Express Newspapers* (1988)
- *X v Y* (1998)
- *Douglas and Jones v Hello! Ltd* (2005)
- *Re S (A Child) (Identification on Publication)* (2004)
- *Ash v McKennitt* (2006)
- *Murray v Express Newspapers* (2008)
- *CTB v Newsgroup* (2012)
- *PJS* (2016)

STRETCH AND CHALLENGE

Despite *Venables and Thompson v News Group Newspapers* (2001) being regarded as an exceptional case justifying an exceptional order, the courts have gone on to make two further orders, in favour of two other notorious criminals, Maxine Carr (see page 208) and Mary Bell. Research these cases. Do you think such an order is likely to be granted to anyone who can claim that their infamy is likely to lead to someone making death threats against them?

Murray v Express Newspapers (2008)

The defendant newspaper took a photograph of the claimant, the young son of the author of the Harry Potter books, JK Rowling, being pushed by his father in a buggy down a street with his mother walking alongside. The photograph was taken covertly using a long-range lens and was later published in the *Sunday Express*. The claimant (represented by his parents as litigation friends) issued proceedings against the *Sunday Express* for breach of privacy and confidence and under the **Data Protection Act 1998**. The court dismissed the claimant's claims.

Figure 20.13 The author JK Rowling has found her privacy and that of her family affected by ECHR

GRADE BOOST

The decision in *Mosley* v *News Group Newspapers* (2008) attracted a lot of criticism from the media. The court was accused of bringing in a new privacy law by the back door, leading to greater restrictions on the freedom of the press to publish stories about the rich and powerful. Do you agree?

Mosley v *News Group Newspapers* (2008)

The defendant newspaper group published a film showing the claimant involved in sex acts with prostitutes. It characterised them as 'Nazi' style. Mosley was the son of a fascist leader, and chairman of an international sporting body. He denied any Nazi element and claimed breach of confidence. The court had to balance the interest of protecting Mosley's private life with the interest of News Group Newspapers' right of freedom of expression. Mosley won his case. The fact that there is no clear law of privacy does not mean that people's privacy right cannot be protected when their privacy has been breached. An individual whose privacy has been interfered with can rely on the common law, breach of confidence and **Article 8 ECHR**. This case clearly confirms that the courts are willing to protect individuals' rights to a private life when there is intrusion by the media which is not justifiable.

Author of a Blog v *Times Newspapers* (2009)

The claimant, a serving police officer, was the author of the Night Jack blog, which described his police work and his opinions on a number of social and political issues relating to the police. He sought to conceal his identity by blogging under a pseudonym. A journalist for *The Times* had accurately identified the claimant. The claimant applied for an injunction to prevent *The Times* publishing his identity. He argued that the newspaper was subject to an enforceable duty of confidence not to reveal his identity and that he had a reasonable expectation of privacy in respect of the information that he was the blog's author, and there was no public interest justification for disclosing his identity. The court held that the information that the claimant was the author of the blog was not protected by breach of confidence, nor did it qualify as information in respect of which the claimant had a reasonable expectation of privacy, since blogging is a public activity. The injunction was refused.

BBC v HarperCollins Ltd (2010)

The publisher HarperCollins intended to publish the autobiography of the driver who performed the role of 'The Stig' on the BBC's *Top Gear* television programme from 2003 until 2010. It had been an important characteristic of The Stig that his identity was not known to the public. The BBC sought an injunction to prevent the publication of the book on the basis that the driver owed the BBC a duty not to disclose confidential information, including that he was The Stig. The court held that anyone who had an interest in knowing the identity of The Stig knew it, and the fact that the driver was The Stig was so generally accessible that the information had lost its confidential character. The BBC was not granted the injunction and HarperCollins released the book.

Hutcheson v News Group Newspapers (2011)

The businessman Christopher Hutcheson attempted to use a super-injunction to prevent the *Sun* newspaper from publishing the fact that he had fathered two children from an affair. The case received significant media coverage because the TV chef Gordon Ramsay was his son-in-law. Mr Hutcheson was not granted an injunction and the court held that there could be no reasonable expectation of privacy in this case.

> **STRETCH AND CHALLENGE**
>
> Research *Napier v Pressdram Ltd* (2009), where an injunction was not granted to the claimant, who was trying to restrain the magazine *Private Eye* from publishing the outcome of a complaint to the Law Society. Do you agree with the decision in this case?

Terry v Persons Unknown (2010)

The Premiership footballer John Terry was not granted a super-injunction to prevent the *News of the World* publishing a story about his private life. The injunction was rejected after the High Court ruled the primary purpose of the injunction was to protect commercial interests, in particular with sponsors, and not to protect his privacy.

Ferdinand v MGN (2011)

The *Sunday Mirror* published an article about an alleged affair between Rio Ferdinand and an interior designer, Ms Storey. Ferdinand described the article as a 'gross invasion of my privacy' and brought legal action in which he sought damages and a worldwide injunction against further publication. Ferdinand said that he had not seen Ms Storey for years at the time of publication, but they had exchanged text messages between that time and his becoming captain of the England football team in 2010. He claimed that there had been a misuse of private information. The Mirror Group Newspapers argued that he had been appointed captain on the basis that he was a 'reformed and responsible' character. The case centred on whether the *Sunday Mirror* had a public interest defence based on **Article 10 ECHR** (the right to freedom of expression), or whether Ferdinand was entitled to privacy in accordance with **Article 8 ECHR** (the right to respect for private and family life). The court ruled in favour of Mirror Group Newspapers, saying: 'Overall, in my judgement, the balancing exercise favours the defendant's right of freedom of expression over the claimant's right of privacy.'

CTB v News Group Newspapers (2011)

A famous married footballer (Ryan Giggs, known in the case as CTB) successfully obtained an injunction restraining the defendants from publishing his identity and allegations of an affair. The court held that there could be no doubt that the subject of the threatened publication was a matter in respect of which CTB had a reasonable expectation of privacy and which he was entitled to **Article 8 ECHR** protection.

Setting the boundaries for privacy and the European Court of Human Rights

> **KEY CASE**
>
> ***Von Hannover* v *Germany* (No. 2) (2012)**
> This case concerned balancing privacy with freedom of expression. In a unanimous decision, the court found that Germany had not failed in its obligation to respect the applicants' **Article 8 ECHR** rights when it refused to grant an injunction against the publication of a photograph taken of Princess Caroline of Monaco and her husband while on holiday at a ski resort in Switzerland.
>
> This case follows on from *Von Hannover* v *Germany* (No. 1) (2005), when the court held that Princess Caroline's **Article 8** rights had been infringed by the publication of photographs of her with her children.
>
> She, with her husband, brought several cases in Germany for an injunction to prevent further publication of three photographs taken while she was on holiday with her family. The German court, relying on the first Von Hannover decision, granted an injunction covering two of the three photographs on the basis that they were wholly in the sphere of private life. However, the first photo showed Princess Caroline and her husband walking and was accompanied by an article commenting on, among other things, the poor health of her father, Prince Rainier of Monaco. The court held that the photo had to be considered in the context of the article and that the subject matter was of general interest as an 'event in contemporary society' and therefore not protected by privacy. Princess Caroline and her husband appealed to the ECtHR, claiming a violation of their **Article 8** rights. They argued that none of the photos, regardless of the accompanying articles, contributed to a debate of public interest in a democratic society but were purely to satisfy the curiosity of readers.

In *Von Hannover (No. 2) (2012)* the court unanimously held that there had not been a violation of **Article 8**. The ECtHR, in its supervisory role, set out relevant criteria when member states are considering how to balance **Article 8** and **Article 10**:

› Whether the information contributes to a debate of general interest. What amounts to 'general interest' will depend on the circumstances of each case but the court suggested that rumoured marital difficulties of a politician or financial troubles of a famous singer are not matters of general interest.
› How well known the person concerned is, and the subject matter of the report.
› The prior conduct of the individual concerned.
› Content, form and consequences of the publication. This may also include the scope of dissemination, the size of the publication and its readership.
› The circumstances in which the photos were taken. Relevant factors include the consent of the subject, their knowledge that the photo was being taken and whether it was taken illegally.

> ***Springer* v *Germany* (2012)**
> The Grand Chamber of the ECtHR found that the **Article 10** rights of the publisher of a German newspaper had been violated by injunctions granted by the German courts. The tabloid had been prevented from publishing articles about the arrest and conviction of a well-known television actor for possession of cocaine. The Grand Chamber found there was a violation of **Article 10**, the right to freedom of expression, and awarded the publisher damages and costs.

STRETCH AND CHALLENGE

In the absence of a tort of invasion of privacy, the existing laws of breach of confidence have served many celebrities in their battles for the right to privacy (e.g. Catherine Zeta Jones in *Douglas and Jones* v *Hello! Ltd* (2005)). Do you think a privacy law is needed or does the law of breach of confidence suffice?

20 Restrictions of the European Court of Human Rights

This topic is not relevant to the WJEC specification and is Eduqas only.

Official secrets

History of official secrets and the Official Secrets Acts

It is often said that the UK is more obsessed with keeping government information secret than any other Western democracy. The British government uses several methods to keep official information secret, including the doctrine of public interest immunity, the deterrent effect of criminal sanctions under the Official Secrets Acts, the civil service code and the civil action for breach of confidence.

Severe restrictions on disclosure of information are found in the **Official Secrets Acts 1911**, **1920**, **1939** and **1989**.

During the 19th century, as government departments grew larger, the problem of confidentiality grew more acute. An 1873 treasury document urged secrecy on all members of government departments and threatened dismissal of those who disclosed any information. In 1878, a need for further safeguards was emphasised when Marvin, who worked for the foreign office, gave details of a secret treaty to a newspaper. He was prosecuted, but it was discovered that no part of the criminal law covered the situation. He had memorised the information and had not stolen any documents so no conviction could be obtained. This led to the passing of the **Official Secrets Act 1889**. This made it an offence to wrongfully communicate information obtained as a result of being a civil servant. The state had the burden of proving both mens rea (intent) and that the disclosure was not in the interests of the state. The Act, therefore, was not strong enough, so in 1911 another **Official Secrets Act** was passed. It has been suggested that its introduction into Parliament was misleading as it was introduced by the Secretary of State for War, not by the Home Secretary, giving the impression that it was largely an anti-espionage measure. **Section 1** dealt largely with espionage but **s2** was aimed not at enemy agents but at civil servants and other Crown employees.

The Act was passed in one afternoon, and **s2** received no debate at all. **Section 2** appeared to create a crime of strict liability and imposed a complete prohibition on the unauthorised disclosure of even trivial official information. It lacked any provision regarding the substance of the information. **Section 2(2)** criminalised the receiver of the information, although there did appear to be a requirement of mens rea. It did not recognise the role of the press in informing the public. There were few prosecutions under **s2** as it seemed to create an acceptance of secrecy in the civil service.

The demise of **s2** was probably due to it being seen as unacceptable in a modern democracy, and in response to the following three decisions.

> ### Aitken (1970)
> Aitken, a reporter, disclosed that the UK government had misled the British people about the amount of aid the UK was giving Nigeria in its war against Biafra. The government said it was supplying about 15 per cent of Nigeria's arms, whereas the true figure was 70 per cent. Aitken disclosed the report to the press. He was prosecuted under **s2**. The judge, Mr Justice Caulfield, had little sympathy with a case brought merely to reduce government embarrassment and which had no national security interest. The facts of the report were available elsewhere. He found that mens rea was needed and directed the jury to acquit. He also stressed the freedom of the press and that **s2** should be pensioned off. All defendants were acquitted. (Under the **1989 Act**, however, they would be guilty of making disclosures about army logistics and deployment which would be likely to jeopardise British defence interests abroad.)

Tisdall (1984)

Tisdall worked in the Foreign Secretary's private office. She discovered proposals to delay the announcement of a delivery of cruise missiles to Greenham Common until after it had occurred, and to make the announcement at the end of Prime Minister's Questions to avoid answering questions. She thought this was morally wrong and leaked it to the *Guardian* newspaper. She pleaded guilty under s2 and received a six-month prison sentence, but the case created adverse publicity for the government.

Ponting (1985)

This case ended the influence of s2. Ponting was a senior Ministry of Defence official who gave a Labour MP information which undermined the truth of ministerial answers to questions he had been asking in Parliament about the sinking of the *Belgrano* warship during the Falklands War. Ponting was prosecuted under s2 and acquitted.

Section 2's lack of credibility may have been a factor in the decision to bring civil as opposed to criminal proceedings against the *Guardian* and *Observer* newspapers for disclosure of allegations in *Spycatcher* (see page 211). Civil proceedings for breach of confidence were less risky, as they had no jury and a temporary injunction could be obtained quickly. However, the government did think that criminal law rather than civil law was in general a more appropriate response to cases such as Ponting (1985), therefore reform was needed of the Official Secrets Act 1911.

Official Secrets Act 1989

The government claimed the Act would usher in a new era of openness, but it does little for freedom of information. It does narrow the wide breadth of s2, although an official who makes a disclosure may face an action for breach of confidence as well as disciplinary proceedings. The Home Secretary at the time said it was 'a great liberalising measure', which must refer to other aspects of the Act. For example, features which were viewed as liberalising included the categorisation of information which makes relevant the substance, the introduction of tests for harm, the mens rea requirements of ss5 and 6 defences, and the decriminalisation of the receiver of the information. However, the Act applies not only to Crown servants but also to journalists, it contains no defence of public interest or of prior disclosure, there is no general requirement to prove mens rea, and there is no right of access to information. What is omitted is as significant as what is included.

The Act narrows the scope of protection of official information by the criminal law to certain categories:

- Security and intelligence
- Defence
- International relations
- Crime

KEY CASE

R v Shayler (2001)
This held that there is no defence of acting in the public interest.

20 Restrictions of the European Court of Human Rights

Table 20.1 Categories of protection of official information

Security and intelligence	
Section 1 covers security and intelligence information. It is a wide category and is not confined only to work done by members of the security services. It is intended to prevent members or former members of the security services, and anyone notified that they are subject to the provisions of s1, from disclosing anything or appearing to relate to the operation of those services. All such members have a lifelong duty to keep silent even if their information might reveal a serious abuse of power in the security services. There is no need to show that any harm will or may flow from disclosure, and so all information, however trivial, is covered.	
Section 1(3)	criminalises disclosure of information relating to the security services by a former or present Crown servant, as opposed to a member of the security services. It includes a test for harm.
Section 1(4)	states that a disclosure is damaging if it damages the work, or any part of, the security and intelligence services, or it is information or a document or other article whose unauthorised disclosure would be likely to cause damage, or which falls within a class of information, documents or articles which would have that effect. This test for damage may, therefore, be easily satisfied.

Defence	
Section 2 covers information relating to defence. The meaning of defence is set out in s2(4)(a), covering the size, shape organisation, logistics, order of battle, deployment, operations, state of readiness and training of the armed forces of the Crown. *R v Shayler* (2002) is a key case.	
Section 2(4)(b)	covers the weapons, stores or other equipment of those forces and the invention, development, production and operation of such equipment and research relating to it.
Section 2(4)(c)	covers defence policy and strategy and military planning and intelligence.
Section 2(4)(d)	covers plans and measures for the maintenance of essential supplies and services that are or would be needed in times of war.
It must be shown that a disclosure is or would likely to be damaging as defined under s2(2) because: '(a) it damages the capability of, or any part of, the armed forces of the Crown to carry out their tasks or leads to loss of life or injury to members of these forces or serious damage to the equipment or installation of those forces; or (b) it endangers the interests of the UK abroad, seriously obstructs the promotion or protection by the UK of those interests or endangers the safety of British citizens abroad; or (c) it is of information or of a document or article which is such that its unauthorised disclosure would be likely to have those effects.' (a) deals with more serious harm, while (b) is much wider.	

International relations	
Section 3 covers information relating to international relations. The harm test under s3(2) is the same as that under s2(2)(b) and (c): 'it endangers the interests of the UK abroad and it is of information or of a document or article which is such that its unauthorised disclosure would be likely to have any of those effects.' This section includes disclosure of any information provided in confidence by the government to a foreign country or international organisation. This section is designed to limit media coverage of foreign policy and diplomacy.	

Crime	
Section 4 is concerned with crime and special investigation powers.	
Section 4(2)	covers information which is likely to result in the commission of an offence or impede the prevention or detection of offences. There is a harm test relating to this information.
Section 4(3)	covers information obtained using interception and security services warrants. There is no harm test under this category.
Section 5 states that it is a specific offence for journalists and editors to publish information which they know falls into one of the protected categories, although the prosecution must prove that they had reason to believe that publication would be damaging to the security services or to the interests of the UK. If charged under s5, editors can testify as to their state of mind and will be entitled to an acquittal if the jury accepts that there was no rational basis for thinking that the disclosure would damage British interests. This defence will not be available if they publish information from former or serving members of the security services (or notified persons), and are charged instead under s1 with aiding and abetting or conspiring with such persons.	
Section 6 states that it is an offence to make, without authority, a damaging disclosure of information in categories 1 to 3 that was communicated in confidence by the UK to another state or an international organisation and disclosed without the authority of that state or organisation. There are also offences relating to the retaining or failure to take care of protected documents and articles and disclosing information which facilitates unauthorised access to protected material. Mere receipt of information is no longer an offence.	
Section 7: a disclosure will not lead to liability under the Act if it is authorised.	
Section 8 states: 'Where a Crown servant or government contractor, has in their possession… any document or other article which it would be an offence under any of the foregoing provisions of the Act for them to disclose… they are guilty of an offence if: being a Crown servant, they retain the document or article; or being a government contractor, they fail to comply with an official direction for the return or disposal of the document or article; or if they fail to take such care to prevent the unauthorised disclosure of the document or article.'	
Section 8(2)	It is a defence for a Crown servant charged with an offence under subsection 8 to prove that, at the time of the alleged offence, they believed they were acting in accordance with their official duty.

> **STRETCH AND CHALLENGE**
>
> Look up **s12 Official Secrets Act 1989**. Who is a Crown servant or government contractor?

Conclusion: Defences

> It is generally a defence for the accused to prove that they did not know that the information fell into the protected category, or that disclosure would be damaging (**1989 ss1(5), 2(3), 3(4), 4(4)(5)**).

> Under **s5**, it is for the prosecution to prove that that the accused knew or had reasonable cause to believe that the information was protected and that disclosure would be damaging (**s5(2)(3)**).

> There is no defence that disclosure was in the public interest except in the limited situation that the information had been previously published.

> **Section 7**: a belief in authorisation will provide a defence.

Therefore, the defences can be summarised as follows:

1. The defendant did not know information fell into a protected category.
2. They had no reason to believe the information would cause harm.
3. They believed in lawful authorisation.

A civil action for breach of confidence could also arise.

> This topic is not relevant to the WJEC specification and is Edquas only.

Contempt of court

Here we are concerned with two conflicting interests: the interest in protecting the administration of justice and in the principle of free speech. The main outcome of criminal contempt is to limit the media from reporting or commenting on matters that are subject to litigation, as it may poison the minds of potential jurors or influence or intimidate potential witnesses.

The development of the common law relating to contempt of court

In deciding whether a publication amounts to a contempt of court, there is a test of whether it creates a substantial risk that justice, either in a particular case or as a continuing process, will be seriously impeded or prejudiced. The test was first formulated in the **Contempt of Court Act 1981**, which the UK government was obliged to pass after the ECtHR held that the old contempt law was so strict that it violated the **Article 10 ECHR** guarantee of freedom of expression. The UK courts had banned the *Sunday Times* from conducting a campaign against Distillers, the manufacturer of the deforming drug thalidomide, and its reluctance to properly compensate victims. There were many outstanding legal actions against Distillers at the time, and the courts took the view that the newspaper campaign would prejudice issues arising during litigation and put unfair pressure on Distillers to settle for more than might otherwise have been awarded. The ECtHR rejected these arguments, saying that thalidomide was a matter of national concern, and the mere fact that litigation was in progress did not alter the right and responsibility of the media to impart information and comment about a public tragedy (see *Sunday Times* v *UK* (1981)).

The **Contempt of Court Act 1981** therefore originated as a liberalising measure, requiring the finding of a substantial risk of serious prejudice.

Contempt of Court Act 1981

Section 1

Conduct will be contempt if it interferes with the administration of justice in particular proceedings, regardless of intent to do so. The starting point is to ask whether the article or publication relates to particular proceedings. If it appears to have a long-term effect on the course of justice generally, without affecting any particular case, it would seem to fall outside the Act.

After establishing that the publication might affect a particular case, a number of tests must be satisfied to establish the strict liability rule. It is not necessary to show that the defendant intended to prejudice proceedings, so no mens rea needs to be proven.

Section 2(3)
Was the article written during the active period? Normally, prejudicial material can only be published negligently or in ignorance of a forthcoming trial while proceedings are deemed to be 'active'.

Criminal cases become active as soon as the first formal steps in launching a conviction are taken, by arrest, issuing a warrant for arrest or issuing a summons to appear in court. Civil cases become active as soon as the case is listed as being ready for trial.

Publication of prejudicial material outside these timeframes will not normally amount to contempt unless it is intended to prejudice some further trial, while publication within the active period will be in contempt if it constitutes a substantial risk of serious prejudice. A case ceases to be active when it has concluded, but it reactivates if an appeal is lodged.

Section 2(2)
Does the article create a substantial risk of serious prejudice to the trial or case? Factors that can create a substantial risk of serious prejudice include:

> words used
> proximity of article to trial
> pictures used
> profile of the person named in the article
> circulation.

Does the article create a substantial risk of serious prejudice to the trial or case? In *AG v News Group Newspapers* (1987), the Court of Appeal said both parts of the test must be satisfied, and showing a slight risk of serious prejudice or a substantial risk of slight prejudice would not be enough.

AG v News Group Newspapers (1987)
Allegations had been made about the cricketer Ian Botham, who was very famous at the time. The court refused to stop the newspaper publishing allegations about his involvement in drug taking on a cricket tour of New Zealand. Botham had brought a libel action against another newspaper over these allegations, which had been published some time before, and the case was due to be tried by a jury ten months after the date of the proposed republication. The court accepted that there was a chance that a new publication in a national newspaper would influence a jury at a later date but, in view of the ten-month delay, the risk was not substantial.

Woodgate and Bowyer (2001)
The *Sunday Mirror* was fined £175,000 for printing information that could have affected the trial of Leeds United footballers Jonathan Woodgate and Lee Bowyer, and which caused the whole court case to be re-run.

Having established a substantial risk, it is necessary to ask whether there is a substantial risk that the effect of such influence will be of a prejudicial nature. It must be shown that the language used, facts disclosed or sentiments expressed would lead an objective observer

STRETCH AND CHALLENGE
1. Compare the *Ian Botham* case with *AG v Hislop and Pressdram* (1991), where a gap of three months between the article and trial did create a substantial risk of serious prejudice.
2. Research *AG v Independent TV News and Others* (1985). What factors were relevant in this case?

to conclude that a substantial risk had been established that a person involved in the proceedings would be prejudiced, before going on to consider whether the effect could be described as serious.

Prejudice and seriousness can be established in several ways:

› An article might influence persons against or in favour of the defendant.
› An article might affect either the outcome of the proceedings or their very existence.
› Proximity of time can affect this part of the test, as can the extent to which the trial concerns a person in the public eye.

If it appears that **s2(2)** is established, it also needs to be established that the **s5** defence does not apply. **Section 5** contains a public interest defence, which ensures that public debate on matters of current controversy can continue even if it reflects upon matters before the courts. **Section 5** exonerates publications that discuss matters of general public interest in good faith if the risk of prejudice is merely incidental.

The defence was used successfully in *AG* v *English* (1985), when it was held that a newspaper article criticising the common practice of doctors allowing deformed babies to die, which was published during the trial of a doctor alleged to have committed manslaughter in these circumstances, amounted to only incidental prejudice.

Section 5 will not protect publications that directly relate to imminent or ongoing jury trials and which criticise witnesses or defendants, set out inadmissible evidence or encourage a particular outcome. The Attorney General determines whether there will be a prosecution for contempt of court.

GRADE BOOST

Does the law of contempt strike a fair balance between these two conflicting interests? If not, how could it be reformed?

Why have a law of contempt?

A law of contempt strikes a balance between:

› a person's right to be treated fairly in court
› a journalist's right to report what is happening in the world.

SUMMARY: RESTRICTIONS OF THE ECHR: DUTY OF CONFIDENTIALITY AND CONTEMPT OF COURT

→ Breach of confidence and privacy: *Kaye* v *Robertson* (1991); *Wainwright* v *Home Office* (2003); *Hosking* v *Runting* (2004)

→ No tort of invasion of privacy in England and Wales but legal controls can be used against the media and others: *Prince Albert* v *Strange* (1849); *Argyll* v *Argyll* (1967); *Coco* v *AN Clark (Engineers) Ltd* (1969); *Stephens* v *Avery* (1988); *HRH Princess of Wales* v *MGN Newspapers Ltd* (1993); *Shelley Films Ltd* v *Rex Features Ltd* (1993); *Fairnie (Deceased) and Others* v *Reed and Another* (1994)

→ Public interest defence: confidential information will not be protected if the public interest outweighs the interest in preserving confidentiality: *AG* v *Guardian Newspapers Ltd (No. 2)* (1990)

→ **Article 8 ECHR** (right to privacy) incorporated into **Human Rights Act 1998**. Privacy must be weighed alongside freedom of speech and expression (**Article 10 ECHR**): *Venables and Thompson* v *News Group Newspapers* (2001); *Associated Newspapers Ltd* v *Prince of Wales* (2006); *Murray* v *Express Newspapers* (2008); *Mosley* v *News Group Newspapers* (2008); *Author of a Blog* v *Times Newspapers* (2009); *BBC* v *HarperCollins Ltd* (2010); *Hutcheson* v *News Group Newspapers* (2011); *Terry* v *Persons Unknown* (2010); *Ferdinand* v *MGN* (2011); *CTB* v *News Group Newspapers* (2011)

→ Setting the boundaries for privacy and ECtHR: *Von Hannover* v *Germany (No. 2)* (2012); *Springer* v *Germany* (2012)

→ **Official Secrets Acts 1911**, **1920**, **1939** and **1989**: *Aitken* (1970); *Tisdall* (1984); *Ponting* (1985)

→ **Official Secrets Act 1989**: scope of protection of official information covers security and intelligence, defence, international relations, crime

→ Defences to the **Official Secrets Act 1989**: defendant did not know information fell into a protected category; had no reason to believe the information would cause harm; believed in lawful authorisation

→ A law of contempt balances a person's right to a fair trial with a journalist's right to report

→ **Contempt of Court Act 1981**: *Sunday Times* v *UK* (1981); *AG* v *News Group Newspapers* (1987); *Woodgate and Bowyer* (2001); *AG* v *English* (1985)

20 Restrictions of the European Court of Human Rights

> **TEST YOURSELF**
>
> 1. What is the test for breach of confidence from the case of *Coco v AN Clark (Engineers) Ltd (1968)*?
> 2. Explain the public interest defence for breach of confidence.
> 3. What are the competing interests with contempt of court laws?
> 4. Explain the significance of s2(2) Contempt of Court Act 1981.
> 5. What official information is covered by the Official Secrets Act 1989?

Obscenity

Under Article 10(1) ECHR, a person has the right to freedom of expression. The Human Rights Act 1998 also makes special reference to the importance of the right to freedom of expression under s12, which stipulates that 'the court must have particular regard to the importance of the Convention right to freedom of expression'. This is, however, a qualified right and can be removed for a legitimate reason, such as the protection of health or morals or for the protection of the reputation or rights of others (Article 10(2)).

What is obscene to one person may not be to another, particularly in a more permissive society. The key concepts of proportionality and margin of appreciation were explained in Chapter 18, and apply to this area of the law. In *Hoare v UK* (1997), the court held that it was a proportionate means of achieving the legitimate aim.

In *Handyside v United Kingdom* (1976) the ECtHR acknowledged that prosecutions under the Act were permissible provided the qualifications in Article 10(2) were properly applied (and proportionate). It was within the UK's 'margin of appreciation'.

This section covers the extent to which there is a right to shock and/or offend under English law and the ECHR.

The law has attempted to provide some clarity.

There are many laws that deal with obscene publications, but for the purposes of the A Level specification two key statutes are used to explain and evaluate the law on obscene publications and the restrictions on Article 10:

- the Obscene Publications Act 1959 (as amended by the Obscene Publications Act 1964)
- the Criminal Justice and Immigration Act 2008.

Obscene Publications Act 1959 as amended

Offence

So, what is 'obscene' according to the Obscene Publications Act 1959 (OPA 1959)? Under s2(1), it is an offence to publish an 'obscene article for gain or not' or to have an obscene article for publication for gain.

Section 1(1) provides the definition of obscene for the purposes of the Act. It says: 'An article shall be deemed to be obscene if its effect or (where the article comprises two or more distinct items) the effect of any one of its items is, if taken as a whole, such as to tend to deprave and corrupt persons who are likely, having regard to all relevant circumstances, to read, see or hear the matter contained or embodied in it.'

Eighteen Plus Adult Explicit Content Warning

Figure 20.14 Obscenity laws aim to protect the public from unsuitable material

The Court of Appeal has held that 'obscenity depends on the article and not upon the author' (*Shaw* v *DPP* (1962)).

'Article' has a wide definition under s1(2) OPA. It means anything 'containing or embodying matter to be read or looked at or both, any sound record, and any film or other record of a picture or pictures' (s1(2)).

'Publication' also has a wide definition under s1(3) OPA. A person 'publishes' an article who '(a) distributes, circulates, sells, lets on hire, gives, or lends it, or who offers it for sale or for letting on hire; or (b) in the case of an article containing or embodying matter to be looked at or a record, shows, plays or projects it or, where the matter is data stored electronically, transmits that data'. Therefore, electronically transmitting data via the internet constitutes a publication.

Difficulties have arisen in relation to internet publications. *R* v *Perrin* (2002) held that viewing a web page in England is reading a publication in this country even if the website is based in another jurisdiction. This case also concerned Article 10 ECHR and held that, under the 'margin of appreciation', 'Parliament was entitled to conclude that the prescription was necessary in a democratic society'.

Defences

There is a defence under s2(5) OPA 1959 that if the defendant proves there was 'no reasonable cause to suspect that the article is obscene'. Section 1(3)(a) OPA 1964 provides a corresponding defence relating to a charge of 'having an obscene article for publication for gain'.

Section 4(1) provides for a 'public good' defence but can only be used where the jury has established that the article is obscene. The defendant must prove that it is for the 'public good'. It provides that a defendant will not be liable 'if it is proved that publication of the article in question is justified as being for the public good on the grounds that it is in the interests of science, literature, art or learning, or of other objects of general concern'. The 'public good' defence does not apply 'where the article in question is a moving picture film or soundtrack', but there is a comparable defence in s4(1A) in relation to a moving picture film or soundtrack where 'the publication is justified as being for the public good on the grounds that it is in the interests of drama, opera, ballet or any other art, or of literature or learning'.

The Obscene Publications Act 1964 amended the OPA 1959, particularly making it an offence to have an obscene publication for gain. The 'gain' can be either for the defendant or another (s2(1) OPA 1959 as amended by OPA 1964). 'Gain' is not defined in the statute but has been taken to cover financial gain as well as other 'gain', such as deriving pleasure from the article.

> ### KEY CASE
>
> #### *R* v *Calder and Boyars* (1969)
> The defendants were charged with having published an obscene book, *Last Exit to Brooklyn*. They argued that it was not obscene because it would deprave only a 'minute lunatic fringe of its readers' and furthermore claimed that the publication was in any case justified as being for the public good in accordance with s4.
>
> The jury should consider the potentially harmful effect of the material: that is, the number of people who would tend to be depraved and corrupted by the article, the strength of the tendency and the nature of the depravity or corruption. They should then balance this against the strength of the literary, sociological or ethical merit of the article and determine whether the publication is on balance for the public good.

The 2019 CPS guidelines now indicate pornography depicting legal acts between consenting adults will no longer be prosecuted under the OPA 1959, provided no serious harm was caused and the likely audience is aged over 18. The CPS also provided clarification on the use of the public good defence.

GRADE BOOST

Remember to include in your answers when qualified rights can be taken away. These are the weakest rights and can be removed when 'prescribed by law, necessary and proportionate in a democratic society in order to fulfil a legitimate aim'.

Evaluative point: there have been calls to repeal the two OPA Acts as there are so few prosecutions under the laws. The CPS has reviewed its guidance regarding the sort of content that justifies prosecution, following a failed prosecution in *Peacock* (2012). Defendant Michael Peacock was charged with six counts of obscene publication. He had produced gay-porn DVDs featuring sexual acts that were legal to perform but illegal to show on film. The jury was unanimous in finding him not guilty on all counts.

STRETCH AND CHALLENGE

Why do you think *Peacock* (2012) is significant? Why do you think the jury decided Mr Peacock was not guilty?

Criminal Justice and Immigration Act 2008

Until 2008 there were no criminal offences dealing specifically with pornography. Section 63(1) provides that it is an offence to be in possession of an 'extreme pornographic image'. The Criminal Justice and Immigration Act 2008 shifts the burden from the producers and distributors of 'extreme pornography' to the viewers who merely have such images in their possession.

The definition of an 'extreme pornographic image' is multifaceted:

› Under s63(3), 'an image is 'pornographic' if it is of such a nature that it must reasonably be assumed to have been produced solely or principally for the purpose of sexual arousal'.
› Under s63(5A) and (6), an image is 'extreme' if it explicitly and realistically portrays specific matters, such as certain violence, and 'it is grossly offensive, disgusting or otherwise of an obscene character'.

Section 65 provides for some general defences which place the burden of proof on the defendant. There is a defence:

› if the accused had 'a legitimate reason for being in possession of the image concerned'
› if the defendant shows that they 'had not seen the image concerned and did not know, nor had any cause to suspect, it to be an extreme pornographic image'. This defence is similar to the 'no reasonable cause to suspect' defence under OPA 1959 and OPA 1964 and the courts will presumably interpret it in the same limited manner.

In relation to an unsolicited image that is not kept by the defendant 'for an unreasonable time'.

Section 66 provides for a specific defence for those who participate in the creation of extreme pornographic images.

The extreme pornography offence does not apply to the British Board of Film Classification (BBFC) classified films (s64(1)).

KEY TERMINOLOGY

general defences: defences that can apply to any crime (with some exceptions), as opposed to 'special defences', which can only apply to certain crimes. For example, diminished responsibility is only available for murder.

Table 20.2 shows the differences between these two key statutes.

Table 20.2 Differences between the key statutes for obscenity

Obscene Publications Act 1959	Criminal Justice and Immigration Act 2008
Makes it an offence to publish an obscene article or have such an article for publication for gain.	Makes it an offence to be in possession of an 'extreme pornographic image'.
Applies to articles generally.	Only applies to images.
Designed to prevent depravity and corruption of the minds of those likely to encounter the article.	Arguably informed by a 'harm to women'.
Defences: 'no reasonable cause to suspect' public good.	Defences: 'no reasonable cause to suspect' legitimate reason for possession unsolicited image participation.

STRETCH AND CHALLENGE

Over a thousand prosecutions under the new extreme pornography legislation have taken place per year, although the law was introduced with a promise that it would *not* lead to the increase of prosecutions and would not criminalise behaviour which was not already unlawful.

Several cases have hit the headlines due to either sensational facts or controversial applications of the law:

- *R v Holland* (2010) (the 'tiger case') is a case that raises concerns about fairness and appropriate charging.
- *R v Dymond* (2010) ('the dead squid case') also has some challenging aspects.

Research these cases to help your evaluation of the law. Do you think Article 10(2) is being appropriately applied in these cases?

These websites are useful for evaluation here:

www.backlash.org.uk

'Prosecuting_the_possession_of_extreme_pornography:_A_misunderstood_and_mis-used_law', www.researchgate.net/publication/293477497

SUMMARY: RESTRICTIONS OF THE ECHR: OBSCENITY

→ **Article 10 ECHR**: qualified right to 'freedom of expression'

→ The **Obscene Publications Act 1959** as amended by the **Obscene Publications Act 1964**: *R v Perrin* (2002); *Hoare v UK* (1997); *Handyside v UK* (1976)

→ 'Obscenity depends on the article and not upon the author': *Shaw v DPP* (1962)

→ **Criminal Justice and Immigration Act 2008** shifts the burden from the producers and distributors of 'extreme pornography' to the viewers

→ **s11 Defamation Act 2013**: a judge decides the remedy, usually damages but can be an injunction

TEST YOURSELF

1. What type of right is Article 10, and when can it be lawfully removed?
2. Explain what happened in the case of *Handyside v UK* (1976).
3. Why is the case of *Peacock* (2012) significant?
4. Summarise some of the main differences between the **Obscene Publications Act 1959** and the **Criminal Justice and Immigration Act 2008**.

Defamation

Defamation is a tort where the claimant is seeking compensation for damage to their reputation.

Defamation cases require a court to balance two competing qualified rights: the right of the claimant to protect their privacy and reputation (**Article 8**), and the right of the defendant to freedom of expression. **Article 10 EHCR** provides for freedom of expression and **Article 8 ECHR** provides for a right to a private and family life, home and correspondence. Both of these are qualified rights, which can be removed for a legitimate reason and when necessary and proportionate.

Defamation can be divided into two parts:

> Libel: the defamation appears in a permanent form.
> Slander: the defamation appears in a non-permanent form.

The main Act for this tort is the **Defamation Act 2013**. As this is a relatively new law, cases brought under the old law may still be relevant.

Under **s11 Defamation Act 2013**, defamation actions are now tried without a jury unless the court orders otherwise. A judge, therefore, decides the remedy, which is usually damages but can also be an injunction.

A number of elements need to be established in order to have a successful claim:

> The statement must be defamatory.
> The statement must refer to the claimant or be taken to refer to the claimant.
> The statement must have been published.
> Publication of the statement has caused or is likely to cause serious harm to the claimant's reputation.

There are also a number of defences that might apply. Each element will now be considered further.

Defamatory statements

There is no statutory or single definition of what constitutes a 'defamatory' statement. Case law provided the original definitions and the modern test can be found in *Sim* v *Stretch* (1936). The courts consider whether the statement would 'tend to lower the plaintiff in the estimation of right-thinking members of society generally'.

Figure 20.15 Technology has increased the potential for libellous statements

The central question in this element is: 'Has the claimant's reputation been adversely affected or put at risk by the statement?' Therefore, a statement will be considered defamatory if reading it would make an ordinary, reasonable person (not their friends and family):

- think less well of the individual referred to
- think the individual lacks the ability to do their job effectively
- avoid the individual
- treat the person as a figure of fun.

This is not concerned with how it made the person referred to feel but the impression it makes or is likely to make on those reading it. No loss or damage, financial or otherwise, needs to be proved in most cases.

What have the courts held to be 'defamatory statements'? See the outcome of the following cases:

Byrne v Deane (1937)
A notice implying that the claimant had informed the police about illegal gambling machines on the premises was held not to be defamatory as a 'right-thinking member of society' would likely have approved of his action of informing the police and would not think less of him as a consequence.

Jason Donovan v The Face (1998)
The pop star successfully sued *The Face* magazine for saying he was gay when he had portrayed himself as heterosexual. It was held to be defamatory to say he had deceived the public about his sexuality as it was implying that he was a liar and a hypocrite.

Berkoff v Burchill (1996)
Actor Steven Berkoff was described as 'hideous-looking' and was compared with Frankenstein's monster by journalist Julie Burchill. The court decided that the article made him an object of ridicule and he was successful in his defamation case.

> **STRETCH AND CHALLENGE**
> Think of some examples of defamatory statements, for example falsely calling someone a paedophile.

> **STRETCH AND CHALLENGE**
> Look up the case of *Stocker v Stocker (2019)* involving posts on social media. How did the Supreme Court approach defamatory statements on social media and how did readers interact with them?

Innuendo

A statement does not have to directly criticise the claimant. It might do so indirectly, by implication. This is known as an innuendo.

Tolley v JS Fry and Sons Ltd (1931)
An amateur golfer's image was used on advertising material promoting chocolates. His amateur status meant that he should not profit from his sport, so the implication that he had been paid to advertise the chocolates was held to be defamatory.

Therefore, a defamatory statement need not directly criticise the claimant. An implied criticism, known as innuendo, can be sufficient.

It is irrelevant whether a defendant intended to publish a statement that adversely affects a claimant's reputation.

Requirement of serious damage to reputation
Section 1(1) Defamation Act 2013 introduced a requirement that the defamatory statement must have caused, or be likely to cause, serious damage to the claimant's reputation. This aims to reduce the number of claims brought over trivial insults or jokes and protects freedom of

expression. Only damage to reputation is covered, not hurt feelings, and media outlets can escape liability by publishing a swift apology. This happened in *Cooke and Another v MGN Ltd (2014)* where a defamatory statement was published but liability was avoided by a complete apology being published in the next edition.

The statement must refer to the claimant or be taken to refer to the claimant. It must be proved by the claimant that an ordinary, reasonable reader or listener would take the statement as referring to them. There are several ways this can happen. The claimant can be named either by their actual name or a fictional name (as in *Hulton v Jones (1910)*), the claimant's picture can be used (*Dwek v Macmillan Publishers Ltd and Others (2000)*) and the statement can refer to the claimant through context (*Hayward v Thompson (1964)*).

Defamatory statements may be made about a group of people, but overly large groups may not be able to claim, as in *Knupffer v London Express Newspapers (1944)*, unless the claimant can be singled out. The courts have not, however, indicated a specific number of people above which a claim would fail. In *Riches v News Group (1986)*, the *News of the World* published an article making allegations about 'Banbury CID'. No officers were mentioned by name but several of the group 'Banbury CID' successfully sued for defamation.

The statement must have been published. This covers more than just the 'traditional' newspaper, magazine or television. It means that the information has passed from the defendant to a person other than the claimant or the defendant's spouse.

Every repetition is a fresh publication and creates a fresh cause of action ('repetition rule'). Repetition by the same publisher will no longer create a fresh claim for defamation (s8 Defamation Act 2013).

STRETCH AND CHALLENGE
What has changed as a result of **s8 Defamation Act 2013** regarding the 'repetition rule'?

Defences to defamation

The main defences are:

- truth: **s2 Defamation Act 2013**
- honest opinion: **s3 Defamation Act 2013**
- responsible publication on a matter of public importance: **s4 Defamation Act 2013**
- absolute privilege
- qualified privilege
- offer of amends.

1. Truth

Covered by **s2 Defamation Act 2013**, this is essentially the same as the old common law defence of 'justification' and provides for a defence to a defamation claim where the defendant can prove that the statement, however damaging to the claimant's reputation, is 'substantially' true; small inaccuracies will not prevent the defence applying. *Gecas v Scottish Television (1992)* will likely still apply even though it was decided under the 'old' law.

The defence of truth was successfully argued in the case of *Stocker v Stocker (2019)*.

2. Honest opinion

Covered by **s3 Defamation Act 2013**, this new defence aims to give greater protection to freedom of expression and replaces the 'old' defence known as 'fair comment' (although some of the old case law might still apply). It allows for statements of opinion (on trivial or important matters), provided that three conditions are met:

> **GRADE BOOST**
> The 'old' defence only applies to matters of public interest, but the new defence under **s3** applies to a commentary on any subject. This offers greater protection for freedom of expression.

1. The statement contained a statement of opinion: *Galloway v Telegraph Group Ltd* (2004).
2. The statement indicates, whether in general or specific terms, the basis of that opinion: *Joseph v Spiller* (2010).
3. An honest person could have held the opinion, on the basis of:
   a) any fact which existed at the time the statement was expressed
   b) anything claimed to be a fact in a privileged statement that was published before the statement that is being complained about.

This condition is a significant change from the old law and now applies an objective test.

Section 3(5) states that the defence will not apply where the claimant can show that the defendant did not honestly hold the opinion they expressed (even if it was an opinion that an honest person could have come to).

3. Responsible publication on a matter of public importance

This is covered by **s4 Defamation Act 2013**. It was previously known as the 'Reynolds' defence' from *Reynolds v Times Newspapers* (1999) and aims to protect the media when they responsibly report on matters of public interest (even if it turns out to be untrue).

The Act provides that it applies to statements of opinion or fact, where:

› the statement complained of was on a matter of public interest (**s4(1)(a)**)
› the defendant reasonably believed its publication was in the public interest (**s4(1)(b)**).

'Matters of public interest' is not defined in the Act.

Reynolds v Times Newspapers (1999) set out ten factors that the court needs to consider and these were reaffirmed in *Flood v Times* (2012):

1. Seriousness of the allegations.
2. Nature of the information: is it a matter of public interest?
3. Source of the information: is it a reliable source?
4. Steps taken to verify the information including getting the other side of the story.
5. Status of the information: is it an old or new allegation?
6. Urgency: is the information perishable or the newspaper in competition with another?
7. Whether comment was gathered from the claimant.
8. Did the article include the gist of the claimant's opinion?
9. Tone of the article (e.g. to raise queries or call for investigations rather than creating statements of fact).
10. Does the article need to be drawn to the public's attention as quickly as possible?

Since the **Defamation Act 2013** came into force, there has been much debate about the status of the factors set out in *Reynolds* (1999), and whether they should be applied as a 'checklist' for courts when considering the new defence under **s4**.

However, the Supreme Court ruling in *Serafin v Malkiewicz* (2020) makes clear the importance of adhering to the two-stage approach of **s4(1)(a)** and **(b)**, employing the language of the section and avoiding referring to the *Reynolds* factors or treating them as a 'checklist' or as constituting 'requirements' of the defence under **s4**. Despite this, the Court did indicate that one or more of the factors will be relevant when assessing whether the defendant was reasonable in believing that publication was in the public interest under **s4(1)(b)**.

The Supreme Court made an interesting comment, in passing, that the interpretation of the defence must ensure that operation of the section generates no violation either of the claimant's right under **Article 8** (right to respect a person's privacy) or of the defendant's right under **Article 10** (freedom of expression) of the **ECHR**.

4. Absolute privilege

Statements covered by absolute privilege cannot be defamatory. This only covers the person making the statement and not subsequent reports of the statement. The following examples are covered:

> Parliamentary proceedings, including Hansard.
> Fair, accurate and contemporaneous reports of court proceedings which are held in public, i.e. statements made in court by individuals and reports by journalists of the court proceedings.
> Communications between solicitor and client.
> Statements made by one spouse to another.

5. Qualified privilege

Like absolute privilege, this defence applies to statements made in certain specified circumstances; it is broader than absolute privilege. It only covers statements made without malice, so a claimant can sue if it can be proved the statement was made maliciously. There is a new provision in **s6 Defamation Act 2013** covering statements published in scientific or academic journals where the statement relates to a scientific or academic matter and, before it was published, independent subject matter 'peer review' took place. This section was aimed at preventing the stifling of legitimate scientific debate following the case of *British Chiropractic Association* v *Singh* (2010).

It also covers fair and accurate reports of proceedings in public of any law-making body in the world – including the UK Parliament.

6. Offer of amends

Section 2 of the Defamation Act 1996 provides for a procedure known as 'offer of amends', which is a written correction or apology along with the payment of compensation.

There is a set procedure:

1. The offer must be made before a defence is lodged.
2. The claimant may accept the offer, in which case the proceedings stop.
3. The parties can then agree on terms that the court can enforce.
4. If the offer is not accepted the defendant can choose a defence.

The defence is not available if the defamation is intentional, i.e. the person making the statement knew it was about the claimant and was false and defamatory.

This defence is useful for cases where stories have been published that are true of the person the publication intends them to refer to but could be taken to refer to someone else and are not true of that person.

Mode of trial and remedies

Section 11 Defamation Act 2013 provides that defamation actions will be tried without a jury unless the court orders otherwise, so a judge will decide the damages as well as the verdict. Claims must usually be brought within a year of publication: there is some discretion to extend the limitation period.

Remedies

There are two main remedies for defamation:

> damages
> injunction.

STRETCH AND CHALLENGE

Research the High Court case of *Lachaux v Independent Print Ltd* (2021). What did the judge, Mr Justice Nicklin, say about the defendants' defence of s4 public interest?

> **STRETCH AND CHALLENGE**
>
> Look up the case of *Vardy* v *Rooney* (2022). Summarise what happened in this case and the court's final ruling in relation to the defamation claim issued by Vardy.

Section 12 Defamation Act 2013 gives the court power, if the claimant wins, to order the defendant to publish a summary of the judgment.

Section 13 Defamation Act 2013 allows the court to order that the operator of a website on which the defamatory statement is posted to remove the statement, or to order that any person who was not the author, editor or publisher of the defamatory statement to stop distributing, selling or exhibiting material containing the statement.

> **SUMMARY: RESTRICTIONS OF THE ECHR: DEFAMATION**
>
> → Defamatory statements: *Sim* v *Stretch* (1936); *Byrne* v *Deane* (1937); *Jason Donovan* v *The Face* (1998); *Berkoff* v *Burchill* (1996)
> → Innuendo: indirect criticism by implication: *Tolley* v *JS Fry and Sons Ltd* (1931)
> → Requirement of serious damage to reputation: s1(1) Defamation Act 2013: *Cooke and Another* v *MGN Ltd* (2014); *Hulton* v *Jones* (1910); *Dwek* v *Macmillan Publishers Ltd and Others* (2000); *Hayward* v *Thompson* (1964); *Knupffer* v *London Express Newspapers* (1944); *Riches* v *News Group* (1986)
> → Defences to defamation: truth (s2 Defamation Act 2013); honest opinion (s3 Defamation Act 2013); responsible publication on a matter of public importance (s4 Defamation Act 2013); absolute privilege; qualified privilege; offer of amends

> **TEST YOURSELF**
>
> 1. What are the elements of a defamation claim?
> 2. What are the main defences to a defamation claim?
> 3. What did the case of *Sim* v *Stretch* (1936) say regarding damage to a claimant's reputation?
> 4. What is the defence of truth under s2 Defamation Act 2013?
> 5. What is the difference between absolute and qualified privilege?

> **EXAM PAST PAPER QUESTIONS**
>
> WJEC – A Level – Unit 3 – June 2019
>
> The local council decided to demolish the community youth centre and sell off the land to developers to build luxury houses. Catrin, who runs the youth centre, organised a protest against the closure. Around two hundred people turned up and set off to march to the council offices, with Catrin in the lead. Some of the marchers carried home-made placards saying: 'Demolish the Council!' As the marchers drew near to the council offices, Sergeant Jones arrived in a police car, accompanied by PC Evans. Sergeant Jones told Catrin that they were marching without police permission, and would have to stop. Catrin refused, so Sergeant Jones arrested her. While this was going on, PC Evans ordered the marchers who were carrying placards to put them down. Some of the marchers waved their placards in defiance, so PC Evans arrested them. The march came to a standstill as the rest of the marchers tried to find out what was happening. Fearing trouble, Sergeant Jones radioed for reinforcements. Several police vans arrived filled with officers, who imposed a tight cordon around the marchers Magistrates' Court.
>
> In light of reported case law and other sources of law, advise Catrin whether the police were acting within their powers to control these public order situations. [50]

20 Restrictions of the European Court of Human Rights

WJEC – A Level – Unit 3 – June 2019

Paul was walking down the street singing happily because he had just been offered a place at college to train as a professional photographer. The noise annoyed PC Clarke who tapped Paul on the shoulder and told him to be quiet. Paul said, 'I'm not doing anything wrong, am I?' PC Clarke replied: 'Let's find out, shall we?' and proceeded to carry out a thorough search of Paul's clothing and bag. In the bag, PC Clarke found an expensive camera. PC Clarke thought that this was highly suspicious, that someone as young as Paul would have such an expensive camera, so he arrested Paul in order to carry out further enquiries. At the police station, Paul was put in a cell while waiting to be interviewed. During that time he made several requests to be allowed to phone his mother and speak to a solicitor, but each time he was told he would have to wait as the police were too busy. After 18 hours in the cell, Paul was interviewed by detectives who were investigating a number of burglaries in the area. Paul explained repeatedly that the camera had been lent to him by the college, but as it was now the middle of the night, he was told that he would have to remain in custody until the police could confirm his story. The police had difficulty contacting the college, so after Paul had spent a total of 46 hours in police custody, it was decided to release him on bail subject to the condition that he should report to the police station the following day.

In the light of reported case law and other sources of law, advise Paul as to the legality of the actions of the police. [50]

WJEC – A Level – Unit 4 – June 2019

Analyse and evaluate whether the tort of breach of confidence provides an adequate solution to the problem of media intrusion in the lives of ordinary citizens. [50]

Eduqas – A Level – Component 3 – October 2021

Public order laws strike a fair balance between freedom of assembly and the need to prevent disorder. Discuss. [25]

Eduqas – AS Level – Component 2 – May 2018

(a) Explain the powers of the police to impose conditions on a procession under s.12 of the Public Order Act 1986. [6]

(b) Explain the provisions and restrictions under Article 10 of the European Convention on Human Rights. [6]

(c) Assess whether the law provides adequate protection to a suspect who has been stopped and searched. [9]

Read the scenario below and answer part (d).

Izzy organised a march to protest against plans to close the hospital's intensive care ward. Sergeant Jones who was escorting the march instructed Izzy and her fellow marchers to turn down a side street away from the hospital grounds and towards the town centre. PC Davies who was assisting Sergeant Jones also instructed Izzy not to display any placards. As the procession wound through the town centre, Izzy and some of the other marchers held up placards showing graphic images of serious injuries. Sergeant Jones found the placards distressing and told Izzy and the marchers to put them down. They refused. One woman was so frightened, she refused to enter the Post Office outside which the protesters had stopped.

(d) Advise Izzy as to whether she has committed any public order offences. [9]

21 The debate relating to the protection of human rights in the UK

Figure 21.1 The HRA was passed in 1998

The **Human Rights Act 1998 (HRA)** was passed by the Labour government following its landslide victory in 1997, based on a promise to 'bring rights home'. As mentioned in previous chapters, the Act incorporated the **ECHR** (and first protocol) into domestic law and came into force in October 2000. According to **s7 HRA**, the **ECHR** is directly applicable in UK courts, with no need to go to the European Court of Human Rights (ECtHR), although it is possible as a last resort.

In practice, the Act was the most important constitutional development for over 300 years, but since it was passed, many people have questioned whether the UK has now made the transition from liberties to rights or whether there is still a need for a Bill of Rights.

Analysis of the Human Rights Act 1998

It is clear that the **HRA** is not the same as, for example, the US Bill of Rights, which entrenches rights and allows courts to strike down legislation. Instead, the **HRA** preserves the doctrine of parliamentary sovereignty, as Parliament alone can decide whether to repeal or amend legislation.

However, incorporation of the **ECHR** into domestic law is a step towards a British Bill of Rights.

The HRA does have drawbacks:

> - The government may proceed with legislation despite any incompatibility with ECHR rights. There is a wide margin of appreciation permitted under the ECHR and most Convention rights are only qualified.
> - The courts cannot strike down or refuse to apply incompatible legislation.
> - The Act is vulnerable to repeal.

There is a clear shift in power since incorporation, with unelected judges having a greater influence over social policy than in the past. However, it could be argued that this means a clearer separation of powers and greater respect for the rule of law as a result of such increased activism by the judiciary.

The Commission for Equality and Human Rights was set up in 2007 and became fully operational in 2009. Its functions include:

> - providing advice and guidance
> - conducting inquiries
> - bringing cases
> - monitoring the ECHR in domestic law
> - scrutinising new laws
> - publishing regular reports.

STRETCH AND CHALLENGE

Research the case of *Othman (Abu Qatada) v UK (2012)*. Was the UK government justified in its anger at the ECHR's decision, which it believed hindered its fight against terrorism and crime?

Figure 21.2 The US Bill of Rights was drawn up in 1791, after the country gained independence from Britain

A Bill of Rights for the UK?

Among Western democracies, only the UK and Israel do not have a Bill of Rights. The USA, South Africa and most of Europe do. However, a Bill of Rights is only as effective as the state that enforces it.

In June 2022 the government introduced the Bill of Rights Bill to Parliament, which would repeal the Human Rights Act 1998 if passed.

What could remain the same with a British Bill of Rights?

These points are based on the Bill of Rights Bill.

> The UK will remain a party to the ECHR and will be obliged under Article 1 to secure to everyone within its jurisdiction the rights and freedoms in Section 1 of the Convention.
> Clause 2 confirms that the Bill gives effect to the same set of Convention rights as the HRA. Arguably, the Bill gives effect to some of those rights in different and in some cases, lesser ways than the HRA.
> Declarations of incompatibility – the courts will continue to be able to make declarations of incompatibility (DOIs).
> Duty of public authorities – Clause 12 of the Bill mirrors s6 HRA and requires public authorities to act compatibly with Convention rights.

Evaluation

Although the government asserted that the Bill enhances human rights protection, it, to some extent, preserves it but arguably diminishes the level and forms of protection when compared to the position under the HRA.

What will change if the Bill is passed?

> **Section 3 HRA**: the Bill contains no similar provision. There will be no requirement for judges to interpret domestic legislation compatibly with human rights, so far as possible to do so. Arguably, this is the Bill taking back parliamentary sovereignty; however, the effect of this may be the issuing of more DOIs since judges are unable to 'correct' the offending legislation first hand.
> **'Living instrument'**: in addition, the Bill seeks to ensure that domestic courts interpret Convention rights in more of a literal, narrow way. This is an attempt to impede the creative or generous interpretations of rights under the ECHR and, rather than viewing the ECHR as a 'living instrument', will force courts to focus on the 'original' meaning of the text of the 1950s Convention.
> **Section 2 HRA**: presently, UK courts are required to 'take into account' ECtHR jurisprudence. Rulings are 'strongly persuasive' but not binding. Section 2 is replaced by Clause 3 of the Bill, which says that the UK Supreme Court is the 'ultimate judicial authority on questions arising under domestic law in connection with the Convention rights'.
> **Challenges to deportation under Article 8**: a higher threshold will be set for foreign national offenders seeking to challenge deportations based on Article 8 of the Bill: the right to a private life. The offender will have to show that deportation would result in manifest harm to a qualifying member of the offender's family that is so extreme that the harm would override the paramount public interest in removing the offender from the UK.
> A new permission stage for human rights challenges. A victim of a human right violation to convince a court that they have suffered a significant disadvantage because of the violation. This could impose a significant barrier to human rights challenges – it remains unlawful for public authorities to act incompatibly with Convention rights but how will that be known if a challenge cannot be made?
> **Evaluative point**: arguably a weakening of human rights protection. Though s3 was rarely used, its removal could generate an increase in declarations of incompatibility. However, if a challenge is difficult to make because of the new permissions stage, this becomes irrelevant and the offending legislation remains.
> The higher threshold for deporting foreign nationals could undermine the protection afforded by Article 8.

STRETCH AND CHALLENGE

Look up the Sewell Convention. What impact would the repeal of the HRA have on this?

Other changes

- Greater weight given to Article 10 (freedom of expression). Clause 4 of the Bill directs the court to give 'great weight' to the importance of freedom of expression but not when there is an exercise of state power in criminal proceedings.
- A move away from positive obligations: Clause 5 prevents UK courts from interpreting Convention rights as imposing positive obligations (i.e. it prevents Convention rights from being interpreted in a way that requires public authorities (or others) to perform positive acts). Again, this change reflects the desire of the government to restrict the interpretation of Convention rights to more literal, conservative readings, again eroding the 'living instrument' sentiment with which the Convention was passed and constraining its ability to adapt to social change.
- Henry VIII clause: Clause 40 of the Bill provides the Lord Chancellor (as Secretary of State for Justice) with the (arguably judicial) power to pass delegated legislation to 'amend or modify any primary legislation or subordinate legislation so as to preserve or restore (to any extent) the relevant judgment of the court'. This is, arguably, a step back from the Constitutional Reform Act 2005, which removed the Lord Chancellor as head of the judiciary and from his judicial role. The power conferred by Clause 40 reverts to what the Lord Chancellor used to do as a judge, and confers a judicial power on the Lord Chancellor, thus diminishing the separation of powers in the UK.

Further potential problems with a Bill of Rights

The Good Friday Agreement includes reference to the HRA and repeal of this could undermine the Northern Ireland peace process.

Devolution settlements (e.g. for the Scottish Parliament) include reference to the ECHR.

Conclusion

On the one hand, the Bill makes sense from the government (political) perspective in the sense that it will make it more difficult to bring domestic human rights claims, especially those viewed by the court of public opinion as 'underserving'. In addition, it asserts the position of the Supreme Court as the 'ultimate authority' and limits its subordination to Strasbourg.

Legally, however, the Bill diminishes human rights protection and, in some ways, its alignment with the rule of law is questionable.

Ultimately, the Bill makes it much more difficult for people to enforce their human rights. More cases will go to Strasbourg and therefore domestic human rights protection is weaker than the present position under the HRA. Devolution settlements and the Good Friday Agreement continue to pose difficulties (see Table 21.1).

Table 21.1 Advantages and disadvantages of a Bill of Rights

Advantages	Disadvantages
Controls the Executive: a Bill of Rights offers a check on the huge powers of the Executive (e.g. the government and its agencies, such as the police, etc.). Courts could refuse to apply legislation that was incompatible with the Bill of Rights.	Not needed: some argue that our rights are adequately protected.
	Inflexible: it would be hard to change.
	Could lead to uncertainty: many Bills of Rights have a loose drafting style.
Judiciary must uphold ECHR: under s3 HRA, judges must interpret all laws to be compatible with human rights BUT only so far as it is possible to do so. This means that an Act that breaches rights in the Convention still prevails, but this would not be the case with a Bill of Rights.	Weak: a Bill of Rights is only as effective as the government that underpins it.
	Increased power to the judiciary: judges are not elected and power would be removed from Parliament.
	Difficult to draft: it is hard to identify what could be included.
Entrenchment: the HRA is not entrenched therefore it can be repealed. A Bill of Rights would be entrenched.	
New rights: the HRA did not bring in any new rights but a Bill of Rights would.	

STRETCH AND CHALLENGE

Summarise the findings of the Independent Report on the Human Rights Act, published by the UK government in December 2021.

GRADE BOOST

It is crucial when you are considering whether the UK needs a Bill of Rights to be aware of the arguments for and against the current protection of human rights in the Human Rights Act 1998 and the current Bill of Rights Bill 2022.

SUMMARY: REFORM OF HUMAN RIGHTS

→ Council of Europe drafted the European Convention on Human Rights and Fundamental Freedoms (1950) (ECHR), ratified by the UK in 1951 and binding from 1953

→ The Human Rights Act 1998 (HRA) incorporated the ECHR into domestic law and came into force in October 2000 and is a step towards a British Bill of Rights
- s7 HRA: ECHR is directly applicable in UK courts
- Drawbacks of the HRA: legislation can still be incompatible with ECHR rights; vulnerable to repeal; unelected judges can now influence social policy

→ The Commission for Equality and Human Rights was set up in 2007 and became fully operational in 2009

→ Advantages of a British Bill of Rights:
- Controls the Executive
- Judiciary must uphold ECHR
- Entrenchment
- New rights

→ Disadvantages of a British Bill of Rights:
- Not needed
- Inflexible
- Could lead to uncertainty
- Ineffective if government is weak
- Increased power to the judiciary
- Difficult to draft

→ British Bill of Rights introduced as a Bill to Parliament in June 2022

TEST YOURSELF

1. What is the Council of Europe?
2. How many members does the Council of Europe have?
3. What is the role of the Commission for Equality and Human Rights?
4. What is a Bill of Rights?
5. Discuss three advantages of a Bill of Rights.
6. Discuss three disadvantages of a Bill of Rights.
7. What plans does the government have to replace the Human Rights Act 1998?
8. What did the Human Rights Act 1998 incorporate into UK law?
9. What does s7 HRA state?
10. What is meant by the doctrine of parliamentary sovereignty and how might a British Bill of Rights impact this?

EXAM SKILLS

Reform of the protection of human rights in the UK is a topic that could feature in its own right. However, when addressing any specific question on the ECHR and/or HRA, you should be fully prepared to discuss reforms of the current law.

EXAM PAST PAPER QUESTIONS

WJEC – A Level – Unit 4 – June 2022
Analyse and evaluate the impact of the Human Rights Act 1998 on the protection of human rights in the UK. [50]

WJEC – A Level – Unit 4 – June 2019
Analyse and evaluate whether the protection of human rights within the United Kingdom would be strengthened by the introduction of a Bill of Rights. [50]

Eduqas – A Level – Component 3 – June 2022
Analyse and evaluate the arguments for and against a Bill of Rights in the United Kingdom. [25]

Eduqas – A Level – Component 3 – June 2019
'The Human Rights Act 1998 is proving to be an effective substitute for a Bill of Rights.'
Discuss. [25]

Contract Law

22 Rules and theory of the law of contract

Origins and definition of contract law

How many contracts have you entered into today? Have they all involved a piece of paper? Did they all require a signature?

A basic definition of a contract is any agreement or promise that is legally binding. It can be written or unwritten so long as it satisfies the requirements of a lawful contract.

Examples could include paying for parking in a pay-and-display car park, buying your lunch in the canteen, or getting on the bus. More traditionally, a contract is the document you sign when you buy a mobile phone, book a holiday or start a new job.

We need contract law to enable society to run freely. If agreements were not legally binding, what would happen if your employer just decided they did not need you any more, or your mobile phone operator just decided to stop offering a service? The law of contract seeks to provide safety for people who are let down by parties who fail to fulfil their promises in a contract.

Laissez-faire/freedom of contract

Modern contract law stems from the **laissez-faire** doctrine, which was first introduced in the 19th century. Laissez faire is the idea that people can make agreements on their own terms and enter into a 'bargain' in their own interests and on their own terms. The ability to form contracts with no government restrictions is a key principle of economics and free-market libertarianism.

This freedom of contract principle can, however, be limited by legislation such as the **Unfair Contract Terms Act 1977** (see page 271) to ensure the notion of fairness is upheld.

> **KEY TERMINOLOGY**
>
> **laissez faire:** contract law term used to indicate that a person should have freedom of contract with minimal state or judicial interference.

The Human Rights Act 1998

The relationship between contract law and the **Human Rights Act 1998 (HRA)** is important, though the obligations on the court are the same as for other areas of the law – to take into account **s3**, which states that 'so far as it is possible to do so, primary legislation and subordinate legislation must be read and given effect in a way which is compatible with Convention rights'.

As with other areas of law, if any aspect of contract legislation is found to be incompatible, the courts can issue a declaration of incompatibility under **s4 HRA**.

The relationship between contract law and the European Union

The European Union (EU) has had a huge impact on contract law in the United Kingdom, because a number of directives have had to be implemented in the field of consumer law. It has to be noted that the impact of the EU is subject to change with the UK leaving the EU, though to date no legislation has been affected.

In 2011, the European Commission published a draft **Common European Sales Law (CESL)**, which was a type of codified contract system for the sale of goods across the EU, with the aim of improving cross-border trade and removing legal barriers between EU member states. This was after it was found that less than one in five consumers (18 per cent) in the EU had made an online purchase with a retailer based in another EU country. Therefore, to encourage cross-border trade, the fear of dealing with other countries needed to be reduced.

The **CESL** proposal was withdrawn in 2015, and a modified proposal was introduced, with the aim of setting 'harmonised EU rules for online purchases of digital content', such as ebooks and apps, as well as the sales of physical goods, such as clothes and furniture. The rationale behind this proposal was to fully unleash the potential of ecommerce and create a digital single market.

The digital single market will still allow traders to rely on their national contract laws, but will also create a set of key mandatory EU contractual rights for cross-border sales, because 27 different sets of laws discourage companies from cross-border trading.

STRETCH AND CHALLENGE

The case of *Shanshal v Al-Kishtaini* (2001) is a good authority on the relationship between contract law and human rights and how a contract cannot deprive a person of their possessions except in the public interest, as contained under the First Protocol of the **European Convention on Human Rights**.

SUMMARY: RULES AND THEORY OF THE LAW OF CONTRACT

→ **Origins and definition of contract law:** any agreement or promise that is legally binding, written or unwritten
→ **Laissez-faire/freedom of contract:** ability to make agreements on own terms
→ Can be limited by legislation, e.g. **Unfair Contract Terms Act 1977**, to ensure fairness
→ **Human Rights Act 1998:** *Shanshal* v *Al-Kishtaini* (2001)
→ **European Union (EU):** draft **Common European Sales Law (CESL)** to improve cross-border trade and remove legal barriers between EU member states
→ Modified proposal for a digital single market

TEST YOURSELF

1. What is meant by a contract?
2. List all the examples of contracts you have entered into in the last week.
3. Explain what is meant by laissez faire.
4. What is the significance of **s3 Human Rights Act 1998** on contract law?
5. What is meant by a 'digital single market', and how is it proposed that this will be achieved?

23 Essential requirements of a contract

Formation of a contract

The law on contract concerns a binding agreement between two parties. It confers obligations on both parties to 'carry out their side of the bargain'. If they do not, it may be **breach of contract**.

The law of contract is mainly about the enforcement of promises, but not all promises will be legally enforceable. To enforce a contract, the courts look for the presence of certain elements. There may be a dispute about whether a contract actually exists. In deciding whether promises or agreements are enforceable, certain elements need to be proved and it must be established that the contract has been formed according to certain rules.

OFFER + ACCEPTANCE + INTENTION TO CREATE LEGAL RELATIONS = BINDING CONTRACT
↓
INVITATION TO TREAT

Figure 23.1 The essential elements of a contract

The process of an agreement begins with an **offer**. For a contract to be formed, this offer must be unconditionally accepted. There must then be valid communication of the offer and the courts must also establish that there is (or was) an intention to create legal relations and consideration.

If these elements are not present, the courts will find that no contract exists between the parties. There cannot be an action for breach of a non-existent contract, as neither party will be bound by the promises they have made. It is therefore essential to determine whether a contract has been formed.

Offer

An offer is an expression of willingness by an **offeree** to enter into a legally binding agreement based on the terms set out in the offer made by the **offeror**. The contract is formed when these terms are accepted.

This seems straightforward. Why, then, does this stage of the contract cause confusion?

The difference between offers and invitations to treat

There is an important distinction in the law of contract between an offer, an invitation to treat and a mere statement of price. An invitation to treat does not constitute an offer.

An invitation to treat is an indication of willingness to deal but not an intention to be bound. A party is inviting offers to be made, which they are then free to accept or reject. A classic example is offering a newspaper for sale in a shop: customers can choose whether or not to buy it.

> **KEY TERMINOLOGY**
>
> **breach of contract:** to break a contract by not following its terms and conditions.
>
> **offer:** in contract law, a proposition put by one person to another person made with the intention that it shall become legally binding as soon as the other person accepts it.
>
> **offeree:** the person to whom an offer is being made and who will consequently accept the offer.
>
> **offeror:** the person making an offer.

241

Example: A display of goods
Goods displayed for sale on the shelves of a supermarket are generally considered invitations to treat. When the customer picks up the goods, this is not acceptance but merely an offer to buy on the part of the customer. If they wish to buy the goods, the customer then takes them to the cash desk, where the sale is agreed on payment and at this point the contract is formed.

> ### *Pharmaceutical Society of Great Britain* v *Boots Cash Chemists Ltd* (1953)
> A Boots pharmacy offered for sale on its shelves in a self-service shop certain goods that by law should only be sold by a registered pharmacist. The Pharmaceutical Society of Great Britain (the body responsible for enforcing this legislation) brought a prosecution against the shop for allowing customers to buy these products by helping themselves, but the Court of Appeal said it had no case. The customer, having selected the goods, made an offer to purchase when they took them to the cash desk, and a registered pharmacist, who had discretion about whether to accept the offer to buy when the goods were presented, supervised at the point of sale. The goods for sale on the shelves were therefore an invitation to treat, not an offer.
>
> ### *Fisher* v *Bell* (1961)
> A flick knife was displayed in a shop window with a ticket reading 'Ejector knife 4s'. It was an offence under the Offensive Weapons Act 1959 to 'offer for sale' prohibited weapons. It was held that the display of the knife was not an offer for sale but rather an invitation to treat, where the customer had the choice of whether or not to go into the shop to offer to buy the knife.

In these cases, it is evident that shopkeepers retain discretion to refuse sale to a person they don't feel comfortable selling to, and customers retain discretion to change their mind by returning the goods to the shelf before the sale.

Example: Lots at an auction
An auctioneer's calls for bids are an invitation to treat and not an offer. Consequently, the bids made by people at an auction are offers that the auctioneer can accept or reject. The acceptance is the fall of the hammer (in an auction without a reserve) and this is the point at which the contract is formed. The auctioneer is acting on behalf of the owner of the goods and the contract is formed between the highest bidder and the owner of the goods. An auction lot may be withdrawn at any time before the hammer falls.

> ### *British Car Auctions* v *Wright* (1972)
> A prosecution for offering to sell an unroadworthy vehicle at an auction failed as it was held that an auction is generally an invitation to treat or make bids. The bidder makes the offer and this offer is only accepted when the hammer falls.
>
> ### *Harris* v *Nickerson* (1873)
> Harris saw an advert in an auction catalogue for some furniture he wanted to bid for. On attending the auction, he found the auctioneer had withdrawn from sale the items he had hoped to buy. Harris sued for breach of contract but failed. The court held that advertising the goods for sale was no more than an invitation to treat and that the contract, in any case, would not be formed until the auctioneer's hammer fell on acceptance of a bid.

23 Essential requirements of a contract

Example: Goods or services advertised for sale in a newspaper or magazine
An advertisement for goods for sale is usually an invitation to treat but it can be an offer, depending on its wording and conditions. There is an important distinction here between a bilateral contract (invitation to treat) and a unilateral contract (offer).

Partridge v *Crittenden* (1968)
An advert in a magazine stated 'Bramble finch cocks and bramble finch hens 25s each'. The person who placed the advert was charged with offering for sale a wild bird, contrary to the **Protection of Wild Birds Act 1954**. The divisional court said he must be acquitted. The advertisement was an invitation to treat, not an offer to sell; with limited stock, the advertiser could not reasonably intend to be bound to sell to all those who might accept. This would be obviously impractical.

Carlill v *Carbolic Smoke Ball Company* (1893)
A business advertised smoke ball 'medicine', promising to pay £100 to any purchaser who used the smoke ball correctly and still got flu. Mrs Carlill used the smoke ball correctly but still got flu. The court upheld her claim for the £100, saying that the promise to pay £100 was indeed an offer that was subsequently accepted by anyone who used the smoke ball correctly and got flu. The wording of the advertisement clearly showed an intention to be bound to anyone accepting it, so it was held that the advertisement was a unilateral contract.

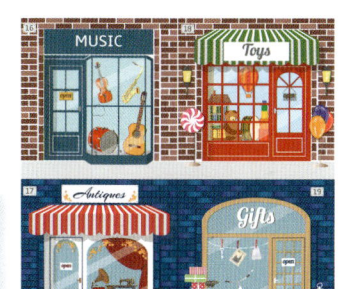

Figure 23.2 Contracts are formed while shopping

> **KEY TERMINOLOGY**
>
> **bilateral contract:** a contract between two parties where each promises to perform an act in exchange for the other party's act.
>
> **unilateral contract:** an offer made in exchange for an act; for example, a reward for lost property.

However, the form and wording of a contract may give rise to an offer in the case of a unilateral contract.

Example: A request for tenders
Public authorities are required to offer for tender for many of their services, and it is also a common practice for private businesses. For example, a company that wants to install new computers invites tenders (quotations) and various installers to respond with different prices and conditions. The company is free to choose any installer they wish, even if it is not the cheapest. Where goods are advertised for sale by tender, the statement is not considered to be an offer but generally an invitation to treat. Any tender then proposed is the offer. If, however, the company has advertised that they will accept the cheapest bid then they are bound to give the work to the lowest bidder.

Harvela Investments v *Royal Trust of Canada* (1986)
The Royal Trust of Canada invited two parties to bid for some land on the understanding that the highest bid would be accepted. Harvela bid $2,175,000 and Sir Leonard Outerbridge bid $2,100,000 or $100,000 more than any other offer. The Royal Trust of Canada accepted Sir Leonard's offer and Harvela successfully sued for breach of contract.

The wording of the invitation to tender made it an offer that could only be accepted by the highest bidder. The referential bid by Sir Leonard (the statement that he would outbid any other party by $100,000) was ineffective, as it defeats the purpose of asking for highest bids. He had thus only bid $2,100,000 compared with Harvela's bid of $2,175,000.

Example: A statement of price
Simply indicating a price that would be found acceptable does not make an offer.

243

Harvey v Facey (1893)

Harvey telegraphed to Facey: 'Will you sell us 'Bumper Hall Pen? Telegraph lowest cash price.' Facey replied: 'Lowest cash price ... £900'. Harvey then telegraphed: 'We agree to buy ... for £900 asked by you. Please send us title deed.'

It was held that Facey's telegram was an invitation to treat, and was not an offer, as it was merely a statement of price.

However, there are occasions where a statement of price can constitute an offer.

Biggs v Boyd Gibbins (1971)

Mr and Mrs Biggs were negotiating with Mr Gibbins over the sale of some property they owned. In the course of the negotiations, they wrote to Mr Gibbins stating: 'For a quick sale I will accept £26,000.' Mr Gibbins replied: 'I accept your offer.' Mr and Mrs Biggs responded: 'I thank you for accepting my price of £26,000.' The Biggs' first letter was deemed to be an offer that Gibbins had accepted.

Rules of an offer

Communication of the offer

To be effective, an offer must be communicated. A person cannot accept an offer if they have no knowledge of it. The rationale is that if a contract is an agreed bargain, there can be no agreement without knowledge.

Taylor v Laird (1856)

Taylor gave up his captaincy of a ship but needed passage back to the UK. He offered to do this by working as an ordinary crew member. His claim for wages was not successful, as the owner of the ship had not received communication of Taylor's offer to work in order to gain passage back to the UK. It was held that in order for an offer to be accepted, there must be knowledge of it.

An offer can be made to one person, but can also be made to the world, and as long as they have knowledge of the offer, anyone can accept it. In **Carlill v Carbolic Smoke Ball Company (1893)**, discussed on page 243, the advert was a unilateral contract, an offer on behalf of the Smoke Ball Company to anyone who satisfied the conditions laid out in it. The company had made the offer generally (to the 'whole world') and Mrs Carlill had accepted it by buying the smoke ball and still getting flu. A unilateral offer, such as the one in **Carlill**, cannot be withdrawn while it is being performed.

If someone had bought the smoke ball and got flu, it would not be fair to void the contract once the series of events had begun.

Errington v Errington and Woods (1952)

A father purchased a house and mortgaged it in his own name for his son and daughter-in-law to live in on the agreement that provided they kept up the repayments, the house would be transferred to them once the mortgage was paid off. After approximately 15 years, the father died and his widow sued for possession of the house. The court held that there was a unilateral contract and, though the son and daughter-in-law were not bound to go on paying, if they did, the father was bound to transfer the property to them in accordance with the promise.

Figure 23.3 Examples of invitations to treat

23 Essential requirements of a contract

The terms of the offer must be certain
The parties to a contract must know what they are contracting to and therefore the terms must not be too vague.

> ### *Guthing* v *Lynn* (1831)
> The buyer of a horse promised to pay the seller an extra £5 'if the horse is lucky for me'. It was held this was too vague to be enforceable.

It is possible to withdraw the offer at any time before the offer is accepted
In principle, there is no legal commitment until a contract has been concluded by the acceptance of an offer and, up to that point, either party is free to change their mind and withdraw from the negotiations.

> ### *Routledge* v *Grant* (1828)
> Grant had offered his house for sale. He had a condition in the offer that it would remain open for six weeks. He took the house off the market after six weeks and the courts held that this was lawful as no one had yet accepted the offer.

The offeror must communicate the withdrawal of the offer to the offeree
An offer remains open and cannot be considered withdrawn until the offeree has received it.

> ### *Byrne* v *Van Tienhoven* (1880)
> See Figure 23.4 for a timeline of this case. By 15 October, B clearly thinks a contract is in place, and the court agrees. The fact that A revoked the order is irrelevant, as B had accepted before receiving the revocation.

Communication of a withdrawal of offer can be by a reliable third party
If the offeror wants to withdraw the offer, this need not be communicated by the offeror themselves but can be done through a reliable third party.

> ### *Dickinson* v *Dodds* (1876)
> Dodds offered to sell his house to Dickinson. The offer was to be 'left open till Friday'. On Thursday afternoon, Dickinson heard from a third party that Dodds had sold the property to someone else. On the Friday morning, Dickinson delivered a formal acceptance to Dodds, and then brought an action for specific performance against Dodds. The court held that the offer made to Dickinson had been withdrawn on the Thursday and was no longer capable of acceptance. This was acceptable as the third party was a reliable source who was shown to be a mutual acquaintance of both parties and who could be relied upon by both parties.

1 October: A posts an order to B for some goods

8 October: A posts a letter revoking the order

11 October: B receives A's order

15 October: B replies, accepting the terms

20 October: B receives A's revocation

Figure 23.4 A timeline of actions relating to the case of *Byrne* v *Van Tienhoven* (1880)

Termination of an offer

It is important to know for how long an offer is valid. The offeror might have tried to withdraw the offer or a long time might have elapsed before the offer was accepted. It would seem unfair and impractical that an offer remains open indefinitely or that an offer cannot be properly terminated. For these reasons, the courts have developed certain rules governing the duration of a valid offer.

The general rule is that an offer can be withdrawn at any time before it is accepted. Once validly accepted, there is a contract and it may be too late to withdraw. This was evidenced above in the case *Routledge* v *Grant* (1828).

However, there are some situations where an offer, once made, can be validly terminated.

Acceptance
Once accepted by a valid means, there is a contract and the offer ceases to be.

Rejection
If the offeree rejects the offer, that is the end of it.

Revocation
An offer can be withdrawn before it has been accepted, provided it is done correctly as highlighted above. The correct ways to revoke are as follows:

- An offer can be withdrawn at any time before it is accepted: *Routledge* v *Grant* (1828).
- Revocation must be communicated or it is unsuccessful: *Byrne* v *Van Tienhoven* (1880).
- Revocation can be communicated by a third party if they are reliable: *Dickinson* v *Dodds* (1876).

If the offeree has started to perform the unilateral contract, it cannot be withdrawn once performance has begun: *Carlill* v *Carbolic Smoke Ball Company* (1893).

Also note the provisions of the Consumer Protection (Distance Selling) Regulations 2000, which allows a 14-day cooling-off period for products bought online.

Counter-offer
If, on responding to an offer, the offeree tries to vary the terms of the contract or tries to introduce a new term, that communication may be classed not as acceptance of the contract but as a counter-offer. A contract is not formed at this stage. The original offeror is free to accept or reject the counter-offer, so a counter-offer is essentially a rejection of the original offer.

> ### *Hyde* v *Wrench* (1840)
> It was held that the 'counter-offer kills the original offer'. Wrench had offered to sell his estate to Hyde for £1,000 and Hyde had responded by offering £950. Wrench rejected this offer. Hyde then decided to offer £1,000 but Wrench refused. Hyde sued for breach of contract. It was decided that by offering £950, Hyde had effectively rejected the original offer of £1,000 and his offer of £950 was a counter-offer, which Wrench had subsequently rejected. It was, however, highlighted that had Wrench's original offer of £1,000 been accepted unconditionally, there would have been a binding contract.

Courts have drawn an important distinction between a counter-offer and a mere request for information. Unlike a counter-offer, a request for information would not terminate the contract as it is not rejecting the original terms of the original offer. This would still mean the offer is open to acceptance by the offeree.

> ### *Stevenson* v *McLean* (1880)
> The plaintiff (the offeree) and defendant (the offeror) agreed terms of a contract to buy iron. The offeree then asked if he could stagger payment and delivery over a two-month period. On hearing nothing back from the offeror, the offeree telegraphed his acceptance to the offeror, only to discover he had sold the iron elsewhere. The plaintiff successfully sued for breach of contract. The judge held that there was no counter-offer, merely an enquiry for further information which should have been answered.

KEY TERMINOLOGY

counter-offer: an attempt to vary the conditions of the original offer. It is therefore not acceptance, and a contract is not formed until the counter-offer is accepted.

Lapse of time

In cases where the offer specifies that it will remain open for a certain duration, the offer automatically terminates after this time has passed. Where no specified time period is laid down, the offer remains open for a 'reasonable time' only. This is fair, as it is unreasonable to expect an offer to remain open indefinitely, especially where business transactions are concerned and an element of certainty is required.

Ramsgate Victoria Hotel v *Montefiore* (1866)

The defendants made an offer in June to buy shares in the plaintiff's company, but heard nothing as they only made an allocation of shares available in November. At that point, the plaintiffs accepted the defendants' offer, but the defendants refused to go ahead, saying too much time had lapsed. The court said that although the offer had not been formally withdrawn, it would expire after 'a reasonable time', particularly given the fluctuating nature of shares, and the time had gone beyond what was reasonable.

Failure of conditions

Offers are normally made with certain conditions attached. If these conditions are not met then the offer cannot be accepted.

Financings Ltd v *Stimson* (1962)

The defendant had bought a car on hire purchase from a car dealer. The car dealer explained that the agreement would only become binding when it was signed by the finance company (Financings Ltd: the plaintiffs). The defendant took the car away and paid a first instalment but returned it two days later, claiming he had changed his mind. His agreement had not yet been signed by the finance company (a 'condition' of the offer) and so the finance company's claim against the defendant failed, as the court held that one of the conditions of the offer had not been met and the defendant had returned the car in time.

Death

An offeree cannot accept an offer once the offeror has died. The decision may be different if the offeree does not know of the offeror's death and if there is no personal involvement. The courts have been divided on this issue.

Bradbury v *Morgan* (1862)

It was held that if the offeree accepts in ignorance of the death of the offeror, a contract might be formed.

> **GRADE BOOST**
>
> Claimants were known as plaintiffs until the **Civil Procedure Rules 1998** came into force on 1 April 1999. Using the word 'plaintiff' when you give examples of older cases shows you are aware of this. However, you should also add a note to explain why you have chosen this terminology.

This case should be contrasted with *Dickinson* v *Dodds* (1876), where it was held that the death of either party to the contract terminates the agreement because there can be no formal acceptance.

The best view is probably that a party cannot accept an offer once they find out about the death of the offeror but that, in certain circumstances, the offer could be accepted if made in ignorance of the offeror's death.

Acceptance

Once an offer has been made by the offeror, the offeree is free to accept the offer. A contract cannot be formed until the offer has been unconditionally accepted. The acceptance must be an acceptance of each of the terms of the offer and must be a 'mirror image' of the offer. It has already been seen that trying to add new terms to the offer is not an acceptance but rather a counter-offer that implies the original offer is rejected. Acceptance can be established where the offeree's words or conduct give rise to an objective presumption that the offeree agrees to the offeror's terms.

Just as there were rules for the establishment of a valid offer, there are also rules for the successful communication of the acceptance.

Rules of acceptance

The acceptance must be unconditional

This is the 'mirror image' rule. It has been established that any attempt to change the terms of the offer is a counter-offer (as in the case *Hyde* v *Wrench* (1840) discussed above). A mere request for further information is not a rejection and the offer can still be accepted following the clarification of this information (*Stevenson* v *McLean* (1880), discussed above).

The acceptance must be communicated to the offeror

It must be a positive act, meaning that silence does not amount to acceptance.

> ### *Felthouse* v *Brindley* (1863)
> A man had negotiated the sale of his horse with his uncle. The uncle wrote to the nephew saying: 'If I hear no more from you, I shall consider the horse to be mine.' The nephew did not respond. The nephew's property went to auction but the auctioneer failed to withdraw the horse from the auction and it sold, despite the nephew's instruction that it be withdrawn. The uncle's action to sue the auctioneer failed as the nephew had never actually accepted his offer.

The offeree has to be aware of the existence of the offer

> ### *Inland Revenue Commissioners* v *Fry* (2001)
> Fry's husband sent the Inland Revenue a cheque for much less than the amount of tax they had asked for. He attached a note stating it was 'in full and final settlement to be accepted when banked'. Because of its postroom procedures of separating cheques from correspondence, the Inland Revenue was ignorant of this offer and, despite cashing the cheque which could, under a unilateral contract, be said to be an acceptance due to a prescribed course of conduct, the court held that the offeree must have knowledge of the offer in order to accept it.

Communication of the acceptance must be made by an authorised person

Generally, this means the offeree, but it has also been established that someone authorised by the offeree can communicate acceptance.

Powell v Lee (1908)

A man had been interviewed for a role as head teacher of a school and the managers subsequently decided he was the best candidate for the job. One of the managers, acting without the authority of the rest, told the man he had been accepted. However, the managers changed their minds and appointed someone else. On discovering this, the man sued for the breach of contract, claiming damages for loss of salary. The courts held that there was no valid contract (and thus no breach) as the intention to contract had not been communicated by an authorised person.

Acceptance can be in any form unless it is a requirement that it be in a specific form

The acceptance can be in any form, including conduct, but if the offeror requires it to be made in a specific form then it is only a valid acceptance if made by that form.

Yates Building Co v Pulleyn Ltd (1975)

A piece of land was offered for sale, with the statement that if purchasers wished to make an option to purchase, it had to be done in writing sent by 'registered or recorded delivery post'. The offeree sent his option by ordinary post and the courts held that the communication was not valid because it did not comply with the method of communication stated in the offer.

Battle of the forms

If Eve makes an offer on her standard terms and Zak accepts on a document containing his standard but clashing terms, no contract has been formed unless Eve acts upon Zak's communication, for example by delivering goods, which means she has impliedly accepted the communication. Zak has effectively made a counter-offer, which has been accepted on the basis of Eve's conduct.

This situation is known as the 'battle of the forms'.

Figure 23.5 Contracts often have standard terms

Butler Machine Tool v Excell-o-Corp (1979)

The plaintiff offered to sell a machine to the defendant. A term of the offer stated that any orders were accepted on the seller's terms and that these would prevail over any conflicting terms in the buyer's order. The defendants ordered the machine on different terms in their own standard form. At the bottom of this form was a tear-off slip for the plaintiff to fill in and send back, with the words: 'We accept your order on the terms and conditions stated thereon.' The plaintiff signed and returned it, writing, 'Your official order … is being entered in accordance with our revised quotation.'

The buyer (defendant) won judgement as the conduct of the parties implied a valid contract had been formed.

In applying this logic, it will be found that in most cases when there is a 'battle of forms', a contract is made as soon as the last of the forms is sent and received without any objections, especially where conduct implies acceptance.

Modern methods of communication

With increased use of instantaneous methods of communication, such as fax, email and internet order forms, the courts have seen a shift in the facts of the cases reaching the courts. The crucial factor appears to be – how instantaneous is the method of communication?

Brinkibon v *Stahag Stahl* (1982)
A telex agreeing to terms and conditions was received out of office hours. The House of Lords accepted that 'instantaneous communications' could only be regarded as effective communication when the office reopened.

Figure 23.6 For digital contracts, acceptance occurs when the digital service has been received by the consumer

While this appears to be a sound decision, it could be argued it will not cover all situations and the intentions of the parties and good business practice must be paramount.

Entores Ltd v *Miles Far East Corp* (1955)
The courts held that the contract is only complete when the acceptance is received by the offeror and the contract is made at the place where the acceptance is received.

Although the principles laid down in the cases above are still likely to be followed, further issues may need to be examined and resolved; for example, the effectiveness of telephone answering services or delays between sending and receiving emails. Therefore, in implementing the **Distance Selling EU Directive 97/7**, the UK enacted the **Consumer Protection (Distance Selling) Regulations 2000** to formalise this area and to offer consumers and sellers protection and clarity.

› These regulations apply to the sale of goods via modern methods of communication, such as fax, telephone, internet, email, TV shopping and mail order.
› Under Regulation 7, the seller is under an obligation to provide the purchaser with minimum information; for example, a description of the goods, the price, arrangements for payment and delivery, and the right to cancel the contract within 14 days.
› Under Regulation 8, written confirmation must also be given.
› If these rules are not followed, the contract is not formed.

In addition, the **Electronic Commerce Directive 2000/31** was implemented in the UK by the **Electronic Commerce (EC Directive) Regulations 2002**. **Article 11** states: 'where a purchaser in accepting a seller's offer is required to give his consent through technological means, such as clicking on an icon, the contract is concluded when the recipient of the service has received, electronically, an acknowledgement of receipt of the recipient's acceptance'.

The postal rule

Where an agreement states or implies the ordinary post is the normal, anticipated or agreed form of acceptance, acceptance takes effect when the letter is posted, not received.

Adams v *Lindsell* (1818)
The defendants offered to sell some goods to the plaintiffs and requested an acceptance by post. On 5 September, the plaintiffs sent a letter of acceptance as specified. On 8 September, the defendants sold the goods to a third party. They received the plaintiffs' letter of acceptance by post on 9 September. The plaintiffs successfully sued for breach of contract and the postal rule was established. It was held that a contract was formed when the plaintiffs posted their letter of acceptance on 5 September and therefore the defendants were in breach.

The postal rule has been extended to cover situations where the letter is never received and not just delayed.

> ### Household Fire Insurance v Grant (1879)
> A letter detailing the allotment of shares was never received, but it was held that there was still a valid agreement once the letter had been posted.

The rationale behind these decisions is that the parties can protect themselves by stating in the offer that it will not be a binding contract until acceptance is received.

The courts have so far refused to extend the postal rule to situations involving telex and email. With these situations, acceptance must be received, rather than merely sent, as per the guidance in the EU directives.

Intention to create legal relations

People make promises with one another every day. It is not practical or fair that every promise can be enforced in the courts. The law has therefore reached a compromise and offered a distinction between two situations in which agreement may be made:

> **Commercial and business agreements**: the presumption is in favour of the intention to create legal relations.
> **Social and domestic agreements**: the presumption is against the intention to create legal relations.

There are, of course, situations where the facts of the case will result in a decision against these presumptions, making the presumption rebuttable.

As we have seen, an offer must be a statement made with the intention of it becoming binding on acceptance. It is also essential that all the parties intend to create legal rules through the formation of the contract. The determination of the parties to create legal rules is an objective test: they need to establish whether reasonable parties to such an agreement would have had an intention to create legal relations.

The courts are not concerned with the subjective test (the state of mind of the parties involved). They will look at the facts as a whole to determine whether intention to create legal relations exists.

Figure 23.7 Postal acceptance occurs when the letter is posted

STRETCH AND CHALLENGE
Consider some of the problems with the postal rule, both in general and in relation to modern methods of communication.

Commercial and business agreements

In commercial and business agreements, courts will presume an intention to create legal rules exists unless there is evidence to the contrary.

> ### Edwards v Skyways Ltd (1969)
> An airline (the defendant) had to make some pilots redundant. One pilot, Edwards (the plaintiff), was given notice of redundancy as per the terms of his contract. After discussions with trade unions, the airline agreed to make ex gratia (voluntary rather than legally obligated) redundancy payments to pilots, but they tried to avoid paying Edwards this payment following his redundancy. The defendant tried to claim that the ex gratia payment was not intended to be binding, but the judge held that, since the agreement to pay was made in commercial dealings, it could be presumed to be an intention to create legal relations.

The courts have also held that offers to give away free gifts to promote a business fall under the same binding presumption.

> ### *Esso Petroleum Company Ltd* v *Commissioners of Customs and Excise* (1976)
> Esso was giving away a free World Cup coin with every four gallons of petrol purchased at its pumps. Millions of these coins were distributed. Customs and Excise tried to claim that the coins were being 'sold' and it could therefore claim purchase tax from the transaction. The courts held that since Esso was trying to gain extra business from the promotion of the free coins, there was an intention to be legally bound by the agreement.

The courts have, however, said that it is possible for the agreement not to contain an intention to be legally binding if this is specifically stated.

> ### *Jones* v *Vernon's Pools Ltd* (1938)
> Vernon's Pools (a type of lottery) inserted a clause onto its coupons (tickets) stating the transaction would be binding in honour only and would not give rise to any legal relationship. The plaintiff sent in his winning coupon but it was lost. He tried to make a claim for his winnings but failed because the insertion of the clause onto the coupon prevented any claim as it negated the intention to create legal relations.

Social and domestic agreements

Figure 23.8 An agreement with a friend is classed as a social and domestic agreement

Generally, social and domestic agreements cover family members, friends and workmates. The courts will presume that legal relations do not exist unless there is evidence to the contrary.

23 Essential requirements of a contract

Balfour v Balfour (1919)
A husband, who lived abroad, promised his wife in England an income of £30 per month. When the wife petitioned for divorce, she tried to claim an ongoing £30 income. Her claim failed on the basis that their agreement was made when their marriage was cordial and that they never intended to sue on it. There was no intention to be legally bound and it was not appropriate for the courts to interfere in situations like this. The courts also commented that if they opened up their jurisdiction to cover such situations, they would likely be inundated by similar claims.

The courts have stated that there is a *rebuttable presumption* that domestic agreements are not intended to create legal relations. This means that if the courts can find evidence of intention, they may also find that a legally binding agreement has been made.

Merritt v Merritt (1970)
The spouses were already separated and made an agreement that the husband would pay the estranged wife an income if she paid the outstanding mortgage. The courts held this agreement to have intention to create legal relations.

KEY TERMINOLOGY

rebuttable presumption: a presumption that is rebuttable is one that can be reversed if the courts find sufficient evidence to do this.

Where the parties have exchanged money, the courts are likely to remove the presumption of intention to create legal relations.

Simpkins v Pays (1955)
A lodger had entered a competition with two members of the household in which he lived. Although the entry was in the householder's name, they each contributed equally to the cost on the understanding that they would share any winnings. When they won, the householder refused to share the winnings. The court found the lodger and the two others to have intention to create legal relations and the householder had to share the winnings equally.

Consideration

The evidence of an agreement alone does not give rise to a legally enforceable contract. A promise without consideration is a gift, while one made for consideration is a bargain. Both parties to the contract must provide consideration if they wish to sue on the contract. Consideration means that each side must promise to give or do something for the other. In *Dunlop v Selfridge (1915)*, consideration was defined as:

> 'An act or forbearance of one party, or the promise thereof, is the price for which the promise of the other is bought, and the promise thus given for value is enforceable.'

As with offer and acceptance, certain rules need to be examined in relation to the issue of consideration.

The rules of consideration

Consideration must be sufficient but not adequate
Here, the courts are saying that the consideration provided need not match in value what is being offered by each party, but the consideration must be sufficient to be legally enforceable. This depends on what the parties were satisfied with when they made the agreement.

> ### *Thomas* v *Thomas* (1942)
> A man had expressed his desire that his wife be allowed to remain in his property on his death for a (very small) payment of £1 per year. The executors did this for some years but later tried to dispossess her. The courts found that the £1 nominal payment was 'sufficient' consideration.

However, in a contrasting case that seems to go against this principle, items that are apparently of no worth have been classed as amounting to valuable and sufficient consideration.

> ### *Chappell* v *Nestlé Company* (1960)
> To promote its chocolate bars, Nestlé had offered a record for sale, for a sum of money plus three chocolate wrappers. The owners of the copyright to the record tried to sue to prevent the promotion as they would receive fewer royalties if the record was offered in return for chocolate wrappers. They failed and the courts held that the wrappers, despite being thrown away on receipt, were valid and sufficient consideration.

The consideration must move from the promisee (the person to whom the promise is made)
This means that only a party that has provided consideration can sue or be sued on the contract.

Existing contractual duty does not constitute consideration
A party simply doing something that they are already bound to do in the contract is not sufficient to amount to consideration.

There are some exceptions to these rules, where courts have reached a different decision. For example, this could apply where a party makes a promise to pay extra and receives an extra benefit from the other party's agreement to complete what they were already bound to do under an existing agreement.

> ### *Williams* v *Roffey Bros and Nicholls Contractors Ltd* (1990)
> Having agreed to refurbish a block of flats, the main contractors (the defendants), fearing that a sub-contractor (the claimant/plaintiff) would fail to meet deadlines and so cause penalties to be incurred on the main contract, offered him extra payments for prompt completion. When the claimant sought to enforce this promise, a unanimous Court of Appeal said that if the defendants doubted whether the claimant subcontractor would perform his contractual obligation, then a further promise by him to perform that contract might be consideration for the defendants' offer of extra money as long as the offer was not obtained by the claimant's fraud or economic duress. There may have been no legal benefit to the defendants, as they were just getting the work they expected done, but they secured the practical benefit of getting the work completed on time without the trouble of hiring a new sub-contractor and risking the claimant's bankruptcy if they sought to recover the costs and penalties.

Part-payment of debt is not consideration
The general rule laid down in **Pinnel (1602)** says that part-payment of a debt can never satisfy the whole debt. Any agreement to accept part-payment in full satisfaction of the debt is unenforceable as there is no consideration. The creditor could always sue for the balance owed.

23 Essential requirements of a contract

> ### D and C Builders v Rees (1965)
> D and C Builders was owed £482 from Mr Rees, for whom they had carried out some work. After D and C waited several months for the payment, Mr Rees offered £300 to settle the debt. Due to the financial difficulties of the builders, they accepted this smaller settlement. The builders then successfully sued for the remainder. The courts held that they were not prevented by their agreement to accept less and could sue for the remainder. The courts also found that they were pressurised into accepting less by Mr Rees taking advantage of their known poor financial situation.

Two exceptions to this general rule have been examined in the courts over the years, where the agreement to pay less than the debt owed can be enforced.

Exception 1: Where something different is added or happens that is sufficient consideration
This could be, for example, an agreement to accept a smaller sum on an earlier date or to accept a payment other than in money, or a lesser sum plus something other than money.

The exception also occurs where part-payment has been made by a third party, as in the case of *Hirachand Punamchand* v *Temple* (1911).

> ### Hirachand Punamchand v Temple (1911)
> A father paid a smaller sum to a money lender than was owed to cover his son's debts. The money lender accepted it in full settlement but later sued for the balance. It was held that the part-payment was valid consideration, and that to allow the moneylender's claim would be a fraud on the father.
>
> This case shows that the courts will find that a promise to accept a smaller sum in full satisfaction will be binding on a creditor, where the part-payment is made by a third party, on condition that the debtor is released from the obligation to pay the full amount.

Exception 2: The doctrine of promissory estoppel
This is an equitable doctrine and has its origins in the *obiter dicta* of Lord Denning in the case of *Central London Property Trust Ltd* v *High Trees House Ltd* (1947). The doctrine provides a means of making a promise binding, in the absence of consideration, in various circumstances. The principle is that if someone (the promisor) makes a promise which another person acts on, the promisor is stopped (or estopped) from going back on the promise, even though the other person did not provide consideration.

For the successful operation of the doctrine, five essential requirements need to be established:

1. The need for an existing contractual relationship between the parties: it is generally considered that promissory estoppel exists to modify existing contractual relationships rather than to make new ones.
2. Need for reliance on the promise: an essential requirement is that the promisee has relied on the promise. In the *High Trees House* (1947) case, the lessees had relied upon the promise not to put the rent back up while the flats were half empty.
3. A 'shield and not a sword': established in the case of *Combe* v *Combe* (1951), this means the doctrine can be used as a defence to a claim and not as a ground for bringing an action.
4. It must be inequitable for the promisor to go back on the promise: the claimant must have agreed to waive (give up) some of their rights under that contract (normally the amount of the debt that has been unpaid). It must also be unfair for the promisor to withdraw the promise. This also covers situations where the promissee has extracted the promise

STRETCH AND CHALLENGE
Research the cases of *Tweddle and Atkinson* (1861), which demonstrates that consideration must move from the promise, and *Collins* v *Godfrey* (1831), which demonstrates that the existing contractual duty does not constitute consideration.

KEY TERMINOLOGY
promissory estoppel: if someone (the promisor) makes a promise that another person acts on, the promisor is stopped (or estopped) from going back on the promise, even though the other person did not provide consideration.

by taking advantage of the promissory estoppel (as in the case of *D and C Builders* v *Rees* (1966)).

5. The doctrine is generally suspensory: this means that the promise is normally time-limited (as in the *High Trees House* case, when the agreement to reduce the rent by half was binding until the flats became full again).

Past consideration is no consideration

This simply means that any consideration given cannot come before the agreement but must come after it. For example, Callum gives Gabi a lift to work in his van. On arrival Gabi promises to give Callum £10 towards the fuel. Callum cannot enforce this promise as his consideration, giving Gabi a lift, is past.

This is a common-sense rule as it prevents people from being forced into contracts on the basis of them being sent goods or services that they have not ordered. It is, essentially, a promise that has not been agreed to by both parties.

> ### *Re McArdle* (1951)
> The plaintiff had carried out work on a house in which his brothers and sister had a beneficial interest. He asked them to contribute to the costs he had incurred in the refurbishment, which they agreed to do. The courts held that this agreement was not enforceable as the work had been completed before any agreement to pay had been made. The promise to pay was not supported by any consideration. The work was therefore 'past' consideration and not valid.

> **EXAM SKILLS**
>
> When applying this area of law to a problem question, plan your question using the identify, define, apply (IDA) structure, as shown in Table 23.1.
>
> Remember that this topic can also come up as an essay question.

Table 23.1 The IDA structure

Introduction:
What are the required elements of an enforceable contract?
Identify the contracts in your scenario – who are the parties and what do the contracts involve?
Make a note of any dates as well that may be important when deciding whether there was a valid acceptance.

Identify	Description	Application
Offer	Describe the requirements of a valid offer, using case law to support. Describe what is meant by an invitation to treat and how these are different to offers.	Are all the requirements of an offer present in the scenario? Are there any invitations to treat? Are there any counter-offers?
Acceptance	Describe the requirements of a valid acceptance, using case law to support. Describe the postal rule. Describe how an acceptance occurs with instant methods of communication.	Are all the requirements of an acceptance present in the scenario? Are there any postal acceptances? When would these take effect?
Consideration	Describe the rule of consideration, using case law to support.	Is there consideration present in the scenario?
Intention	Describe the effect of a social arrangement, using case law to support. Describe the effect of a commercial arrangement, using case law to support.	Are the contract(s) in the scenario social or commercial in nature? What effect does this therefore have on whether the contract is enforceable?

Conclusion:
Has a valid contract been formed?

Privity of contract

The basic rule is that a contract cannot confer rights or impose obligations arising under it on any person or agent except the parties to it. This means that only the parties to a contract should be able to sue or enforce their rights. It is called privity of contract.

> ### *Tweddle* v *Atkinson* (1861)
> A father and a father-in-law contracted to give the plaintiff a sum of money. Because the contract was made between the father and father-in-law, the plaintiff could not enforce the contract, even though he was to benefit from the money.

This rule can leave some parties without a remedy so, over the years, the courts have developed exceptions in both the common law and statute to enable third parties to have rights to a contract, and now the privity rule has limited application.

KEY TERMINOLOGY

privity of contract: a doctrine which allows the parties to a contract to sue each other, but does not allow a third party to sue.

Contracts (Rights of Third Parties) Act 1999

This Act enables third parties to enforce rights under a contract, if the contract was made after 11 May 2000. Section 1 of the Act allows a third party to enforce terms of a contract in one of two situations:

> **s1(1)(a)**: if the third party is specifically mentioned in the contract as someone authorised to enforce the term; or
> **s1(1)(b)**: if the contract purports to confer a benefit upon them.

Section 1(2) of the Act contains an exception to the second situation: that the third party cannot enforce their rights if 'it appears that the parties did not intend the term to be enforceable by the third party'.

STRETCH AND CHALLENGE

Research the case of *BBC v HarperCollins* (2010) (see page 215), which concerned The Stig from the TV show *Top Gear*. He wanted to release an autobiography, but there was a contract to keep his identity a secret. Why was The Stig allowed to publish an autobiography?

> ### *Nisshin Shipping* v *Cleaves* (2003)
> Cleaves was a company of brokers which negotiated for shipowners to loan their ships to charterers. Although Cleaves was not a party to any of the contracts, the charterers had agreed to pay a commission to Cleaves. The court held that under the 1999 Act, the clauses of the contract purported to confer a benefit on the brokers, and therefore there was a presumption that there was an intention for that term to be enforceable.

Other statutory exceptions

Other statutory exceptions have developed over the years and these can be used as an alternative to the 1999 Act, although the 1999 Act covers most situations.

> **Married Women's Property Act 1882** allows the beneficiary to life insurance to enforce the terms, even though they are not parties to the contract.
> **Road Traffic Act 1988** requires all drivers to take out third-party liability insurance.
> **Law of Property Act 1925** stipulates that privity of contract does not apply to restrictive covenants relating to land.

> **GRADE BOOST**
>
> Have a look at the case of *Jackson v Horizon Holidays Ltd* (1975), where Lord Denning ruled that the plaintiff was entitled to damages after a holiday went wrong, not just for himself but also for his family because he had entered into the contract for their benefit as well.

Common law exceptions

There are also common law exceptions to the general privity of contract rule that have been developed for convenience and flexibility.

Collateral contracts

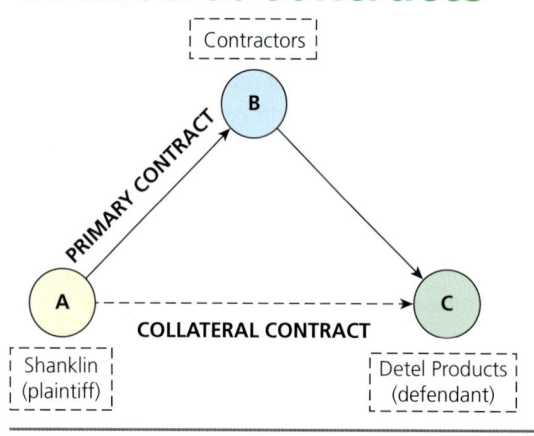

Figure 23.9 The contracts in *Shanklin Pier* v *Detel Products Ltd* (1951)

This is a contract between one party and two others, where the court will find that a collateral contract between the two others evades the privity rule only where there is an intention to create a collateral contract.

> ### *Shanklin Pier* v *Detel Products Ltd* (1951)
>
> The plaintiffs (A) had employed contractors (B) to paint their pier. They told the contractors to buy paint made by the defendants (C), who had said that the paint would last for seven years. It only lasted for three months. The court decided that the plaintiffs could sue the defendants on a collateral contract. They had provided consideration for the defendants' promise by entering into an agreement with the contractors, which entailed the purchase of the defendants' paint.

Agency

This refers to a situation where someone has made a contract on behalf of someone else. The **agent** may contract on behalf of his principal with a third party, thereby bringing the third party into a contractual relationship.

> ### *Scruttons Ltd* v *Midland Silicones* (1962)
>
> A contract (called a bill of lading) limited the liability of a shipping company to $500 per package. The defendant was a stevedore, a company that unloaded and loaded ships at a dock. It had contracted with the shipping company to unload the plaintiff's goods on the basis that they were to be covered by the exclusion clause in the bill of lading. The plaintiffs were ignorant of the contract between the shipping company and the stevedores. Owing to the stevedore's negligence, the cargo was damaged, and when sued, they pleaded the limitation clause in the bill of lading. The House of Lords held that the stevedore could not rely on the clause as there was no privity of contract between the plaintiffs and defendants.

23 Essential requirements of a contract

Trusts

A trust is an equitable obligation to hold property on behalf of another.

Les Affréteurs Réunis v Leopold Walford (1919)
A broker (C) negotiated a charter party by which the shipowner (A) promised the charterer (B) to pay the broker a commission. It was held that B was trustee of this promise for C, who could thus enforce it against A.

Table 23.2 Privity of contract: An evaluation

Advantages of privity of contract	Disadvantages of privity of contract
Free will: parties should be free to make contracts with whoever they wish and should only incur rights and obligations when they have agreed to be part of a contract.	Extended litigation: the privity rule could lead to a chain of contract claims.
Unjust: it is unjust to allow a party to sue if they themselves cannot be sued.	Intention of the parties: the privity rule does not necessarily reflect the intentions of the parties, who may wish a third party to have rights and obligations.
Restrictive: the privity rule restricts the rights of the parties to modify or terminate the contract.	
Indefinite liability: the exceptions, particularly the Contracts (Rights of Third Parties) Act 1999, expose contractors to indefinite liability by unlimited third parties.	Lots of exceptions: the sheer number of statutory and common law exceptions makes it legally complex.

SUMMARY: ESSENTIAL REQUIREMENTS OF A CONTRACT

- **Offer** has to be distinguished from an **invitation to treat**
- Offer must be communicated
- Terms of offer must be certain
- Offer can be withdrawn at any time before acceptance:
  - Offeror must communicate the withdrawal of the offer to the offeree:
  - Communication of withdrawal of an offer can be by a reliable third party
- An offer can be terminated by:
  - acceptance
  - rejection
  - revocation
  - death
  - counter-offer
  - lapse of time
  - failure of conditions
- Acceptance must be unconditional
- Acceptance must be communicated to offeror
- Offeree must be aware of the existence of the offer
- Communication of acceptance must be by an authorised person
- Acceptance can be in any form unless it is a requirement that it must be in a specific form
- Instant communication: acceptance is valid once received
- Postal rule: acceptance takes effect when the letter is posted
- Intention to create legal relations:
  - Social and domestic arrangements: there is a presumption that an intention to create legal relations **does not** exist, but can be rebutted if there is money involved
  - Commercial and business arrangements: there is a presumption that an intention to create legal relations **does** exist
- Both parties must give consideration if they wish to sue on a contract
- Consideration must be sufficient, but need not be adequate
- Consideration must move from the person to whom the promise is made
- Existing contractual duty does not constitute consideration
- Part-payment of a debt is not consideration
- Past consideration is not consideration
- Privity of contract: idea that only the parties to a contract have rights under it: *Tweddle v Atkinson* (1861), *BBC v HarperCollins* (2010)
- Contracts (Rights of Third Parties) Act 1999 enables third parties to enforce rights under a contract: *Nisshin Shipping v Cleaves* (2003)
- Other statutory exceptions are Married Women's Property Act 1982, Road Traffic Act 1988, Law of Property Act 1925
- **Common law exceptions**:
  - Collateral contracts: *Shanklin Pier v Detel Products Ltd* (1951)
  - Agency: *Scruttons Ltd v Midland Silicones* (1962)
  - Trusts: *Les Affreteurs Reunis v Leopold Walford* (1919)
- **Advantages**
  - Free will
  - Unjust
  - Restrictive
  - Indefinite liability
- **Disadvantages**
  - Extended litigation
  - Intention of the parties
  - Lots of exceptions

TEST YOURSELF

1. What is the difference between an offer and an invitation to treat?
2. Give three examples of invitations to treat.
3. Explain the ways in which an offer can be terminated.
4. If an offer was accepted via email, at what point would the acceptance be effective?
5. What is the significance of the case *Adams* v *Lindsell* (1818)?
6. When might the court find that there has been intention to create legal relations in a social agreement?
7. Outline the five rules of consideration.
8. What is meant by 'privity of contract'?
9. In what circumstances does the **Contracts (Rights of Third Parties) Act 1999** allow third parties to be able to enforce rights under a contract?
10. What are the advantages of privity of contract?

EXAM PAST PAPER QUESTIONS

WJEC – A Level – Unit 3 – June 2019

On Thursday Anna visited Olivia's make-up and beauty salon, The Beauty Zone, because she wanted to have eyelash extensions done for a 21st birthday party that she was attending on the following Saturday. When Olivia had finished, Anna was so delighted with her new eyelashes that she said she would give Olivia an extra £40 as a tip. When Anna looked in her purse she realised she did not have enough money with her to pay the tip she had promised, but said she would call in with it after the party on the Monday to give it to her. On Monday, Anna phoned Olivia to tell her that she no longer intended on giving her the tip of £40. Olivia, in reliance on Anna's promise, bought a new dress on the Saturday and is pressing Anna to pay the tip.

Advise Anna as to whether there was consideration, applying your knowledge of legal rules and principles. [50]

WJEC – A Level – Unit 4 – June 2019

Analyse and evaluate the importance of the doctrine of privity of contract. [50]

Eduqas – A Level – Component 3 – May 2022

The law surrounding offer and acceptance of a contract is out of date and in urgent need of reform. Discuss. [25]

Eduqas – AS Level – Component 2 – May 2022

(a) Explain the doctrine of promissory estoppel. [6]
(b) Explain the effect of a counter offer on a contract. [6]
(c) Assess the importance of distinguishing between an offer and an invitation to treat in the formation of a valid contract. [9]

Eduqas – AS Level – Component 2 – May 2019

(b) Explain the elements of a valid contract. [6]
(c) Assess the significance of the postal rule of acceptance to the formation of valid contracts. [9]

Read the scenario below and answer part (d).

Ann, Rebecca, her daughter, and Ann's paying lodger, Tim, regularly take part in playing and entering magazine competitions. Ann, Rebecca and Tim all contribute to the cost of entering the competitions, such as paying for postage; however, the entries were always made in Ann's name. One day Ann receives a letter stating that her competition entry has been successful; Ann tells Rebecca and Tim the good news but refuses to share the prize with Tim. Tim wishes to sue Ann for his share.

(d) Advise Tim as to whether there is an intention to create legal relations on these facts. [9]

Eduqas – A Level – Component 3 – May 2019

The rules for communication of offer and acceptance have developed with changes in society; however some areas of the law are still unclear. Discuss. [25]

24 Express and implied terms

The difference between representations and terms

The terms of a contract set out the obligations under a contract. Terms can be express or implied. Terms can also be classified according to their importance, as conditions, warranties and innominate terms.

Terms need to be distinguished from mere representations, which have no liability attached to them because they have just induced a party to enter into the contract. These are usually made orally before the contract has been made. Sometimes these representations can be terms, and whether they are a representation or a term depends on the intention of the parties.

However, if a representation has been false and has wrongly induced the other party to enter the contract, this is a misrepresentation and it will attach liability to the party making it.

Figure 24.1 The terms of a contract set out the obligations of both parties

> **KEY TERMINOLOGY**
>
> **term:** a statement made during contract negotiations that is intended to be a part of the contract, binding the parties to it.
>
> **express terms:** contract terms laid down by the parties themselves.
>
> **implied terms:** contract terms that are assumed, either by common law or statute.
>
> **representation:** a statement made during contract negotiations that is not intended to be a part of the contract.

Express terms

Whether a precontractual statement is a representation or a term will depend on the intention of the parties. Whatever the case, if the parties wish it to be part of the contract, it must be incorporated. This is straightforward if it is written into the contract but can prove more complicated if it is not. To combat this, the courts have developed some guidelines, as follows.

The importance of the statement

Bannerman v White (1861)

In a transaction for the purchase of hops, White asked whether the hops had been treated with sulphur. Bannerman said that the hops had not been treated, believing this to be the truth. However, it was discovered that sulphur had been used. White sued because he would not have entered into the contract if he had known beforehand that sulphur had been used.

The court agreed that the statement about the sulphur was incorporated into the contract because had it not been for that statement, White would not have entered into the contract.

Figure 24.2 The sale of hops demonstrated the importance of the statement in *Bannerman* v *White* (1861)

The knowledge and skill of the person making the statement

If the person making the statement has expert knowledge or skills, clearly the courts will be more willing to interpret it as a term rather than a representation.

Dick Bentley Productions Ltd v Harold Smith (Motors) Ltd (1965)

The claimant, Dick Bentley Productions, was looking for a 'well-vetted' Bentley car. The defendant, a car dealer, stated that he had one for sale that had recently had its gearbox and engine replaced, and since then had only done 20,000 miles.

After the car had been purchased, problems began to emerge and it also emerged that the car had in fact done 100,000 miles since the replacements. The court held that the statement was a term because the claimant relied on the expertise of the car dealer in good faith.

KEY TERMINOLOGY

held: decided; the decision of the court.

The timing of the statement

The more time that elapses between the statement being made and the contract being concluded, the less likely the courts will be to consider the statement a term.

Routledge v McKay (1954)

This case concerned the sale of a motorbike. Both parties were private individuals with no specialist knowledge. The seller believed the motorbike had been manufactured in 1942 but it turned out to have been manufactured in 1930. The claim that the date of manufacture was a term failed because the interval between the statement being made and the contract concluded suggested that the statement was not a term.

Agreements in writing

There is a presumption that any statement made before the contract which was then not incorporated into a written contract was a mere representation and not a term. If the parties intended it to be a term, it would have been included in the written documents.

24 Express and implied terms

> **KEY CASE**
>
> **Arnold v Britton (2015)**
> This case concerned leases for holiday chalets in a caravan park in Swansea, Wales. The term in question concerned the amount that needed to be paid for the service charge and maintenance of the caravan site.

Figure 24.3 To be considered a term, a statement should be made close to the conclusion of the contract, as in *Routledge v McKay* (1954)

> **STRETCH AND CHALLENGE**
>
> Research ***Duffy v Newcastle United Football Co Ltd* (2000)**, which concerned the opportunity for season ticket holders to buy their seats. Discuss the following questions:
>
> 1. Why was the promotional material not deemed to constitute terms?
> 2. Why did the fans argue that they should have been deemed terms?

Interpretation of express terms

When determining the meaning of an express term, judges often have to discover the parties' intentions. This has been the subject of some debate in the courts in recent years.

In its decision, the Supreme Court laid down some guidance on how terms should be interpreted, favouring a literal interpretation of contracts.

> Commercial common sense should not be used to undervalue the language of the contract.
> A court is more likely to move away from the natural meaning of the words if the drafting is bad.
> Just because a contract has worked out badly for one party, it does not justify departing from the wording of the contract.
> In construing a contract, the courts can only take into account facts and circumstances known to both sides at the time the contract was made.
> If an event occurs which the parties had not contemplated, but it is clear what their intention would have been had they done so, the court can give effect to that intention.

This is the most recent decision in relation to the interpretation of contracts and it seems that a **literal approach** is favoured over business sense.

Figure 24.4 *Arnold v Britton* (2015) is the key case for interpretation of express terms

263

> **KEY TERMINOLOGY**
>
> **literal approach:** the judge takes the literal and grammatical meaning of a word, even if this leads to absurdity.
>
> **purposive approach:** this allows the judge to look at the 'spirit of the law' and what Parliament intended when it passed the law. It is a more modern method of interpretation.

> **STRETCH AND CHALLENGE**
>
> Research some cases that have come before the court concerning the interpretation of terms. Discuss whether a literal or a more purposive approach was taken in each:
> - *Martinez* v *Ellesse International SpA* (1999)
> - *Pink Floyd Music Ltd* v *EMI Records* (2010)
> - *Investors Compensation Scheme Ltd* v *West Bromwich Building Society* (1998)

This approach contrasts with Lord Neuberger's comments in the slightly earlier case of *Marley* v *Rawlings* (2014), where a more purposive approach was favoured. Lord Neuberger stated that the court must identify the intention of the parties by identifying the meaning of the relevant words in light of:

1. the natural and ordinary meaning of those words
2. the overall purpose of the document
3. any other provisions in the document
4. the facts known or assumed by the parties at the time that the document was executed
5. common sense.

Implied terms

Terms implied by fact

An implied term is not laid down in the contract but is assumed by both parties to have been included had they thought about it. The leading case on this is the Supreme Court decision in *Marks and Spencer* v *BNP Paribas* (2015).

> **KEY CASE**
>
> **Marks and Spencer v BNP Paribas (2015)**
> This case concerned the refund of rent to Marks and Spencer after it terminated a lease for the property from the landlord, BNP Paribas. This refund was not expressly provided for in the contract but Marks and Spencer argued that it was an implied term. The Supreme Court ruled that Marks and Spencer was not entitled to the refund because the commercial contract was so detailed that the Supreme Court would respect the bargain struck and avoid interfering with the contract.

The Supreme Court judgment in *Marks and Spencer* v *BNP Paribas* (2015) clarified the law in relation to whether to imply a term into a contract. The Supreme Court suggested that the following guidelines should be used:

- A term can only be implied if, without the term, the contract would lack commercial or practical coherence.
- A term may also be implied if it is strictly necessary for business efficacy. The requirement for necessity is quite important, as this is a more stringent requirement than the previous approach, which required the proposed term to be 'reasonable and equitable'.
- A term should also satisfy the test of business necessity. It must be so obvious that it goes without saying. This is what was previously known as the 'officious bystander test'.

The business efficacy test and the officious bystander tests have been used in determining whether a term should be implied since *Equitable Life Assurance Society* v *Hyman* (2000), where it was held that the term also had to be:

- capable of clear expression
- compatible with any express terms of the contract.

The officious bystander

In *Shirlaw* v *Southern Foundries* (1926), the officious bystander test was clarified by MacKinnon LJ:

> 'That which, in any contract, is left to be implied need not be expressed in something as obvious that it goes without saying so that, if while the parties were making their bargain, an officious bystander were to suggest some express provision for it in the agreement, they would testily suppress him with a common "Oh, of course!".'

Business efficacy
This is a term which one side alleges must be implied to make the contract work.

> ### The Moorcock (1889)
> The Court of Appeal held that a contract to use the defendant's jetty to unload the claimant's boat contained an implied term that the boat would be moored safely at the jetty. It held that such a term would be necessary for business efficacy, otherwise the claimant 'would simply be buying an opportunity for danger'. The term had been breached because the boat was permitted to be moored when the water level was too low, and therefore the actions for damages for breach of contract were successful.

KEY TERMINOLOGY

damages: an award of money that aims to compensate the innocent party for the financial losses they have suffered as a result of the breach.

This was further clarified in Reigate v Union Manufacturing Co (1918) by Sutton LJ:

> 'A term can only be implied if it is necessary in the business sense to give efficacy to the contract: i.e. if it is such a term that it can confidently be said that if at the time the contract was being negotiated someone had said to the parties, "What will happen in such a case?", they would both have replied "Of course so and so will happen, we did not trouble to say that, it is too clear."'

This is still the law, despite attempts to unify it into one test of reasonableness in the case of Attorney General of Belize v Belize Telecom (2009).

Consumer Rights Act 2015: Implied terms

There are certain terms which the law says have to be included, regardless of whether the parties want them or intended to include them.

The law surrounding this used to be governed by the Sale of Goods Act 1979, the Unfair Terms in Consumer Contracts Regulations 1999 and the Supply of Goods and Services Act 1982. However, these Acts have now been repealed and the law is now contained in the Consumer Rights Act 2015.

The Consumer Rights Act 2015 protects consumers against unfair terms, prevents companies excluding liability for negligence and also implies that certain terms automatically go into consumer contracts.

Figure 24.5 All goods that are purchased from shops have to satisfy the terms of the Consumer Rights Act 2015

Supply of goods
This includes physical goods, as well as digital content such as downloads, software and pre-installed content.

Section 9: Satisfactory quality
This is the expectation that the goods will not be faulty or damaged, and this is judged by what a reasonable person would consider satisfactory. There is also the consideration that it includes 'all the other relevant circumstances'. This means any statement about the specific characteristics of the goods made by the trader in an advert or on a label, so the goods can be unsatisfactory if this was drawn to the consumer's attention before the contract was made.

Section 9(3) outlines the aspects that should be considered when judging satisfactory quality:

- Fitness for all the purposes for which goods of that kind are usually supplied
- Appearance and finish
- Freedom from minor defects
- Safety
- Durability

Section 10: Fit for purpose
This section provides that goods should be fit for the purpose they are supplied for as well as any specific purpose made known to the retailer.

This term does not apply if the consumer did not rely, or it is unreasonable for the consumer to rely, on the skill or judgement of the trader.

Section 11: As described
This means that the goods must match any description, models or samples shown at the time of purchase. This term obviously does not apply if any differences were brought to the attention of the consumer prior to purchase.

Bringing a claim
Sections 19–24 set out the remedies that apply if the statutory rights for goods contained in **ss9–11** are not met. A consumer must bring the claim against the retailer, not the manufacturer (see Table 24.1).

Table 24.1 The remedies available to the consumer at certain times

Time	Remedy
Date of purchase	**Section 20** gives the consumer a legal right to reject goods that are of unsatisfactory quality, unfit for purpose or not as described to get a full refund, but this is limited to within 30 days of purchase.
30 days	**Section 23** provides that the consumer has to give the retailer one opportunity to repair or replace any goods outside the 30 days. If the attempt to repair is unsuccessful, the consumer can claim a refund or a price reduction.
6 months	If a fault is discovered within six months of purchase, it is presumed to have been there since purchase, unless the retailer can prove otherwise. If the fault is discovered after six months, the burden is on the consumer to prove that the product was faulty at the time of delivery. The consumer then has six years to take a claim to the small claims court.

Under **s28**, the retailer is responsible for the goods until they are in the possession of the consumer. This means that the retailer is liable for the service provided by the courier it employs.

If a retailer fails to deliver the goods within 30 days, the consumer has the right to terminate the purchase and get a full refund, even if the timing of the delivery was not essential.

As well as those statutory remedies available under the **Consumer Rights Act 2015**, the consumer can still pursue other **common law** and **equitable** remedies as an alternative or in addition. These could include:

- damages
- specific performance
- a right to treat the contract as ended.

Supply of services
This includes services for dry cleaning, entertainment, work done by professionals (including solicitors, estate agents and accountants), building work, fitted kitchens, double glazing and home improvements.

KEY TERMINOLOGY

common law (also case law or precedent): law developed by judges through decisions in court.

equitable: fair.

24 Express and implied terms

Section 49: Reasonable care and skill
The legislation does not provide a definition of what 'reasonable care and skill' means. It is thought that whether a person has met the standard of reasonable care and skill will depend on whether they have met industry codes of practice or standards.

Section 50: Binding information
Any information that is given to the consumer before the service is provided and that is relied upon by the consumer is binding. This applies to information that is given both orally and in writing.

Section 51: Reasonable price
Where the price is not agreed beforehand, the service must be provided for a reasonable price. The explanatory notes to the legislation give an example:

'If a homeowner engages a plumber to fix an urgent leak, they may not take the time to discuss the price before fixing the problem. The price might not be in the contract if the plumber did not know the problem before they arrived to fix it. If the leak was fixed in ten minutes and with only a £50 replacement part, £1,000 is unlikely to be a reasonable price to pay.'

Section 52: Reasonable time
Unless a timescale has been agreed, the legislation states that the service must be carried out within a reasonable time frame after the contract has been agreed.

Figure 24.6 Supply of services under the Consumer Rights Act 2015 includes work provided by tradespeople on home improvements

Bringing a claim
If the service does not satisfy the criteria in **ss49–52**, statutory remedies are available.

- **Section 55**: the trader should either redo the element which is inadequate or perform the whole service again at no extra cost.
- **Section 56**: where repeat performance is not possible, the consumer can claim a price reduction. This could be up to 100 per cent of the cost and the trader should refund the consumer within 14 days of agreeing that a refund is due.

Consumer Rights Act 2015: Unfair terms

This legislation also provides guidance on consumer rights in relation to unfair terms contained in contracts. The protection offered by this statute is far greater than the protection offered by the **Unfair Contract Terms Act 1977**, which is discussed on page 271.

Section 62

This stipulates that an unfair term under the Act is not binding on the consumer.

A term is unfair if, contrary to the requirement of good faith, it causes a significant imbalance in the parties' rights and obligations under the contract to the detriment of the consumer.

Key terms of a contract should be assessed for fairness unless they are prominent and transparent, or if they are terms that relate to the main subject matter of a contract, or if the assessment is of the price payable under the contract. A term would be regarded as prominent and transparent if it is 'expressed in plain and intelligible language and (in the case of written terms) is legible'.

Schedule 2

This outlines the so called 'grey list' of terms which may be regarded as unfair. These can include but are not limited to:

- fees and charges hidden in the small print
- something that tries to limit the consumer's legal rights
- disproportionate default charges
- excessive early termination charges.

Consumer Contracts (Information, Cancellation and Additional Charges) Regulations 2013

These **Regulations** cover online shopping and bring into UK law the **Consumer Rights Directive** from the EU. It also supersedes the Distance Selling Regulations.

The **Regulations** require traders to give certain information before entering into a contract and covers all contracts entered into after 13 June 2014. They cover the sale of goods online, over the phone, from a catalogue or face to face somewhere that is not the business premises of the trader (e.g. the consumer's home), and aim to protect consumers from unfair practices.

A trader should provide the following key information:

1. A description of the goods, services or digital content, including how long any commitment will last on the part of the consumer.
2. The total price of the goods, service or digital content or how the price will be calculated.
3. How the consumer will pay for the goods or services and when they will be provided.
4. All additional delivery charges and other costs.
5. Details of who pays the cost of returning items if there is a right to cancel.
6. Details of any right to cancel. The trader also needs to provide, or make available, a standard cancellation form to make cancelling easy.
7. Information about the seller, including their geographical address and contact details and the address and identity of any other trader for whom the trader is acting.
8. Information on the compatibility of digital content with hardware and other software that the trader is aware of.

GRADE BOOST

The concept of good faith is similar to the test outlined in the previous law of **Consumer Contracts Regulations 1999**, so the case law that helped to identify unfair terms still stands as good law:

- *Aziz* v *Caixa d'Estalvis de Catalunya* (2013)
- *Interfoto Picture Library Ltd* v *Stiletto Visual Programmes Ltd* (1989)
- *Director General of Fair Trading* v *First National Bank* (2001)

If you are answering a problem question in this area, you will need to establish whether the contract is between a consumer and a business or between two businesses.

Cancelling goods

Cancellation rights under the **Regulations** are more generous than if goods or services were bought from a shop (see Table 14.2).

Table 24.2 Consumer rights when cancelling goods

Time	The consumer's rights
Date of purchase	The right to cancel starts the moment the consumer places their order and ends 14 days from the day the goods are received.
14 days	The consumer has a further 14 days to return the goods to the trader.
28 days	The trader has another further 14 days to give a refund from the date they receive the goods back or the consumer providing evidence of having returned the goods.

The exceptions to the rules on cancellations are for:

› CDs, DVDs or software if the seal has been broken on the wrapping
› perishable items
› tailor-made or personalised items.

Cancelling services

The consumer has 14 days to cancel, though they must pay for any service they have used up to the point of cancellation.

In relation to digital content, the consumer must acknowledge that once a download has started, they lose their right to cancel. Retailers must supply digital content within the 14-day cancellation period unless the consumer has given their consent for a longer period.

Exclusion clauses

An **exclusion clause** is when one party to the contract attempts to exclude all liability or to limit liability for breaches of the contract. The law has tried to control the use of these clauses, by common law and by statute, as they are unfair to the consumer.

Common law

Generally, the use of exclusion clauses is disapproved of, especially where they are made by a party with considerably stronger bargaining power than the other. To regulate exclusion clauses, the courts ask two questions:

1. Has the clause been incorporated into the contract? This can be done by signature, reasonable notice or through previous course of dealing.
2. Does the clause cover the alleged breach?

KEY TERMINOLOGY

exclusion clause: an attempt by one party to a contract to exclude all liability or to limit liability for breaches of the contract.

Figure 24.7 Incorporation by signature

269

Incorporation by signature

If the contract has been signed at the time of making the contract, it is assumed that the contents become terms of the contract, regardless of whether the parties have read the terms, so long as there is no evidence of fraud or misrepresentation.

L'Estrange v Graucob (1934)

This case concerned the rental of a vending machine. The claimant had signed the contract without reading it, not realising there was a clause within the contract that excluded liability for the product. The claimant had no form of redress when the machine became faulty as she was deemed to be bound by the contract by signing the contract.

Incorporation by reasonable notice

If a party gives separate written terms at the time the contract is made, those terms only become part of the contract if the consumer has had reasonable notice that they exist.

Parker v South Eastern Railway (1877)

A cloakroom ticket had details of the cloakroom opening hours and also the words 'See back'. On the back was a limitation clause, which claimed that the company was only liable for £10 for the loss of any property left with them. When the claimant tried to claim for his lost £24 bag, his action failed because he was deemed to have had reasonable notice of the limitation clause.

Figure 24.8 A ticket could contain a limitation clause

In deciding whether reasonable notice had been given, the courts will look at the time the notice was given. That is, it should be given at the same time the contract was made, or before.

Olley v Marlborough Court Ltd (1949)

The terms of the contract, including exclusion clauses, were on the back of a hotel door, which guests would not have seen until they got to their room, by which time the contract had already been completed. This was deemed to be too late to be classed as 'reasonable notice'.

The form in which the notice is given is also important. It should be the case that any notice of exclusion clauses is given in a document that the claimant would reasonably expect to contain contractual terms.

> ### Chapelton v Barry UDC (1940)
> Exclusion clauses were printed on the back of a ticket that was given in return for the purchase of a deckchair on a beach. This was deemed to be more like a receipt and therefore a reasonable person would not expect it to contain contractual terms.

In recent times, the courts have held that the more unusual or onerous a term, the greater the degree of notice is required to incorporate it.

> **STRETCH AND CHALLENGE**
> The concept of notice was discussed in the more recent case of *O'Brien v MGN (2001)*, which concerned a newspaper competition involving scratch cards. Research this case and discuss whether reasonable notice of the rules was given to consumers.

Incorporation by a previous course of dealing

If two parties have previously made contracts with each other, and those contracts contained an exclusion or limitation clause, then it is assumed that those same exclusion clauses apply to subsequent transactions, even if they had not been incorporated in the usual way.

Figure 24.9 Exclusion clauses from previous contracts can be assumed to apply

> ### Spurling v Bradshaw (1956)
> The parties had been doing business together for several years and on the occasion in question did not receive the documentation containing the exemption clauses until the contract had been concluded. The claimant lost his action on the basis that, although reasonable notice had not been given on this occasion, the parties had had enough dealings in the past to warrant the clause incorporated on this occasion.

If it is decided that an exemption or limited clause has been incorporated correctly, the courts will decide if the clause covers the breach. If the words of the clause are ambiguous then the courts will interpret them in a way which is least favourable to the party relying on them. This will help protect the consumer from deliberately vague and ambiguous language in contracts. This is known as the *contra proferentem* rule.

Unfair Contract Terms Act 1977

Statutory control for exclusion and limitation clauses lies in the **Unfair Contract Terms Act 1977** for non-consumer contracts only. There is protection for consumers in the **Consumer Rights Act 2015**, as outlined on page 268.

The purpose of the **Unfair Contract Terms Act 1977** is to provide an element of control over exclusion and limitation clauses, and applies only to liability arising in the course of a business and in relation to liability from one business to another. Its main provisions are as follows.

Section 2: Exclusion of liability for negligence

- **Section 2(1)**: a business cannot exclude or restrict liability for death or personal injury arising from negligence.
- **Section 2(2)**: a business can exclude or restrict liability for other types of loss if it is reasonable to do so. The test for reasonableness is laid down in **s11**.

Section 3: Exclusion of liability for breach of contract

Subject to the **s11** reasonableness test, a business cannot:

- exclude or restrict liability for breach of contract
- provide substantially different performance to that reasonably expected
- provide no performance at all.

Section 6: Exclusion of liability in contracts for sale of goods

Clauses that are implied by statute, such as those in the **Consumer Rights Act 2015**, cannot be excluded.

Section 11: Reasonableness test

The court should ask itself whether the term in question is a:

> 'fair and reasonable one to be included having regard to the circumstances which were, or ought reasonably to have been, known to or in the contemplation of the parties when the contract was made'.

Schedule 2

Factors to take into consideration when applying the reasonableness test are as follows:

1. The strength of the bargaining positions of the parties, taking into account alternative suppliers available to the purchaser.
2. Whether the customer received an inducement to accept the term, for example, whether they were given the opportunity to pay a higher price without the exclusion clause.
3. Whether the customer knew or ought to have known of the term and whether such terms are in general use in a particular trade.
4. Where exclusion relates to non-performance of a condition, whether it was reasonably practicable to comply with the condition.
5. Whether the goods were made or adapted to the special order of the customer. One of the first cases to be brought before the courts under the **Unfair Contract Terms Act 1977** was *George Mitchell (Chesterhall) Ltd* v *Finney Lock Seeds Ltd* (1983).

George Mitchell (Chesterhall) Ltd v *Finney Lock Seeds Ltd* (1983)

The claimant was a farmer who purchased 30 lb cabbage seeds from the defendants for £192. The claimant planted the cabbage seeds over 63 acres and invested a lot of time on the crops. The seeds only produced a small green leaf not fit for human consumption. The contract contained a clause which limited liability to the price of the seeds. The claimant had lost £60,000 plus interest on the defective seeds.

The Court of Appeal held that the clause was unreasonable as the buyer would not have been aware of the fault whereas the seller would have been.

Importance of terms

When a term of a contract has been breached, it is important to distinguish what type of term has been breached. Contractual terms can either be conditions, warranties or innominate terms.

Conditions

A condition is a term of a contract which is so important to the contract that a failure to perform the condition would render the contract meaningless. If a condition has been breached, the claimant is entitled to the fullest range of remedies: damages or repudiation or both.

Any term implied by statute is also regarded as a condition, in terms of the effect of its breach.

Figure 24.10 Identifying what is a condition, warranty or innominate term is important when a contract is breached

> **KEY CASES**
>
> The key cases for conditions in a contract are:
> *Poussard* v *Spiers and Pond* (1876) An opera singer who missed an opening night was in breach of a condition.
> *The Mihalis Angelos* (1970) A ship that was not ready to load was in breach of a condition despite the fact that it had caused no loss to the defendant.
> *Bunge Corp* v *Tradax Export SA* (1981) Breaching a notice period for the loading of goods on a lorry was a breach of a condition as there is a special need for certainty in commercial contracts.

Warranties

A warranty is a term of a contract which is minor. If a warranty has been breached, the injured party can sue for damages but not repudiation (rejection of the contract). Warranties are regarded as obligations that are secondary to the major purpose of the contract.

> **KEY CASE**
>
> The key case for warranties is *Bettini* v *Gye* (1876), where an opera singer who missed rehearsals was not in breach as this did not go to the root of the contract.

Innominate terms

An innominate term is a term of a contract which cannot be identified as either warranty or condition, and so is identified as innominate until the contract has been breached. The idea is that a contract will only be repudiated (rejected) in the event of a breach if it is fair to both sides.

It is uncertain what the remedy will be until the extent of the breach has been considered and the judge declares the appropriate remedy.

KEY TERMINOLOGY

remedy: an award made by a court to the innocent party in a civil case to 'right the wrong'.

> **KEY CASES**
>
> The key cases for innominate terms are:
> *Hong Kong Fir Shipping Co Ltd* v *Kawasaki Ltd* (1962) The court looked at the effect of the breach before classifying the term as either a warranty or condition. The question asked was: 'Has the breach substantially deprived the innocent party of the whole benefit of the contract?'
> *Schuler AG* v *Wickman Machine Tool Sales Ltd* (1973) The court in this case held that the term concerning the amount of visits a salesperson should make was a warranty and not a condition.

SUMMARY: EXPRESS AND IMPLIED TERMS

Express terms
➔ Incorporated by:
- being written into the contract, or
- making a statement prior to the contract's conclusion

➔ Guidelines:
- How much importance is placed on the statement
- Knowledge and skill of the person making the statement
- Timing of the statement

Implied terms: By fact
➔ Leading case: *Marks and Spencer* v *BNP Paribas* (2015)
➔ The term:
- is implied if, without it, the contract would lack commercial or practical coherence
- must be necessary for business efficacy: *The Moorcock* (1889)
- must satisfy the officious bystander test: *Shirlaw* v *Southern Foundries* (1926)

Implied terms: By law
➔ Consumer Rights Act 2015: Sale of goods
- Section 9: satisfactory quality
- Section 10: fit for purpose
- Section 11: as described

➔ Consumer Rights Act 2015: supply of services
- Section 49: reasonable care and skill
- Section 50: binding information
- Section 51: reasonable price
- Section 52: reasonable time

Unfair terms: By law
➔ Consumer Rights Act 2015: unfair terms
- Section 62: any term that is unfair under the Act is not binding

➔ Consumer Contracts (Information, Cancellation and Additional Charges) Regulations 2013
- Outlines key information that should be provided to consumers entering into contracts online, over the phone or from a catalogue
- The consumer has the right to cancel within 14 days after ordering

Exclusion clauses: Common law
➔ Exclusion clauses must be incorporated:
- by signature
- by reasonable notice
- by a previous course of dealing

➔ The exclusion clause has to cover the breach:
- *contra proferentem* rule

Exclusion clauses: Statute
➔ Unfair Contract Terms Act 1977 applies only to non-consumer contracts
- Section 2: exclusion of liability for negligence
- Section 3: exclusion of liability for breach of contract
- Section 6: exclusion of liability in contracts for sale of goods
- Section 11: reasonableness test

TEST YOURSELF

1. Explain the difference between representations and terms.
2. Outline the three ways in which an express term can be incorporated into a contract.
3. Why is the literal interpretation the preferred method of interpretation for contracts?
4. What is the significance of *Marks and Spencer* v *BNP Paribas* (2015)?
5. What redress is available for consumers who are bringing a claim for defective goods under the Consumer Rights Act 2015?
6. What redress is available for consumers who are bringing a claim for unsatisfactory services provided under the Consumer Rights Act 2015?
7. Outline three key pieces of information that must be provided to a consumer under the Consumer Contracts (Information, Cancellation and Additional Charges) Regulations 2013.
8. Under the Consumer Contracts (Information, Cancellation and Additional Charges) Regulations 2013, what rights does a consumer have to cancel their purchase after 14 days?
9. Outline the three ways in which an exclusion clause can be incorporated into a contract.
10. What is the purpose of the Unfair Contract Terms Act 1977?
11. Explain what is meant by a warranty.

EXAM PAST PAPER QUESTIONS

WJEC – Unit 3 – June 2022

Fiona bought a new pond filter system from Pond Life Ltd who assured her that it would be perfect for improving the quality of the water in her garden fish pond. Fiona arranged for Jack to install the filter system. Jack missed two appointments, for which Fiona had taken time off work. When he finally turned up for the third appointment, Jack damaged the mosaic garden tiles around the pond when he dropped his tools whilst installing the filter system. Though Jack properly installed the filter system, it was of poor quality and failed to improve the water quality of the pond leading to several fish dying. Pond Life Ltd refused to accept any responsibility. Jack also pointed out that Fiona had signed a "completion of work" form, which included a statement that he would not be liable for any damage resulting from the installation work.

Advise Fiona whether there has been a breach of any implied or express terms for the purchase and installation of the filter system, applying your knowledge of legal rules and principles. [50]

Eduqas – A Level – Component 3 – June 2022

Analyse and evaluate the regulation of exclusion clauses. [25]

Eduqas – A Level – Component 2 – June 2019

Daniel, a talented amateur photographer who was sometimes paid to take photographs, took a very expensive camera to be repaired by Emma, who often repaired Daniel's cameras for him. As Daniel was leaving Emma's shop, Emma handed him a piece of paper which had a repair number on it to identify Daniel's camera and which also contained the following clause: "Liability for any breach of contract is limited to £50 and, in any event, there is no liability for any breach not reported within 24 hours of the camera's collection."

As a result of Emma's negligent work when repairing the camera, the camera was ruined. Daniel did not discover this until a few days later when he went to use the camera. When he took it back to Emma, she refused to pay for the camera, claiming that she was protected by her contract with him.

Advise Daniel whether Emma can refuse to pay him for the camera, applying your knowledge and understanding of legal rules and principles. [25]

Eduqas – AS level – Component 2 – June 2018

The Bear Hotel was preparing for a very large party on Saturday. On Monday, they sent an email to Bubbles & Fizz asking for a written quote for the price of a large quantity of champagne. Bubbles & Fizz emailed back that they would send a letter as the Bear Hotel had requested. Bubbles & Fizz's letter arrived on Tuesday. In the letter, Bubbles & Fizz offered to supply the champagne for a price of £5,000 and asked the Bear Hotel to reply by letter to accept their offer. The Bear Hotel immediately replied by email, "We will pay £4,500." Bubbles & Fizz then telephoned to state that the price was not negotiable, but that they could still supply the champagne for £5,000, and also to ask on what day delivery was required. The Bear Hotel replied "Friday" and Bubbles & Fizz asked the Bear Hotel to send a letter confirming acceptance. The Bear Hotel sent a letter, posted on Tuesday night, which arrived at Bubble & Fizz on Thursday. On Wednesday, Bubble & Fizz sent an email stating that they could not now supply the champagne on Friday. The Bear Hotel had to find another supplier for the champagne on Thursday. However, the price was then £7,000 because the order was at such short notice.

Advise the Bear Hotel as to whether they are entitled to claim against Bubbles & Fizz. [9]

25 Misrepresentation and economic duress

What is a misrepresentation?

A misrepresentation is an untrue or false statement of law or fact made by one party, which induces the other party to enter into an agreement or contract.

If a representation is falsely made, it can be a misrepresentation and can cause the contract to be voidable.

Legal definition

A misrepresentation is:

> a statement of material fact (*Bisset* v *Wilkinson* (1927), *Edgington* v *Fitzmaurice* (1885))
> made by one party to a contract to the other party (*Peyman* v *Lanjani* (1985)) to the contract
> during the negotiations leading up to the formation of the contract (*Roscorla* v *Thomas* (1842))
> which was intended to operate and did operate as an inducement (*JEB Fasteners Ltd* v *Marks Bloom & Co Ltd* (1983), *Attwood* v *Small* (1838)) to the other party to enter the contract
> but which was not intended to be a binding obligation (*Couchman* v *Hill* (1947)) under the contract, and which was untrue or incorrectly stated.

> **STRETCH AND CHALLENGE**
>
> Research the following cases and discuss their influence on representation.
> - *Bisset* v *Wilkinson* (1927), *Edgington* v *Fitzmaurice* (1885)
> - *Peyman* v *Lanjani* (1985)
> - *Roscorla* v *Thomas* (1842)
> - *JEB Fasteners Ltd* v *Marks Bloom & Co Ltd* (1983), *Attwood* v *Small* (1838)
> - *Couchman* v *Hill* (1947)

Fraudulent misrepresentation

Where fraudulent misrepresentation is alleged, fraud must also be proved. *Derry* v *Peak* (1889) showed that if a person makes a false statement which they do not believe to be true at the time, this is a fraudulent misrepresentation. However, this case has now been overturned by statute, as codified in the Companies Act 2006. See also the case of *Thomas Witter Ltd* v *TBP Industries Ltd* (1996).

> **KEY CASE**
>
> **Thomas Witter Ltd v TBP Industries Ltd (1996)**
> The defendants owned a business which the claimant wished to buy. During the negotiations the defendants gave the claimant the accounts of the business and also estimated future profits. However, the defendants did not indicate that some accounts had been prepared on a different basis from other accounts.
>
> Within six months the claimant claimed that they had been lured into buying the business by the representations made in the management accounts. The court held that these misrepresentations were not made fraudulently. There was no evidence of dishonesty since they believed that the statements in the accounts were true, although the misrepresentations were made negligently.

25 Misrepresentation and economic duress

If fraudulent misrepresentation is found the damages will be awarded according to the tort of deceit and are also available under s2(1) Misrepresentation Act 1967. The equitable remedy of rescission is also available (that is, to void the contract as if it had never happened).

The defendant is responsible for all losses, including any consequential loss, providing a causal link between the fraudulent misrepresentation and the claimant's loss.

Negligent misrepresentation

There are three requirements:

1. The party making the statement must be in possession of the particular type of knowledge for which the advice is required.
2. There must be sufficient proximity between the two parties that it is reasonable to rely on the statement.
3. The party to whom the statement is made relies on the statement and the party making the statement is aware of that reliance.

Damages will be applied according to the standard tort measure of negligence or under s2(1) Misrepresentation Act 1967. The equitable remedy of rescission is also available.

KEY CASE

Hedley Byrne v Heller & Partners (1964)
An advertising agency checked a prospective client's creditworthiness with its bank. The bank sent a letter apparently stating that the client would be safe to work with, so the agency sued the bank when it lost money after the client went into liquidation. The court held that damages may be recovered for a negligent misrepresentation where advice has been sought, a financial loss has been incurred and where there is a special relationship between the parties.

KEY TERMINOLOGY

rescission: to unmake a contract or transaction, to return the parties to the position they would be in if it had never happened.

STRETCH AND CHALLENGE

Read Lord Denning's judgment in *Esso Petroleum Co Ltd v Mardon* (1976). Do you agree with his judgment?

Figure 25.1 In the Esso case there was no action for misrepresentation as the statement was an estimate of future sales rather than a statement of fact

Innocent misrepresentation

Any misrepresentation not made fraudulently was historically classed as an innocent misrepresentation, regardless of how it was made.

Since the emergence of the Hedley Byrne principle and the passing of the **Misrepresentation Act 1967**, the only misrepresentations that can be claimed to be made innocently are those where a party makes a statement with an honest belief in its truth, for example, where the party merely repeats inaccurate information, the truth of which they are unaware.

The main remedy for innocent misrepresentation is the equitable remedy of rescission. Damages are also available under **s2(1) Misrepresentation Act 1967**.

Misrepresentation under statute

Section 2(1) Misrepresentation Act 1967

This states:

> 'Where a person has entered into a contract after a misrepresentation has been made to him by another party thereto and as a result thereof he has suffered loss, then if the person making the misrepresentation would be liable to damages in respect thereof had the misrepresentation been made fraudulently, that person shall be so liable notwithstanding that the misrepresentation was not made fraudulently unless he proves that he had reasonable grounds to believe and did believe up to the time the contract was made that the facts represented were true.'

In other words, a party who has been a victim of a misrepresentation has an action available without having to prove either fraud or the existence of a special relationship under the Hedley Byrne criteria. The burden of proof is reversed, so that the person making the statement has to prove that they were not negligent.

GRADE BOOST

Research these key cases for misrepresentation and find out the facts and judgments in both. How were the cases eventually resolved?

- *Howard Marine and Dredging Co Ltd* v *A Ogden and Sons (Evacuations) Ltd* (1978)
- *Spice Girls Ltd* v *Aprilia World Service* (2002)

STRETCH AND CHALLENGE

Consider what type of misrepresentation is involved in the following examples:
- Mo is selling his motorcycle to Anisha. Anisha asks what capacity the engine is. Mo, after looking at the registration documents, tells her that it is a 600cc. Unknown to Mo, the documents are incorrect.
- Sundus, a salesperson, tells Bryn that a carpet can be cleaned with bleach, without checking the manufacturer's specification, which would have revealed that it cannot.
- Harry, who has no qualifications at all, tells prospective employers at an interview that he has a degree in marketing.
- Michelle recently purchased 'beefburgers' from her local supermarket, only to later discover in the newspaper that that brand actually contained horsemeat.

Section 2(2) Misrepresentation Act 1967

Under **s2(2) Misrepresentation Act 1967**, the judge has the discretion to decide which remedy to apply. Rescission will therefore not be available if the judge has decided that damages are a more appropriate remedy.

EXAM SKILLS

Ensure you are able to analyse and evaluate misrepresentation and economic duress, but also be able to apply the legal rules and principles of misrepresentation and economic duress to given scenarios.

25 Misrepresentation and economic duress

Economic duress

A contract may be set aside because extreme coercion has rendered it commercially unviable (economic duress). Five conditions need to be satisfied for there to be a finding of duress:

1. Pressure was exerted on the contracting party: *North Ocean Shipping Co* v *Hyundai Construction Co [The Atlantic Baron]* (1979).
2. Pressure was illegitimate: *Atlas Express Ltd* v *Kafco (Importers and Distributors) Ltd* (1989).
3. The pressure induced the claimant to enter the contract: *Barton* v *Armstrong* (1975).
4. The claimant had no choice but to enter the contract: *Universe Tankships* v *International Transport Workers' Federation* (1983).
5. The claimant protested at the time or shortly after the contract was made: *North Ocean Shipping Co* v *Hyundai Construction Co [The Atlantic Baron]* (1979).

Figure 25.2 Key cases for misrepresentation: *Howard Marine* (1978) and *Spice Girls Ltd* (2002)

SUMMARY: MISREPRESENTATION AND ECONOMIC DURESS

Misrepresentation
→ Definitions:
- a false statement in a contract that can cause the contract to be voidable
- a statement of material fact made by one party to a contract to the other party during the negotiations of the contract which was intended to operate and did operate as an inducement to the other party to enter the contract, but which was not intended to be a binding obligation under the contract, and which was untrue or incorrectly stated

Fraudulent misrepresentation
→ Fraud must be proved: *Derry* v *Peak* (1889) but overturned by **Companies Act 2006**
→ Remedies:
- Damages according to tort measure of deceit
- Damages under **s2(1) Misrepresentation Act 1967**
- Equitable remedy of rescission

Negligent misrepresentation
→ Hedley Byrne principle: *Hedley Byrne* v *Heller & Partners* (1964)
→ Three requirements:
  1. Knowledge
  2. Proximity
  3. Reliance
→ Remedies:
- Damages according to tort measure of negligence
- Damages under **s2(1) Misrepresentation Act 1967**
- Equitable remedy of rescission

STRETCH AND CHALLENGE

Discuss the benefits of bringing a case of misrepresentation under statute as opposed to the common law. Conclude with an evaluation of the law on misrepresentation and whether it provides consumers with an adequate remedy.

EXAM SKILLS

An exam question on misrepresentation/economic duress may require you to explain an aspect of the topic for AO1 and/or apply an aspect of the topic, for example to a hypothetical scenario for AO2, and/or evaluate an aspect of the topic for AO3.

279

Innocent misrepresentation
→ **Misrepresentation Act 1967**: only claims where a party believes their untrue statement to be true
→ Remedies:
- Equitable remedy of rescission
- Damages under **s2(1) Misrepresentation Act 1967**

Misrepresentation under statute
→ **Section 2(1) Misrepresentation Act 1967**
→ No need to prove fraud or special relationship under the Hedley Byrne criteria
→ Person making statement must prove they were not negligent
→ *Howard Marine and Dredging Co Ltd* v *A Ogden and Sons (Evacuations) Ltd* (1978) and *Spice Girls Ltd* v *Aprilla World Service* (2002)
→ Section 2(2) Misrepresentation Act 1967: judge decides remedy

Economic duress
→ Extreme coercion renders contract commercially unviable (economic duress)
→ Five conditions:
1. Pressure on contracting party: *North Ocean Shipping Co* v *Hyundai Construction Co [The Atlantic Baron]* (1979)
2. Illegitimate pressure: *Atlas Express Ltd* v *Kafco (Importers and Distributors) Ltd* (1989)
3. Pressure induced claimant to enter contract: *Barton* v *Armstrong* (1975)
4. Claimant had to enter contract: *Universe Tankships* v *International Transport Workers' Federation* (1983)
5. Claimant protested quickly: *North Ocean Shipping Co [The Atlantic Baron]* v *Hyundai Construction Co* (1979)

TEST YOURSELF

1. What is meant by misrepresentation?
2. What are the different types of misrepresentation?
3. Name a case that illustrates negligent misrepresentation.
4. Name a case that illustrates fraudulent misrepresentation.
5. What remedies are available for misrepresentation?
6. What is meant by economic duress?
7. What conditions must be satisfied for a finding of economic duress?
8. Discuss two problems with the law on misrepresentation.

EXAM PAST PAPER QUESTIONS

WJEC – A Level – Unit 4 – 2019
Analyse and evaluate how well the law on economic duress protects a party from unfair pressure from another party. [50]

WJEC – A Level – Unit 4 – 2022
Analyse and evaluate the extent to which the Misrepresentation Act 1967 protects buyers against negligent statements made by sellers. [50]

Eduqas – A Level – Component 2 – 2019
Ben had wanted to buy a caravan. He went to see the stock of second-hand caravans at 'Colin's Caravans'. Ben liked the look of a blue 'Sunshine Traveller' caravan. However, Ben was very anxious not to purchase a caravan which had ever been involved in an accident. He made that clear to Colin, who told him that, in his opinion the caravan in which Ben was interested had never been in an accident. Ben purchased the caravan and had it redecorated inside with leopard print wallpaper, to suit his personal taste. He then discovered that the caravan had once been involved in a serious accident. Ben paid £15,000 for the caravan. As it had been involved in a serious accident, it was only worth £7,000.

Advise Ben whether he can take action for misrepresentation and the remedies available to him, applying your knowledge and understanding of legal rules and principles. [25]

26 Discharge of a contract

The most obvious way a contract is discharged is when all parties have performed their obligations, but there are other ways for a contract to be discharged.

DISCHARGE OF CONTRACT			
AGREEMENT	BREACH	PERFORMANCE	FRUSTRATION

Figure 26.1 The different ways of discharging a contract

Discharge by agreement

This is where the parties agree to terminate a contract, so that one or both parties are released from their obligations. There are two types of discharge by agreement.

Bilateral discharge
The assumption is that both parties are to gain a fresh but different benefit from a new agreement.

Unilateral discharge
The benefit is only to be gained by one party, who is therefore trying to convince the other party to let them off the obligations arising under the original agreement.

Discharge by breach

This is where a party fails to perform an obligation, performs an obligation defectively or indicates in advance that they will not be performing an agreed obligation under a contract. There are two types of discharge by breach.

Actual breach
This is where a party to a contract does not perform their obligations under the contract at all.

Anticipatory breach
This is where a party to a contract indicates in advance that they will not be performing their obligations as agreed.

Discharge by performance

This is where all obligations under the contract have been met, and the obligations should match the requirements of the contract exactly. *Cutter* v *Powell* (1795) found that if a contract requires entire performance and a party fails to perform the contract in its entirety, they are entitled to nothing from the other party under the contract.

There are ways in which this rule can be limited.

Substantial performance
If a party has done substantially what was required under the contract, then the doctrine of substantial performance can apply. The party can recover the amount appropriate to what has been done under the contract.

> **STRETCH AND CHALLENGE**
>
> Research these key cases relating to actual breach:
> - *Platform Funding Ltd* v *Bank of Scotland plc* (2008)
> - *Pilbrow* v *Pearless de Rougemont & Company* (1999)
> - *Modahl* v *British Athletic Federation Ltd* (1999)
> - *Abramova* v *Oxford Institute of Legal Practice* (2011)

> **STRETCH AND CHALLENGE**
>
> Research these key cases relating to anticipatory breach:
> - *Frost* v *Knight* (1872)
> - *Avery* v *Bowden* (1855)
> - *Fercometal Sarl* v *Mediterranean Shipping Company* (1989)
> - *White and Carter Ltd* v *McGregor* (1962)

281

> **STRETCH AND CHALLENGE**
>
> Research these key cases relating to substantial performance:
> - *Dakin & Company* v *Lee* (1916)
> - *Hoeing* v *Isaacs* (1952)
> - *Bolton* v *Mahadeva* (1972)

> **STRETCH AND CHALLENGE**
>
> Research the key case *Sumpter* v *Hedges* (1898) in relation to acceptance of part performance.

> **STRETCH AND CHALLENGE**
>
> Research these key cases relating to prevention of performance:
> - *Planche* v *Colburn* (1831)
> - *Startup* v *Macdonald* (1843)

Severable contracts

A contract is severable when payment becomes due at various stages of performance, rather than in one lump sum at the end when the performance is completed; for example, when major building work is taking place. In these cases, the price for each stage can be claimed when that stage is completed.

Acceptance of part performance

Where one of the parties has performed the contract but not completely, if the other side has shown a willingness to accept the part performed, then the strict rule in *Cutter* v *Powell* (1795) will not apply. An example could be when a service has not been fully carried out or where only half a delivery has been made.

Prevention of performance

If the other party prevents a party from carrying out their obligations because of some act or omission, then the rule in *Cutter* v *Powell* (1795) cannot apply.

Discharge by frustration

This is where something happens, through no fault of the parties, to make the performance of the contract impossible. The contract is said to be frustrated.

> *Taylor* v *Caldwell* (1863)
>
> An action failed because performance of the contract had become impossible when a building where a concert was due to take place burnt down.

Frustration usually occurs in three main types of circumstance.

Impossibility

Performance has become impossible. This might be because of the destruction of something essential for the contract's performance, the death of either party, the unavailability of the parts or because the method of performance becomes impossible.

Illegality

This is where a change in the law after the contract is formed has made its performance illegal. This can often happen in times of war when laws may change without notice.

Commercial sterility

This is where the commercial purpose of the contract has disappeared as a result of the intervening event. This is also sometimes known as 'pointless'.

The Law Reform (Frustrated Contracts) Act 1943 outlines the legal consequences when a contract has been frustrated. Section 1(2) stipulates that:

> 'all sums paid or payable to any party in pursuance of the contract before the time when the parties were so discharged shall, in the case of sums so to be paid, be recoverable from him as money received by him ceases to be payable'.

This means that a person can recover money paid under a contract prior to the frustrating event. **Section 1(3)** stipulates that:

'where any party to the contract has obtained a valuable benefit, other than a payment of money before the time of discharge, this shall be recoverable from him by the said other party a sum not exceeding the value of the said benefit'.

This means that where a party has obtained a valuable benefit other than money, the party receiving the benefit can be ordered to pay a just sum in return for the benefit.

SUMMARY: DISCHARGE OF A CONTRACT

→ **Discharge by agreement:** parties agree to terminate a contract
  - **Bilateral discharge:** parties get a different benefit from a new agreement
  - **Unilateral discharge:** benefit is only to be gained by one party
→ **Discharge by breach:** a party fails to perform an obligation or does it defectively
  - **Actual breach:** a party does not perform their obligations at all: *Platform Funding Ltd v Bank of Scotland plc* (2008), *Pilbrow v Pearless de Rougemont & Company* (1999), *Modahl v British Athletic Federation Ltd* (1999), *Abramova v Oxford Institute of Legal Practice* (2011)
  - **Anticipatory breach:** a party indicates in advance that they will not be performing their obligations: *Frost v Knight* (1872), *Avery v Bowden* (1855), *Fercometal Sarl v Mediterranean Shipping Company* (1989), *White and Carter Ltd v McGregor* (1962)
→ **Discharge by performance:** all obligations under the contract have been met: *Cutter v Powell* (1795)
→ **Substantial performance:** if a party has done substantially what was required under the contract: *Dakin & Company v Lee* (1916), *Hoeing v Isaacs* (1952), *Bolton v Mahadeva* (1972)
→ **Severable contracts:** payment due at various stages of performance
→ **Acceptance of part performance:** one of the parties has performed the contract but not completely but the other party will accept this: *Sumpter v Hedges* (1898)
→ **Prevention of performance:** one party prevents the other from carrying out their obligations: *Planche v Colburn* (1831), *Startup v Macdonald* (1843)
→ **Discharge by frustration:** performance of the contract becomes impossible: *Taylor v Caldwell* (1863)
→ Three reasons for frustration:
  - Impossibility
  - Illegality
  - Commercial sterility
→ **Law Reform (Frustrated Contracts) Act 1943** outlines the legal consequences when a contract has been frustrated

STRETCH AND CHALLENGE

Research these key cases relating to discharge by frustration:
- *Robinson v Davidson* (1871)
- *Nickoll and Knight v Ashton Edridge & Company* (1901)
- *Pioneer Shipping Ltd v BTP Tioxide Ltd* (1981)
- *Metropolitan Water Board v Dick Kerr & Company Ltd* (1918)
- *Krell v Henry* (1903)
- *Herne Bay Steamboat Company v Hutton* (1903)

EXAM SKILLS

Highlight the scenario before you start writing so that you can establish which type of discharge may be relevant. When applying the law, focus on the type of discharge that applies in the scenario, but don't be afraid to explain why the others do not apply.

TEST YOURSELF

1. What are the two types of discharge by agreement?
2. Explain the significance of the case of *Cutter v Powell* (1795).
3. Explain how a contract can be discharged where one of the parties substantially performs what was required under the contract.
4. What does it mean for a contract to be discharged by frustration?
5. What is meant by 'commercial sterility'?
6. Explain the two types of discharge by breach.
7. When does part performance of obligations under a contract discharge the contract?
8. Summarise the provisions under the **Law Reform (Frustrated Contracts) Act 1943**.
9. What is the significance of the case of *Startup v Macdonald* (1843)?
10. Name the four ways in which a contract can be discharged.

EXAM PAST PAPER QUESTIONS

WJEC – Unit 3 – June 2022

Active Athletics stadium in Newport was to host the annual race event on 10th, 11th and 12th October 2019. As the event would attract more crowds than usual, Active Athletics contracted with Builders R Us for them to build a bigger car park close to the stadium. As part of the contract, Builders R Us were required to re-lay and widen the existing car park. The new car park was to be completed by 7th October 2019. A deposit of £40,000 was payable by Active Athletics before the 7th September 2019 and the balance of £80,000 was payable on the 7th October 2019. Mr King, a local resident, decided to make some money out of the forthcoming event, and knowing that visitors to the event would be looking for accommodation, he let out his house in Newport for £2,000 for the 3 days of the event to Mrs Mann. Mrs Mann paid a deposit of £800 on entering into the contract with Mr King and the balance was due on 10th October 2019. During the first week of October 2019 Newport experienced exceptionally heavy rain. The stadium, which was next to the local river, was flooded so the athletics event had to be cancelled. The event could not be rescheduled. The area is no longer suitable for any development. Builders R Us are claiming the balance of the money they say is due. They say that their labour costs for the new car park amount to £50,000 and they wish to recover this from Active Athletics. Mrs Mann has also informed Mr King that as the event has been cancelled she no longer wants to stay at his house in Newport.

Advise Active Athletics as to their liability to Builders R Us and also advise Mr King who is seeking to recover the balance of £1,200 from Mrs Mann. [50]

Eduqas – AS Level Component 2 – May 2022

Read the scenario below and answer part (d).

> Naomi has spent many months organising the wedding of her daughter, Bridget, to Jim, in May 2020. 'The Willows' in Mansfield has been booked for the reception. However, following a serious argument, Bridget and Jim decide not to get married. Naomi contacts 'The Willows' and informs them of her need to cancel the booking.

(d) Advise Naomi as to how she might discharge the contract. [9]

Eduqas – A Level Component 2 – June 2022

Sunrise Holidays agreed to rent Rose Cottage, a seaside holiday home in Cornwall, which it owns, to David and Kate and their two children, for the two weeks of their summer holiday in July. David and Kate paid the price of the holiday in full. There was very wet weather just before the holiday, as a result of which there was a substantial leak of water through the cottage roof. This made Rose Cottage uninhabitable until it dried out and repairs were carried out. These would not be completed until after the period for which David and Kate had rented the cottage. David and Kate believed that the cottage had not been properly maintained and this was the cause of the damage. As a result of the flooding, Sunrise Holidays telephoned and cancelled David and Kate's holiday at Rose Cottage, claiming that the contract had been frustrated. David and Kate had already travelled to Cornwall. They then booked an alternative cottage from Cosy Cottages, but as they were booking late there was limited choice and they had to pay an additional £300. In addition, Kate and the children complained that they were too far from the sea and could not enjoy the water sports had they stayed in Rose Cottage.

Advise David and Kate of the rights and remedies against Sunrise Holidays, applying your knowledge and understanding of legal rules and principles. [25]

Eduqas – A Level – Component 3 – June 2019

Analyse and evaluate whether the law on discharge of contracts should be reformed. [25]

27 Remedies

A remedy is a 'solution' in a civil case; it is an award made by a court to the innocent party. Two types of remedy need to be considered:

1. Common law remedy of damages
2. Equitable remedies.

Common law remedy of damages

The common law remedy of damages is available 'as of right' if it is established that a contract is breached. Damages in contract law are an award of money to financially compensate the injured party. The purpose of damages in contract law is to put the victim, so far as it is possible and so far as the law allows, in the same position they would have been in had the contract not been broken but had been performed in the manner and at the time intended by the parties.

When a contract is breached, a party may suffer pecuniary (financial) loss or non-pecuniary loss.

Pecuniary losses
These are the financial losses that result from a breach of contract.

Non-pecuniary losses
These are other losses, such as mental distress, disappointment, hurt feelings or humiliation. Traditionally, these have not been compensated in contract law (unlike tort), but recently this rule has been relaxed for contracts that are specifically for pleasure, relaxation and peace of mind.

Limitations on the awarding of damages
Tests of causation
A person will only be liable for losses caused by their breach of contract. The defendant's breach must be an effective and intervening act between the breach of contract and the loss incurred to break the chain of causation (as in the case of *Quinn v Burch Brothers (Builders) Ltd* (1966)).

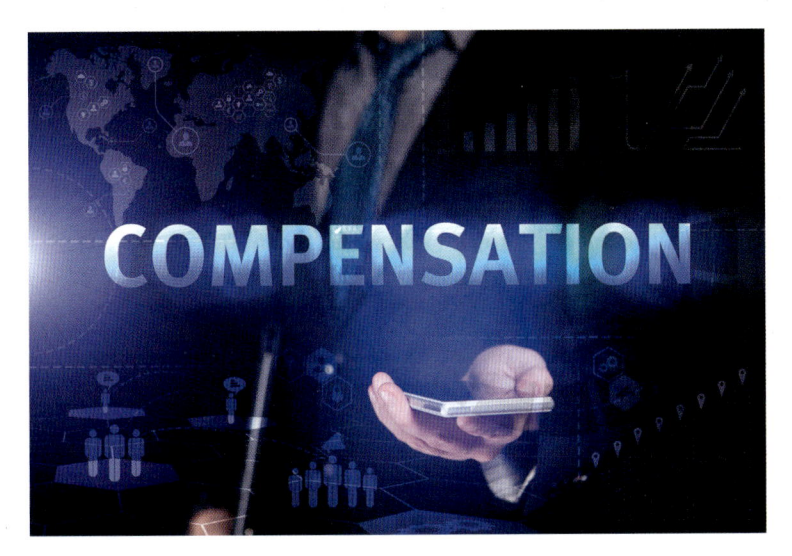

KEY TERMINOLOGY

remedy: an award made by a court to the innocent party in a civil case to 'right the wrong'.

STRETCH AND CHALLENGE

Explain the purpose of damages in contract law.

STRETCH AND CHALLENGE

Research the cases of *Jarvis v Swans Tours Ltd* (1973) and *Farley v Skinner* (2001) and explain how they relate to damages for non-pecuniary losses.

Figure 27.1 Compensation is a form of damages

Remoteness

Some losses are considered too remote (removed) from the breach of contract to be expected to be compensated by the defendant. A defendant will only be liable for such losses as were 'reasonably foreseeable' as arising from the breach. This was demonstrated in *Hadley v Baxendale* (1854) and later in *Transfield Shipping v Mercator Shipping [The Achilleas]* (2008).

Mitigation of loss

Claimants are under a duty to mitigate their loss; they cannot recover damages for losses which could have been avoided if they had taken reasonable steps. For example, in *Pilkington v Wood* (1953), the claimant (plaintiff) sued his conveyancing solicitor for not noticing that his house had a defective title, making it hard to sell at the original value. Claimants cannot just sit back and allow losses to increase. If there is something they can do to reduce the impact or loss, and there are reasonable steps they can take, then they are under an obligation to do so.

> **KEY TERMINOLOGY**
>
> **mitigation of loss:** lessening or reducing a loss.

Calculating loss

Once it has been established that the defendant is liable for the loss, the court needs to calculate the sum of damages owed by the defendant to the claimant. Claimants choose to base their claim on either loss of expectation or reliance loss. It is more common to base the claim on loss of expectation; claimants cannot claim under both.

Loss of expectation

If this is the basis for the claim, the courts will aim to put claimants in the position they would have been in had the breach not occurred. The claimant would have expected a certain result from the contract so the damages will compensate for the loss of this expectation, as in *Golden Victory* (2007).

Ways to quantify the loss of expectation may include the following:

- The difference in value between the goods or services of the quality indicated in the contract and those actually delivered, where they are of inferior value.
- The difference between the contract price and the price obtained in an 'available market' (such as for a car, as in *Charter v Sullivan* (1957)).
- Loss of profit.
- Loss of a chance, for example of employment, as in *Chaplin v Hicks* (1911).

Reliance loss

Where this is the basis for calculating damages, the courts will seek to put the claimant in the position they were in before the contract was made, as in *Anglia Television Ltd v Reed* (1972).

Equitable remedies

Unlike common law remedies, which are 'as of right', equitable remedies are discretionary.

Where common law remedies are inadequate to compensate the claimant, there are, instead, equitable remedies. They are provided at the discretion of the court and take into account the behaviour of both parties and the overall justice of the case.

There are four main equitable remedies:

- injunction
- specific performance
- rescission
- rectification.

> **KEY TERMINOLOGY**
>
> **discretionary:** it is a choice of the court whether to award or not.

Injunction

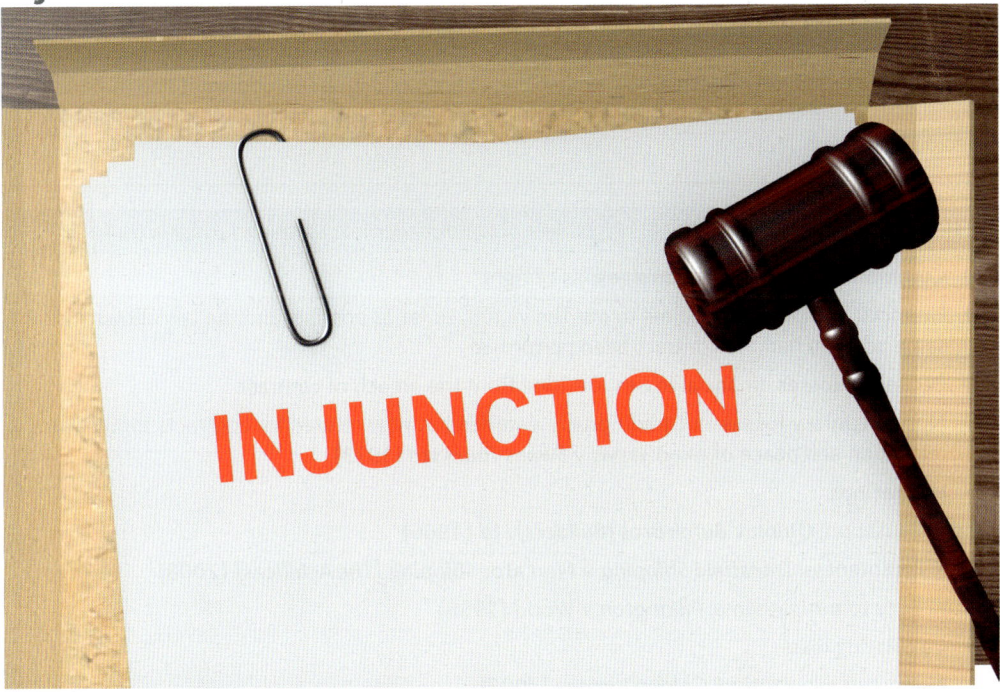

Figure 27.2 An injunction is another remedy in contract law

An injunction normally compels the defendant not to do a something in particular (called a prohibitory injunction). In *Warner Brothers Pictures Inc v Nelson* (1937), an actress was initially prevented from working for any company other than Warner Brothers for two years but was eventually permitted other, non-acting employment. However, where the action has already taken place, the court may instead order a mandatory injunction compelling the party to do something. This would normally be an order that the defendant take action to restore the situation to that which existed before the defendant's breach.

> **KEY TERMINOLOGY**
>
> **prohibitory injunction:** an order not to do something.
>
> **mandatory injunction:** an order to do something.

Specific performance

An order of specific performance compels one side of the contract to perform their obligations. This is a rarely awarded remedy and is only awarded where:

- damages would be inadequate (*Beswick v Beswick* (1968))
- the contract has been made fairly (*Walters v Morgan* (1861))
- the award of specific performance would not cause great hardship or unfairness for the defendant (*Patel v Ali* (1984)).

This supports the equitable nature of specific performance as a remedy.

Rescission

This remedy places parties back in their pre-contractual position. If this is not possible, rescission is not granted. It is mainly granted as a remedy in misrepresentation cases. This is known as *restitutio in integrum*. *Clarke v Dickson* (1858) is the most quoted case on this.

Rectification

This is an equitable remedy under which a written document can be altered to correct a mistake. It will be granted when a written agreement contradicts the actual agreement made by the parties: *Craddock Brothers Ltd v Hunt* (1923).

EXAM SKILLS

This topic is likely to feature as an essay style question requiring you to analyse and evaluate the remedies or assess them (depending on the specification and mark allocation). You will therefore be required to consider the availability of both common law and equitable remedies but also to critique the extent to which they provide an adequate solution with reference to decided case law.

SUMMARY: REMEDIES

→ **Common law remedy of damages**: 'as of right'
→ **Financial compensation**: aims to put the victim, so far as possible and the law allows, in the same position had the contract been performed
→ **Pecuniary losses**: financial losses resulting from the breach of contract
→ **Non-pecuniary losses**: not traditionally awarded but now relaxed for contracts for pleasure, relaxation and peace of mind: *Jarvis* v *Swans Tours Ltd* (1973)
→ **Limitations**:
  - Causation: *Quinn* v *Burch Bros (Builders) Ltd* (1966)
  - Remoteness: *Transfield Shipping* v *Mercator Shipping [The Achilleas]* (2008)
  - Duty to mitigate loss: *Pilkington* v *Wood* (1953)
→ Calculating loss:
  1. Loss of expectation: *Golden Victory* (2007)
  2. Reliance loss: *Anglia Television Ltd* v *Reed* (1972)
→ **Equitable remedies are discretionary**:
  - Injunctions
  - Specific performance
  - Rescission
  - Rectification

TEST YOURSELF

1. What is the purpose of the common law remedy of damages in the law of contract?
2. What is a 'pecuniary' loss?
3. What is a 'non-pecuniary' loss?
4. Explain what is meant by causation in the law of contract.
5. In relation to remoteness of loss, what losses will a defendant be liable for? Name two cases that demonstrate this.
6. What is 'mitigation of loss'?
7. What is equitable remedy and when is such a remedy available?
8. What are the four main equitable remedies?
9. Which type of injunction compels a defendant not to do something?
10. What is the equitable remedy of rectification?

EXAM PAST PAPER QUESTIONS

Eduqas – AS Law – Component 2 – October 2020
(c) Assess the various forms of remedies available for breach of contract. [9]

Eduqas – A Level – Component 3 – October 2020
1.1 Discuss the extent to which the remedies available for a breach of contract provide consumers with an adequate solution. [25]

Criminal Law

28 Rules and theory of criminal law

Definition of a crime

There are lots of ways to define a 'crime', but we can certainly say that it is a wrong against an individual, society and the state, which should be punished.

In *Proprietary Articles Trade Association* v *Attorney General for Canada* (1931), Lord Atkin stated his definition of crime:

> 'The criminal quality of an act cannot be discerned by intuition (made out by "gut feeling"); nor can it be discovered by reference to any standard but one: is the act prohibited by penal consequences?'

The state (the government) develops a code of behaviour for the whole of society to adhere to, in order to maintain social control and standards in society. Those who commit crimes are prosecuted by the state (as opposed to in civil law, where actions are taken by individuals). The Crown Prosecution Service (CPS) will conduct most of these proceedings.

Most criminal law is laid down by Parliament but some criminal law offences are found in case law and common law.

Figure 28.1 Criminal law defines criminal offences

Examples of common law offences

Over many years, judges have developed certain offences and may still find it necessary to do so on occasion. However, in *Knuller* v *DPP* (1973), the House of Lords stated that it did not feel it was in its remit to create offences and that this should be left to Parliament wherever possible. Parliament will step in and provide statutory guidelines when it feels it is necessary to bring the law into line with policy.

Murder

Murder is the best-known example of a common law offence. It is not defined in any statute but judges often imposed a death penalty for murder until Parliament passed the **Murder (Abolition of the Death Penalty) Act 1965**.

Conspiracy to corrupt public morals

> *Shaw* v *DPP* (1962)
> The defendant published a book with the names, pictures and services offered by prostitutes and was convicted of conspiracy to corrupt public morals. There was no alternative statutory offence for the defendant to be convicted of, so the judges created this offence in this case.

Marital rape

> **KEY CASE**
>
> ***R v R* (1991)**
> An 18th-century precedent stated that a husband could not be guilty of raping his wife. In this case, the House of Lords held that the status of women in society had changed and that they had now achieved equality with men so they should not be regarded as a form of chattel (belonging). If a wife does not consent to sex, her husband can now be found guilty of rape.

Elements of a crime

For a defendant to be found guilty of a crime, two elements must be present: **actus reus** and **mens rea**. These terms come from the Latin phrase *actus non facit reum nisi mens sit rea*: 'the act itself does not constitute guilt unless done with a guilty mind'. The general **presumption** is that a defendant must have committed a guilty act while having a guilty state of mind. A presumption is a starting point for the courts, which presume certain facts to be true unless the evidence points to the contrary and rebuts the presumption.

Burden of proof

The prosecution has to convince the judge or jury that the defendant is criminally liable. This is a 'golden thread' that runs through the UK legal system: that a person is presumed innocent until proved guilty. ***Woolmington v DPP* (1935)** stressed the fact that the prosecution has to prove the case beyond reasonable doubt in any criminal trial.

'Beyond reasonable doubt' is a very high standard of proof. The judge or jury must be left with hardly a shadow of doubt in their minds that the defendant committed the crime. Otherwise, the defendant must be found not guilty.

The original phrase 'beyond all reasonable doubt' has been used for more than 200 years, but the Judicial Office has told judges not to use this phrase any longer because jurors don't understand what it means. Instead, they should ask if the jury is 'satisfied that they are sure'. The old phrase still stands but judges must now start with the new phrase.

Actus reus

The term actus reus has a wider meaning than 'an act'. The actus reus can be:

- a voluntary action
- an omission
- a state of affairs.

The actus reus is different for each crime, so for murder it is unlawful killing but for theft it is the dishonest appropriation of property belonging to another. The defendant must have committed the act or omission voluntarily. If the act is done involuntarily, the defendant will not be guilty.

> **KEY TERMINOLOGY**
>
> **actus reus:** 'the guilty act' that must be present for a defendant to be found guilty of a crime. It can be a voluntary action, an omission or a state of affairs.
>
> **mens rea:** 'the guilty mind' that must be present for a defendant to be found guilty of a crime. It can include intention, recklessness or negligence.
>
> **presumption:** a starting point for the courts, which presume certain facts to be true unless there is a greater balance of evidence to the contrary that disproves the presumption.

Figure 28.2 An action as a result of being chased or stung by a swarm of bees may not be voluntary

A voluntary action

> ### Hill v Baxter (1958)
> The court gave examples of involuntary acts, such as reflex actions after being hit on the head with a hammer or being stung by a swarm of bees. The criminal law is only concerned with fault.

An omission

A failure to act does not usually result in someone being found criminally liable in English law. Lord Justice Stephen said: 'It is not a crime to cause death or bodily injury, even intentionally, by any omission.'

However, there are some exceptions to this rule. A person will be held criminally liable for failing to act where:

- there is a duty created by statute
- they have a contractual duty to act
- there is a duty imposed by their official position
- they have voluntarily accepted responsibility for another person
- they have created a dangerous situation
- there is a special relationship, such as with a family member.

A state of affairs

Here, the defendant has not acted voluntarily but has nonetheless been convicted of a crime. They are 'being' rather than 'doing' offences.

For someone to have committed the actus reus, in some crimes there must also be a consequence. For example, for murder someone has to end up dead. The defendant's act must have produced the unlawful killing.

These concepts are explored in more detail in Chapter 29.

Mens rea

Mens rea translates as 'guilty mind'. There are different levels of mens rea. From highest to lowest, they are:

- intention
- recklessness
- negligence.

The levels of mens rea are explained in more detail on page 297.

Intention

This was defined by the courts in *R v Mohan* (1975) as 'a decision to bring about, in so far as it lies within the accused's power, [the prohibited consequence], no matter whether the accused desired that consequence of his act or not'.

The defendant's motive is irrelevant when deciding intention. There are two types of intention:

- **Direct intention:** the defendant wants a result and carries out an act to achieve it. Generally, this is easier to prove based on the circumstances of the crime.
- **Indirect/oblique intention:** the defendant doesn't want the outcome but realises that in acting as they do, that there is a possibility that it will happen.

> **STRETCH AND CHALLENGE**
>
> Research the facts of *Larsonneur* (1933) and *Winzar v Chief Constable of Kent* (1983) and discuss what the state of affairs were in these cases. See page 301 for a detailed discussion on crimes of strict liability.

> **GRADE BOOST**
>
> Research the following cases, and discuss whether there was a duty to act in these cases:
> - *Pittwood* (1902)
> - *Dytham* (1979)
> - *Stone and Dobinson* (1977)
> - *Gibbins and Proctor* (1918)
> - *Khan* (1988)

Recklessness

A definition of recklessness is a situation where the defendant knows that there is a risk that their actions will lead to harm but goes on to take the risk regardless. This is a lower form of mens rea than intention.

Negligence

See Chapter 29, page 296 for more information about the concept of mens rea and negligence.

> **STRETCH AND CHALLENGE**
>
> For the meaning of intention, research and discuss the following cases:
> - *Hyam* v *DPP* (1975)
> - *Moloney* (1985)
> - *Hancock and Shankland* (1986)
> - *Nedrick* (1986)
> - *Woollin* (1998)
> - *Matthew and Alleyne* (2003)

Codification of the criminal law

In most countries, criminal law is codified: they have a coded or written document that details each part of the criminal law. In the UK, criminal law is found in numerous statutes and in common law. It can be difficult for lawyers, let alone lay people, to find the law and keep up to date with it. But surely it is important that we should know the criminal law if we can be deprived of our liberty if we break it.

The Law Commission Act 1965 established the Law Commission (see page 13), which was given the task of codifying the criminal law. However, it found the task impossible. Eventually, with help from senior academics, a draft criminal code was published in 1989, which incorporated the criminal law as well as suggestions for reform. However, Parliament has never legislated on this and it remains in draft form.

Figure 28.3 The UK criminal law is laid down in different statutes and common law

28 Rules and theory of criminal law

See Chapter 7, Criminal Process: Structure and sentencing for more information on bail and remand in custody, the workings of the CPS and the trial process.

SUMMARY: RULES AND THEORY OF CRIMINAL LAW

→ A crime is a wrong against an individual, society and the state which should be punished by the state: *Proprietary Articles Trade Association v Attorney General for Canada* (1931)

→ The Crown Prosecution Service (CPS) conducts most of these proceedings

→ **Common law offences**: only Parliament should create offences and provide statutory guidelines: *Knuller v DPP* (1973)

→ **Murder**: not defined in any statute. Death penalty abolished in Murder (Abolition of the Death Penalty) Act 1965

→ **Conspiracy to corrupt public morals**: *Shaw v DPP* (1962)

→ **Marital rape**: *R v R* (1991)

→ **Actus reus**: 'the guilty act' must be present for a defendant to be found guilty of a crime
   - A voluntary action: *Hill v Baxter* (1958)
   - An omission or failure to act is criminally liable under certain conditions. Duty to act: *Pittwood* (1902), *Dytham* (1979), *Stone and Dobinson* (1977), *Gibbins and Proctor* (1918), *Khan* (1988)
   - A state of affairs: *Larsonneur* (1933), *Winzar v Chief Constable of Kent* (1983)

→ **Mens rea**: 'the guilty mind' must be present for a defendant to be found guilty of a crime
   - Direct or indirect (oblique) intention: *Mohan* (1975), *Hyam v DPP* (1975), *Moloney* (1985), *Hancock and Shankland* (1986), *Nedrick* (1986), *Woollin* (1998), *Matthew and Alleyne* (2003)
   - Recklessness
   - Negligence

→ **Burden of proof**: the prosecution has to convince the judge or jury that the defendant is criminally liable but they are presumed innocent until proved guilty: *Woolmington v DPP* (1935)

→ **Beyond reasonable doubt**: the judge or jury must be sure that the defendant committed the crime to be found guilty

→ Law Commission Act 1965 established the Law Commission to codify criminal law, but 1989 criminal code remains in draft form

GRADE BOOST
Remember that the rules set out in this section apply to all the offences you will learn about in criminal law.

TEST YOURSELF

1. What does the term actus reus mean?
2. What does the term mens rea mean?
3. Who has the burden of proof?
4. What does beyond all reasonable doubt mean?
5. What is the 'golden thread' running throughout criminal law?
6. Where is the definition of murder found?
7. What is meant by a state of affairs offence?
8. Give three situations where a person will be held criminally liable for failing to act.
9. What are the two different types of intention?
10. What are the three types of mens rea?

29 General elements of criminal liability

The burden and standard of proof

In a criminal case, the burden of proving guilt is on the prosecution. The standard to which it needs to prove this guilt is 'beyond reasonable doubt'. The standard of proof is higher in a criminal case than in a civil one, as the impact on a defendant of being found guilty of a criminal offence is much greater. It also supports the principle of 'innocent until proven guilty' and Article 6 ECHR (right to a fair trial).

Elements of crime

As we saw in Chapter 28, there are generally two elements required for the commission of a criminal offence: actus reus (the guilty act) and mens rea (the guilty mind). There are exceptions, which are explored in the section on strict liability (see page 301).

Once this is established, causation needs to be proved, which looks at the link between the result and the conduct of the defendant.

This topic will consider:

> actus reus
> omission
> mens rea
> factual causation
> legal causation
> strict liability.

> **KEY TERMINOLOGY**
>
> **causation (or 'chain of causation'):** connecting the actus reus and the corresponding result. For there to be criminal liability, there must be an unbroken chain of causation. There are two types of causation: legal and factual.

> **GRADE BOOST**
>
> The standard of proof in a civil case is 'on the balance of probabilities', and the burden of proof is on the claimant.

Actus reus

This consists of all the elements of a crime other than the mens rea. Actus reus may consist of the following elements.

Conduct

The action requires a particular conduct (behaviour) but the consequence of that behaviour is insignificant. An example is perjury, where a person lies under oath. It is irrelevant whether the lie is believed or affects the case; it is the conduct of lying that is sufficient as the actus reus.

Result

The action requires a particular end result. An example is murder, when the crime requires the result of the victim dying. It also requires causation to be proved.

State of affairs

For these crimes, the actus reus consists of 'being' rather than 'doing'; for example, 'being' in charge of a vehicle while under the influence of alcohol or drugs. There is a link with strict liability (see page 301).

The following cases each demonstrate a 'state of affairs' crime.

R v Larsonneur (1933)

Mrs Larsonneur, a French national, was brought to the UK from Ireland in police custody, against her will: she had no desire to come to the UK. She was arrested on arrival in the UK for being an illegal alien. The fact she had not wanted to come to the UK, nor had any power over her transfer, was irrelevant as she was 'found' or 'being' illegally in the UK. She was found guilty.

Winzar v CC Kent (1983)

The defendant was found drunk in a hospital and slumped on a chair. The police were called and removed him to the street, where they charged him with being 'drunk on the highway', contrary to the Licensing Act 1872.

These crimes are also known as absolute liability offences and are considered in the section on strict liability on page 301.

Omission

This is a 'failure to act'. The general rule is that it is not an offence to fail to act unless someone is under a duty to act. A person could walk past a random person drowning in a fountain and be under no legal obligation to help them get out.

Duty to act

A person can only be criminally liable if they have failed to act when under a legal duty to do so and the crime is capable of being committed by omission. There are recognised situations where a person is under a duty to act.

1. Statute

If a statute requires an action, it is unlawful not to do so. For example, under s6 Road Traffic Act 1988, failing to provide a breath sample or a specimen for analysis is an offence.

A further example is found in the Education Act 1996 where a parent can be found guilty of an offence of failing to ensure their child of compulsory school age attends school regularly.

2. Contract

Individuals may be contracted to act in a particular way and if they fail to act when under this contractual duty, they may be liable for an offence. The case of R v Pitwood (1902) illustrates this.

> **KEY CASE**
>
> **R v Pitwood (1902)**
> A carter was killed after Pitwood, a level-crossing keeper, failed to close the crossing gate when he went on lunch. He had a contractual duty to ensure the crossing gate was closed and his failure to act led to the death of the carter.

3. Duty arising out of a special relationship

Certain family relationships, such as parent–child and spouses, result in a duty to act. The case of R v Gibbins and Proctor (1918) demonstrates this.

> **KEY CASE**
>
> **R v *Gibbins and Proctor* (1918)**
> The defendant and his lover failed to feed his daughter, who was living with them. She died of starvation. The woman, despite the child not being hers, was living in the same household and had taken the defendant's money to feed the child. She was therefore under a duty to act (to feed and care for the child). They were both found guilty of murder.

4. Duty arising out of a person assuming responsibility for another

If a person chooses to take care of another person who is infirm or incapable of taking care of themselves, they are under a duty to do so without negligence. The case of *R v Stone and Dobinson* (1977) illustrates this.

> **KEY CASE**
>
> **R v *Stone and Dobinson* (1977)**
> Stone's younger sister, Fanny, came to live with Stone and Dobinson. Fanny suffered from anorexia and, despite some weak attempts by Stone and Dobinson to get her help, she eventually died. The jury found that a duty was assumed from electing to take care of a vulnerable adult. They should have made more of an effort to get her help and were found guilty of manslaughter.

5. Defendant has inadvertently created a dangerous situation, becomes aware of it, but fails to take steps to rectify it

> **R v *Miller* (1983)**
> The defendant was squatting in a flat. He fell asleep without extinguishing his cigarette. When he awoke, he realised the mattress was alight but merely moved to the next room and went back to sleep. His failure to act and call for help caused hundreds of pounds' worth of damage. He was convicted of arson.

The difference between a positive act and an omission

It is generally not a crime to fail to act, unless someone is under a duty to do so.

For example, doing nothing while somebody drowns is an omission, but holding that person's head under the water so that they drown is a positive act. In *Airedale NHS v Bland* (1993), the removal of a feeding tube from a patient to allow him to die naturally was held to be an omission and therefore not a criminal act. Contrast this with euthanasia, where an act such as administering a deliberate overdose to terminate a person's life would be classed as a positive act and therefore a criminal offence.

Mens rea

> **KEY TERMINOLOGY**
>
> **strict liability:** a group of offences, usually regulatory in nature, that only require proof of actus reus, not mens rea.

The general presumption is that a defendant must have committed a guilty act while having a guilty state of mind. Mens rea refers to the mental element of the definition of a crime. If Parliament intended mens rea in an offence, it will often include mens rea words in the statute such as 'intentionally', 'recklessly' and 'negligently'. If Parliament deliberately left out a mens rea word then the offence may be considered to be one of strict liability.

The mens rea differs according to the crime. For example, the mens rea of murder is malice aforethought, which has come to mean an intention to kill or cause grievous bodily harm (GBH) whereas the mens rea of assault is intentionally or recklessly causing the victim to apprehend the application of immediate unlawful force.

Coincidence of actus reus and mens rea

The general rule is that to be guilty of a criminal offence requiring mens rea an accused must possess the required mens rea when performing the actus reus, and it must relate to that particular act or omission. This is also known as the contemporaneity rule. For example, Bob is planning to kill his colleague tomorrow, but kills him by accident today. This does not make Bob guilty of murder. There are two ways the courts have taken a flexible approach to this question: by continuing acts and single transaction of events.

1. Continuing acts
It is not necessary for mens rea to be present at the start of the actus reus as long as at some point in a continuous act, mens rea appears. The case of *Fagan v Metropolitan Police Commissioner* (1969) demonstrates this point.

> *Fagan v Metropolitan Police Commissioner* (1969)
>
> Fagan accidentally parked his car on a police officer's foot when asked by the officer to park the car near the curb. Fagan did not mean to drive his car on the officer's foot. However, when asked to move, he refused. It was at this point that mens rea was formed and driving onto the officer's foot and remaining there was a continuing act.

Under the doctrine of transferred malice, mens rea may be transferred from an intended victim to an unintended one. This is shown in the case of *Latimer* (1986), where the defendant hit victim number one with his belt but it recoiled off him, injuring victim number two, an innocent bystander. The defendant had committed the actus reus of the offence with the necessary mens rea. The mens rea (intention to harm the person he aimed at) could be transferred to the actual victim.

2. Single transaction of events
The courts have held that as long as there is one unbroken transaction of events, actus reus and mens rea need not occur at the same time. For example, if Rhidian attempts to murder Trystan by beating him to death, has not succeeded but thinks he is dead, then actually kills Trystan by running him over, Rhidian will still be guilty of murder. A similar situation arose in the case of *Thabo Meli* (1954).

Types of mens rea

There are various types of mens rea, but for the purposes of the A Level specification, intention, recklessness and negligence are considered here. The mens rea for a particular offence is either defined in the relevant statute, as it is with s47 assault occasioning actual bodily harm, or through case law, as is the case with oblique intent.

Intention
Intention is always subjective: in order to find that a defendant had intention, the court must believe that the particular defendant on trial desired the specific consequence of their action. Consider intention in relation to the offence of murder. The mens rea of murder is malice aforethought. Despite the term 'malice', no malice needs to be present. For example, a murder could be committed out of love or compassion, as in the case of helping a terminally ill relative to die. No 'aforethought' is required either: murder can be committed on the spur of the moment with no prior planning. According to *Vickers* (1957), the mens rea of murder can be implied from an intention to cause grievous bodily harm (GBH). A defendant does not need to have intended to kill. The definition has therefore been interpreted as an intention to kill or cause GBH.

KEY CASE

Thabo Meli (1954)
The defendants had attempted to kill the victim by beating him up but he was not dead. They then disposed of what they thought was his corpse over a cliff. The victim died as a result of the fall. The court held that there was one transaction of events and as long as the defendants had the relevant mens rea at the beginning of the transaction, it could coincide with the actus reus when that occurred.

Figure 29.1 Actus reus and mens rea do not need to be simultaneous if they are part of a chain of events

KEY TERMINOLOGY

subjective: an assumption relating to the individual in question (the subject).

There are two types of intention: direct and oblique.

› Direct intention is where the defendant has a clear foresight of the consequences of their action and specifically desires that consequence. For example, Megan stabs Lauren because she desires the consequence of Lauren's death.
› Oblique (or indirect) intention is less clear than direct intent. Here, the defendant may not actually desire the consequence of the action (e.g. death), but if they realise that the consequence will happen as a virtual certainty, they can be said to have oblique intention. This area of law has evolved through case law. The current direction on oblique intent comes from the case of *Nedrick* (1986) as confirmed in *Woollin* (1998), when the judge stated that 'the jury should be directed that they were not entitled to find the necessary intention for a conviction of murder unless they felt sure that death or serious bodily harm had been a virtual certainty (barring some unforeseen intervention) as a result of the defendant's actions and that the defendant had appreciated that such was the case, the decision being one for them to be reached on a consideration of all the evidence'.

STRETCH AND CHALLENGE

The area of oblique intent has developed through case law over the years to the current direction. Explore the following cases and consider their facts, how the law has changed and why:

- *S8 Criminal Justice Act 1967*: 'natural and probable consequence'
- *R v Maloney* (1985): 'natural consequence of the action'
- *Hancock and Shankland* (1986): 'degrees of probability'
- *Nedrick* (1986)
- *Woolin* (1998)

KEY TERMINOLOGY

objective: a test that considers not the particular defendant in question, but what another average, reasonable person would have done or thought if placed in the same position as the defendant.

Recklessness

This type of mens rea concerns the taking of an unjustified risk. The standard used to be **objective** recklessness – also known as Caldwell recklessness after a case of that name – in which the court would ask what a reasonable person might have foreseen, not the particular defendant.

The first use of the phrase 'subjective recklessness' was in the *Cunningham* (1957) case. It is sometimes referred to as Cunningham recklessness, where the court asks the question: 'Was the risk in the defendant's mind at the time the crime was committed?' Following the case of *R v G and another* (2003), recklessness is now almost purely a subjective concept, so that the prosecution must prove that the defendant realised they were taking a risk.

KEY CASES

Cunningham (1957)
A defendant moved a gas meter in order to steal the money within. This caused gas to leak and caused injury to the victim who inhaled it. The defendant won his appeal and the court replaced objective recklessness with subjective recklessness: it has to be proved that the particular defendant (the subject) foresaw the risk and took the action, and not just what the reasonable person might have foreseen.

R v G and another (2003)
Two boys aged 11 and 12 set fire to newspapers in a wheelie bin outside a shop. The fire spread to the shop and other buildings, causing significant damage. They were convicted of arson as, at the time, arson required the objective Caldwell standard of recklessness and the risk would have been obvious to a reasonable person, even if it was not to the young boys. On appeal, it was decided that the objective standard was not appropriate and the subjective characteristics of the boys such as their age and immaturity should be considered by the courts. Caldwell objective recklessness was overruled and replaced with subjective recklessness.

29 General elements of criminal liability

Figure 29.2 Starting a fire that could harm people is classed as recklessness

Negligence
Negligence consists of falling below the standard of the ordinary reasonable person. The test is objective and has traditionally been associated with civil law. It now has some relevance in criminal law with gross negligence manslaughter.

Causation

Causation relates to the causal relationship between conduct and result and is an important aspect of the actus reus of an offence. There needs to be an unbroken and direct chain of causation between the defendant's act and the consequences of that act. There must not be a novus actus interveniens that breaks the chain of causation, or there will be no criminal liability for the resulting consequence. There are two types of causation: factual and legal.

Factual causation
This is tested using the 'but for' test and the de minimis rule.

1. The 'but for' test
This test asks 'but for' the conduct of the defendant, would the victim have died as and when they did? If the answer is no then the defendant will be liable for the death.

> **R v White (1910)**
> White poisoned his mother but she died of a heart attack before the poison had a chance to take effect. He was not liable for her death.

STRETCH AND CHALLENGE
Explore the cases of *Cunningham* (1957) and *Caldwell* (1982). What were the facts of the case and what did they rule in relation to negligence?

GRADE BOOST
Remember that, occasionally, some subjective characteristics of the defendant can be considered with an objective test (such as age and gender) that may have an effect on the way they reacted.

KEY TERMINOLOGY
novus actus interveniens: an intervening act that is so independent of the original act of the defendant that it succeeds in breaking the chain of causation. There may be liability for the initial act.

KEY CASE
R v Pagett (1983)
An armed defendant was trying to resist arrest and held his girlfriend in front of him as a human shield. He shot at the police and they shot back, killing the girlfriend. It was held that 'but for' his action of holding her as a human shield, she would not have died as and when she did. This was despite the fact it was not him who shot her.

2. The de minimis rule

De minimis means insignificant, minute or trifling. This test requires that the original injury caused by the defendant's action must be more than a minimal cause of death. *Pagett* (1983) also illustrates this.

Legal causation

This is tested using the impact of the injury, the 'thin skull' test and novus actus interveniens.

1. The injury must be the operating and substantial cause of death

This test considers whether the original injury inflicted by the defendant is, at the time of death, still the operating and substantial cause of death.

> **R v *Smith* (1959)**
>
> A soldier had been stabbed, was dropped twice on his way to the hospital, experienced a delay in seeing a doctor and subsequently given poor medical treatment. The court held that these other factors were not enough to break the chain of causation. At the time of his death, the original wound was still the 'operating and substantial' cause of death.

> **R v *Jordan* (1956)**
>
> This case took a different stance to the Smith case. The defendant stabbed the victim. While in hospital, the victim was given an antibiotic to which he was allergic and died. The defendant was acquitted of murder because, at the time of death, the original stab wound had almost healed and the death was attributable not to that injury but to the antibiotic. The courts said that negligent medical treatment could only break the chain of causation where it is 'palpably wrong'.

In this context, palpably wrong means seriously wrong and so independent of the original act that it is possible to break the chain of causation. In *R v Jordan* (1956), it was seen as a novus actus interveniens and the original stab wound was no longer the 'operating and substantial' cause of death.

2. The 'thin skull' test

A defendant has to take their victim as they find them, meaning that if the victim dies from some unusual or unexpected physical or other condition, the defendant is still responsible for the death. For example, if during a fight the defendant hits the victim with a punch that would not normally cause anything more than soreness and bruising, but due to the victim having an unusually thin skull they die, the defendant is still liable for the death.

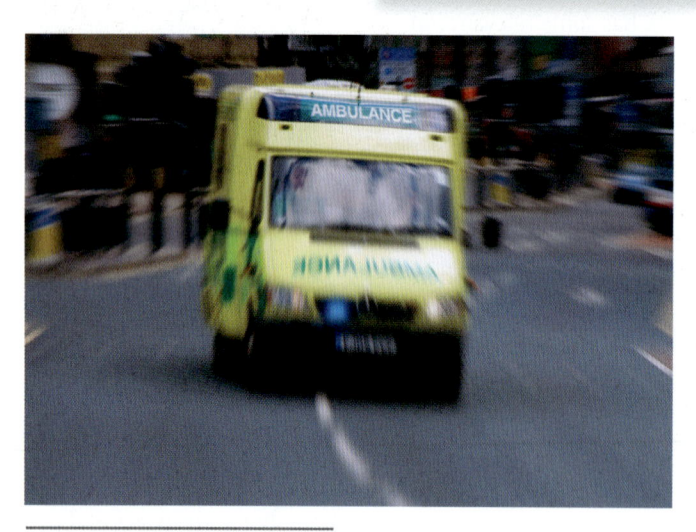

Figure 29.3 The acts of third parties can break the chain of causation

> **R v *Blaue* (1975)**
>
> The defendant stabbed a woman who happened to be a Jehovah's witness. As a result of her beliefs, she refused a blood transfusion which would have saved her life. The defendant argued he should not be responsible for her death as the transfusion could have saved her life and she refused it. The court disagreed and said he must take his victim as he finds them.

3. Novus actus interveniens (new intervening act)
For an intervening act to break the chain of causation, it must be unforeseeable and random. It is sometimes likened to an 'act of God'. The case of *R v Jordan* (1956) is an example of a novus actus interveniens.

> **EXAM SKILLS**
>
> When applying the law on general elements of liability to a scenario-style question, it is important to define the actus reus and mens rea of each offence using legal authority to support your definition. You then need to apply the actus reus and mens rea of each offence to the facts with supporting authority and draw a conclusion. Remember, you may also have to incorporate a defence if applicable.
>
> The concepts explored in this section will be needed for each of the offences studied at AS/A Level. You will need to revisit this section when revising homicide, property offences and non-fatal offences.

> **STRETCH AND CHALLENGE**
>
> A more recent case that looks at this issue is *Cheshire* (1991). Find out about this case and what the court said in relation to causation.

Strict liability

Most crimes require both actus reus and mens rea. However, there is a group of offences known as strict liability, where only the actus reus needs to be proved to establish liability. With these offences, there is no need to prove mens rea for at least one element of the actus reus and liability is imposed without fault on the part of the defendant. As a result, some people feel strict liability offences are unfair but, as they cover relatively minor crimes, it is generally accepted that they are needed to allow society to run smoothly. They tend to cover regulatory offences such as food hygiene, parking offences and polluting the environment. For strict liability offences, the defence of mistake is not available.

There is also a group of crimes known as absolute liability offences. These require proof of actus reus only but are not concerned with whether the actus reus is voluntary.

(See the section about elements of crime on page 294, which refers to these offences as 'state of affairs' crimes and demonstrates through the cases of *Winzar* (1983) and *Larsonneur* (1933) that the actus reus need not be controlled by the defendant).

Figure 29.4 Judges use different aids to identify a strict liability offence

Although most strict liability offences are statutory offences, Parliament does not always make it clear whether mens rea is required. It is therefore for judges to decide whether an offence should be one of strict liability. Judges start with the presumption that mens rea is always required and no offence is strict liability. They then consider four factors to confirm or rebut this presumption.

The four Gammon factors

The case of *Gammon (HK) Ltd v Attorney General* (1985), where builders had failed to follow exact plans and part of the building they had constructed collapsed, confirmed that the starting point for a judge is to presume that mens rea is always required before a person can be found guilty of a criminal offence. This case laid down four Gammon factors the courts need to consider in determining if an offence is one of strict liability.

Judges also use statutory interpretation to interpret statutes to determine if Parliament intended the offence to be one of strict liability. Judges have to use aids of interpretation such as the literal, golden, mischief and purposive approaches to determine if an offence was intended to be one of strict liability. They also have to use rules of language and the presumption that mens rea is required.

> **GRADE BOOST**
>
> Though punishments are usually small for strict liability offences, the case of *Gammon* (1985) is an exception. In this case the penalty was a fine of up to $250,000 or three years' imprisonment.

1. Is the offence regulatory in nature or a true crime?

If the offence is regulatory in nature (meaning not criminal, minor or with no moral issue involved) the offence is more likely to be classed as strict liability. A case that considered this question is *Sweet* v *Parsley* (1970).

> #### *Sweet* v *Parsley* (1970)
> Ms Sweet sublet her property to a group of tenants, retaining a room for herself but hardly spending any time there. The police searched the property and found cannabis. Ms Sweet was convicted under **s5 Dangerous Drugs Act 1965** (now replaced), of 'being concerned in the management of premises used for the smoking of cannabis'. She appealed, alleging that she had no knowledge of the circumstances and indeed could not have reasonably been expected to have such knowledge. On appeal, her conviction was overturned, with Lord Reid acknowledging that strict liability was only appropriate for 'quasi-crimes' where no real moral issue was involved. Ms Sweet's conviction had caused her to lose her job and had damaged her reputation. It was felt that strict liability was inappropriate and the offence should be classed as a 'true crime' requiring mens rea. She did not have any mens rea so her conviction was quashed.

2. Does the offence relate to an issue of social concern?

This is an issue of concern to general society at a given time. Issues of social concern can shift over time but tend to relate to offences such as selling alcohol or cigarettes to minors, pollution and public safety. It is felt that imposing strict liability for crimes that relate to issues of social concern will promote extra vigilance and care on the part of defendants to not commit the offence. Of course, this is only appropriate for regulatory offences, and the distinction drawn in *Sweet* v *Parsley* (1970) is still applicable.

> #### *Harrow London Borough Council* v *Shah* (1999)
> The defendants were convicted of selling National Lottery tickets to a child under 16. It did not matter that they believed the child to be over 16: the offence was committed as soon as they had sold the lottery ticket to a person under 16. The courts felt this offence related to an issue of social concern.

3. Did Parliament intend to create an offence of strict liability by using certain words in a statute?

Although there is no official list of words that point towards a crime being one of strict liability, Parliament uses some words when drafting statutes that point to mens rea being required. 'Mens rea words' include intentionally, recklessly and knowingly. Other words have generally been interpreted by judges as pointing towards no mens rea being required. These include possession and cause.

> #### *Alphacell* v *Woodward* (1972)
> The defendants were charged with causing polluted matter to enter a river. The pumps that prevented the pollution from overflowing into the river had become clogged with leaves and, as a result, the matter leaked into the river. It was irrelevant that the defendants had no idea the pumps were clogged with leaves and had not wanted any contamination to enter the river. They had caused the polluted matter to enter the river and were therefore liable.

29 General elements of criminal liability

4. The gravity of the punishment

The more serious the criminal offence and punishment that can be imposed, the less likely it is to be one of strict liability. This reflects the fact that with strict liability, defendants can be convicted without fault. This can be problematic as the associated small penalties do not always act as a *deterrent*. On the other hand, as in the case of *Callow v Tillstone* (1900), the damage to a small business's reputation can be far greater than the impact of a small fine.

> ### *Callow* v *Tillstone* (1900)
> A butcher was convicted of 'exposing unfit meat for sale'. The butcher was found guilty even though he had taken reasonable care not to commit the offence by having the carcass inspected by a vet, who said it was safe to eat.

KEY CASE

Cundy v *Le Cocq* (1884)
The defendant was convicted of unlawfully selling alcohol to an intoxicated person, contrary to s13 Licensing Act 1872. It was held that it was not necessary to consider whether the defendant knew, should have known or should have used reasonable care to detect that the person was intoxicated. As soon as the defendant sold the alcohol to the drunken person, he was guilty of the offence.

KEY TERMINOLOGY

deterrent: something that discourages a particular action.

STRETCH AND CHALLENGE

Many of the cases in this section overlap to demonstrate more than one factor. For example, *Alphacell* v *Woodward* (1972) can be used to show how some words to indicate strict liability were intended by Parliament but it was also an issue of social concern (pollution). Think about the other cases described in this section and how they may demonstrate more than one of the factors.

GRADE BOOST

Think of cases to demonstrate the ways that courts have protected society through the imposition of strict liability. Use these cases to provide the evaluation required for higher marks.

- Sale of unfit meat: *Callow* v *Tillstone* (1900)
- Pollution: *Alphacell* v *Woodward* (1972)
- Dangerous buildings: *Gammon (HK) Ltd* v *Attorney General* (1985)
- Food hygiene: *Callow* v *Tillstone* (1900)

Table 29.1 Advantages and disadvantages of strict liability

Advantages	Disadvantages
Time and cost of proving mens rea: mens rea can be difficult to prove, and if it had to be proved for every offence, the courts would be clogged with cases and some guilty individuals may escape conviction. This in turn would increase court costs.	Possibility of injustice: liability is imposed without fault on the part of the defendant. Individuals may have taken all reasonable steps to avoid the behaviour and be unaware they are committing the illegal act yet still face conviction. The injustice is magnified further with absolute liability offences, as in the case of *Larsonneur* (1933).
Protection of society by promoting a higher standard of care: as strict liability offences are easy to prove, individuals may take more care when acting in certain situations, thereby protecting society from harmful behaviour.	Role of judges: judges are interpreting what they think Parliament intended in an Act. This gives judges an increased role and there is a risk of inconsistency in the imposition of strict liability.
The ease of imposing strict liability acts as a deterrent: individuals are deterred from carrying out the offending behaviour in the knowledge that a prosecution is likely to result in a conviction, due to only having to prove the actus reus.	Is strict liability actually a deterrent? As a result of the small penalties imposed for strict liability, some argue that it does not act as a deterrent. For example, large businesses may continue to carry out the offending behaviour (such as pollution), paying the small fines and not changing their practices. In addition, to act as a deterrent it is argued that a person ought to have knowledge that what they are doing is wrong, so they could have taken steps to prevent it. This is not always the case with strict liability offences.
Proportionality of the punishment appropriate for strict liability: strict liability offences tend to carry small penalties. This is appropriate as defendants may be unaware they are committing the offence or have taken all reasonable steps to avoid doing so.	Does strict liability breach the European Convention on Human Rights (ECHR)? There has been some debate over whether, according to Article 6(2) ECHR, everyone should be presumed innocent until proven guilty according to law. *R v G* (2008) appears to allow the imposition of strict liability.

Proposal for reform

The Law Commission proposed a Criminal Liability (Mental Element) Bill (1977), where the onus would be on Parliament, if it wished to create an offence of strict liability, to make this clear in the Act of Parliament. It is Parliament's responsibility to decide the nature of criminal liability and to provide a clear indication to judges of whether it intended to create a crime with no requirement of mens rea. This would prevent some of the confusion and inconsistency of judicial decisions.

303

EXAM SKILLS

Strict liability as an aspect of this topic is likely to feature as a question in its own right. It lends itself to an explanation and evaluation of the current law.

STRETCH AND CHALLENGE

A harsh sentence is more likely to be a deterrent from committing crime. Explain how deterrence is linked to theories of punishment.

Explore the following cases and consider how the question of strict liability in relation to human rights was dealt with by the courts:

- *Hansen* v *Denmark* (1995)
- *Salabiaku* v *France* (1988)

SUMMARY: GENERAL ELEMENTS OF CRIMINAL LIABILITY

→ A criminal case has to be proved by the prosecution beyond reasonable doubt
→ Actus reus and mens rea needed for the commission of a criminal offence
→ **Factual causation:**
  - 'But for' test: *R* v *White* (1910)
  - De minimis rule: *R* v *Pagett* (1983)
→ **Legal causation:**
  - The injury must be the operating and substantial cause of death: *R* v *Smith* (1959), *Jordan* (1956)
  - The thin skull test: *R* v *Blaue* (1975)
  - Novus actus interveniens: *R* v *Pagett* (1983)
  - Contemporaneity rule: coincidence of actus reus and mens rea:
    - Continuing acts: *Fagan* v *MPC* (1969)
    - Single transaction of events: *Thabo Meli* (1954)
  - Transferred malice: *Latimer* (1986)
  - Actus reus: guilty act
  - Conduct crimes: perjury
  - Result crimes: murder
  - State of affairs crimes: *R* v *Larsonneur* (1933)
→ **Omissions**
  - Omissions: not a crime to fail to act unless under a duty to act:
    - Statute: **Road Traffic Act 1988**: breath sample
    - Contract: *R* v *Pitwood* (1902)
    - Duty arising out of a special relationship: *R* v *Gibbins and Proctor* (1918)
    - Duty arising out of a person assuming responsibility for another: *R* v *Stone and Dobinson* (1977)
    - Defendant has inadvertently created a dangerous situation, becomes aware of it, but fails to take steps to rectify it: *Miller* (1983)
→ **Mens rea**
→ Direct and oblique intention: virtual certainty test: *Nedrick* (1986), *Woollin* (1998)
→ Recklessness: subjective: *R* v *G and another* (2003)
→ Negligence
→ Strict liability crimes do not require proof of mens rea for at least one element of the actus reus
→ Tends to cover regulatory offences, e.g. food hygiene, parking offences, polluting
→ Offences tend to be statutory but require statutory interpretation by judges, as Parliament doesn't always make it clear whether an offence is strict liability
→ Starting point for judges is presumption that mens rea is always required: *Gammon (HK) Ltd v Attorney General* (1985)
→ Presumption can be rebutted by considering four Gammon factors:
  - Is the offence regulatory in nature or a true crime? *Sweet* v *Parsley* (1970)
  - Does the offence relate to an issue of social concern? *Harrow London Borough Council* v *Shah* (1999)
  - Did Parliament intend to create an offence of strict liability by using certain words in a statute? e.g. intentionally, knowingly. Non mens rea words include possession, cause: *Alphacell* v *Woodward* (1972), *Cundy* v *Le Cocq* (1884)
  - The gravity of the punishment: *Callow* v *Tillstone* (1900), *Gammon (HK) Ltd* v *Attorney General* (1985)

- **Advantages of strict liability**:
  - Reduces time and cost of proving mens rea
  - Protection of society by promoting a higher standard of care
  - Ease of imposing strict liability acts as a deterrent
  - Proportionality of appropriate punishment
- **Disadvantages of strict liability**:
  - Possibility of injustice
  - Role of judges in interpreting statutes can lead to inconsistency
  - Small penalties may reduce deterrence
  - Does strict liability breach the European Convention on Human Rights? *R v G* (2008)
  - Proposals for reform: Criminal Liability (Mental Element) Bill (1977)

TEST YOURSELF

1. Phil is squatting in a house. One night, he gets drunk while smoking a cigarette and falls asleep by a pile of old newspapers. Phil wakes up to discover the papers alight but just moves to the next room and goes back to sleep. The house suffers fire damage and Phil is charged with arson. Is Phil guilty of an offence?
2. What is the presumption regarding mens rea?
3. Explain the 'de minimis' test.
4. When does negligent medical treatment break the chain of causation according to *R v Jordan* (1956)?
5. When might a person be liable for an omission in criminal law?
6. What is the two-stage test for oblique intention? What case established this?
7. What is a novus actus interveniens?
8. Which rule does the case of *R v Blaue* (1975) demonstrate?
9. What are the four Gammon factors for establishing a case of strict liability?
10. Name two advantages and two disadvantages of strict liability.

EXAM PAST PAPER QUESTIONS

Eduqas – June 2019 – Question 3: Criminal Law Section
(a) Explain the 'but for' test in causation.   [6]
(b) Explain when an intervening act might break the chain of causation.   [6]
(c) Assess whether the current law on intention is uncertain and unjust.   [9]
Read the scenario below and answer part (d).

Sam is on holiday and is sitting by the side of the pool at his hotel. The pool is empty apart from one swimmer, Ethan. Ethan jumps out of the pool and goes to the diving board and attempts to dive in. Unfortunately, he misjudges his dive and he hits his head on the side of the swimming pool, knocking him unconscious he sinks to the bottom of the pool. Sam sees all of this happen but he does nothing. Ethan drowns.

(d) Advise Sam as to whether he would be liable for failure to act on these facts.   [9]

30 Offences against the person

At A Level, the topic of 'Offences against the person' is split into non-fatal offences and fatal offences. These aspects of the topic are likely to feature separately on the exam.

Non-fatal offences against the person

The majority of offences do not result in death. There are five non-fatal offences against the person that need to be considered. These are mainly derived from the **Offences against the Person Act 1861**. From least to most serious, these are:

1. assault
2. battery
3. **s47** actual bodily harm (ABH)
4. **s20** grievous bodily harm (GBH)
5. **s18** grievous bodily harm (GBH) with intent.

It is important to be aware of the actus reus and mens rea of each offence with case law to support.

It is also important to appreciate the hierarchical relationship between the offences, as it will affect any **plea bargaining**. Plea bargaining is an agreement between prosecution and defence in a criminal case that the charge will be reduced if the defendant pleads guilty. For example, a defendant charged with a **s20** offence will be offered the opportunity to plead guilty to the lesser **s47** offence. On the face of it, this seems unfair and not in the interests of justice, but the courts rely upon defendants pleading guilty.

The CPS charging standards (see page 311) provide guidance to prosecutors for what injuries constitute which non-fatal offence. They do not, however, have any legal significance and are merely there to guide.

> **KEY TERMINOLOGY**
>
> **plea bargaining:** the defendant pleads guilty to a lesser offence in return for a lower sentence to save court time and make the trial more predictable.
>
> **common law (also case law or precedent):** law developed by judges through decisions in court.
>
> **summary offence:** the least serious offences, triable only in the Magistrates' Court.

Assault

Assault is not defined in an Act of Parliament, as it is a **common law** offence.

Section 39 Criminal Justice Act 1988 provides that assault is a **summary offence** with a maximum sentence on conviction of six months' imprisonment or a fine.

Actus reus

The actus reus of assault is any act which causes the victim to apprehend the immediate infliction of violence, such as raising a fist, pointing a gun or threatening somebody. In the case of *Logdon v DPP (1976)*, as a joke, the defendant pointed a gun at the victim. She was frightened until he told her it was a replica gun. The court held that the victim had apprehended immediate physical violence, and the defendant had been at least reckless as to whether this would occur.

Words can amount to an assault, as can silent telephone calls. In *R v Ireland, Burstow (1997)* the defendant made silent telephone calls to three women and these were held to be sufficient to cause the victim to apprehend the immediate infliction of unlawful force. In *Constanza (1997)* threatening letters were held to amount to an assault.

Words can also take away liability for assault as in *Tuberville v Savage* (1669), where the accused put his hand on his sword and said, 'If it were not assize time I would not take such language from you.' (At the time of the *Tuberville* case, periodic criminal courts called assizes were held across the UK, where judges would travel to various areas to try cases. In this case, it meant the judges were in town.) The threat was the hand being placed on the sword, which could have amounted to an assault. However, because he coupled this with the statement that he would not use his sword as it was assize time, the words took away liability for the assault.

The threat has to be 'immediate', although this has been interpreted liberally by the courts as can be evidenced by the cases of *Ireland* (1997), *Constanza* (1997) and *Smith* (1983).

> ### *Smith* v *Chief Superintendent of Woking Police Station* (1983)
> The victim was in her nightdress in her downstairs window. The defendant, who had trespassed on to her property, was staring at her through the window and, even though the door was locked and she was behind the window, it was deemed to be sufficiently 'immediate' for an assault.

Mens rea

The mens rea of assault, as defined in *R v Savage, Parmenter* (1992), is that the defendant must have either intended to cause the victim to fear the infliction of immediate and unlawful force, or must have seen that such fear would be created (subjective recklessness).

Recklessness is now generally subjective. As we saw in Chapter 29, it must be believed that the defendant in question foresaw the consequence of their action but took the risk anyway. This is also known as Cunningham recklessness, from the case of *R v Cunningham* (1957). Caldwell recklessness (objective) has all but been abolished following the decision in *R v G and another* (2003).

GRADE BOOST
It is important for the exam that you are be able to explain the actus reus and mens rea of each offence, and appreciate the subtle differences and overlaps between them. You should support with case law and then apply each element to the facts of a problem scenario.

Battery

As with assault, battery is not defined in an Act of Parliament; it is a common law offence. **Section 39 Criminal Justice Act 1988 (CJA 1988)** provides that battery is a summary offence with a maximum sentence on conviction of six months' imprisonment or a fine.

Although assault and battery are two separate and distinct offences, they can sometimes be charged together as 'common assault'.

Actus reus

The actus reus of battery is the application of unlawful physical force on another. It is accepted that a certain amount of physical force happens in daily life (*Collins v Wilcock* (1984)), such as walking down a busy street where people may bump into one another. For it to be a battery, the force must be unlawful.

The application does not need to be direct, as in the case of *Haystead v DPP* (2000), where the defendant punched a woman, causing her to drop her child. It was held to be indirect battery of the child. The case of *Fagan v Metropolitan Police Commissioner* (1969) is similar; see Chapter 29, page 297 for details.

The term 'physical force' implies that a high level of force needs to be applied, but this isn't the case. In the case of *Thomas* (1985), it was held that touching the hem of a girl's skirt while she was wearing it was akin to touching the girl herself. The victim also need not be aware that they are about to be struck; therefore, striking someone from behind will constitute battery. Contrast this with assault, where the victim must fear the application of unlawful force and so therefore must be aware of it.

Unlike assault, a battery can be committed by omission where there is a duty to act. In DPP v Santana-Bermudez (2004), the defendant was asked by a police officer searching him whether he had any 'needles or sharps' on him. He failed to inform her and when she searched him she pricked her finger on a hypodermic needle in his pocket. It was held that his failure to inform her of the presence of the needle was sufficient to satisfy the actus reus.

Mens rea

The mens rea of battery is intention or subjective recklessness to apply unlawful force on another, as confirmed in R v Venna (1976).

s47 Actual bodily harm (ABH)

The statutory offence of actual bodily harm (ABH) is set out in s47 Offences Against the Person Act 1861, which provides that it is an offence to commit an assault occasioning actual bodily harm.

Although the statute only refers to assault, the offence may also be committed by a battery. It is in fact far more common for offences under s47 to be committed by battery than by an assault.

ABH is a triable either way offence (see page 55). The maximum sentence for ABH is five years' imprisonment.

Actus reus

The actus reus for ABH can be broken down into three elements:

1. assault or battery
2. occasioning
3. actual bodily harm.

1. Assault or battery

The first element of ABH requires proof of the actus reus of either an assault or battery as defined above.

2. Occasioning

The assault or battery must occasion actual bodily harm. The chain of causation therefore needs to be established between the defendant's act and the harm caused. For there to be criminal liability, there must be an unbroken chain of causation. This is usually easy to prove, but see the case of R v Roberts (1971):

> ### R v Roberts (1971)
> A woman jumped from a moving car, injuring herself, and the question was whether choosing to jump from the moving car had broken the chain of causation. She jumped as the defendant was making sexual advances towards her, including touching her clothes. It was held that the defendant had committed a battery by touching the woman's clothes and that had caused her to jump out of the moving car, thereby injuring herself. It was stated that the victim's reaction (jumping from the car) did not break the chain of causation if it was reasonably foreseeable, provided it was not so 'daft or so unexpected that no reasonable man could be expected to foresee it'. If this was the case then it could constitute a novus actus interveniens (as explained in Chapter 29).

Figure 30.1 Battery can be committed by omission

KEY TERMINOLOGY

occasion(ing): to bring about or to cause.

GRADE BOOST

You should state what the mens rea of assault or battery actually is:

- **Assault**: intention or subjective recklessness to cause the victim to apprehend the infliction of immediate unlawful violence.
- **Battery**: intention or subjective recklessness to apply unlawful force on the victim.

3. Actual bodily harm

The definition of what constitutes ABH was clarified in the case of *Miller* (1954) as 'hurt or injury calculated to interfere with health or comfort'; that is, ABH can be physical or psychological harm. It can include cutting someone's hair, as in *DPP v Smith* (2006). The case of *Chan Fook* (1994) also makes the point that the injury needs to be more than 'transient or trifling'. The word 'actual' in this context means that, though the injury doesn't need to be permanent, it should not be so trivial as to be insignificant.

> **KEY CASE**
>
> **R v Savage (1992)**
> A woman went into a bar and saw her ex-partner's new girlfriend. She went up to her and said, 'Nice to meet you, darling' and threw beer from her glass over her. While doing so, she accidentally let go of the glass, which broke and cut the other woman's wrist. She argued that she had only the mens rea of battery (throwing the beer) but the court held that this was irrelevant. No additional mens rea was required for the actual bodily harm (the glass cutting the woman's wrist). As long as she had the mens rea for battery then the mens rea of ABH was satisfied.

Figure 30.2 Having the mens rea for battery meant that there was mens rea for ABH in *R v Savage*

Mens rea

The mens rea of battery is the same as for assault or battery. There is no requirement to prove any extra mens rea for the ABH, as per *Roberts* (1971) and confirmed in *R v Savage* (1992).

s20 Grievous bodily harm (GBH)

The statutory offence of grievous bodily harm (GBH) is set out in **s20 Offences Against the Person Act 1861**, which provides that it is an offence to maliciously inflict grievous bodily harm or wound the victim.

Grievous is defined in *DPP v Smith* (1961) as 'really serious harm' and confirmed in *Saunders* (1985). In *R v Brown and Stratton* (1998), injuries such as bruising, broken nose, missing teeth and concussion were held to be grievous bodily harm.

GBH is a triable either way offence. The maximum sentence for GBH is five years' imprisonment, but this has been criticised as being the same as for the lesser offence of ABH.

> **KEY TERMINOLOGY**
>
> **wounding:** to break both layers of the skin, usually resulting in bleeding.
>
> **maliciously:** interpreted as meaning with intention or subjective recklessness.
>
> **indictable:** the most serious offences, triable only in the Crown Court.

Actus reus

GBH can be proved by either showing an infliction of GBH or a *wounding* of the victim. It is important to choose the charge carefully as being either infliction of GBH or a wound.

1. Infliction of GBH

> **KEY CASES**
>
> **Clarence (1888)**
> A husband passed a sexually transmitted disease to his wife by having intercourse with her. It was ruled that 'inflict' required an assault or battery and, as she had consented to sexual intercourse, neither of these was present. This is now considered to be bad law.
>
> **M'Loughlin (1838)**
> A scratch or break to the outer skin is not sufficient if the inner skin remains intact.

The term 'inflict' has caused difficulty in the courts over the years. In *Clarence* (1888), the term was given a very restrictive meaning but, more recently, in *Dica* (2004) the meaning was widened to include recklessly transmitting HIV to an unaware victim as being 'infliction' of GBH.

A similarly wide approach is demonstrated in *R v Halliday* (1889), where a husband frightened his wife to the extent that she jumped out of their bedroom window to escape. The court held that her injuries had been directly inflicted by the defendant even though she had voluntarily jumped from the window.

The case of *R v Bollom* (2003) established that the age and characteristics of the victim are relevant to the extent of the injuries sustained.

2. Wounding

A wound requires a breaking in the continuity of the skin, usually resulting in bleeding. In *Moriarty v Brooks* (1834), it was held that both the dermis and the epidermis must be broken; however, in *JCC (A Minor) v Eisenhower* (1984), an internal rupture of blood vessels in the victim's eye as a result of being shot with a pellet gun was not held to amount to wounding within s20.

Mens rea

The mens rea for GBH is defined by the word *maliciously*.

The case of *Mowatt* (1967) decided that it does not need to be established whether or not the defendant intended or was reckless as to the infliction of GBH or a wound as long as it can be proved that he intended or was reckless to cause some physical harm. This was further clarified in the case of *DPP v A* (2000), where it was held to be sufficient to prove the defendant intended or foresaw that some harm might occur and it was not necessary to show the defendant intended or foresaw that serious harm would occur.

s18 Grievous bodily harm (GBH) with intent

The statutory offence of grievous bodily harm with intent is set out in s18 Offences Against the Person Act 1861, which provides that it is an offence to intend to maliciously wound or cause grievous bodily harm. Section 18 is an *indictable* offence. The maximum sentence for s18 Offences Against the Person Act 1861 is life imprisonment, reflecting the gravity of s18 in comparison to s20 of the same Act.

Actus reus

Like the actus reus for s20, the actus reus for s18 is either maliciously wounding or causing grievous bodily harm. It refers to the term 'cause' as opposed to 'inflict' and though they are not the same (*R v Ireland, Burstow* (1997)) they have been taken to mean that causation is required. The meaning of 'wound' and causing 'grievous bodily harm' are the same as for s20.

Mens rea

The key difference between s20 and s18 is that s18 can only be proved with intention (direct or oblique) whereas s20 can be established with recklessness or intention to cause some harm.

The mens rea has two aspects:

1. The defendant must 'maliciously' wound or cause grievous bodily harm.
2. The defendant must have specific intent to either cause grievous bodily harm to the victim or to resist or prevent the lawful apprehension or detainer of any person.

Charging standards

The CPS has issued guidelines known as charging standards for the offences against the person, to ensure greater consistency. It details types of injury (e.g. swelling, graze, black eye, etc.) and the charge that should follow if such injuries are present.

Evaluation of non-fatal offences against the person

Many reports have suggested reforms to this area of law:

> 'Criminal Law Revision Committee, Fourteenth Report, Offences Against the Person' (1980)
> 'Legislating the Criminal Code: Offences Against the Person and General Principles, Law Commission Report' (1993)
> 'Violence: Reforming the Offences Against the Person Act 1861', Home Office Consultation Paper with draft Bill (1998)
> 'Reform of Offences Against the Person', Law Commission (2015) Law Com No. 361.

The main criticisms are:

> The law is out of date – issues such as infliction of GBH through disease such as an STD and 'bodily harm' including injury to mental health have only recently been covered by the law.
> There is inconsistency between offences, for example, the same sentence for ABH and GBH (yet life imprisonment for s18), and for assault and battery, and the same mens rea for ABH as with assault/battery.
> Use of language – the language used in the Offences Against the Person Act 1861 is old-fashioned and does not reflect the modern use of language. For example, the words 'malicious' and 'grievous'.

The 2015 report sets out many recommendations for reforming the law for non-fatal offences against the person, including:

> a clearer hierarchy of offences against the person: there should be clearer distinctions between the injuries inflicted, blameworthiness of the defendant and penalties
> using modern and accessible language
> adding a new offence of 'aggravated assault' for low-level injuries
> replacing common law battery with physical assault.

STRETCH AND CHALLENGE

The leading case is now *R v Savage* (1992), while *DPP v Parmenter* (1992) confirmed this point. Find out more about the *DPP v Parmenter* case.

GRADE BOOST

Section 18 is a crime of specific intent, meaning that it can only be proved with intention as the mens rea.

Section 47 and s20 are both basic intent offences as they can be proved with either intention or recklessness.

Section 18 is a specific intent offence (as required by *R v Belfon* (1976)) and requires intention to maliciously cause grievous bodily harm, thus reflecting the severity of the injuries and culpability of the defendant.

STRETCH AND CHALLENGE

Have a look at the charging standards on the CPS website and make a list of the likely injuries for each of the offences mentioned in this section.

> **EXAM SKILLS**
>
> This topic is frequently examined as a problem scenario. You will need to be able to explain and/or apply the criminal liability of the parties involved. More than one non-fatal offence is likely to feature in the exam.
>
> You might also be required to analyse and evaluate the effectiveness of the law in this area and consider proposals for reform.

> **SUMMARY: NON-FATAL OFFENCES AGAINST THE PERSON**
>
> → **Assault**:
> - Actus reus: apprehension of immediate infliction of unlawful violence. Common law offence: **s39 Criminal Justice Act 1988**
> - Mens rea: intention or subjective recklessness to cause the victim to fear the infliction of immediate unlawful force
>
> → **Battery**:
> - Actus reus: application of unlawful physical force. Common law offence: **s39 Criminal Justice Act 1988**
> - Mens rea: intention or subjective recklessness to apply unlawful force on another
>
> → **ABH**: **s47 Offences Against the Person Act 1861**
> - Actus reus: 1. assault or battery, 2. occasioning, 3. actual bodily harm
> - Mens rea: the same as for assault or battery; no additional mens rea required for the actual bodily harm
>
> → **GBH**: **s20 Offences Against the Person Act 1861**
> - Actus reus: malicious infliction of grievous bodily harm or wounding (breaking of the skin)
> - Mens rea: intention or subjective recklessness to inflict 'some' harm
>
> → **GBH with intent**: **s18 Offences Against the Person Act 1861**
> - Actus reus: malicious wounding or causing grievous bodily harm. Indictable offence; maximum life imprisonment
> - Mens rea: specific intent crime; intention to maliciously cause grievous bodily harm
>
> → **CPS charging standards**: provides guidance for prosecutors about the possible injuries for each non-fatal offence. This should aid consistency in charging decisions.

> **TEST YOURSELF**
>
> 1. List the five non-fatal offences against the person, in a hierarchy from least to most serious.
> 2. What is the actus reus of assault?
> 3. Can words negate liability for an assault? Use case law to support.
> 4. What is the mens rea of battery?
> 5. How have the courts defined 'actual bodily harm'?
> 6. What is the key difference between the mens rea for **s20** and **s18 Offences Against the Person (OAP) Act 1861**?
> 7. What is the maximum sentence on conviction for **s18 OAP Act 1861**?
> 8. What is a 'wound' for the purposes of **s20 OAP Act 1861**?
> 9. What is the mens rea for **s20 OAP Act 1861**?

10. Consider the criminal liability of the parties in the following scenario:

    Karina decides to end her relationship with David after a few months, due to his controlling behaviour. David sent hundreds of messages every day to Karina and made silent telephone calls. Once, he was caught standing outside her house during the early hours of the morning. His behaviour is causing her to feel concerned for her safety.

    Karina then started to date Matthew. One day, Matthew and Karina were walking along the street when they were approached by David. Outraged by this new relationship, David shoves Karina out of the way and punches Matthew in the face, causing bruising, a black eye and a fractured eye socket. Karina stumbles backwards and falls into Dr Gerth who is walking by. He falls over and cuts his hand on the pavement.

Fatal offences against the person

Murder

This is the most serious of all the offences of *homicide*. The definition of murder is not contained in statute; indeed, it is a common law offence, the definition of which was outlined by Lord Justice Coke in the 17th century: 'the unlawful killing of a reasonable person in being and under the King's (or Queen's) Peace and with malice aforethought, express or implied'.

Causation is an essential element that needs to be proved in murder cases, because it is a result crime. It has to be proved that the defendant caused the death of the victim in fact and in law. Table 30.1 summarises this idea.

> **KEY TERMINOLOGY**
>
> **homicide:** the killing of one person by another, deliberately or not.

Figure 30.3 Murder is a common law offence

Table 30.1 Summary of causation

Actus reus		Mens rea	
A human being is dead.		Intention to kill or cause grievous bodily harm.	
The defendant caused the death IN FACT.		Intention can be direct or indirect (oblique).	
The defendant caused the death IN LAW.			

Actus reus

1. A human being is dead

A person is a human being when it can exist independently of its mother (**AG's reference No. 3 of 1994**). Therefore, a person who kills an unborn child may be criminally liable under the law, but it will not be for a homicide offence. There is much controversy over what constitutes 'dead', but it would seem that the courts favour the definition of 'brain-dead' and this was confirmed in the case of **R v Malcherek and Steel (1981)**.

2. The defendant caused the death in fact (factual causation)

a) The 'but for' test

This test asks 'but for' the conduct of the defendant, would the victim have died as and when they did? If the answer is no then the defendant will be liable for the death. The example case is **R v White (1910)** (see page 299).

b) The de minimis rule

De minimis means insignificant, minute or trifling. This test requires that the original injury caused by the defendant's action must be more than a minimal cause of death. The example case is **R v Pagett (1983)** (see page 299).

3. The defendant caused the death in law (legal causation)

a) The injury must be the operating and substantial cause of death

This test considers whether the original injury inflicted by the defendant is, at the time of death, still the operating and substantial cause of death; that the chain of causation has not been broken by another event. An example case is **R v Smith (1959)**, contrasted with **R v Jordan (1956)** (see page 300).

b) The 'thin skull' test

A defendant has to take their victim as they find them. If the victim dies from some unusual or unexpected physical or other condition, the defendant is still responsible for the death. For example, if during a fight the defendant hits the victim with a punch that would not normally cause anything more than soreness and bruising, but because the victim has an unusually thin skull, they die, the defendant is still liable for the death. An example case is **R v Blaue (1975)** (see page 300).

c) Foreseeable intervening act

If the intervening act is foreseeable, courts have concluded that it will not be enough to break the chain of causation. However, if the intervening act is so extraordinary as to **not** be foreseeable, it can break the chain of causation, as in R v Roberts (1971) (see page 308).

Mens rea

The mens rea for murder is defined as 'malice aforethought', which has come to mean either an intention to kill or an intention to cause grievous bodily harm. The term malice aforethought causes confusion as there is neither a requirement for the defendant's actions to be malicious, nor for there to be any premeditation.

Intention for murder

```
                    INTENTION TO KILL
                           or
         INTENTION TO CAUSE GRIEVOUS BODILY HARM
                     DPP v SMITH (1961)
              • The word 'grievous' means 'serious'.
              • The test of intention is subjective:
                it is what the defendant intended,
                not what the 'reasonable man' intended.
```

Direct intention
The defendant wants the victim to die and does what is necessary to achieve it.

Indirect intention (oblique intention)
The defendant foresees the consequences but does not want the consequences to happen.
R v Moloney (1985)
The defendant and his stepfather were messing around with a shotgun. Moloney pulled the trigger as a dare and killed his stepfather.

Figure 30.4 Direct and indirect (oblique) intention of murder or grievous bodily harm

This can either be direct or indirect (oblique):

› Direct intention is where the consequence is the defendant's main aim or purpose. For example, Omar shoots Mirwa because he wants to kill her.
› Oblique intention is less straightforward (but is still acceptable as the mens rea of murder). This is where a defendant, in order to achieve their primary aim or purpose, may also cause something else to happen. For example, if a defendant wishes to shoot someone who is located behind a window, his direct intention is to shoot the victim but he also knows he must break the window in order to do so. He can, therefore, be said to have obliquely intended to break the window.

A two-part legal test for oblique intention was set down by the Court of Appeal case of R v Nedrick (1986) and approved by the House of Lords in R v Woollin (1998):

1. Was the result a virtually certain consequence of the defendant's conduct?
2. Did the defendant foresee that the result was a virtually certain consequence of their conduct?

If the answer to both questions is yes, then the defendant has oblique intention and this is sufficient for a conviction of murder.

> **STRETCH AND CHALLENGE**
>
> Look up the case of R v Cheshire (1991). This case also involved the question of whether substandard medical treatment was enough to break the chain of causation. Did the court agree with R v Smith (1959) or R v Jordan (1956)?

Table 30.2 Timeline of decisions on oblique intention

Year	Case	Outcome
1975	Hyam v DPP	Where there is foresight there will always be intention.
1986	R v Hancock and Shankland	The greater the probability of a consequence, the more likely the consequence was foreseen, and therefore also intended.
1986	R v Nedrick	The judge directed that a jury can infer intention where death or grievous bodily harm is a virtual certainty of the defendant's actions and the defendant appreciates this to be the case.
1998	R v Woollin	The wording was changed so that a jury is entitled to find intention where death or grievous bodily harm is a virtual certainty of the defendant's actions. It is a question of evidence, not law.
2003	R v Matthews and Alleyne	It followed the direction taken in Woollin (1998) and the virtual certainty test now seems to be the standard approach to take.

KEY CASES

R v Hancock and Shankland (1986)
The defendants were striking miners who threw a concrete block from a bridge to block the road below. It killed a passing taxi driver. The defendants were convicted of murder, which was later quashed on appeal when the court concluded that the greater the probability of a consequence, the more likely the consequence was foreseen, and therefore also intended.

R v Nedrick (1986)
The defendant was convicted of murder after throwing paraffin through the letterbox of a woman against whom he had a grudge. The woman's 12-year-old son died in the attack. An appeal was allowed and Nedrick was then convicted of manslaughter. The court held that the jury should consider how probable the consequence was and whether it was foreseen by the defendant. The jury may then infer intention if they are confident that the defendant realised the consequence was a virtual certainty and the defendant appreciated this to be the case.

R v Woollin (1998)
The defendant was a father who lost his temper with his three-year-old son when he choked on his food. He insisted he had not wanted the child to die, but the court held that it was a reasonably foreseeable consequence of his actions.

R v Matthews and Alleyne (2003)
This case concerned an 18-year-old who had been robbed and thrown over a bridge by two youths. The boy had told the youths that he could not swim before they pushed him. He drowned, and the court found that was a reasonably foreseeable consequence of the defendants' actions.

Criticisms of the law on murder

> The mandatory life sentence does not allow the court to take account of, for example, killing out of compassion.
> No precise definition of when 'death' occurs.
> Intention includes an intention to cause GBH but the conviction is the same (murder).
> No clear definition of intention. Problems with oblique intent.
> Cases of euthanasia.

Reform proposals for the law on murder

Reform of murder and the mandatory life sentence have been considered several times. The key reports are:

> Law Commission, Draft Criminal Code
> Law Commission Report, *Partial Defences to Murder* (Law Com No. 290, 2004)

> Law Commission Consultation Document, *A New Homicide Act for England and Wales?* (Law Com CP No. 177, 2005)
> Law Commission Final Report, *Murder, Manslaughter and Infanticide* (Law Com CP No. 304, 2004).

STRETCH AND CHALLENGE
Research these reform proposals. What have they suggested in terms of reforms to the structure and/or sentencing of homicide offences?

STRETCH AND CHALLENGE
If courts tend to conclude that indirect intention is still intention, think about cases of assisted suicide. Here, the person foresees that their actions will bring about the death of the person, even though that is not the result they would want. Look at the cases of *Diane Pretty* (2002) and *Debbie Purdy* (2009). Do you agree with the courts' decisions in these cases?

Research the case of *Re A (Conjoined Twins)* (2000), when a lifesaving operation for one conjoined twin would kill the other twin. Do you think this constitutes murder?

Voluntary manslaughter

Voluntary manslaughter is the crime where a defendant has committed murder but is relying on a special (and partial) defence contained in the Homicide Act 1957 and the Coroners and Justice Act 2009. If the special defence is proved, the charge of murder will be reduced to manslaughter, and the judge will have discretion in terms of sentencing the defendant. The burden of proof is on the defence to prove that the defence applies to them.

Such a defence may be:

> loss of control
> responsibility
> suicide pact.

Loss of control

This offence is now contained in the Coroners and Justice Act 2009 (CJA 2009), which replaced the old defence of provocation under the Homicide Act 1957.

Elements of the defence
1. 'Loss of control'
s54(i) Coroners and Justice Act 2009:

> Defendant must have lost their self-control at the time of the actus reus.
> The loss of control here need not be sudden, which means that women with a 'slow-burn' reaction will not be treated less fairly (*Ahluwalia* (1992)). Under the old defence of provocation, the loss of control had to be 'sudden'.
> Cumulative loss of self-control may be possible: *R v Dawes, Hatter and Bowyer* (2013).
> Defendant must not be acting in a 'considered desire for revenge', and a delay between the trigger (see below) and the loss of control may be considered as evidence of a desire for revenge.
> Whether the defendant 'lost their self-control' is a question to be decided by the jury.

2. 'By a qualifying trigger'
s55(i) Coroners and Justice Act 2009:

> This can be from a fear of serious violence from the victim.
> This is a new concept that protects women who have been subjected to continuous domestic violence by their abusive partners, or a homeowner who protected their property by killing a burglar.
> The test is subjective, which means it is how the defendant fears, not how the 'reasonable man' or someone else in their position would fear the serious violence. It has been suggested, however, that the victim has to be the source of violence, and the defendant has to fear that the violence is directed towards them.

KEY TERMINOLOGY
special defence: a defence that can only be used by a defendant being prosecuted for the offence of murder.

partial defence: the use of a defence that has the effect not of completely acquitting the defendant but allowing a reduction in the charge and sentence given to the defendant.

GRADE BOOST
When applying the law to a problem question, take each element of the offence and apply it to the problem question. Work your way methodically through this list of 'ingredients', applying them to the scenario and remembering to use appropriate legal authority throughout. You may then need to apply a special defence (considered below) or a general defence (considered in a later chapter).

s55(ii) Coroners and Justice Act 2009:

› Things are said or done of an extremely grave character, causing the defendant a justifiable sense of being seriously wronged.
› This is a narrow approach, because although the sense of being wronged is subjective, it has to be justified, which is an objective test and one that can only be determined by the jury.
› The Court of Appeal observed in *R v Clinton, Parker and Evans* (2012) that this requires an objective evaluation. The things said or done must be 'extremely grave' (very serious) and they must have made the defendant justifiably feel 'seriously wronged'. This requirement removes the possibility of using the defence for trivial matters such as in the case of *R v Doughty* (1986) (decided under the old law of provocation), where the persistent crying of a baby was held to be within the scope of 'things said or done').

s55(iii) Coroners and Justice Act 2009:

› A combination of the first and second triggers.

These triggers cannot be used if the defendant incited the victim to say or do what they did to provide an excuse to use violence

Sexual infidelity

Under the old law of provocation, sexual infidelity was an accepted ground of provocation. However, **s55(6)(c)** of the **CJA 2009** states that 'the fact that a thing done or said constituted sexual infidelity is to be disregarded'.

The case of *R v Clinton, Parker and Evans* (2012) is important on this issue as the court held that where sexual infidelity alone was the trigger then the defence is not permitted. However, where sexual infidelity was 'an essential part of the context' then the defence may be available. For example:

› if a victim tells the defendant he is having an affair and she kills him, the defence of loss of control is not available
› however, if the victim tells the defendant he is having an affair, and makes serious and grave insulting remarks about her compared with his new lover, and then she kills him, she may have the defence of loss of control.

> *'A person of D's sex and age, with a normal degree of tolerance and self-restraint and in the circumstances of D, might have reacted in the same or in a similar way to D'*

› This objective test asks whether a person of the defendant's sex and age (subjective characteristics), with an ordinary level of tolerance and self-restraint, and in similar circumstances, might have acted in the same or a similar way to the defendant **(s54(1)(c))**.
› The new defence seems to have followed *A-G for Jersey v Holley* (2005).
› It is thought that where abnormal characteristics are present, it is more likely that the defendant will rely on the defence of diminished responsibility.

Burden of proof

The prosecution must disprove the defence of loss of control beyond reasonable doubt.

Other significant cases
› *R v Jewell* (2014)
› *R v Workman* (2014) and *R v Barnsdale-Quean* (2014)
› *R v Dawes, Hatter and Bowyer* (2013).

Effect of this defence
The use of this defence has implications of discrimination against women. The so-called battered woman's syndrome was brought to light in the cases of *Thornton* (1996) and

Ahluwalia (1992), which both involved women who killed their husbands after they had endured years of abuse. In both cases there seemed to be a 'cooling off period', which means the element of 'sudden' loss of control was not satisfied.

It was raised in these cases that a sudden loss of control is a male reaction and takes no account of the fact that women react to provocation in different ways. Helena Kennedy QC described the female reaction as 'a snapping in slow motion, the final surrender of frayed elastic'. Because of this criticism, the courts seemed to become more lenient and, in the case of *Ahluwalia* (1992), an appeal was allowed and the defence of diminished responsibility accepted instead. More encouraging was the judge's approach in the appeal for *Thornton* (1996), where the concept of 'battered woman's syndrome' was accepted and could be taken into account when considering whether there had been a sudden and temporary loss of control. Under the new defence, this is still relevant because, although the loss of control need not be sudden, a time delay is relevant in deciding whether there had been a loss of control.

Figure 30.5 Victims of domestic violence might have a defence to sudden and temporary loss of control in light of 'battered woman's syndrome'

STRETCH AND CHALLENGE

Consider the cases of *R v Doughty* (1986), *R v Pearson* (1992) and *R v Brown* (1972), which were decided under the old defence of provocation. How do you think they would have been decided under the new defence?

R v Doughty (1986): under the new defence, persistent crying of a baby does not equate to circumstances of an extremely grave character for trigger (ii).

R v Pearson (1992): acts of third parties would be irrelevant for trigger (i), but may be relevant for trigger (ii).

R v Brown (1972): the new Act is not clear about the situation where a mistake has been made, but this will be resolved by the courts in due course.

STRETCH AND CHALLENGE

Look up some of the criticisms of the law on loss of control. These will be required for an essay question that requires you to analyse and evaluate the law.

Diminished responsibility

The defence of diminished responsibility was created because of the limitations of the other mental capacity defence – insanity. It recognises that some defendants commit crime because of their mental illness, but does not return a verdict of 'not guilty by reason of insanity' as with the defence of insanity, therefore providing at least some justice for the victim.

The defence of diminished responsibility was not entirely replaced by the **CJA 2009**. It remains in **s2 Homicide Act 1957** but has been amended by **s52 CJA 2009**. The new definition includes the phrasing 'abnormality of mental functioning'. The purpose was to clarify the law but no changes were made to the applicability of the defence. The **new** definition means that one of the essential elements of the defence is a recognised medical condition. The old case law is expected to still be helpful in determining what may count as an 'abnormality of mental functioning'.

Elements of the defence

1. **Section 2(1) Homicide Act 1957** as amended by **s52 CJA 2009**:
   The defendant is suffering from an abnormality of mental functioning which (a) arose from a recognised medical condition.

Before 2009, the **Homicide Act 1957** referred to 'abnormality of the mind'. The new wording in **CJA 2009** has clarified and modernised the law (in line with developments in medical science) and should allow for a wider range of mental illnesses to fall within the scope of the defence.

R v Martin (Anthony) (2001) would probably have succeeded under this defence because the defendant was suffering from a paranoid personality disorder when he killed an intruder in his home (see page 353 for details of this case).

> **KEY CASE**
>
> *R v Byrne* (1960)
> This case defined abnormality of the mind as 'a state of mind so different from that of ordinary human beings that the reasonable man would term it abnormal'. The test is objective and for the jury to decide.

The requirement of a 'recognised medical condition' narrows the defence and requires expert medical opinion to be considered during the criminal trial. This has allowed for some physical conditions that cause an abnormality of mental functioning to be included, for example, epilepsy, sleep disorders and diabetes.

2. **Section 2(1)(b)** as amended: the abnormality of mental functioning must have substantially impaired the defendant's ability to do one of more of the things mentioned in **s52(1A)**.

(1A) Those things are:

(a) understand the nature of their conduct; or
(b) form a rational judgement; or
(c) exercise self-control.

This is a much more specific element of the crime and it makes clear what aspects of the mental functioning must be affected.

The word 'substantial' was considered in the case of *R v Golds* (2014).

3. **Section 52(1)(c)** as amended: must provide an explanation for the defendant's acts and omissions in doing or being a party to the killing.

Under **s2(1B)** the abnormality of mental functioning must be a significant contributory factor to the killing.

If *R v Dietschmann* (2003) were to be decided under the new defence, it is unclear whether the case would have got past the first hurdle of depression being recognised as a medical condition. However, it does not matter if drink or drugs are involved; the key question is whether the medical condition overrides that and is a significant contributor to the killing.

> *R v Dietschmann* (2003)
> The defendant was suffering from depression, but was also drunk when he killed his victim. Even though the abnormality was the depression, the court accepted diminished responsibility because, even though he may not have killed had he been sober, the depression was a substantial cause.

> **STRETCH AND CHALLENGE**
>
> Look up the case of *Sally Challen* (2020): this led to the coercive control being relevant to the defence of diminished responsibility (in her case) and also loss of control. It builds upon and supports a more sophisticated analysis of the criminal law's understanding of the impact of domestic violence on the mental capacity of defendants. It arguably also aligns the partial, special defences with the new offence of coercive controlling behaviour in an intimate relationship (**s76 Serious Crime Act 2015**).

> **GRADE BOOST**
> Research the law on intoxication and diminished responsibility. Does the law distinguish between voluntary intoxication and alcohol dependency syndrome?

> **GRADE BOOST**
> Look up the case of *R v Ahluwalia* (1992). On what grounds did her appeal on the basis of the defence of diminished responsibility succeed after her original defence of provocation (now loss of control) had failed?

> **STRETCH AND CHALLENGE**
>
> Look up some of the criticisms of the law on diminished responsibility. These will be required for an essay question that requires you to analyse and evaluate the law.
>
> Another special defence to murder is that of suicide pact. It is for the defence to prove on the balance of probabilities that this defence applies. Look at the case of *R v H* (2003).
>
> Do you think that the reversal of the burden of proof disadvantages the defendant, who is already likely to be distressed, or is it necessary to prevent disguised suicide pacts, for example, those who assist someone to die when they will benefit from their death?

> **GRADE BOOST**
>
> You need to be prepared for an essay question on the elements of defence topic as well as a problem question. The contemporary nature of this topic makes it likely to be examined and you need to show an awareness of the changes to the law and approaches, and how they will affect defendants relying on these defences.

> **KEY TERMINOLOGY**
>
> **suicide pact**: a partial defence to murder contained in **s4 Homicide Act 1957** whereby, if a surviving person of a pact for two people to die can prove that they both intended to die, the charge will be reduced to voluntary manslaughter.
>
> **constructive manslaughter**: the death of a person is caused by an unlawful and dangerous criminal act.
>
> **gross negligence manslaughter**: the death of a person is caused by civil negligence.

Involuntary manslaughter

Involuntary manslaughter is where a defendant has committed the actus reus of murder but does not have the mens rea. While the defendant did not intend to kill or cause GBH they were still to blame, in some way, for the death, and if that blame is serious enough, this warrants a criminal conviction.

There are two forms of involuntary manslaughter relevant to the specification:

1. manslaughter by an unlawful and dangerous act (constructive manslaughter)
2. gross negligence manslaughter.

Unlawful and dangerous act manslaughter (constructive manslaughter)

All common elements of murder are present.

Actus reus

It has to be an unlawful act, not an omission.

> ### *R v Lowe* (1973)
> This involved the commission of the offence of child neglect, and the neglect caused the child's death.

The act has to be criminal, not civil. This was held in the case of *R v Franklin* (1883) and in the more recent case of *R v D* (2006).

> ### *R v D* (2006)
> Having suffered years of domestic abuse from her husband, the victim committed suicide. Prior to the suicide, her husband had cut her forehead when he struck her with his bracelet. This was held to be enough of an unlawful criminal act because it constituted an offence under **s20 Offences Against the Person Act 1861**.

It also has to be a dangerous act. The test is whether a reasonable person would foresee that the act would cause harm.

> ### *R v Church* (1966)
> The court held that the test has to be whether a 'sober and reasonable person would realise the risk' of their act.

It does not matter what form that harm takes, as long as some harm is foreseeable, as in *R v JM and SM* (2012). The defendant must have the same knowledge as the sober and reasonable person.

> ### *R v Dawson* (1985)
> The victim was a 60-year-old with a serious heart condition. The defendants were not to know about this condition and neither was a sober and reasonable person, therefore, the act could not be dangerous.
>
> ### *R v Watson* (1989)
> The victim was an 87-year-old man. The court held that the defendants should be reasonably expected to know that the man would be frail and easily scared. Therefore, the act was dangerous.

The case of *DPP v Newbury and Jones* (1976) provides the direction for the jury on the issue of dangerousness and the objective test. In his judgment Lord Salmon said:

> 'In judging whether an act was dangerous the test is not did the accused recognise that it was dangerous but would all sober and reasonable people recognise its danger … it is unnecessary to prove that the accused knew that the act was unlawful or dangerous.'

Causation

It must be established that the unlawful and dangerous act was the cause of the death.

> ### *R v Johnstone* (2007)
> The victim was subjected to a series of taunts, which involved spitting and shouting (not deemed to be a dangerous act) and stones and wood being thrown (deemed to be a dangerous act). The victim suffered a heart attack brought on by stress. The defendants could not be convicted of constructive manslaughter because it was not clear whether it was the dangerous act that brought on the heart attack, and thus caused the death of the victim.

If the victim intervenes in the chain of causation with a voluntary act, this will be sufficient to break the chain of causation.

> ### *R v Kennedy (No. 2)* (2007)
> The court held that a drug dealer can never be held responsible for the death of a drug user.

But contrast this case with *R v Cato* (1976):

> ### *R v Cato* (1976)
> The drug dealer injected heroin into the victim, so in this case the defendant would have been liable for the manslaughter of the victim.

Mens rea

This is the mens rea of the unlawful act. For example, if the unlawful act was **s18 Offences Against the Person Act 1861**, then the mens rea would be intention.

STRETCH AND CHALLENGE

Consider the case of *R v Lamb* (1967), where the defendant pointed a gun at his friend as a joke. The defendant had no intention of hurting the victim but one of the bullets slipped out and killed his friend. Can you identify (a) the unlawful act and (b) the mens rea of that act? Based on this, is the defendant guilty of constructive manslaughter?

Gross negligence manslaughter

Negligence is usually covered under the civil law but there is some negligent behaviour (leading to death) that is so severe as to require punishment under the criminal law.

The test was laid down in the case of *R v Adomako* (1994).

As with constructive manslaughter, all common elements of murder are present.

Duty of care

A duty of care is established under the 'neighbourhood principle' contained in *Donoghue v Stevenson* (1932) (see page 112 for details of this case). Whether or not a duty of care is owed is a matter for the jury to decide using the 'neighbourhood principle'.

A few key exceptions arose in *R v Willoughby* (2004), where it was held that there will almost always be a duty of care between doctor and patient.

Gross negligent breach of that duty

Whether or not the breach of the duty amounts to gross negligence is a matter for the jury to decide, though in the case of *R v Bateman* (1925), Lord Hewart CJ suggested that it 'showed such disregard for life and safety of others as to amount to a crime against the state and conduct deserving punishment'.

Risk of death

As well as being expressed in *R v Adomako* (1994), this provision was further confirmed in *R v Misra and Srivastava* (2005) where doctors failed to diagnose a post-operation infection which led to the death of the patient. The lack of diagnosis, and the subsequent lack of treatment, was held to constitute a risk of death.

> **STRETCH AND CHALLENGE**
>
> Look up some of the criticisms of the law on constructive manslaughter. These will be required for an essay question where you are asked to analyse and evaluate the law.

> **KEY CASE**
>
> **R v Adomako (1994)**
> The defendant was a doctor who had inserted a ventilator tube into a patient's mouth, but the patient died from lack of oxygen when the tube became detached from the machine. Adomako had not realised quickly enough that his patient was dying, and he appealed to the House of Lords against his conviction of gross negligence manslaughter. Lord Mackay in the House of Lords held that there were several elements that had to be satisfied to uphold the conviction:
> - duty of care
> - gross negligent breach of that duty
> - risk of death.

> **GRADE BOOST**
>
> Research the case of *R v Bawa-Garba* (2016) on the offence of involuntary manslaughter by gross negligence. Do you agree with the outcome of the original trial and the appeal?

> **SUMMARY: FATAL OFFENCES AGAINST THE PERSON**
>
> → **Murder**
> - 'The unlawful killing of a reasonable person in being and under the King's (or Queen's) Peace and with malice aforethought, express or implied.' LJ Coke
> - Actus reus elements:
>   - Human being: independent of mother: *AG's Reference No. 3 of 1994*
>   - Death: *R v Malcherek and Steel* (1981)
>   - Causation in fact: 'but for test' *R v White* (1910); de minimis rule: *Pagett* (1983)
> → Legal causation:
>   - injury as the operative and substantial cause of death: *R v Smith* (1959), *R v Jordan* (1956)
>   - 'thin skull test': *R v Blaue* (1975)

- foreseeable intervening act: *R v Roberts* (1971)
- Mens rea elements: malice aforethought: intention to kill OR intention to cause GBH: *DPP v Smith* (1961)
- Direct intention
- Oblique intention: *R v Woollin* (1998): virtual certainty test

→ **Voluntary manslaughter**
- Murder elements + Special defence: **Homicide Act 1957** and **Coroners and Justice Act 2009**
- Partial defence:
  - Loss of control
  - Diminished responsibility
  - Suicide pact
- Loss of control: **s54 Coroners and Justice Act 2009**:
  - Loss of control
  - Qualifying trigger
  - Reasonable person
  - Prosecution to disprove
- Diminished responsibility: **s2 Homicide Act 1957** as amended by **s52 Coroners and Justice Act 2009**:
  - Abnormality of mental functioning
  - Arising from a recognised medical condition
- Abnormality of mental functioning must be a significant contributory factor to the killing
- The abnormality of mental functioning must have substantially impaired the defendant's ability to:
  - understand the nature of their conduct; or
  - form a rational judgement; or
  - exercise self-control
- Defence to prove on the balance of probabilities, using expert evidence

→ **Involuntary manslaughter**
- Actus reus of murder + either unlawful and dangerous act OR gross negligence
- Unlawful and dangerous act manslaughter
- Elements of actus reus of murder
- Unlawful act: act not omission; criminal act not civil
- Dangerous act: reasonable person
- Causation
- Mens rea is the mens rea of the unlawful act

→ **Gross negligence manslaughter**
- *Adomako* (1994)
- Elements of actus reus of murder
- Duty of care
- Grossly negligent breach of that duty of care
- Risk of death
- Suicide pact

TEST YOURSELF

1. What offences are covered by the term 'homicide'?
2. What is the actus reus of murder?
3. When does death occur? Make reference to case law.
4. What is the test for oblique intention? Make reference to case law.
5. What case provides the definition of gross negligent manslaughter?
6. What is a partial defence?
7. Where is the law on loss of control contained?
8. What are the elements of the defence of loss of control?
9. What are the elements of the defence of diminished responsibility?
10. Is sexual infidelity to be disregarded when considering loss of control? Explain your answer fully.

EXAM PAST PAPER QUESTIONS

WJEC – Unit 3 – Sample Assessment Materials

A charity which helps ex-offenders began renovating an old house in an affluent suburb and turning it into a hostel for former prisoners. Many of the people who lived nearby were opposed to the hostel, as they feared that its presence would affect the value of their own houses and make them harder to sell. One local resident, David, decided to take matters into his own hands. Under cover of darkness, he broke into the hostel and began to damage the renovation work and throw paint over the walls. Suddenly one of the charity workers Mary appeared with her mobile phone in her hand, ready to call the police. To stop her, David punched her as hard as he could, knocking her unconscious. Thinking he had killed her, David tried to make it look as if Karen had died in an arson attack, setting fire to a heap of rags before running from the burning building. It so happened that Mary's phone had already connected with the emergency services before she fell unconscious, and the ambulance and fire brigade were there within minutes. Mary was brought out alive from the building, but died when the ambulance taking her to hospital was involved in a serious road accident.

Advise David as to whether he may be criminally liable for the death of Mary, applying your knowledge and understanding of legal rules and principles. [50]

Eduqas – AS Level – Component 2 – May 2019

(a) Explain the 'but for' test in causation. [6]

(b) Explain when an intervening act might break the chain of causation. [6]

(c) Assess whether the current law on intention is uncertain and unjust. [9]

Eduqas A Level – Component 2 – June 2019

Joe is a member of his school's mixed hockey team. The team's captain, Kevin, constantly criticises Joe in front of the other members of the team for being overweight and slow. During a particularly difficult game against another school, Joe lost the ball to Kim, a girl from the opposing team, who promptly scored a goal. Kevin ran over to Joe, shouting furiously, "You idiot, even a girl can play better than you!" Joe felt upset and humiliated and when Kate next moved in to tackle him, he lost all control and struck her hard on the leg with his hockey stick. After the game was over, Kate noticed a swelling in her leg, and showed it to her sports teacher, Linda. Linda said that it was probably just a bad bruise, but advised Kate to rest her leg and see her doctor in the morning. Kate ignored this advice and went out to party where she danced all night. However, that night Kate collapsed and was taken to hospital, where she died. It was later discovered that her death was due to a blood clot caused by the blow to her leg, and that her life could have been saved if she had received early medical treatment.

Advise Joe whether he may be criminally liable for Kate's death, applying your knowledge and understanding of legal rules and principles. [25]

31 Property offences

This topic of property offences covers three separate offences:

- theft
- robbery
- burglary.

Prior to the **Theft Act 1968**, this area of law was covered by common law and was complex. The **Theft Act 1968** effectively codified the law of some property offences. It has, however, continued to evolve through the interpretation of various parts of the Act by judges deciding certain cases. Since the original 1968 Act, there have been two further statutory updates: the **Theft Act 1978** and the **Theft (Amendment) Act 1996**, which amends the 1968 and 1978 Acts.

Figure 31.1 Theft involves the dishonest appropriation of someone else's property with intention to permanently deprive

Theft

This is defined in **s1 Theft Act 1968**:

> 'A person is guilty of theft if he dishonestly appropriates property belonging to another with the intention of permanently depriving the other of it.'

The actus reus elements of theft are:

1. appropriation (**s3**)
2. property (**s4**)
3. belonging to another (**s5**).

The mens rea elements of theft are:

1. intention to permanently deprive (**s6**)
2. dishonesty (**s2** and Ghosh test; see page 330).

The maximum sentence for theft is seven years' imprisonment.

Each element will be considered in turn.

Actus reus of theft

1. Appropriation

This element is defined in **s3(1) Theft Act 1968**:

> 'Any assumption by a person of the rights of an owner amounts to an appropriation, and this includes where he has come by the property (innocently or not) without stealing it, any later assumption of a right to it by keeping or dealing with it as owner.'

This means that the defendant has physically taken an object from its owner (e.g. a handbag or tablet computer). The defendant is assuming some or all their rights. This aspect has been interpreted widely and includes assuming any rights of the owner (e.g. moving, touching, destroying, selling, etc.). They are doing something with the property that the owner has a right to do (**bundle of rights**) and that no one else has the right to do without the permission

> **KEY TERMINOLOGY**
>
> **bundle of rights:** the owner of a property has a bundle of rights over their own property, so they have the right to do anything with it (e.g. destroy it, throw it away or do something random with it).

of the owner. One right is sufficient, as seen in *R v Morris* (1923), when the defendant switched the price on an item in a shop, intending to pay the lower price. Even though he did not make it to the checkout, the price switch and the placement of the goods in his trolley was considered to be an 'appropriation', as owners have the right to price their own goods.

Section 3(1) also covers situations where someone does not steal property (e.g. they are lent a bracelet by a friend) but then assumes the rights of the owner by refusing to return it. The 'appropriation' takes place once the person decides to keep it.

An appropriation can still take place even if the victim consents to the property being taken, as in *Lawrence v MPC* (1972). Viscount Dilhorne said:

> 'Parliament by the omission of these words (consent) has relieved the prosecution establishing that the taking was done without the owner's consent.'

Keith LJ said: 'An act may be an appropriation notwithstanding that it is done with the consent of the owner.' This principle was followed in *R v Gomez* (2000).

In *R v Hinks* (2000), the defendant's charge of theft was upheld regardless of it being a gift, as the defendant had 'appropriated' the money. This has the advantage of protecting vulnerable people.

> **STRETCH AND CHALLENGE**
>
> Research and summarise the key cases of *Lawrence v MPC* (1971) and *R v Gomez* (1993). What legal principles were established?

> **STRETCH AND CHALLENGE**
>
> How does *R v Hinks* (2000) demonstrate protection of vulnerable people regarding the interpretation of 'appropriation'?

> **STRETCH AND CHALLENGE**
>
> Look at the following scenarios and decide if an appropriation has taken place and, if so, when it takes place:
>
> 1. Terry borrows a bike from Abdul. After a month, Terry decides to sell the bicycle. Has Terry appropriated the bicycle?
> 2. Matthew is shopping in a store. He swaps the label on a shirt he intends to buy for that of a lower priced item. Has Matthew appropriated the shirt?
> 3. Tom's glasses fall from his jacket on to the pavement. Meera picks up the glasses and hands them back to Tom. Has Meera appropriated the glasses?

2. Property

This element is defined in s4 Theft Act 1968:

> 'Property includes money and all other property, real or personal, including things in action and other intangible property.'

Property may seem easy to define at first but there are some issues that need to be considered in further detail.

Things that can be stolen (so count as property) include:

- money (physical existence rather than its value)
- personal property
- real property
- intangible property
- things in action.

Real property includes land and buildings, although s4(2) provides that land, and things forming part of the land and severed from it (e.g. flowers, picked crops), cannot normally be stolen, except in the circumstances laid down in that section.

Intangible property means property that does not exist in a physical sense, such as copyright or patents.

A 'thing in action' (or a 'chose in action') is a technical term describing property that does not exist in a physical sense but which provides the owner with legally enforceable rights.

> **KEY TERMINOLOGY**
>
> **real property:** land and buildings.
>
> **intangible property:** property that does not physically exist, such as copyright or patents.
>
> **thing (or chose) in action:** property that does not exist in a physical sense but which provides the owner with legally enforceable rights (e.g. a bank account, investments, shares and intellectual property such as patents).

Examples include a bank account in credit where the bank refuses the customer their money, investments, shares and intellectual property such as patents. People have legal rights over these things but they cannot physically hold them.

> **GRADE BOOST**
> Recently, the cryptocurrency Bitcoin has been considered as a 'thing in action'.

R v Williams (2001)
The defendant was convicted of theft of the credit balances in his victim's bank accounts after he dishonestly tricked customers into overpaying him via cheque. The reduction of their bank credit balance (the 'thing in action') constituted theft.

The courts have, however, decided that some things are not 'property' within the definition. In *Oxford* v *Moss* (1979), it was held that seeing unopened exam questions was not theft as they were not 'property' but 'information'.

Electricity is treated separately under the Act. It is considered intangible property that cannot be stolen, but if a person (s11) 'dishonestly uses electricity without authority or dishonesty causes it to be wasted or diverted' then they may be liable for an offence.

Things that cannot be stolen are set out in s4(3) and s4(4) of the Act and cover situations where a person picks mushrooms, flowers, fruit or foliage growing wild on land. This is not to be treated as theft unless it is done for reward, sale or other commercial purpose (s4(3)). Section 4(4) relates to tamed or untamed wild animals.

A human body cannot normally be stolen. However, *R* v *Kelly and Lindsay* (1998) held that although a dead body is not normally property, the body parts in this case could be as their 'essential character and value has changed'.

> **STRETCH AND CHALLENGE**
> Look at the following scenarios and decide if it involves 'property' capable of being stolen:
> - Olivia takes her dog Clarence for a walk and picks some flowers growing wild on the side of the road, takes them home and puts them in a vase in her living room.
> - Jelani goes for a run and sees some apples in Farmer Silver's field. She hops over the gate and picks some apples to take home to her children.
> - Josh is a student in a college. He is due to sit a Media exam and knows the exam paper is on the desk in his classroom under a pile of paper. During the lesson, when his teacher is out of the room, he goes to the front of the class and sneaks a look at the paper. He takes a picture of it on his mobile phone.

> **GRADE BOOST**
> Can illegal drugs be stolen? Can a drug dealer be the victim of a theft? Research *R* v *Smith* (2011) on this issue.

> **STRETCH AND CHALLENGE**
> Research the position regarding cheques and the problems they have caused the law in this area.
>
> When considering 'information', what about trade secrets? How did the Law Commission in its consultation paper 'Legislating the Criminal Code: Misuse of Trade Secrets' (1997) suggest dealing with this matter?

3. Belonging to another
'Property shall be regarded as belonging to any person having possession or control of it, or having in it any proprietary right or interest.'

It includes:
- where a person owns the property but also where they have possession or control over it or a proprietary right or interest over it
- property belonging to someone under civil law and covers mere possession without rights of ownership. For example, a hired wedding suit is not owned by the person hiring it but they are in control of it at the time they are in possession of it. If someone takes the hired suit from the hiree (person who hired it), they can be said to have appropriated property belonging to the hiree, even though the hiree does not actually own the suit.

A person can, therefore, be liable for stealing their own property (*R* v *Turner No. 2* (1971)). In this case, Turner had taken his car to a garage to be repaired. After the repairs had been completed, he drove the car away from outside the garage, without paying. The garage was 'in possession' of his car at the time he took it, consequently making him liable for stealing his own car.

Even if property is legally obtained, there is still an obligation to use it in a particular way. **Section 5(3)** states:

> 'Where a person receives property from, or on account of another, and is under an obligation to the other to retain and deal with that property or its proceeds in a particular way, the property shall be regarded (as against him) as belonging to the other.'

If you gave your teacher a deposit for a class trip but the teacher spent that money on a set of textbooks for the class, the teacher has not 'used the money in the right way' so has committed theft. This section also covers things like charity collections.

In *R v Hall* (1972), the Court of Appeal said that each case depended on its facts. In this case, there was no obligation to use the deposit money in a particular way as it was paid into a general account.

What about situations where property is passed to the defendant by mistake, for example, the overpayment of wages? **Section 5(4)** provides that property which is passed to the defendant by mistake is to be treated as 'belonging to' the original owner and, therefore, once the defendant realises the mistake and refuses to return the property, a theft takes place. The failure to return the property, on realising the mistake must be deliberate, was defined in *Attorney General's Reference (No. 1 of 1983)* (1985).

Mens rea of theft

The mens rea of theft comprises two elements: intention to permanently deprive and dishonesty.

Intention to permanently deprive

The defendant must intend to permanently deprive the other of the property, regardless of whether the other is actually deprived of the property. This is covered in **s6 Theft Act 1968**:

> 'A person ... is regarded as having the intention of permanently depriving ... if his intention is to treat the thing as his own to dispose of regardless of the other's rights ... (B)orrowing or lending ... may amount to so treating it if, but only if, the borrowing or lending is for a period and in circumstances making it equivalent to an outright taking or disposal.'

Borrowing without permission (e.g. joyriding a car) without the intention to permanently deprive is not theft. There are other offences for dealing with situations like this, for example, the offence of 'taking without consent' (TWOC).

Section 6(1) covers situations where the property is 'borrowed' temporarily. This is not normally theft because there is no intention to permanently deprive. But, in *R v Lloyd* (1985), the court held that borrowing could fall within the remit of **s6** if the property was borrowed 'until the goodness, the virtue, the practical value ... has gone out of the article'. In this case, the defendant, who worked in a cinema, removed films to make pirate copies. He returned the films a few hours later, after the copying process had taken place. The 'temporary deprivation' of the films, in this case, was not sufficient for a conviction of theft.

> **GRADE BOOST**
>
> Research *R v Marshall* (1998) on this issue.

However, in *R v Velumyl* (1989), the defendant was convicted after he, without lawful authority, took cash from his employer's safe and lent it to his friend, intending for the cash to be repaid the following Monday. However, a spot-check took place before the money was returned, and it was discovered missing. He was convicted of theft on the basis that he intended to permanently deprive the owner of the exact notes and coins despite intending to return items of the same value.

Figure 31.2 Theft requires dishonesty and an intention to permanently deprive

Dishonesty

Section 2 Theft Act 1968 does not define dishonesty but gives examples of what is not dishonest. It says:

> (1) 'A person's appropriation of property belonging to another is not to be regarded as dishonest:
>
> (a) if he appropriates the property in the belief that he has in law the right to deprive the other of it, on behalf of himself or of a third person; or
>
> (b) if he appropriates the property in the belief that he would have the other's consent if the other knew of the appropriation and the circumstances of it; or
>
> (c) except where the property came to him as trustee or personal representative) if he appropriates the property in the belief that the person to whom the property belongs cannot be discovered by taking reasonable steps.'

Section 2(2): 'A person's appropriation of property belonging to another may be dishonest notwithstanding that he is willing to pay for the property.'

All the tests above are subjective: they are decided on the basis of what the defendant believes, rather than what the reasonable person should know or believe (objective).

If the **s2(1)** circumstances do not apply, then the court directs the jury to the common law test for dishonesty to decide whether the defendant has acted dishonestly.

This test used to come from the case of *R v Ghosh* (1982), but in the recent civil case of *Ivey v Genting Casinos (UK) Ltd* (2017), the Supreme Court moved away from the Ghosh test and adopted a different approach to determine dishonesty. *Ivey* (2017) therefore now provides the common law test for dishonesty, and has since been followed in the case of *R v Barton and Booth* (2020).

Ivey (2017) established a largely objective test for dishonesty:

› Firstly, the jury decides the state of the individual's subjective, genuine knowledge or belief as to the facts.
› Secondly, the jury decides whether the defendant's conduct was objectively dishonest by the standards of ordinary decent people.

STRETCH AND CHALLENGE

Research the decision in *R v Lavender* (1994) on the issue of permanent deprivation.

STRETCH AND CHALLENGE

Research the Law Commission report entitled 'Fraud' (2002) and summarise some of the criticisms of this element of the law of theft.

Robbery

This offence is similar to theft but involves the use of force to facilitate the theft. Burglary (see page 332) involves intrusion into property in order to steal. It is important to understand these key differences between the three property offences.

Robbery is defined in s8(1) Theft Act 1968:

> 'A person is guilty of robbery if he steals, and immediately before or at the time of doing so, and in order to do so, he uses force on any person or puts or seeks to put any person in fear of being then and there subjected to force.'

It is an indictable offence so is triable on indictment in the Crown Court. It is a more serious offence than theft and can carry a maximum sentence on conviction of life imprisonment.

Some have called it aggravated theft as it involves the offence of theft plus force or the threat of force.

The actus reus elements of robbery are:

1. actus reus of theft
2. uses force or there is a threat of force in order to steal
3. immediately before or at the same time as stealing
4. on any person.

The mens rea elements of robbery are:

1. mens rea of theft
2. intention to use force in order to thieve.

Actus reus of robbery

1. Theft
All the elements of theft must be present for there to have been a robbery. If one element is missing there is no robbery. This was confirmed in *R v Robinson* (1977).

To recap, the elements of theft defined in s1 Theft Act 1968 are:

> dishonestly
> appropriates
> property
> belonging to another
> with the intention to permanently deprive the other of it.

2. Intentional force
This element distinguishes robbery from theft. Examples of 'force' could be shoving someone in order to take their handbag or punching someone to take their mobile phone. A threat of force is also sufficient, for example, waving a knife at someone and demanding they hand over their wallet.

However, the force must be used in order to steal AND be immediately before or at the time of the theft. Once the theft is complete, there is a robbery. This was confirmed in *Corcoran v Anderton* (1980) where the theft had not been completed (the woman kept hold of her bag and did not let the attackers take it), so there was only an attempted robbery.

Force (or threat of) used in order to steal
> Whether there is sufficient force (or threat of it) to steal is a question for the jury to decide. It can include a small amount of force, as confirmed in *Dawson and James* (1976) and *R v Clouden* (1987).

> **STRETCH AND CHALLENGE**
>
> Should there be different 'degrees' of robbery? Research some of the criticisms of the law. How could the law be reformed?

- Force can be indirectly applied to the victim, for example, if applied via property. In *R v Clouden* (1987), the defendant had wrenched a shopping bag from the victim's hand. This conduct was sufficient to amount to force for the purposes of the offence of robbery.
- However, it may not be considered to be 'force' as required for robbery if, for example, a mobile phone fell out of a person's hand or if the defendant grabbed a laptop from a person's lap. In *P v DPP* (2012), it was held that snatching a cigarette held by the victim would not amount to force.
- It is not a requirement that the force be applied; mere fear of force through a threat or gesture is sufficient. For example, saying 'I have a knife which I will stab you with unless you give me your wallet' would be sufficient for fear of force.
- It is important to remember that the force (or threat of it) must be used in order to steal. For example, a defendant pushes a woman to the ground intending to rape her and she offers him her designer watch if he stops. If he takes the watch, there is both force and theft but it would not amount to robbery. This is because the force used was intended to rape her and not to steal.

3. Force used immediately before or at the time of the theft

The question of how 'immediate' is immediate has been debated in the courts. The courts confirmed in *R v Hale* (1979) that if the act of theft continues when the force is used then it can be a robbery.

> ### *R v Hale* (1979)
> Two defendants forced their way past a woman into her house. One put his hand over her mouth while the other went upstairs and took a jewellery box. Before they left the house, they tied up the woman. The Court of Appeal held that there was force (the defendant putting his hand over the victim's mouth) immediately before the theft (the taking of the jewellery box). They also considered that, as a continuing act, tying up the woman before leaving the house with the jewellery box could also constitute force for the purposes of robbery. The 'appropriation' was ongoing. This rationale was followed in *R v Lockley* (1995).

> **STRETCH AND CHALLENGE**
>
> What if the threat is not 'real'? For example, if the defendant uses fingers inside his jacket to make it look like he has a gun? Research *R v Bentham* (2005) on this issue.

4. On any person

The theft does not have to happen to the person being threatened. For example, in an armed bank robbery, a random customer in the bank that is being held up would be in fear of force being used against them but the money stolen would be the bank's property. This would still be a robbery.

Mens rea of robbery

The mens rea of robbery is mens rea of theft (dishonesty and intention to permanently deprive the other of the property) plus the intention to use force to steal.

Burglary

The offence of burglary is generally considered to be someone breaking into a private residence and stealing property from it. **Section 9 Theft Act 1968** makes it clear that it goes further than this. **Section 9 Theft Act 1968** defines the offence:

'(1) A person is guilty of burglary if—

he enters any building or part of a building as a trespasser and with intent to commit any such offence as is mentioned in subsection (2) below; or

having entered any building or part of a building as a trespasser he steals or attempts to steal anything in the building or that part of it or inflicts or attempts to inflict on any person therein any grievous bodily harm.

(2) The offences referred to in subsection (1)(a) above are offences of stealing anything in the building or part of a building in question, of inflicting on any person therein any grievous bodily harm, and of doing unlawful damage to the building or anything therein.'

There are in fact **two** offences of burglary under s9(1)(a) and s9(1)(b). There is also an offence under s10 Theft Act 1968 of aggravated burglary.

The maximum sentence on conviction for burglary is 14 years if the burglar has entered a dwelling, or maximum of ten years if the burglar has entered any other building. Aggravated burglary carries a maximum of life imprisonment.

According to *R v Flack* (2013), the word 'dwelling' is to be interpreted by the jury without guidance from the judge.

Burglary under s9(1)

A person is guilty of burglary under s9(1)(a) if they enter a building, or any part of a building, as a trespasser, with intent to commit theft, inflict grievous bodily harm (GBH) on any person in the building or commit criminal damage.

The actus reus has three elements:

1. entry
2. into a building or part of a building
3. as a trespasser.

Burglary under s9(1)(b) adds another element to the actus reus:

1. actus reus of theft or GBH, or attempt at theft or GBH inside it.

Under s9(1)(a) the mens rea has two elements:

1. intention or recklessness as to trespass
2. ulterior intent (the intention to commit theft, GBH or damage the building or its contents).

Section 9(1)(b) amends the second element of mens rea:

› mens rea for theft or GBH, or attempt at theft or GBH inside it.

The main differences between the two offences of burglary is:

› under s9(1)(a) the intention must be formed by the defendant at the time of entry.
› under s9(1)(b) the intent to commit the ulterior offence can come later, as what the defendant intends on entry is not relevant.
› s9(1)(a) covers unlawful damage.
› s9(1)(b) does not.

Actus reus of burglary

The common elements of actus reus will now be explored in turn.

1. Entry

This element has been defined by the courts in case law. It is not defined in statute.

› *R v Collins* (1973) held there had to be an 'effective and substantial entry'.
› In *R v Brown* (1985) the definition was changed to just require an 'effective entry', removing the requirement for a 'substantial entry'. In this case, there was a partial entry as the defendant only put his head and shoulders through an open window to steal property from inside and this was considered to be an 'effective' entry.
› In *R v Ryan* (1996) the requirement of an 'effective' entry was not followed.

R v Ryan (1996)
The defendant had attempted to enter a house through a window but was found trapped half-inside the house by the homeowner. His head and one arm were inside the house but he was unable to reach any property to steal. His conviction for burglary was upheld even though it was not an 'effective' entry. There is no requirement for the theft to have been completed to be a conviction under **s9(1)(a)**.

What if a defendant does not physically enter the building but uses some other means to access the inside of the building? Using an instrument such as a fishing rod through an open window in order to steal something from inside may amount to 'entry' for the purposes of burglary.

2. A building or part of a building

The defendant must enter a building or part of a building as a trespasser. A 'building' is not defined in the Act but has been given a wide definition. It includes traditional structures such as flats, factories, shops and houses, but sheds and outbuildings are also considered to be 'buildings'. **Section 9(3) Theft Act 1968** says that a 'building' includes 'inhabited vehicles or vessels', covering things like caravans and houseboats. Tents, being temporary structures, are not included, therefore, stealing something from a tent is theft and not burglary.

What about more temporary structures that have been used for storage or work, such as a container or a portacabin? There have been some cases on the issue. *B and S v Leathley (1979)* held that an outdoor freezer connected to an electric supply was a building.

However, in *Norfolk Constabulary v Seekings and Gould (1986)*, a lorry trailer with wheels, connected to the electric supply, was not considered to be a building.

A burglary can also take place from part of a building. This covers situations where a defendant is in a part of a building that they do not have permission to be in. They would therefore be a trespasser in that part. For example, customers in a supermarket have the right to be in the shop but become trespassers if they enter a part of the building (e.g. a storeroom or staff room) where they are not permitted to be. It would, therefore, be theft of an item from a supermarket shelf but burglary from the storeroom.

Figure 31.3 CCTV in shops helps to deter theft

R v Walkington (1979)
The defendant entered a shop as a customer but then went behind the partitioned counter to access the till. He became a trespasser at that point and was charged with burglary. He was permitted to be in the shop but not in the counter area, where he was a trespasser. He had the intention to steal from the till and so this was burglary.

3. As a trespasser
Trespassing is a civil law concept. A trespasser is a person who does not have permission to be in a building or part of the building (as in *R v Walkington* (1979), above).

If a defendant has permission to enter the building or part of the building then they are not a trespasser, as seen in *R v Collins* (1973). It must be shown that the defendant was aware they were trespassing or that they were subjectively reckless in doing so.

It might be that a person has permission to enter but goes beyond that permission, as in *R v Smith and Jones* (1976). This covers a range of situations where a person stays beyond their permission (e.g. they have a ticket to enter an art show but stay after closing and steal a sculpture).

Mens rea of burglary
The mens rea under s9(1)(a) is different to that under s9(1)(b).

Mens rea under s9(1)(a)
It needs to be proved that:

1. the defendant had intention or subjective recklessness to trespass, and
2. the defendant, at the time of entry, intended to commit one of the offences listed in s9(2). Known as ulterior offences, these are theft, inflicting GBH or unlawful damage to the building or anything in it. The intention must exist at the time of entry. If the intent is not present upon entry, subsequent formation of ulterior intent will not amount to burglary.

Provided the defendant enters with the relevant intention, the full offence of burglary is committed at the point of entry; the defendant need not actually go on to commit the ulterior offence.

Mens rea under s9(1)(b)
This section is different and easier to prove. As with s9(1)(a), it needs to be proved that the defendant had intention or subjective recklessness to trespass. There is no need to prove any mens rea on entering the building. However, it must be proved that, once inside, there was actual or attempted offending of the ulterior offence.

GRADE BOOST
As we saw in Chapter 29, the subjective recklessness element required for entering as a trespasser is called Cunningham recklessness, after *R v Cunningham* (1957).

STRETCH AND CHALLENGE
Research *R v Smith and Jones* (1976). What were the facts? How had the defendant exceeded his permission and become a 'trespasser'?

EXAM SKILLS
This topic is frequently examined as a problem scenario. You will need to be able to explain and/or apply the criminal liability of the parties involved. You will need to determine if the offence of theft, robbery and/or burglary has been committed. More than one property offence may feature so be careful with identifying the correct burglary offence under s9(1)(a) or (b).

You might also be required to analyse and evaluate the effectiveness of the law in this area and consider proposals for reform.

SUMMARY: PROPERTY OFFENCES

→ **Theft: s1 Theft Act 1968**
- Maximum sentence seven years' imprisonment
- Triable either way offence
- Actus reus has three elements:
    1. Appropriation (**s3**): bundle of rights: *R v Morris* (1923), *Lawrence v MPC* (1972), *R v Gomez* (2000), *R v Hinks* (2000)
    2. Property (**s4**): real property, intangible property, things in action, *Oxford v Moss* (1979), things that cannot be stolen
    3. Belonging to another (**s5**): possession or control, proprietary right or interest, own property: *R v Turner No. 2* (1971), obligation to use in a particular way, mistake
- Mens rea:
    - Dishonesty: **s2** and *Ivey* test
    - Intention to permanently deprive (**s6**): *Lloyd* (1985), *Velumyl* (1989)

→ **Robbery: s8 Theft Act 1968**
- Maximum sentence life imprisonment
- Indictable offence
- Actus reus:
    - Actus reus of theft: **s1 Theft Act 1968**
    - Uses force or there is a threat of force in order to steal: *Corcoran v Anderton* (1980), *Dawson and James* (1976), *Clouden* (1987)
    - Immediately before or at the same time as stealing: *Hale* (1979)
    - On any person
- Mens rea of robbery:
    - Mens rea of theft
    - Intention to use force in order to thieve

→ **Burglary: s9(1)(a) and s9(1)(b) Theft Act 1968**
- Maximum sentence 14 years' imprisonment
- Triable either way offence
- Burglary under **s9(1)(a)**: a person is guilty if they enter a building, or any part of a building, as a trespasser, with intent to commit theft, inflict GBH on any person in the building or commit criminal damage
- Actus reus of burglary under **s9(1)(a)** has three elements:
    1. entry: *R v Collins* (1973), *R v Brown* (1985), *Ryan* (1996)
    2. (into a) building: *B and S v Leathley* (1979), or part of a building: *Walkington* (1979)
    3. as a trespasser: *Walkington* (1979), permission to enter: *Collins* (1972), *Smith and Jones* (1976)
- Mens rea of burglary under **s9(1)(a)** has two elements:
    1. intention or recklessness as to trespass
    2. ulterior intent: intention to commit theft, GBH or damage to the building or its contents
- Burglary under **s9(1)(b)**: guilty if, having entered a building or part of a building as a trespasser, someone steals, attempts to steal or inflicts or attempts to inflict GBH on any person inside

- Actus reus of burglary under **s9(1)(b)** has four elements:
    1. entry: *R v Collins* (1973), *R v Brown* (1985), *Ryan* (1996)
    2. (into a) building: *B and S v Leathley* (1979), or part of a building: *R v Walkington* (1979)
    3. as a trespasser: *R v Walkington* (1979), permission to enter: *R v Collins* (1972), *R v Smith and Jones* (1976)
    4. Actus reus of theft/GBH, or attempted theft/GBH inside
- Mens rea of burglary under **s9(1)(b)** has two elements:
    1. intention or recklessness as to trespass
    2. mens rea for theft/GBH or attempt theft/GBH inside

TEST YOURSELF

1. What is the maximum sentence for theft?
2. What are the elements of the actus reus of theft?
3. What are the elements of the mens rea of theft?
4. Can you steal your own property? Explain with reference to case law.
5. Explain the two types of burglary.
6. What is the maximum sentence for burglary?
7. With the offence of robbery, what must the force or threat of force be used for?
8. What are the elements of the mens rea of robbery?
9. When must the force or threat of force in order to steal take place for the offence of robbery?
10. Explain the common law test for dishonesty following the case of *Ivey* (2017).

EXAM PAST PAPER QUESTIONS

WJEC – June 2019 – Unit 3

Caroline and Lisa are lecturers in a Further Education College. They share a staff room with two other members of staff. Caroline is preparing mock exam papers for her students and needs a stapler to staple them together, she can't find hers but sees a stapler on Lisa's desk, and she uses it and puts it back on her own desk. Later in the day, Lisa, when looking for her stapler, sees Caroline's purse on her desk with a £50 note sticking out of it. Lisa is very short of money this month due to an expensive car repair bill, so she takes the £50 note. Josie, one of Caroline's students comes into the staff room to find Caroline, to ask her a question about the forthcoming exam. No one is in the staff room, but Josie sees on Caroline's desk the mock exam papers, she quickly takes one, rushes to the photocopier, photocopies it and puts the original back on Caroline's desk. As she is leaving the staff room, Caroline returns. Josie, concerned that Caroline may have seen her take the exam paper, rushes past Caroline and knocks against her so hard that Caroline falls to the floor, bruising her arm.

Advise Caroline, Lisa and Josie as to their potential criminal liability under the Theft Act 1968, applying your knowledge of legal rules and principles. [50]

32 Capacity defences

Criminal law defences: Insanity

The M'Naghten rules were devised by the House of Lords following the case of *M'Naghten* in 1843.

The defendant should be presumed sane unless, at the time of the offence, they can prove they were:

1. labouring under such a defect of reason
2. caused by a disease of the mind
3. that they did not know either the nature and quality of the act or, if they did know it, that they didn't know what they were doing was wrong.

1. Defect of reason

The courts have stated that there needs to be a complete absence of the power to reason. Absentmindedness or confusion is not sufficient. In *Clarke* (1972), a woman was accused of theft from a supermarket, but it was said that she was acting absentmindedly due to depression and diabetes. The court said the rules on insanity do not apply to those who retain the power to reason but don't use it in moments of confusion or absentmindedness.

Figure 32.1 The case of *Clarke* (1972) confirmed that absentmindedness is NOT a defect of reason for the defence of insanity

> **KEY CASE**
>
> **M'Naghten (1843)**
> Daniel M'Naghten had become so obsessed with the Prime Minister, Robert Peel, that he decided to shoot him. He missed, and shot and killed the Prime Minister's secretary, Edward Drummond, instead. He was found to be suffering from extreme paranoia and was found not guilty by reason of insanity.

2. Disease of the mind

This can be either a mental or physical disease that affects the mind. It is a legal term and not a medical one. Medical conditions such as schizophrenia are covered but so are many other conditions that would not be defined as being diseases of the mind in any medical sense; however, it must be caused by an **internal factor**.

In *R v Quick* (1973), the condition was caused by an external factor, the drug insulin. Therefore, the defendant could rely on the defence of automatism and **not** insanity.

Voluntary intoxication

Where the defendant voluntarily takes an intoxicating substance which causes a temporary psychotic episode, the defence of insanity **cannot** be used. This is because the intoxicating substance is an external factor. The key cases of *R v Coley* (2013) and *R v Harris* (2013) illustrate this point well.

3. Nature and quality of the act

This refers to the physical character of the act. There are two ways in which the defendant would not know the physical character of the act:

1. they are in a state of unconsciousness or impaired consciousness; or
2. they are conscious but do not understand or know what they are doing, due to their mental condition.

If the defendant can show that either of these applied at the time of the act then this part of the M'Naghten rules is satisfied. Both defendants in *Kemp* (1956) and *Burgess* (1991) were in a state of lost consciousness, and the more recent case of *Oye* (2013) indicates a defendant not knowing the nature and quality of their act.

> **R v Oye (2013)**
>
> Oye was behaving strangely at a café and the police were called. On their arrival, Oye began throwing plates at the police, so he was arrested and taken to a police station. He continued to behave strangely, including drinking water out of a toilet cistern. When he was moved to the custody suite, he became angry and punched an officer in the face, breaking her jaw. Oye was charged with assault occasioning actual bodily harm and two accounts of affray.
>
> Oye argued in his defence that he had believed the police were demons and agents of evil spirits. At his trial, medical evidence stated that Oye had had a psychotic episode and that he had not known what he was doing and/or that what he was doing was wrong. Despite this evidence and the judge directing the jury on the defence of insanity, Oye was found guilty. The Court of Appeal substituted a verdict of not guilty by reason of insanity.

STRETCH AND CHALLENGE

Research the following cases where non-psychiatric illnesses such as arteriosclerosis, epilepsy, diabetes and sleepwalking have been classified as a disease of the mind – *R v Kemp* (1957); *Bratty v AG for Northern Ireland* (1963); *R v Sullivan* (1984); *R v Hennessy* (1989) and *R v Burgess* (1991)).

STRETCH AND CHALLENGE

To prepare for a discussion of the other conditions that can amount to a disease of the mind, research the key cases of *R v Kemp* (1956), *Sullivan* (1984), *Hennessy* (1989) and *Burgess* (1991). Ensure you know the facts of these key cases and how the defence of insanity worked in each of them.

> **KEY CASE**
>
> ### R v Coley (2013)
> The defendant, who was a regular cannabis user, attacked his neighbour and her partner with a knife. On arrest, he said he had blacked out and had no memory of what had happened. A psychiatric report suggested that he could have suffered a brief psychotic episode brought on by the taking of cannabis. The judge refused to accept the defence of insanity and Coley was convicted of attempted murder. The Court of Appeal upheld his conviction as the situation was one of voluntary intoxication and the abnormality was caused by an external act.

The defendants must prove they did not know what they were doing was legally wrong. If the defendant knows the nature and quality of the act and that it is legally wrong, they cannot use the defence of insanity, even if they have a mental illness, as in **R v Windle (1952)**.

> ### R v Windle (1952)
> The defendant gave his wife an overdose of aspirin. When the police arrived he said, 'I suppose they'll hang me for this!' This last statement was evidence that he knew what he was doing was wrong and he was hanged.

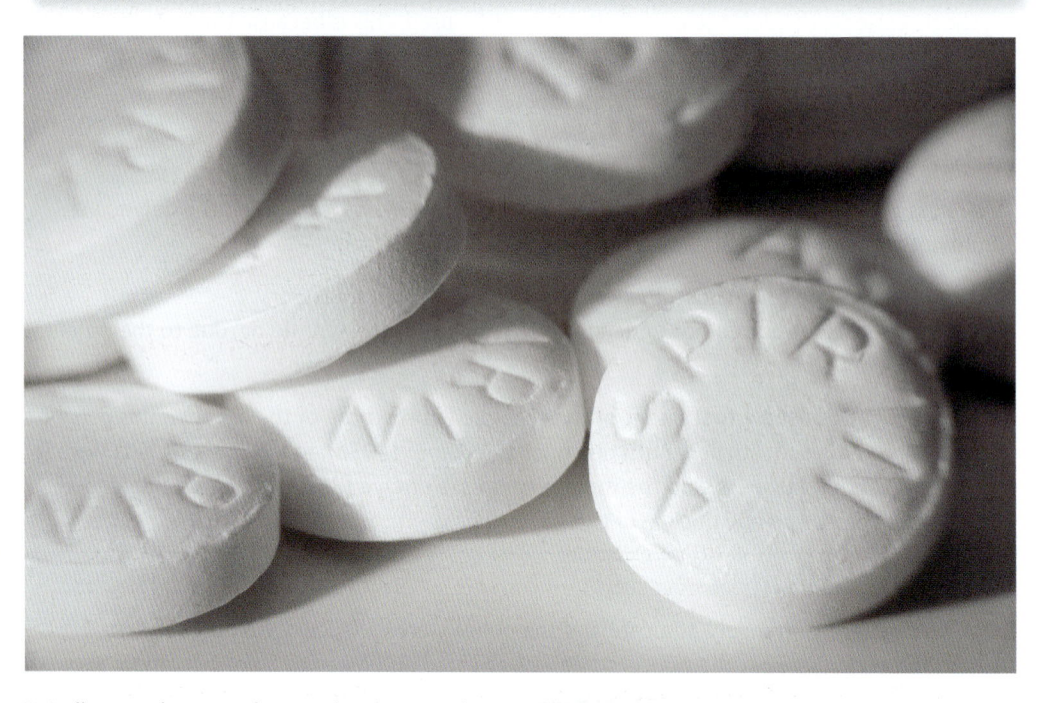

Figure 32.2 Windle knew that the overdose of aspirin would be fatal for his wife and had no defence

Windle was shown to know what he was doing was wrong and knew the punishment in law for his actions. The same logic was followed in **R v Johnson (2007)**.

> ### R v Johnson (2007)
> The defendant forced his way into his neighbour's flat and stabbed him. He was charged with wounding with intent to do grievous bodily harm under the **Offences Against the Person Act 1861**. During his trial, two psychiatrists gave evidence that he was suffering from paranoid schizophrenia and hallucinations; however, both psychiatrists agreed that, despite these conditions, Johnson did know the nature and quality of his acts, and knew that what he had done was legally wrong. Johnson was convicted of wounding with intent. At the Court of Appeal, his conviction was upheld. The defence of insanity was not available in this case as Johnson knew the nature and quality of his acts and that they were legally wrong (that is, he knew that the act was contrary to law).

The verdict

When a defendant successfully proves the defence of insanity, the jury must return a verdict of 'not guilty by reason of insanity'. Prior to 1991, the only punishment was a hospital order, which was not appropriate for those who had conditions such as diabetes and epilepsy.

The **Criminal Procedure (Insanity and Unfitness to Plead) Act 1991** introduced new orders available to extend the options available to a judge. A judge can now impose a:

- hospital order without time limit (mandatory for murder)
- hospital order with time limit
- guardianship order
- supervision and treatment order
- absolute discharge.

Problems with the defence of insanity

- One of the main issues with the defence of insanity is that the definition of insanity was set in *M'Naghten*, a case dating back to 1843. At this time, medical knowledge was limited and, with advances in medical knowledge of mental health disorders, a more modern definition should now be used.
- Another issue is that the definition of insanity is a legal definition and not a medical one. Some defendants who should be regarded as insane are not (e.g. *R v Byrne* (1960)).
- On the other hand, defendants who have physical diseases like diabetes or even those who sleepwalk are considered insane (e.g. *R v Hennessy* (1989) and *R v Burgess* (1991)).
- Furthermore, the defendant has to prove insanity, which may breach **Article 6 European Convention on Human Rights** (the defendant is innocent until proven guilty).
- There is also a stigma to being labelled insane, yet it is the only defence available to many defendants.
- It is the jury's job to decide whether the defendant is insane, and they are not really qualified to do this.

Reforming the defence of insanity

There have been several attempts at reforming the defence of insanity.

- **1953**: the Royal Commission on Capital Punishment suggested those with irresistible impulses would have been covered, but it never became law. Instead, the government introduced the defence of diminished responsibility, but this is only available for murder charges.
- **1975**: the Butler Committee suggested it should be replaced by verdict of 'not guilty on evidence of mental disorder, but this never became law.
- **1989**: draft Criminal Code suggested a defendant should be not guilty on evidence of severe mental disorder or handicap, but it never became law.
- **1991**: the **Criminal Procedure (Insanity and Unfitness to Plead) Act** gave judges more discretion on disposals where the defendant uses the defence of insanity.
- **2013**: the Law Commission's paper 'Criminal Liability: Insanity and Automatism' proposed abolishing both defences and realigning them, but this has not been implemented.

STRETCH AND CHALLENGE

Research the case of *Loake* v *CPS* (2017) where the question of whether the defence of insanity applies to all offences was considered.

Links with automatism

Insanity is also known as insane automatism; automatism is also known as non-insane automatism.

Insanity is caused by an internal factor; automatism is caused by an external factor.

The verdict for insanity is 'not guilty by reason of insanity' and usually results in some form of treatment order. A successful plea of automatism will lead to a complete acquittal.

Criminal law defences: Automatism

For automatism to work as a defence, the actions of the defendant must be completely involuntary. In *Bratty v Attorney General for Northern Ireland* (1963), it was defined as:

'an act done by the muscles without any control by the mind, such as a spasm, a reflex action or a convulsion; or an act done by a person who is not conscious of what he is doing such as an act done whilst suffering from concussion or whilst sleepwalking.'

There are two types of automatism:

1. Insane automatism is where the case of automatism is a disease of the mind within the M'Naghten rules. In such cases, the defence is insanity and the verdict is not guilty by reason of insanity.
2. Non-insane automatism is where the cause is external and where the defence succeeds it is a complete defence and the defendant is not guilty.

Figure 32.3 Sleepwalking can be defined as automatism

Non-insane automatism

This is a defence because the actus reus is not voluntary and the defendant does not have the required mens rea for the offence. For automatism to work as a defence, it must be caused by an external factor that makes the defendant totally lose control over their actions. Examples of external causes include a blow to the head, being attacked by bees or a prolonged sneezing fit.

In *Hill v Baxter* (1958), the issue of no fault when the defendant was in an automatic state through an external cause was approved. The court approved the earlier decision in *Kay v Butterworth* (1945) that a person should not be convicted if, through no fault of their own, they lose control due to an external cause. In this case, the judge said:

'A person should not be made liable at the criminal law who, through no fault of his own, becomes unconscious when driving, as, for example, a person who has been struck by a stone or overcome by a sudden illness, or when the car has been put temporarily out of his control owing to his being attacked by a swarm of bees.'

In *T* (1990), it was accepted that exceptional stress can be an external factor that may cause automatism, although the defence was not successful in this case.

In *Attorney General's Reference (No. 2 of 1992)* (1993) reduced or partial control of one's actions is not sufficient to constitute non-insane automatism.

Figure 32.4 Loss of control due to sudden illness is a defence

342

Attorney General's Reference (No. 2 of 1992) (1993)

The defendant was a lorry driver who had been driving for several hours when he began to drive along the hard shoulder of the motorway. He drove along it for approximately half a mile, whereupon he hit a broken-down car and killed two people. He pleaded the defence of non-insane automatism, arguing that he was suffering from a condition called 'driving without awareness', which puts a driver in a trance-like condition. He was found not guilty by the jury. On a referral by the Attorney General to the Court of Appeal, on a point of law, the court ruled that because his condition only caused partial loss of control, the defence of automatism could not be used.

Figure 32.5 The defence of non-insane automatism was dismissed at appeal in *Attorney General's Reference (No. 2 of 1992)* (1993)

External factors: Automatism and diabetes

In *R v Quick* (1973), hypoglycaemia was caused by an external factor as the defendant had taken his insulin but not eaten and then drunk alcohol. He was able to use automatism as a defence.

In *R v Hennessy* (1989), hyperglycaemia was caused by an internal factor (his diabetes), as he had not taken his insulin. He had to rely on the defence of insanity.

Self-induced automatism

The defence is unlikely to be available if the accused caused the automatism themselves.

R v Bailey (1983)

The defendant was in a hypoglycaemic state as he had taken his insulin but not eaten. He then attacked his ex-girlfriend's new boyfriend with an iron bar. He knew the risks, as he had been feeling unwell, so his actions were regarded as reckless, and there was insufficient evidence to successfully raise the defence of automatism.

> **STRETCH AND CHALLENGE**
>
> Compare *T* **(1990)** with *Burgess* **(1991)**. What are the differences in these cases?

In *R v Hardie* **(1985)** (see page 346), the defendant had taken Valium, which would normally have a calming effect but instead it made him very agitated, and he set his ex-girlfriend's flat on fire. He was allowed to use the defence of automatism as he had thought that the Valium would calm him down, which is its normal effect, so therefore he had not been reckless.

If the automatism is caused by drink or drugs, the defence will not be available.

Proposals for reform

One of the main problems with the defence of automatism is that in each case it has to be decided whether the situation is one of insane or non-insane automatism.

In 2013, the Law Commission published a paper on the defences of insanity and automatism. The paper pointed out that the two defences are closely related and that if the defence of insanity is reformed then the defence of automatism must be reformed at the same time.

> **EXAM SKILLS**
>
> Ensure you are able to analyse and evaluate the defence of insanity and automatism and that you are also able to apply the legal rules and principles of the defence of insanity and automatism to given scenarios.

Criminal law defences: Intoxication

This defence covers intoxication by alcohol, drugs or other substances (e.g. glue-sniffing).

As a general rule, if a person is voluntarily intoxicated and commits a crime, there is no defence.

Intoxication is relevant as to whether or not the defendant has the required mens rea for the offence. If the defendant does not have the required mens rea because of their intoxicated state, they may not be guilty; however, this depends on whether the intoxication was voluntary or involuntary and whether the offence charged is one of specific or basic intent.

Voluntary intoxication and specific intent offences

These are crimes where intention is required in addition to the basic offence.

For example, **s18 Offences Against the Person Act 1861** is grievous bodily harm (GBH) or malicious wounding with intention to cause GBH.

Voluntary intoxication can negate the mens rea for a specific intent offence. If the defendant is so intoxicated that the mens rea for the offence is not formed, they are not guilty.

Figure 32.6 Intoxication can negate the mens rea for an offence

DPP v Beard (1920)

The defendant had been charged with murder. He argued in his defence that he was too intoxicated to have formed the mens rea for the murder. He was convicted but, on appeal, Lord Birkenhead stated the rule that still applies today:

> 'If he was so drunk that he was incapable of forming the intent required, he could not be convicted of a crime which was committed only if the intent was proved.'

R v *Sheehan and Moore* (1975) is a good example of where it was held that the defendants were so drunk that they did not have the mens rea for murder.

R v Sheehan and Moore (1975)

The defendants had thrown petrol over a tramp and set fire to him. They were too drunk to have formed any intent to kill or cause GBH. Therefore, as they did not have the mens rea for murder, they were able to use intoxication as a defence. However, they were found guilty of manslaughter as that is a basic intent offence.

This usually means the charge is reduced rather than escaping liability. For example, in *R v Lipman* (1970) (see page 348), where he killed his girlfriend while hallucinating on the drug LSD, he was convicted of manslaughter instead of murder.

Also bear in mind *AG for Northern Ireland v Gallagher* (1963), where it was held that drunken intent is still intent. The defendant bought a knife to kill his wife and drank a large amount of whisky to give him the courage to do it. He was convicted of murder.

Voluntary intoxication and basic intent offences

Where the offence is one of basic intent, intoxication is **not** a defence. This is because, as is shown in *DPP v Majewski* (1977), voluntarily becoming intoxicated is considered a reckless course of conduct, and recklessness is enough to constitute the necessary mens rea.

KEY CASE

DPP v Majewski (1977)
The defendant had taken large amounts of drugs and alcohol before attacking the landlord of the pub where he was drinking, and then police officers who arrived after receiving a call from the landlord. The House of Lords held that getting drunk is a reckless course of conduct and recklessness is sufficient to constitute the necessary mens rea for assault.

R v Fotheringham (1989)

The defendant had been out drinking. On his return home, he climbed into bed with the 14-year-old babysitter who was sleeping in his bed. He started to have sexual intercourse with her in the mistaken belief that it was his wife. On appeal, his conviction for rape was upheld. Rape is a crime of basic intent and therefore his drunken mistake could not be relied on in his defence.

Involuntary intoxication

This covers situations where the defendant did not know they were taking an intoxicating substance, for example, spiked drinks. It also covers situations where prescribed drugs have the unexpected effect of making the defendant intoxicated.

It was said in *R v Pearson* (1835) that 'If a party be made drunk by stratagem, or the fraud of another, he is not responsible.' Therefore, there may be defence for basic and specific intent crimes.

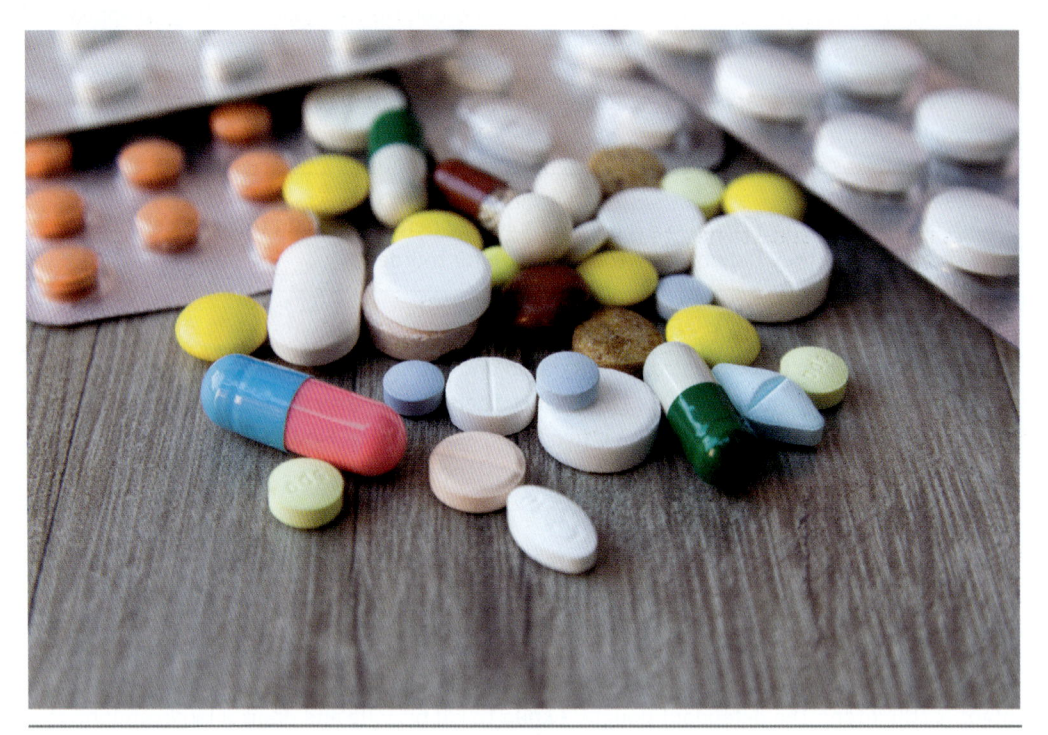

Figure 32.7 Prescribed drugs can have unexpected effects

R v Hardie (1985)

The defendant set light to a wardrobe after consuming some Valium tablets that had been prescribed to his girlfriend. He took the Valium because he was feeling stressed that his partner had asked him to leave their home. He was charged with arson.

At his trial, he stated that he remembered nothing about starting the fire due to his intoxicated state, but accepted that he must have started it as he was the only one in the room when it started. The trial judge directed the jury that, as the defendant had voluntarily consumed the Valium, his intoxication could be no defence to the crime.

Hardie successfully appealed that he had not been reckless. It was held that the actions in this case did not necessarily amount to voluntary intoxication. Parker LJ said:

> 'Valium is wholly different in kind from drugs which are liable to cause unpredictability or aggressiveness ... if the effect of a drug is merely soporific or sedative the taking of it, even in some excessive quantity, cannot in the ordinary way raise a conclusive presumption against the admission of proof of intoxication for the purpose of disproving mens rea ... The jury should have been directed that if they came to the conclusion that, as a result of the Valium, the appellant was, at the time, unable to appreciate the risks to property and persons from his actions, they should then consider whether the taking of the Valium was itself reckless.'

Compare *R v Hardie* (1985) with *R v Allen* (1988).

> ### R v Allen (1988)
> Allen had consumed some homemade wine, which had a much greater effect on him than he anticipated. He committed several sexual assaults and claimed he was so drunk he did not know what he was doing. He argued that he had not voluntarily placed himself in that condition, as the wine was much stronger than he realised. The court held that the intoxication was still voluntary even though he had not realised the strength of it. The crime of sexual assault is one of basic intent and therefore the appellant was unable to rely on his intoxicated state to negate the mens rea.

The test, therefore, is: 'Did the defendant have the necessary mens rea when they committed the offence?' If the answer is 'yes', then the defendant will be guilty.

Figure 32.8 Intoxication can still be voluntary even where the defendant had not realised the strength of the alcohol

> ### R v Kingston (1994)
> The defendant's coffee was drugged by a couple who were in dispute with him over business matters and wanted to blackmail him. The defendant was invited to abuse a 15-year-old boy who had been set up by the blackmailers. The defendant abused the boy and was photographed doing so by the blackmailers. The House of Lords upheld his conviction for sexual assault, saying:
>
> > 'There is no principle of English law which allows a defence based on involuntary intoxication where the defendant is found to have the necessary mens rea for the crime. The prosecution had established the defendant had the necessary intent for the crime – a drunken intent is still intent.'

Intoxicated mistake

If the defendant makes a mistake due to intoxication, it will depend on what the mistake was as to whether the defence is available. Where the mistake means the defendant did not have the necessary mens rea for the offence, they have a defence when the offence is one of specific intent. However, where the offence is one of basic intent, there is no defence, as seen in *Lipman* (1970).

Figure 32.9 Intoxication was not a defence to manslaughter in *R* v *Lipman* (1970)

R v *Lipman* (1970)

The appellant had taken LSD. He was hallucinating and believed he was being attacked by snakes and descending to the centre of the earth. While in this state, he killed his girlfriend by cramming bed sheets into her mouth. The court held that his intoxication could be used to demonstrate that he lacked the mens rea for murder, as murder is a crime of specific intent. His intoxication, however, could not be a defence to manslaughter, as that is a crime of basic intent.

R v *O'Grady* (1987)

O'Grady was an alcoholic and had spent the day drinking large quantities of alcohol with two friends. The friends then went to O'Grady's house to sleep. O'Grady claimed he was woken by one of the friends hitting him on the head. He said that he picked up some broken glass and started hitting his friend in order to defend himself. He said he only recalled hitting him a few times. O'Grady then said the fight ended and he cooked them both some food before going back to sleep. In the morning, he found his friend dead. The death was caused by loss of blood: the friend had 20 wounds to his face in addition to injuries to his hands and a fractured rib. There was also severe bruising to his head, brain, neck and chest.

O'Grady was convicted of manslaughter. His appeal was dismissed and the conviction upheld because a defendant is not entitled to rely, as far as self-defence is concerned, upon a mistake of fact which has been induced by voluntary intoxication.

32 Capacity defences

The judge said:

> 'There are two competing interests. On the one hand, the interest of the defendant who has only acted according to what he believed to be necessary to protect himself, and on the other hand, that of the public in general and the victim in particular who, probably through no fault of his own, has been injured or perhaps killed because of the defendant's drunken mistake. Reason recoils from the conclusion that in such circumstances a defendant is entitled to leave the court without a stain on his character.'

The ruling in *O'Grady* (1987) was confirmed in *R v Hatton* (2005).

Figure 32.10 A defendant's drunken mistake cannot be relied on for the purposes of self-defence

R v Hatton (2005)

The defendant had drunk over 20 pints of beer. He and the victim went back to Hatton's flat. In the morning, Hatton found the victim dead with injuries caused by being hit with a sledgehammer. Hatton said he couldn't remember what had happened but thought that the victim had tried to attack him and that he was defending himself. Hatton was convicted of murder. The Court of Appeal upheld his conviction and stated that the decision in *O'Grady* (1987) was not limited to basic intent crimes but also applied to specific intent crimes. A defendant's drunken mistake cannot be relied on for the purposes of self-defence.

Problems with the defence of intoxication

- The decision in *DPP v Majewski* (1977) is that a person is reckless and therefore guilty if they get drunk, but this does not comply with the principle that the actus reus and mens rea of a crime must coincide.
- Usually, if recklessness is sufficient for the mens rea, the defendant needs to be aware of the risk, but this is not the case with intoxication.
- Where there is a lesser offence, the charge will be reduced to a basic intent crime, but where there is no lesser offence, the defendant escapes liability.

STRETCH AND CHALLENGE

Research the case of *R v Taj* (2018), which discusses common law defences and drunken mistake.

EXAM SKILLS

Ensure you are able to analyse and evaluate the defence of intoxication and that you are also able to apply the legal rules and principles of the defence of intoxication to given scenarios.

GRADE BOOST

Research the Law Commission's 2009 report 'Intoxication and Criminal Liability' for recommendations for reform of the law of intoxication. Ensure you can fully discuss the proposals for reform in this area, looking back at the Butler Committee proposals in 1975 and the Law Commission proposals in 1993 and 1995.

Figure 32.11 Duress can involve the use of force

Criminal defences: Necessity defences of duress and duress of circumstances

This defence exists where the defendant is put under considerable pressure to commit a crime or face death or serious injury to them or another for whom they feel responsible, and the defendant is faced with a terrible dilemma. The problem is that the defendant commits the actus reus with the mens rea, so the defence takes the circumstances into account.

Duress can be used as a defence to all crimes **except** murder, manslaughter and perhaps treason.

The defence takes two different forms:

1. Duress by threats: this consists of direct threats to the defendant to commit a crime or face death or serious personal injury to themselves or another.
2. Duress of circumstances: this consists of external circumstances that the defendant believes constitute a serious threat.

There are some similarities to the defence of necessity (see page 356).

> **KEY CASES**
>
> ### DPP for Northern Ireland v Lynch (1975)
> It was originally held in this case that the defence of duress was available to a secondary party on a charge of murder. The defendant was ordered by Meehan, a member of the terrorist group the IRA, to drive a car. The defendant did not know Meehan personally but knew of his reputation and knew that he would be shot if he did not comply. Three armed men got into the car and the defendant drove them as directed. The three men then shot and killed a policeman. The defendant was convicted of murder, the trial judge having ruled that the defence of duress was not available in the circumstances. The Court of Appeal dismissed the appeal and the defendant appealed to the House of Lords, where his appeal was allowed, ruling that the defence of duress is available to a participant to murder who does not personally do the act of killing.
>
> ### R v Howe and others (1986)
> However, in this case the House of Lords ruled that the defence in *DPP for Northern Ireland v Lynch* (1975) was not available to anyone charged with murder, even if they were only a secondary party and had not done the killing themselves.

Howe and Bailey, aged 19, and Bannister, aged 20, were acting under orders of Murray, aged 35. The charges related to two murders. The first murder related to 17-year-old Elgar, who was being tortured. Howe and Bannister kicked and punched Elgar and were told they would receive similar treatment if they did not do as Murray ordered. Elgar might have died of his injuries if Bailey hadn't then strangled him. The second killing took place the following night at the same location, when Murray ordered Howe and Bannister to strangle a 19-year-old man and they complied. The House of Lords, upholding their convictions for murder, said that the defence of duress is not available for murder, for either the principal or secondary offender.

R v Gotts (1982)
A 16-year-old boy was ordered by his father to kill his mother, otherwise his father would shoot him. He stabbed his mother, causing serious injuries, but she survived. He was charged with attempted murder and the trial judge ruled that the defence of duress was not available to him. He pleaded guilty and then appealed the judge's ruling. His appeal was dismissed and his conviction upheld. The House of Lords held that the defence of duress was not available for attempted murder. Lord Griffiths said:

> 'We face a rising tide of violence and terrorism against which the law must stand firm, recognising that its highest duty is to protect the freedom and lives of those that live under it. Attempted murder requires proof of an intent to kill, whereas in murder it is sufficient to prove an intent to cause really serious injury. It cannot be right to allow the defence to one who may be more intent upon taking a life than the murderer.'

1. Duress by threats

The courts have to consider the seriousness of the harm that the accused has been threatened with and the criminal behaviour they commit.

In deciding if the defence should succeed, the jury must consider a two-stage test laid down in *R v Graham* (1982) and approved of in *R v Howe* (1987):

› Subjective test: did the defendant feel they had to act the way they did because they reasonably believed they would face death or serious personal injury?
› Objective test: would a sober person of reasonable firmness with the same characteristics as the defendant respond in the same way as the defendant?

KEY CASE

R v Graham (1982)
The defendant lived in a flat with his wife, Mrs Graham (the victim), and his gay lover, King. The defendant suffered from anxiety attacks for which he was prescribed Valium. King was of a violent disposition and both the defendant and his wife were frightened of him and had experienced violence from him. On one occasion, King attacked Mrs Graham with a knife and the defendant intervened, sustaining cuts to his hands. As a result of the attack, Mrs Graham went to stay with the defendant's mother. King and the defendant began drinking heavily and the defendant also took a large quantity of Valium. King then told the defendant it was time to get rid of Mrs Graham for good. Together, they devised a plan.

The defendant phoned up Mrs Graham and told her that he had cut his wrists and to come round straight away. When she arrived, King strangled her with a wire. The defendant helped by holding onto the wire. He then helped King to dispose of the body. King pleaded guilty to murder and was sentenced. The defendant raised the defences of duress and intoxication. In relation to duress, the defendant raised an argument which was supported by medical evidence that his anxiety and intake of Valium would have made him more susceptible to threats. He was still found guilty. On appeal, his conviction was upheld on the grounds that the fact that a defendant's will to resist has been eroded by the voluntary consumption of drink or drugs or both should not be taken into account.

The threat must be of death or serious personal injury. The cumulative effect of threats can be considered by the court, as in *R v Valderrama-Vega* (1985).

Figure 32.12 Courts have to consider the seriousness of the harm that the accused has been threatened with

R v Valderrama-Vega (1985)
The defendant had been convicted of importing drugs. He had done so because he had received threats of serious violence against him and his family if he did not comply. There were also threats to reveal his homosexual activities to his wife. He also received financial rewards for his action. The trial judge refused to allow the defence of duress to be put before the jury. The defendant appealed his conviction. The appeal was allowed. Threats to reveal his homosexuality alone would be insufficient to support the defence of duress but could be taken into account when coupled with threats of serious personal violence, as was the case here.

The threat must be unavoidable
- In *R v Gill* (1963), the defendant had the opportunity to inform the police between the threats and carrying out the crime, so could not use the defence.
- In *R v Hudson and Taylor* (1971), the defence was allowed because the threat was still operating when the defendants were giving evidence in the court, as they believed it could be carried out immediately.
- *R v Hasan* (2005) stated the current law, which takes a stricter approach, as in *Gill* (1963). Here the defendant joined a criminal gang so was unable to use the defence when he was threatened because he should have realised that could happen.

The threat must be operative at the time of committing the crime

R v Abdul-Hussain (1999)
The defendants were Shi'ite Muslims who had fled from Iraq to Sudan because of the risk of punishment and execution due to their religion. They feared they would be sent back to Iraq so they hijacked a plane, which landed in the UK. The defendants were charged with hijacking and pleaded the defence of duress. The trial judge ruled that the defence could not be used as they were not in sufficiently close and immediate danger, so they were convicted. The Court of Appeal quashed their convictions, holding that the threat need not be immediate, but it had to be imminent in the sense that it was 'hanging over them'.

2. Duress of circumstances

This defence was first recognised in *R v Willer* (1986) and confirmed in *R v Conway* (1988).

> ### R v Willer (1986)
> The defendant's car was surrounded by a gang of youths, who threatened him. He drove along the pavement as his only route of escape but was convicted of reckless driving. The Appeal Court allowed duress of circumstances.

> ### R v Conway (1988)
> Two men ran towards the defendant's car. The defendant's passenger had been shot at a few weeks earlier so he considered the two men to be a threat. He drove off and was charged with reckless driving. His appeal was successful and duress of circumstances was allowed as a defence.

In *R v Martin* (1989), the court stated that the two-stage test in *R v Graham* (1982) for duress by threats also applies to duress of circumstances.

> ### R v Martin (1989)
> The defendant had driven while disqualified from driving. He claimed he did so because his wife threatened to commit suicide if he did not drive their son to work. His wife had previously attempted suicide and the son was late for work and she feared he would lose his job if her husband did not get him to work. Martin pleaded guilty to driving while disqualified following a ruling by the trial judge that the defence of duress of circumstances was not available to him. On appeal, his conviction was quashed, as the defence of duress should have been available to him. It did not matter that the threat of death arose through suicide rather than murder.

In *R v Pommell* (1995), the court ruled that the defence was available to all offences except murder, manslaughter and treason.

> ### R v Cairns (1999)
> The defendant had been driving a car. It was surrounded by a group of youths, one of whom threw himself on the bonnet. The defendant, feeling threatened, drove off and the man on the bonnet was injured. The court said, when establishing the defence of duress of circumstance, the defendant needed only to show a reasonable and genuine perception of a threat of serious physical injury, not necessarily that the threat was genuine.

Problems with duress

> The defence is not available for murder but there are situations where it might be necessary and unjust to not allow it.
> *R v Hasan* (2005) has narrowed the circumstances in which the defence can be available, which may mean it is not available to those who need it.
> A defendant's low IQ is not considered by the court following *R v Bowen* (1996).
> *R v Hudson and Taylor* (1971) shows that even where the defendant is surrounded by police protection, they may not consider this more powerful than the threat.

Criminal defences: Self-defence

This defence not only covers the actions needed to defend oneself from an attack, but also actions taken to defend another person. The defences of self-defence and defence of another are common law defences; in addition, there is also a statutory defence.

Figure 32.13 Reasonable force can be used in self-defence

Section 3 Criminal Law Act 1967: Statutory defence

'A person may use such force as is reasonable in the circumstances in the prevention of crime or in assisting in the lawful arrest of offenders or suspected offenders, or of persons unlawfully at large.'

The amount of force that can be used in self-defence, defence of another or in the prevention of crime is set out in **s76 Criminal Justice and Immigration Act 2008**.

Factors taken into account when deciding whether the force used was reasonable in the circumstances include:

› a person acting for a legitimate purpose may not be able to weigh to a nicety the exact measure of necessary action; and
› evidence of someone having only done what they honestly and instinctively thought was necessary for a legitimate purpose constitutes strong evidence that only reasonable action was taken by that person for that purpose.

Section 76 allows that a person facing an attack is under stress and cannot be expected to work out the exact amount of force needed in the circumstances. If there is evidence that the person 'honestly and instinctively' thought the level of force was reasonable to protect themselves or another, or to prevent a crime, this is strong evidence that the action was reasonable in the circumstances.

However, if the force is used after all danger is over (e.g. for revenge or retaliation), this defence is not available.

> ### *Hussain and another* (2010)
> The defendant's house was broken into and he and his family were threatened by armed men. The defendant and one of his sons managed to escape and chased the armed men as they ran from the house. They caught one of the men and beat him up. It was held that they could not use the defence of self-defence as all danger to them from the original attack was over.

Householder cases

Section 43 Crime and Courts Act 2013 has amended **s76 Criminal Justice and Immigration Act 2008** to allow for a wider defence to householders where an intruder enters their property. In such cases, the degree of force will only be regarded as unreasonable where its use was 'grossly disproportionate'.

To be a householder case, the:

› force must be used by the defendant while in, or partly in, a building that is a dwelling
› defendant must not be a trespasser
› defendant must have believed the victim to be a trespasser.

Self-defence and excessive force

The amount of force used to defend oneself or another must be reasonable. If the force is excessive the defence will fail.

> ### *R v Clegg* (1995)
> Clegg was a soldier on duty in Northern Ireland. A car, with its headlights on full beam, sped towards him at the checkpoint he was manning. One of the soldiers with Clegg shouted for the car to stop, but it did not. Clegg fired three shots at the car and a further shot as the car passed him. The final shot hit and killed a passenger in the back of the car. Clegg could not use self-defence as a defence because evidence showed that the car had gone past him by the time he fired the last shot so there was no danger when he fired the shot. The force was regarded as excessive and his murder conviction was upheld. In 1999, Clegg's case was sent back to the Court of Appeal by the Criminal Cases Review Commission and his conviction was quashed, as new evidence cast doubt on whether Clegg actually fired the fatal shot.
>
> ### *R v Martin (Anthony)* (2001)
> Martin shot two burglars who had broken into his remote farmhouse, killing one of them. Evidence showed that the burglars were leaving when Martin shot them, and that the one who died had been shot in the back. Martin was found guilty of murder. He appealed, arguing he should have been allowed to use the defence of self-defence as he was suffering from a paranoid personality disorder which made him think he was in a very dangerous situation. His appeal was rejected by the Court of Appeal, which held that personality disorders could not be taken into account when considering the defence of self-defence. His conviction was, however, subsequently reduced to manslaughter on the grounds of diminished responsibility.

Relevance of the defendant's characteristics

As seen in *R v Martin* (2002), the Court of Appeal rejected the defendant's appeal, holding that personality disorders could not be taken into account when considering the defence of self-defence.

This decision was followed in *R v Cairns* (2005), where the court held that, when deciding whether the defendant had used reasonable force in self-defence, it was not appropriate to take into account whether the defendant was suffering from a psychiatric condition.

The law in *R v Martin* (2002) and *R v Cairns* (2005) was upheld in *R v Oye* (2013) (see page 339).

> **GRADE BOOST**
> Visit the Crown Prosecution Service (CPS) website (www.cps.gov.uk) and read the CPS paper 'Self-defence and the Prevention of Crime' (2011). What were the findings in this paper?

Mistaken use of force in self-defence

In *R v Williams (Gladstone)* (1987), the defendant had to have a 'genuine' mistaken belief which may or may not be reasonable.

> ### R v Williams (Gladstone) (1987)
> The defendant witnessed what he thought was a fight and intervened, saying he was a police officer and trying to make an arrest. In fact, one of the people involved had just mugged a woman and the other was trying to arrest him. The defendant was prosecuted for assaulting the victim but the jury was told he could only use the defence of mistaken force in self-defence if it was reasonable. On appeal, the court said that the jury should have been told that if they believed it was a genuine mistake, they should decide the case on this basis, and Williams was able to use the defence of protection of others.

EXAM SKILLS
Ensure you are able to:
- analyse and evaluate all of the criminal law defences
- apply the legal rules and principles of the various defences to given scenarios.

Also, remember that exam scenario questions can often feature several defences; for example, a homicide scenario question could feature the defences of loss of control and diminished responsibility.

Criminal defences: Necessity

This topic is not relevant to the WJEC specification and is Eduqas only.

This is a very limited defence, as the courts have generally not been prepared to accept it.

Defendants are placed in a position where they believe they have to commit an offence to prevent a worse evil from happening. The original case where necessity was raised is the key case of *R v Dudley and Stephens* (1884).

Although there is not much move to recognise this as a defence in criminal cases, there has been more recognition of its availability in civil cases.

Re F (Mental Patient: Sterilisation) (1990)

F was a 36-year-old woman. She had a serious mental disability caused by an infection when she was a baby. She had been a voluntary in-patient at a mental hospital since the age of 14. She had the verbal capacity of a child of two and the mental capacity of a child of four. When she developed a sexual relationship with a fellow patient, her mother and medical staff at the hospital were concerned that she would not cope with pregnancy and childbirth and would not be able to raise a child herself. Methods of contraception other than sterilisation were not practical for her so they sought a declaration that it would be lawful for her to be sterilised. F was incapable of giving valid consent since she did not appreciate the implications of the operation.

The declaration was granted. It would be lawful for the doctors to operate without her consent.

KEY CASES

R v Dudley and Stephens (1884)
Four people were shipwrecked miles from land. Three weeks later, the two defendants, being the stronger men, killed and ate the cabin boy in order to survive. They were rescued four days later and were charged with murder on their return to England. They used necessity as a defence. Although that defence was not allowed, the usual sentence of death was lowered to six months' imprisonment in recognition that they were faced with a terrible dilemma.

Re A (Conjoined Twins) (2000)
Mary and Jodie were conjoined twins, joined at the pelvis. Jodie was the stronger of the two and capable of living independently. However, Mary was weaker and was completely dependent on Jodie for her survival. According to medical evidence, if the twins were left as they were, Mary would eventually be too much of a strain on Jodie and they would both die. If they operated to separate them, this would inevitably lead to Mary's death, but Jodie would have a strong chance of living an independent life. The parents refused consent for the operation to separate them. The doctors applied to the court for a declaration that it would be lawful and in the best interests of the children to operate.

The High Court granted the declaration on the grounds that the operation would be the same as a withdrawal of support, that is, an omission rather than a positive act and also that the death of Mary, although inevitable, was not the primary purpose of the operation. The parents appealed to the Court of Appeal but the appeal was dismissed. The operation could be lawfully carried out by the doctors.

Figure 32.14 Necessity is rarely successful as a defence, as in the case of R v Dudley and Stephens (1884)

Four circumstances were developed where necessity would be permissible:

1. Where an act was done only to avoid consequences which could not otherwise be avoided.
2. The consequences would have inflicted inevitable and irreparable evil.
3. No more was done than was reasonably necessary for the purpose.
4. The evil inflicted was not disproportionate to the evil avoided.

The defence of necessity was also considered in *R v Shayler* (2001) where a further criterion for the defence to be available was added to those in *Re A* (2000): the evil must be directed towards the defendant or to someone for whom they had responsibility.

R v Shayler (2001)
The defendant was a member of MI5 who had disclosed official secrets. He argued it was out of necessity to improve the efficiency of MI5, but he did not fulfil the criteria for necessity, so therefore he could not use the defence.

Following **Southwark London Borough Council v Williams (1971)**, Lord Denning stated that allowing the defence of necessity would 'open a door that no man could shut' and would give an excuse for all types of behaviour.

Although there are questions about this defence, the Law Commission in the **Draft Criminal Code** states: 'We are not prepared to suggest that necessity should in every case be a justification; we are equally unprepared to suggest that necessity should in no case be a defence.'

Figure 32.15 Shayler could not fulfil the criteria for necessity as the evil was not directed at him

Criminal defences: Mistake

To use mistake as a defence, the defendant must have made a mistake in the facts and not a mistake in the law: 'Ignorance of the law is no excuse', as stated in **R v Reid (1973)**.

There are several points to note here for the defence to work:

- The mens rea of the offence must be made negative by the mistake.
- The defence can be used where the defendant's actions can be excused or justified in some way.
- A statute may also specifically provide for instances where the defendant has a 'lawful excuse'.

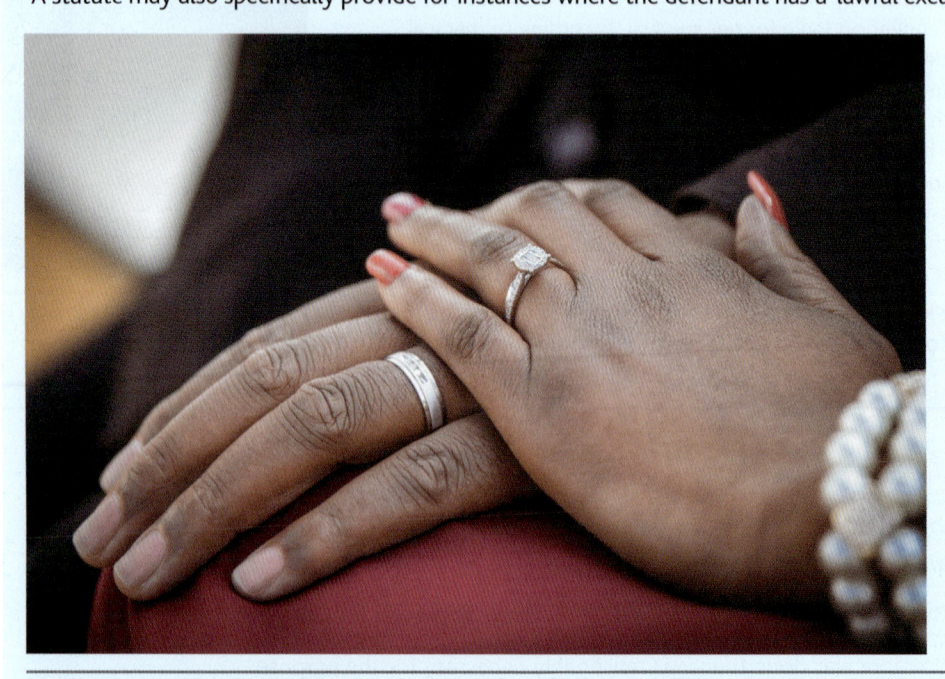

Figure 32.16 Mistake was a defence against bigamy in *R v Tolson* (1889)

The mistake must be reasonable, as shown in the following cases, along with **R v Williams (Gladstone) (1987)** (see page 356).

32 Capacity defences

R v Tolson (1889)
The defendant thought her husband was dead and married someone else. Her husband returned and she was prosecuted for bigamy. She appealed and her conviction was quashed as her actions were considered to be natural and legitimate by the court and in no way immoral. The court allowed the defence of mistake but did stress that the mistake had to be both reasonable and honest.

DPP v Morgan (1976)
The defendant was a senior officer in the RAF and told three of his junior officers to go to his house and have sex with his wife. He assured them that it would be fine, despite their concerns. They followed his orders, despite the woman's severe protests, resulting in their prosecution. At their trial, the judge told the jury that their belief in the wife's consent had to be reasonable. On appeal, the court said that the judge's direction was incorrect and that the belief only had to be genuine and not necessarily reasonable. Their convictions were still upheld.

Mistake and intoxication

Mistake cannot be used as a defence where the defendant is voluntarily intoxicated. In R v O'Grady (1987) (see page 348), the court held that an intoxicated mistake regarding how much force could be used in self-defence did not provide a defence.

R v Fotheringham (1989) (see page 345) is another example.

Criminal defences: Consent

Consent is often used as a defence to non-fatal offences against the person. It can never be a defence to murder or serious injury.

Figure 32.17 Consent cannot be a defence to fatal offences against the person

R v Donovan (1934)
The defendant caned a 17-year-old girl for sexual gratification, causing bruising. He was convicted of indecent assault and common assault. On appeal, his conviction was quashed, as the victim had consented to the act.

R v Slingsby (1995)
The defendant was charged with involuntary manslaughter. The defendant and victim had taken part in 'vigorous sexual activity', which the victim had consented to. During the activity a ring worn by the defendant caused small cuts to the victim, which led to blood poisoning, from which she later died. The victim's consent meant there was no battery or assault, so the defendant was not guilty of manslaughter as there was no unlawful act.

There must be true consent. In R v Tabassum (2000), the defendant had persuaded women to allow him to measure their breasts for the purpose of compiling a database for sale to doctors. While the women were aware of the act, they had only consented because they thought that the defendant had a medical qualification or training.

> **GRADE BOOST**
> See also **R v Konzani (2005)** for more about consent and HIV.

A victim submitting through fear does not mean that consent is real. In **R v Olugboja (1982)**, the victim and her friend had been raped by the defendant's friend. When the defendant tried to have sex with her, she submitted. The defendant claimed that this was consent but the Court of Appeal held there was a difference between real consent and mere submission.

In **R v Dica (2004)**, consent was given to sexual intercourse without knowledge of the fact that the defendant was HIV positive. The Court of Appeal held that there was no consent to the risk of the infection.

Implied consent

The courts will consider that some injuries are impliedly consented to by everyone in society. In **R v Wilson v Pringle (1987)**, the court held that ordinary 'jostlings' of everyday life were not battery. Sports injuries during properly conducted games and sports also fall into this category.

R v Barnes (2004)
The defendant made a tackle on the victim during an amateur football game. The victim suffered a serious leg injury. The defendant's conviction under **s20 Offences Against the Person Act 1861** was quashed on appeal. The Court of Appeal said that where an injury is caused during a match, a criminal prosecution should be kept for those situations where the conduct was sufficiently bad to be properly categorised as criminal.

Exceptions

The question is whether it is in the public interest to allow an exception or not.

In **Attorney General's Reference (No. 6 of 1980) (1981)**, where two men had agreed to fight in the street to settle their differences following an argument, the Court of Appeal held that consent could not be a defence to such an action as it was not in the public interest.

It is now accepted that consent is not a defence to a **s47 Offences Against the Person Act 1861** offence unless it falls within one of the exceptions listed in **Attorney General's Reference (No. 6 of 1980) (1981)**:

Figure 32.18 There is implied consent to sports injuries if the conduct is not criminal

› properly conducted games and sports
› lawful chastisement or correction
› reasonable surgical interference
› dangerous exhibitions.

The list is not exhaustive and the courts have also recognised tattooing, rough horseplay, ear-piercing and male circumcision as valid exceptions.

Consent to minor injuries

The question is whether it is in the public interest to allow such an exception or not.

In **R v Brown (1993)**, the House of Lords held that consent was not a defence to gay sadomasochistic acts, even though they were all adults and the injuries inflicted were minor and transitory.

Compare this with **R v Wilson (1997)**, where the Court of Appeal held that, where a defendant had branded his initials on his wife's bottom with a hot knife at her request, this was not an unlawful act, even though she had to have medical treatment for the burns caused. The court held it was not in the public interest that such consensual behaviour should be criminalised.

> **STRETCH AND CHALLENGE**
>
> The issue of whether consent will be allowed or not seems to come down to a debate about public policy. Should the state intervene in activities between consenting adults in the privacy of their own homes? Do you think the decision in **R v Brown (1993)** was correct?

Mistaken belief in consent

Provided the defendant genuinely believes the victim has consented, there is a defence to an assault even if they are mistaken in this belief.

> ### R v Jones (1986)
> Two boys aged 14 and 15 were thrown into the air by older boys. One suffered a broken arm and the other ruptured his spleen. The defendants argued that they believed that the two boys had consented to the activity. On appeal, their convictions for offences under **s20 Offences Against the Person Act 1861** were quashed. The court decided that a genuine mistaken belief in consent could be a defence and that this fell into the recognised exception of rough horseplay.

The courts have proposed a case-by-case approach, which could make the law very uncertain.

Figure 32.19 Euthanasia is currently illegal in the UK

Consent and euthanasia

No one can consent to their own death. This means that, if a terminally ill person wants to die, they must take their own life. If anyone kills them, it is murder. Even if someone helps them to take their own life, that person is guilty of the offence of assisting suicide. This was decided in **R (on the application of Pretty) v DPP (2001)**.

SUMMARY: CAPACITY DEFENCES

Insanity and automatism

→ **Definition:** *M'Naghten* (1843):
- defect of reason
- disease of the mind
- not knowing nature and quality of act or they are doing wrong

→ **Insanity** and automatism overlap

→ For **insanity**, defence must prove, on the balance of probabilities, defendant has a defect of reason due to disease of the mind:
- Verdict not guilty by reason of insanity
- Judge can make one of four orders

→ For **automatism**, defendant must raise the defence and the prosecution must disprove it:
- Must be caused by an external factor
- If not guilty, defendant is free (unlike insanity)

Intoxication

→ Specific intent crimes: **voluntary intoxication**:
- If defendant has mens rea, they are guilty: *R v Gallagher* (1963)
- If defendant has no mens rea, they are not guilty

→ Specific intent crimes: **involuntary intoxication**:
- If defendant has mens rea, they are guilty: *R v Kingston* (1994)
- If defendant has no mens rea, they are not guilty: *R v Hardie* (1984)

→ Specific intent crimes: **drunken mistake**:
- If the mistake negates mens rea, the defendant is not guilty
- If the mistake is about the need to defend oneself, it is not a defence and the defendant will be guilty, in both specific and basic intent offences: *R v O'Grady* (1987), *R v Hatton* (2005)

→ Basic intent crimes: **voluntary intoxication**:
- Defendant is guilty as becoming intoxicated is a reckless course of conduct: *R v Majewski* (1977)

→ Basic intent crimes: **involuntary intoxication**:
- Defendant is not guilty as they have not been reckless: *Hardie* (1984)

→ Basic intent crimes: **drunken mistake**:
- Defendant is guilty as it is a reckless course of conduct

Duress

→ Can be by threats or circumstances

→ Available for all offences except murder (*R v Howe* (1987)) and attempted murder (*R v Gotts* (1992))

→ Threat must be serious (death or serious injury), but can consider cumulative effect of other threats with threat of injury: *R v Valderrama-Vega* (1985)

→ Two tests: objective and subjective: *R v Graham* (1982)

→ Threat does not need to be immediate but it must be imminent; duress not available where:
- defendant joins a criminal gang they know is violent: *R v Sharp* (1987), *R v Hasan* (2005)
- defendant puts themselves in a position where they foresaw, or should have foreseen, the risk of being subject to compulsion

Consent
→ Not a defence for murder or **s18 Offences Against the Person Act 1861**; generally not a defence to the offences in **s20** and **s47 Offences Against the Person Act 1861**, but there are exceptions (e.g. properly conducted sports, surgery, tattoos)
→ Allowed as a defence for battery
→ There must be true consent: *R v Tabassum* (2000)
→ Can be implied to the everyday 'jostlings' of life: *R v Wilson and Pringle* (1987)

Necessity and self-defence
→ **Definition**: circumstances force a person to act to prevent a worse evil
→ Doubts whether necessity is a defence in its own right, but forms basis of other defences
→ Must be reasonable force to defend oneself or another. If the force is excessive, the defence will fail
→ Defence of necessity is only recognised as duress of circumstances in criminal law: *Dudley v Stephens* (1884)
→ Civil cases recognise defence of necessity: *Re A (Conjoined Twins)* (2000)

TEST YOURSELF

1. What case gives the definition of insanity?
2. What are the elements of the defence of insanity?
3. What examples of non-psychiatric illnesses have been classified as a disease of the mind?
4. The **Criminal Procedure (Insanity and Unfitness to Plead) Act 1991** provides orders available to a judge where there has been a successful defence of insanity. What are they?
5. For automatism to work as a defence, it must be caused by what type of factor?
6. For what types of crimes can voluntary intoxication be used?
7. What is the key case for voluntary intoxication and basic intent crimes?
8. What is the key case for the defence of necessity?
9. When can the defence of consent be used?
10. What are the different types of duress?

EXAM PAST PAPER QUESTIONS

WJEC – A Level – Sample Assessment Materials
Analyse and evaluate the extent to which the law accepts duress as a defence to a criminal charge. [50]

33 Preliminary offences of attempt

An attempt is where a person tries to commit an offence but for some reason fails to complete it. Attempt is defined in **s1 Criminal Attempts Act 1981**:

> 'if, with intent to commit an offence to which this section applies, a person does an act which is more than merely preparatory to the commission of the offence, he is guilty of attempting to commit the offence'.

The actus reus of the offence is: a person does an act which is more than merely preparatory to the commission of an offence.

The mens rea is: with intent to commit that offence.

Actus reus of attempt

Before the definition in the **Criminal Attempts Act 1981**, two main tests came from the courts:

> Last act test: had the defendant done the last act they could do before committing the crime?
> Proximity test: were the defendant's acts 'so immediately connected' to the actus reus of the offence as to justify liability for attempt?

The courts have now held these common law tests to be irrelevant. The important point is whether the defendant has done an act which is 'more than merely preparatory'.

More than merely preparatory

The act has to be more than merely preparation for the main crime. There have been many cases on the meaning of 'merely preparatory' but there is no single clear principle that comes from them.

Attorney General's Reference (No. 1 of 1992) (1993)

The defendant dragged a girl to a shed with the intent of raping her. He lowered his trousers and assaulted the girl but did not rape her. His conviction for attempted rape was upheld. It was held that the defendant need not have performed the last act before the crime proper, nor need he have reached the 'point of no return'.

R v Gullefer (1990)

The defendant jumped onto a greyhound racetrack to try to stop a race so it could be declared void and he could claim back the money he had bet. His conviction for attempting to steal was quashed because his action was merely preparatory to committing the offence and he had not 'embarked on the crime proper'.

Figure 33.1 The defendant's actions in *R v Gullefer* (1990) was not more than merely preparatory

R v Geddes (1996)

The defendant was found in the boys' toilets in a school in possession of a large knife, some rope and masking tape. He had no right to be in the school. He had not spoken to or contacted any pupils.

The Court of Appeal asked two questions:

> Had the accused moved from planning or preparation to execution or implementation?
> Had the accused done an act showing that he was actually trying to commit the full offence, or had he only got as far as getting ready, or putting himself in a position, or equipping himself to do so?

Geddes' conviction for attempted false imprisonment was quashed on appeal.

R v Campbell (1990)

The defendant was outside a post office with an imitation gun, wearing sunglasses and with a threatening note in his pocket. His conviction for attempted robbery was quashed on appeal.

Going beyond more than merely preparatory
The following cases show where a defendant has gone beyond more than merely preparatory.

R v Boyle and Boyle (1987)

The defendants were found standing next to a door with a broken lock and hinge. Their conviction for attempted burglary was upheld. Trying to gain entry was an attempt, and they were embarking on the crime proper.

R v Tosti (1987)

The defendant, intending to burgle premises, took metal-cutting equipment with him and hid it behind a nearby hedge. He then examined the padlock on the door but did not damage the padlock. He was found guilty of attempted burglary.

R v Jones (1990)

The defendant's partner told him she wanted to end their relationship because she was seeing someone else (the victim). The defendant bought a gun, got into the victim's car wearing a crash helmet, obscuring his face, and pointed the gun at the victim. The victim grabbed the gun and threw it out of the window. The defendant's conviction for attempted murder was upheld.

Mens rea of attempt

All inchoate offences are crimes of specific intent. To attempt a crime the defendant must intend to bring about the result. This will even be the case where recklessness may be sufficient for the offence. If the prosecution cannot prove intention, then the defendant is not guilty of attempt.

R v Easom (1971)
The defendant picked up a bag in a cinema, looked through it and put it back without taking anything. There was no evidence that the defendant had intended to permanently deprive and therefore they could not be guilty of attempted theft.

R v Husseyn (1977)
The defendant and another man were seen hanging around the back of a van. When approached by the police they ran off. The defendant was convicted of attempting to steal equipment that was in the van. The Court of Appeal quashed his conviction.

However, see *Attorney General's Reference (Nos 1 and 2 of 1979)* (1980), where the Court of Appeal decided that if a defendant had a conditional intent (they intended stealing if there was anything worth stealing), they could be charged with an attempt to steal.

Mens rea of attempted murder
For attempted murder, the prosecution must prove an intention to kill (to cause GBH is not enough for attempted murder, it must be to kill). This is shown in *R v Whybrow* (1951), where the defendant wired up his wife's bath and caused her to have an electric shock. He was convicted of attempted murder.

Is recklessness enough to satisfy the mens rea of attempt?

R v Millard and Vernon (1987)
The defendants pushed many times against a fence on a stand at a football ground. The prosecution said they were trying to break it, and they were convicted of criminal damage, but the Court of Appeal quashed their convictions. It was held that recklessness is not enough for the mens rea for attempted criminal damage.

Attorney General's Reference (No. 3 of 1992) (1994)
The defendant threw a petrol bomb towards a car with four men inside. The bomb missed and harmlessly hit a wall. He was acquitted at first because the judge said that it had to be proved that the defendant intended to damage property and to endanger life. On appeal, the Court of Appeal said that the trial judge was wrong. While it was necessary to prove he intended to damage property, it was only necessary to prove that he was reckless as to whether life would be endangered. He was therefore convicted of attempting to commit arson with intent to endanger life.

Attempting the impossible
Section 1(2) Criminal Attempts Act 1981 says:

> 'A person may be guilty of attempting to commit an offence ... even though the facts are such that the commission of the offence is impossible.'

STRETCH AND CHALLENGE
Research the House of Lords decision on impossibility in *Anderton v Ryan* (1985), overruled a year later in *R v Shivpuri* (1986). Do you think the House of Lords was correct to overrule its previous decision in *Anderton v Ryan*?

33 Preliminary offences of attempt

Figure 33.2 Attempting the impossible poses a legal problem

Problems with the law on attempt

It is not always clear in deciding the dividing line between what is merely preparatory and what is an attempt. Due to the wording in the **Criminal Attempts Act 1981**, which states that the defendant must do an act, that attempt cannot be committed by an omission (a failure to act). Should a defendant be guilty where it is impossible for them to commit the full offence?

> **SUMMARY: PRELIMINARY OFFENCES OF ATTEMPT**
>
> → An attempt is where a person tries to commit an offence but fails to complete it: defined in **s1 Criminal Attempts Act 1981**
> → Actus reus: a person does an act which is more than merely preparatory to the commission of an offence
> → Mens rea: person has intent to commit that offence
> → Problems with the law on attempt:
>   • Not always clear what is merely preparatory and what is an attempt

> **EXAM SKILLS**
>
> Ensure you are able to analyse and evaluate the preliminary offences of attempt and that you are also able to apply the legal rules and principles of the preliminary offences of attempt to given scenarios.

> **GRADE BOOST**
>
> Should a defendant be guilty where it is impossible for them to commit the full offence?
>
> Research the findings of the Law Commission's 2009 report 'Conspiracy and Attempts'. In what ways, if any, did the **Criminal Attempts Act 1981** improve on the common law? Is further reform now required?

> **TEST YOURSELF**
>
> 1. Where is the definition of an attempt found?
> 2. What is meant by 'more than merely preparatory'?
> 3. What cases can you cite to illustrate the 'more than merely preparatory' test?
> 4. What level of mens rea is required for an offence of attempt?
> 5. What does **Section 1(2) Criminal Attempts Act 1981** say about attempting the impossible?

Case index

A and X and others v Secretary of State for the Home Department (2004) 92, 173
Abramova v Oxford Institute of Legal Practice (2011) 281
Abu Hamza (2006) 73
Adams v Lindsell (1818) 250
Addie v Dumbreck (1929) 156
Adler v George (1964) 27
AG for Jersey v Holley (2005) 318
AG for Jersey v Holley (2005) 36, 37
AG for Northern Ireland v Gallagher (1963) 345
AG of Belize v Belize Telecom (2009) 265
AG v Dallas (2012) 84
AG v Davey and Beard (2013) 80
AG v English (1985) 222
AG v Guardian Newspapers Ltd (No. 2) (1990) 211, 212
AG v Hislop and Pressdram (1991) 221
AG v Independent TV News and Others (1985) 221
AG v News Group Newspapers (1987) 221
AG v PYA Quarries Ltd (1958), 130, 131
Agricultural Horticultural and Forestry Industry Training Board v Aylesbury Mushrooms Ltd (1972) 22
Airedale NHS Trust v Bland (1993) 37
Al-Khawaja and Thaery v UK (2009) 39
Alcock v Chief Constable of South Yorkshire Police (1991) 115, 119
Alderson B in Blyth v Birmingham Waterworks (1865) 115
Alphacell v Woodward (1972) 302, 303
American Cyanamid v Ethicon (1975) 167
Anderson (2003) 173
Anderton v Ryan (1985) 36, 366
Anglia Television Ltd v Reed (1972) 286
Argyll v Argyll (1967) 210
Armsden v Kent Police (2000) 116
Arnold v Britton (2015) 263
Arrowsmith v Jenkins (1963) 193
Arthur JS Hall and Co v Simons (2000) 88, 89, 112
Ash v McKennitt (2006) 213
Associated Provincial Picture Houses Ltd v Wednesbury Corporation (1947) 23
Atlas Express Ltd v Kafco (Importers and Distributors) Ltd (1989) 279
Attorney General's Reference (No. 1 of 1983) (1985) 329
Attorney General's Reference (No. 1 of 1992) (1993) 364
Attorney General's Reference (No. 2 of 1992) (1993) 342, 343
Attorney General's Reference (No. 3 of 1992) (1994) 366
Attorney General's Reference (No. 3 of 1994) (1997) 314

Attorney General's Reference (No. 6 of 1980) (1981) 360
Attorney General's Reference (Nos 1 and 2 of 1979) (1980) 366
Attwood v Small (1838) 276
Austin and Another v Commissioner of Police of the Metropolis (2007) 192
Austin v London Borough of Southwark (2010) 36
Author of a Blog v Times Newspapers (2009) 214
Avery v Bowden (1855) 281
B and S v Leathley (1979) 334
Bailey v Armes (1999) 152
Baldaccino v West Wittering (2008) 157
Balfour v Balfour (1919) 39, 253
Bannerman v White (1861) 262
Barnett v Chelsea & Kensington Hospital Management Committee (1968) 113, 118
Barton v Armstrong (1975) 279
BBC v HarperCollins Ltd (2010) 215
Beard v London General Omnibus (1900) 149
Beatty v Gillbanks (1882) 185
Bellinger v Bellinger (2003) 173
Berkoff v Burchill (1996) 228
Bernstein v Skyviews and General Ltd (1977) 126
Beswick v Beswick (1968) 287
Bettini v Gye (1876) 273
Bibby v Chief Constable of Essex Police (2000) 193
Biggs v Boyd Gibbins (1971) 244
Biguzzi v Rank Leisure plc (1999) 45
Bisset v Wilkinson (1927) 276
Blyth v Birmingham Waterworks Co (1856) 111
Bolam v Friern Hospital Management Committee (1957) 117
Bolton v Mahadeva (1972) 282
Bolton v Stone (1951) 115
Bottomley v Todmorden Cricket Club (2003) 155
Bourhill v Young (1943) 114
Bradbury v Morgan (1862) 247
Bratty v AG for Northern Ireland (1963) 339, 342
Brinkibon v Stahag Stahl (1982) 250
British Car Auctions v Wright (1972) 242
British Chiropractic Association v Singh (2010) 231
British Railways Board v Herrington (1972) 156
Brock v DPP (1993) 26
Bromley London Borough Council v Greater London Council (1982) 93
Bunge Corp v Tradax Export SA (1981) 273
Burnie Port Authority v General Jones Pty Limited (1994) 143

Bushell's case (1670) 77
Butler Machine Tool v Excell-o-Corp (1979) 249
Byrne v Deane (1937) 228
Byrne v Van Tienhoven (1880) 245, 246
C v Director of Public Prosecutions (1994) 59
Caballero v UK (2000) 69
Callow v Tillstone (1900) 303
Cambridge Water Co Ltd v Eastern Counties Leather plc (1994) 130, 142
Campbell v MGN (2004) 212
Caparo v Dickman (1990) 112, 113
Carlill v Carbolic Smoke Ball Company (1893) 243, 244, 246
Catholic Church Welfare Society v Institute of the Brothers of the Christian Schools (2012) 150
Central London Property Trust Ltd v High Trees House Ltd (1947) 255
Century Insurance v Northern Ireland Road Transport (1942) 148
Chapelton v Barry UDC (1940) 271
Chaplin v Hicks (1911) 286
Chappell v Nestlé Company (1960) 254
Charing Cross Electric Supply Co v Hydraulic Power Co (1914) 144
Charter v Sullivan (1957) 286
Cheeseman v DPP (1990) 26
Clarke v Dickson (1858) 287
Coco v AN Clark (Engineers) Ltd (1968) 210, 223
Collins v Godfrey (1831) 255
Collins v Wilcock (1984) 307
Combe v Combe (1951) 255
Conway v George Wimpey & Co (1951) 124
Conway v Rimmer (1968) 36
Conway v Wimpey (1951) 149
Cooke and Another v MGN Ltd (2014) 229
Corcoran v Anderton (1980) 331
Couchman v Hill (1947) 276
Council of Civil Service Union v Minister for the Civil Service (1984) 93
Coventry and Others v Lawrence (2014) 139, 141
Cox v Ministry of Justice (2016) 147
Craddock Brothers Ltd v Hunt (1923) 287
Crown River Cruises Ltd v Kimbolton Fireworks Ltd (1996) 137
CTB v News Group Newspapers (2011) 215
CTB v Newsgroup (2012) 213
Cundy v Le Cocq (1884) 303
Cunningham v Harrison (1973) 165
Customs and Excise v Cure and Deeley Ltd (1962) 23
Cutter v Powell (1795) 281, 282
D and C Builders v Rees (1965) 255, 256
Daborn v Bath Tramways (1946) 116

Case index

Dakin & Company v Lee (1916) 282
Damilola Taylor case (2002) 71
Darnley v Croydon Health Services NHS Trust (2018) 113
Davis v Johnson (1979) 30
Dawson and James (1976) 331
Debbie Purdy (2009) 317
Derbyshire County Council v Times Newspapers (1993) 172
Diane Pretty (2002) 317
Dick Bentley Productions Ltd v Harold Smith (Motors) Ltd (1965) 262
Dickinson v Dodds (1876) 245, 246, 247
Director of Public Prosecutions (DPP) v Jones (1999) 37
Donnelly v Joyce (1972) 165
Donoghue v Stevenson (1932) 38, 112, 323
Douglas and Jones v Hello! Ltd (2005) 174, 213, 216
DPP for Northern Ireland v Lynch (1975) 351
DPP v A (2000) 310
DPP v Beard (1920) 345
DPP v Clarke (1992) 188
DPP v Fiddler (1992) 188
DPP v Jones (1998) 186, 187
DPP v Majewski (1977) 345, 349
DPP v Morgan (1976) 359
DPP v Newbury and Jones (1976) 322
DPP v Orum (1988) 188
DPP v Redmond-Bate (1999) 193
DPP v Santana-Bermudez (2004) 308
DPP v Smith (2006) 309
Duffy v Newcastle United Football Co Ltd (2000) 263
Duncan v Jones (1936) 193
Dunlop v Selfridge (1915) 253
Dunnett v Railtrack (2002) 47, 49
Dwek v Macmillan Publishers Ltd and Others (2000) 229
Edgington v Fitzmaurice (1885) 276
Edwards v Skyways Ltd (1969) 251
Elliot v Grey (1960) 28
Entores Ltd v Miles Far East Corp (1955) 250
Equitable Life Assurance Society v Hyman (2000) 264
Errington v Errington and Woods (1952) 244
Esso Petroleum Co Ltd v Commissioners of Customs and Excise (1976) 252
Esso Petroleum Co Ltd v Mardon (1976) 277
Fagan v Metropolitan Police Commissioner (1969) 297, 307
Fairnie (Deceased) and Others v Reed and Another (1994) 211
Farley v Skinner (2001) 285
Felthouse v Brindley (1863) 248
Fercometal Sarl v Mediterranean Shipping Company (1989) 281
Ferdinand v MGN (2011) 215
Financings Ltd v Stimson (1962) 247
Fisher v Bell (1961) 242
Fitzpatrick v Sterling Housing Association Ltd (2000) 38

Fletcher v Bealey (1884) 167
Flood v Times (2012) 230
Foster v Warblington UDC (1906) 136
Foy v Chief Constable of Kent (1984) 191, 193
Froom v Butcher (1976) 162
Frost v Knight (1872) 281
Galloway v Telegraph Group Ltd (2004) 230
Gammon (HK) Ltd v Attorney General (1985), 301, 303
Garry Weddell (2008) 69
Gecas v Scottish Television (1992) 229
Gee v Metropolitan Railway (1873) 118
General NHS Trust and Steel v Joy and Halliday (2004) 47
George Mitchell (Chesterhall) Ltd v Finney Lock Seeds Ltd (1983) 272
Ghaidan v Godin-Mendoza (2004) 9, 32, 173
Gillan and Quinton v the UK (2010) 195
Gillick v West Norfolk and Wisbech Area Health Authority (1985) 38
Glasgow Corporation v Taylor (1992) 152, 153
GM Crops (2000) 77
Golden Victory (2007) 286
Goodwin v UK (2002) 11
Goswell v Commissioner of Police the Metropolis (1998) 202
Guthing v Lynn (1831) 245
H v Ministry of Defence (1991) 47
Hadley v Baxendale (1854) 286
Haley v London Electricity Board (1965) 114
Hall v Simons (2000) 36
Halsey v Esso Petroleum Co Ltd (1961) 137
Halsey v Milton Keynes General NHS Trust (2004) 45, 47, 49
Handyside v United Kingdom (1976) 172, 223
Hanif and Khan v UK (2011) 80
Hansen v Denmark (1995) 304
Harris v Nickerson (1873) 242
Harrison v Duke of Rutland (1893) 193
Harrow London Borough Council v Shah (1999) 302
Harvela Investments v Royal Trust of Canada (1986) 243
Harvey v Facey (1893) 244
Haseldine v Daw (1941) 152, 154
Haystead v DPP (2000) 307
Hayward v Thompson (1964) 229
Healthcare at Home Limited v The Common Services Agency (2014) 156
Hedley Byrne v Heller & Partners (1964) 277
Herne Bay Steamboat Company v Hutton (1903) 283
Herrington v British Railways Board (1972) 36
Hickman v Maisey (1900) 189
Hill v Baxter (1958) 291, 342
Hilton v Thomas Burton (Rhodes) Ltd (1961) 149
Hirachand Punamchand v Temple (1911) 255
Hoare v UK (1997) 223
Hoeing v Isaacs (1952) 282
Hollywood Silver Fox Farm Ltd v Emmett (1936) 139

Hong Kong Fir Shipping Co Ltd v Kawasaki Ltd (1962) 273
Hosking v Runting (2004) 209
Household Fire Insurance v Grant (1879) 251
Howard Marine and Dredging Co Ltd v Ogden and Sons (Evacuations) Ltd (1978) 279
HRH Princess of Wales v MGN Newspapers Ltd (1993) 210, 211
Hubbard v Pitt (1976) 189
Hughes v Lord Advocate (1963) 118
Hulton v Jones (1910) 229
Hunter and Others v Canary Wharf Ltd (1997) 134, 135, 137, 140
Hunter and Others v London Docklands Corporation (1997) 134, 137, 140
Hussain and another (2010) 355
Hutcheson v News Group Newspapers (2011) 215
Hyam v DPP (1975) 292, 316
Hyde v Wrench (1840) 246, 248
Inland Revenue Commissioners v Fry (2001) 248
Investors Compensation Scheme Ltd v West Bromwich Building Society (1998) 264
Iqbal v London Transport Executive (1973) 148
Isle of Wight Council v Plat (2017) 28
Ivey v Genting Casinos (UK) Ltd (2017) 330
Jarvis v Swans Tours Ltd (1973) 285
Jason Donovan v The Face (1998) 228
JCC (A Minor) v Eisenhower (1984) 310
JEB Fasteners Ltd v Marks Bloom & Co Ltd (1983) 276
Jolley v London Borough of Sutton (2000) 118, 154
Jonathan Aitken (1970) 217
Jones v Vernon's Pools Ltd (1938) 252
Joseph v Spiller (2010) 230
Kay v Butterworth (1945) 342
Kay v Lambeth London BC (2006) 39
Kent v Griffiths (2001) 113
Kent v Metropolitan Commissioner (1981) 185
Keown v Coventry Healthcare NHS Trust (2006) 157
Khorasandjian v Bush (1993) 136, 137
Kleinwort Benson Ltd v Lincoln City Council (1998) 37
Knupffer v London Express Newspapers (1944) 229
Krell v Henry (1903) 283
L'Estrange v Graucob (1934) 270
Lachaux v Independent Print Ltd (2021) 231
Latimer v AEC Ltd (1953) 116
Lawrence v MPC (1972) 327
Leeds City Council v Price (2006) 173
Les Affréteurs Réunis v Leopold Walford (1919) 259
Limpus v London General Omnibus (1863) 149
Lion Laboratories v Evans and Express Newspapers (1988) 213
Lister and Others v Helsey Hall (2002) 152
Logdon v DPP (1976) 306

369

London Borough of Islington v Elliott and Morris (2012) 167
London Street Tramways v LCC (1898) 36
Lord Janner (2015) 74
M'Loughlin (1838) 310
Magor and St Mellons Rural District Council v Newport Corporation (1950) 28
Malone v Laskey (1907) 136, 137
Malone v Metropolitan Police Commissioner (1979) 172, 205
Malone v UK (1985) 204, 205
Manchester City Council v Pinnock (No. 2) (2011) 39
Marks and Spencer v BNP Paribas (2015) 264
Marley v Rawlings (2014) 264
Martinez v Ellesse International SpA (1999) 264
Matthew and Alleyne (2003) 292
Maya Evans (2010) 190
McCann v UK (1995) 172
McIlkenny v Chief Constable of the West Midlands (1980) 93
McLoughlin v O'Brien (1983) 114
Merritt v Merritt (1970) 39, 253
Metropolitan Water Board v Dick Kerr & Company Ltd (1918) 283
Michael v Chief Constable of South Wales Police (2015) 114
Miles v Forest Granite Co (Leicestershire) Ltd (1918) 142
Miller v Jackson (1977) 139, 140
Modahl v British Athletic Federation Ltd (1999) 281
Montgomery v Lanarkshire (2015) 112
Moriarty v Brooks (1834) 310
Morris v Murray (1991) 159, 160
Morris v UK (2002) 39
Mosley v News Group Newspapers (2008) 214
Moss v McLachlan (1985) 191
Mowatt (1967) 310
Moy v Pettman Smith (2005) 89
Muir v Keay (1875) 30
Mulcahy v Ministry of Defence (1996) 114
Mullin v Richards (1998) 117
Murray v Express Newspapers (2008) 213
Nagy v Weston (1966) 193
Napier v Pressdram Ltd (2009) 215
Nettleship v Weston (1971) 113, 115, 116
Newsgroups Newspapers v Sogat (1982) 185
Nichols v Marsland (1876) 144
Nickoll and Knight v Ashton Edridge & Company (1901) 283
Nicol v DPP (1996) 193
Nisshin Shipping v Cleaves (2003) 257
Norfolk Constabulary v Seekings and Gould (1986) 334
North Ocean Shipping Co v Hyundai Construction Co [The Atlantic Baron] (1979) 279
O'Brien v MGN (2001) 271
O'Hara v UK (2000) 198

OBG Ltd v Allan (2007) 212
Olley v Marlborough Court Ltd (1949) 270
Osman v DPP (1999) 196
Othman (Abu Qatada) v UK (2012) 174
Oxford v Moss (1979) 328
Paris v Stepney Borough Council (1951) 116
Parker v South Eastern Railway (1877) 270
Partridge v Crittenden (1968) 243
Patel v Ali (1984) 287
Pepper v Hart (1993) 30, 36
Perry v Kendrick's Transport Ltd (1956) 144
Peters v Prince of Wales Theatre (1943) 144
Peyman v Lanjani (1985) 276
Pharmaceutical Society of Great Britain v Boots Cash Chemists Ltd (1953) 242
Phipps v Rochester (1955) 152, 153
Pilbrow v Pearless de Rougemont & Company (1999) 281
Pilkington v Wood (1953) 286
Pink Floyd Music Ltd v EMI Records (2010) 264
Pinnel's Case (1602) 254
Pioneer Shipping Ltd v BTP Tioxide Ltd (1981) 283
PJS v News Group Newspapers (2016) 181, 213
Planche v Colburn (1831) 282
Platform Funding Ltd v Bank of Scotland plc (2008) 281
Poplar Housing v Donoghue (2001) 174
Poussard v Spiers and Pond (1876) 273
Povey v Rydal School (1970) 165
Powell v Kempton (1899) 30
Powell v Lee (1908) 249
Prince Albert v Strange (1849) 210
Proprietary Articles Trade Association v Attorney General for Canada (1931) 289
Quinn v Burch Brothers (Builders) Ltd (1966) 285
R (Laporte) v Chief Constable of Gloucestershire (2007) 192, 193
R (on the application of Baroness Jenny Jones and others) v the MPC (2019) 190
R (on the application of Haw) v Secretary of State for the Home Department (2006) 190
R (on the application of Kadhim) v Brent London Borough Housing Benefit Review Board (2001) 37
R (on the application of Pretty) v DPP (2001) 361
R (Roberts) v Commissioner of the Police of the Metropolis (2015) 195
R v A (2001) 173
R v Abdroikov (2007) 80
R v Abdul-Hussain (1999) 352
R v Adomako (1994) 323
R v Ahluwalia (1992) 317, 319
R v Alexander and Steen (2004). 84
R v Allen (1988) 347
R v Bailey (1983) 343
R v Banks (2011) 80
R v Barnes (2004) 360

R v Barnsdale-Quean (2014) 318
R v Barton and Booth (2020) 330
R v Bateman (1925) 323
R v Bawa-Garba (2016) 323
R v Belfon (1976) 314
R v Bentham (2005) 332
R v Blaue (1975) 301, 314
R v Bollom (2003) 310
R v Bowen (1996) 353
R v Boyd (2002) 39
R v Boyle and Boyle (1987) 365
R v Bristol (2007) 196
R v Brown (1972) 319
R v Brown (1985) 333
R v Brown (1993) 360
R v Brown and Stratton (1998) 309
R v Burgess (1991) 339, 341, 344
R v Byrne (1960) 320, 341
R v C (2004) 39
R v Cairns (1999) 353, 356
R v Calder and Boyars (1969) 224
R v Caldwell (1982) 36, 299
R v Campbell (1990) 365
R v Canale (1990) 201
R v Cato (1976) 322
R v Chan Fook (1994) 309
R v Cheshire (1991) 301, 315
R v Church (1966) 321
R v Cilliers (2017) 79
R v Clarence (1888) 310
R v Clarke (1972) 339
R v Clegg (1995) 355
R v Clinton, Parker and Evans (2012) 318
R v Clouden (1987) 331
R v Coley (2013) 339, 340
R v Collins (1973) 333, 335
R v Connor and Rollock (2002) 84
R v Constanza (1997) 307
R v Conway (1988) 353
R v Cunningham (1957) 298, 299, 307, 335
R v D (2006) 321
R v Dallas (2012) 81
R v Dawes, Hatter and Bowyer (2013) 317, 318
R v Dawson (1985) 322
R v Dica (2004) 37, 310, 360
R v Dietschmann (2003) 320
R v Donovan (1934) 359
R v Doughty (1986) 318, 319
R v Duarte (1990) 204
R v Dudley and Stephens (1884) 356, 357
R v Dymond (2010) 226
R v Dytham (1979) 292
R v Easom (1971) 366
R v Flack (2013) 333
R v Ford (1989) 82
R v Fotheringham (1989) 345, 359
R v Fraill (2011) 80
R v Fraser (1987) 81
R v G and another (2003) 36, 298, 307
R v Geddes (1996) 365
R v Ghosh (1982) 330

370

Case index

R v Gibbins and Proctor (1918) 292, 295, 296
R v Gill (1963) 352
R v Golds (2014) 320
R v Goldstein (2006)
R v Gomez (2000) 327
R v Gotts (1982) 351
R v Gough (1993)
R v Graham (1982) 351
R v Grant (2005) 200, 201
R v Gullefer (1990) 364
R v Hale (1979) 332
R v Hall (1972) 329
R v Hall (1994) 206
R v Halliday (1889) 310
R v Hancock and Shankland (1986) 292, 298, 316
R v Hardie (1985) 344, 346
R v Harris (2013) 339
R v Hasan (2005) 352, 353
R v Hatton (2005) 349
R v Hennessy (1989) 339, 341, 343
R v Hinks (2000) 327
R v Holland (2010) 226
R v Horncastle (2009) 39
R v Horseferry Road Justices, ex parte Siadatan (1990) 188
R v Howe and others (1986) 351
R v Hudson and Taylor (1971) 352, 353
R v Husseyn (1977) 366
R v Inhabitants of Sedgley (1831) 30
R v Ireland, Burstow (1997) 306, 307, 314
R v James and Karimi (2006) 37
R v Jewell (2014) 318
R v JM and SM (2012) 322
R v Johnson (1997) 133
R v Johnson (2007) 340
R v Johnstone (2007) 322
R v Jones (1986) 361
R v Jones (1990) 365
R v Jordan (1956) 300, 314, 315
R v Karakaya (2005) 84
R v Kelly and Lindsay (1998) 328
R v Kemp (1957) 339
R v Kennedy (No. 2) (2007) 322
R v Khan (Sultan) (1996) 204, 205
R v Khan & Khan (1988) 292
R v Kingston (1994) 347
R v Konzani (2005) 360
R v Lamb (1967) 322
R v Larsonneur (1933) 291, 295, 301, 303
R v Latimer (1986) 297
R v Lavender (1994) 331
R v Lavinia Woodward (2017)
R v Lipman (1970) 345, 348
R v Lloyd (1985) 329
R v Lockley (1995) 332
R v Lord Chancellor (2017) 52
R v Lowe (1973) 321
R v Lowrie (2004) 133
R v M'Naghten (1843), 339, 341
R v Malcherek and Steel (1981) 314
R v Marshall (1998) 329

R v Martin (1989) 353, 356
R v Martin (Anthony) (2001) 320, 355
R v Matthews and Alleyne (2003) 316
R v Mental Health Tribunal ex parte H (2001) 173
R v Millard and Vernon (1987) 366
R v Miller (1954) 309
R v Miller (1983) 296
R v Mirza (2004) 84
R v Misra and Srivastava (2005) 323
R v Mohan (1975) 291
R v Moloney (1985) 292, 298
R v Morris (1923) 327
R v Nedrick (1986) 292, 298, 315, 316
R v O'Grady (1987) 348, 349, 359
R v Olugboja (1982) 360
R v Ong (2001) 133
R v Owen (1992) 83
R v Oye (2013) 339, 356
R v Pagett (1983) 299, 314
R v Pearson (1835) 346
R v Pearson (1992) 319
R v Perrin (2002) 224
R v Pittwood (1902) 292, 295
R v Ponting (1985) 77, 93, 218
R v Pryce (2013) 84
R v Quick (1973) 339, 343
R v R (1991) 9, 36, 38, 290
R v Reid (1973) 358
R v Rimmington (2006) 133
R v Roberts (1971) 308, 315
R v Robinson (1977) 331
R v Ruffell (1991) 132
R v Ryan (1996) 333, 334
R v Samuel (1988) 104, 200, 201
R v Saunders (1985) 309
R v Savage, Parmenter (1992) 307, 309
R v Secretary of State ex parte Brind (1990) 172
R v Shayler (2001) 218, 357
R v Sheehan and Moore (1975)
R v Shivpuri (1986) 36, 366
R v Slingsby (1995) 359
R v Smith (1959) 300, 314, 315
R v Smith (2003) 82
R v Smith (2011) 328
R v Smith (Morgan) (2001) 37
R v Smith and Deane (2016) 80
R v Smith and Jones (1976)
R v Stagg (1994) 206
R v Stone and Dobinson (1977) 292, 296
R v Sullivan (1984) 339
R v Tabassum (2000) 359
R v Taylor (1950) 37
R v Taylor and Taylor (1993) 84
R v Thomas (1985) 307
R v Thornton (1996) 319
R v Tolson (1889) 359
R v Tosti (1987) 365
R v Turner No. 2 (1971) 328
R v Twomey and others (2009) 82
R v Valderrama-Vega (1985) 351, 352

R v Velumyl (1989) 329
R v Venna (1976) 308
R v Vickers (1957) 297
R v Walkington (1979)
R v Wang (2005) 77
R v Watson (1989) 322
R v White (1910) 299, 314
R v Whybrow (1951) 366
R v Willer (1986) 353
R v Williams (2001) 328
R v Williams (Gladstone) (1987) 356, 358
R v Willoughby (2004) 323
R v Wilson (1997) 361
R v Windle (1952) 340
R v Woollin (1998) 292, 298, 315, 316
R v Workman (2014) 318
Rae v Marrs (1990) 155
Ramsgate Victoria Hotel v Montefiore (1866) 247
Re A (Conjoined Twins) (2000) 317, 357
Re F (Mental Patient: Sterilisation) (1990) 356
Re McArdle (1951) 256
Re P and Others (2009) 173
Re Pinochet Ugarte (1999) 93
Re Polemis & Furness, Withy & Co Ltd (1921) 118
Re S (A Child) (Identification on Publication) (2004) 213
Read v J Lyons & Co Ltd (1947) 142
Ready Mixed Concrete Ltd v Minister of Pensions (1968) 147, 148
Reigate v Union Manufacturing Co (1918) 265
Reynolds v Times Newspapers (1999) 230
RHM Bakeries v Strathclyde Regional Council (1985) 143
Riches v News Group (1986) 229
Rickards v Lothian (1913) 142
Rigby v Chief Constable of Northamptonshire (1985) 128
Robinson v Chief Constable of West Yorkshire Police (2018) 112
Robinson v Davidson (1871) 283
Robinson v Kilvert (1888)
Roe v Minister of Health (1954) 115
Roles v Nathan (1963) 154
Romford Jury (1993) 81
Rondel v Worsley (1969) 36, 89
Rookes v Barnard (1964) 165
Roscorla v Thomas (1842) 276
Rose v Plenty (1975) 149
Routledge v Grant (1828) 245, 246
Routledge v McKay (1954) 262
Royal College of Nursing v DHSS (1981) 27
Rylands v Fletcher (1868) 109, 110, 128, 141, 142, 143, 159
Salabiaku v France (1988) 304
Sally Challen (2020) 320
Sander v UK (2000) 82
Sarah Tisdall (1984) 218
Sayers v Harlow UDC (1957) 161
Schuler AG v Wickman Machine Tool Sales Ltd (1973) 273

371

Scott v Avery (1855) 48
Scruttons Ltd v Midland Silicones (1962) 258
Serafin v Malkiewicz (2020) 230
Shanklin Pier v Detel Products Ltd (1951) 258
Shannon Matthews (2008) 70
Shanshal v Al-Kishtaini (2001) 240
Shaw v DPP (1962) 224, 289
Shelley Films Ltd v Rex Features Ltd (1993) 210, 211
Shirlaw v Southern Foundries (1926) 264
Sim v Stretch (1936) 227
Simmons v Castle (2012) 38
Simpkins v Pays (1955) 253
Singh v London Underground (1990) 47
Smith v Chief Superintendent of Woking Police Station (1983) 307
Smith v Leech Brain & Co (1962) 118
Smith v Stages (1989)
Smoldon v Whitworth and Nolan (1997) 160
Southport Corporation v Esso Petroleum (1954) 124
Southwark London Borough Council v Williams (1971) 358
Spice Girls Ltd v Aprilia World Service (2002) 279
Springer v Germany (2012) 216
Spurling v Bradshaw (1956) 271
St Helen's Smelting Co v Tipping (1865) 138
Stannard v Gore (2012) 143
Staples v West Dorset District Council (1995) 155
Star Energy Weald Basin Limited v Bocardo SA (2010) 124, 125
Startup v Macdonald (1843) 282
Steel v UK (1998) 193
Steinfeld and Keidan v Secretary of State for International Development (2018) 173
Stephens v Avery (1988) 210, 211
Stevenson v McLean (1880) 246, 248
Stevenson, Jordan and Harrison v MacDonald and Evans (1952) 147
Stocker v Stocker (2019) 228, 229
Stone v Smith (1647) 124
Storey v Ashton (1869) 148, 149
Sturges v Bridgman (1879) 139
Sumpter v Hedges (1898) 282
Sunday Times v UK (1979) 172, 173
Sunday Times v UK (1981) 220
SW v UK (1996) 39
Sweet v Parsley (1970) 302
T (1990) 342, 344
Taylor v Caldwell (1863) 282
Taylor v Laird (1856) 244
Terry v Persons Unknown (2010) 215
Thabo Meli (1954) 297
The Commissioner of Police for the Metropolis v Thompson and Hsu (1997) 202
The Mihalis Angelos (1970) 273
The Moorcock (1889) 265
Thomas v NUM (1985) 93
Thomas v Thomas (1942) 254
Thompson and Venables v UK (1999) 61, 62
Three Rivers District Council v Bank of England (No. 2) (1996) 30
Tolley v JS Fry and Sons Ltd (1931) 228
Tomlinson v Congleton Borough Council (2003) 156, 157
Transco plc v Stockport Metropolitan Borough Council (2004) 142, 143
Transfield Shipping v Mercator Shipping [The Achilleas] (2008) 286
Tuberville v Savage (1669) 307
Tweddle and Atkinson (1861) 255, 257
UCB v Halifax (SW) Ltd (1999) 45
Ullah v Special Adjudicator (2004) 173
United States v Ghislaine Maxwell (2022) 81
Universe Tankships v International Transport Workers' Federation (1983) 279
Vardy v Rooney (2022) 232
Vidal-Hall v Google (2015) 212
Von Hannover v Germany (No. 2) (2012) 216
Wagon Mound (No. 1) (1961) 118, 130, 131, 138, 140, 142
Wainwright v Home Office (2003) 209
Walker v Crystal Palace Football Club (1909) 147
Walters v Morgan (1861) 287
Ward v James (1966) 47
Warner Brothers Pictures Inc v Nelson (1937) 287
West v Shepherd (1964) 165
Wheat v Lacon & Co (1966) 152
Wheeler v Saunders Ltd (1994) 138
White and Carter Ltd v McGregor (1962) 281
Whitehouse v Lemon (1976) 74
Whiteley v Chappel (1968) 27
Williams v Roffey Bros and Nicholls Contractors Ltd (1990) 254
Wilson v Pringle (1987) 360
Wilson v Secretary of State for Trade and Industry (2003) 30
Windle v DPP (1996) 187
Winzar v Chief Constable of Kent (1983) 291, 295, 301
Witter Ltd v TBP Industries Ltd (1996) 276
Wood v Leadbitter (1845) 127
Woodgate and Bowyer (2001) 221
Woodward v Hutchings (1977)
Woolmington v DPP (1935) 290
X v Y (1998) 213
Y v the Netherlands (1985) 174
Yates Building Co v Pulleyn Ltd (1975) 249
Yewens v Noakes (1880) 144
YL v Birmingham City Council (2008) 174
Young v Bristol Aeroplane Co (1944) 37

Glossary

acquittal: the defendant has been found not guilty and will go free.

Act of Parliament (statute): a source of primary legislation that comes from the UK legislature

actus reus: 'the guilty act' that must be present for a defendant to be found guilty of a crime. It can be a voluntary action, an omission or a state of affairs.

admissible: useful evidence which cannot be excluded on the basis that it is immaterial, irrelevant or violating the rules of evidence.

aggravating factor: a factor relevant to an offence that has the effect of increasing the sentence. Examples include the defendant having previous convictions, or if a weapon was used in the offence.

appropriate adult: a parent, guardian or social worker who must be present when a youth under the age of 17 is being interviewed in police custody, or on trial at the youth court. Their role is to make sure the young person understands legal terminology, is aware of their rights and is comforted and reassured.

bail hostel: a place of residence for people on bail who cannot give a fixed address, run by the Probation Service.

bail: the defendant is allowed to be at liberty rather than prison before their court hearing, as long as they agree to particular conditions, such as regularly reporting to a police station.

beyond reasonable doubt: the standard of proof that is required in criminal cases. For a defendant to be guilty, the judge or jury must be convinced that there is no doubt that the defendant is guilty.

bilateral contract: a contract between two parties where each promises to perform an act in exchange for the other party's act.

binding precedent: a previous decision that has to be followed.

breach of contract: to break a contract by not following its terms and conditions.

Brexit: the common name given to Britain's exit from the European Union and is widely used by the media when referring to issues surrounding the negotiations.

bundle of rights: the owner of a property has a bundle of rights over their own property, so they have the right to do anything with it (e.g. destroy it, throw it away or do something random with it).

burden of proof: the responsibility placed on one party in a case to prove the allegation or claim. In criminal cases, this lies with the prosecution to prove that the defendant is guilty.

cab rank rule: a barrister is obliged accept any work in a field in which they are competent to practice, at a court at which they normally appear and at their usual rates.

case stated: appeals on the grounds that there has been an error of law or the magistrates have acted out of their jurisdiction. Can be used by both the prosecution and defence.

causation (or chain of causation): connecting the actus reus and the corresponding result. For there to be criminal liability, there must be an unbroken chain of causation. There are two types of causation: legal and factual.

chambers: office space where barristers group together to share clerks (administrators) and operating expenses.

charge: the decision that a suspect should stand trial for an alleged offence.

claimant: the person bringing the action. Before 1 April 1999, this person was known as the plaintiff.

common law (also case law or precedent): law developed by judges through decisions in court.

constructive manslaughter: the death of a person is caused by an unlawful and dangerous criminal act.

contempt of court: a criminal offence punishable by up to two years' imprisonment for anyone who is disobedient or discourteous to a court of law.

conviction: the defendant has been found guilty and the case will proceed to the sentencing stage.

counter-offer: an attempt to vary the conditions of the original offer. It is therefore not acceptance, and a contract is not formed until the counteroffer is accepted.

cross-examination: questioning of a witness in court by the opposing counsel.

custom: rules of behaviour which develop in a community without being deliberately invented.

damages: an award of money that aims to compensate the innocent party for the financial losses they have suffered as a result of the breach.

declaration of incompatibility: issued under s4 Human Rights Act 1998, this gives senior judges the power to question the compatibility of legislation with human rights. The declaration is sent to Parliament. It does not allow judges to strike out laws.

defendant: the person defending the action (e.g. the person accused of a crime).

delegated legislation (secondary or subordinate legislation): law created by a body other than Parliament but with the authority of Parliament, as laid down in primary legislation.

deterrent: something that discourages a particular action.

devolution: the transference of power from central government to regional or local government (e.g. the formation of the Welsh Government, the Northern Ireland Assembly and the Scottish Parliament).

discretionary: it is a choice of the court whether to award or not.

duty solicitor: solicitors who work in private practice but have secured a contract with the Legal Aid Agency to provide criminal advice to people who have been arrested. The person in custody will have the assistance of whoever is on the rota for that day.

early administrative hearing: the first appearance at magistrates' court for all defendants suspected of a summary or indictable offence. This hearing considers legal funding, bail and legal representation.

entrenched: a firmly established piece of law which is difficult, or unlikely, to change (e.g. the US Bill of Rights). The UK has no laws that are entrenched.

equitable: fair.

examination in chief: the defence or prosecution questioning a witness in court by their own counsel.

exclusion clause: an attempt by one party to a contract to exclude all liability or to limit liability for breaches of the contract.

Executive: the government.

express terms: contract terms laid down by the parties themselves.

first instance (trial court): a court in which the first hearing of a case takes place. It is distinguished from an appellate court, which hears appeal cases.

First Tier Tribunal: part of the legal system that aims to settle the 'first instance' stage of legal disputes. It is split into seven chambers or specialist areas.

foreseeable: events the defendant should be able to have predicted could happen.

general defences: defences that can apply to any crime (with some exceptions), as opposed to 'special defences', which can only apply to certain crimes; for example diminished responsibility is only available for murder.

gross negligence manslaughter: the death of a person is caused by civil negligence.

hearsay: second-hand evidence which is not what the witness knows personally but is something they have been told.

held: decided; the decision of the court.

homicide: the killing of one person by another, deliberately or not.

House of Lords: the name of the Upper House in Parliament, which is the legislative chamber. Confusion arose before the establishment of the Supreme Court, as the highest appeal court was also called the House of Lords.

implied terms: contract terms that are assumed, either by common law or statute.

indictable: the most serious offences, triable only in the Crown Court.

Inns of Court: Barristers must join Inner Temple, Middle Temple, Gray's Inn or Lincoln's Inn. The Inns provide accommodation and education and promote activities.

institutional racism: a public or private body's operation or policies and procedure are deemed to be racist.

intangible property: property that does not physically exist, such as copyright or patents.

judicial precedent (case law): a source of law where past judges' decisions create law for future judges to follow.

judicial review: the process of challenging the legality of a decision, action or failure to act by a public body such as a government department or court.

laissez-faire: contract law term used to indicate that a person should have freedom of contract with minimal state or judicial interference.

lay (person): someone who is not legally qualified.

legislative reform order: a Statutory Instrument which can amend an Act of Parliament without the need for a parliamentary Bill.

literal approach: the judge takes the literal and grammatical meaning of a word, even if this leads to absurdity.

litigation: the process of taking a case to court.

maliciously: interpreted as meaning with intention or subjective recklessness.

mandatory injunction: an order to do something.

margin of appreciation: the discretion given to each EU member state to interpret ECHR rights.

mens rea: 'the guilty mind' that must be present for a defendant to be found guilty of a crime. It can include intention, recklessness or negligence.

mitigation of loss: lessening or reducing a loss.

no win, no fee: an agreement between a solicitor and a client whereby the client will only pay the legal fees if the case is won.

Non-pecuniary damages: damages that are not wholly money-based.

novus actus interveniens: an intervening act that is so independent of the original act of the defendant that it succeeds in breaking the chain of causation. There may be liability for the initial act.

obiter dicta: 'things said by the way'. This is not binding and is only persuasive.

objective: a test that considers not the particular defendant in question, but what another average, reasonable person would have done or thought if placed in the same position as the defendant.

occasion(ing): to bring about or to cause.

offer: in contract law, a proposition put by one person to another person made with the intention that it shall become legally binding as soon as the other person accepts it.

offeree: the person to whom an offer is being made and who will consequently accept the offer.

offeror: the person making an offer.

on the balance of probabilities: the standard of proof in a civil case where the burden is on the claimant to establish that it is more likely than not the defendant did what they are claiming.

original precedent: a decision in a case where there is no previous legal decision or law for the judge to use.

parliamentary sovereignty: Dicey's principle that Parliament has absolute and unlimited power, and that an Act of Parliament overrules any other source of law.

Parole Board: a body set up under the Criminal Justice Act 1967 to hold meetings with an offender to decide whether they can be released from prison after serving a minimum sentence. They complete a risk assessment to determine whether it is safe to release the person back into the community. If they are safe to be released, they will be released on licence with conditions and close supervision.

partial defence: the use of a defence which has the effect not of completely acquitting the defendant but allowing a reduction in the charge and sentence given to the defendant.

Pecuniary damages: damages that can be easily calculated in money terms.

per incuriam: 'made by mistake'. Before the 1966 Practice Statement this was the only situation in which the House of Lords could depart from its previous decisions.

persuasive precedent: previous decision that does not have to be followed.

plea bargaining: the defendant pleads guilty to a lesser offence in return for a lower sentence to save court time and make the trial more predictable.

pre-sentence report: a report that helps the court to decide whether there are any factors in the defendant's history which may affect the sentencing.

presumption: a starting point for the courts, which presume certain facts to be true unless there is a greater balance of evidence to the contrary that disproves the presumption.

primary legislation: law made by the legislature, which in the UK is Parliament. Acts of Parliament are primary legislation.

privity of contract: a doctrine which allows the parties to a contract to sue each other, but does not allow a third party to sue.

Privy Council: the final appeal court for most Commonwealth countries.

procedural ultra vires: where the procedures laid down in an enabling Act for making a Statutory Instrument have not been followed (e.g. consultation was required but not carried out). Literal meaning: 'beyond the powers'.

prohibitory injunction: an order not to do something.

promissory estoppel: if someone (the promisor) makes a promise that another person acts on, the promisor is stopped (or estopped) from going back on the promise, even though the other person did not provide consideration.

proportionate: relates to the concept of 'proportionality'. This means that the restriction on the human right must be the least restrictive option to meet the legitimate aim.

proximate relationship: (in tort law) how close the defendant and victim are physically or emotionally.

pupillage: a one-year apprenticeship in which a pupil works alongside a qualified barrister, who is known as the pupil master.

purposive approach: this allows the judge to look at the 'spirit of the law' and what Parliament intended when it passed the law. It is a more modern method of interpretation.

Queen's Counsel (QC): an appointed senior barrister who has practised for at least 10 years. They can wear silk gowns, hence 'to take silk'.

ratio decidendi: 'the reason for the decision'. This is the binding element of precedent, which must be followed.

real property: land and buildings.

rebuttable presumption: a presumption that is rebuttable is one that can be reversed if the courts find sufficient evidence to do this.

remedy: an award made by a court to the innocent party in a civil case to 'right the wrong'.

representation: a statement made during contract negotiations that is not intended to be a part of the contract.

rescission: to unmake a contract or transaction, to return the parties to the position they would be in if it had never happened.

reserved powers model: under this model, the Senedd is allowed to legislate on matters that are not reserved to the UK Parliament. Matters that remain reserved to the UK Parliament include defence and foreign affairs.

retrospective effect: laws that operate affecting acts done before they were passed.

rights of audience: the right to appear as an advocate in any court.

rule of law: the state should govern its citizens in accordance with rules that have been agreed upon.

secret soundings: the old appointments process whereby information on a potential judge would be gathered over time, informally, from leading barristers and judges.

sentence: the punishment given to someone who has been convicted of an offence. It can be imprisonment, a community sentence or a suspended sentence or discharge.

separation of powers: state power is separated into three types, Executive, judicial and legislative, with each type exercised by different bodies or people.

special defence: the use of a defence which has the effect not of completely acquitting the defendant but allowing a reduction in the sentence given to the defendant.

stare decisis: to stand by the previous decisions.

statute (Act of Parliament): a source of primary legislation that comes from the UK legislature.

strict liability: a group of offences, usually regulatory in nature, that only require proof of actus reus, not mens rea.

subjective: an assumption relating to the individual in question (the subject).

substantive ultra vires: where delegated legislation goes beyond what Parliament intended.

suicide pact: a partial defence to murder contained in s4 Homicide Act 1957 whereby, if a surviving person of a pact for two people to die can prove that they both intended to die, the charge will be reduced to voluntary manslaughter.

summary offence: the least serious offences, triable only in the magistrates' court.

super injunction: a type of injunction that prohibits the publication of information and also prohibits the reporting of the fact that the injunction even exists.

surety: a sum of money offered to the court by a person known to the suspect which guarantees the suspect's attendance at court when required.

tenancy: a permanent place for a barrister in chambers.

term: a statement made during contract negotiations that is intended to be a part of the contract, binding the parties to it.

thing (or chose) in action: property that does not exist in a physical sense but which provides the owner with legally enforceable rights (e.g. a bank account, investments, shares and intellectual property such as patents).

tort: a civil wrong committed by one individual against another, such as injury caused by negligence.

tortfeasor: someone who has committed a tort.

trespasser: a visitor who has no permission or authority to be on the occupier's land.

triable either way: an offence that can be tried in either a magistrates' court or in the Crown Court.

unilateral contract: an offer made in exchange for an act; for example, a reward for lost property.

uplift fee/success fee: additional fee in a no win, no fee case, of up to 100 per cent of the legal representative's basic fee, which is payable if the case is won. If the case is not won, the losing party will not have to pay any fees.

Upper Tribunal: hears appeals from the First Tier Tribunal, and in some complex cases will act within a first instance jurisdiction.

vicarious liability: in the civil law of tort, a third party (e.g. an employer) can be held responsible for a tort committed by another (e.g. an employee).

vis major: Latin for 'a superior force'. Used in civil cases to denote an act of God or loss resulting from natural causes, such as a hurricane, tornado, or earthquake, and without the intervention of human beings.

wounding: to break both layers of the skin, usually resulting in bleeding.

Index

absolute privilege 231
accessibility, in courts 58
Access to Justice Act (1999) 16, 87, 100–1, 103
acquittal 60, 219, 342
Acts of Parliament (statute) 1–2, 4, 10–11
   statutory interpretation 26–32
actual bodily harm (ABH) 308–9
actus reus 290–1, 294–7
   actual bodily harm (ABH) 308–9
   assault 306–7
   attempt 364–5
   battery 307–8
   burglary 333–5
   grievous bodily harm (GBH) 310–11
   involuntary manslaughter 321–2
   murder 314–15
   robbery 331–2
   theft 326–9
admissible evidence 71, 201
adult offenders, sentencing 65–6
advisory committees 15–16
advocacy 88
aggravated trespass 129
airspace, trespass in 125
All England Law Reports (All ER) 35
alternative dispute resolution (ADR) 47–9
Anti-Terrorism, Crime and Security Act (2001) 10
appeals
   civil cases 43
   criminal cases 59
   see also Court of Appeal
arbitration 48–9
Arbitration Act (1996) 48–9
arrest 197–9
assault 306–7
assisted suicide 317, 361
attempt 364–7
attempted murder 366
Auld Review 16
automatism 341–4
bail 67–70
Bail Act (1976) 68–70, 72
bail hostel 69
barristers 88–9
battery 307–8
beyond reasonable doubt 56
   see also standard of proof
bilateral contract 243
Bill of Rights *see* British Bill of Rights
Bills 2
binding element 35–6
binding precedent 35
Bloody Sunday inquiry 16
breach of confidence 210–12
breach of confidentiality 208–12

breach of contract 241, 273
breach of the peace 190–1
British Bill of Rights 174, 235–7
British Sign Language Act (2022) 2
Budget statement 10
bugging devices 204
bundle of rights 326–7
burden of proof 56, 290, 294, 318–19
burglary 332–5
byelaws 19
cab rank rule 88
cannabis 19
capacity defences 338–63
Caparo test 113
case law *see* judicial precedent (case law)
case stated 59
cause groups 12
chambers 88
Chancery Division 43
children
   occupiers' liability to 153–4
   see also youth offenders
Children and Social Work Act (2017) 2
Civil Aviation Act (1982) 139
Civil Contingencies Act (2004) 19
civil courts
   alternative dispute resolution (ADR) 47–9
   appeals 43
   juries 46–7
   procedure 44–6
   structure and hierarchy 42
   tribunals 50–2
Civil Liability Act (2018) 166
civil liberties 170
Civil Partnership Act (2004) 173
Civil Procedure Rules (1998) 44, 47, 51, 128
claimant 42
codification 10, 13–14, 292
collateral contracts 258
Common European Sales Law (CESL) 240
common law 34, 220, 289–90, 306
Communications Act (2003) 133, 174
Companies Act (2006) 276
conciliation 48–9
conditional bail 68–9
conditional discharge 63
conditional fee arrangements (CFAs) 103–4
confidence, breach of 210
confidentiality 208–10
consent
   as criminal defence 359–61
   tort law 159–61
constitution 4, 170
Constitutional Reform Act (2005) 6–7, 39, 92, 94, 237
Consumer Protection (Distance Selling) Regulations (2000) 246, 250

Consumer Rights Act (2015) 155, 265–8, 272
contempt of court 80–1, 220–2
Contempt of Court Act (1981) 83–4, 172, 220–2
contract law
   acceptance 248–9
   battle of the forms 248–50
   breach of contract 241, 273
   common law exceptions 258
   consideration 253–4
   discharge 281–3
   express terms 261–4
   formation of contract 241–59
   implied terms 264–72
   innominate terms 273
   interpretation 263–4
   invitations to treat 241–4
   misrepresentation 276–80
   offers 241–7
   origins and definition 239–40
   postal rule 250–1
   privity of contract 257, 259
   promissory estoppel 255
   rebuttable presumption 253
   remedies 285–8
   social and domestic agreements 252–3
   statutory exceptions 257
   termination of offer 245–7
   terms 261–73
   unfair terms 268, 271–2
   warranties 273
Contracts (Rights of Third Parties) Act (1999) 257
contributory negligence 161–2
conveyancers 90
conviction 59, 71
Coroners and Justice Act (2009) 14, 66, 317–19
coroners' court 78
Council on Law Reporting 35
councils 19
county court 35, 42–4
court hierarchy 34–5
Court of Appeal 34, 37, 43, 59–60, 212
Courts Act (1971) 57
Courts Act (2003) 95–6
Courts Act (2022) 96
Courts and Legal Services Act (1990) 87, 90, 103
Covert Human Intelligence Sources (Criminal Conduct) Act (2021) 205–6
Crime and Courts Act (2013) 65, 94, 355
Crime and Disorder Act (1998) 55
Criminal Appeal Act (1995) 59, 60
Criminal Attempts Act (1981) 364, 367
Criminal Justice Act (1967) 64
Criminal Justice Act (1988) 307

376

Index

Criminal Justice Act (2003)   11, 14, 16, 66, 79, 82, 199, 306
Criminal Justice and Courts Act (2015)   79–80, 83–4
Criminal Justice and Immigration Act (2008)   225–6, 354–5
Criminal Justice and Public Order Act (1994)   69, 129, 186–7, 195
criminal law
   actual bodily harm (ABH)   308–9
   actus reus   290–1, 294–7, 306–11, 314, 321–2, 326–9, 331–2, 333–5, 364–5
   assault   306–7
   attempted murder   366
   battery   307–8
   burden of proof   290, 294, 318–19
   burglary   332–5
   capacity defences   338–63
   causation   299, 313–14, 322
   common law offences   289–90
   criminal liability   290–2, 294–304
   definition of a crime   289
   grievous bodily harm (GBH)   309–11
   gross negligence manslaughter   323
   involuntary manslaughter   321
   mens rea   29, 290–2, 296–9, 307–11, 322, 329–30, 332, 335, 365–6
   murder   289, 313–17
   offences against the person (fatal)   313–23
   offences against the person (non-fatal)   306–11
   offences of attempt   364–7
   robbery   331–2
   special defence   317–21
   strict liability   296, 301–3
   theft   326–30
   voluntary manslaughter   317–21
criminal process
   acquittal   60
   appeals   59
   bail   67–70
   closing speeches   57
   conviction   59, 71
   court hierarchy   55–6, 59
   defence   57, 59–60
   indictable offences   55
   juries   77
   plea bargaining   306
   prosecution   56, 60
   summary offences   55, 306
   trail process   56
   triable either way   55–6
   see also criminal law; Crown Prosecution Service (CPS); sentencing
cross-examination   56
Crown Court   35, 55–7, 59–60, 60–1, 78, 106
   layout   58
   role of   57–8
Crown Prosecution Service (CPS)   70–4
Crown Prosecution Service Inspectorate Act (2000)   71
custody, youth offenders   63–4

customs   4
damages   163–6, 285
   see also remedies
defamation   227–32
   defamatory statements   227–9
   defences to   229–31
   remedies   231–2
Defamation Act (1996)   231
Defamation Act (2013)   46, 78, 227–32
defence, criminal process   57, 59–60, 317–21
defences
   capacity defences   338–63
   to defamation   229–31
   partial defence   317–21
   special defence   317–21
   tort law   159–62
defendant   42
delegated legislation   4, 19–24
   controls   21–3
   devolution   20–1
detention   199–200
deterrence   61, 303
devolution   5, 20–1
Dicey, A.V., theory of parliamentary sovereignty   4–6
diminished responsibility   319–21
direct action   12
direct interference   123–4
display of goods   242–3
Domestic Violence, Crimes and Victims Act (2003)   14
drafting errors   27
duress   350–3
duty of care   112–15, 153, 156–7, 323
duty solicitor   104–5
early administrative hearing   55
Education Act (1996)   295
emergency laws   19
Emergency Powers Act (1920)   19
employee status   146–7
employment tribunals   50, 52
enabling Acts   19, 22
equality   6
Equality Act (2010)   101, 195
European Convention on Human Rights (ECHR)   11, 31, 170–2, 234–6
   Article 2   172, 213
   Article 5   67–8, 176, 194, 201
   Article 6   45, 84, 176, 178–9, 341
   Article 8   173, 179–80, 194, 195, 200, 204–5, 212, 215–16, 227, 236
   Article 10   13, 172, 176, 180–1, 183–5, 212, 215–16, 220, 223–4, 227, 237
   Article 11   13, 182, 183–5
   Article 14   173
   restrictions on   183–232
European Court of Human Rights (ECtHR)   6, 11, 35, 62, 172, 216, 234
European Directive on Alternative Dispute Resolution   48–9
European Union (EU)   5
   and contract law   240

euthanasia   296, 316, 361
evidence, admissible   71, 201
examination in chief   56
Executive   6–7
fair trial, right to   178–9
Family Division   43
fault-based liability   109
Finance Act (2017)   2
first tier sentencing   63
Fraud Act (2006)   14
freedom of expression   180–1, 223–4, 227
Gender Recognition Act (2004)   11
golden rule   27, 29
goods and services   265–72
   see also contract law
government, separation of powers   6–7
   see also Parliament
Government of Wales Act (1998)   20
Government of Wales Act (2006)   20–1
Green Paper   2
grievous bodily harm (GBH)   309–11
gross negligence manslaughter   323
Hansard   30–1
harassment   136–7
hearsay   71
High Court   5, 22, 34, 42–4, 59
Highways Act (1980)   193
homicide
   involuntary manslaughter   321
   murder   289, 313–17
   voluntary manslaughter   317–21
Homicide Act (1957)   317, 319
homosexuality   9
House of Commons   1, 3, 7
House of Lords   1, 3, 7, 34, 36, 39
human rights   5, 6, 11, 13, 31, 170–5, 234–7
   absolute rights   171, 176
   civil liberties   170
   fair trial   178–9
   freedom of expression   180–1, 223–4, 227
   liberty and security   67–8, 177
   limited rights   171, 176
   privacy   179–80, 204, 208–16, 227
   qualified rights   171, 176, 204
   rights, freedoms or liberties   172
   see also European Convention on Human Rights (ECHR)
Human Rights Act (1998)   5, 6, 31, 35, 55, 82, 170–2, 173–5, 181, 183, 185, 198, 212, 234–7, 239
hung jury   78
Hunting Act (2004)   3
independent contractors   150, 154–5
injunctions   166–8, 214–15, 287
innuendo   228–9
Inquiries Act (2005)   15
insanity   338–44
institutional racism   16
Interception of Communications Act (1985)   204
interrogation   199–200
intoxication   344–9

Investigatory Powers Act (2016) 206–7
invitations to treat 241–4
involuntary manslaughter 321
Joint Committee on Statutory Instruments (JCSI), 22
judges
   constitutional position 9
   dismissal and termination 93
   hierarchy of 92
   independence 93
   skills and role of 9–10, 26, 37–8, 92
   see also judiciary; sentencing
Judicial College Guidelines (JCG) 166
judicial precedent (case law) 4, 9, 34–40
   advantages and disadvantages 39
   binding element 35–6
   court hierarchy 34–5
   law reporting 35
   process 36–8
judicial review 5, 22, 56
Judicial Review and Courts Act (2022) 56
judiciary 6–7, 88, 89, 92–4
juries 83–4
   challenging 81–2
   civil cases 46–7
   criminal cases 78
   eligibility 79
   hung jury 78
   tampering 82
Juries Act (1974) 2, 78–80, 82
Justices of the Peace Act (1361) 95
Justices of the Peace Act (1979) 97
Justices of the Peace Act (1997) 95
Kay's law 67
King's Bench Division 43, 59
King's Counsel (KC) 89
laissez-faire doctrine 239
language
   changes and ambiguity 26
   rules of 30
Law Commission 13–15, 292
Law Commission Act (1965) 13, 292
Law Commission Act (2009) 15
Law of Property Act (1925) 257
Law Reform (Frustrated Contracts) Act (1943) 282–3
Legal Aid 100–6
Legal Aid, Sentencing and Punishment of Offenders Act (2012) 38, 62, 65–6, 68–9, 101–6, 129
Legal Aid Agency 101, 105
legal executives 90
Legislative and Regulatory Reform Act (2006) 19, 22–3
legislative competence 21
Legislative Competence Orders 21
legislative process 3
legislative reform orders 19
legislature 6–7
Leveson inquiry 16
liberty, right to 67–8, 177
life sentences 66

literal rule 27, 29, 263–4
litigation 42
lobbying 12
Local Government Act (1972) 134
Lord Chancellor 92
loss of control 317–19
magistrates 95–9
Magistrates' Court 35, 55–7, 58, 60, 62, 95–9, 105
Magistrates' Courts Act (1980) 130
malice, acts of 138–9, 297
   see also mens rea
Malicious Communications Act (1988) 133
marital rape 290
marital status 9
Marriage Act (1994) 2
Married Women's Property Act (1882) 257
media influence 10–11
media intrusion 213–15
mediation 48–9
Members of Parliament (MPs) 1–2, 4, 11
mens rea 29, 290–2, 296–9
   actual bodily harm (ABH) 309
   assault 307
   attempt 365–6
   battery 308
   burglary 335
   grievous bodily harm (GBH) 310–11
   involuntary manslaughter 322
   murder 315–16
   robbery 332
   theft 329–30
mischief rule 27–8, 29
misrepresentation 276–80
Misrepresentation Act (1967) 277–8
Misuse of Drugs Act (1971) 19
misuse of private information 212
monarchy 1–3, 7, 19
Montesquieu 6–7
murder 289, 313–17
negligence 111–21, 140, 165–6, 299
   see also contributory negligence; gross negligence manslaughter
negotiation 48–9
noise 135–8
non-pecuniary losses 285
Northern Ireland Act (1998) 21
Northern Ireland Assembly 5, 20
novus actus interveniens 299, 301
obiter dicta 35–6
Obscene Publications Act (1959) 223–6
obscenity 223–6
obstruction of police 193
Occupiers' Liability Act (1957) 152–6, 157
Occupiers' Liability Act (1984) 14, 152, 156–7
offences against the person see actual bodily harm (ABH); assault; battery; grievous bodily harm (GBH); homicide
Offences Against the Person Act (1861) 64, 306, 308–9, 321, 344, 360
Offensive Weapons Act (1959) 242
official secrets 217–20

Official Secrets Act (1920) 27, 217
Official Secrets Act (1989) 217, 217–18
Old Bailey 57
original precedent 34
paralegals 90
parenting order 63
Parliament 1–2
   Bills 2
   law reform 9, 10
   legislative process 3
   pressure groups 11–13
   see also Acts of Parliament (statute); Scottish Parliament; Welsh Parliament
Parliament Acts (1911) (1949) 3
parliamentary sovereignty 4
Parole Board 64
partial defence 317–21
pecuniary losses 285
plea bargaining 306
Police, Crime, Sentencing and Courts Act (2022) 58, 61, 66, 67, 79, 184–5, 190
Police Act (1996) 193
Police Act (1997) 205
Police and Criminal Evidence Act (1984) 15, 62, 67, 104, 194–203
Police and Justice Act (2006) 63
police bail 67–8
police powers 194–203
Police Reform Act (2002) 201
Police Reform and Social Responsibility Act (2011) 190
postal rule 250–1
powers, separation of 6–7, 9
premises searches 196–7
pressure groups 11–13
primary legislation 19
privacy, right to 179–80, 204, 208–16, 227
Private Members' Bills 2, 11
private nuisance 134–41
privity of contract 257, 259
Privy Council 19, 37
procedural ultra vires 22–3
promissory estoppel 255
proof
   burden of 56, 290, 294, 318–19
   standard of 42, 56, 202, 290, 294
property offences
   burglary 332–5
   robbery 331–2
   theft 326–30
prosecution 56, 60
   see also criminal process
Prosecution of Offences Act (1985) 71
Protection From Harassment Act (1997) 137
Protection of Freedom Act (2012) 200
Protection of Wild Birds Act (1954) 243
protests 182–93
provocation 318
Public Bills 2
public inquiries 15–16
public interest test 71–2, 211, 230
public nuisance 130–4

Index

public order   183–93
Public Order Act (1986)   184, 187–8
purposive approach   28–9
racism   16, 189
rape   9, 290
ratio decidendi   35
rebuttable presumption   253
recklessness   292, 298–9, 366
referral order   63
reform
   advisory committees   15–16
   agencies   11
   judicial precedent (case law)   9
   Law Commission   13–15
   legal profession   90
   parliamentary   9, 10–11
   pressure groups   11–13
   Private Members' Bills   11
   problems with   16–17
Regulation of Investigatory Powers Act (2000)   205–6
rehabilitation   61
religious hatred   189
remedies
   contract law   285–8
   defamation   231–2
   tort law   108, 163–8, 277
remedy   42, 194, 273
Rent Act (1977)   38
reparation   61, 63
reporting   35
representation   89–90
rescission   277
reserved powers model   21
restoritative justice   108
retribution   61, 108
retrospective effect   39
Road Traffic Act (1930)   28, 160, 257, 295
robbery   331–2
Royal Assent   3
Royal Commissions   15
rule of law   5–6
   breaches of   6
'Sarah's Law'   11
Scotland Act (1998)   21
Scottish Parliament   5, 20
secondary legislation *see* delegated legislation

self-defence   354–6
Senior Courts Act (1981)   46
sentencing   57, 60, 66
   adult offenders   65–6
   aims of   60–1
   life sentences   66
   mitigating factors   66
   youth offenders   61–4, 66
Sentencing Act (2020)   61–5
Sentencing Council   66
separation of powers   6–7, 9
Serious Crime Act (2007)   14
Sexual Offences Act (2003)   9
Silk Commission   21
small claims   42
solicitors   87–8
sources of law   1–2
special defence   317–21
standard of proof   42, 56, 202, 290, 294
stare decisis   34
statute *see* Acts of Parliament (statute)
statutory instruments (SIs)   19, 22–3
statutory interpretation   26–32
stop and search   195–6
strict liability   109, 146, 296, 301–3
strike action   190–1
subordinate legislation *see* delegated legislation
substantive ultra vires   23
suicide   321
   assisted   317, 361
summary offences   55, 306
Supply of Goods and Services Act (1982)   14
Supreme Court   7, 21, 26, 34, 39, 43, 59, 94
Supreme Court Act (1981)   57, 78
Supreme Court Act (1984)   78
surveillance   204–8
tenders   243–4
Terrorism Act (2000)   195, 199
theft   326–30
Theft Act (1968)   326–35
'thin skull' test   300
tort law   108, 133
   consent   159–61
   contributory negligence   161–2
   criticisms   110
   damages   163–6
   defences   159–62

   direct interference   123–4
   injunctions   166–8
   negligence   111–21, 140, 165–6
   occupiers' liability   152–7
   primary and secondary victims   119–20
   private nuisance   134–41
   public nuisance   134–5
   remedies   108, 128, 140, 163–8, 277
   strict liability   109, 146
   tort action   108–9
   trespass to land   123–8
   vicarious liability   146–51
trade associations   11–12
tradespeople   154–5
trespassers   108, 186–7
   burglary   335
   in common law   156
   in criminal law   129–33
   in tort law   123–8
tribunals   50–2
Tribunals, Courts and Enforcement Act (2007)   14, 51–2, 90, 92
Tribunals and Inquiries Act (1958)   50
ultra vires   19, 22–3
Unfair Contract Terms Act (1977)   14, 239, 268, 271–2
unilateral contract   243
Universal Declaration of Human Rights (UDHR)   170
University College London Act (1996)   2
vicarious liability   146–51
visitors, occupiers' liability   152–5
voluntary manslaughter   317–21
voting, right to   6
Wales, law reform   16
Wales Act (2014)   21
Wales Act (2017)   21, 51
welfare state   100
Welsh Parliament   5, 20
   devolution   20–1
White Paper   2
Woolf reforms   42, 44–5
Woolf Report   16
youth offenders
   custody   63–4
   sentencing   61–4, 66
youth rehabilitation orders (YROs)   62–3

Photo credits

Photos reproduced by permission of: **p.1** *l* Arcaid Images/Alamy Stock Photo, *r* PA Images/Alamy Stock Photo, *b* © Maksym Yemelyanov/stock.adobe.com; **p.5** © nito/stock.adobe.com; **p.7** *t* Crown Copyright, *tl* Crown Copyright, *tr* © Imageplotter/Alamy Stock Photo, *l* © Ian Shaw/Alamy Stock Photo, *b* © adrian looby/Alamy Stock Photo; **p.12** © RobertoBarcellona/Shutterstock.com; **p.20** © travelwitness/stock.adobe.com; **p.21** © lazyllama/Shutterstock.com; **p.23** © klublu/stock.adobe.com; **p.26** © Victor Moussa/stock.adobe.com; **p.28** © Araya Jirasatitsin/Shutterstock.com; **p.31** © Steven May/Alamy Stock Photo; **p.34** © Zerbor/stock.adobe.com; **p.35** © ESB Professional/Shutterstock.com; **p.38** © Africa Studio/stock.adobe.com; **p.47** © fizkes/stock.adobe.com; **p.48** *(1)* © Kzenon/stock.adobe.com, *(2)* © Bacho Foto/stock.adobe.com, *(3)* © Rawpixel.com/stock.adobe.com, *(4)* © Portrait Image Asia/Shutterstock.com; **p.52** © Andrey Popov/stock.adobe.com; **p.57** © Tupungato/Shutterstock.com; **p.78** © Vicky Jirayu/Shutterstock.com; **p.83** © Adam Gregor/stock.adobe.com; **p.84** © moodboard/stock.adobe.com; **p.88** © Spiroview Inc/Shutterstock.com; **p.89** *t* © Angelina Dimitrova/Shutterstock.com, *c* © David Levenson/Alamy Stock Photo; **p.91** © Flamingo Images/Shutterstock.com; **p.93** © hafakot/Shutterstock.com; **p.111** © Tom Gowanlock/Shutterstock.com; **p.114** © Jason/stock.adobe.com; **p.117** © javiindy/stock.adobe.com; **p.120** © Travel-Fr/Shutterstock.com; **p.123** © urmosilevente/stock.adobe.com; **p.125** © Thampapon/Shutterstock.com; **p.126** © seeshooteatrepeat/Shutterstock.com; **p.127** © oliophotography/stock.adobe.com; **p.129** *t* © Louise McGilviray/stock.adobe.com, *b* © NEIL ROY JOHNSON/Shutterstock.com; **p.131** © ABB Photo/Shutterstock.com; **p.132** © moomsabuy/Shutterstock.com; **p.134** © Syda Productions/stock.adobe.com; **p.135** © QQ7/stock.adobe.com; **p.136** © Darryl Sleath/Shutterstock.com; **p.138** © Tinka Mach/stock.adobe.com; **p.140** © Lesterman/Shutterstock.com; **p.147** © jirsak/stock.adobe.com; **p.148** © Andrei Korovin/Shutterstock.com; **p.149** © Brian Jackson/stock.adobe.com; **p.152** © Doraemon9572/Shutterstock.com; **p.157** © BrandonKleinPhoto/Shutterstock.com; **p.159** © OceanProd/stock.adobe.com; **p.160** © Sergey Nivens/stock.adobe.com; **p.161** © Kkulikov/Shutterstock.com; **p.167** © Scott Maxwell/ LuMaxArt/Shutterstock.com; **p.172** © Elenarts/Shutterstock.com; **p.174** © hidesy/Shutterstock.com; **p.176** © Branislav Cerven/Shutterstock.com; **p.178** © BillionPhotos.com/stock.adobe.com; **p.179** © Kitreel/Shutterstock.com; **p.180** © alexskopje/Shutterstock.com; **p.182** © pcruciatti/Shutterstock.com; **p.184** © Koca Vehbi/Shutterstock.com; **p.186** © whitejellybeans/Shutterstock.com; **p.187** © 1000 Words/Shutterstock.com; **p.190** © Cavan-Images/Shutterstock.com; **p.191** © jovannig/stock.adobe.com; **p.192** © 1000 Words/Shutterstock.com; **p.196** © Solid Web Designs LTD/Shutterstock.com; **p.197** © BortN66/stock.adobe.com; **p.200** © kaninstudio/stock.adobe.com; **p.204** *c* © titikul_b/stock.adobe.com, *b* © Robert Lucian Crusitu/Shutterstock.com; **p.206** © Andrey Popov/Stock.adobe.com; **p.210** © Everett Collection/Shutterstock.com; **p.211** © mark reinstein/Shutterstock.com; **p.214** © s_bukley/Shutterstock.com; **p.223** © pikepicture/Shutterstock.com; **p.227** © Adam Gregor/stock.adobe.com; **p.234** © David Carillet/Shutterstock.com; **p.235** © Cory Woodruff/Shutterstock.com; **p.249** © NothingIsEverything/Shutterstock.com; **p.250** © vasabii/Shutterstock.com; **p.252** © Adam Gregor/stock.adobe.com; **p.261** © fizkes/stock.adobe.com; **p.262** © alter_photo/stock.adobe.com; **p.263** *t* © Irma07/Shutterstock.com, *b* © Joggie Botma/stock.adobe.com; **p.265** © Joggie Botma/stock.adobe.com; **p.267** © denphumi/stock.adobe.com; **p.269** © Bits and Splits/stock.adobe.com; **p.270** © sumire8/stock.adobe.com; **p.271** © megaflopp/stock.adobe.com; **p.273** © megaflopp/stock.adobe.com; **p.277** © Sorbis/Shutterstock.com; **p.279** *l* © VanderWolf Images/stock.adobe.com, *r* © Featureflash Photo Agency/Shutterstock.com; **p.285** © Sergey Dudyrev/Shutterstock.com; **p.287** © hafakot/Shutterstock.com; **p.289** © fotofabrika/stock.adobe.com; **p.290** © jkcDesign/stock.adobe.com; **p.292** © DOC RABE Media/stock.adobe.com; **p.297** © Andrei Nekrassov/stock.adobe.com; **p.299** © Tfrancis/Shutterstock.com; **p.300** © JaneHYork/Shutterstock.com; **p.301** © Best Vector Elements/Shutterstock.com; **p.308** © Roman Milert/Shutterstock.com; **p.309** © Ixepop/Shutterstock.com; **p.313** © Liukov/Shutterstock.com; **p.314** *tl* © nasirkhan/Shutterstock.com, *tr* © BeRad/Shutterstock.com; **p.319** © Oleg Golovnev/Shutterstock.com; **p.326** © Mike_shots/Shutterstock.com; **p.330** © Daniel Jędzura/stock.adobe.com; **p.334** © Sunday Stock/Shutterstock.com; **p.338** © Shine Nucha/Shutterstock.com; **p.340** © Shane Maritch/Shutterstock.com; **p.342** *t* © Africa Studio/stock.adobe.com, *b* © eggeeggjiew/stock.adobe.com; **p.343** © sezer66/Shutterstock.com; **p.344** © AlenKadr/stock.adobe.com; **p.346** © VonaUA/Shutterstock.com; **p.347** © Paweł Michałowski/stock.adobe.com; **p.348** © mrjo_7/stock.adobe.com; **p.349** © Vgstockstudio/Shutterstock.com; **p.350** © Erce/Shutterstock.com; **p.352** © milankubicka/stock.adobe.com; **p.354** © antoniodiaz/stock.adobe.com; **p.357** © Melkor3D/Shutterstock.com; **p.358** *t* © jat306/stock.adobe.com, *c* © Qualivity/Shutterstock.com; **p.359** © TungCheung/Shutterstock.com; **p.360** © efks/stock.adobe.com; **p.361** © Koldunov/Shutterstock.com; **p.364** © Juhku/stock.adobe.com; **p.367** © tomertu/stock.adobe.com.